Breaking Through
College Reading

SIXTH EDITION

Brenda D. Smith

PROFESSOR EMERITUS, GEORGIA STATE UNIVERSITY

Longman

New York   San Francisco   Boston
London   Toronto   Sydney   Tokyo   Singapore   Madrid
Mexico City   Munich   Paris   Cape Town   Hong Kong   Montreal

TO MY MOTHER AND FATHER

Vice President and Editor-in-Chief: Joseph Opiela
Senior Acquisitions Editor: Steven A. Rigolosi
Development Editor: Bennett Morrison
Marketing Manager: Melanie Criag
Supplements Editor: Donna Campion
Media Supplements Editor: Nancy Garcia
Technical Reviewer: Jacqueline Stahlecker
Production Manager: Ellen MacElree
Project Coordination, Text Design, and Electronic Page Makeup: Nesbitt Graphics, Inc.
Cover Designer/Manager: Nancy Danahy
Photo Researcher: Photosearch, Inc.
Manufacturing Buyer: Lucy Hebard
Printer and Binder: Quebecor World/Dubuque
Cover Printer: Phoenix Color Corp.

For permission to use copyrighted material, grateful acknowledgment is made to the
copyright holders on pp. 517–519, which are hereby made part of this copyright page.

Library of Congress Cataloging-in-Publication Data
Smith, Brenda D., 1944–
    Breaking through : college reading / Brenda D. Smith. —6th ed.
        p.   cm.
    Includes index.
    ISBN 0-321-05103-3 (student ed.) — ISBN 0-321-05104-1 (instructor's ed.)
        1. Reading (Higher education)   2. Study skills.   I. Title.

    LB2395.3 .S62 2001
    428.4'071'1—dc21

                                                                        2001029756

Please visit our website at http://www.ablongman.com/smith

ISBN 0-321-05103-3 (Student Edition)
ISBN 0-321-05104-1 (Instructor's Edition)

3 4 5 6 7 8 9 10—QWD—04 03 02

Brief Contents

Detailed Contents

CHAPTER 5

Supporting Details and Organizational Patterns   151

What Is a Detail?   152

Patterns of Organization   163

CHAPTER 6

Textbook Learning 211

Expect Knowledge to Exist 212

Annotating 212
When to Annotate 212
How to Annotate 212

Notetaking 214
When to Take Notes 214
How to Take Notes 215

Summarizing 217
When to Summarize 217
How to Summarize 217

Outlining 221
When to Outline 221
How to Outline 221

Mapping 225
When to Map 225
How to Map 225

Take Organized Lecture Notes 227

SUMMARY POINTS 228

CHAPTER 8

Efficient Reading   287

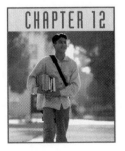

Preface

The Goals of the Sixth Edition

The new features in this sixth edition are designed to build a community of learners who reflect, network, organize, and share. They focus on connecting academic and everyday reading activities, sharing the responsibilities for learning through group interaction, and developing independence in researching the Internet. In the new **Everyday Reading Skills** features, students apply academic skills to eleven everyday activities such as reading newspapers, magazines, advertisements, reference materials, fiction and nonfiction books, workplace mail, and the Internet. In **Collaborative Problem Solving**, students brainstorm together and share in teaching and learning by using creative and critical thinking skills to respond to four group challenges that reflect the chapter's instruction. The **Explore the Net** exercises now include specific websites, and they have been expanded to include new questions. A variety of new **Reader's Tip** boxes briefly highlight strategies for thinking and reading, as well as strategies for studying in many different academic disciplines. Two new appendixes have been added: **Making Sense of Figurative Language and Idioms**, an ESL section, and **Weekly Vocabulary Lessons** which focuses on linking and learning words through word parts or word families. The new features in *Breaking Through*, Sixth Edition, tap additional resources to expand academic horizons and make learning relevant, current, and fun.

As the community of learners develops, so does each individual. The ultimate goal of *Breaking Through* is for students to become successful independent learners. The techniques are to teach, to model, and to offer practice in the reading and study skills most essential for understanding and retaining the material in freshman college tests. Further goals are to motivate students to achieve success and to help students draw on previous knowledge in order to integrate new and old ideas.

This sixth edition includes many new practice exercises and fifteen new, longer reading selections. *Personal Feedback* questions are included in the chapters to encourage students to communicate academic and personal concerns to the instructor. *Comprehension Questions* are labeled as *main idea, detail,* or *inference* to help students evaluate strengths and weaknesses. A **Progress Record for Reading Selections** has been added at the very end of the text for keeping track of student performance on the comprehension and vocabulary questions following the reading selections at the ends of chapters. *Vocabulary Preview* and *Vocabulary Enrichment* sections introduce and follow the reading selections to reinforce vocabulary-building skills. These selections are also followed by *React, Reflect,* and *Think Critically* questions to stimulate thought and encourage thoughtful written responses. The *Explore the Net* feature at the end of each selection offers students an opportunity to seek additional information on a related subject by searching the Internet.

Organization

The sixth edition of *Breaking Through* opens with a chapter on motivation, attitude, and action. Success starts with a vision and is built on determination, perseverance, and activity. Chapter 2 moves to theories of reading and the strategies used by successful readers. To control the process, readers must understand it. Reading is thinking and interacting with the printed page in three stages: before, during, and after the process. Chapter 3 is devoted to vocabulary. It deals with context clues, word parts, analogies, and the use of the dictionary, thesaurus, and glossaries. Explanations and exercises are included.

Understanding the main idea, the most important reading comprehension skill, begins with models and practice exercises in Chapter 4 and extends into Chapter 5 with attention to supporting details, organizational patterns, and the beginning stages of notetaking. Chapter 6 explains annotating, notetaking, outlining, and mapping.

Chapter 7 offers advice on multiple-choice and true-false test-taking, as well as essay responses. Heightened awareness and insight into expectations can give students a winning edge and help improve test scores. The efficient reading discussion in Chapter 8 presents techniques for rate improvement and provides exercises to assess student reading rates.

Chapter 9 recognizes college students as analytical reasoners and problem solvers, with exercises provided to help students develop and refine analytical reasoning skills. Chapter 10, on implied meaning, and Chapter 11, on critical reading, focus on unstated attitudes and assumptions. These chapters are designed to help students become more aware of suggested meaning and to be more critical of what they read. Success in college depends on being able to transfer reading skills to daily textbook assignments. Chapter 12 includes models of outlining and notetaking activities and contains two longer textbook selections for transferring skills, studying content, and demonstrating learning.

Special Features of the Sixth Edition

- Eleven new **Everyday Reading Skills** features give tips and practice on how to research the Internet and how to read newspapers, magazines, advertisements, reference materials, fiction and nonfiction books, and workplace mail.
- **Collaborative Problem Solving** questions at the end of eleven chapters provide collaborative application and critical thinking opportunities for students to present to the class.
- **Explore the Net** activities suggest subjects related to the longer readings as topics for research on the Internet. Detailed instructions on how to use the Internet are presented in Chapter 1 and tips on evaluating Internet information appear in Chapter 11.
- **Reader's Tip** boxes condense advice for readers into practical hints for quick reference. Reader's Tips that appear with icons feature reading and studying tips for different academic disciplines.
- Fifteen **new high-interest reading selections** reflect the cultural diversity and evolving interests of student readers. For a complete list of reading selections, please see the inside front cover.
- **New practice exercises** are interspersed throughout the text.
- **Summary Points** summarize the key concepts of each chapter in a concise, easy-to-read format.
- The appendixes have been expanded to five. **Making Sense of Figurative Language and Idioms**, an ESL section, provides practice on recognizing popular expressions. The addition of **Weekly Vocabulary Lessons** offers an extended vocabulary plan for learning new words through word parts or word families.

Continuing Features

- Reading selections and practice exercises are taken from actual freshman-level college textbooks.
- Three reading levels in most chapters permit individualization of assignments to meet student needs.
- Textbook reading selections cover a variety of college courses, including history, communication, psychology, sociology, literature, science, criminal justice, and management.
- "Connect" articles help students relate old knowledge to new ideas.
- Skills are presented in the recommended teaching order, but each chapter is self-contained to provide flexibility in teaching.
- An explanation of the thinking strategies involved in reading includes a discussion of the stages of reading, schema theory, and metacognition.
- Five strategies are presented for organizing material for later study. (Separate lecture material for notetaking practice is provided in the Instructor's Manual.)
- Test-taking strategies include advice on multiple-choice, true-false, and essay exams.
- Selections are followed by multiple-choice, true-false, and sentence completion questions on both the literal and the interpretive levels of comprehension.
- Selections are followed by ten vocabulary words that are presented with contextual clues and line references to their location in the passage. (Vocabulary quizzes are provided in the Instructor's Manual for further practice.)
- **React, Reflect, and Think Critically questions** prompt personal interaction with the material.
- **Personal Feedback** questions offer opportunities for self-assessment and communication of academic and personal concerns.
- **Comprehension questions** are labeled as *main ideas, detail,* or *inference* to help students evaluate their own strengths and weaknesses.
- Instruction on **main idea** and **supporting details** is expanded into two Chapters (4 and 5).
- **Vocabulary-building** instructions and exercises are presented in a separate early chapter, followed by reinforcing vocabulary enrichment activities for the longer reading selections.

Teaching and Learning Package

Each component of the teaching and learning package has been crafted to ensure that the course is a rewarding experience for both instructors and students.

Book-Specific Supplements

- The **Annotated Instructor's Edition (AIE)** is an exact replica of the student text, with the answers provided on the write-in lines in the text. (0-321-05104-1)
- The **Instructor's Manual**, prepared by the author, offers teaching tips, sample syllabi, and other teaching resources (0-321-05105-X)
- The printed **Test Bank** for *Breaking Through*, Sixth Edition, prepared by Linda Arthur of Georgia Southern University, offers a series of skill and reading quizzes for each chapter, formatted for ease of copying and distribution. (0-321-05106-8). The **Longman Electronic Test Bank for Developmental Reading** is also available. The electronic test bank offers more than

3,000 questions in all areas of reading, including vocabulary, main idea, supporting details, patterns of organization, language, critical thinking, analytical reasoning, inference, point of view, visual aids, and textbook reading. With this easy-to-use CD-ROM, instructors simply choose questions from the electronic test bank, then print out the completed test for distribution. To order a copy of the electronic test bank, please contact your Longman sales consultant.

For additional quizzes, readings, and Internet-based activities, be sure to visit *Breaking Through Online* at **http://www.ablongman.com/smith.**

The Longman Developmental Reading Package

In addition to the book-specific ancillaries discussed above, Longman offers many other supplements to instructors and students. All of these supplements are available either free or at greatly reduced prices.

For Additional Reading and Reference

- **The Dictionary Deal.** Two dictionaries can be shrinkwrapped with any Longman Reading title at a nominal fee. *The New American Webster Handy College Dictionary* is a paperback reference text with more than 100,000 entries. *Merriam Webster's Collegiate Dictionary*, Tenth Edition, is a hardback reference with a citation file of more than 14.5 million examples of English words drawn from actual use. For more details on ordering a dictionary with this text, please contact your Longman sales representative.
- **Penguin Quality Paperback Titles.** A series of Penguin paperbacks is available at a significant discount when shrinkwrapped with any Longman title. Some titles available are Toni Morrison's *Beloved,* Julia Alvarez's *How the Garcia Girls Lost Their Accents,* Mark Twain's *Huckleberry Finn,* Frederick Douglas's *Narrative of the Life of Frederick Douglas,* Harriet Beecher Stowe's *Uncle Tom's Cabin,* Dr. Martin Luther King, Jr.'s *Why We Can't Wait,* and plays by Shakespeare, Miller, and Albee. For a complete list of titles or more information, please contact your Longman sales consultant.
- ***The Pocket Reader,* First Edition.** This inexpensive volume contains 80 brief readings (1-3 pages each) on a variety of themes: writers on writing, nature, women and men, customs and habits, politics, rights and obligations, and coming of age. Also included is an alternate rhetorical table of contents. 0-321-07668-0.
- ***The Longman Textbook Reader.*** This supplement, for use in developmental reading courses, offers five complete chapters from Addison Wesley/Longman textbooks: computer science, biology, psychology, communications, and business. Each chapter includes additional comprehension quizzes, critical thinking questions, and group activities. For information on how to bundle the free *Longman Textbook Reader* with *Breaking Through,* please contact your Longman sales representative.
- ***Newsweek* Alliance.** Instructors may choose to shrinkwrap a 12-week subscription to *Newsweek* with any Longman text. The price of the subscription is 57 cents per issue (a total of $6.84 for the subscription). Available with the subscription is a free "Interactive Guide to *Newsweek*"—a workbook for students who are using the text. In addition, Newsweek provides a wide variety of instructor supplements free to teachers, including maps, Skill Builders, and weekly quizzes. For further information on the Newsweek Alliance, please contact your Longman sales representative.

● **Florida Adopters:** *Thinking Through the Test,* **by D. J. Henry.** This special workbook, prepared specially for students in Florida, offers ample skill and practice exercises to help student prepare for the Florida State Exit Exam. To shrinkwrap this workbook free with your textbook, please contact your Longman sales representative. Also available: Two laminated grids (one for reading, one for writing) that can serve as handy references for students preparing for the Florida State Exit Exam.

Electronic and Online Offerings

● **Reading Roadtrip Multimedia Reading and Study Skills Software, Version 2.0 and Online Version.** This innovative and exciting multimedia reading CD-ROM takes students on a tour of 15 cities and landmarks throughout the United States. Each of the 15 modules corresponds to a reading or study skill (for example, finding the main idea, understanding patterns of organization, and thinking critically). All modules contain a tour of the location, instruction and tutorial, exercises, interactive feedback, and mastery tests. To order the Reading Road Trip 2.0 CD-ROM with *Breaking Through,* or to order passwords that grant access to the Reading Road Trip Website (**http://www.ablongman.com/readingroadtrip**), speak to your Longman sales representative.

● **The Longman English Pages Website.** Both students and instructors can visit our free content-rich Website for additional reading selections and writing exercises. From the Longman English pages, visitors can conduct a simulated web search, learn how to write a resume and cover letter, or try their hand at poetry writing. Stop by and visit us at **http://www.ablongman. com/englishpages.**

● **The Longman Electronic Newsletter.** Twice a month during the spring and fall, instructors who have subscribed receive a free copy of the Longman Developmental English E-Newsletter in their e-mailbox. Written by experienced classroom instructors, the newsletter offers teaching tips, classroom activities, book reviews, and more. To subscribe, visit the Longman Basic Skills Website at **http://www.ablongman.com/basicskills**, or send an e-mail to **BasicSkills@ablongman.com**

● ***Teaching Online: Internet Research, Conversation, and Composition,* Second Edition.** Ideal for instructors who have never surfed the Net, this easy-to-follow guide offers basic definitions, numerous examples, and step-by-step information about finding and using Internet sources. Free to adopters. 0-321-01957-1.

● ***Researching Online,* Fifth Edition.** A perfect companion for a new age, this indispensable supplement helps students navigate the Internet. Adapted from *Teaching Online,* the instructor's Internet guide, *Researching Online* speaks directly to students, giving them detailed, step-by-step instruction for performing electronic searches. Available free when shrinkwrapped with *Breaking Through.* Contact your Longman sales consultant for information on how to order.

For Instructors

● **CLAST Test Package, Fourth Edition.** These two 40-item objective tests evaluate students' readiness for the CLAST exams. Strategies for teaching CLAST preparedness are included. Free with any Longman English title. Reproducible sheets: 0-321-01950-4. Computerized IBM version: 0-321-01982-2. Computerized Mac version: 0-321-01983-0.

● **TASP Test Package, Third Edition.** These 12 practice pre-tests and post-tests assess the same reading and writing skills covered in the TASP examination. Free with any Longman English title. Reproducible sheets: 0-321-01959-8. Computerized IBM version: 0-321-01985-7. Computerized Mac version: 0-321-01984-9.

Acknowledgments

I would like to thank several people for their contributions to this book. First, Steven Rigolosi, my acquisitions editor, is constantly talking with teachers and seeking to meet student needs. Steve is inventive, creative, and generous in sharing new ideas with me. I appreciate his support and dedication on this project. Second, I had the pleasure of working with two developmental editors on this book. I began the project with my long-time developmental editor and buddy, Susan Moss. Susan and I have worked together on many projects, and I appreciate her talent, focus, and enthusiasm. I continued and completed the project with Ben Morrison. I appreciate his helpful suggestions and his careful attention to detail. Third, I benefited from the ideas of two energetic and intelligent researchers on this revision: Both Lisa Moore and Donna Cassidy assisted in making this an interesting and challenging edition. Fourth, many thanks go to my daughter, Julie Smith, for her research contributions. I would also like to acknowledge the help and suggestions that I received from the following people who reviewed the fifth and sixth editions of the text:

Linda Black
St. John's River Community College

Linda S. Edwards
Chattanooga State Technical Community College

Marianne Errico
Georgia Perimeter College

Patricia Grega
University of Alaska, Anchorage

Paulette Jacques
Northwestern Connecticut Community College

Emily Johnson
Georgia Perimeter College

Bette D. Kalash
Borough of Manhattan Community College

Melinda Schomaker
Georgia Perimeter College

Carla Thomson
Palomar College

Dorothy Traughber
Murray State College

—*Brenda D. Smith*

Student Success

- Are you a winner?
- What is the can-do spirit?
- Do you set high standards?
- Do you plan for success?
- How can you manage time efficiently?
- What are the behaviors of success?
- How can fellow students be learning resources?
- What student responsibilities determine success in college?

Everyday Reading Skills: Searching the Internet

Think Success

Are you mentally ready to go to college? Do you have a desire to achieve? Have you set goals for yourself, and are you ready to plan for achieving those goals? College life and college work are fun, but they require extra effort. Begin by cultivating an attitude for success.

Most of this book focuses on strategies for reading college texts. Before you concentrate on the books, however, take a look at yourself and your dreams. You are now shaping your future. To become a winner and reap the rewards, you must first think like a winner. Studies show that not only do college graduates enjoy more social and self-esteem benefits, but they also earn more than those with only high school diplomas. In 1998 the median annual income for full-time year-round workers with bachelor's degrees was $51,405 for men and $36,559 for women; the income for workers with only high school degrees was $31,477 and $22,780, respectively.[1]

This chapter will help you shape your thinking and behaviors by presenting the thoughts and describing the actions of successful people. Working on yourself can be as important as working on the books.

Set Goals

Entering college is a major turning point in life. College offers freedom, variety, and increased responsibility. Success in college requires a commitment of time, money, and energy. College is an investment in the future that requires a sacrifice in the present.

Build a team of caring people to support you as you go after your goals. Begin with your instructor. Respond thoughtfully to the Personal Feedback sections that appear throughout this text and pass them in to your instructor. Share your dreams, enthusiasm, and anxieties in order to build a learning partnership and strengthen your determination. This partnership will be only as strong as each of you allow it to be. Your instructor is not a mind reader, so reveal who you really are. Move beyond the academic and respond to questions regarding your habits, responsibilities, joys, and stresses. Your instructor wants to know you as a person and wants to help you be successful.

For this first Personal Feedback section, think about your feelings as you begin your college career, and then respond to the questions.

PERSONAL Feedback 1   Name _____

1. What three dreams and/or influences motivated you to come to college?

(a) _____

(b) _____

(c) _____

---

[1]National Center for Education Statistics, U.S. Department of Education, *Digest of Education Statistics, 1999*, Table 386. <http://nces.ed.gov/fastfacts/display.asp?id=77>

2. In five years what do you hope to be doing both professionally and personally?

   (a) Professionally: _____

   _____

   (b) Personally: _____

   _____

3. Explain three anxieties that you have as you begin college.

   (a) _____

   (b) _____

   (c) _____

4. What will you do to celebrate on the day you receive your college degree or certificate? _____

Create a Positive Attitude

Your dreams are your goals. Hold them in a corner of your mind as you go through college. On rough days, think of the dreams and picture the excitement of achieving your goals. Imagine your graduation celebration and think about those who will join in the fun. Allow your dreams to renew your enthusiasm and keep you focused on your goals. Let motivation overshadow your anxieties. Program your mind to think of success rather than failure. Don't worry about why something *cannot* be done. Instead, think about how it *can* be accomplished. What you think of yourself determines what you will become.

Seek Excellence

All of us would like to do well. Some people, however, set higher goals and eventually achieve more than others. What explains the difference? In his book *Live Your Dreams*, Les Brown offers a blueprint for success that starts with high expectations. Although he was born into poverty, adopted and raised by a single mother, and at one time was labeled "educable mentally retarded," Les Brown became a disc jockey, a three-term Ohio legislator, and an acclaimed public speaker. He energizes audiences around the country in professional seminars and on television, sharing his dreams and summarizing his strategies for success. He recognizes the difficulties faced by many, but passes along George Washington Carver's advice that we should judge people not by what they have, but by what they have had to overcome to succeed. The following is an excerpt from Brown's book.

MAKING CHOICES FOR SUCCESS

FIX YOUR FOCUS

Whatever dream you decide to go after, whether it is a family, or a career goal, you must consciously decide that it is your *life's mission*. Benjamin Disraeli said, "The secret of success is constancy to purpose." You must go at it obsessively and set high standards for yourself along the way. There is no room for compromise when you are charting a course for your life or your career.

I spoke to a group of sharp young people not long ago, and when I finished, some of the fellows came up and said they were interested in becoming professional speakers. They invited me to go out with them that evening to have a good time. These fellows looked as though they knew how to have a *serious* good time. I had planned to work on my delivery that night by listening to my tape of my speech. I tape my speeches and listen to them later so I can study what works and what does not work with a particular audience. In effect, I listen to the audience listening to me.

I was tempted to go with these fellows, and back when I was their age I probably would have given in to that temptation and gone. But I have become more disciplined and more committed to my craft.

A friend of mine, Wes Smith, wrote a humor book called *Welcome to the Real World,* and in it he offered advice to fresh high school and college graduates. He had a line in the book that pertains to the situation I faced that night. It said, "Having a drink with the boys after work every night is a bad idea. Notice that the boss doesn't do it. That is why *he* is the boss and *they* are still the boys."

Wes told me that he wrote that line with one particular group of hard-partying young businessmen in mind, and five years after the book came out, he ran into one of them. The guy volunteered that he'd read that line in Wes's book and decided never to go drinking after work again. It paid off, he said. He had risen to a vice-presidency at a savings and loan.

In my drive to become a public speaker, I developed that kind of *focus,* too. There is not a lot of time for hard partying if you are pursuing greatness. It was not that these young fellows were not serious about their interest in professional speaking, but they were just as serious about having a good time. I don't believe they were focused on their goals. They were seeking a profession but they were not on a mission to make a dramatic difference in the world. I am. You should be too.

Rather than the party crowd, I prefer to seek out people with knowledge that might be useful. I like to find out what books successful and intelligent people are reading. I want access to the information that contributes to their success and intelligence.

SEEK SUPPORT

I have come to believe that, to a certain degree, when the student is ready, the teacher appears. I first met Mike when I attended a meeting at which he spoke. I was impressed with his intelligence and articulate presentation. We became friends and Mike came to see things in me that I did not see in myself. Through his patience and example, he helped me reach a higher level. It has not always been easy for either of us. Mike is hard on me sometimes, and I have been known to be a somewhat inattentive pupil.

When I became a program director at the radio station, I hired Mike to work as my news director. I was still undisciplined at that time in my life, and I liked to sneak out of the office to shoot pool now and then. Mike made me feel guilty about it, so I would duck down and duck-walk past his office window. Sometimes he'd catch me in the parking lot and say, "Brown! Where are you going?" I wanted to be broadcasting at that point, but I wasn't committed enough to be in the building all day long being focused on my goal. I was creative, but I didn't like to keep my nose to that grindstone.

Mike convinced me that there were greater possibilities for my humble gifts than being a radio entertainer. He had a greater vision of what I could do to help others, and he has stayed with me to keep me on the path that he first envisioned. He developed the nine principles for life enrichment. He is a beacon that lights my way.

I believe that as you grow in consciousness you begin to attract people who facilitate your growth. Be on the lookout for these sorts of people, the masters, the mentors and the people who see things for you that you do not see for yourself. Find those who can look at your performance objectively and critically but positively.

We all need to have friends who hold our feet to the fire and challenge us. You need mutually enhancing relationships. As my relationship with Mike developed, he imparted some of his work habits to me. Look for the sort of friends who help you work on your weaknesses, not just those who feed your habits and congratulate you on your strong points.

—*Live Your Dreams* by Les Brown

No one says that achievement is easy. Set your goals high and boost yourself out of your comfort zone to seek your dreams. Persistence and a willingness to do the work that others are reluctant to do will make the difference.

PERSONAL Feedback 2

Name _____

1. Identify three people on your personal support team.

    (a) _____

    (b) _____

    (c) _____

2. Define the word *mentor*. Describe one of your mentors.

    Mentor: _____

    Who? _____

3. What are three things you want to learn from this reading course?

    (a) _____

    (b) _____

    (c) _____

4. What grade do you realistically seek in this course?

    Grade: _____

    Explain: _____

5. List four responsibilities you have as a college student who wants to be a high achiever with excellent grades.

    (a) _____

    (b) _____

    (c) _____

    (d) _____

6. Name one of your high school teachers who you thought was an

    excellent instructor. _____

(continued)

7. What do you expect from a college instructor? List four responsibilities of a good instructor.

   (a) _____

   (b) _____

   (c) _____

   (d) _____

8. Define Les Brown's use of the word *focus*. _____

Plan for Success

A business maxim known as Parkinson's law states that work expands to fill the time available for its completion. Have you ever had all Saturday to finish an assignment and found that it did in fact take all day, whereas if you had planned to finish it in four hours, you probably could have done so?

Time is limited, and everyone has only twenty-four hours in a day, even the president of the United States. Does the president get more done than you do? The key to success is to plan and use the minutes and hours wisely. Establish a routine and stick to it. Plan for both work and play.

Manage Your Time

Alan Lakein, a time management consultant, works with businesspeople all over the country. In his book *How to Get Control of Your Time and Your Life,* he offers the following daily method of planning for achievement.

MAKING THE MOST OF PRIORITIES

The main secret of getting more done every day took me several months of research to discover. When I first started delving into better time use, I asked successful people what the secret of their success was. I recall an early discussion with a vice-president of Standard Oil Company of California who said, "Oh, I just keep a 'To Do' list." I passed over that quickly, little suspecting at the time the importance of what he said. I happened to travel the next day to a large city to give a time management seminar. While I was there I had lunch with a businessman who practically owned the town. He was chairman of the gas and light company, president of five manufacturing companies, and had his hand in a dozen other enterprises. By all standards he was a business success. I asked him the same question of how he managed to get more done and he said, "Oh, that's easy—I keep a To Do List."

ONLY A DAILY LIST WILL DO

People at the top and people at the bottom both know about To Do Lists, but one difference between them is that the people at the top use a To Do List every single day to make better use of their time; people at the bottom know about this tool but don't use it effectively. One of the real secrets of getting more done is to make a To Do List every day, keep it visible, and use it as a guide to action as you go through the day.

Because the To Do List is such a fundamental time planning tool, let's take a closer look at it. The basics of the list itself are simple: Head a piece of paper "To Do," then list those items on which you want to work; cross off items as they are completed and add others as they occur to you; rewrite the list at the end of the day or when it becomes hard to read.

Some people try to keep To Do Lists in their heads but in my experience this is rarely as effective. Why clutter your mind with things that can be written down? It's much better to leave your mind free for creative pursuits.

WHAT BELONGS ON THE LIST

Are you going to write down everything you have to do, including routine activities? Are you only going to write down exceptional events? Are you going to put down everything you *might* do today or only whatever you decided you *will* do today? There are many alternatives, and different people have different solutions. I recommend that you do not list routine items but do list everything that has high priority today and might not get done without special attention.

Don't forget to put the A-activities for your long-term goals on your To Do List. Although it may appear strange to see "begin learning French" or "find new friends" in the same list with "bring home a quart of milk" or "buy birthday card," you want to do them in the same day. If you use your To Do List as a guide when deciding what to work on next, then you need the long-term projects represented, too, so you won't forget them at decision time and consequently not do them.

Depending on your responsibilities, you might, if you try hard enough, get all the items on your To Do List completed by the end of each day. If so, by all means try. But probably you can predict in advance that there is no way to do them all. When there are too many things to do, conscious choice as to what (and what not) to do is better than letting the decision be determined by chance.

I cannot emphasize strongly enough: You must *set priorities.* Some people do as many items as possible on their lists. They get a very high percentage of tasks done, but their effectiveness is low because the tasks they've done are mostly of C-priority. Others like to start at the top of the list and go right down it, again with little regard to what's important. The best way is to take your list and label each item according to ABC priority, delegate as much as you can, and then polish off the list accordingly.

—*How to Get Control of Your Time and Your Life* by Alan Lakein

exercise 1

Answer the following questions and make a To Do List.

1. What does the author believe is the difference between the To Do List of people at the top and those of people at the bottom? _____

_____

_____

2. Prior to reading this passage, what method have you used to keep up with things you need to remember to do? _____

_____

3. What kinds of things does the author say belong on a To Do List? _____

   _____

4. How can you indicate levels of priority on your To Do List? _____

   _____

5. Why do you think a student would feel that it is not necessary to keep a

   daily To Do List? _____

   _____

6. Make out your own To Do List today. In the left margin, indicate priorities. Keep your list in a notepad or in your assignment book so that it is always handy.

   Example

A	(1)	Pay rent
B	(2)	Change oil in car
A	(3)	Call Maria
C	(4)	Buy dictionary
B	(5)	Get breakfast foods

   To Do List

   _____ (1) _____

   _____ (2) _____

   _____ (3) _____

   _____ (4) _____

   _____ (5) _____

   _____ (6) _____

   _____ (7) _____

Plan Your Week

Organize yourself every week. Project your schedule for next week and put it on the time chart at the end of this chapter (see page 28). Be specific about each item and note what you anticipate studying when listing a study time. Be realistic about your activities and plan recreation as well as work time.

The majority of your activities will remain routine. For example, your class hours are probably the same each week. Put them on the chart first. If you have a job, plug in your work hours. If you work while attending college, you will have even fewer minutes to waste and thus you must become a superefficient time manager. Put in your mealtimes and your bedtime. If you can't live without a favorite television show, plug that in as well. Don't pretend that you are going to be studying and then not live up to your expectations.

Lay out your life the way you would like to live it for the week, and then try to stick to the plan. At the beginning of each week, adjust your plan for any changes that you foresee. Use your weekly schedule as a goal.

Reader's TIP   Time Savers

Using time wisely becomes a habit. Analyze your current problems according to the following principles of time management to gain greater control of yourself and your environment.

1. Plan. Keep an appointment book by the day and hour. Write a daily To Do List.
2. Start with the most critical activity of the day and work your way down to the least important one.
3. Ask yourself, "What is the best use of my time right now?"
4. Don't do what doesn't need doing.
5. Concentrate completely on one thing at a time.
6. Block out big chunks of time for large projects.
7. Make use of five-, ten-, and fifteen-minute segments of time.
8. Keep phone calls short or avoid them.
9. Listen well for clear instructions.
10. Learn to say "No!" to yourself and others.
11. Wean yourself from TV. Business executives do not watch soap operas.
12. Strive for excellence, but realize that perfection may not be worth the cost.

Study the Syllabus

On the first day of class almost every professor distributes a syllabus. This valuable learning tool is an outline of the goals, objectives, and assignments for the entire course. The syllabus includes examination dates and an explanation of the grading system. Depending on the professor, the syllabus may be a general overview or a more detailed outline of each class session. Keep your syllabus for ready reference; it is your guide to the professor's plan for your learning. Sophisticated students do not use class time to ask questions about test dates or details they could find by looking at the syllabus.

exercise 2   Review the following history syllabus and answer the questions.

United States History Syllabus

Class: 9–10 daily   10-Week Quarter: 1/4–3/12
Dr. J. A. Johnson   Office Hrs.: 10–12 daily
Office: 422G   Phone: 562-3367
                         E-mail: jajlsp.edu

Required Texts
(1) *A People and a Nation* by Norton et al.
(2) One paperback book on immigration selected from the list for a report.

Course Content

This course is a survey of United States history from the early explorations to the present. The purpose is to give you an understanding of the major forces and events that have interacted to make modern America.

Method of Training

Thematic lectures will be presented in class. You are expected to read and master the factual material in the text as well as take careful notes in class. Tests will cover both class lectures and textbook readings.

Grading

Grades will be determined in the following manner:

Tests (3 tests at 20% each)
Final Exam
Written Report

Tests will include both multiple-choice or identification items and two essay questions.

Important Dates

Test 1: 1/22   Final Exam: 3/18
Test 2: 2/11   Written Report: 3/10
Test 3: 3/3   Makeup Test (with permission): 3/16

Written Report

Your written report on immigration should answer one of the three designated questions and reflect your reading of a book from the list. Each book is approximately 200 pages long. Your report should be at least six typed pages. More information to follow.

Assignments

Week 1: Ch. 1 (pp. 1–27), Ch. 2 (pp. 28–49), Ch. 3 (pp. 50–68)
Week 2: Ch. 4 (pp. 69–86), Ch. 5 (pp. 87–103), Ch. 6 (pp. 104–122)
Week 3: Ch. 7 (pp. 123–139), Ch. 8 (pp. 140–159), Ch. 9 (pp. 160–176), Ch. 10 (pp. 177–194)

Test 1: Chaps. 1–10

Week 4: Ch. 11 (pp. 195–216), Ch. 12 (pp. 217–236), Ch. 13 (pp. 237–253)

Week 5: Ch. 14 (pp. 254–272), Ch. 15 (pp. 273–288), Ch. 16 (pp. 289–304), Ch. 17 (pp. 305–320)

Week 6: Ch. 18 (pp. 321–344), Ch. 19 (pp. 345–358), Ch. 20 (pp. 359–375)

Test 2: Chaps. 11–20

Week 7: Ch. 21 (pp. 376–391), Ch. 22 (pp. 392–410), Ch. 23 (pp. 411–428)

Week 8: Ch. 24 (pp. 429–450), Ch. 25 (pp. 451–466), Ch. 26 (pp. 467–484), Ch. 27 (pp. 486–504)

Week 9: Ch. 28 (pp. 505–520), Ch. 29 (pp. 521–533), Ch. 30 (pp. 534–553)

Week 10: Ch. 31 (pp. 554–569), Ch. 32 (pp. 570–586), Ch. 33 (pp. 587–599)

Test 3: Chaps. 21–28
Final Exam: Chaps. 1–33

1. What is the stated purpose of this history course? _____
   _____

2. How will your grade be determined? _____
   _____

3. How many pages do you have to read during the first week? _____
   Second week? _____ Third week? _____

4. On the average, how many pages should you read each day for the first
   week? _____

5. Will you have any pop quizzes? _____

6. Does the final exam count more than the individual tests? _____
   _____

7. What questions might you ask about the tests? _____
   _____

8. Do you have questions that are not answered by this syllabus? _____
   _____

PERSONAL feedback 3   Name _____

1. When did you receive the syllabus for this reading course? Where
   is it now? _____
   _____

2. When is your next test and how much does it count toward your
   final grade? _____
   _____

3. What material does your next major exam cover? Will the questions be multiple choice or essay? _____
   _____

4. Is there a penalty for turning work in late? _____
   _____

5. What is the purpose of this course? _____
   _____

(continued)

6. What questions do you have about how your final grade will be determined? _____

_____

7. What questions do you have about the syllabus or the course?

_____

_____

Use a Calendar to Decode a Syllabus

Students who just glance at the course syllabus might think there is no immediate assignment because the first test is four weeks away. Wrong! These students will find themselves falling behind by the second class session because of their "slow start" or "no start" strategy. Avoid this pitfall. As soon as the course begins, use your calendar along with the syllabus to divide your work according to the days and weeks of the course.

Be cautious of unlimited freedom, because it could become the freedom to fail. Some professors make short-term goal setting entirely the student's responsibility. For example, such a professor would say that the syllabus clearly states the exam will cover the first twelve textbook chapters. Period. No interim goals are provided. Thus it is up to students to take control and design their own detailed learning plan.

To make a learning plan, use a calendar with your syllabus, and break up all your reading assignments according to the number of days and weeks available. Mark exam dates and assignment deadlines. Plan to finish textbook and supplemental reading several days before test dates so you can use the last few days for study only. Total the pages assigned and divide to determine how many pages you should read each day. Write these on your calendar and give yourself a projected weekly page average. Do the same scheduling for term papers, critiques, or special projects. Mark the date you need to start special assignments, divide the work into small steps, and indicate your projected goals for each day. Use your calendar of expected achievements to stay on schedule in each of your classes.

Reader's TIP Making a Learning Schedule

Use your assignment calendar to devise a learning schedule. Mark important dates for this class.

- Enter all test dates and due dates for papers.
- Divide reading assignments in the textbook and record as daily and weekly goals. Leave several days for study and review before tests.
- Record dates for completing extra reading.
- Analyze assigned projects and create daily or weekly goals.
- Designate dates for completing the first draft of written reports.

Act Successful

Successful people share certain observable characteristics. Study those characteristics and discover the accompanying behaviors. Then imitate the behaviors of successful people. The following example demonstrates students behaving in the opposite manner.

College Professor "Takes" American History

In order to prepare for a course to assist students in learning history, I "took" American History 113. I put the word *took* in quotation marks because I skipped the hard part; I did not take the exams. I did, however, attend class, take notes, observe, and learn.

Since the university operated on the quarter system at that time, classes meet for ten weeks with an extra week for exams. My particular class met on Tuesdays and Thursdays from 10:50 to 1:05, which means the class lasted for two hours and fifteen minutes. I attended all but one class.

I had an excellent professor who seemed concerned that students learn and make good grades. In fact, after the first class, I would have been astonished if any student could fail. To my amazement, the professor actually distributed a list of ten questions from which he would choose the two essay questions on the first exam. After talking with students in other classes, I learned that this was not unusual; many professors distributed lists of possible exam questions.

As the course progressed, I noticed that some students were their own worst enemies. I could see opportunities for learning that students were ignoring. I began taking notes on student behaviors, as well as my regular notes on the history lectures. From my observations, not just of a few class sessions, but of the entire duration of the course, I formed some opinions about why some students make A's and others barely pass or even fail. For example, I observed that many students skipped class or came late; some took very sketchy lecture notes; students rarely talked to each other; and many students did not seem to have grasped clearly defined expectations. Although my observations were made only in a history course, after talking to other students and professors, I believe that the behaviors necessary for success apply to most college courses. I wanted to say to some individuals, "You are shooting yourself in the foot." Some of the suggestions outlined below are simple and obvious, yet many students ignored them.

Attend Class

"I missed the last class. Did we do anything?" Does this sound familiar? Although the class lasted almost two and a half hours and covered too much to repeat, some students seem unconvinced that an absence puts them at a disadvantage. In my history class, the professor used the exam questions as a guide to the lectures. I was astounded at how many students skipped classes. Even though 40 students were registered for the course, no more than 33 ever showed up at any one session. At the session after the midterm, only 17 students were present. I asked myself, "Why would a student pay for a course, yet not take advantage of the instruction?" Professors cannot teach students who are not there.

Assume some of the responsibility for your class sessions. If your interest is not sufficiently stimulated, move beyond blaming it all on the professor. Ask questions and participate in class discussions. Arrive prepared so class sessions will be more meaningful. Talk with other students. Suggest ideas to the professor. Every class period can be significant if you, the professor, and other class members participate in making it meaningful.

Be on Time for Class

Professors usually begin with important reminders about test questions, assignments, or papers, and then give an overview of what will be discussed in class that day. If you come late, you arrive for the details and miss the "big picture." You put yourself at a disadvantage and must scramble to catch up. In my history class, sometimes as many as seven students arrived late, strolling into class with sodas and snacks, suggesting they did not make a prompt arrival their first priority.

Be Aware of Essential Class Sessions

Always strive for a solid beginning, a "fast start," rather than a shaky one. At the first class meeting students usually ask questions to clarify the syllabus, and the professor responds with important, unwritten details that can help you improve your grades. For example, does your history professor expect you to memorize dates, to understand the causes and effects of social change, or to critique historical interpretations? Goals such as these will be explained on the first day.

Students who do not attend the last class before an exam put themselves at an extreme disadvantage. By this time, the professor has usually written the exam and feels pressured to cover anything that he or she will ask on the test that has not been discussed previously in class. Student questions usually prompt a brief but extremely helpful review that pinpoints essential areas of study. Hearing the professor comment, "That's not really important," helps you eliminate study areas and save time. In addition, be sure you have studied enough before this session so that you know which things you need to clarify.

Never miss an exam unless you are on your death bed! The exam makeup may be in a noisy study area or scheduled two weeks later. This could mean you receive academic feedback too late to use it to improve. "Makeup" is just what the word implies, trying to move from behind to regain a position. Unfortunately, I observed that some students did not start studying or take the course seriously until after the first exam. Be sure to be in class when exams are returned. Listen to the professor's description of a good answer. Learn from the professor's responses to other students. Find out what you did right, what you did wrong, and exactly what is expected. Also, find out who made the best grades and ask those students how they studied. The exam and subsequent discussions help you understand expectations and set your future learning goals.

Be Equipped for Success

Some students arrive on the first day of class without paper and end up writing lecture notes on the back of the syllabus. Others arrive prepared to get organized and learn. Every college student should have the equipment listed in Exercise 3. Put a check mark next to each item of equipment that you have with you.

exercise 3

_____ Assignment calendar with large daily spaces

_____ Three-ring notebook for organizing papers

_____ Spiral notebook for lecture notes

_____ Three-ring plastic hole puncher for putting handouts in notebook

_____ Notebook paper

_____ Notebook dividers (at least five) or flags for organizing by topic

_____ Some sort of container in which to keep the following:

_____ pencil	_____ regular pen
_____ erasable pen	_____ highlighter
_____ correction fluid	_____ small pencil sharpener
_____ small stapler	_____ small "Post-it" notes
_____ small binder clips	

Mark Your Text

Get the most from your books and use them as learning tools. Read your textbooks with a pen or highlighter in hand and mark information that you will most likely need to know later. A well-marked textbook is much more of a treasure than an unmarked one, a treasure that you may want to keep as a reference for later courses.

Don't miss an opportunity to learn by being reluctant to mark in your text. Marking your text actively involves you in reading and studying. Some books, such as this one, are workbooks. The small amount of money that you receive in a textbook resale may not be worth what you have lost in active involvement. Use this book to practice, to give and get feedback, and to keep a record of your progress.

Communicate with Your Instructor

Don't be an anonymous student. Let your professor know who you are. Get your money's worth and more. Make a special effort to speak to your professor about assignments you found interesting or something you did not understand. Overcome your fear and seek help when you need it. Contrary to popular opinion, good students are more likely to seek help than weak ones. Visit during office hours. Professors want their students to be successful.

Review Your Lecture Notes

Review your lecture notes after each class session. Recite to yourself what the professor said. Identify gaps of knowledge and seek clarification. This kind of review reinforces your learning and reminds you of what the professor thinks is important. Unfortunately, most students wait until test time to review notes, thus missing these easy opportunities to solidify learning. Your own notebook is a valuable resource; use it.

Network with Other Students

Use the other students in the classroom as learning resources. For the first four weeks of my history class, almost none of the students spoke to each other. I was amazed. Even when I arrived five or ten minutes early to observe behavior, no one spoke. Most stared straight ahead, some read the history text, and some read the newspaper. After the first exam, however, students started to compare scores and to talk about correct answers.

Research with college students all over the country has shown that students who are part of a study group are less likely to drop out of school. However, many bright college students are loners. They do not know how to network and think that studying in groups is cheating. In fact, study groups teach students to collaborate and to form academic bonds. Networking is important for all students, including older, returning students who may initially feel out of the mainstream. Put fellow students on your learning team.

Begin your team building on the first day of class. In each course, ask for the name, telephone number, and e-mail address of at least two other students. Write this information in your text or lecture notebook so you won't lose it. These names and numbers are insurance policies. If you are absent or are unclear on an assignment, call a classmate for clarification, homework, and lecture notes. Students *can* help other students. Begin your network right now with two people. Don't be bashful.

Classmate ＿＿＿＿＿＿   Phone ＿＿＿＿＿＿   E-mail ＿＿＿＿＿＿

Classmate ＿＿＿＿＿＿   Phone ＿＿＿＿＿＿   E-mail ＿＿＿＿＿＿

Collaborate to Divide Work

Find a "study buddy" to share the work. In my history class, only two essay questions would be chosen for the exam from the list of ten distributed on the first day. The professor expected answers to include information from the lectures, as well as details from the history text. To be thoroughly prepared for the exam, each student should have a study outline answering each of the ten questions. Such an assignment presents an obvious opportunity to cut work in half. Why not get a study buddy and each prepare five possible essay answers and share? Seize every opportunity to collaborate and divide work efficiently.

Look at an "A" Paper

When exams are returned, always find out the correct answers. For essay responses, always ask to see an "A" paper. Ask the professor or a top-scoring student to allow you "an opportunity to read an excellent paper." Who would deny such a request? Analyze the "A" paper to determine how you can improve. Ask yourself, "What is this student doing that I'm not doing?" Even if you made an "A" yourself, read another paper. Maybe your next exam response will earn an

"A+." In my history class, I noticed that the good students sought examples, but the weak students slipped out of the room without seeking any help or insight from others.

Use Technology to Communicate

Do you need to meet face to face to study together? Conflicting class and work schedules make getting study groups together difficult. The telephone, the fax machine, and e-mail can eliminate some of those barriers. Outlines, lecture notes, and mathematics problems can be discussed and sent back and forth rapidly. You and your study buddy can communicate without wasting time commuting.

Consider a Tape Recorder

If your professor talks fast and you have trouble taking notes, try using a tape recorder. Do not use the recorder as an excuse to postpone the organizing and priority setting involved in notetaking. Instead, use the audio replay as another sensory tool for learning. The tiny tape recorders now available make this option fairly convenient. One history student said she listened to the replays while driving her car or fixing dinner.

Pass the First Test

Always overprepare for the first exam. Success on the first exam builds confidence, allays fears, and saves you from trying desperately to come from behind.

Watch Videos

Visual learning is powerful. Find videos on subjects covered in your text. Use the college library, the public library, and well-stocked video stores. If you are studying the Great Depression, check out a video of newsreel clips or watch *The Grapes of Wrath*, a drama set in that period based on the classic novel by John Steinbeck. For an introductory psychology course, check the college library for a movie on Sigmund Freud or theories of personality.

Predict Exam Questions

Predict both essay questions and multiple-choice items for exams. Not all professors provide possible essay questions and study guides. On your own you can review your textbook's table of contents and turn major headings into possible essay questions. Turn chapter titles into essay questions. Consider subheadings and boldface print a ripe source of multiple-choice items. Review lecture notes for any indication the professor has given about areas of special importance. Ask previous students about the professor's exams. The format and questions on a major exam should not come as a total shock to you. Predict and be prepared.

Get Moving Now

Phillip C. McGraw, a professional psychologist, has worked with clients in strategic life planning for over twenty years. He advised Oprah Winfrey during the highly publicized "mad cow" lawsuit and appears regularly on her television show. In his book *Life Strategies*, McGraw explains his ten laws of life. The fifth law seems particularly appropriate as you turn your dreams and knowledge into actions to achieve academic success.

LIFE LAW #5: LIFE REWARDS ACTION

Your Strategy: Make careful decisions and then pull the trigger. Learn that the world couldn't care less about thoughts without actions.

The responses and results that you receive from anyone, in any situation, are triggered by the stimuli you provide. The stimuli are your behaviors. This is the only way people can get to know you, and decide whether to reward or punish you. If you behave in a purposeless, meaningless, unconstructive way, you get inferior results. If you behave in purposeful, meaningful, constructive ways, you get superior results. That is how you create your own experience. When you choose the behavior (the action), you choose the consequences. The better the choices, the better the results; the better the behavior, the better the results. But the bottom line is that, if you do nothing, you get neither. Life rewards action.

People don't care about your intentions. They care about what you do.

Procrastination—mere intention—is the bane of human existence. Assigned to a geriatric rotation while serving my internship at a V.A. psychiatric hospital, I had the opportunity to do "therapy" with a number of elderly veterans whose life circumstances had led them to our hospital. I put the word *therapy* in quotation marks, because in most of these encounters the patient was the teacher, and, in all honesty, I was the student.

These men, from all walks of life and all levels of education and sophistication, taught this young doctor some important things in life. Paramount among those lessons was that every single one of them, approaching the end of his life, wished that he had done things that he had not. One regretted that he had never returned to the Philippines to visit the grave of an army buddy; another had dreamed of publishing his detective stories, but "never got up the guts" to send off any manuscripts; another wished that he had spent more time with his teenage granddaughter before her tragic death in a car accident.

Every one of them, in one way or another, said, "Doc, don't waste it, son. When it's over, it's over." With the wisdom of age and experience, each told me that he had intended so much more than he had ever done. They talked not only of actions not taken and opportunities lost, but of *timing*. It is true that life presents windows of opportunity. Very often, the window of opportunity will be open for a time, but then slam shut forever. As you evaluate your life in the areas and the categories in which you feel moved to take action, recognize that you have to seize the opportunities when they present themselves, and create them when they do not.

The time-honored formula for taking purposeful action goes like this:

Be
Do
Have

What the formula says is BE committed, DO what it takes, and you will HAVE what you want. *The difference between winners and losers is that winners do things losers don't want to do.* Notice the word *do* in that statement.

My dad's life was a lesson about action. At the age of seventy-one, thirty years after earning his Ph.D. in psychology, he enrolled in the seminary with the intention of earning a Master of Divinity degree. The problem was exhaustion: his heart was so bad he could only walk fifty feet at a time, so he had to get to campus thirty minutes before class. Then, from the parking lot, he had mapped out a route as complicated as any pass pattern in the NFL: fifty steps to the park bench and rest; thirty-seven steps to the tree stump and rest, and so on, every day, all to go 150 yards. But he saw it through. Ultimately, after two years and I don't know how many rest breaks, my dad stepped onto the dais to receive his diploma, and the whole arena erupted in cheers. So don't tell me about how hard it is to do things.

—*Life Strategies* by Phillip C. McGraw

PERSONAL Feedback 4   Name _____

1. What procrastination tactics do you use to delay homework?

   _____

2. Describe a personal intention that you regret not putting in action.

   _____

3. What specific activities do you think academic winners do that academic losers do not want to do? _____

   _____

4. Why might speaking up in class be considered risk taking? _____

   _____

5. What are the rewards for speaking up in class? _____

   _____

6. Describe a situation in which you have sought help individually from a college instructor. _____

   _____

Summary Points

- To become a winner, think like a winner.
- Formulate a dream that you turn into reality.
- Create the self-image of a star. Believe in your possibilities, and feel "born to win."
- Imitate the characteristics and behaviors of successful students.
- Decode your syllabus on the first day and keep it for ready reference.
- Use a calendar to list your test dates, as well as daily and weekly learning goals.
- Beware of unlimited freedom.
- Attend class on time and participate in making it successful.
- Ask to read the papers of top-scoring students.
- Talk to fellow students about class assignments.
- Review lecture notes after each class and seek clarification from fellow students.
- Ask someone to be your study buddy.
- Use technology to help you learn.
- Predict exam questions.
- Remember that life rewards action.

PERSONAL Feedback 5

Name _____

Name _____

Address _____

_____

Home Phone _____

E-mail address _____

Other classes this term and class hours: _____

_____

_____

_____

Place of work _____

Work schedule _____

Work phone _____

Explain any special concerns about this course or your learning that might be helpful to your instructor. _____

_____

_____

_____

List any questions that you would like to ask your instructor.

_____

_____

_____

COLLABORATIVE PROBLEM SOLVING

Form a five-member group and select one of the following questions. Brainstorm and then outline your major points on a transparency. Choose a member to present the group findings to the class.

▶ Make a list of the top ten ways college students waste time.

▶ Make a list of the top ten lifestyle (nutritional and fitness) errors made by college students.

▶ Make a list of the top ten ways to overcome procrastination.

▶ Write instructions for getting an e-mail address on your campus.

EXPLORE THE NET

If your college offers free e-mail addresses for students, sign up for the service. If not, investigate the following for a free address:

Hotmail

www.hotmail.com

Bigfoot

www.bigfoot.com

Excite

www.excite.com

Begin the course by opening the lines of communication with your "team members."

● Send an e-mail message to your instructor, just to say, "Hi! I am happy to be in your course, and I want to do well."

● Create a group address list of at least two classmates and send them e-mail messages. Say, "Do you remember me? Let's stay in touch to clarify assignments."

EVERYDAY READING SKILLS

Searching the Internet

The **Internet** is an electronic system of more than 25,000 computer networks initially developed by the U.S. Defense Department in the 1960s. It is the backbone for an information network called the **World Wide Web (WWW)** or, simply, "the Web."

The WWW is similar to an enormous library; the Web sites are like books, and the Web pages are like the pages in the books. These pages can contain written text, photographs, graphics, music, sound effects, movies, and animation. Although learning to use the Internet can be intimidating and frustrating at first, you can very quickly become a proficient navigator.

For finding your way on the Web, you need specific directions, just as you need an address and zip code to mail a letter. A **uniform resource locator (URL)** provides those directions. A URL is similar to an e-mail address, except that it routes you to a source of information called a *Web page* or *Web site* rather than to the mailbox of an individual person. URLs are made up of several parts, as shown in the following address for the Web site for the Emory University Health Sciences Center Library:

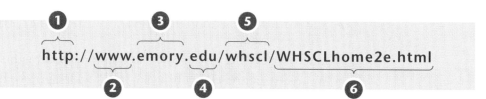

The following is a key to the numbered components of the sample URL.

1. **Protocol** This is standard for web addresses and indicates *Hypertext Transfer Protocol*, the type of language computers on the Internet use to communicate with each other. (Note that most browsers will automatically add the protocol "http://" before the address once you type it.)
2. **Server name** This indicates the computer network over which you will "travel" to reach the desired location. In most cases, this will be the World Wide Web.
3. **Domain name** This is a name registered by the Web site owner.
4. **Domain type** This indicates the category to which the site owner belongs.
5. **Directory path** This indicates a particular location within the Web site's host computer.
6. **File name** This indicates a specific file within the host's directory

Such an address will take you to the site's **home page,** which you can think of as the main terminal through which you can reach other areas of the site. Like e-mail addresses, URLs must be typed with no mistakes.

Locate a Web Site

After you have entered the URL and reached the desired Web site, get an overview of what the site has to offer by scanning headlines, graphics, buttons, animation, category headings, and tables of contents. These will give you an idea of how the site is organized and where to go to find what you want. Look for the following elements to help find your way:

- **Headlines and Topic Headings** These provide a quick overview of what the site has to offer. By clicking on them, you often move automatically to a subsequent section of the site, which might mean moving to another part of the same page or jumping to a new page or file within the same site.
- **Graphics** (including photos) As with headlines, at a glance these enable you to understand how a site is organized. Clicking on them usually moves you to the section of the site they represent.
- **Buttons** These are often shown next to headings or graphics; clicking them moves you to the desired location.
- **Hypertext Links** Usually referred to simply as **links**, these phrases appear as bold blue, underlined text. Clicking on them not only moves you from one page to another within the site, but can also send you to other related Web sites. The words chosen and underlined as the link generally describe the information you are likely to find at that destination.

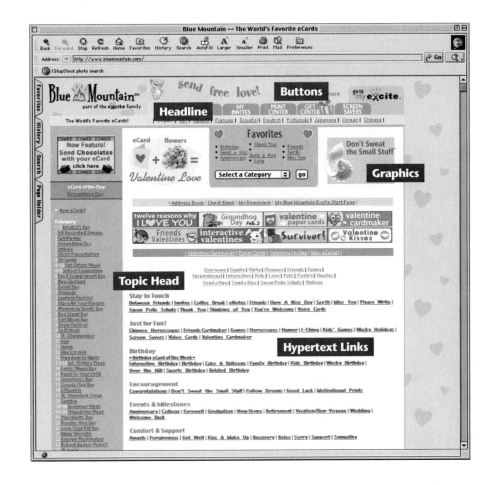

| exercise 1 | Research to locate the following on the Empire State Building. First, go to the Empire State Building's Web site (www.esbnyc.com) and examine the different headings. Then go to the appropriate pages to answer the following questions. |

1. When did construction on the Empire State Building begin? _____

   _____

2. How much does it cost to go up to the observatories? _____

   _____

   _____

3. What time does the Empire State Building Observatory typically close?

   _____

4. List two of the museum's famous visitors: _____

   _____

Conduct a Search

The most intimidating part of navigating the Internet may be learning how to find the information you want. You do this by conducting a *search* for your topic. There are several steps that can help organize your search and make it more rewarding:

1. Make a Plan

Locating information on the Web requires using a **search engine,** which is a program that looks throughout the Internet for information. Several different companies offer their own versions. They can be found at such Web sites as Yahoo, AltaVista, Excite, Go.com, or Lycos (a partial listing of available search engines follows). Thus, once you are connected to the Internet, you type in www.yahoo.com or just yahoo.com to get to the search engine.

No matter which one you choose, you will need to enter a keyword(s) or phrase in a search text box to describe the information you want. The search engine searches the Internet for sites that contain that word or phrase and displays a list of the first 10 to 25 sites (called *hits*). The more specific your description the better. For example, entering "Star-Spangled Banner" will result in a large list of sites about the history of the song.

Popular Search Engines and Their URLs

Excite
www.excite.com

Go.com
www.go.com

Webcrawler
www.webcrawler.com

Yahoo
www.yahoo.com

Lycos
www.lycos.com

2. Search and Search Again

Your initial search may be so specific that you get very few hits or it may be so general that you get thousands, many of which are not appropriate to your research. Either way, you may have to try several searches before finding what you need. Making a list of any key terms that relate to your topic can be helpful. *Star-Spangled Banner, Francis Scott Key,* and *the National Anthem,* for example, are all related topics that might help get you started. Scan a few of the hits your initial search produces to find other related terminology, names, and events that could be helpful.

For a comparison, use the following different search engines to look up Cleopatra, the Egyptian queen. Record the number of hits you find for each of the following:

Yahoo   _____

Excite   _____

Go.com   _____

3. Read Selectively

It is usually not practical to read all the available information the Internet has to offer on a given subject. Read selectively to narrow the scope of your research. After a search, scan the list of hits to find keywords related to your research. The sites that contain the most appropriate information are usually listed first. A summary of each site may also be included. When you go to a particular Web site, read titles, subtitles, links, tables of contents, outlines, or introductory paragraphs to determine if the information is appropriate to your research.

Reader's TIP Limiting Your Search

- Enter **"AND"** or a + sign between each word of your search. For example, using the words *Apple Computer* for your search will turn up thousands of hits that include not only sites about the company, but also sites related to apple (the fruit) and sites about computers in general. Using *AND* in your key phrase (*Apple AND Computer*) will return sites that only contain both words in the phrase.
- Enter **"OR"** to broaden a search. *Apple OR Computer* will return sites that contain information about either apples or computers.
- Enter **"NOT"** to exclude items. *Apple AND Computer NOT fruit* will exclude sites that mention fruit and computers.
- Use quotation marks when you want only hits that contain the exact phrase such as "Apple Computer Financial Report for 2001."

4. Record Your Sources

As you progress in your search, keep track of keywords and phrases you have used as well as the results they produce. When you find a site to which you would like to return or one that you would like to use as a reference in your research, there are several options:

- *Write down* the URL next to the term used to find it so you can return to it later.

- *Print* the Web site material. You will have a hard (paper) copy to keep that usually lists the URL at the top of the printout.
- *Bookmark* or save the site. **Bookmarking** (or adding to *Favorites*, depending on your particular Web browser) lets you automatically return to the Web site with just one or two mouse clicks. If you will not have access to the same computer in the future, saving (or *exporting*, depending on your Web browser) a copy of the text of the Web page to disk will enable you to take it with you for reference on a different computer.

Reader's TIP Using Institutional Indexes

Indexes are *databases* that categorize articles according to topics for easy access. Check with your library for the following popular college databases that are paid for by your institution:

Galileo
Periodical Abstracts
Newspaper Abstracts
Lexis-Nexis Academic Universe
MLA Bibliography
ABI Inform
Psyc FIRST
Social Science Abstracts
ERIC
MEDLINE

exercise 3

Using the search engine of your choice, locate three Web sites with information on the European Union. List each site and briefly describe the focus of the information.

1. _____

2. _____

3. _____

WEEKLY TIME CHART

Time	Sunday	Monday	Tuesday	Wednesday	Thursday	Friday	Saturday
8–9							
9–10							
10–11							
11–12							
12–1							
1–2							
2–3							
3–4							
4–5							
5–6							
6–7							
7–8							
8–9							
9–10							
10–11							
11–12							

Stages of Reading

- What is reading?
- Do you know when you don't know?
- What is schema?
- What do good readers think about as they read?
- How can you remember what you read?

Everyday Reading Skills: Reading News and Feature Stories in the Newspaper

What Is the Reading Process?

In the past, experts thought of reading comprehension as a *product*. They assumed that if you could pronounce the words fluently, you would automatically be able to comprehend. Instruction focused on practicing and checking for the correct answers rather than on explaining comprehension skills. Newer approaches, by contrast, teach reading comprehension as a *process* in which you use your understanding of different skills or stages to achieve an understanding of the whole. Students are taught how to predict upcoming ideas, activate existing knowledge, relate old information with new, form a main idea, and make inferences.

Stages of Reading

Good reading is divided into the following three thinking stages:

- **Before reading:** *Preview* to find out what the material is about, what you already know about the topic, and what you need to find out while reading.
- **During reading:** *Anticipate* upcoming information, visualize and integrate old and new knowledge, and assess your own understanding in order to make adjustments.
- **After reading:** *Recall and react* to what you have learned.

During the past fifty years, many experts have devised study skills strategies that break these three thinking stages into small steps. A historical example is SQ3R, which was devised by Francis P. Robinson at Ohio State University. The letters stand for Survey, Question, Read, Recite, and Review. Any of the study systems can be successful, but all are designed systematically to engage the reader in thought *before, during,* and *after* reading.

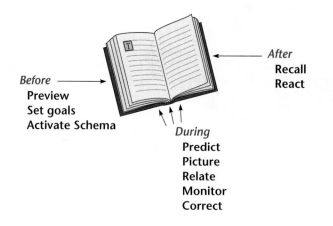

Before
Preview
Set goals
Activate Schema

After
Recall
React

During
Predict
Picture
Relate
Monitor
Correct

Stage One: Previewing

Previewing is a method of assessing the material, your knowledge of the subject, and your goals for reading. Try to connect with the topic and get an overview of the assignment before starting on the first paragraph. At the beginning of each new course, preview the table of contents of your new textbooks to get an overview of the scope of the material. Before reading a chapter, use the signposts such as subheadings, boldface or italic type, and summaries to anticipate what you will be learning.

Reader's TIP   Questions for Previewing

Use the following questions as guides to energize your reading and help you become an active learner:

1. What is the topic of the material?
2. What do I already know about the subject?
3. What is my purpose for reading?
4. How is the material organized?
5. What will be my plan of attack?

Signposts for Previewing. Consider the following typical features of college textbooks when previewing.

Learning Questions. Many textbook chapters start with questions designed to heighten your interest and stimulate your thinking. Such questions directly relate to what the material covers and thus help you set goals.

Title. The title of a book, chapter, or article is the first clue to its meaning. Some titles are designed to be clever to attract attention, but most try to communicate the important thought in the text. Identify the *who, what,* or *why* of the title to anticipate the content of the material and its importance to you.

Introductory Material. For an overview of a textbook, read the table of contents and the preface. The first highlights the book's contents, and the second gives the author's perspective on the subject. Many texts have a detailed outline that serves as a table of contents for each chapter. Others list probing questions that are answered in each chapter, or they begin with a summary of the chapter. Regardless of the specific feature provided, be sure to read the material to anticipate the content.

Subheadings. Subheadings are the titles of the sections within chapters that, like the major titles, describe the content. Usually subheadings appear in bold or italic type and outline the author's message. Turn the subheadings into questions to anticipate what you will need to know from the reading. For example, the subheadings in a marketing text, "Estimating Revenue Potential" and "Simulated Market Test," could be changed to "How Do You Estimate Revenue Potential?" and "What Is a Simulated Market Test?"

Italics, Boldface, and Numbers. Italic and bold type highlight words that merit special emphasis. These are usually terms that you will need to define and remember. Numbers are also used to list important details that you may need to learn.

Visual Aids or Marginal Notations. A biology professor at a major university tells his students to at least look at the illustrations and read the captions in the assigned material before coming to class, even if they don't read the assignment. He wants his students to have a visual overview. Authors use photos, charts, and graphs to enhance meaning, heighten interest, and help readers visualize information. Additional notations and definitions may be added in the page margins to further simplify the material for the reader.

Concluding Summary or Review. Most textbook chapters end with a summary of the most important points, which may be several paragraphs or a list of the important ideas. Regardless of its form, the summary helps you recall the material and reflect on its importance.

exercise 1

Read the table of contents of this text and glance through the chapters. Notice the format of the chapters and selectively scan the subheadings. Preview the text to answer the following questions:

1. How many major chapters are in this book? _____

2. Other than the obvious differences of topics covered, how does the organizational format of Chapter 3 differ from the format of Chapter 4?

   _____

   _____

3. What is the purpose of "Explore the Net"? _____

   _____

4. What is the purpose of Summary Points? _____

   _____

5. In which chapter would you find information on drawing conclusions?

   _____

6. In the chapter on the main idea, what are other words that are sometimes used to mean the same as main idea? _____

   _____

7. Name five college subjects represented in the longer selections at the end of the chapters. _____

8. In which chapter would you learn more about patterns of organization?

   _____

9. What is the purpose of Chapter 12? _____

   _____

10. In which chapter would you find hints on time management? _____

exercise 2

To get an overview of this chapter, look at the questions on the first page. Read the Summary Points on page 43 and scan to understand the subheadings and the boldfaced and italicized words. Preview the chapter to answer the following questions:

1. What is metacognition? _____

2. What is a schema? _____

   _____

3. What five thinking strategies do good readers use during reading? _____

_____

4. What college subjects are represented by the longer reading selections at the end of this chapter? _____

The Power of Prior Knowledge. Experts say that prior knowledge is the most important factor in reading comprehension. Thus, if you know very little about a subject, the initial reading in that area will be difficult. The good news, however, is that the more you know, the easier it is for you to read and learn. Every new idea added to your framework of knowledge about a subject makes the next reading assignment on the topic a little bit easier.

Students who already know a lot about history may think that American history assignments are easy. But students who perhaps excel in science and know little history might disagree. Because of prior knowledge, most students would probably agree that senior-level college courses are much easier than freshman survey courses.

PERSONAL Feedback 1   Name _____

1. What was your favorite subject in high school and why? _____

_____

_____

2. What magazines do you like to read? _____

_____

3. What sections do you like to read in the newspaper? _____

_____

4. What magazines did your family subscribe to during your high school years? _____

5. What is the best book you have read? _____

_____

6. What television programs do you watch regularly? _____

_____

7. How does prior knowledge seem to relate to your areas of greatest interest? _____

_____

Previewing to Activate Schemata. Your prior knowledge on a subject is a schema. According to theory, a **schema** (plural, *schemata*) is the skeleton of knowledge in your mind on a particular subject. As you expand your knowledge, the skeleton grows. Here's another way to think about a schema: A schema is like a computer chip in your brain that holds everything you know on a particular subject. You pull it out when the need arises, add to it, and then return it to storage.

Your preview of the material will help you know which "computer chips" to activate. It is your responsibility to call on what you already know and blend it with the new ideas. If you embellish the new thoughts with your past experience, your reading will become more meaningful.

Students tend to know more than they think they know. No matter how unfamiliar the topic may seem, you can probably provide some small link from your own experience. The written material provides the signals. It becomes *your* task to pick up those signals and use them to retrieve prior knowledge and form a link of understanding with the next text.

EXAMPLE Read the following sentence and activate your schema. Identify a knowledge link. Briefly describe an idea or image that comes to mind.

> Cuba became an obsession of American policy makers in 1959, when Fidel Castro and rebels of his 26th of July Movement ousted America's longtime ally Fulgencio Batista.
>
> —*A People and a Nation* by Mary Beth Norton et al.

EXPLANATION You may know little Cuban history, but you probably know that Miami, Florida, has a large and flourishing Hispanic population, begun by people who left Cuba. Do you know why they left Cuba? Link this knowledge of Cubans in Florida to the new information.

Stage Two: Integrating Knowledge

If you watch two students reading silently, can you tell which student comprehends better? Probably not. The behaviors of good silent readers are thinking behaviors that cannot be observed or learned by watching others. These behaviors, however, need not be mysterious to college students.

Knowing About Knowing. A myth in reading, probably inspired by the speed reading craze, is that good readers begin an assignment, race through it, and never stop until the last period. In fact, however, *good readers work hard* to assimilate the information they read. If they do not understand or if they get confused, they go back and reread to resolve the confusion. Good readers also understand the processes involved in reading and consciously control them. This awareness and control of the reading processes is called **metacognition,** which one expert defines as "knowing about knowing."[1]

Some students don't know when they don't know. They continue to read even though they are not comprehending. Poor readers tolerate such confusion because they either don't realize that it exists or don't know what to do about it.

---

[1]Ann L. Brown, "The Development of Memory: Knowing, Knowing About Knowing, and Knowing How to Know," in *Advances in Child Development and Behavior* (vol. 2), ed. H. W. Reese (New York: Academic Press, 1975).

Poor readers focus on facts, whereas good readers try to assimilate details into a larger cognitive pattern. Good readers monitor their own comprehension. In other words, they supervise their own understanding of the material. They recognize inadequate comprehension and interrupt their reading to seek solutions.

Five Thinking Strategies of Good Readers. In order to find out what good readers do, Beth Davey studied the research on good and poor readers. She discovered that good readers, both consciously and subconsciously, use the following five thinking strategies.[2]

1. Predict: Make Educated Guesses. Good readers make predictions about thoughts, events, outcomes, and conclusions. With the arrival of each new character in an Agatha Christie murder mystery, the reader makes a guess about who the culprit might be. Textbook predictions, although a little less dramatic, are equally important. While reading the facts in a science text, for example, you may be anticipating the concluding theory.

As you read, your predictions are confirmed or denied. If they prove invalid, you make new predictions. For example, in reading an economics text, you might predict that inflation hurts everyone. But after further reading, you discover that real estate investors make money by selling at the inflated prices. Thus your initial prediction proved invalid, and you readjusted your thinking on inflation. Your predictions involve you with the author's thinking and helped you learn.

EXAMPLE What are your predictions for the rest of the section based on these beginning sentences of a textbook paragraph?

> An industry that has been rocked by the Web is automobile retailing. Sites such as Auto-by-Tel, Microsoft Carpoint, and Autoweb.com provide the ultimate in convenience for car buyers. First, buyers can visit sites such as Edmunds to find out how much dealers actually pay for the cars. Armed with this information, buyers then go to these Web sites and . . .
>
> —*Marketing Management* by Russell Winer

EXPLANATION The rest of this section explains how buyers can bid on and order cars online. The Web has revolutionized car buying and is leaving the traditional dealer behind.

2. Picture: Form Images. For good readers, the words and the ideas on the page trigger mental images that relate directly or indirectly to the material. Because these mental images depend on the reader's experience, visualization is a highly individualistic process. One learner might read about Maine and picture the countryside and the rockbound coast, whereas another, with no experience in the area, might visualize the shape and location of the state on a map. Images are like movies in your head. You form a visualization to enhance the message in the text. Fiction quickly moves you into a new world of enjoyment or terror through visualization. Expository or textbook writing may require more imagination than fiction, but the images created also strengthen the message.

---

[2]Adapted from Beth Davey, "Think Aloud—Modeling the Cognitive Processes of Reading Comprehension," *Journal of Reading*, 27 (Oct. 1983): 44–47.

EXAMPLE Describe your visualizations for the following sentence.

> A dress so loud it hurts my eyes. There are yellows and oranges enough to throw back the light of the sun. I feel my whole face warming from the heat waves it throws out. Earrings gold, too, and hanging down to her shoulders. Bracelets dangling and making noises when she moves her arm . . .
>
> —*Everyday Use for Your Grandmama* by Alice Walker

EXPLANATION Imagine a woman dressed in yellows and oranges that are perhaps too bright with long earrings and dangling bracelets. Depending on prior knowledge, you may visualize someone you know.

3. Relate: Draw Comparisons. When you relate your existing knowledge to the new information in the text, you are embellishing the material and making it part of your framework of ideas. A phrase or a situation may remind you of a personal experience that relates to the text. For example, a description of ocean currents may remind you of a strong undertow you once fought while swimming. Such related experiences help you digest the new experience as part of something you already know.

EXAMPLE Describe a previous experience that the following excerpt brings to mind.

> A few years ago country singer Garth Brooks tried to prevent his latest album from being sold to any chain or store that also sells used CDs. His argument was that the used-CD market deprived labels and artists of earnings. His announcement came after Wherehouse Entertainment, Inc. started selling used CDs side by side with new releases, at half the price.
>
> —*Economics Today*, 1999–2000 Edition, by Roger Leroy Miller

EXPLANATION Have you ever bought used CDs? If so, did the store also sell new releases? Is this example similar to the used textbook market at your college bookstore?

4. Monitor: Check Understanding. Monitor your ongoing comprehension to test your understanding of the material. Keep an internal summary of the information as it is presented and how it relates to the overall message. Your summary will build with each new detail as long as the author's message is consistent. If, however, certain information seems confusing or erroneous, stop and seek a solution to the problem. Monitor and supervise your own comprehension. Remember that poor readers continue to read even when confused, but good readers seek to resolve the difficulty. Good readers demand complete understanding and know whether it has been achieved.

EXAMPLE What is confusing about the following sentence?

> "Another such victory like that on July 1," wrote Richard Harding Davis, "and our troops must retreat."
>
> —*America and Its People*, Third Edition, by James Martin et al.

EXPLANATION The words *retreat* and *victory* refer to opposite ideas. Usually the defeated army retreats. Davis must mean that the victory was too costly, and thus was hardly a victory at all. Thus Davis is speaking sarcastically, but a second reading might be necessary to figure this out.

5. Correct Gaps in Understanding. Do not accept gaps in your reading comprehension. They may signal a failure to understand a word or a sentence. Stop and resolve the problem so you can continue to synthesize and build your internal summary. Seek solutions to confusion. Usually, this means rereading a sentence or looking back at a previous page for clarification. If an unknown word is causing confusion, the definition may emerge through further reading. Changing predictions is also a corrective strategy. For example, while reading a geography textbook you may be predicting that heavy rains saved a country from famine, but, as the conclusion emerges, it seems that fertilizers and irrigation were the saviors. If you cannot fill the gaps yourself, seek help from the instructor or another student.

EXAMPLE   How could you seek to better understand the following paragraph?

> Contemporaries cited more pressing needs. "We are a new country," a Boston doctor reminded his son, who wished to pursue a scientific career. "We have, as it were, just landed on these shores; there is a vast deal to be done; and he who will not be doing, must be set down as a drone."
> —*Biology: A Journey into Life,* Second Edition, by Karen Arms and Pamela Camp

EXPLANATION   Did the father want his son to study science or not? Do you know the meaning of *contemporaries* and *drone*? Do you understand the phrase *pressing needs*? Is the father's attitude in contrast with attitudes today and thus unexpected? After using the correction strategies of defining and rereading, you will unravel that the father said no to science.

Applying All Five Thinking Strategies. The following passage illustrates the use of the five thinking strategies. Some of the reader's thoughts appear as handwritten comments in the margins. Keep in mind that each person reacts differently. This example merely represents one reader's attempt to integrate knowledge.

EXAMPLE   Do the handwritten thoughts also represent your thoughts?

A BREATH FOR FASHION

In 1800s? Nineteenth-century doctors were taught that men and women breathed differently: men

What is a diaphragm? used their diaphragms to expand their chests, whereas women raised the ribs near the

How did they breathe? top of the chest. Finally, a woman doctor found that women breathed in this way be-

Is it healthy? cause their clothes were so fashionably tight that the diaphragm could not move far

Are they victims of enough to admit air into the lungs. Some women even had their lower ribs removed sur-

fashion? gically so that they could lace their waists more tightly.

> —*Biology: A Journey into Life,* Second Edition, by Karen Arms and Pamela Camp

EXPLANATION   The handwritten comments model the reader's conscious and subconscious thoughts. Such an analysis may seem artificial and intrusive, but be aware that you do incorporate thinking strategies like these into your reading. The following exercises are designed to make you more aware of this interaction.

exercise 3

For the following passages, answer the questions and make a conscious effort to use the five strategies as you read:

1. Predict (develop hypotheses).
2. Picture (develop images).
3. Relate (link prior knowledge with new ideas).
4. Monitor (clarify ongoing comprehension).
5. Use corrective strategies (solve comprehension problems).

Passage 1

LANGUAGE PREFERENCES OF NEWBORNS

Eight 2-day-old infants who were born into monolingual English homes and eight 2-day-old infants who were born into monolingual Spanish homes were tested to determine whether they could discriminate between their own and another language. A contingent reinforcement procedure was used, in which infants learned to control the presentation of audio recordings of women speaking in either Spanish or English by sucking on a pacifier that was connected to a computer. The harder and longer the infants sucked, the longer they could control the length of time they heard the voices. After spending about 12 minutes learning how to control the voices through sucking, twelve of the sixteen infants showed the expected pattern: they activated the recordings in their native language for longer periods than they did the recordings in the foreign language (Moon, Cooper, & Fifer, 1993). The two days over which the infants were exposed to their native language after birth may have influenced their preferences, but the researchers believe that it is more likely that their prenatal experiences determined their preferences for their native language.

—*Exploring Child Development* by Richard Fabes and Carol Lynn Martin

1. What results did you predict? _____

2. Where would you envision these newborns were tested? _____

   _____

3. Do you know anyone who read and played music for an unborn child during pregnancy? Explain why you would or would not recommend either.

   _____

4. Why do you think the intensity of sucking on the pacifier was used as a

   measure? _____

5. Underline any part of the passage that you found confusing or needed to

   reread.

Passage 2

MONETARY POLICY

"It's as good as gold." That familiar cliché has been misleading for at least a decade. Had you invested $100 in a mutual fund made up of the Standard & Poor's 500 stock index 10 years ago, today you would have approximately $350. If you had put $100 into gold 10 years ago, today it would be worth $70.

—*Economics Today*, 1999–2000 Edition, by Roger Leroy Miller

1. How did you predict the cliché "It's as good as gold" would be contradicted?

   _____

2. How did you figure out the meaning of *cliché*? _____

   _____

3. Do you know anyone who has made money on the stock market recently?
   What was the stock? _____

4. Approximately how much better was stock than gold in the last decade?

   _____

5. Underline any part of the passage that you found confusing.

Stage Three: Recalling

Recall is your review of what you have read. Recall is self-testing and can be a silent, oral, or written recitation. When you recall, you take an additional few minutes to tell yourself what you have learned before you close the book. Poor readers tend to finish the last paragraph of an assignment, sigh with relief, and close the book without another thought. Study strategies developed by experts, however, stress the importance of a final recall or review stage. The experts emphasize that this final step improves both comprehension and memory.

As a part of monitoring your comprehension, maintain a running summary as you read. The end of an assignment is the time to give voice to this internal summary and review the material for gaps of knowledge. You can do the recall step in your head or on paper. To recall, talk to yourself and test your understanding. Pull the material together under one central idea or generalization, and then review the relevant details and commit them to memory.

Do not neglect this last stage. From a metacognitive point of view, you are adding related ideas to existing schemata and creating new knowledge networks or "computer chips" for storage. Recall makes a difference in what you retain from your reading.

How to Recall. The recall stage of reading can be either an internal, organized conversation with yourself or a written reorganization. What method you choose depends on the difficulty of the material or your purpose for learning. Keep in mind that the goal is self-testing. Rather than waiting for the professor's inquiry, answer your own question, "What did I get from this material?"

Reader's TIP   React and Reflect

After recalling what an author has said, evaluate its significance for you by answering the following questions:

- Did I enjoy the reading? Why or why not?
- Was the selection well written? Explain specifics.
- Do I agree or disagree with the author? Why or why not?
- How many of the ideas am I going to accept?

Feel free to accept or reject ideas according to your prior knowledge and the logic of the presentation. Your response is subjective, but as a critical thinker, you should base it on what you already know and what you have just found out.

EXAMPLE Read the following passage and decide what it is about and whether you agree or disagree with the author.

> Access is a very important resource for an interest group. As we have noted, a person who makes a campaign contribution will often say something like this: "I don't want any special promise from you; all I want is the right to come and talk to you when I need to." This seemingly modest request may in fact be significant. Access is power.
>
> —*American Democracy* by Fred Harris

EXPLANATION What is your position on the issue of access and power? You may agree with the author's position. The message is that if you can manage to talk to a powerful political figure, you have an excellent chance of influencing decisions. Because face-to-face contact can be convincing, access probably does give power.

exercise 4 Read the following passages and decide whether you agree or disagree with their messages. You are giving your *reactions* to the ideas, so there are no right or wrong answers. Think and react.

Passage 1

GENDER DIFFERENCES

Men and women differ with respect to gossip. It isn't that one group gossips and the other does not. [It is the subjects of their talks.] "When most men talk to their friends or on the phone," Tannen says, "they may discuss what's happening in business, the stock market, the soccer match, or politics." "For most women, getting together and talking about their feelings and what is happening in their lives is at the heart of friendship."

Men and women differ when it comes to lecturing and listening. Experimental studies support Tannen in finding that "men are more comfortable than women in giving information and opinions and speaking in an authoritative way to a group, whereas women are more comfortable than men in supporting others."

—*You Just Don't Understand: Women and Men in Conversation* by Deborah Tannen

1. What is the message? _____

_____

2. Why do you agree or disagree with these assertions of gender differences on gossip, lecturing, and listening?

   (a) Gossip? _____

   (b) Lecturing? _____

   (c) Listening? _____

Passage 2

TEACHING BABIES TO SWIM

Drowning is one of the most common accidents of childhood. In addition to falling into swimming pools, rivers, and lakes, children have drowned by toppling into toilets or buckets with just a few inches of water in them. In an effort to "drownproof" them, some parents enroll their children in infant swimming programs. Other parents enroll their infants in these programs because they believe that there is a critical period for learning to swim.

These programs should be viewed with caution for several reasons. The YMCA Division of Aquatics and the American Academy of Pediatrics recommend that parents wait until children are 3 years old before enrolling them in organized aquatic programs.

—Richard Fabes and Carol Lynn Martin, *Exploring Child Development*

1. What is the message? _____

_____

2. Do you agree or disagree and why? _____

3. What is missing in this argument? _____

_____

Assess Your Progress as a Learner

This textbook creates an artificial environment for you to learn about your own reading. Normally after reading, you do not answer ten comprehension questions and ten vocabulary questions. You read, reflect, and move on. In this book, however, the questions are provided to help you monitor your thinking. To improve your skills, reflect seriously on what you are getting right and what you are getting wrong. Getting a quick homework or classwork grade is part of the process, but it is not the real purpose. Understanding and improving are the goals, and they require your active participation as a learner. Assume responsibility for your own improvement.

Levels of Reading Comprehension

In order to give you more insight into your strengths and weaknesses, the comprehension questions at the end of each long reading selection in this text are labeled *main idea, detail,* and *inference.* These question types represent different levels of sophistication in reading that can be ranked and defined as follows:

1. Literal—What did the author say? These are detail questions about the facts, and the answers are clearly stated within the material. This is the beginning level of reading comprehension, the least sophisticated level. You might be able to answer detail questions but not understand the overall meaning of the passage.

Example: Africanized honeybees can remain agitated for 8 hours (True or False)

2. Interpretive—What did the author mean by what was said? These are main idea and inference questions. In order to answer, you must interpret the facts along with the author's attitude, using implied meaning to make assumptions and draw conclusions. At this level, you are considering both what is stated and what is unstated in order to figure out what the author is trying to say.

Example: In the college student's quoted observations, the phrase "gut classes" means classes that are: (a) difficult, (b) challenging, (c) easy, or (d) interesting.

3. Applied—How does the author's message apply to other situations? These are questions that call for reaction, reflection, and critical thinking. This is the highest level of sophistication and involves analyzing, synthesizing, and evaluating. You are putting together what was said with what was meant and applying it to new situations and experiences. You are attempting to make wider use of what you have just learned.

Example: How could terrorists use hypnotism to sabotage Pentagon security?

Use the questions in this book as diagnostic information. What do your responses tell you about yourself? What kinds of questions do you always answer correctly? What do your errors tell you about your reading? Learn from your mistakes and begin to categorize your own reading strengths and weaknesses. Throughout the course, refer back to previous work as a reference for your own development. Keeping records and reflecting on your own learning are essential parts of your improvement plan.

PERSONAL Feedback 2   Name _____

1. Why do you think students are reluctant to engage in stage three of reading, which is recalling what they have read? _____

   _____

2. What have you learned in this chapter that is positive about your reading habits?_____

   _____

3. What three immediate changes would you suggest for your own reading improvement?

   (a) _____

   (b) _____

   (c) _____

4. What did you learn in this chapter about the reading process that surprised you? _____

   _____

5. What myths did you have about reading that no longer seem to be true? _____

6. What is keeping you from becoming an excellent reader? _____

_____

7. What questions would you like to ask your instructor about the reading process? _____

_____

Summary Points

- Reading comprehension includes understanding an author's words, as well as what they suggest, and adding appropriate details.
- Good readers understand the processes of reading and consciously control them.
- Good readers anticipate content, structure, and purpose.
- Good readers activate their schemata by tapping previous knowledge.
- Good readers predict, picture, relate, monitor, and use corrective strategies.
- After reading, good readers pull the material together as one central idea and review the relevant details.
- Good readers evaluate the significance of what they have read, and they accept or reject new ideas.
- Good readers keep records of their own learning progress.

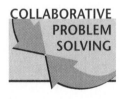

COLLABORATIVE PROBLEM SOLVING

Form a five-member group and select one of the following questions. Brainstorm and then outline your major points on a transparency. Choose a member to present the group findings to the class.

▶ Make a list of five questions about your college at the literal level.

▶ Make a list of five questions about your college at the interpretive level.

▶ Make a list of five questions about your college at the applied level.

▶ Explain how recalling, connecting, and reacting help you remember what you have read.

THINKING BEFORE READING

Preview the selection for clues to content. What do you already know about hypnosis? Activate your prior knowledge. Anticipate the author's ideas and your purpose for reading. Think!

Is hypnosis fake?

Would you be a good candidate for hypnosis? Why or why not?

If you were hypnotized, what posthypnotic suggestion would you like to receive?

I'll read this to find out_____

VOCABULARY PREVIEW

Are you familiar with these words?

focuses	selective	distracting	suggestible	babble
speculating	anesthesia	posthypnotic	regulating	squiggly

When is a posthypnotic suggestion actually given?

Is a stock purchase considered a speculation in the market?

Your instructor may give a true-false vocabulary review before or after reading.

THINKING DURING READING

As you read, use the five thinking strategies of a good reader: predict, picture, relate, monitor, and correct. Answer the questions in the margins that reflect your active thinking.

Reader's TIP   Reading and Studying Psychology

- Seek to understand abstract terms and confusing concepts through the concrete examples that illustrate them.
- Relate psychological theories to yourself and visualize people you know as examples.
- Memorize key terms with definitions and an example, especially for multiple-choice tests.
- Test yourself by turning each boldface heading into a question and recite your answer.
- Because much of psychology is about theories, connect the names of researchers with their theories. Learn characteristics and examples for each theory.
- Compare and contrast theories. For example, how do the social learning theorists differ from the behaviorists?
- Reduce your notes to visual diagrams. For example, to study personality theories, draw charts to list the comparative elements.

Hypnosis

Hypnosis has been known and used for many hundreds of years, since ancient times. But not until the last one hundred years has scientific study begun to help us understand hypnosis.

WHAT IS HYPNOSIS?

Several different things happen when a person is hypnotized. A hypnotized person doesn't make plans or control his or her own actions or thoughts. People in deep hypnosis, for example, don't seem to think anything unless the hypnotist tells them to. People in lighter hypnosis will sit waiting for the hypnotist to tell them what to do. Also, a hypnotized per-
5   son focuses attention in a very selective way. Things that would normally be distracting, such as a loud noise, aren't distracting. Attention is focused on the things the hypnotist says to focus on.

What are you visualizing?

Hypnotized people are very suggestible. If the hypnotist says, "There's a rhinoceros here, see it," they can see it. If the hypnotist points to a chair and says, "You cannot see
10   this," then they don't see it. Instead of dealing with reality themselves, they allow the hypnotist to tell them what is real and what is not. Hypnotized people will act out roles they usually don't perform. For example, the hypnotist can suggest that the person is really only one year old. The hypnotized person then will crawl around, babble like a baby, and act the way babies are supposed to act. Hypnotized people can be programmed by a
15   suggestion of the hypnotist to forget all they have seen or heard while hypnotized.

Do you know anyone who has been hypnotized?

Not all hypnotized people will show all these effects. There are different levels of hypnosis. People usually have to practice by being hypnotized several times in order to reach the deeper levels. Hypnosis is not sleep. The brain waves of hypnotized people are like those of people who are awake. If you feel like speculating, consider this: The brain waves
20   of people most easily hypnotized often show right cortex activation.

BEING HYPNOTIZED

Different techniques are used by hypnotists. Usually they ask the subject to concentrate on something. The subject has to cooperate. The hypnotist asks the subject to give up some control over the moment-to-moment events in the subject's life and turn over this control to the hypnotist. The hypnotist asks the subject to imagine things under the con-
25   trol of the hypnotist.

Some people are more easily hypnotized than others, some are never hypnotized. Some fall into deep hypnosis readily; most can attain some degree of hypnosis with practice. No one knows clearly why there are these differences. It is possible, however, to predict who will or will not be hypnotized by giving a test of suggestibility. For example, the
30   subject is asked to stand with eyes closed. After a few seconds, the experimenter says: "You're beginning to sway a little bit." Then the experimenter watches to see if the subject sways. (The experimenter must be prepared to catch the ones who really get into it.) People who show some effects from the suggestions of the experimenter are more easily hypnotized.

How could hypnotism be used positively?

35   Can you hypnotize someone against the person's will? Probably not. If the person had a lot of past experience with hypnosis, and you knew what cues set off the hypnosis, you might be able to arrange for the cues to happen and the person would go under. But that would be rare.

Would you be easy or difficult to hypnotize?

THE EFFECTS OF HYPNOSIS

Hypnosis is well known for the really dramatic effects that can sometimes be achieved.
40   Surgeons have successfully used it to suggest that the person can feel no pain. They have removed an appendix with no anesthesia. Hypnotists often suggest things such as: "Watch out for that charging rhinoceros." Then the hypnotized subject ducks and runs.

The person swears he can see and hear the animal. One hypnotist held up a piece of chalk and said: "This is a burning cigarette." He touched the arm of the subject with it, and a red mark appeared, just as if the subject had been burned. People can often re-member things under hypnosis that they can't remember in the normal state. This may be due to their increased focus of attention.

Another effect is gained by making a posthypnotic suggestion, so that the subject does something after coming out of the hypnosis. The subject is hypnotized and told: "After you wake up, watch what I do. When I scratch my ear, jump up and shout: 'The building is on fire!' Then sit down. You won't remember that I told you this. Okay, now when I count to three, wake up." Then later, in the middle of a class, for example, the hypnotist casually scratches an ear. Up jumps the subject and shouts: "The building is on fire!" Then the subject looks all around, sees the amused faces, gets red with embarrass-ment, and sits down. "Why did you do that?" asks the hypnotist. "I don't know," says the subject.

Are hypnotized subjects faking it? Not in any usual sense of the word "faking." When the subject is acting like a one-year-old, the subject really believes that he or she is one year old. Of course, some people do fake it, but an experienced hypnotist can distinguish them from the truly hypnotized subjects.

Can you use hypnosis to get people to do things they wouldn't do under different conditions? For example, will people violate their own ethical principles? It has hap-pened—not always, not predictably, but in a few cases. Under deep hypnosis a subject pulled a trigger on a gun that would have killed another person if it had been loaded. People have stuck their hands into pits of snakes they thought were dangerous.

Is it dangerous to play around with hypnosis? Yes. It's dangerous because the subject can become emotional or very dependent on you, and you aren't trained to deal with that. Will a person go under and never come out? No.

Could hypnotism help solve crimes?

Could evil people manipulate others through hypnotism?

WHAT'S GOING ON IN HYPNOSIS?

There are several theories. The old one was that hypnosis was a form of sleep, but re-search has shown this isn't true. Some researchers say: "It's a role the person plays, just like the role of mother, student, or lover. The role has certain things you're supposed to do, and other people expect you to do them. When you're hypnotized, you play the hypnotized role, doing what you think hypnotized people are supposed to do." This may be part of it, but some theories go further.

75   Hypnosis raises important questions about the organization of the human brain. We know there are levels of organization in the brain. As you read this, for example, a lower part of your brain is regulating your body temperature without your thinking about it. Another part is organizing all these little squiggly patterns on paper into words that make sense. Way up high, you are thinking. Some theorists have said that what happens in
80   hypnosis is that levels in the brain become disconnected. The subject's conscious level is restricted to the things the hypnotist suggests; nothing else is allowed into that consciousness. If the subject's arm is hurt, and the hypnotist says, "No, it's not," the subject doesn't experience the pain at the conscious level. It might as well not exist. All we are aware of is what we are conscious of. In hypnosis, goes this theory, the content of your
85   conscious brain comes under the direction of the hypnotist. Why this happens, or how it happens, is not known.

Do you believe this?

(1,237 words)

—*Psychology: What It Is/How to Use It* by David Watson

THINKING AFTER READING

RECALL   Self-test your understanding. Your instructor may choose to give a true-false review.

REACT   If you were a smoker, would you try hypnosis to help you stop smoking?

_____

_____

REFLECT   Describe three positive uses of hypnosis.

(1) _____

(2) _____

(3) _____

THINK CRITICALLY   How could terrorists use hypnotism to sabotage Pentagon security? Write your answer on a separate sheet of paper.

Name _____

Date _____

COMPREHENSION QUESTIONS

Answer the following with *a, b, c,* or *d,* or fill in the blank. In order to help you analyze your strengths and weaknesses, the question types are indicated.

Main Idea _____ 1. The author's primary purpose in this passage is

    a. to explain hypnosis and its effects.
    b. to encourage the use of hypnosis for adjustment problems.
    c. to explain why people want to be hypnotized.
    d. to summarize the need for hypnosis in modern society.

Detail _____ 2. Scientific study shows that hypnotized persons are all of the following *except*

    a. highly suggestible.
    b. concentrated in their attention.
    c. asleep.
    d. willingly controlled by the hypnotist.

Inference _____ 3. The author believes that

    a. everyone can be hypnotized.
    b. most people can be hypnotized who want to be.
    c. people can be hypnotized who don't want to be.
    d. most people fall into deep hypnosis readily.

Detail _____ 4. Under hypnosis people have been known to do all of the following *except*

    a. act in a manner harmful to their own bodies.
    b. violate their own ethical principles.
    c. never come out of the hypnotic state.
    d. imitate an animal behavior.

Inference 5. Some theorists believe that a person does not feel pain under hypnosis because _____

Inference _____ 6. According to the passage, it can be concluded that

    a. hypnosis is harmful and should not be used.
    b. hypnosis can be beneficial.
    c. hypnosis has been used only during the past hundred years.
    d. hypnotists are illegitimate hucksters.

Inference _____ 7. The author implies that a person who is easily hypnotized

    a. has a vivid imagination.
    b. is less intelligent than one who is difficult to hypnotize.
    c. has inadequate brain regulation.
    d. wants to maintain control.

Answer the following with *T* (true), *F* (false), or *CT* (can't tell).

Inference _____ 8. Posthypnotic suggestion can make a person engage in an atypical action while not under hypnosis.

Inference _____ 9. Hypnosis is more popular in the United States for entertainment than for relief of pain.

Inference _____10. Hypnosis is an example of mind over matter.

VOCABULARY

Answer the following with *a, b, c,* or *d* for the word or phrase that best defines the boldface word used in the selection. The number in parentheses indicates the line of the passage in which the word is located.

_____ 1. "**focuses** attention" (5)

    a. applies
    b. concentrates
    c. suggests
    d. recalls

_____ 2. "a very **selective** way" (5)

    a. general
    b. amateurish
    c. strict
    d. discriminating

_____ 3. "would normally be **distracting**" (5)

    a. diverting
    b. unsafe
    c. inspiring
    d. frightening

_____ 4. "are very **suggestible**" (8)

    a. sensible
    b. sensitive
    c. ignorant
    d. easily influenced

_____ 5. "**babble** like a baby" (13)

    a. misbehave
    b. converse intelligently
    c. make meaningless sounds
    d. play

_____ 6. "feel like **speculating**" (19)

    a. pondering
    b. talking
    c. changing
    d. remembering

_____ 7. "with no **anesthesia**" (41)

    a. doctor
    b. mental concern
    c. painkillers
    d. antibodies

_____ 8. "a **posthypnotic** suggestion" (48)

    a. before hypnosis
    b. after hypnosis
    c. during hypnosis
    d. nonhypnotic

_____ 9. "is **regulating** your body temperature" (77)

    a. increasing
    b. decreasing
    c. controlling
    d. simplifying

_____10. "little **squiggly** patterns" (78)

    a. straight
    b. meaningful
    c. organized
    d. twisted

ASSESS YOUR LEARNING

Review questions that you did not understand, found confusing, or answered incorrectly. Seek clarification. Indicate beside each item the source of your confusion and notice the question type. Beside confusing vocabulary items, make notes to help you remember the new word. Use your textbook as a learning tool.

EXPLORE THE NET

● Investigate the hypnosis-related conferences that are coming to an area near you. Would you be interested in attending a conference on reducing stress, stopping smoking, improving athletic performance, or relieving migraines? Select a conference with a focus that you would enjoy and find out the costs and the projected benefits. Try the following sites or conduct your own search.

National Guild of Hypnotists

www.ngh.net

World Hypnosis Organization

www.ngh.net

● Investigate the risks involved with hypnosis. Which risks would be of greatest concern to you and might impact your decision to attend a conference?

Hypnotica

www.rdoublel.com/hypnosis/faq.htm#safe

How Hypnosis Can Help You

www.theoaktree.com/hypover.htm

For additional readings and exercises, visit the *Breaking Through* Web site:

www.ablongman.com/smith

SELECTION 2   ⚗   **SCIENCE**

THINKING BEFORE READING

Preview the selection for clues to content. Activate your schema and anticipate what you will learn.

Why can bee stings be fatal to some people?

Could you escape from killer bees by jumping into water?

What animals or insects have been introduced into an unnatural environment and become pests?

I'll read this to find out _____

_____

VOCABULARY PREVIEW

Are you familiar with these words?

decades	invaded	agitated	sluggish	zippier
preliminary	dominant	intruding	squadron	continuous

How do a millenium and a decade differ?

Are blue eyes or brown eyes dominant?

What does the prefix *in* in *invaded* and *intruding* mean?

Your instructor may give a true-false vocabulary review before or after reading.

THINKING DURING READING

As you read, use the five thinking strategies of a good reader: predict, picture, relate, monitor, and correct. Answer the questions in the margins that reflect your active thinking.

⚗ **Reader's TIP   Reading and Studying Science**

- Master a concept by explaining it in your own words.
- Draw your own scientific models and diagram the processes to reinforce learning them.
- Use illustrations as a reading and review tool before exams.
- Use chapter summaries as study checklists to be sure you have reviewed all the chapter material.
- Think like a scientist at the textbook Web site by participating in virtual research activities.
- Use mnemonics to memorize. Remember the example—**M**any **P**eople **F**ind **P**arachuting **A**larming—to remember the five kingdoms, which are monera, protista, fungi, plantae, and animalia.
- Know the theories you are applying in the lab and their significance.
- Blend lecture, lab, and textbook notes.

The Killers Are Coming! The Killers Are Coming!

How far were they in United States in 2002?

In 1990, descendants of "killer" bees that flew out of South America a few decades earlier buzzed across the border between Mexico and Texas. By 1995, they had invaded 13,287 square kilometers of Southern California and were busily setting up colonies.

How can people escape?

5   When provoked, the bees behave in a terrifying way. For example, thousands flew into action simply because a construction worker started up a tractor a few hundred yards away from their hive. Agitated bees flew into a nearby subway station and started stinging passengers on the platform and inside the trains. They killed one person and injured a hundred others. Not too long ago, they put a couple of tree trimmers in Indio, California, in the hospital; they also killed two people in Texas and two in Arizona.

10   Where did these bees come from? In the 1950s some queen bees had been shipped from Africa to Brazil for selective breeding experiments. Why? It happens that honeybees are big business. In addition to being a source of nutritious honey, bees are rented to commercial orchards where their collective pollinating activities may make a significant contribution to the production of fruit. For example, if you position a screened cage around an

Do bees mean big money?

15   orchard tree that has blossomed out less than 1 percent of the tree's flowers will set fruit. Put a hive of honeybees in the same cage, and 40 percent of the flowers will set fruit.

Compared to their relatives in Africa, bees in Brazil are rather sluggish pollinators and honey producers. By cross-breeding the two varieties, researchers thought they might be able to come up with a strain of mild-mannered but zippier bees. They put local bees and

20   imported bees together inside netted enclosures complete with artificial hives. Then they let nature take its course.

What are the genetic dangers?

Twenty-six African queen bees escaped. That was bad enough. Then beekeepers got wind of preliminary experimental results. After learning that the first few generations of offspring were more energetic but not overly aggressive, they imported hundreds of

25   African queens and encouraged them to mate with the locals. And they set off a genetic time bomb.

Before long, African bees became established in commercial hives—and in wild bee populations. And their traits became dominant. The "Africanized" bees do everything other bees do, but they do more of it faster. Their eggs develop into adults more quickly.

Will the honeybees become extinct?

30   Adults fly more rapidly, outcompete other bees for nectar, and even die sooner.

When something disturbs their hives or swarms, Africanized bees become extremely agitated. They can remain that way for as long as eight hours. Whereas a mild-mannered honeybee might chase an intruding animal fifty yards or so, a squadron of Africanized bees will chase it a quarter of a mile. If they catch up to it, they collectively can sting it to death.

35   Doing things faster means having a continuous supply of energy and efficient way of using it. An Africanized bee's stomach can hold thirty milligrams of sugar-rich nectar—which is enough fuel to fly sixty kilometers. That's more than thirty-five miles!

How can they be stopped?

(507 words)

—*Biology: The Unity and Diversity of Life*, Eighth Edition, by Cecie Starr and Ralph Taggart

THINKING AFTER READING

RECALL   Self-test your understanding. Your instructor may choose to give a true-false review.

REACT   Why would government regulations allow the introduction of killer bees into Brazil? Would this be allowed in California? _____

_____

REFLECT   What was the sequence of events that got the bees from California? _____

_____

_____

THINK CRITICALLY   What environmentally sound suggestions would you make for ridding the United States of this killer bee population? Write your answer on a separate sheet of paper.

Name _____

Date _____

COMPREHENSION QUESTIONS

Answer the following with *a, b, c,* or *d,* or fill in the blank. In order to help you analyze your strengths and your weaknesses, the question types are indicated.

Main Idea _____ 1. The best statement of the main idea of this selection is

    a. "Africanized" bees are killing native bees and destroying crops.
    b. Aggressive "Africanized" bees are moving into the United States.
    c. Cross-breeding bees can enhance fruit production.
    d. Bees resulting from cross-breeding are highly aggressive.

Detail _____ 2. The passage states that bees have been sighted in all the following states *except*

    a. Texas.
    b. California.
    c. New Mexico.
    d. Arizona.

Inference _____ 3. In the examples, the author implies that the killer bees attack

    a. only when threatened.
    b. when provoked but not necessarily threatened.
    c. only those who threaten the hive.
    d. equipment as well as people.

Detail _____ 4. The bees were transported from Africa to South America

    a. accidentally in cargo.
    b. naturally by air currents during a hurricane.
    c. in the same manner in which they entered the United States.
    d. deliberately for breeding.

Detail _____ 5. In comparison to the local Brazilian bees, the "Africanized" bees do all of the following *except*

    a. fly faster.
    b. die sooner.
    c. fly longer.
    d. spend more time in their eggs before birth.

Inference _____ 6. The importation and cross-breeding of the African bees set off a

genetic time bomb that resulted in _____

_____

Inference _____ 7. The author implies that the Africanized bees

    a. attack in groups.
    b. produce more energy than Brazilian honeybees.
    c. attack and eat Brazilian honeybees.
    d. eat more than Brazilian honeybees.

Answer the following with *T* (true) or *F* (false).

Detail _____ 8. According to the passage, putting a bee hive in a screened cage around an orchard tree will increase flower production by 39%.

Detail _____ 9. The first few generations of offspring of the cross-breeding Brazilian and African bees did not accurately predict the later descendant bees that invaded California and Texas.

Detail _____10. Africanized honeybees can remain agitated for eight hours.

VOCABULARY

Answer the following with *a, b, c,* or *d* for the word or phrase that best defines the boldface word used in the selection. The number in parentheses indicates the line of the passage in which the word is located.

_____ 1. "a few **decades** earlier" (1)
a. 5-year periods
b. 10-year periods
c. 20-year periods
d. 100-year periods

_____ 2. "**invaded** 13,287 kilometers" (2)
a. cut up
b. flown past
c. surrounded
d. spread over

_____ 3. "**Agitated** bees flew" (6)
a. disturbed
b. diseased
c. wounded
d. quick

_____ 4. "**sluggish** pollinators" (17)
a. forgetful
b. maladaptive
c. unfocused
d. lazy

_____ 5. "**zippier** bees" (19)
a. livelier
b. more dangerous
c. larger
d. happier

_____ 6. "**preliminary** experimental results" (23)
a. illegal
b. preparatory
c. unfounded
d. hidden

_____ 7. "traits became **dominant**" (28)
a. known
b. troubled
c. governing
d. undesirable

_____ 8. "chase an **intruding** animal" (33)
a. uninvited
b. sick
c. slow
d. small

_____ 9. "a **squadron** of Africanized bees" (33)
a. leader
b. invasion force group
c. spy unit
d. straight line

_____10. "**continuous** supply of energy" (35)
a. uninterrupted
b. harmful
c. overworked
d. limiting

ASSESS YOUR LEARNING

Review confusing questions, seek clarification, and make notes in your text to help you remember new information and vocabulary.

CONNECT

Read the following passage about Africanized honeybees. If you owned a landscape or lawn maintenance company, what would you do to help your employees avoid being stung by an Africanized honeybee? List and explain five steps that you would take to protect your workers.

The Do's and Don'ts of Dealing with Killer Bees

Jerry Fink
Las Vegas Sun, May 15, 2000

The sting of the Africanized honeybee is the same as the European bee, but Africanized bees will attack by the hundreds or thousands when protecting their hives. This is the reason they are considered dangerous and potentially lethal, especially to the very young, elderly and small animals.

Bees are especially attracted to lawnmowers, dogs barking, weed eaters or other noises. They are also attracted to bright flashing lights. This is why when emergency vehicles respond to a bee incident, they do not use lights or sirens.

If you see an attack . . . . Call 911 immediately. Advise the person to seek shelter in a building or vehicles.

Do not scream or wave your arms at the person because this will attract the bees to you. If it appears the person is lying on the ground unconscious, do not try to rescue him. The bees will leave because the person is not moving and they will attack you instead.

If attacked . . . . Run as fast as you can from the bees; in most cases you can outrun them.

Cover your face with your hands. Do not scream or wave your arms, as this will keep the bees attacking.

Look for shelter, such as a building or vehicle. Swimming pools are not a good place to hide because the bees will wait for you to come up for air and attack again.

If someone has been stung several times, he should seek medical attention. If the person becomes dizzy, has difficulty breathing or their lips and fingernails turn blue, call 911 immediately. The person may be suffering an allergic reaction to the stings and might need immediate medical attention.

EXPLORE THE NET

● Locate and copy a map showing where Africanized bees can currently be found in the United States. Try the following sites, or conduct your own search.

Africanized Bees in the Americas

www.stingshield.com/!ahbtitl.htm

Africanized Honeybees: Quarantine Map

agnews.tamu.edu/bees/quaran.htm

● Locate information on safety precautions that can be used to prevent being stung by an Africanized bee.

GEARS

gears.tucson.ars.ag.gov/ahb/index.html

Africanized Honeybee Alert

www.fortbend.lib.tx.us/extension/ahbfaq.htm

For additional readings and exercises, visit the *Breaking Through* Web site:

www.ablongman.com/smith

SELECTION 3 🌐 SOCIOLOGY

THINKING BEFORE READING

Preview the selection for clues to content. Activate your schema and anticipate what you will learn.

Why are you sometimes reluctant to speak up in class?

Do students sitting in the front row participate in class discussions more than those in the back row?

In your classes have you noticed a difference in male and female class participation?

This selection will probably say _____

VOCABULARY PREVIEW

Are you familiar with these words?

epidemic	engulfed	plague	ignited	constructive
commitment	prestigious	chord	sidetracked	dynamics

Can a plague reach epidemic proportions?

What does the prefix *en* in *engulfed* mean?

What is a prestigious car to drive?

Your instructor may give a true-false vocabulary review before or after reading.

THINKING DURING READING

As you read, predict, picture, relate, monitor, and correct. Answer the questions in the margins that reflect your active thinking.

> 🌐 **Reader's TIP   Reading and Studying Sociology**
> - Use the chapter outline, learning objectives, and introductory anecdotes to stimulate your schema and curiosity before reading.
> - Use the summaries, key terms, and discussion questions to review your learning after reading.
> - Think broadly about society and social organizations. Search for the historical reasons for human behaviors and organizational structures. Make cause-and-effect connections between history, culture, and social organizations.
> - Compare and contrast customs and social behaviors across cultures.
> - Remain open-minded and be tolerant of cultural differences. Avoid biased value judgments.
> - Think objectively and scientifically to evaluate the problems of society.

Problems in Schools

What school violence has been in the news lately?

Several hundred thousand students and at least one thousand teachers are physically assaulted on school grounds every year. About one-fourth of students attending school in central cities voice fear of being attacked in or around the school. And government studies as well as news reports suggest that thousands of young people routinely bring guns
5 and other deadly weapons to school (U.S. Bureau of Justice Statistics, 1991).

Disorder spills into schools from the surrounding society. Our nation is among the most violent in the world, with disorder of epidemic proportions in poor communities. In short, schools do not create the problems of violence, but they do have the power to effect change for the better.

Will this school be exceptional?

10 Take the case of Malcolm X Elementary School: Malcolm X is in a poor neighborhood of Washington, D.C., that residents call "the jungle" because, as one local police officer observed, "it's all about survival here." Engulfed by the urban ills that plague this country, most students at Malcolm X live in poor, single-parent families and contend with prostitution, drugs, and daily violence.

Picture the uniforms.

15 Yet, entering Malcolm X school is like entering another world: All the boys wear white shirts and red ties, and all the girls wear plaid jumpers. The hallways are clean and quiet; classrooms are orderly. The extraordinary achievement of Malcolm X is that students are learning—not out of fear, but because they want to.

Why can't all schools do as well?

What accounts for this remarkable school? As most of the staff sees it, the key is atti-
20 tude. Skillful and committed teachers have ignited in students a sense of pride and a hunger to achieve. Principal John Pannell, son of a West Virginia school-bus driver, states his simple philosophy: "If we don't have high expectations for these children, who will?" For their part, most students feel that teachers really care about them. Beaming at her second-grade class, Avis Watts adds, "This is their lifeline really; they know that they'll be
25 fed, loved, and everything else in this school" (Gup, 1992).

While schools like Malcolm X may be the exception, they demonstrate the power of education to bring constructive change to even the most disadvantaged students. The key to such success appears to lie in commitment to children, teaching skills, firm disciplinary policies, and the ability of school officials to enlist the support of parents and the
30 larger community.

STUDENT PASSIVITY

Are the students silent?

35   If some schools are plagued by violence, many more are filled with passive, bored students. Some of the blame for passivity can be placed on television (which now consumes more of young people's time than school does), on parents (who do not foster a desire to learn), and on students themselves. But schools, too, play a part, since our educational system itself generates student passivity (Coleman, Hoffer, & Kilgore, 1981).

COLLEGE: THE SILENT CLASSROOM

40   Here are the observations of a bright and highly motivated first-year student at a prestigious four-year college. Do they strike a familiar chord?

> I have been disappointed in my first year at college. Too many students do as little work as they can get away with, take courses that are recommended by other students as being "gut" classes, and never challenge themselves past what
> 45   is absolutely necessary. It's almost like thinking that we don't watch professors but we watch television. (Forrest, 1984:10)

This is an old study. Has behavior changed?

Passivity is also common in colleges and universities. Martha E. Gimez (1980) describes college as the "silent classroom" because the only voice heard is usually the teacher's. Sociologists tend not to conduct research on the college classroom—a curious
50   fact considering how much time they spend there. A fascinating exception is a study at a coeducational university where David Karp and William Yoels (1976) found that—even in small classes—only a handful of students said anything at all during the typical class period. Karp and Yoels concluded that passivity is a classroom norm, and that students even become irritated if one of their number is especially talkative.

55   Gender also affects classroom dynamics. Karp and Yoels found that in coeducational classes taught by a man, male students carried on most classroom discussion. With women as instructors, however, the two sexes were more equal in terms of participation. Why? Perhaps because women instructors directed questions to women students as frequently as to men, while male teachers favored their male students.

60   Students offered Karp and Yoels various explanations for classroom passivity, including not having done the assigned reading or fearing that they might sound unintelligent to teachers and other students. To them, passivity is mostly their own fault. Yet long before they reach college, Karp and Yoels point out, students learn to view instructors as "experts" who serve up "truth." Thus they find little value in classroom discussion and
65   perceive that the student's proper role is to quietly listen and take notes. This perception squares with the finding of Karp and Yoels that only 10 percent of class time is devoted to discussion.

What is the ratio in my classes?

Students also realize that instructors generally come to class ready to deliver a prepared lecture. Lecturing allows teachers to present a great deal of material in each class,
70   but only to the extent that they avoid being sidetracked by student questions or comments (Boyer, 1987). Early in each course, most instructors single out a few students who are willing and able to provide the occasional, limited comments they desire. Taken together, such patterns form a recipe for passivity on the part of most college students.

Why would I avoid speaking up?

How would discussion enhance my classes?

Yet faculty can bring students to life in their classrooms: The key is actively involving
75   them in learning. One recent study of classroom dynamics, for example, linked higher levels of student participation to four teaching strategies: (1) calling on students by name when they volunteer, (2) positively reinforcing student participation, (3) asking analytical rather than factual questions and giving students time to answer, and (4) asking for students' opinion even when they do not volunteer (Auster & MacRone, 1994).

Do my professors do this?

(981 words)

—*Sociology,* Eighth Edition, by John J. Macionis

THINKING AFTER READING

RECALL Self-test your understanding. Your instructor may choose to give a true-false review.

REACT Why do college students allow the classroom to be silent? _____

_____

_____

REFLECT What are the factors that make Malcolm X Elementary School outstanding? _____

_____

THINK CRITICALLY Why do many educators believe that school uniforms contribute to academic achievement?

Name _____

Date _____

COMPREHENSION QUESTIONS

Anwer the following with *a, b, c,* or *d,* or fill in the blank. In order to help you analyze your strengths and your weaknesses, the question types are indicated.

Main Idea _____ 1. The best statement of the main idea of this selection is

    a. Violence disrupts education and encourages passivity.
    b. Successful schools hire dedicated teachers who expect student commitment.
    c. Television has fostered student passivity and silence in the college classroom.
    d. Although schools have many problems, teachers and students have the power to effect change.

Inference 2. The author believes that the problems of violence are not created

by the schools but are created by _____

_____

Detail _____ 3. According to the passage, the success of Malcolm X Elementary School involves all of the following *except*

    a. higher expectations for students.
    b. higher teacher salaries.
    c. firm discipline.
    d. a student desire to learn.

Inference _____ 4. In the college student's quoted observations, the phrase "gut" classes means classes that are

    a. difficult.
    b. challenging.
    c. easy.
    d. interesting.

Detail _____ 5. In coeducational college classes taught by a male, Karp and Yoels found that

    a. males are less likely than females to participate.
    b. females are more likely than males to participate.
    c. males are more likely than females to participate.
    d. males and females participate equally.

Detail _____ 6. In the Karp and Yoels study, students blamed passivity on

    a. the lecture format.
    b. poorly prepared instructors.
    c. previous high school experiences.
    d. themselves.

Inference _____ 7. The author implies all of the following except

    a. students are trained to value lecture over discussion.
    b. college courses should shift to 10 percent lecture and 90 percent discussion.
    c. teaching techniques can be used to stimulate class discussion.
    d. the small group of students who participate tends to be the same individuals.

Answer the following with *T* (true) or *F* (false).

Detail _____ 8. According to the passage, more teachers than students are assaulted on schools grounds.

Detail _____ 9. Karp and Yoels found that students do not always welcome the class participation of their fellow students.

Inference _____ 10. The author implies that classroom participation enhances student learning.

VOCABULARY

Answer the following with *a*, *b*, *c*, or *d* for the word or phrase that best defines the boldface word used in the selection. The number in parentheses indicates the line of the passage in which the word is located.

_____ 1. "**epidemic** proportions" (7)

    a. unbelievable
    b. unrealistic
    c. contagious
    d. widespread

_____ 2. "**Engulfed** by urban ills" (12)

    a. overwhelmed
    b. prompted
    c. motivated
    d. silenced

_____ 3. "**plague** this country" (12–13)

    a. push
    b. power
    c. trouble
    d. lead

_____ 4. "**ignited** in students" (20)

    a. rewarded
    b. lit
    c. chosen
    d. witnessed

_____ 5. "bring **constructive** change" (27)

    a. helpful
    b. steady
    c. slow
    d. institutional

_____ 6. "**commitment** to children" (28)

    a. discipline
    b. challenge
    c. recognition
    d. dedication

_____ 7. "**prestigious** four-year college" (40–41)

    a. coeducational
    b. distinguished
    c. unnamed
    d. diverse

_____ 8. "strike a familiar **chord**" (41)

    a. sound
    b. difficulty
    c. calling
    d. quotation

_____ 9. "**sidetracked** by student questions" (70)

     a. angered
     b. moved off course
     c. left out of control
     d. embarrassed

_____ 10. "classroom **dynamics**" (75)

     a. problems
     b. rules
     c. theories
     d. interactions

ASSESS YOUR LEARNING

Review confusing questions, seek clarification, and make notes in your text to help you remember new information and vocabulary.

EXPLORE THE NET

● Search the Internet for articles on reducing school violence. Make a list of ten strategies that are recommended and cite your sources.

Clearinghouse on Urban Education

www.eric-web.tc.columbia.edu/digests/dig115.html

Office of Juvenile Justice and Delinquency Prevention

www.ojjdp.ncjrs.org/resources/school.html

● What is the impact of television violence on behavior? Search for an engaging article on the issue and state why you agree or disagree with the author's premise.

Impact of Televised Violence

www.ksu.edu/humec/impact.htm

Continuing the Discussion: Does TV Kill?

www.pbs.org/wgbh/pages/frontline/teach/tvkillguide.html

For additional readings and exercises, visit the *Breaking Through* Web site:

www.ablongman.com/smith

Reading News and Feature Stories in the Newspaper

What do you usually read first in your daily newspaper? You probably already have a pattern for reading your favorite parts. To help you locate different topics, newspapers are divided into *sections*: national and international news; local or regional news; sports; entertainment and the arts (including movies and television); classified ads; plus any other categories the editors believe are appropriate for the local community. The front page always carries the most important stories from all the categories. Those articles are often continued in the appropriate sections where other articles related to the lead story may also be found. Some newspapers include an index on the front page to help you locate high-interest articles or regular sections.

Understand the Evolution of Newspaper Style

To appreciate the organization of a newspaper, you must first understand that the evolution of the journalistic style of newspaper writing developed as a response to the telegraph machine, a new technology which could break down at any time.

As protection against a communication breakdown or a deadline cut off as well as to ensure that readers received the most important parts of the news story, reporters got into the habit of including only the most important points in the first paragraphs. The major and minor details of the story were then placed in the following paragraphs in *descending* order of importance. Thus the **inverted pyramid** format of news writing was invented. Although technology has improved dramatically, this format has continued.

Recognize the Variety of Newspaper Articles

Newspapers expand far beyond headline news and include all of the following elements:

News Stories. **News stories** are the front page articles that objectively report facts in descending order of importance. The **lead** is the first paragraph that catches the reader's attention, summarizes the essential points of the story, and establishes a focus. The lead contains the 5 *W*'s and one *H*: Who, What, When, Where, Why, and How? Think of the first paragraph as a condensed version of the event.

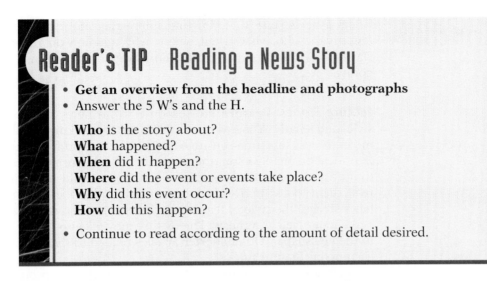

Reader's TIP Reading a News Story

- **Get an overview from the headline and photographs**
- Answer the 5 W's and the H.

  Who is the story about?
  What happened?
  When did it happen?
  Where did the event or events take place?
  Why did this event occur?
  How did this happen?

- Continue to read according to the amount of detail desired.

Subsequent paragraphs present details in a hierarchy of importance. A news story has no ending, but rather tapers down from major to minor details. As you read further, more complete information is given about these five basic questions. Your level of interest will determine how far you read for more details. The following is an example of the inverted pyramid format in a news story.

THE MONROE REPORTER

25¢   Monroe's Hometown Newspaper   Tuesday, April 25, 2000

TWISTER HITS LYNCHBURG

Most important points

Lynchburg—A tornado slammed into his southern Virginia community early yesterday, leaving more than 400 people homeless and injuring more than 75. Two people were killed when their mobile home was hurled down an embankment.

Major details

The twister hit around 7:15 A.M. Wednesday, tearing the steeple off the Edgewood First Presbyterian Church, ripping glass out of storefronts, and overturning several cars at the Edgewood Forest Center next door. Arbor Park, a residential development directly across the street, was untouched.

Minor details

The storm system, which stretched from Georgia and the Carolinas to southern Maryland dumped over 6 inches of rain on Lynchburg and the surrounding area in less than 3 hours. Flooding and tornado-related damage are expected to top $1 million. The governor's office immediately declared the region a disaster area and called in the National Guard for assistance.

Select a news story that you find interesting and clip it from the newspaper. Identify the who, what, when, where, why, and how on a separate sheet of paper. On the news clipping itself, draw an inverted pyramid over the most important points.

Feature Stories. **Feature stories** differ from news stories in their timeliness, style, and length. Whereas news stories cover breaking headlines, a feature story might discuss less time-sensitive issues such as a profile of an actor or an important local businessperson, the reopening of a historical hotel, or a new lifestyle trend. In other words, articles such as these would have similar impact if you read them today or five days from now. Unlike the inverted pyramid style of news stories, the style of feature stories is characterized by a beginning, middle, and end, as well as a thesis. The feature may take up one or two complete pages of the newspaper. Other shorter articles related to the same primary topic often accompany feature stories.

Feature stories are usually found in the section appropriate to their subject. In the previous examples, an actor's profile would be found in *arts/entertainment*, the profile of a local businessperson would be in the *business section*, the refurbishing of a landmark hotel would be in *local news*, and new trends would be in the *lifestyle* or *living section*. They add a fresh angle to previous news by including overlooked or undisclosed information. The *exposés* are based on in-depth investigation to reveal or "expose" shocking or surprising information such as abuses of power or the quality of public education in your area.

Reader's TIP   Reading a Feature

- How does the angle or focus of a feature story differ from that of a straight news story?
- How credible are the sources cited?
- Is it factual or sensationalized?
- Does the reporter show a bias?
- Does the reporter judge or do you decide?

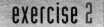

Locate a feature story that interests you and clip it from the newspaper. What is the angle of the story and why is it being printed now? Circle any credible sources that are cited and underline sentences or phrases that show a positive or negative bias by the reporter.

3

Vocabulary

- What are context clues?
- What are roots, prefixes, and suffixes?
- How do you use the dictionary?
- Do words have "families"?
- What is a glossary?
- Why use a thesaurus?
- What comparisons form analogies?

Everyday Reading Skills: Joining a Mailing List or Newsgroup

Learning New Words

Recognizing the meaning of words is essential to understanding what you read. If you have a weak vocabulary and stumble over unknown words when you read, you will lose your train of thought and end up concentrating on words rather than on meaning. A poor vocabulary severely limits your reading comprehension and speed.

Research tells us that you are already phenomenally successful at vocabulary acquisition. On the average, you have learned 3,000 to 5,000 words each year from kindergarten through twelfth grade. Experts estimate that only 300 new words are systematically taught each year by a teacher, so congratulate yourself that independently you have learned approximately 2,700 words every year! Were you afraid of new words? Apparently not, because during each of those years, you encountered 15,000 to 30,000 unknown words and you survived. That makes you a very efficient vocabulary builder. Continue to expand your vocabulary knowledge using those skills that have already made you an expert.

To the college reader, being able to recognize a large number of words is more important than being able to use each one of them. Studies show that we use only about 20 percent of the words we know. The average high school graduate recognizes about 50,000 words and uses only 10,000, whereas the average college graduate recognizes around 70,000 words and uses approximately 15,000. This means that during your years in college you probably will learn about 20,000 new words.

The English language contains about one million words. This number includes technical words in all disciplines, many of which the average person would never use. As a college student, however, you are becoming an expert in a particular field and a mini-expert in several areas. Each time you take a course in a new discipline, you are faced with a vocabulary unique to that subject. It takes a little time and a lot of effort to master these new words. After overcoming this initial shock of vocabulary adjustment for each new course, the reading becomes easier and comprehension improves.

PERSONAL Feedback 1   Name _____

1. What is your present system for remembering new words?

   _____

   _____

   _____

2. For the ten vocabulary items following the selection in Chapter 2 on hypnosis (p. 49), why do you think the line numbers were given for the words? _____

   _____

3. Why do instructors say that studying Latin is a useful way to increase your vocabulary? _____

   _____

4. What is the last new word you can remember learning? _____

   _____

5. What is a word that you frequently encounter but do not completely understand? _____

6. On a scale of 1 to 10, with 10 meaning *excellent at the college level,* how would you rate your vocabulary at present? _____

7. What do you feel are the benefits of having a large vocabulary?

   _____

   _____

8. List ten adjectives that describe you. Stretch your vocabulary and go beyond simple one- and two-syllable words. _____

   _____

   _____

Remembering New Words

Use Association

Certain new words, especially college-level words, are hard to remember because you don't hear them every day and can't easily work them into a typical conversation. To latch on to a new word, form an association with it. Try to remember the word in the context in which it was used. Visualize the word or a situation pertaining to the word. Always try to think of a new word in a phrase, rather than in isolation. For example, do you know the word *surrogate?* Perhaps you encountered the word in psychology class when studying Harlow's experiments on the need for love in infants. The surrogates were wire models substituted for real monkey mothers to test the infant monkey's attraction. To remember the word *surrogate,* think of it in the phrase *surrogate mother* and visualize the infant monkey cuddling up to a wire artificial mother for love and affection. This association creates an indelible picture in your mind.

Use Concept Cards

You can also use concept cards to help you remember vocabulary. *Concept* means idea. On a concept card you expand the definition of a single word into a fully developed idea. You are creating an episode for the new word by providing a sentence, a picture, and a source reference.

Keep a concept card file of new words. Include more than the usual "mystery word" on the front of the card and the definition on the back. Use the technique of association, and on the front of the card write the word within a meaningful phrase or sentence, or both. Also on the front, note where you encountered the new word. On the back of the card, write the definition, and, to add a further memory link, draw a picture that illustrates the way you are using the word in your phrase or sentence. See the illustration at the top of the next page for an example.

FRONT

BACK

surrogate mother

The baby monkey preferred
the terry cloth surrogate mother

Passage text on love

Def: <u>substitute</u>, as in the wire
mothers in the monkey love
experiments

When making concept cards, your limits depend only on your creativity and talent. For example, in *Vocabulary Cartoons*, a book by Sam, Max, and Bryan Burchers, the authors link the sounds within words to exaggerated visual images. The resulting cartoons, as shown below, depict the links and suggest the definitions by using sound associations and visual images, along with humor, to improve memory.

Practice Your New Words

Review your concept cards regularly. Look at the word on the front and quiz yourself on the definition. When you feel you have a clear understanding of the meaning, use your new word in writing or in conversation.

HOVEL
(HUV ul)
a small, miserable dwelling;
an open, low shed
Link: **SHOVEL**

"The mice's HOVEL was an old, rusted SHOVEL."

EDIFICE
(ED uh fis)
a building, especially one of imposing
appearance or size
Link: **ATE A FACE**

HE ONLY EATS THE FINEST BUILDINGS!

"The Great Kong ATE the north FACE of the EDIFICE."

Notice the words around you. As you begin to pay attention to unfamiliar terms in print and in conversations, you will more than likely discover that you encounter more interesting words.

Unlocking the Meaning of New Words

Use Context Clues

To figure out the meaning of a new word, do not immediately go charging off to the dictionary and record a definition as if it were one more addition to a giant notebook list of words. Contrary to what you may have heard, the dictionary is a *last* resort when you aren't sure what a word means. Instead, first try to figure out the meaning from the **context clues** in the sentence or paragraph in which the word is used.

Use Knowledge of Word Parts

Another way to discover the meaning of a word is to examine its parts. Do you recognize any prefixes, suffixes, or roots, such as *pseudo* (meaning *false*) or *nym* (meaning *name)* in the word *pseudonym?* If you know these word parts, you can easily figure out that *pseudonym* means a false name rather than a real one. Samuel Clemens's use of the name Mark Twain is an example of a pseudonym.

Use the Glossary and the Dictionary

If a word is unique to a subject area, such as the marketing term *promotional mix,* refer to the glossary in the back of the textbook for a definition that pertains specifically to that field. If all else fails and you can't understand what you are reading without a definition of the word, then go to the dictionary. But if the word is not essential to your general comprehension, skip it entirely or come back to it later. Your purpose for reading is to get meaning, not to collect vocabulary words. As you read more and encounter more new words, your vocabulary will naturally expand. Make a habit of noticing new words and try to remember them by association.

Types of Context Clues

The first line of attack on a new word is to try to figure out the meaning from its *context,* or the way it is used in the sentence or paragraph. There are several types of context clues. The following examples show how each type can be used to figure out word meaning.

Definition

The unknown word is defined within the sentence or paragraph.

EXAMPLE   The explorers landed in an *alien* environment, a place both foreign and strange to their beloved homeland.

EXPLANATION The definition is set off by a comma following the phrase in which the word appears. *Alien* means *strange* or *foreign*.

exercise 1

For each of the context clue exercises in this section, mark *a, b, c,* or *d* for the meaning closest to that of the boldface word. Do not use your dictionary.

_____ 1. The CIA was engaged in **covert** activities in South America that were not made public.

    a. foreign
    b. dishonest
    c. dangerous
    d. hidden

FRONT   BACK

covert operations
in South America

CIA activities

hidden or secret

_____ 2. The meeting was brief, and the message was **concise** and to the point.

    a. laborious
    b. lengthy
    c. short
    d. important

_____ 3. If we have to have a pet around the house, get one that is **docile** and easy to manage.

    a. gentle
    b. short
    c. sick
    d. young

_____ 4. The professor gave an **ultimatum** about tardiness, saying today would be the last time anyone would be allowed to enter class late.

    a. final demand
    b. new proposal
    c. lecture
    d. choice

_____ 5. Checking the references in the bibliography for errors was **tedious** and uninteresting.

a. educational
b. necessary
c. exhausting
d. boring

Elaborating Details

Descriptive details suggest the meaning of the unknown word.

EXAMPLE The natives were *hostile* when the settlers approached their village. They lined up across the road and drew their weapons. The settlers were afraid to go farther.

EXPLANATION As described in the sentences after the word, *hostile* must mean *unfriendly.*

exercise 2

_____ 1. Because she had only a few minutes to spare, the professor gave the paper a **cursory** reading.

a. careful
b. hasty
c. thoughtful
d. modest

_____ 2. No one was completely sure of the politician's position on the tax cut question because the answer was so **ambiguous**.

a. confusing
b. silly
c. late
d. incomplete

_____ 3. The edge of a dangerous cliff is a **precarious** position for a summertime picnic lunch.

a. exciting
b. lovely
c. risky
d. scenic

_____ 4. The winds and thunder **foreshadowed** the terrible storm that was to come.

a. stalled
b. intercepted
c. foretold
d. lessened

_____ 5. Wishing to save her money, she was **frugal** and sought out the bargain items on sale.

a. thrifty
b. clever
c. sly
d. determined

Elaborating Examples

An anecdote or example before or after the word suggests the meaning.

EXAMPLE The bird's appetite is *voracious.* In one day he ate enough worms to equal three times his body weight.

EXPLANATION Because the bird ate an extraordinary amount, *voracious* means extremely *hungry* or *greedy.*

exercise 3

_____ 1. The dancer's movements were not rehearsed, but were a **spontaneous** response to the music.

  a. planned
  b. simple
  c. unpremeditated
  d. smooth

_____ 2. The embargo will **restrict** previously flourishing trade with the country and stop the goods from entering the seaport.

  a. promote
  b. enlist
  c. renew
  d. confine

_____ 3. The **affluent** members of the community live in big homes with swimming pools.

  a. powerful
  b. wealthy
  c. athletic
  d. political

FRONT

affluent people

BACK

_____ 4. Because the employer had never heard of the three companies listed as references, she was **dubious** about the applicant's previous work history.

    a. relaxed
    b. unconcerned
    c. doubtful
    d. hopeful

_____ 5. The ophthalmologist gave a favorable **prognosis**, saying that in two weeks her vision would be clear and she would no longer need the dark glasses.

    a. forecast
    b. prescription
    c. warning
    d. notification

Comparison

A similar situation suggests the meaning of the unknown word.

EXAMPLE

The smell of the flower was as *compelling* as a magnet's pull on a paper clip.

EXPLANATION Because a magnet will pull a paper clip to it, the comparison suggests that the smell of the flower had an attraction. *Compelling* means *attracting*.

exercise 4

_____ 1. I am as **skeptical** about its chances of success as I am about my chances of winning the lottery.

    a. doubtful
    b. confident
    c. remorseful
    d. hopeful

_____ 2. Confirming an appointment before leaving the office is as **prudent** as never letting your gas tank go lower than one-quarter full.

    a. annoying
    b. reckless
    c. rewarding
    d. wise

_____ 3. Like cursing in a public place, **gauche** behaviors reflect unfavorably on those who engage in them.

    a. loud
    b. crude
    c. mean
    d. unreasonable

_____ 4. Because there is always a first time for everything, each of us is a **novice** at some point in our lives.

    a. fool
    b. master
    c. manager
    d. beginner

_____ 5. If the climber is actually a circus performer, it is **plausible** that he attempted such a dangerous feat on the tall building.

    a. doubtful
    b. impossible
    c. terrible
    d. believable

Contrast

An opposite situation suggests the meaning of the unknown word.

EXAMPLE

In America, she is an *eminent* scientist, even though she is virtually unknown in England.

EXPLANATION *Even though* are signal words indicating that an opposite is coming. Thus *eminent* means the opposite of *unknown;* it means *well known* or *famous.*

exercise 5

_____ 1. Unlike **introverted** people, very talkative folks love crowds and conversation.

    a. quiet
    b. loud
    c. friendly
    d. hostile

_____ 2. His favorites were not the old stories of days gone by, but the works of more **contemporary** authors.

    a. intelligent
    b. recent
    c. revolutionary
    d. meaningful

_____ 3. He did not mean to cause the problem. While looking for his hat, the young man **inadvertently** knocked over the lamp.

    a. purposely
    b. knowingly
    c. unintentionally
    d. suddenly

_____ 4. Now that she is an adult college student who is in control of her emotions, she no longer engages in the **infantile** outbursts that marked her behavior as a child.

    a. immature
    b. sudden
    c. angry
    d. short

_____ 5. Although she had a crush on him all fall, Maria's interest in him began to **wane** when he asked two other girls to the holiday party.

a. grow
b. lessen
c. accelerate
d. intensify

> **WANE**
> (wain)
> to decrease gradually
> Link: **RAIN**
>
> *"Snowmen WANE in the RAIN."*

exercise 6

Use context clues to write the meanings of the following words that are frequently used in business textbooks.

1. With less time to shop and more people online, **e-commerce** is cutting into mall shopping profits. _____ Selling over the internet

2. When you call a **broker** to buy stocks, a fee for the broker is added to the cost. _____ Agent that helps cut w/ stock decl

3. **Consumers** who buy product in the marketplace today are demanding better quality from manufacturers. Customers

4. The **competition** of having different companies offer similar products in the marketplace tends to bring prices down. _____ bus. rivaly

5. To interest you in purchasing products, advertisers rely heavily on implied meaning as one of their **tactics**. Strategies

6. In government, the **fiscal** year for allocating budgeted money ends on June 30 and begins on July 1. _____ financial

7. Fads run in **cycles**, so frequently an old fad goes out of style and is repeated twenty years later. _____ continual, recur. _____

8. In order to secure a loan, the borrower may list her house or car as **collateral** to protect the lender in case full repayment is not received. _____
_____ Something of personal value, expensive _____

9. If you know a manufacturer to contact, you can save money by buying carpeting **wholesale** rather than at the full retail value in stores. _____
_____ At cost _____

10. During periods of high **inflation** more money is needed to buy fewer products, and people are not rewarded for saving money. _____
_____ full _____ in value or when so prices go up _____

Multiple Meanings of a Word

Some words are confusing because they have several different meanings. For example, the dictionary lists over thirty meanings for the word *run*. To determine the proper meaning, use the context of the sentence and paragraph in which the word occurs. Many of the multiple-meaning words are simple words that are used frequently. If you are puzzling over an unusual use of a common word, consider the context and be aware that the word may have a new meaning.

exercise 7

The boldface words in the following sentences have multiple meanings. Write a sentence in which the word is used differently than in the example.

1. Sally cannot **bear** to be in the house alone at night. _____
_____

2. The committee voted to **ditch** the residency requirement. _____
_____

3. The water in the mountain **spring** was cool and clean. _____
_____
_____

4. The owners suspected a dead animal was causing the **foul** odor from the basement. _____
_____

5. Mr. Robinson served on the **board** of directors for the school. _____
_____

6. The new principal will get to the **root** of the problem. _____

7. The swimmers ate only a **light** lunch because the meet was scheduled for early afternoon. _____

8. If we **pool** our money, we can afford the sofa. _____

9. The red pen had a **fine** point. _____

10. Her loud sneeze was the first sign of a **cold**. _____

Word Parts

Many words that at first may seem totally foreign to you are actually made up of words that you already know. One authority claims that learning approximately 30 key word parts will help you unlock the meaning of about 14,000 words. Although this claim may be exaggerated, it emphasizes the importance of roots, prefixes, and suffixes. Word parts are clues to the meaning of new words.

Look at the following family of words. Some may be familiar, and some may be new to you. You probably know the meaning of the first two words and thus can deduce that *ped* means *foot*. Try to figure out the meaning of the other *ped* words by applying your knowledge of closely related words.

Pedal: lever pressed by the foot

Pedestrian: person walking on foot

What do the following words mean? Use the clues to write the definitions.

quadruped: _____ (Hint: quadruplets?)

centipede: _____ (Hint: turn of the century?)

pedometer: _____ (Hint: speedometer?)

Roots

The **root** is the stem or basic part of the word. The roots that we use are derived primarily from Latin and Greek. For example, *port* is a root derived from Latin meaning *to carry,* as in the word *porter.* *Thermo* is a Greek word meaning *heat,* as in *thermometer.* In both cases, additional letters have been added to the word, but the meaning of the word has not changed. Knowing the definition of the root helps unlock the meaning of each word.

EXAMPLE

The root forms *duc, duct,* and *duce* mean *to lead.* This root branches out into a large word family. Use the root to supply appropriate words to complete the following three sentences.

1. If the factory is ready, the new line of furniture will go into _____ in September.

2. The company is trying to cut down overhead in order to _____ expenses.

3. Legitimate business expenses can be _____ from your taxes if you keep the proper receipts.

EXPLANATION The correct answers are *production*, *reduce*, and *deducted*.

exercise 8

The following exercises include frequently used roots. Use the root to supply an appropriate word to complete the sentences in each group.

grad, gred, gres: take steps, go, degree

1. The seniors will _____ from high school the first week in June.

2. The mountain trail began as a _____ climb and became steeper toward the top.

3. If we continue to work through lunch and all afternoon, we should make enough _____ on our project to finish by five o'clock.

port: carry

4. If we could _____ fewer goods into this country, our balance of payments would improve.

5. She wanted a _____ radio so she could listen to the game while riding in the boat on the lake.

6. Private contributions and volunteers _____ the efforts of the Salvation Army.

7. The organized _____ to and from the game will be by bus.

cred: believe

8. We could not believe what we saw; the feat was _____.

9. Some law schools in the country are not fully _____ by the state, and their courses do not transfer to other schools.

10. Derogatory remarks were made about his performance in an effort to _____ him.

Prefixes

A **prefix** is a group of letters with a special meaning that are added to the beginning of a word. For example, *ex* means *out of* and *im* means *into*. Adding these two prefixes to *port* gives two words that are opposite in meaning. *Export* means to send something out of the country, whereas *import* means to bring something in. Again, knowing the prefixes can help you identify the meaning.

EXAMPLE   The prefix *trans* means *across, over,* and *beyond.* Write a word beginning with *trans* to complete each of the following three sentences.

transcend ←   → transform
transcribe ←   trans   → transcontinental
transgress ←   → translucent

1. The radio station can now _____ programs to a wider audience.

2. Since she did not speak French, he acted as a _____ while she conducted business in Paris.

3. When the business _____ was completed, the two executives shook hands.

EXPLANATION   The correct answers are *transmit, translator,* and *transaction.*

exercise 9   The following exercises include frequently used prefixes. Use the prefix to supply an appropriate word to complete the sentences in each group.

dis: take away, not, deprive of

1. After catching criminals, the police carefully _____ them to remove any items that could be used as weapons.

2. Because of missing the review in the last class before the final exam, the student was at a _____ in studying for the test.

3. Hospital employees are instructed to use special containers to _____ of used needles.

mis: wrong, bad

4. Because the child _____ in the restaurant, he was not allowed to go again.

5. The answer was not a lie, but it did _____ the truth.

6. Because of the lawyer's error, the judge declared a _____ and court was adjourned.

pre: before

7. Even a fortune-teller could not have _____ the fun we had scuba diving.

8. Police recommend alarm systems as a type of crime _____ .

9. The student was so _____ with her mathematics assignment that she did not hear the doorbell ring.

10. If you order by phone, you will need a credit card to _____ for the concert tickets.

Suffixes

A **suffix** is a group of letters with a special meaning that are added to the end of a word. A suffix can alter the meaning of a word as well as the way the word can be used in the sentence. For example, the *er* in *porter* means the *person who* and makes the word into the name of a person. But adding *able*, which means *capable of*, to *port*, does not change the meaning as much as it changes the way the word can be used in the sentence. Some suffixes, therefore, have more meaning than others, but all alter the way the word can be used in a sentence.

EXAMPLE   The suffix *ist* means *one who* or *that which*. Write a word ending with *ist* to complete each of the following three sentences.

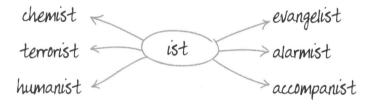

1. If you have a toothache, go to your _____ immediately.

2. The _____ played the piano with such force that the floorboards shook.

3. The picture was painted by a well-known American _____ .

EXPLANATION   The correct answers are *dentist*, *pianist*, and *artist*.

exercise 10   The following exercises include frequently used suffixes. Use the suffix to supply an appropriate word to complete the sentences in each group.

ion, sion, tion: act of, state of, result of

1. To honor his birthday, we invited his friends to a party and had a big

   _____ .

2. If you don't clean out the wound and use a bandage, you are likely to get an

   _____ .

3. The _____ bridge was held in the air by cables descending from two towers on either side of the river.

4. Use your _____ to visualize the festive atmosphere of music and outdoor dining.

ship: office, state, dignity, skill, quality, profession

5. After breaking her leg and thus missing two weeks of class, the student was advised to apply for a _____ withdrawal and get a fresh start the next semester.

6. The university also offered merit _____ that were not based on financial need.

7. The infantry soldier demonstrated excellent _____ by hitting the red mark with a bullet at each shot.

less: without

8. Because the show was boring, I became _____ and could not sit still.

9. A baby lamb is _____ against fierce and determined predators.

10. He suffered from insomnia and spent many _____ nights walking the halls.

The Dictionary

Use the dictionary as a last resort for finding the definition of a word while you are reading, unless the word is crucial to your understanding. Remember, stopping in the middle of a paragraph breaks your concentration and causes you to forget what you were reading. Mark unknown words with a dot in the margin, and then, when you have finished reading, look the words up in the dictionary.

Dictionaries contain more than just the definition of a word. They contain the pronunciation, the spelling, the derivation or history, the parts of speech, and the many different meanings a word may have. An entry may also include an illustration or give context examples of the use of the word in a phrase. Consider the following entry.

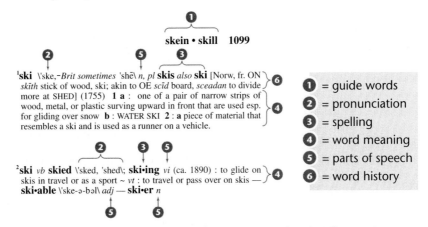

Source: Reprinted with permission from *Merriam-Webster's Collegiate Dictionary, Tenth Edition.* © 2000 by Merriam-Webster, Incorporated.

Guide Words

The two words at the top of each dictionary page are called *guide words*. They represent the first and last word on the page. The words in the dictionary are in alphabetical order, you can use the guide words to determine quickly if the word you are looking for is on that particular page. The guide words for the sample entry are *skein* and *skill*.

Pronunciation

Each word is divided into sounds after the boldface main entry. Letters and symbols are used to indicate special sounds. A key to understanding the special sounds appears at the bottom of one of the two pages open to you.

Spelling

Spellings are given for the plural form of the word (if the spelling changes) and for any special endings. This is particularly helpful when letters are dropped or added to form the new word. In the sample entry, the plural of *ski* can be spelled correctly in two ways, either *skis* or *ski*. The first spelling is usually the preferred one.

Word Meaning

Frequently, a word has many meanings. For example, *car* means automobile as well as the cargo part of an airship. In such a case, the dictionary uses a number to indicate each new meaning. In the sample entry, notice that a ski can be a narrow strip of wood or a piece of material that resembles a ski.

Parts of Speech

For each meaning of a word, the part of speech is given in abbreviated form. For example, *n* means *noun, adj* means *adjective, adv* means *adverb*, and *vi* or *vt* means *verb*. Other abbreviations are listed in the section in the front of your dictionary. In the example, *ski* is both a noun and a verb.

Word History

The original language in which the word appeared is listed after the pronunciation or at the end of the entry. For example, *L* stands for Latin and *Gk* stands for Greek. Usually, the original meaning is also listed. *Ski* is derived from the Norwegian (Nor) word *skith*, which means "stick of wood."

exercise 11

Use the dictionary page that follows to label the statements as either *T* (true) or *F* (false).

_____ 1. The *manual alphabet* for the deaf was created in 1864.

_____ 2. A *mantra* is used in Hinduism.

_____ 3. A *manticore* has the head of a man and the body of a bull.

_____ 4. A devilfish can be called a *manta ray*.

_____ 5. The word *manure* can be either a noun or a verb.

_____ 6. The *Mantoux test* was named for a French physician.

_____ 7. The *mantis* is a divine insect used by religious cults.

_____ 8. A hearing-impaired person would probably know that pointing only the index finger upward represents the letter *Z*.

_____ 9. The word *mantilla* has a Spanish derivation.

cloth or blanket used in southwestern U.S. and Latin America usu. as a cloak or shawl **2** [AmerSp, fr. Sp; fr. its shape] : DEVILFISH 1

man–tai·lored \'man-ˌtā-lərd\ *adj* (1922) : made with the severe simplicity associated with men's coats and suits

manta ray *n* (1936) : DEVILFISH 1

man·teau \man-ˈtō, ˈman-ˌ\ *n* [F, fr. OF *mantel*] (1671) : a loose cloak, coat, or robe

man·tel \'man-t⁰l\ *n* [ME, fr. MF, fr. OF, mantle] (15c) **1 a** : a beam, stone, or arch serving as a lintel to support the masonry above a fireplace **b** : the finish around a fireplace **2** : a shelf above a fireplace

man·tel·et \'mant-lət, 'man-t⁰l-ət, ˌman-t⁰l-'et\ *n* [ME, fr. MF *mantlet*, dim. of *mantel*] (14c) **1** : a very short cape or cloak **2** *or* **mant·let** \'mant-lət\ : a movable shelter formerly used by besiegers as a protection when attacking

man·tel·piece \'man-t⁰l-ˌpēs\ *n* (1686) **1** : a mantel with its side elements **2** : MANTEL 2

man·tel·shelf \-ˌshelf\ *n* (ca. 1828) : MANTEL 2

man·tic \'man-tik\ *adj* [Gk *mantikos*, fr. *mantis*] (1850) : of or relating to the faculty of divination : PROPHETIC

man·ti·core \'man-ti-ˌkōr, -ˌkȯr\ *n* [ME, fr. L *mantichora*, fr. Gk *mantichōras*] (14c) : a legendary animal with the head of a man, the body of a lion, and the tail of a dragon or scorpion

man·tid \'man-təd\ *n* [NL *Mantidae*, group name, fr. *Mantis*, genus name] (1895) : MANTIS

man·til·la \man-ˈtē-yə, -ˈti-lə\ *n* [Sp, dim. of *manta*] (1717) **1** : a light scarf worn over the head and shoulders esp. by Spanish and Latin-American women **2** : a short light cape or cloak

man·tis \'man-təs\ *n, pl* **man·tis·es** *or* **man·tes** \'man-ˌtēz\ [NL, fr. Gk, lit., diviner, prophet; akin to Gk *mainesthai* to be mad — more at MANIA] (1658) : any of an order or suborder (Mantodea and esp. family Mantidae) of large usu. green insects that feed on other insects and clasp their prey in forelimbs held up as if in prayer

man·tis·sa \man-ˈti-sə\ *n* [L *mantisa, mantissa* makeweight, fr. Etruscan] (ca. 1847) : the part of a logarithm to the right of the decimal point

¹man·tle \'man-t⁰l\ *n* [ME *mantel*, fr. OF, fr. L *mantellum*] (13c) **1 a** : a loose sleeveless garment worn over other clothes : CLOAK **b** : a mantle regarded as a symbol of preeminence or authority ⟨invested his people with the ~ of universal champions of justice —Denis Goulet⟩ **2 a** : something that covers, enfolds, or envelops **b** (1) : a fold or lobe or pair of lobes of the body wall of a mollusk or brachiopod that in shell-bearing forms lines the shell and bears shell-secreting glands — see CLAM illustration (2) : the soft external body wall that lines the test or shell of a tunicate or barnacle **c** : the outer wall and casing of a blast furnace above the hearth; *broadly* : an insulated support or casing in which something is heated **3** : the back, scapulars, and wings of a bird **4** : a lacy hood or sheath of some refractory material that gives light by incandescence when placed over a flame **5 a** : REGOLITH **b** : the part of the interior of a terrestrial planet and esp. the earth that lies between the lithosphere and above the central core **6** : MANTEL

²mantle *vb* **man·tled; man·tling** \'mant-liŋ, 'man-t⁰l-iŋ\ *vt* (13c) : to cover with or as if with a mantle : CLOAK ⟨the encroaching jungle growth that *mantled* the building —Sanka Knox⟩ ~ *vi* **1** : to become covered with a coating **2** : to spread over a surface **3** : BLUSH ⟨her rich face *mantling* with emotion —Benjamin Disraeli⟩

man–to–man \'man-tə-'man\ *adj* (1902) **1** : characterized by frankness and honesty ⟨a ~ talk⟩ **2** : of, relating to, or being a system of defense (as in football or basketball) in which each defensive player guards a specified opponent

Man·toux test \ˌman-ˈtü-, ˌmän-\ *n* [Charles *Mantoux* †1947 Fr. physician] (ca. 1923) : an intracutaneous test for hypersensitivity to tuberculin that indicates past or present infection with tubercle bacilli

man·tra \'män-trə *also* 'man- *or* 'mən-\ *n* [Skt, sacred counsel, formula, fr. *manyate* he thinks; akin to L *mens* mind — more at MIND] (1808) : a mystical formula of invocation or incantation (as in Hinduism); *also* : WATCHWORD 2 — **man·tric** \-trik\ *adj*

man·trap \'man-ˌtrap\ *n* (1788) : a trap for catching humans : SNARE

man·tua \'man(t)-ə-ˌwə, 'man-tə-wə\ *n* [modif. of F *manteau* mantle] (1678) : a usu. loose-fitting gown worn esp. in the 17th and 18th centuries

Manu \'mä-(ˌ)nü\ *n* [Skt] : the progenitor of the human race and giver of the religious laws of Manu according to Hindu mythology

¹man·u·al \'man-yə-wəl, -yəl\ *adj* [ME *manuel*, fr. MF, fr. L *manualis*, fr. *manus* hand; akin to OE *mund* hand and perh. to Gk *marē* hand] (15c) **1 a** : of, relating to, or involving the hands ⟨~ dexterity⟩ **b** : worked or done by hand and not by machine ⟨a ~ transmission⟩ ⟨~ computation⟩ ⟨~ indexing⟩ **2** : requiring or using physical skill and energy ⟨~ labor⟩ ⟨~ workers⟩ — **man·u·al·ly** *adv*

²manual *n* (15c) **1** : a book that is conveniently handled; *esp* : HANDBOOK **2** : the prescribed movements in the handling of a weapon or other military item during a drill or ceremony ⟨the ~ of arms⟩ **3 a** : a keyboard for the hands; *specif* : one of the several keyboards of an organ or harpsichord that controls a separate division of the instrument **b** : a device or apparatus intended for manual operation

manual alphabet *n* (ca. 1864) : an alphabet esp. for the deaf in which the letters are represented by finger positions

manual training *n* (1880) : a course of training to develop skill in using the hands and to teach practical arts (as woodworking and metalworking)

ma·nu·bri·um \mə-ˈnü-brē-əm, -ˈnyü-\ *n, pl* **-bria** \-brē-ə\ *also* **-bri·ums** [NL, fr. L, handle, fr. *manus*] (ca. 1848) : an anatomical process or part shaped like a handle: as **a** : the cephalic segment of the sternum of humans and other mammals **b** : the process that bears the mouth of a hydrozoan : HYPOSTOME

man·u·fac·to·ry \ˌman-yə-ˈfak-t(ə-)rē, ˌma-nə-\ *n* (1647) : FACTORY 2a

¹man·u·fac·ture \ˌman-yə-ˈfak-chər, ˌma-nə-\ *n* [MF, fr. ML *manufactura*, fr. L *manu factus*, lit., made by hand] (1567) **1** : something made from raw materials by hand or by machinery **2 a** : the process of making wares by hand or by machinery esp. when carried on systematically with division of labor **b** : a productive industry using mechanical power and machinery **3** : the act or process of producing something

²manufacture *vb* **-tured; -tur·ing** \-ˈfak-chə-riŋ, -ˈfak-shriŋ\ *vt* (1683) **1** : to make into a product suitable for use **2 a** : to make from raw

materials by hand or by machinery **b** : to produce according to an organized plan and with division of labor **3** : INVENT, FABRICATE **4** : to produce as if by manufacturing : CREATE ⟨writers who ~ stories for television⟩ ~ *vi* : to engage in manufacture — **manufacturing** *n*

man·u·fac·tur·er \-ˈfak-chər-ər, -ˈfak-shrər\ *n* (1719) : one that manufactures; *esp* : an employer of workers in manufacturing

man·u·mis·sion \ˌman-yə-ˈmi-shən\ *n* [ME, fr. MF, fr. L *manumission-, manumissio*, fr. *manumittere*] (15c) : the act or process of manumitting; *esp* : formal emancipation from slavery

man·u·mit \ˌman-yə-ˈmit\ *vt* **-mit·ted; -mit·ting** [ME *manumitten*, fr. MF *manumitter*, fr. L *manumittere*, fr. *manus* hand + *mittere* to let go, send] (15c) : to release from slavery **syn** see FREE

¹ma·nure \mə-ˈn(y)ur\ *vt* **ma·nured; ma·nur·ing** [ME *manouren*, fr. MF *manouvrer*, lit., to do work by hand, fr. L *manu operare*] (15c) **1** *obs* : CULTIVATE **2** : to enrich (land) by the application of manure — **ma·nur·er** *n*

²manure *n* (1549) : material that fertilizes land; *esp* : refuse of stables and barnyards consisting of livestock excreta with or without litter — **ma·nu·ri·al** \-ˈn(y)ur-ē-əl\ *adj*

ma·nus \'mā-nəs, 'mä-\ *n, pl* **ma·nus** \-nəs, -ˌnüs\ [NL, fr. L, hand] (1826) : the distal segment of the vertebrate forelimb from carpus to terminus

¹man·u·script \'man-yə-ˌskript\ *adj* [L *manu scriptus*] (1597) : written by hand or typed ⟨~ letters⟩

²manuscript *n* (1600) **1** : a written or typewritten composition or document as distinguished from a printed copy; *also* : a document submitted for publication **2** : writing as opposed to print

¹Manx \'man(k)s\ *adj* [alter. of *Maniske*, fr. (assumed) ON *manskr*, fr. *Mana* Isle of Man] (1630) : of, relating to, or characteristic of the Isle of Man, its people, or the Manx language

²Manx *n* (1672) **1** : the Celtic language of the Manx people almost completely displaced by English **2** *pl in constr* : the people of the Isle of Man **3** : MANX CAT

Manx cat *n* (1859) : any of a breed of shorthaired tailless domestic cats

¹many \'me-nē\ *adj* **more** \'mōr, 'mȯr\; **most** \'mōst\ [ME, fr. OE *manig*; akin to OHG *manag* many, OCS *mŭnogŭ* much] (bef. 12c) **1** : consisting of or amounting to a large but indefinite number ⟨worked for ~ years⟩ **2** : being one of a large but indefinite number ⟨~ a man⟩ ⟨~ another student⟩ — **as many** : the same in number ⟨saw three plays in *as many* days⟩

²many *pron, pl in constr* (bef. 12c) : a large number of persons or things ⟨~ are called⟩

³many *n, pl in constr* (12c) **1** : a large but indefinite number ⟨a good ~ of them⟩ **2** : the great majority of people ⟨the ~⟩

man–year \'man-ˈyir\ *n* (1916) : a unit of the work done by one person in a year composed of a standard number of working days

many·fold \ˌme-nē-ˈfōld\ *adv* (14c) : by many times ⟨aid to research has increased ~⟩

many–sid·ed \ˌme-nē-ˈsī-dəd\ *adj* (1570) **1** : having many sides or aspects **2** : having many interests or aptitudes — **many–sid·ed·ness** *n*

many–val·ued \ˌme-nē-ˈval-(ˌ)yüd, -yəd\ *adj* (1934) **1** : possessing more than the customary two truth-values of truth and falsehood **2** : MULTIPLE-VALUED

Man·za·nil·la \ˌman-zə-ˈnē-yə, -ˈni-lə\ *n* [Sp, dim. of *manzana* apple] (1843) : a pale very dry Spanish sherry

man·za·ni·ta \ˌman-zə-ˈnē-tə\ *n* [AmerSp, dim. of Sp *manzana* apple] (1846) : any of various western No. American evergreen shrubs (genus *Arctostaphylos*) of the heath family with alternate leaves

Mao·ism \'maú-ˌi-zəm\ *n* (1950) : the theory and practice of Marxism-Leninism developed in China chiefly by Mao Tse-tung — **Mao·ist** \'maú-ist\ *n or adj*

Mao·ri \'maú(ə)r-ē\ *n, pl* **Maori** *or* **Maoris** (1843) **1** : a member of a Polynesian people native to New Zealand **2** : the Austronesian language of the Maori

---

\ə\ abut \ᵊ\ kitten, F table \ər\ further \a\ ash \ā\ ace \ä\ mop, mar
\aú\ out \ch\ chin \e\ bet \ē\ easy \g\ go \i\ hit \ī\ ice \j\ job
\ŋ\ sing \ō\ go \ȯ\ law \ȯi\ boy \th\ thin \th\ the \ü\ loot \ú\ foot
\y\ yet \zh\ vision \à, ᵏ, ⁿ, œ, œ̄, ᵫ, ᵬ\ \'\ see Guide to Pronunciation

Word Origins

Words have ancestors. Some of the ancestors are words that were borrowed from other languages. *Shampoo*, for example, comes from a Hindi word meaning *to press*, and *moccasin* comes from the Algonquian Indian word for *shoe*. Other word ancestors include mythology, literature, people, places, and customs. The origin of the word *sadist*, which refers to a person who enjoys inflicting pain on others, is attributed to the Marquis de Sade, an eighteenth-century French author who wrote with pleasure about such cruelty.

Etymology

The study of word origins is called **etymology**. An etymologist traces the development of a word back to its earliest recorded appearance. In dictionaries, the etymology of a word is usually given in brackets. The extent to which the word origin is explained varies from one dictionary to another. Note the information on the etymology of the word *mentor* in the following dictionaries:

This entry is from the small paperback edition of the *American Heritage Dictionary:*

men·tor (mĕn′tôr′, -tər) *n.* A wise and trusted counselor or teacher. [< Gk. *Mentōr,* counselor of Odysseus. See men-*.]

Source: Reprinted with permission from
*American Heritage Dictionary of the English
Language, Third Paperback Edition.*

This entry is from the textbook-size edition of *Webster's New Collegiate Dictionary:*

¹**men·tor** \'men-,tȯr, -tər\ *n* [L, fr. Gk *Mentōr*] **1** *cap* : a friend of Odysseus entrusted with the education of Odysseus' son Telemachus **2 a** : a trusted counselor or guide **b** : TUTOR. COACH — **men·tor-ship** \-,ship\ *n*
²**mentor** *vt* (1983) : to serve as a mentor for

Source: Reprinted with permission from *Merriam-
Webster's Collegiate Dictionary, Tenth Edition.* © 2000
by Merriam-Webster, Incorporated.

In both cases, the entries give information on the origin, but the second explains the mythological background more clearly. Both of these dictionaries are abridged, which means that information has been condensed. An abridged dictionary is adequate for most college use. In special cases, however, you may desire information more on the origin or the past use of a word. If so, an unabridged, or unshortened, dictionary is necessary, but its large size dictates that you must go to it rather than carry it around with you. Note the entry for *mentor* in the unabridged *Webster's Third New International Dictionary:*

men·tor \'men-,tȯ(ə)r, -ȯ(ə), -ntə(r)\ *n* -s [after *Mentor,* tutor of Telemachus in the Odyssey of Homer, fr. L, fr. Gk *Mentōr*] **1** : a close, trusted, and experienced counselor or guide ⟨every one of us needs a ∼ who, because he is detached and disinterested, can hold up a mirror to us —P.W.Keve⟩ ⟨was much more than a ∼; he supplied decisions —Hilaire Belloc⟩ ⟨has been my ∼ since 1946 —Lalia P. Boone⟩ ⟨regarded by patrons . . . as a personal friend as well as fashion ∼ —N.Y. State *Legislative Committee on Problems of the Aging*⟩ **2** : TEACHER, TUTOR, COACH ⟨a writer of monographs, and a ∼ of seminars —*Atlantic*⟩ ⟨although he had never accepted a pupil . . . she persuaded him to become her ∼ —*Current Biog.*⟩ ⟨one of the game's most successful young ∼s —*Official Basketball Guide*⟩

Source: Reprinted with permission from
*Webster's Third New International® Dictionary,
Unabridged.* © 1997 by Merriam-Webster, Inc.

Your college library probably has several unabridged dictionaries in the reference room. Other excellent choices for etymological research include the *Random House Dictionary of the English Language* and the *American Heritage Dictionary of the English Language.*

Why Study Etymology? The more you know about a word, the easier it is to remember. The etymology gives you the history of a word, which can help you establish new relationships on your "computer chip," or schema, for that word. "Meeting the ancestors" can also help you create a rich visual image of the word by using the background information. For example, the word *trivial* means "of little worth or importance." It comes from the Latin words *tri* for *three* and *via* for *way,* which combine to mean "the crossing of three roads" in Latin. The Romans knew that people would stand and talk at such an intersection. Because many strangers would be listening to the conversations, it was advisable to talk only of small, or trivial, matters. This history of *trivial* can increase your enjoyment of the word while enhancing your ability to remember the definition.

exercise 12

Many English words have their roots in the names of characters in Greek mythology. The words represent a particular characteristic or predicament of the mythological person or creature. Read the entries here to discover their mythological origins, and answer the questions that follow.

> **am·a·zon** \'a-mə-ˌzän, -zən\ *n* [ME, fr. L, fr. Gk *Amazōn*] (14c) **1** *cap*
> : a member of a race of female warriors of Greek mythology **2** : a tall strong often masculine woman

Source: Reprinted with permission from *Merriam-Webster's Collegiate Dictionary, Tenth Edition.*
© 2000 by Merriam-Webster, Incorporated.

1. *Amazon* means _____

2. Explain the myth. _____

> **nar·cis·sism** \'när-sə-ˌsi-zəm\ *n* [G *Narzissismus,* fr. *Narziss* Narcissus, fr. L *Narcissus*] (1822) **1** : EGOISM, EGOCENTRISM **2** : love of or sexual desire for one's own body — **nar·cis·sist** \'när-sə-sist\ *n or adj* — **nar·cis·sis·tic** \ˌnär-sə-'sis-tik\ *adj*

> **nar·cis·sus** \när-'si-səs\ *n* [L, fr. Gk *Narkissos*] **1** *cap* : a beautiful youth in Greek mythology who pines away for love of his own reflection and is then turned into the narcissus flower **2** *pl* **nar·cis·si** \-'si-ˌsī, -(ˌ)sē\ *or* **nar·cis·sus·es** *or* **narcissus** [NL, genus name, fr. L, narcissus, fr. Gk *narkissos*]: DAFFODIL; *esp* : one whose flowers have a short corona and are usu. borne separately

Source: Reprinted with permission from *Merriam-Webster's Collegiate Dictionary, Tenth Edition.*
© 2000 by Merriam-Webster, Incorporated.

3. *Narcissism* means _____

4. Explain the myth. _____

_____

Textbook Glossary

Textbooks use words that are not found in the dictionary. This may sound strange, but it is true. For example, what does *loss leader* mean? Each word is listed separately in the dictionary, but the two words are not listed together and defined. Looking up *loss* and then looking up *leader* will not give you a correct definition of the term as it is used in the field of marketing. However, the glossary in the back of the marketing textbook defines the term as "a product whose price has been cut below cost to attract customers to a store." The textbook **glossary** defines words and phrases as they apply to particular fields of study. Consult it before using the dictionary for words that seem to be part of the terminology of the discipline.

exercise 13

The following exercise will give you an idea of the types of words and the amount of information presented in a glossary. Notice that many of the words take on a special meaning within the particular field of study. Use the marketing glossary on the next page to answer the questions with *T* (true) or *F* (false).

_____ 1. Being upset after deciding to buy a Toyota rather than a BMW is called *cognitive dissonance.*

_____ 2. A *brokerage allowance* is a marked-up price.

_____ 3. In *cannibalization,* a new product outsells a similar existing product in the same company.

_____ 4. A *buyer's market* is an advantageous time to sell a house.

_____ 5. *Cartels* are illegal in the United States.

_____ 6. In *comparative advertising,* rivals are mentioned.

_____ 7. In a sales presentation, the *close* asks for action.

_____ 8. Both a *cash discount* and *cash rebate* save the customer money.

_____ 9. A *break-even analysis* shows the profit made on an item.

_____ 10. The *business cycle* is the calendar year.

Thesaurus

Dr. Peter Mark Roget, an English physician, collected lists of related words as a hobby, and in 1852 the lists were published in a **thesaurus**, or treasury of words. In the book, he related words because they were synonyms such as *illegal* and *unlawful,* as well as antonyms such as *peaceful* and *warlike.* This book, still called *Roget's Thesaurus* because of the man who first had the idea, has been revised frequently through the addition of new words and the deletion of obsolete ones.

Roget's Thesaurus is not a dictionary. In fact, you would probably not use it while reading. Instead, it is a valuable source for writers who are stuck on using a particular word again and again and want a substitute. For example, if you are writing a history term paper and have already used the noun *cause* twice in one paragraph and hesitate to use it again, consult *Roget's Thesaurus* for other options. You will find noun alternatives such as *origin, basis, foundation, genesis,* and *root.* If you need a verb for *cause,* you will find synonyms that include *originate, give rise to, bring about, produce, create, evoke,* and many others. Probably

brand name   The pronounceable part of the brand. **(322)**

breakdown approach   An approach to estimating sales potential that assumes a product's sales potential varies with the country's general level of business activity. **(255)**

breakeven analysis   A method used to determine the level of sales at which total revenue will equal total cost, given the product's per-unit selling price. **(616)**

broadcast media   The communications channels that sell advertising time to marketers; radio and television. **(529)**

brokerage allowance   A reduction from list price granted to brokers for the marketing functions they perform. **(633)**

build-up approach   An approach to estimating sales potential that begins with an estimate of the number of units of the product category a typical buyer in a typical sales territory will buy, then multiplying that number by the number of potential buyers in the territory, and doing the same for all the other territories; adding the figures provides an estimate of market potential; estimating the share of that market potential the firm will capture at a given level of marketing effort provides an estimate of sales potential. **(255)**

business cycle   The sequence of changes that occur in an economy's overall level of business activity—prosperity, recession, depression, and recovery. **(33)**

buyclasses   The three basic types of industrial buying: new task buying, modified rebuy buying, and straight rebuy buying. **(184)**

buyer's market   An environment in which supply is greater than demand. **(18)**

buying center   The people who determine what will be purchased to fill an organization's needs and from whom the products will be purchased. **(188)**

buyphases   The problem-solving steps used by industrial buyers primarily in new task buying: recognizing a need; specifying the need; searching for potential suppliers; inviting, acquiring, and analyzing vendor proposals; selecting the vendor and placing the order; and following up. **(185)**

cannibalization   The situation that exists when a firm's new product experiences increased sales mainly due to the decreasing sales of its established product or products. **(298)**

cartel   A group of firms in different countries (or a group of countries) that agrees to share markets, limit output, and set prices; illegal in the United States. **(707)**

cash discount   A reduction in a product's list price that rewards customers for paying their bills promptly. **(632)**

cash rebate   A type of manufacturer's couponing effort in which the buyer requests a return of a portion of the price directly from the manufacturer. **(637)**

catalog retailing   A type of nonstore retailing in which the retailer offers its merchandise in a catalog that includes ordering instructions, and the customer orders by mail or phone or at a catalog counter in a retail store. **(408)**

catalog showroom   A discount retail facility whose customers preshop by catalog and then select merchandise from samples displayed in the showroom. **(406)**

channel conflict   Disagreement among members of a marketing channel as to their respective roles and functions; horizontal conflict occurs between members at the same level, and vertical conflict occurs between members at different levels. **(378)**

channel leader   The marketing channel member in an administered VMS who exerts power over the other channel members and can influence their decisions and actions. **(382)**

close   The point in a sales presentation at which the salesperson attempts to clinch the sale, to get action by asking the prospect for the order. **(566)**

cognitive dissonance   A state of psychological tension or postpurchase doubt that a consumer experiences after making a difficult purchasing choice. **(140)**

combination export manager   A domestic agent middleman that serves as the export department for several noncompeting manufacturers, contacting foreign customers and negotiating sales for manufacturer-clients for a commission. Similar to a selling agent in domestic commerce. **(721)**

combination store   A retail store that is larger than a superstore and offers even more diversified merchandise and services; a combination food and drugstore with roughly half the selling space devoted to nonfood items. **(404)**

communication   The process of influencing others' behavior by sharing ideas, information, or feelings with them; occurs when a sender transmits a message, a receiver receives it, and the sender and receiver have a shared meaning. **(480)**

comparative advertising   Advertising in which the marketer compares its brand to rival brands identified by brand name. **(519)**

competitive bidding   The practice of prospective sellers competing by submitting their prices for goods or services to an industrial buyer who is shopping around. **(645)**

over a hundred words are listed as relating to *cause,* but not all of them are synonymous. Select the one that fits your need in the sentence, adds variety to your writing, and maintains the same shade of meaning that you desire.

The words in a thesaurus are listed in alphabetical order, and familiar dictionary abbreviations are used for parts of speech. The following is an example from *Roget's Thesaurus* showing the entry for the word *influence.*

> **influence,** *n. & v.* —*n.* influentialness; IMPORTANCE, POWER, mastery, sway, dominance, AUTHORITY, control, ascendancy, persuasiveness, ability to affect; reputation, weight; magnetism, spell; conduciveness; pressure. *Slang,* drag, pull. —*v.t.* affect; move, induce, persuade; sway, control, lead, actuate; modify; arouse, incite; prevail upon, impel; set the pace, pull the strings; tell, weigh. *Ant.,* see IMPOTENCE.

Source: Reprinted with permission from Morehead and Morehead, *The New American Roget's College Thesarus.*

If a word is printed in small capitals such as *IMPORTANCE, POWER,* and *AUTHORITY,* it means that you can find additional synonyms by looking that particular word up in its alphabetical order. Explanations sometimes appear in brackets and not every word in the dictionary is listed.

Reader's TIP   Using an Electronic Thesaurus

Your word-processing program probably has a thesaurus. In Word Perfect, for example, the thesaurus is found in the *Tools* pull-down menu, as one of the *Language* options. To use this, select the word for which you want alternatives by dragging the cursor over the word to highlight it and then clicking on the thesaurus. An array of words will appear, usually both in the *Meanings* box and in the *Replace with Synonyms* box as indicated in the figure here displaying alternatives for the word *right.* Click and highlight a different word other than *just,* which is presently highlighted in the *Meanings* box, and you will get a different array of synonyms. For example, click on the word *sane* in the following illustration and your synonym options will be *normal, rational, sound, reasonable,* and *wise.* This one word *right* has forty-nine synonym alternatives on this computer thesaurus in Microsoft Word. By moving the down arrow situated to the right of the word *claim,* you will uncover the word *Antonyms* and the words *wrong, incorrect, erroneous,* and *lenient* will appear as options. Thus your computer thesaurus has many more words than appear at first glance. Search and choose an option that fits the context of your sentence.

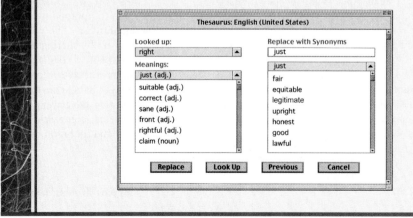

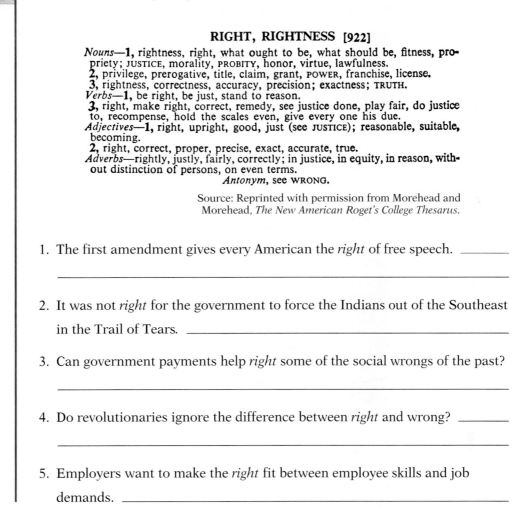

exercise 14 Use the following entry for *right* in *Roget's Thesaurus* to select an alternate word that fits the meaning of *right* in the sentences.

RIGHT, RIGHTNESS [922]

Nouns—**1,** rightness, right, what ought to be, what should be, fitness, propriety; JUSTICE, morality, PROBITY, honor, virtue, lawfulness.
2, privilege, prerogative, title, claim, grant, POWER, franchise, license.
3, rightness, correctness, accuracy, precision; exactness; TRUTH.
Verbs—**1,** be right, be just, stand to reason.
3, right, make right, correct, remedy, see justice done, play fair, do justice to, recompense, hold the scales even, give every one his due.
Adjectives—**1,** right, upright, good, just (see JUSTICE); reasonable, suitable, becoming.
2, right, correct, proper, precise, exact, accurate, true.
Adverbs—rightly, justly, fairly, correctly; in justice, in equity, in reason, without distinction of persons, on even terms.
Antonym, see WRONG.

Source: Reprinted with permission from Morehead and Morehead, *The New American Roget's College Thesarus.*

1. The first amendment gives every American the *right* of free speech. _____

    _____

2. It was not *right* for the government to force the Indians out of the Southeast in the Trail of Tears. _____

3. Can government payments help *right* some of the social wrongs of the past?

    _____

4. Do revolutionaries ignore the difference between *right* and wrong? _____

    _____

5. Employers want to make the *right* fit between employee skills and job demands. _____

Analogies

An **analogy** is a comparison that mimics a previously stated relationship. Perhaps an example is the best explanation. Study the following example:

EXAMPLE *Apple* is to *fruit* as *potato* is to _____.

EXPLANATION The first step in solving an analogy is to pinpoint the initial relationship. What is the relationship between *apple* and *fruit*? Because an apple is a member of the fruit group, you might say that it is one part of a larger whole. To complete the analogy, you must establish a similar relationship for *potato*. In what larger group does a potato belong? *Vegetable* is the answer.

Analogies are challenging and can be very difficult. They test logical thinking as well as vocabulary. Working through analogies is an experience in problem solving.

The following list explains the many different relationships that can be expressed in analogy. Study both the list and the examples.

Reader's TIP   Categories of Relationships for Analogies

Synonyms: Similar in meaning
Start is to *begin* as *end* is to *finish.*

Antonyms: Opposite in meaning
Retreat is to *advance* as *tall* is to *short.*

Function, use, or **purpose:** Identifies what something does. Watch for the object (noun) and then the action (verb).
Car is to *drive* as *towel* is to *absorb.*

Classification: Identifies the larger group association
Mosquito is to *insect* as *gasoline* is to *fuel.*

Characteristics and descriptions: Shows qualities or traits
Sour is to *lemon* as *sweet* is to *sugar.*

Degree: Shows variations of intensity
Walking is to *running* as *cool* is to *frozen.*

Part to whole: Shows the larger group
Pupil is to *school* as *sailor* is to *navy.*

Cause and effect: Shows the reason (cause) and the result (effect)
Work is to *success* as *virus* is to *illness.*

exercise 15

Study the following analogies to establish the relationship of the first two words. Record that relationship, using the categories just outlined. Then choose the word that duplicates that relationship to finish the analogy.

_____ 1. *Leg* is to *table* as *wheel* is to _____.

Relationship? <u>Part to whole</u>

a. chair
b. car
c. motor
d. steer

_____ 2. *Soft* is to *firm* as *peaceful* is to _____.

Relationship? <u>Antonyms</u>

a. pillow
b. kind
c. sleep
d. aggressive

_____ 3. *Turnip* is to *vegetable* as *walnut* is to _____.

Relationship? <u>Classification</u>

a. wood
b. fuel
c. house
d. glass

_____ 4. *Selling* is to *profit* as *germ* is to _____.

Relationship? _Cause + effect_

    a. vaccination
    b. carelessness
    c. wealth
    • d. disease

_____ 5. *Kind* is to *considerate* as *courage* is to _____.

Relationship? _Synonyms_

    a. soldier
    • b. bravery
    c. fear
    d. fighting

_____ 6. *Towel* is to *absorb* as *oven* is to _____.

Relationship? _function_

    a. safety
    b. speed
    • c. cook
    d. kitchen

_____ 7. *Tiny* is to *small* as *happy* is to _____.

Relationship? _Degree_

    a. good
    • b. exhilarated
    c. peace
    d. emotion

_____ 8. *Soft* is to *pillow* as *humid* is to _____.

Relationship? _Characteristics_

    • a. swamp
    b. trip
    c. camp
    d. trees

_____ 9. *Work* is to *success* as *study* is to _____.

Relationship? _Cause + effect_

    a. history
    • b. knowledge
    c. professor
    d. college

_____ 10. *Needle* is to *sew* as *bulb* is to _____.

Relationship? _function_

    a. lamp
    • b. illuminate
    c. electricity
    d. table

Easily Confused Words

Many pairs of words cause confusion because they sound exactly alike or almost alike, but they are spelled and used differently. *Principal* and *principle* are examples of this confusion. A common error is to write, "The new school principle is Mrs. Thompson." Remember, the *al* word is the person, or "pal," and the *le* word is the rule. To keep most of these words straight, memorize and associate. Study the following words that sound similar and learn their differences.

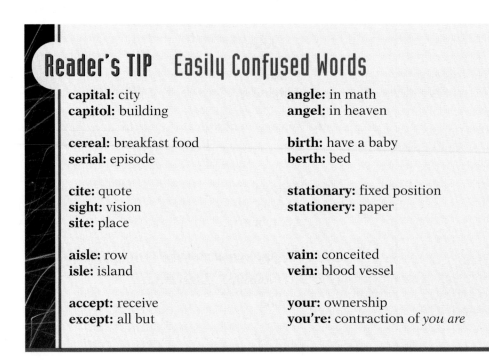

Reader's TIP   Easily Confused Words

capital: city
capitol: building

cereal: breakfast food
serial: episode

cite: quote
sight: vision
site: place

aisle: row
isle: island

accept: receive
except: all but

angle: in math
angel: in heaven

birth: have a baby
berth: bed

stationary: fixed position
stationery: paper

vain: conceited
vein: blood vessel

your: ownership
you're: contraction of *you are*

exercise 16

Circle the correct boldface word to fit the context of each sentence.

1. The letter was written on official university (**stationary, stationery**).

2. The geometry problem involved one right (**angle, angel**).

3. Atlanta is the (**capital, capitol**) of Georgia.

4. The cheapest room on the ship contains only one tiny (**birth, berth**).

5. Eat a bowl of (**cereal, serial**) in the morning.

6. Look for your friend in the second (**aisle, isle**) of the lecture hall.

7. The professor told the students to (**cite, sight, site**) the author's exact words in the paper.

8. Read all of the chapters (**accept, except**) the last two.

9. The swim coach wants to know when (**your, you're**) ready.

10. To draw blood, she stuck the needle in my (**vain, vein**).

PERSONAL feedback 2   Name _____

1. After reading this chapter, how will you change your system for remembering new words? _____

_____

2. Why do you enjoy or dislike studying words? _____

_____

3. Why is it not recommended that you look up unknown words as you read? _____

_____

4. What is one word that your instructor uses frequently that you were not previously accustomed to hearing? _____

_____

5. List ten adjectives to describe characteristics that you would like in a spouse. Again, stretch your vocabulary beyond easy words.

_____

_____

Vocabulary Enrichment

Most of the longer textbook reading selections in this text are followed by a Vocabulary Enrichment section with additional practice for the strategies presented in this vocabulary chapter (see p. 129 for an example). Expanding and enriching your vocabulary goes beyond one lesson and a single chapter. It is an exciting, lifelong activity.

Ten Weekly Vocabulary Lessons

Use the ten weekly vocabulary lessons in Appendix 5 of this textbook to expand your vocabulary. Each lesson follows a structural approach and links words through shared prefixes, roots, and suffixes. The words are organized into different clusters or families to enhance memory, to organize your learning, and to emphasize that most new words are made up of familiar old parts. Strengthen your vocabulary by identifying your old friends in the new words. Then apply your knowledge of word parts to unlock and remember the meanings of the new words.

Your instructor may choose to introduce the words at the beginning of the week, assign review items for practice, and quiz your knowledge of the words at the end of the week. Learn over 200 words through this easy word family approach.

Summary Points

- Use context clues from a passage to figure out the meaning of new words.
- Visualize associations to remember new words.
- Put the word, the definition, a sentence, a picture, and the source on concept cards.
- Consider the context to figure out the correct meaning of multiple-meaning words.
- Use word parts such as roots, prefixes, and suffixes to help unlock the meaning of new words.
- Find much more than just the definitions of words in the dictionary.
- Locate words that are part of the terminology of the discipline in the textbook glossary.
- Use a thesaurus for suggestions to alternate word options when writing.
- To solve an analogy, first determine the category of the relationship.

COLLABORATIVE PROBLEM SOLVING

Form a five-member group and select one of the following questions. Brainstorm and then outline your major points on a transparency. Choose a member to present the group findings to the class.

▶ Make a list of the ten words that have multiple meanings.

▶ Create a list of ten words that begin with the prefix *pre*.

▶ Create five analogies, one for each of the following relationships: synonyms, antonyms, function, part to whole, cause and effect.

▶ Create a list of ten words that end with the suffix *ous*.

EXPLORE THE NET

Use your e-mail and the Internet to increase your vocabulary. Check out the following sites to receive a free vocabulary word each day.

www.wordcommand.com/wordoftheday.htm

www.mailbits.net/free/get/word.asp

Visit the following sites and select an activity to share with your classmates

Wordsmyth

www.wordsmyth.net/

Word Safari

www.home.earthlink.net/~ruthpett/safari/index.htm

For additional readings and exercises, visit the *Breaking Through* Web site:

www.ablongman.com/smith

EVERYDAY READING SKILLS
Joining a Mailing List or a Newsgroup

Subscribe to a Mailing List

A **mailing list** is a list of e-mail addresses of individual people who have subscribed to a periodic mailing distribution on a particular topic. The program that handles the subscription requests for a mailing list is called an **electronic mailing list**. The two most popular are *LISTSERV* and Majordomo. These lists distribute information in two format types, *discussion groups* and *announcements*.

In the discussion group format, the subscribers share a common interest or membership in a particular group. Any member of the mailing list may e-mail ideas or questions that are then distributed to the entire list of subscribers. In the announcement format, a single writer broadcasts a periodical e-mail to a willing audience. Many of these are written in newsletter style.

Mailing lists are helpful in a number of ways. They can answer specific questions that relate to the group focus, report on recent developments in a particular field, or provide entertainment with daily messages. However, be aware that your membership on a mailing list continues until you request to be removed. When you subscribe, you also want to know how to unsubscribe.

Reader's TIP   Subscribing to a Mailing List

- Use a mailing list search engine such as
  www.liszt.com/,
  tile.net/lists/,
  or
  www.lsoft.com/lists/listref.html
  to find directories of mailing lists.

- Type in keywords or phrases appropriate to your interest or research needs to find specific mailing lists.

- To subscribe to an electronic mailing list (the majority of mailing lists found through these search engines are of this type), send an e-mail to the desired list. In the body of the e-mail, type SUBSCRIBE NAME OF THE LIST your name. Use your first and last name after the name of the list, and leave the subject line blank.

Popular Electronic Mailing Lists

DietCity
Description: The most popular *LISTSERV* list; a resource for diet and nutrition information on the Web.
To subscribe: E-mail the command SUBSCRIBE DIETCITY your name to

LISTSERV@LISTSERV.EDIETS.COM.

Merriam Webster's Word of the Day
Description: A daily dose of vocabulary building.
To subscribe: E-mail the command SUBSCRIBE MW-WOD your name to

LISTSERV@LISTERV.WEBSTER.M-W.COM.

Newsletter for Campus Life
Description: The newsletter for Campus Life magazine online.
To subscribe: E-mail the command SUBSCRIBE CAMPUS-LIFE your name to

LISTSERV@LISTSERV.aol.COM.

Fantasy Sports Center Newsletter
Description: An update on the current sports scoop.
To subscribe: E-mail the command SUBSCRIBE FANTASYSCOOPS-L your name to

LISTSERV@LISTSERV.aol.COM.

Quote-A-Day
Description: A daily e-mail with four to five profound and sometimes humorous quotes on a variety of subjects.
To subscribe: send a blank e-mail to

join-quote@MightyCool.com.

 Follow the steps just listed to explore mailing lists that may be of interest to you. Record the addresses of two mailing lists that you would consider joining and explain why each interests you.

1. _____

2. _____

Participate in a Newsgroup

A **newsgroup** is a topic-specific site where you can review information posted by others on a particular subject. These postings include news, opinions, discussions, questions, and even binary files such as images, sound, and software. You can participate in the newsgroup by submitting your own postings. Newsgroups can be valuable research resources because you can draw on the knowledge of experts who participate in them and have access to the latest wire service news reports. Newsgroups differ from mailing lists in that you do not need to join in advance to participate.

Newsgroups

Environmental Science
scientific issues relating to the environment:

www.deja.com/group/sci.environment

Shakespeare
a forum for discussing different issues relating to the works and the man:

www.deja.com/group/humanities.lit.authors.shakespeare

Reader's TIP   Posting on a Newsgroup

- Type in keywords and phrases appropriate to your topic of interest through a newsgroup search engine such as these:
  www.liszt.com/news/,
  www.deja.com/usenet,
  or
  www.aol.com/netfind/newsgroups.html.

- Explore the newsgroups that most closely relate to your search criteria by reading the newsgroup without posting for a while (known as "lurking") and by reading the newsgroup's frequently asked questions (FAQ).

- Either post or subscribe to the newsgroup by clicking on the appropriate icon.

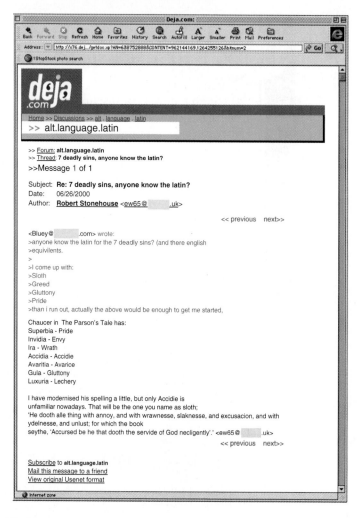

European Union

a discussion on the EU and political integration in Europe:

www.dejanews.com/=liszt/dnquery.xp?query=~g%20talk.politics.european-union

For help with a research topic from a newsgroup, make your questions very specific in order to get other participants to respond by e-mail. For example, "Can someone suggest a research topic about modern European history?" is too general, whereas "Can someone suggest sites for a comparison of the social and economic conditions in Europe leading up to World War I and World War II?" is a more narrow topic and more likely to receive a response. Tip: You can invoke interest in others to read your posting by including an interesting *subject* heading.

exercise 2

Enter a newsgroup and ask a specific question. First, decide on a topic that interests you or a topic you are researching for a college course. Then find a newsgroup about this topic. Form a specific question to ask newsgroup members. Record your question and print any responses that you get from the group.

Question _____

Main Idea

4

- What is a main idea?
- What is a topic?
- How do you recognize the difference between general and specific ideas?
- What is a stated main idea?
- What is an unstated main idea?

Everyday Reading Skills: Selecting a Book

What Is a Main Idea?

The **main idea** of a passage is the core of the material, the particular point the author is trying to convey. The main idea of a passage can be stated in one sentence that condenses specific ideas or details in the passage into a general, all-inclusive statement of the author's message. In classroom discussions, all of the following words are sometimes used to help students understand the meaning of the main idea:

thesis

main point

central focus

gist

controlling idea

central thought

Whether you read a single paragraph, a chapter, or an entire book, many experts agree that your most important single task is to understand the main idea of what you read.

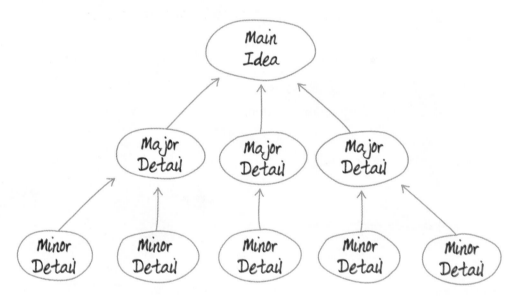

Recognize General and Specific Words

The first step in determining the main idea of a selection is to look at the specific ideas presented in the sentences and try to decide on a general **topic** or subject under which you can group these ideas. Before tackling sentences, begin with words. Pretend that the sentence ideas in a selection have been reduced to a short list of keywords. Pretend also that within the list is a general term that expresses an overall subject for the keywords. The general term encompasses or categorizes the key ideas and is considered the topic of the list.

EXAMPLE   The following list contains three specific ideas with a related general topic. Circle the general term that could be considered the subject of the list.

satin

wool

fabric

silk

EXPLANATION Satin, wool, and silk are different types of fabric. Thus *fabric* is the general term or classification that could be considered the subject or topic.

exercise 1

Circle the general term or subject for each of the following related groups of ideas.

1. chimpanzees	2. cirrus	3. oats	4. Alps	5. shrimp
orangutans	clouds	wheat	Appalachians	crustacean
apes	cumulus	corn	mountains	crab
gorillas	stratus	grain	Rockies	lobster

Recognize General and Specific Phrases

Topics of passages are more often stated as phrases rather than single words. The following list contains a phrase that is a general topic and three specific ideas related to the topic. Circle the general topic that could be the subject.

EXAMPLE

Turn on the ignition.

Press the accelerator.

Insert the key.

Start the car.

EXPLANATION The first three details are involved in starting a car. The last phrase is the general subject or topic.

exercise 2

Circle the phrase that could be the topic for each list.

1. totaling yearly income
   subtracting for dependents
   filing an income tax return
   mailing a 1040 form

2. paying fees
   buying books
   starting college
   going to class

3. picking up seashells
   vacationing at the beach
   walking in the surf
   riding the waves

4. pushing paper under sticks
   piling the logs
   building a fire
   striking a match

exercise 3

Read the lists of specific details and write a general phrase that could be the subject or topic for each group.

1. separate the white and dark clothes

   add one cup of detergent

   insert quarters into the machine

   General topic? _____

2. dribble the ball

   pass ball down court

   shoot a basket

   General topic? _____

3. release the brake

   turn key in ignition

   press on gas pedal

   General topic? _____

4. switch on power

   select a program

   load a disk into the drive

   General topic? _____

5. boil water in a large pot

   add salt and oil

   empty noodles into water

   General topic? _____

Recognize the General Topic for Sentences

Paragraphs are composed of sentences that develop a single general topic. The next practice exercises contain groups in which the sentences of a paragraph are listed numerically. After reading the sentences, circle the phrase that best expresses the topic or general subject of the sentences.

EXAMPLE

1. The law of demand is illustrated in an experiment conducted by the makers of M&M candy.
2. For a twelve-month period, the price of M&Ms remained the same in 150 stores, but the number of M&Ms in a package increased, which dropped the price per ounce.
3. In these stores, sales immediately rose by 20 to 30 percent.

Candy Maker's Experiment

M&Ms Drop in Price

M&Ms Prove the Law of Demand

EXPLANATION The first phrase is too broad. The second relates a detail that is an important part of the experiment. The third links the candy with the purpose of the experiment and thus most accurately states the subject of the sentences.

Circle the phrase that best describes the topic or subject for each group of sentences.

exercise 4

Group 1

1. To provide a favorable climate for growing grapes, the winter temperature should not go below 15° F, and the summers should be long.
2. During the growing season, rainfall should be light.
3. A gentle movement of air is required to dry the vines after rains, dispel fog, and protect the vines from fungus disease.

Protecting Grapes from Disease

Appropriate Temperatures for Growing Grapes

Appropriate Climates for Growing Grapes

Group 2

1. For example, faced with fewer expansion opportunities within the United States, Wal-Mart opened new stores abroad and foreign sales reached $7.5 billion in three years.
2. As more and more companies engage in international business, the world is becoming a single, interdependent global economy.
3. In a plan to become a transglobal giant, Chrysler, one of America's apple pie auto companies, merged with Germany's Daimler-Benz to become DaimlerChrysler.

International Auto Mergers

A Global Economy

Wal-Mart Expansion

Group 3

1. After accidents, suicide is the second leading cause of death among adolescents.
2. In a national survey, 42 percent of the 8th through 10th grade girls reported contemplating suicide sometime in their lives.
3. In the last forty years, the suicide rate among young men 15 to 19 years of age has quadrupled.

Prevention of Suicides

Increase in Adolescent Suicides

Reasons for Teen Suicides

Group 4

1. Some scientists believe that the vestigial diving response offers proof that humans evolved from aquatic animals.
2. If you submerge your face in water, your pulse rate is likely to drop and your metabolic rate decreases.

3. This slowdown suggests a vestigial diving response that would allow humans to remain submerged longer.

Human Science

Vestigial Linkage to Aquatics

Lowering the Metabolic Rate

Group 5

1. Simply drinking water is the best way to prevent dehydration from sweating.
2. Taking salt tablets before drinking water can dehydrate the body even more by extracting water from body tissue.
3. Plain water is better than beverages containing sugar or electrolytes because it is absorbed faster.

Salt Tablets versus Water

Value in Plain Water

Preventing Dehydration

exercise 5

Read the following groups of three sentences and then write a phrase that best states the subject or general topic for the sentences.

Group 1

1. The albatross is one of the few birds that is designed to live at sea and it seldom visits land.
2. Because it has special glands that excrete salt, it can drink seawater and eat salty fish.
3. The albatross's unusually long wings provide the lift for it to glide almost endlessly in high winds over rough seas.

General topic? _____

Group 2

1. Once children begin to speak and understand words, their progress is remarkably fast.
2. Most children begin speaking at 1 year of age and speak only 2 to 3 words.
3. By age 2, they speak about 50 words and understand 200 to 300 words.

General topic? _____

Group 3

1. Dr. Sylvia Castillo of Stanford University founded the National Network of Hispanic Women.
2. This organization publishes a national newsletter that focuses on the successes of Hispanic women in academia and business.
3. The organization has become an important voice for Hispanic issues relating to gender.

General topic? _____

_____

Recognize General and Supporting Sentences

Read the sentences in each of the following groups. The sentences are related to a single subject with two of the sentences expressing specific support and one sentence expressing the general idea about the subject. Circle the number of the sentence that best expresses the general subject. Then read the three topic phrases and circle the phrase that best describes the subject of the sentences.

EXAMPLE

1. An accountant who prefers to work alone rather than as a team member may be an important part of the organization but will not become a leader.
2. A CEO who steers a company into increased profits but exhibits poor people skills by yelling at employees and refusing to listen will not keep her job.
3. To reach the top in the workplace, companies now demand a high level of emotional intelligence (EI), which refers to skills in adaptability, self-control, conflict management, and teamwork.

IQ No Longer Matters

The Importance of Emotional Intelligence

Polite Changes in the Workplace

EXPLANATION The third sentence best expresses the general subject. The other two sentences offer specific supporting ideas. The second phrase, "The Importance of Emotional Intelligence," best describes the general subject of the material. The first phrase is not really suggested, and the last phrase is one of the details that is mentioned.

exercise 6

Circle the number of the sentence that best expresses the general subject. Then read the three topic phrases and circle the phrase that best describes the subject of the sentences.

Group 1

1. African American and Hispanic teens are not as likely to use tobacco as Caucasian adolescents.
2. Each day approximately three thousand teens start smoking, and eventually one third of those teens will die from smoking.
3. Despite the proven danger, in the past decade tobacco usage among teens has increased.

Tobacco Usage Among Teens

Dangers Face Teens

Harms of Smoking

Group 2

1. Berry Gordy, an ex-boxer and Ford auto worker, borrowed $700 from his family and successfully began to manufacture and sell his own records on the Hitsville USA (later called "Motown," for "motor town") label.
2. The next year Smokey Robinson and the Miracles recorded "Shop Around," which was Gordy's first big million-copy hit.

3. Gordy signed an 11-year-old boy to record for him under the name of Stevie Wonder.

   Gordy's Success

   Stevie Wonder at Motown

   The Recording Artists at Motown

Group 3

1. The czarina believed that the devious and politically corrupt Rasputin, known as the "mad monk," was the only one who could save her son.
2. The son of Nicholas II was afflicted with hemophilia, a condition in which the blood does not clot properly.
3. In Russia during the reign of Nicholas II, hemophilia played an important historical role.

   Rasputin's Charm

   Hemophilia

   Influence of Hemophilia on Russia

Group 4

1. The success of Norman Rockwell's illustrations is based on the simple formula of drawing ordinary people doing ordinary things that make us laugh at ourselves.
2. Rockwell used humor to poke fun at situations but never at people.

3. Rockwell painted the people and children in the neighborhood, first from real life and, in later years, from photographs.

Rockwell's Neighborhood

Rockwell's Successful People Formula

Art from Photographs

Group 5

1. By 2000 the world's population moved past 6 billion people, and by 2050 it is expected to reach 9 billion.
2. The global statistics on population growth and the availability of food are alarming.
3. Biotechnologists estimate that the land available for raising crops will decrease by half in the next fifty years.

Biotechnical Agriculture

Feeding the Poor

Population Growth and Hunger

exercise 7

For each group of sentences, write a phrase that states the topic, and then circle the number of the sentence that best expresses the main idea.

Group 1

1. Four hundred Navajos were recruited as marine radio operators, and the codes based on the Navajo language were never broken by the enemy.
2. During World War II, over 25,000 Native Americans served in the armed forces and made amazing contributions toward the war effort.
3. The most famous Indian GI was a Pima Indian, the marine Ira Hayes, who helped plant the American flag on Iwo Jima.

General topic? _____

Group 2

1. One of the earliest and most lasting attempts to explain dreams was Freud's theory that they are products of the mind that can be interpreted and understood.
2. More specifically, Freud believed that dreams are disguised attempts at the fulfillment of wishes that the individual finds unacceptable at the conscious level.
3. Although modern cognitive psychologists reject many of Freud's ideas, they still note that aspects of his dream theory have cognitive validity.

General topic? _____

Group 3

1. Use soap or a liquid sanitizer to wash your hands frequently, and definitely wash them before eating.
2. In developing countries, avoid uncooked food, use bottled water, and peel fruit before eating it.
3. Certain tips can protect travelers from the health risks of traveling abroad.

General topic? _____

exercise 8	Each of the following sentence groups contains three specific supporting sentences. Write a general sentence that states the overall *message* for each group. In addition, write a phrase that briefly states the general *topic* of that sentence.

Group 1

1. The battered woman does not want to believe the man she loves is actually violent.
2. She doesn't want to face the possibility that he may be violent for the rest of their lives together.
3. She wants to hold on to the hope that someday he will quit drinking and the relationship will change.

—*Marriages and Families in a Diverse Society* by Robin Wolf

General sentence stating the main idea? _____

_____

General topic? _____

Group 2

1. Periodic washing or dusting is a substitute for natural cleansing by rainfall and should be performed whenever the leaves show an appreciable amount of dust.
2. Regular inspection for pests and diseases is a part of maintenance that is commonly overlooked, to the decline and ruin of many beautiful plants.
3. To prevent plants from becoming lopsided, it is advisable to turn them a quarter turn every few weeks so that a different section of foliage faces the light.

—*Practical Horticulture*, Fourth Edition, by Laura Williams Rice and Robert P. Rice, Jr.

General sentence stating the main idea? _____

_____

_____

General topic? _____

Group 3

1. A colleague of mine gave a lecture in Beijing, China, to a group of Chinese college students.
2. The students listened politely but made no comments and asked no questions after her lecture.
3. Later, she learned that Chinese students show respect by being quiet and seemingly passive.

—*Messages* by Joseph DeVito

General sentence stating the main idea? _____

_____

General topic? _____

Differentiate Topic, Main Idea, and Supporting Details

We have said that a topic is a word or phrase that describes the subject or general category of a group of specific ideas. Frequently, the topic is stated as the title of a passage. The main idea, in contrast, is a complete sentence that states the topic and *adds the writer's position or focus on the topic*. The supporting details are the specifics that develop the topic and main idea.

Read the following example from a textbook paragraph and label the topic, the main idea, and a supporting detail.

EXAMPLE

Topic   The Body Signaling Feeling

Main Idea   Some signals of body language, like some facial expressions, seem to be "spoken" universally.

Detail   When people are depressed, it shows in their walk, stance, and head position.

—*Psychology* by Carole Wade and Carol Tavris

exercise 9

Compare the items within each group and indicate which is the topic (T), the main idea (MI), and the specific supporting detail (D).

Group 1

___D___   1. Much in this American document comes from England's Magna Carta, which was signed in 1215.

___T___   2. British Roots in American Government

___MI___   3. The American Constitution has its roots in the power of past documents.

Group 2

_____   1. Children are highly valued in African American families.

___T___   2. Valuing Children.

_____   3. Like Latinos, African Americans view "children as wealth," believing that children are important in adding enjoyment and fulfillment to life.

—*Marriage and Families in a Diverse Society* by Robin Wolf

Group 3

_____   1. The Fate of Mexican Americans

_____   2. Some welcomed the Americans; many others, recognizing the futility of resistance, responded to the American conquest with ambivalence.

_____   3. The 80,000 Mexicans who lived in the Southwest did not respond to the Mexican War with a single voice.

—*America and Its People*, Third Edition, by James Martin et al.

Group 4

_____   1. Her early research led to an understanding of how viruses infect the plant and destroy its tissues.

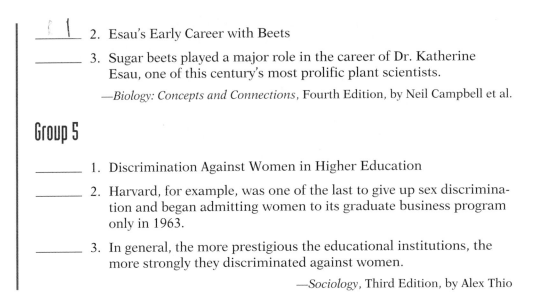

_____ 2. Esau's Early Career with Beets

_____ 3. Sugar beets played a major role in the career of Dr. Katherine Esau, one of this century's most prolific plant scientists.

—*Biology: Concepts and Connections*, Fourth Edition, by Neil Campbell et al.

Group 5

_____ 1. Discrimination Against Women in Higher Education

_____ 2. Harvard, for example, was one of the last to give up sex discrimination and began admitting women to its graduate business program only in 1963.

_____ 3. In general, the more prestigious the educational institutions, the more strongly they discriminated against women.

—*Sociology*, Third Edition, by Alex Thio

Questioning for the Main Idea

To determine the main idea of a body of material, ask questions in the following three basic areas. The order may vary according to how much you already know about the subject. Usually, you decide on the general topic first, sometimes from the title and sometimes by considering the details. If you are familiar with the material, constructing a main idea may seem almost automatic. If the material is unfamiliar, however, you may need to connect the key thoughts to formulate a topic and then create your main idea statement.

1. Establish the Topic

Question: Who or what is this about? What general word or phrase identifies the subject? The topic should be broad enough to include all the ideas, but narrow enough to focus on the direction of the details. For example, identifying the topic of an article as "College Costs," "Change in College," or "Changing to Cut College Costs," might all be correct, but the last may be the most pointed and descriptive for the article.

2. Identify the Key Supporting Terms

Question: What are the important details? Look at the details that seem significant to see if they point in a particular direction. What aspect of the subject do they address? What seems to be the common message? In a passage on college costs, the details might describe benefits of larger classes, telecommunication networks, and video instruction. A common thread is that each idea relates to changes targeted at cutting the costs of college instruction.

3. Focus on the Message of the Topic

Question: What is the main idea the author is trying to convey about the topic?

This statement should be:

- A complete sentence,
- Broad enough to include the important details, and
- Focused enough to describe the author's slant.

In the example about cutting college costs, the main idea might be "Several colleges experiment with ways to cut costs."

Stated Main Ideas

Research shows that readers comprehend better when the main idea is directly stated, particularly when it is stated at the beginning of a passage. Such an initial main idea statement, **thesis statement**, or **topic sentence** is a signpost for readers, briefing them on what to expect. This thesis or main idea statement overviews the author's message and connects the supporting details. Read the following example and use the three-step method to determine the main idea.

EXAMPLE

Polygraph tests have been viewed as an invasion of privacy and criticized on ethical, legal, and scientific grounds. The physiological changes thought to reveal deception could result from anxiety about being interrogated, anger at being asked to take the test, or fear from pondering the consequences of "failing" the test. You might react in any of these ways if you were "hooked up" to a polygraph.

—*Psychology* by Stephen F. Davis and Joseph J. Palladino

1. Who or what is the topic of this passage? _____

2. Underline the key terms.

3. What point is the author trying to make? _____

_____

EXPLANATION The topic of this passage is "Polygraph Tests." The details give specifics about how physiological changes caused by anxiety, anger, or fear can show up the same way on a polygraph test as a lie response. The author states the main idea in the first sentence.

Textbook authors do not always state the main idea in the first sentence. Stated main ideas may be the beginning, middle, or concluding sentence of a passage. Therefore, do not think of stating the main idea only as a search for a particular sentence. Instead, rely on your own skill in answering the three questions about topic, details, and focus. Connect the details to form your own concept of the main idea, and, if a specific sentence in the paragraph restates it, you will recognize it as the main idea.

exercise 10

Apply the three-question technique to identify the topic, key terms, and main idea of the following passages, all of which have stated main ideas.

Passage 1

Mowing must be done correctly for the turf to look its best. Mowing is essentially a pruning operation done on grass. It removes a portion of the photosynthesizing part of the plant, which in turn lessens the supply of carbohydrates going to the roots for growth and respiration. Thus roots are as affected by mowing as the blades of the grass. Cutting that removes more than 30 percent of the blade is detrimental to the roots because of the abrupt drop in carbohydrate flow.

— *Practical Horticulture,* Fourth Edition, by Laura Williams Rice and Robert P. Rice, Jr.

1. Who or what is the topic of this passage? _____
2. Underline the key terms.
3. What point is the author trying to make? _____
   _____

Passage 2

Henry Dreyfuss, in his *Symbol Sourcebook,* points out some of the positive and negative meanings associated with various colors and some cultural comparisons. For example, red in China is used for joyous and festive occasions, whereas in Japan it signifies anger and danger. Blue signifies defeat for the Cherokee Indian, but virtue and truth for the Egyptian. In the Japanese theater, blue is the color for villains. Yellow signifies happiness and prosperity in Egypt, but in tenth-century France yellow colored the doors of crimi- nals. Green communicates femininity to certain American Indians, fertility and strength to Egyptians, and youth and energy to the Japanese. Purple signifies virtue and faith in Egypt, grace and nobility in Japan.

—*Essentials of Human Communication* by Joseph DeVito

1. Who or what is the topic of this passage? _____
2. Underline the key terms.
3. What point is the author trying to make? _____
   _____

Passage 3

Statistics for 1996 reveal that 247 infants (under the age of 1) were victims of homicide, as were 320 persons aged 75 and over. Persons aged 20 to 24 were the most likely to be murdered. Murder perpetrators were also most common in the 20- to 24-year-old group. Firearms are the weapon of choice in most murders. Few murders are committed by strangers, and, geographically, murder is most common in the southern states. Uniform Crime Reports (UCR) statistics on murder describe the yearly incidence of all willful and unlawful homicides within the United States.

—*Criminal Justice Today,* Third Edition, by Frank Schmallenger

1. Who or what is the topic of this passage? _____
2. Underline the key terms.
3. What point is the author trying to make? _____

_____

_____

Passage 4

Many people wonder how they can tell whether or not someone else is sexually attracted to them. Shotland and Craig discovered that when people first meet a person in whom they are sexually interested, they exhibit a particular pattern of behavior. In their study, pairs of male and female college students who had just met were videotaped having a conversation. Afterward, the researchers asked the subjects whether their interest in the other person had been sexual or just friendly. The researchers then matched reports of sexual interest to specific behaviors in the videotapes. They found that behaviors that exhibit sexual interest include long eye contact; playing with inanimate objects; asking questions; giving long answers; discontinuing eating, drinking, or reading; being the first to speak after a pause; doing most of the talking; and, especially, mentioning that one has noticed the other person before this meeting. Although these behaviors, such as asking questions, also tend to occur when a person has only a friendly interest in the partner, they occur to a greater degree when sexual interest is present. When the interest is simply friendly rather than sexual, eye contact is briefer; fidgeting is less; answers to questions tend to be shorter; and the person tends to continue eating, drinking, or even reading when the other person is present. However, because friendly and sexually interested behavior fall at two ends of a continuum and the difference between them is a matter of degree, interpreting behaviors can be difficult.

—*Marriage and Families in a Diverse Society* by Robin Wolf

1. Who or what is the topic of this passage? _____
2. Underline the key terms.
3. What point is the author trying to make? _____

_____

Passage 5

Alcoholism has an impact that extends beyond the chemically dependent family member. The other family members become caught up in the addiction process in their attempt to cope with the chaotic family life that alcoholism produces. The alcoholic is known as the "dependent" because he or she is dependent on a chemical substance. The spouse typically takes on the role of the "enabler" (sometimes called "co-dependent") who tries to help the alcoholic and thereby unwittingly engages in behavior that allows the alcoholic to continue drinking. The enabler attempts to save the alcoholic from experiencing the consequences of addictive behavior. For example, if the alcoholic is drunk or hung over and does not show up at a family barbecue attended by extended kin, the enabler will make excuses for the alcoholic and might say that the alcoholic has the flu. Thus the alcoholism is kept secret and the alcoholic is protected from the anger of relatives.

—*Marriages and Families in a Diverse Society* by Robin Wolf

1. Who or what is the topic of this passage? _____

2. Underline the key terms.

3. What point is the author trying to make? _____

_____

Unstated Main Ideas

Research shows that only about half of the paragraphs in textbooks have directly stated main ideas. This should not be a problem if you understand the three-question technique for locating the main idea. The questions guide you in forming your own statement so that you are not dependent on finding a line in the text.

When the main idea is not directly stated, it is said to be *implied*, which means it is suggested from the thoughts that are revealed.

In this case, the author has presented a complete idea, but for reasons of style and impact has not chosen to express it concisely in one sentence. As a reader, it is your job to connect the details systematically and focus the message.

In the passage here, the main idea is not stated, but it may be determined by answering the three questions that follow.

EXAMPLE In Australia and Belgium, nonvoters are subject to fines; not only the fine itself but the clear expectation that everyone is legally required to vote helps generate 90+ percent turnout rates. In Italy, nonvoters are not fined, but "Did Not Vote" is stamped on their identification papers, threatening nonvoters with the prospect of unsympathetic treatment at the hands of public officials should they get into trouble or need help with a problem.

—*The New American Democracy*, Election Update Edition, by Morris Fiorina and Paul Peterson

1. Who or what is the topic of this passage? _____

(This gives you the general topic or heading.)

2. What are the key terms or details? _____

_____

3. What idea is the author trying to convey about nonvoting? _____

_____

(This is the main idea the author is trying to communicate.)

EXPLANATION The sentence stating the main idea might very well have been the first, middle, or last sentence of the paragraph. Having it stated, however, was not necessary for understanding the passage. In many cases, readers spend time searching for a single sentence that encapsulates the meaning rather than digesting the information and forming ideas. Instead, answer these three questions: "Who or what is this about?" "What are the key terms?" and "What point is the author trying to make?" This passage is about penalties for not voting. The key terms are *"giving fines in Australia and Belgium, and stamping 'Did Not Vote' on identification papers in Italy."* The author's main idea is that in *"some countries nonvoters are penalized to encourage voting."*

exercise 11

Passage 1

Marilyn, a Southwest Airlines flight attendant, takes the mike as her plane backs away from the Houston terminal. "Could y'all lean in a little toward the center aisle please?" she chirps in an irresistible Southern drawl. "Just a bit, please. That's it. No, the other way, sir. Thanks."

Baffled passengers comply even though they have no idea why.

"You see," says Marilyn at last, "the pilot has to pull out of this space here, and he needs to be able to check the rearview mirrors."

Only when the laughter subsides does Marilyn launch into the standard aircraft safety speech that many passengers usually ignore.

—*Business Essentials*, Third Edition, by Ronald Ebert and Ricky Griffin

1. Who or what is the topic of this passage? _____
2. Underline the key terms.
3. What point is the author trying to make? _____
   _____

Passage 2

Children have more taste buds than adults do, which may explain why they are often so picky about eating "grown-up" foods. Even among adults, individuals differ in their sensitivity to taste. Indeed, recent studies have shown that people can be divided into one of three groups: nontasters, medium tasters, and supertasters. Compared to most, supertasters use only half as much sugar or saccharin in their coffee or tea. They also suffer more oral burn from eating the active ingredient in chili peppers. Using videomicroscopy to count the number of taste buds on the tongue, researchers have found that nontasters have an average of 96 taste buds per square centimeter, medium tasters have 184, and supertasters have 425.

—*Psychology*, Second Edition, by Saul Kassin

1. Who or what is the topic of this passage? _____
2. Underline the key terms.
3. What point is the author trying to make? _____
   _____

Passage 3

If the person is extremely important, you had better be there early just in case he or she is able to see you ahead of schedule. As the individual's status decreases, it is less important for you to be on time. Students, for example, must be on time for conferences with teachers, but it is more important to be on time for deans and still more important to be on time for the president of the college. Teachers, on the other hand, may be late for conferences with students but not for conferences with deans or the president. Deans, in turn, may be late for teachers but not for the president. Business organizations and other hierarchies have similar rules.

—*Human Communication*, Sixth Edition, by Joseph DeVito

1. Who or what is the topic of this passage? _____

   _____

2. Underline the key terms.
3. What point is the author trying to make? _____

   _____

Passage 4

Try as she might, Marie Antoinette (1755–1793) found insufficient diversion in her life at the great court of Versailles. When she was fourteen, she had married the heir to the French throne, the future Louis XVI. By the age of nineteen she was queen of the most prosperous state in continental Europe. Still she was bored. Unpopular as a foreigner from the time she arrived in France, Marie Antoinette suffered a further decline in her reputation as gossip spread about her gambling and affairs at court. The public heard exaggerated accounts of the fortunes she spent on clothing and jewelry. In 1785 she was linked to a cardinal in a nasty scandal over a gift of a diamond necklace.

This Austrian-born queen may not have been more shallow or spendthrift than other queens, but it mattered that people came to see her that way. The queen's reputation sank to the nadir when it was reported that she dismissed the suffering of her starving subjects with the haughty retort that if they had no bread, "Let them eat cake."

—*The Unfinished Legacy* by Mark Kishlansky et al.

1. Who or what is the topic of this passage? _____
2. Underline the key terms.
3. What point is the author trying to make? _____

   _____

Passage 5

A mother had a son who threw temper tantrums: lying on the floor, pounding his fists, kicking his legs, and whining for whatever he wanted. One day while in a supermarket he threw one of his temper tantrums. In a moment of desperation, the mother dropped to the floor, pounded her fists, kicked her feet, and whined, "I wish you'd stop throwing temper tantrums! I can't stand it when you throw temper tantrums!" By this time, the son had stood up. He said in a hushed tone, "Mom, there are people watching! You're embarrassing me!" The mother calmly stood up, brushed off the dust, and said in a clear, calm voice, "That's what you look like when you're throwing a temper tantrum." Sometimes, traditional approaches such as bribing, threatening, ignoring, or giving in seem so natural that we overlook the possibility that something different, such as embarrassment, might work too.

—*The Creative Problem Solver's Toolbox* by Richard Fobes

1. Who or what is the topic of this passage? _____
   _____

2. Underline the key terms.

3. What point is the author trying to make? _____
   _____

Differentiating Distractors

To gain insight into recognizing a correctly stated main idea, categorizing incorrect responses can be helpful. When stating the topic or main idea of a passage, it is easy to make the mistake of creating a phrase or a sentence that is either too broad or too narrow. The same two types of errors occur when students are answering main idea questions on standardized tests. A phrase that is too broad is too general and thus would suggest the inclusion of much more than is actually stated in the passage. A phrase that is too narrow is a detail within the passage. It may be an interesting and eye-catching detail, but it is not the subject of the passage.

EXAMPLE

After reading the following passage, decide which of the suggested titles within the passage is correct (C), too broad (TB), or a detail (D).

One interesting research finding shows that listeners can accurately judge the socioeconomic status (whether high, middle, or low) of speakers from 60-second voice samples. In fact, many listeners reported that they made their judgments in fewer than 15 seconds. Speakers judged to be of high status were also rated as being of higher credibility than speakers rated middle and low in status. Listeners can also judge with considerable accuracy the emotional states of speakers from vocal expressions.

—*Human Communication*, Sixth Edition, by Joseph DeVito

_____ 1. Importance of Voice

_____ 2. Speaking

_____ 3. Making Judgments by Voice

_____ 4. Emotional States of Speakers

EXPLANATION The third response most accurately describes the topic of the passage. The first two are too broad and would include much more than is in the paragraph. The last response is a detail that is part of one of the experiments with listeners.

exercise 12

Read the following passage and label the suggested titles within the passage as correct (C), too broad (TB), or as a detail (D).

Passage 1

In California, Mexican Americans were outnumbered and vulnerable to discrimination. During the early years of the Gold Rush, Mexican Americans were robbed, beaten, and lynched with impunity. The 1850 Foreign Miners' Tax imposed a $20 a month tax on Mexican American miners, even though the Treaty of Guadalupe Hidalgo had granted them citizenship. Many Mexicans were forced to sell land to pay onerous taxes that fell heaviest on the Spanish speakers.

—*America and Its People*, Third Edition, by James Martin et al.

_____ 1. Treaty of Guadalupe Hidalgo

_____ 2. Discrimination

_____ 3. Foreign Miners' Tax During the Gold Rush

_____ 4. Discrimination Against Mexican Americans in California

Passage 2

Humpback whales strain their food from seawater. Instead of teeth, these giants have an array of brushlike plates called baleen on each side of their upper jaw. The baleen is used to sift food from the ocean. To start feeding, a humpback whale opens its mouth, expands its throat, and takes a huge gulp of seawater. When its mouth closes, the water squeezes out through spaces in the baleen, and a mass of food is trapped in the mouth. The food is then swallowed whole, passing into the stomach, where digestion begins. The humpback's stomach can hold about half a ton of food at a time, and in a typical day, the animal's digestive system will process as much as 2 tons of krill and fish.

—*Biology: Concepts and Connections*, Fourth Edition, by Neil Campbell et al.

_____ 1. Humpback Whales

_____ 2. Baleen for Teeth

_____ 3. The Digestive System of the Humpback Whale

_____ 4. How Whales Filter Food

Passage 3

Interestingly, Tom Peters, author of the classic management book *In Search of Excellence*, believes that women may have an enormous advantage over men in future management situations. He predicts that networks of relationships will replace rigid organizational structures, and star workers will be replaced by teams made up of workers at all levels who are empowered to make decisions. Detailed rules and procedures will be replaced by a flexible system

that calls for judgments based on key values and a constant search for new ways to get the job done. Strengths often attributed to women—emphasizing interrelationships, listening, and motivating others—will be the dominant virtues in the corporation of the future.

—*Modern Management*, Eighth Edition, by Samuel Certo

———— 1. Values of Organizations

———— 2. Teams Replace Star Workers

———— 3. Future Management Advantages for Women

———— 4. Women at Work

Getting the Main Idea of Longer Selections

Because of the bulk of material included in a book, understanding the main idea of longer selections such as chapters and articles seems more difficult than understanding a single paragraph. Longer selections have several major ideas contributing to the main point and many paragraphs of supporting details. To pull the ideas together under one central theme, an additional step is necessary: Simplify the material by organizing paragraphs or pages into manageable subsections and then deciding how each subsection contributes to the whole.

The following questions can help you determine the central theme for a longer selection:

1. What is the significance of the title? What does the title suggest about the topic?
2. How do the first paragraphs suggest the topic or thesis?
3. Under what subsections can the paragraphs and ideas be grouped?
4. How do these subsections support the whole?
5. What is the overall topic?
6. What point is the author trying to convey?

Search the Internet for articles on acupuncture. Select an article that interests you, and on a separate sheet of paper, provide answers to the six questions just listed pertaining to getting the main idea of longer reading selections.

PERSONAL Feedback 1

Name _____

1. Describe the theme or main idea of a movie that you have seen recently, one that you liked, and give reasons for your positive evaluation.

   Movie Title: _____

   Theme or Main Idea: _____

   _____

   Reasons for Positive Evaluation: _____

   _____

2. Was there anything you did not understand about the main idea?

   _____

3. This chapter includes a longer reading selection on sleep. Approximately how many hours of sleep do you get each night? _____

   _____

4. What time do you usually go to bed? _____

5. What time do you get up? _____

6. Breakfast sends an early supply of glucose to the brain. When do you eat breakfast, and what do you eat for breakfast? _____

   _____

7. Typically what, when, and where do you eat the other meals of the day? _____

   Lunch: _____

   Dinner: _____

8. Exercise is recommended to reduce stress. What exercise do you get on a regular basis, and when do you do it? _____

   _____

9. Do you typically go out on weeknights? If so, typically when and where do you go? _____

   _____

10. Evaluate your energy level and concentration ability. _____

    _____

    _____

Summary Points

- Getting the main idea is the most important skill in reading.
- The main idea may be stated directly within a passage or it may be implied.
- To find the topic of a passage ask, "Who or what is the subject?"
- To find the main idea of a passage ask, "What point is the author trying to make?"
- The main idea of a passage should always be stated by the reader in a complete sentence.
- To get the main idea of longer selections, break the material into subsections and determine how they support the whole.

COLLABORATIVE PROBLEM SOLVING

Form a five-member group and select one of the following questions. Brainstorm and then outline your major points on a transparency. Choose a member to present the group findings to the class.

► Why is prior knowledge the best single predictor of reading comprehension?

► Why is comprehension better when the main idea is stated at the beginning of a test passage?

► Describe a passage that you might write that would have the main idea stated at the end.

► Why should the main idea of a passage be stated in a sentence rather than a phrase? Give examples.

THINKING BEFORE READING

Preview for content, activate your schema, and anticipate what you will learn.

Did you dream last night?

What dream or dreams have you had recently?

Can you explain the meaning of any of your dreams?

I think this will tell me _____.

VOCABULARY PREVIEW

Are you familiar with these words?

unconscious	paradox	convenient	symbolizes	bullied
idling	depriving	ascribed	critical	synchronized

Which word has the same root as *chronological*?

What is the definition of the prefix in *unconscious*?

Is the phrase *jumbo shrimp* a paradox?

Your instructor may give a true-false vocabulary review before or after reading.

THINKING DURING READING

Refer to the
Reader's Tip
for Psychology on page 44.

As you read, use the five thinking strategies of a good reader: predict, picture, relate, monitor, and correct.

Sleeping and Dreaming

The time when we are most obviously unconscious is when we are asleep. Yet we have dreams during that time. This implies that something is going on in our brain.

Is all sleep the same? Are there stages in sleep? When do humans dream? How can you tell if a person is dreaming? Why do people have dreams, anyway? These are the
5   questions to be answered in this section.

Researchers have learned more about sleep and dreaming in the past twenty-five years than in all of history up to that time. One major reason for this is the discovery that when people are asleep there are changes in the activity of their brain and eyes. These changes can be recorded.

10   Beth Smith lies down to sleep after a hard day. She drifts off. At first she is in a light kind of sleep. Her brain waves, if recorded on a brain-wave machine, show a pattern that is definitely different than when she is awake. After less than an hour, two things happen to Beth. Her brain waves change, so that they now look pretty much the way they do when she is awake. Yet she is still asleep. Also, although her eyelids are closed, her eyes
15   begin to move about rapidly under the lids. This lasts for twenty minutes. Then Beth returns to the sleep of easy brain waves and no eye movement.

Basically, there are two kinds of sleep. One is Rapid Eye Movement (REM) sleep. In this, the brain waves are similar to those of a waking person, and the eyes move about rapidly under the closed lids. The other kind of sleep is Non-Rapid Eye Movement sleep.
20   You can guess what that's like, right? Stop for a moment and describe REM and non-REM sleep to yourself.

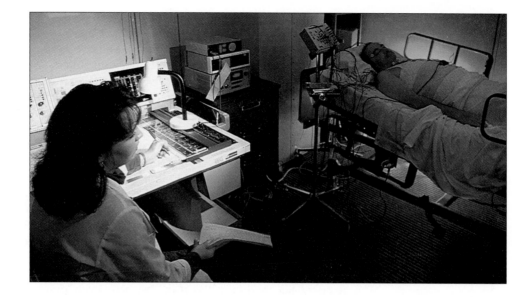

REM sleep is also called *paradoxical sleep.* A paradox is something that seems contradictory within itself. What is the paradox about REM sleep? That the sleeper's brain waves would lead you to believe the person is awake, but in fact the person is asleep.

25   Now, the interesting thing is this. Suppose Beth is showing non-REM sleep. We wake her up and say: "Wake up, Beth! What are you dreaming?"

"Uh . . . nothing," Beth mumbles.

Disappointed, we let her go back to sleep. Later on, Beth begins to show REM sleep. Again, we wake her up. "What are you dreaming, Beth?"

30   "Uh . . . this man has ridden a camel into Mom's office. It's too big. The camel fills up the whole office. The man riding him is an Arab." She goes on with her dream.

Dreaming happens mainly in REM sleep. This is very convenient for researchers. They get volunteers to sleep in a bed in the laboratory. An electronic sensing device that registers eye movement is placed on the eyelids of the volunteers. Thus the researcher can tell

35   exactly when the volunteer is showing REM sleep.

"Wake up, volunteer! What are you dreaming?"

WHAT HAS BEEN LEARNED ABOUT DREAMING?

Everyone dreams about 20 percent of the time they are sleeping—that is, they show REM sleep about that much. Even people who say they never dream show about 20 percent REM sleep. If these "nondreamers" do their sleeping in a laboratory where the researcher can

40   wake them up, it turns out that they dream as much as others. They just don't remember the dreams in the morning, perhaps because memories for dreams fade fast and they are slow waking up.

People go back and forth between REM and non-REM sleep during the night. If something happens in their environment while they are sleeping, people may fit this into

45   the dream. Did you ever have the experience of someone calling you in the morning, but at first you thought it was part of a dream?

Events in daily life sometimes occur in symbolic form in dreams. For example, a boy was having a lot of difficulty on the school playground because a bigger boy kept bullying him. That night the smaller boy dreamed of being alone and unarmed in the African grass

50   country, facing a lion. The lion symbolizes the bully. At other times the dreaded event from daily life simply occurs in a dream in its real-life form—the boy dreams of being bullied by the bigger boy. How and when dream symbols are used is not yet understood.

WHY DO WE DREAM?

Do people actually need to dream? Or is it just the brain "idling its motor"? It's possible that dreams are unimportant, just an accidental part of REM sleep.

55   One experimenter waked volunteers each time they started REM sleep. This meant that he was also depriving them of their dreams. When they showed non-REM sleep, he let them sleep on. Notice that by itself this experiment wouldn't prove much, even if effects did occur. Why? Because the effects might result from just being waked up all the time, rather than from just not being allowed to dream. The experimenters realized this,
60   so they used a second group of volunteers. These were waked exactly as much as the first group, but no attention was paid to whether it was REM or non-REM sleep. Thus any differences could be ascribed to lack of REM sleep periods in the one group.

There were differences. People who were deprived of most of their REM sleep for three nights in a row became irritable and somewhat disrupted in their actions. When on
65   the fourth night they were allowed to sleep on, so they could have REM sleep, they had it about 30 percent of the time instead of the usual 20 percent. Apparently they were "catching up" on their REM sleep. It looks as though people do, indeed, need REM sleep. The critical question is: Is it the REM sleep that they need or the dreams? Do we have REM sleep because it brings dreaming, or is dreaming just an accidental aspect of the
70   needed REM sleep? We don't know.

Why do people dream, then? We don't know that either. It does seem that REM sleep is necessary. But are dreams? What do they accomplish? Some theorists have suggested that we use dreaming to solve emotional problems, some have suggested that memories are stored in the brain during sleep time and dream time. Some even suggest this is a way
75   of keeping our two eyes synchronized. Tomorrow we may know the answer. The discovery of rapid eye movements during dreaming has opened up the world of dreams for research. Notice that the researchers here do something interesting. They go from an observable behavior—the eye movements—to an internal condition—the dream. The discovery of REM sleep helps bridge the gap between mental processes and the outside world.

(1,124 words)

—*Psychology: What It Is/How to Use It* by David Watson

THINKING AFTER READING

RECALL   Self-test your understanding. Your instructor may choose to give you a true-false review.

REACT   Why are sleep and dreaming important research topics for psychologists?

_____

_____

REFLECT   Describe and try to interpret one of your recent or recurring dreams. _____

_____

THINK CRITICALLY   Would you predict any correlation between a good night's sleep and a good quality of life? Why or why not? Write your answer on a separate sheet of paper.

MAIN IDEA

Answer the following questions concerning the selection.

1. Who or what is the topic of the selection? _____

2. What point is the author trying to make? _____

_____

Name _____

Date _____

COMPREHENSION QUESTIONS

Answer the following with *a, b, c,* or *d,* or fill in the blank. In order to help analyze your strengths and weaknesses, the question types are indicated.

Main Idea _____ 1. The best statement of the main idea of this selection is

    a. People become irritable when they do not have an adequate amount of dreaming.
    b. Through the discovery of REM, researchers have begun to learn about sleeping and dreaming, but many questions remain unanswered.
    c. Sleep is an observable behavior, whereas dreaming is an internal condition reflecting the mental processes.
    d. Dreams follow an irregular pattern, with people moving back and forth between REM and non-REM sleep all during the night.

Detail _____ 2. During REM sleep a person experiences

    a. different brain waves than when awake.
    b. the same brain waves as when awake.
    c. eye movement under closed lids.
    d. both *b* and *c.*

Inference 3. REM sleep is called paradoxical sleep because _____

_____

Detail _____ 4. Dreaming occurs

    a. during REM and non-REM sleep.
    b. mainly during REM sleep.
    c. only during non-REM sleep.
    d. as people go back and forth between REM and non-REM sleep.

Detail _____ 5. Some people probably cannot remember dreams because

    a. they awaken in the middle of a dream.
    b. they are nondreamers.
    c. they experience only 20 percent REM sleep.
    d. they are slow waking up.

Inference _____ 6. The author implies that dreams do all of the following *except*

    a. symbolically reflect real-life problems.
    b. include experiences in the environment.
    c. relieve tension and irritability.
    d. normally occur in the last two hours of sleep.

Detail _____ 7. According to the passage, after several nights of interrupted REM sleep, people need to

    a. sleep longer.
    b. dream a greater percentage of the next sleeping time.
    c. have a higher percentage of non-REM sleep.
    d. sleep more frequently for brief periods of time.

Answer the following with *T* (true), *F* (false), or *CT* (can't tell).

Inference _____ 8. Research shows that dreams are unimportant and just an accidental part of REM sleep.

Inference _____ 9. The author feels that the discovery of rapid eye movement is the most significant finding thus far in dream research.

Inference _____ 10. Dreams help people store memories.

VOCABULARY

Answer the following with *a, b, c,* or *d* for the word or phrase that best defines the boldface word as used in the selection. The number in parentheses indicates the line of the passage in which the word is located.

_____ 1. "most obviously **unconscious**" (1)

    a. alert
    b. daydreaming
    c. half-knowing
    d. not aware

_____ 2. "the **paradox** about REM" (23)

    a. mystery
    b. error
    c. contradictory truth
    d. reasoning

_____ 3. "**convenient** for researchers" (32)

    a. logical
    b. easy to use
    c. necessary
    d. cooperative

_____ 4. "**symbolizes** the bully" (50)

    a. warns
    b. summarizes
    c. represents
    d. suspects

_____ 5. "**bullied** by the bigger boy" (51–52)

    a. intimidated
    b. befriended
    c. joined
    d. recognized

_____ 6. "**idling** its motor" (53)

    a. exhausting
    b. running without power
    c. withdrawing
    d. renewing

_____ 7. "**depriving** them of" (56)

    a. irritating
    b. educating
    c. encouraging
    d. preventing

_____ 8. "**ascribed** to lack of" (62)

    a. convened
    b. remembered
    c. attributed
    d. returned

_____ 9. "The **critical** question is" (68)

    a. first
    b. general
    c. crucial
    d. most frequent

_____ 10. "keeping our two eyes **synchronized**" (75)

    a. working simultaneously
    b. working vigorously
    c. focused
    d. slightly crossed

VOCABULARY ENRICHMENT

A. An acronym is an invented word formed by the initial letters of a compound term. REM, for example, is pronounced as a word that rhymes with *them,* rather than pronouncing the three letters separately to indicate rapid eye movement. Write an A beside the following letters that are pronounced as words and thus are acronyms.

_____ 1. HUD   _____ 3. FBI   _____ 5. NAFTA

_____ 2. UNICEF   _____ 4. CIA   _____ 6. radar

B. Study the following easily confused words, and circle the one that is correct in each sentence.

conscience: sense of right or wrong   **its:** ownership or possessive
conscious: awareness of self   **it's:** contraction of *it is*

to: toward
too: more than enough
two: the number 2

7. Let your (conscience, conscious) be your guide when faced

   with temptation.

8. Don't tell me (its, it's) already the end of the month.

9. Many professors assign (to, too, two) much homework for one night.

C. Use the context clues in the following sentences to write the meaning of the boldface psychology terms.

10. Relaxation exercises can be used to reduce test **anxiety.** _____

   _____

11. After years of practice, we **condition** ourselves to always wash our

   hands before meals. _____

12. With the birth of the second child, the first child's desire for a bottle was

   a sign of **regression.** _____

13. Saying that you are too busy to call a sick friend is only **rationalizing.**

   _____

14. Television has become more **permissive** in treating sexual topics openly

   during prime time. _____

15. Compliments can be effective in **reinforcing** desired behaviors. _____

   _____

ASSESS YOUR LEARNING

Review confusing questions, seek clarification, and make notes in your text to help you remember new information and vocabulary.

CONNECT

Read the following passage about getting too little sleep. Describe a situation in which your actions have been adversely affected by lack of sleep. List five tips or bits of advice that you would offer other students for getting an adequate amount of sleep each night that would include REM sleep.

Effects of Skipping Sleep Can Be a Real Eye-opener

Nanci Hellmich
USA Today, March 22, 1999, p. 6D

Ongoing research is showing that when people don't get enough sleep, they build up what experts call a "sleep debt." The debt accumulates night after night: If you get one hour less sleep than you need each night for eight nights in a row, your brain will need sleep as desperately as if you had stayed up all night, says pioneer sleep researcher William Dement of Stanford University.

Tired people are more likely to make math errors, drop things and become emotionally distant from their families, friends and colleagues, he says.

"In the simplest terms, a large sleep debt makes you stupid," says Dement, author of a new book, *The Promise of Sleep*, with Christopher Vaughan (Delacorte Press).

The consequences of lack of sleep can be annoying and expensive, Dement says. He once had a patient who was so sleepy, she loaded dirty dishes into the clothes dryer instead of the dishwasher. She didn't realize her error until she turned on the machine and heard the dishes breaking.

 EXPLORE THE NET

● What are some interpretations of the meaning of water, animals, and flying in dreams?

Dreams and Nightmares

www.redrival.com/nightmare/

Dream Lover Inc.

www.dreamloverinc.com/

● What have scientists learned from sleep deprivation studies? List and explain three findings not covered in this reading selection.

National Sleep Foundation

www.sleepfoundation.org/

Sleepnet.com

www.sleepfoundation.org/

For additional readings and exercises, visit the *Breaking Through* Web site:

www.ablongman.com/smith

THINKING BEFORE READING

Preview the selection for clues to content. Activate your schema and anticipate what you will learn.

When have you experienced the effects of economic prejudice?

When have you felt economic prejudice toward someone else?

I'll read this to find out. _____

VOCABULARY PREVIEW

Are you familiar with these words?

agile	despaired	absentmindedly	coincidence	fidgeted
dismay	muster	gaunt	vile	crumpled

What is the opposite of *gaunt*?

Where do you find *crumpled* paper?

Your instructor may give a true-false vocabulary review before or after reading.

THINKING DURING READING

As you read, use the five thinking strategies of a good reader: predict, picture, relate, monitor, and correct.

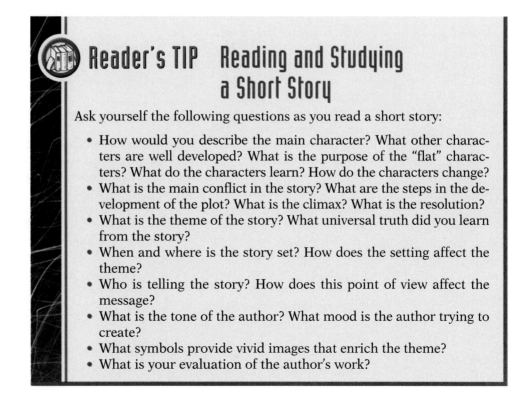

Reader's TIP   Reading and Studying a Short Story

Ask yourself the following questions as you read a short story:

- How would you describe the main character? What other characters are well developed? What is the purpose of the "flat" characters? What do the characters learn? How do the characters change?
- What is the main conflict in the story? What are the steps in the development of the plot? What is the climax? What is the resolution?
- What is the theme of the story? What universal truth did you learn from the story?
- When and where is the story set? How does the setting affect the theme?
- Who is telling the story? How does this point of view affect the message?
- What is the tone of the author? What mood is the author trying to create?
- What symbols provide vivid images that enrich the theme?
- What is your evaluation of the author's work?

The Scholarship Jacket

The small Texas school that I attended carried out a tradition every year during the eighth grade graduation: a beautiful gold and green jacket, the school colors, was awarded to the class valedictorian, the student who had maintained the highest grades for eight years. The scholarship jacket had a big gold S on the left front side, and the winner's
5   name was written in gold letters on the pocket.

My oldest sister Rosie had won the jacket a few years back, and I fully expected to win also. I was fourteen and in the eighth grade. I had been a straight A student since the first grade, and the last year I had looked forward to owning that jacket. My father was a farm laborer who couldn't earn enough money to feed eight children, so when I was six I
10   was given to my grandparents to raise. We couldn't participate in sports at school because there were registration fees, uniform costs, and trips out of town; so even though we were quite agile and athletic, there would never be a sports school jacket for us. This one, the scholarship jacket, was our only chance.

In May, close to graduation, spring fever struck, and no one paid any attention in
15   class; instead we stared out the windows and at each other, wanting to speed up the last few weeks of school. I despaired every time I looked in the mirror. Pencil thin, not a curve anywhere, I was called "Beanpole" and "String Bean," and I knew that's what I looked like. A flat chest, no hips, and a brain, that's what I had. That really isn't much for a fourteen-year-old to work with, I thought, as I absentmindedly wandered from my history class
20   to the gym. Another hour of sweating in basketball and displaying my toothpick legs was coming up. Then I remembered my P.E. shorts were still in a bag under my desk where I'd forgotten them. I had to walk all the way back and get them. Coach Thompson was a real bear if anyone wasn't dressed for P.E. She had said I was a good forward and once she even tried to talk Grandma into letting me join the team. Grandma, of
25   course, said no.

I was almost back at my classroom door when I heard angry voices and arguing. I stopped. I didn't mean to eavesdrop; I just hesitated, not knowing what to do. I needed those shorts and I was going to be late, but I didn't want to interrupt an argument between my teachers. I recognized the voices: Mr. Schmidt, my history teacher, and Mr.
30   Boone, my math teacher. They seemed to be arguing about me. I couldn't believe it. I still remember the shock that rooted me flat against the wall as if I were trying to blend in with the graffiti written there.

"I refuse to do it! I don't care who her father is, her grades don't even begin to compare to Martha's. I won't lie or falsify records. Martha has a straight A plus average and
35   you know it." That was Mr. Schmidt and he sounded very angry. Mr. Boone's voice sounded calm and quiet.

"Look, Joann's father is not only on the Board, he owns the only store in town; we could say it was a close tie and—"

The pounding in my ears drowned out the rest of the words, only a word here and
40   there filtered through. ". . . Martha is Mexican. . . . resign. . . . won't do it. . . . " Mr. Schmidt came rushing out, and luckily for me went down the opposite way toward the auditorium, so he didn't see me. Shaking, I waited a few minutes and then went in and grabbed my bag and fled from the room. Mr. Boone looked up when I came in but didn't say anything. To this day I don't remember if I got in trouble in P.E. for being late or how
45   I made it through the rest of the afternoon. I went home very sad and cried into my pillow that night so Grandmother wouldn't hear me. It seemed a cruel coincidence that I had overheard that conversation.

The next day when the principal called me into his office, I knew what it would be about. He looked uncomfortable and unhappy. I decided I wasn't going to make it any
50   easier for him so I looked him straight in the eye. He looked away and fidgeted with the papers on his desk.

"Martha," he said, "there's been a change in policy this year regarding the scholarship jacket. As you know, it has always been free." He cleared his throat and continued.

"This year the Board decided to charge fifteen dollars—which still won't cover the com-
55 plete cost of the jacket."

I started at him in shock and a small sound of dismay escaped my throat. I hadn't expected this. He still avoided looking in my eyes.

"So if you are unable to pay the fifteen dollars for the jacket, it will be given to the
next one in line."

60 Standing with all the dignity I could muster, I said, "I'll speak to my grandfather
about it, sir, and let you know tomorrow." I cried on the walk home from the bus stop.
The dirt road was a quarter of a mile from the highway, so by the time I got home, my
eyes were red and puffy.

"Where's Grandpa?" I asked Grandma, looking down at the floor so she wouldn't ask
65 me why I'd been crying. She was sewing on a quilt and didn't look up.

"I think he's out back working in the bean field."

I went outside and looked out at the fields. There he was. I could see him walking between the rows, his body bent over the little plants, hoe in hand. I walked slowly out to
him, trying to think how I could best ask him for the money. There was a cool breeze
70 blowing and a sweet smell of mesquite in the air, but I didn't appreciate it. I kicked at a
dirt clod. I wanted that jacket so much. It was more than just being a valedictorian and
giving a little thank you speech for the jacket on graduation night. It represented eight
years of hard work and expectation. I knew I had to be honest with Grandpa; it was my
only chance. He saw me and looked up.

75 He waited for me to speak. I cleared my throat nervously and clasped my hands behind my back so he wouldn't see them shaking. "Grandpa, I have a big favor to ask you,"
I said in Spanish, the only language he knew. He still waited silently. I tried again.
"Grandpa, this year the principal said the scholarship jacket is not going to be free. It's
going to cost fifteen dollars and I have to take the money in tomorrow, otherwise it'll be
80 given to someone else." The last words came out in an eager rush. Grandpa straightened
up tiredly and leaned his chin on the hoe handle. He looked out over the field that was
filled with the tiny green bean plants. I waited, desperately hoping he'd say I could have
the money.

He turned to me and asked quietly, "What does a scholarship jacket mean?"

85 I answered quickly; maybe there was a chance. "It means you've earned it by having
the highest grades for eight years and that's why they're giving it to you." Too late I real-

ized the significance of my words. Grandpa knew that I understood it was not a matter of money. It wasn't that. He went back to hoeing the weeds that sprang up between the delicate little bean plants. It was a time-consuming job; sometimes the small shoots were
90 right next to each other. Finally he spoke again.

"Then if you pay for it, Marta, it's not a scholarship jacket, is it? Tell your principal I will not pay the fifteen dollars."

I walked back to the house and locked myself in the bathroom for a long time. I was angry with Grandfather even though I knew he was right, and I was angry with the
95 Board, whoever they were. Why did they have to change the rules just when it was my turn to win the jacket?

It was a very sad and withdrawn girl who dragged into the principal's office the next day. This time he did look me in the eyes.

"What did your grandfather say?"
100 I sat very straight in my chair.

"He said to tell you he won't pay the fifteen dollars."

The principal muttered something I couldn't understand under his breath, and walked over to the window. He stood looking out at something outside. He looked bigger than usual when he stood up; he was a tall gaunt man with gray hair, and I watched
105 the back of his head while I waited for him to speak.

"Why?" he finally asked. "Your grandfather has the money. Doesn't he own a small bean farm?"

I looked at him, forcing my eyes to stay dry. "He said if I had to pay for it, then it wouldn't be a scholarship jacket," I said and stood up to leave. "I guess you'll just have to
110 give it to Joann." I hadn't meant to say that; it had just slipped out. I was almost to the door when he stopped me.

"Martha—wait."

I turned and looked at him, waiting. What did he want now? I could feel my heart pounding. Something bitter and vile tasting was coming up in my mouth; I was afraid I
115 was going to be sick. I didn't need any sympathy speeches. He sighed loudly and went back to his big desk. He looked at me, biting his lip, as if thinking.

"Okay, damn it. We'll make an exception in your case. I'll tell the Board, you'll get your jacket."

I could hardly believe it. I spoke in a trembling rush. "Oh, thank you, sir!" Suddenly I
120 felt great. I didn't know about adrenaline in those days, but I knew something was pumping through me, making me feel as tall as the sky. I wanted to yell, jump, run the mile, do something. I ran out so I could cry in the hall where there was no one to see me. At the end of the day. Mr. Schmidt winked at me and said, "I hear you're getting a scholarship jacket this year."

125 His face looked as happy and innocent as a baby's, but I knew better. Without answering I gave him a quick hug and ran to the bus. I cried on the walk home again, but this time because I was so happy. I couldn't wait to tell Grandpa and ran straight to the field. I joined him in the row where he was working and without saying anything I crouched down and started pulling up the weeds with my hands. Grandpa worked
130 alongside me for a few minutes, but he didn't ask what had happened. After I had a little pile of weeds between the rows, I stood up and faced him.

"The principal said he's making an exception for me, Grandpa, and I'm getting the jacket after all. That's after I told him what you said."

Grandpa didn't say anything, he just gave me a pat on the shoulder and a smile. He
135 pulled out the crumpled red handkerchief that he always carried in his back pocket and wiped the sweat off his forehead.

"Better go see if your grandmother needs any help with supper."

I gave him a big grin. He didn't fool me. I skipped and ran back to the house whistling some silly tune.

(1,952 words)

—"The Scholarship Jacket" by Marta Salinas from *Nosotras: Latina Literature Today*

THINKING AFTER READING

RECALL   Self-test your understanding. Your instructor may choose to give you a true-false review.

REACT   What was so forceful about Grandpa's argument, "If you have to pay for it, it's not a scholarship jacket"? _____

_____

_____

REFLECT   Why is earning the scholarship jacket not only a personal goal, but also a symbol of achievement for Martha and her family? _____

_____

_____

THINK CRITICALLY   Express your opinion on the statement, "The rich and poor are treated differently," and give specific examples in the areas of education, business, medicine, and law. Organize your response into five paragraphs and write on a separate sheet of paper.

MAIN IDEA

What is the principal issue that concerns the author in this story? _____

_____

_____

Name _____

Date _____

COMPREHENSION QUESTIONS

Answer the following with *a, b, c,* and *d,* or fill in the blank. In order to help you analyze your strengths and weaknesses, the question types are indicated.

Main Idea _____ 1. The best statement of the main idea of this selection is:

    a. Martha won the scholarship jacket because of her high grades.
    b. The Board acted without prejudice in awarding the scholarship jacket.
    c. Mr. Schmidt felt that Martha deserved the jacket.
    d. Despite prejudice, Martha's hard work and her grandfather's thoughtful response won her the scholarship jacket.

Detail _____ 2. Martha did not participate in sports at school because

    a. she was not good at athletics.
    b. she did not like athletics.
    c. sports at school cost too much money.
    d. she was too busy studying.

Inference _____ 3. The Board decided to charge $15 for the scholarship jacket because

    a. they wanted Joann to have it.
    b. the cost of the jacket had gone up.
    c. they wanted to give more than one.
    d. the school was establishing a new scholarship.

Inference _____ 4. Mr. Boone wanted to keep Martha from winning the jacket because

    a. Joann was the best student in his class.
    b. she did not deserve the jacket.
    c. she was Mexican and from a poor family.
    d. Joann's family had more status than Martha's.

Detail _____ 5. The scholarship jacket was all of the following except

    a. awarded each year.
    b. given to the valedictorian.
    c. a gold and black jacket.
    d. similar to the athletic jackets.

Inference _____ 6. All of the following are true about Mr. Schmidt except

    a. he got angry when Mr. Boone suggested the jacket go to Joann.
    b. he felt that Martha deserved the jacket because she had the best grades.
    c. he was happy when Martha got the jacket.
    d. he resigned over the conflict.

Inference _____ 7. Martha's grandfather would not pay the $15 for the jacket because

    a. he did not want Martha to wear a jacket from such a school.
    b. he could not get $15.
    c. he felt that Martha had already earned the jacket.
    d. he thought the jacket was too expensive.

Answer the following with *T* (true) or *F* (false).

Detail _____ 8. Martha's real name was Marta.

Inference _____ 9. The principal and Mr. Schmidt demonstrated higher ethical standards than Mr. Boone and the Board.

Inference _____ 10. The reader can conclude that the principal made an exception for Martha because he felt she was treated unfairly.

VOCABULARY

Answer the following with *a, b, c,* or *d* for the word or phrase that best defines the boldface word used in the selection. The number in parentheses indicates the line of the passage in which the word is located.

_____ 1. "quite **agile** and athletic" (12)

    a. awkward
    b. quick
    c. nimble
    d. clumsy

_____ 2. "**despaired** every time" (16)

    a. gave up hope
    b. yelled
    c. felt good
    d. laughed

_____ 3. "**absentmindedly** wandered" (19)

    a. preoccupied
    b. purposely
    c. carefully
    d. intentionally

_____ 4. "a cruel **coincidence**" (46)

    a. joke
    b. planned meeting
    c. accident
    d. remark

_____ 5. "**fidgeted** with the papers" (50–51)

    a. worked
    b. nervously moved
    c. wrote notes
    d. filed

_____ 6. "sound of **dismay**" (56)

    a. laughter
    b. joy
    c. fear
    d. hope

_____ 7. "could **muster**" (60)

    a. face
    b. gather
    c. fake
    d. confront

_____ 8. "a tall **gaunt** man" (104)

    a. attractive
    b. heavy
    c. evil
    d. thin

_____ 9. "**vile** tasting" (114)

    a. sweet
    b. unpleasant
    c. salty
    d. sour

_____ 10. "**crumpled** red handkerchief" (135)

    a. wrinkled
    b. old
    c. unusual
    d. ordinary

VOCABULARY ENRICHMENT

A. Use the indicated prefix to write words that complete each sentence in the groups.

dis: not, take away, deprive of

1. Because the daughter would not finish college, the family threatened to _____ her in the will.

2. The soldier's cowardice brought _____ on the whole regiment.

3. Because of the severe injury to his spinal cord, the man is now completely _____ and cannot work.

con, com, co: with, together

4. The minister looked out at the _____ and asked them to stand and sing a hymn.

5. Our plane was late arriving in Atlanta, and thus we were unable to make our scheduled _____ to Miami.

6. If all members would _____ their efforts and lend a hand, the job could be finished in half the time.

ad: to, toward

7. If the tape is no longer _____ , it will not stick to the package.

8. To gain public recognition for the new product, the company had to _____ on the radio.

9. Some people say they are _____ to chocolate chip cookies because they can't stop eating them.

B. Use the context clues in the sentence to write the meaning of the boldface words.

10. **Narratives** never preach, but rather deliver a message to our emotions, senses, and imagination through a powerful shared experience. _____
   _____
   _____

11. The **theme** of the story about a college tennis champion might be that the journey to the top, including the hard work and discipline, was more meaningful than the final victory. _____
   _____

12. Poisoned apples and talking mirrors may not seem realistic in a modern telephone conversation, however, in the context of the Snow White, we

easily find both **plausible.** _____

_____

13. E. M. Forster said that "The king died, and the queen died," is a narrative, but changing this to "The king died, and the queen died of grief," creates a **plot.** _____

_____

14. The **suspense** of a narrative is based on conflict, which perhaps starts out as mild and intensifies as each incident occurs. _____

_____

_____

15. Good writers select incidents and details that give **unity** to the story and advance the central theme. _____

_____

ASSESS YOUR LEARNING

Review confusing questions, seek clarification, and make notes in your text to help you remember new information and vocabulary.

EXPLORE THE NET

● Locate and read an article on Latino culture. Describe how this culture is influencing the traditional American way of life. Comment on the Latino contributions in food, music, television, and radio industries. Also, explain why you think these expressions of Latino culture are becoming popular in today's society.

www.williamsinference.com/2614latino.html

● Latinos are the fastest growing segment of the U.S. population, and thus their political and economic power is rapidly increasing. Locate an article that addresses the challenges hindering this power. Explain three of the biggest challenges, and discuss how each can be overcome.

www.iminorities.com/hispanic/politics/archives/millennium999.html

● *Chicano* is a word meaning Mexican-American. The story "The Scholarship Jacket" can be found in the anthology *Growing Up Chicano.* In addition to literature, another form of chicano expression includes murals. Locate and view chicano murals and explain why you think the artists choose to use the side of a building to display their paintings. How is the artist's message enhanced by that decision?

www.sparcmurals.com/present/cmt.cl.html

For additional readings and exercises, visit the *Breaking Through* Web site:

www.ablongman.com/smith

THINKING BEFORE READING

Preview for clues to the content. Activate your prior knowledge. Anticipate what is coming and think about your purpose for reading.

In what city is the Martin Luther King, Jr., homeplace and national memorial?

Where did Martin Luther King, Jr., make the "I have a dream" speech?

What world leader inspired Martin Luther King, Jr.'s nonviolent tactics?

I want to learn _____

VOCABULARY PREVIEW

Are you familiar with these words?

sweltering	centennial	oppressive	podium	resonant
galvanized	spurious	dire	recanted	compelled

What is a *centenarian*?

At what temperature do you *swelter*?

How do *compel*, *repel*, and *expel* differ?

Your instructor may give a true-false vocabulary review before or after reading.

THINKING DURING READING

As you read, use the five thinking strategies of a good reader: predict, picture, relate, monitor, and correct.

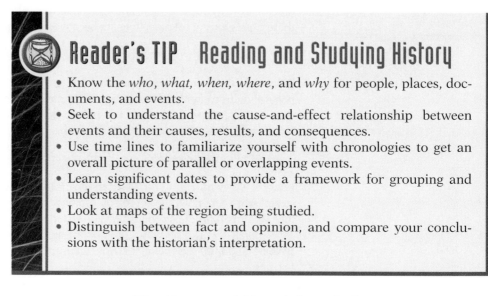

Reader's TIP Reading and Studying History

- Know the *who*, *what*, *when*, *where*, and *why* for people, places, documents, and events.
- Seek to understand the cause-and-effect relationship between events and their causes, results, and consequences.
- Use time lines to familiarize yourself with chronologies to get an overall picture of parallel or overlapping events.
- Learn significant dates to provide a framework for grouping and understanding events.
- Look at maps of the region being studied.
- Distinguish between fact and opinion, and compare your conclusions with the historian's interpretation.

The Dream of Nonviolent Reform

Perspiring in the sweltering heat of a Washington August afternoon, Martin Luther King, Jr., looked down from the steps of the Lincoln Memorial at the largest assembly ever congregated in the United States. Well over 200,000 people, 70 percent of them blacks, jammed the mile-long mall that swept away to the Washington Monument. Angry yet

5   hopeful, they had come to the nation's capital in 1963, the centennial of the Emancipation Proclamation, to personify black demands for equality in society. But the speakers and singers who preceded King had not been particularly effective, the heat and humidity were oppressive, and the great crowd was starting to thin around the edges. As he mounted the podium, King sensed this restlessness and the need for a focus. At first his

10 deep voice was husky, but it soon became resonant with a purpose that quieted and transfixed the multitude and the millions of television viewers. King's eloquence dramatized the anguish of black history. One hundred years after slavery, he pointed out, the black was still "an exile in his own land." It was the future, however, that mattered. "I have a dream," he cried repeatedly, as he sketched his vision of freedom, justice, and har-

15 mony. At the end of his speech King prophesied that one day all people would be able to join together in singing the words of an old Negro spiritual: "Free at last! Free at last! Thank God Almighty, we are free at last." There was an awed silence, then an ear-shattering roar: the crowd was applauding wildly. King had galvanized the massive assembly. At that moment he stood at the crest of a mounting wave of African-American

20 protest. Yet, as King must have known, his dream would have an agonizing birth. Just five years after his Washington address, he lay dead on the balcony of a Memphis motel, the victim of the violence he had devoted his life to overcoming.

. . .

The poor People's March was set for June 1968, but the whirlwind pace King had kept since the beginning of the decade allowed him only occasional participation in the

25 planning. One of the detours took him to Memphis, where a garbage strike threatened to evolve into a racial encounter of crisis proportions. Local black leaders wanted King to organize a peaceful demonstration, but once again he had difficulty working with Black Power militants. Uncontrollable black looters, arsonists, and street fighters were another source of difficulty. On March 28, they had transformed a nonviolent march into an orgy

30 of destruction that had provoked an even greater measure of police brutality. As a self-styled "riot preventer," King was sick at heart. If Memphis exploded, he feared, the approaching summer of 1968 would be chaos. Already, black leaders like Harlem congressman Adam Clayton Powell were arousing the urban masses and, as part of their campaign, making references to "Martin Loser King" and his Uncle Tom tactics. Nonvio-

35 lence, King felt, was on trial in Memphis.

On April 3, 1968, on the eve of the crucial Memphis march, King addressed a capacity crowd at the Masonic Temple located in that city. His mood was strangely somber and introspective. "Like anybody," he mused, "I would like to live a long life." But longevity, he added, was not his chief concern; he would rather do God's will. Some of his aides
40 were reminded of the great Washington rally of 1963, where King had expressed his belief that "if a man hasn't discovered something that he will die for, he isn't fit to live!" The following evening, on the way to yet another mass meeting, King walked onto the balcony of his hotel room and leaned over the railing to talk with a colleague. A moment later he crumpled to the ground. An assassin's bullet, fired from a hotel room across the
45 street, had pierced his skull. The killer, arrested two months later and identified as James Earl Ray, was a white drifter with a long criminal record.

Following Ray's confession, investigations of King's murder continued until 1977. Exhaustive reviews of the evidence seemed to prove conclusively that Ray had acted alone in the assassination, and there was no conspiracy. The research did reveal that the Federal
50 Bureau of Investigation, under orders of its director, J. Edgar Hoover, had complicated the last six years of King's life with a program of systematic harassment on the spurious grounds that he was under the influence of the Communist party. The conspiracy theory surrounding King's death reemerged in the 1990's when James Earl Ray, in prison and in dire health, recanted his confession. Talk of Ray being brought to trial—there had been
55 none due to his confession—ended abruptly when Ray died in early 1998.

The murder of Martin Luther King, Jr., moved the American people as had few events in recent years. The immediate response in all but the most prejudiced white minds was shame. Millions of whites felt compelled to apologize to black people as a whole and went to their churches for services honoring King. But even among the mourners, white
60 and black eyes did not meet easily. Everyone seemed to recognize that, with King's death, a powerful influence for interracial compassion and understanding had been eliminated—the basis of ordered change and reform.

(878 words)

—From *These Beginnings*, Sixth Edition, Volume Two, by Roderick Nash and Gregory Graves

THINKING AFTER READING

RECALL Self-test your understanding. Your instructor may choose to give you a true-false review.

REACT Aside from their stated reasons, why do you think the FBI would spend six years tracking Dr. King? _____

_____

REFLECT What seemed to be the differences in philosophy among the civil rights leaders? _____

_____

THINK CRITICALLY Why was Martin Luther King, Jr.'s birthday made a national holiday? _____

_____

MAIN IDEA

1. What is the topic of the first paragraph? _____

2. What is the topic of the last paragraph? _____

_____

Name _____

Date _____

COMPREHENSION QUESTIONS

Answer the following with *a, b, c,* or *d,* or fill in the blank. In order to help you analyze your strengths and weaknesses, the question types are indicated.

Main Idea   _____ 1. The best statement of the main idea of the selection is

a. King started the civil rights movement with his "I have a dream" speech in Washington.
b. Though his life was taken violently, King was a moving speaker and a major force in the nonviolent movement for civil rights.
c. King was killed violently by a drifter.
d. King controlled the violence in Memphis but was killed for doing so.

Detail   _____ 2. The primary reason over 200,000 people had congregated in Washington in 1963 was

a. to hear Dr. King speak.
b. to urge legislators to pass the Emancipation Proclamation.
c. to show strength in demanding equal treatment for African Americans in society.
d. to honor Lincoln for freeing the slaves.

Detail   _____ 3. In his "I have a dream" speech, King's major thrust is to

a. recall the hardships of the past.
b. blame society for prejudice and hatred.
c. ask God for forgiveness and strength.
d. focus on the possibilities of the future.

Inference   _____ 4. The author implies that

a. Black Power militants did not agree with King's tactics.
b. King and Black Power militants shared the same philosophy and strategies.
c. Adam Clayton Powell supported King's tactics.
d. little friction existed among the different leaders supporting civil rights.

Inference   5. King felt that nonviolence was on trial in Memphis because _____

_____

_____

_____

Inference   _____ 6. The author suggests all of the following *except*

a. King was willing to die for his cause.
b. King had a premonition that he would not live a long life.
c. King knew that fighting for his cause was dangerous.
d. King was willing to back off from his nonviolent stand to get the support of other civil rights leaders.

Detail _____ 7. The author indicates that evidence suggests that

      a. Ray acted alone.

      b. Ray was part of a conspiracy.

      c. J. Edgar Hoover was involved in King's death.

      d. Ray was not the man who fired the shots from the hotel room.

Answer the following with *T* (true) or *F* (false).

Inference _____ 8. After King's death, the American people realized that he was indeed the "riot preventer."

Detail _____ 9. The garbage strike in Memphis was in June 1968.

Detail _____ 10. Ray was brought to trial after he revoked his confession.

VOCABULARY

Answer the following with *a*, *b*, *c*, or *d* for the word or phrase that best defines the boldface word as used in the selection. The number in parentheses indicates the line of the passage in which the word is located.

_____ 1. "**sweltering** heat" (1)

      a. never ending

      b. hot and humid

      c. permanent

      d. oncoming

_____ 2. "the **centennial** of the Emancipation Proclamation" (5–6)

      a. 10-year celebration

      b. 50-year celebration

      c. 100-year celebration

      d. 1,000-year celebration

_____ 3. "heat and humidity were **oppressive**" (7–8)

      a. suffocating

      b. surprising

      c. brief

      d. energizing

_____ 4. "mounted the **podium**" (9)

      a. stairway

      b. top of the monument

      c. steps

      d. speaker's stand

_____ 5. "**resonant** with a purpose" (10)

      a. sensitive

      b. hoarse

      c. forceful and loud

      d. repetitious

_____ 6. "**galvanized** the massive assembly" (18–19)

      a. stopped

      b. excited

      c. frightened

      d. shamed

_____ 7. "on **spurious** grounds" (51–52)

      a. false

      b. evil

      c. criminal

      d. socialistic

_____ 8. "in **dire** health" (53–54)

      a. fair

      b. uncertain

      c. questionable

      d. terrible

_____ 9. "**recanted** his confession" (54)

      a. emphasized

      b. questioned

      c. regretted

      d. took back

_____ 10. "**compelled** to apologize" (58)

      a. nervous

      b. obliged

      c. angered

      d. manipulated

VOCABULARY ENRICHMENT

A.   Use the indicated root to write words to complete each sentence in the groups.

voc, vok: voice, call

  1. His remarks angered her, and it seemed that, despite our mediation, further conversation would only _____ an argument.

  2. The opera star did not appear in the third act because of damage to her _____ cords.

  3. To increase his _____, the student learned a new word each day.

gress, grad, gred: step, degree

  4. If he can take one additional night course this year, he hopes to _____ from college by June.

  5. The company was looking for _____ young employees rather than meek applicants.

  6. The progress was so _____ that we could hardly see any success on a daily basis.

spec, spect: see, watch

  7. The grand finale of the fireworks display was quite a _____.

  8. With the growing audiences, tennis has become a profitable _____ sport.

  9. When buying cuts of meat at the grocery store, look for the government _____ sticker.

B.   Use context clues and mark *a, b, c,* or *d* for the meaning closest to that of the boldface word.

  _____ 10. High blood pressure and shortness of breath can **signify** danger to a person with heart disease.

       a. indicate
       b. simplify
       c. curtail
       d. admonish

  _____ 11. To complete the work on schedule, the committee needs more **diligent** members like you.

       a. convincing
       b. hard-working
       c. older
       d. talkative

  _____ 12. The criminal cannot be convicted on accusation alone. We need **tangible** evidence of his guilt that can be presented in court.

       a. sizable
       b. tremendous
       c. actual
       d. movable

C. Study the following easily confused words, and circle the one that is correct in each sentence.

thorough: careful   **straight:** not curving   **loose:** not tight
threw: tossed   **strait:** narrow passage of water   **lose:** misplace
through: by means of

13. Do a (**thorough, threw, through**) job on your term paper if you want to make a good grade.

14. Rush (**straight, strait**) from here to the library.

15. My tooth is (**loose, lose**).

ASSESS YOUR LEARNING

Review confusing questions, seek clarification, and make notes in your text to help you remember new information and vocabulary.

EXPLORE THE NET

- The assassination of Dr. King, like that of President John F. Kennedy, is an event shrouded in mystery and intrigue. Search for information regarding the assassination of Dr. King. Find at least two articles on the topic. Explain whether you think his death was a conspiracy and support your decision with facts found in your articles.

  www.usdoj.gov/crt/crim/mlk/part2.htm#over

  www.abcnews.go.com

  www.washingtonpost.com

- Dr. King's *I Have A Dream Speech* is his most famous oration. Locate a copy of the speech and read it. Write down information regarding the delivery of the speech as well as some of the dreams mentioned in it. If you can access the recorded copy of the speech on the History Channel Web site, write down how hearing the live version brings the words to life.

  www.web66.coled.umn.edu/new/MLK/MLK.html

  www.historychannel.com/speeches

- Locate and read Dr. King's *Letter from the Birmingham Jail.* He said it was the longest letter he had ever written. Write a summary of the letter that includes the circumstances that compelled him to write the letter, the audience for whom the letter is intended, and the main points Dr. King wants to convey.

  www.geocities.com/Athens/Forum/9061/afro/birmingham.html

For additional readings and exercises, visit the *Breaking Through* Web site:

  www.ablongman.com/smith

PERSONAL Feedback 2
Name _____

1. Review your responses on the three longer reading selections. Summarize and comment on your error patterns. _____
   _____
   _____

2. What selection, short or long, has held your attention the best? Why do you think it did so? _____
   _____
   _____

3. What are your major responsibilities other than going to college?
   _____
   _____
   _____

4. Did you receive any scholarships for college? If so, describe how you qualified for them. _____
   _____
   _____

5. Describe your mode of transportation and your average traveling time to class. _____
   _____
   _____

6. What unforeseen difficulties have you already encountered this term that have interfered with your ability to study? _____
   _____
   _____

EVERYDAY READING SKILLS

Selecting a Book

The next time you are in the market for a good read, enter a bookstore, feast your eyes on the colorful array of books, and remind yourself, "Don't judge a book by its cover." Like groceries and clothing, books are products—and the packaging matters. Book jackets are slick marketing tools designed by experts to entice you to make a purchase through pictures, testimonials, and exaggeration. Cut through the hype and decide if the book will be of interest to you. The introductory material on the cover can be helpful, but remember that exciting covers can be wrapped around boring books.

THE
Depth
OF THE
Howard Wells

By *New York Times* bestselling author, Lou Franklin

"A torrid tale of international intrigue and mystery"
San Francisco Chronicle

"Splendid characters bring a privileged Texas family to life"
Maria Garcia, columnist

"A wealthy and powerful family threatened by
mistrust and greed"
Washington Post

*R*enowned *New York Times* bestselling author Franklin unravels the secrets of the oil rich Howard family in a mystery that begins with the murder of Jeff Howard's former mistress and ends up reaching into the sordid past of an international jetsetter and national hero. Never has the truth been told in such riveting detail or has a family seemed more real. The scandals and the financial crises weave a tapestry of trouble for the Howard family and those who have benefited from their vast wealth.

exercise 1

Refer to the preceding figure to answer the following questions.

1. Is this book on the *New York Times* Best Sellers List? _____

2. What is the book about? _____

3. Who wrote "Never has the truth been told in such riveting detail"? _____
   _____

4. Which of the three review quotes seems most positive and why? _____

_____

_____

Reader's TIP   Selecting a Book

After locating a book that looks interesting, further investigate using these strategies.

- Read the book jacket. Do the quotes from reviewers seem valid or clipped out of context? Do the blurbs introducing the book entice you? Has the author written other books that you have enjoyed? If the book is nonfiction, what are the author's credentials?
- Read the first page and at least one other page. Do you like the writing style? Is it comfortable for you to read? Does the first page grab your attention?
- If nonfiction, look at the illustrations and read the captions. Are you intrigued?
- If nonfiction, review the table of contents and scan the index. Is this material that you want to learn more about?

Consult Best-Seller and Book Club Lists

If you want to know what books other people are buying, consult a best-seller list. Your bookstore or your city newspaper may publish one. If not, the *New York Times* Best Sellers List is nationally respected. Such lists are sometimes divided into best-selling fiction and nonfiction, and then further divided into hardbound books—which are published first and cost more—and paperbacks. Similar to a listing of top-grossing movies, a ranking on a best-seller list indicates quantity, but not necessarily quality.

Bookstores usually have special displays to help you make reading selections; these might say, "Hot Summer Reading," "Books for the Beach," "New Releases," "New Fiction," and "Paperback Favorites." Such display selections are based on sales popularity and the judgment of bookstore personnel. In addition, book clubs sometimes list recommendations, and Oprah's Book Club reading selections are especially popular. The latter are books the talk show host has picked for a television review broadcast. Before you purchase a book, consider that your local library may have the same book available to borrow at no charge.

Sample a Variety of Fiction and Nonfiction

Fiction is writing that has been invented by the imagination. The **novel,** the literary form for the imaginative and pleasurable stories of contemporary fiction, is longer than a short story but presents the same elements of plot, character, theme, setting, and tone.

Nonfiction is a piece of writing based on true events. Some are historical works in which dialogue may be invented based on known facts about the actual people and events of a given time period. Such books are difficult to distinguish from fiction.

Other nonfiction books are not novels at all because they lack both plot and characters. They generally are divided into chapters by ideas and then are further divided by subheadings. The label of *nonfiction* includes biographies and books about travel, art, music, decorating, computers, cooking, and other special interests.

exercise 2

Visit a local bookstore and pretend you have $100 to spend on books. Review both fiction and nonfiction books and make your choices. Record the title and author of each book you select, as well as a one- or two-sentence summary of what you think the book will be about and why you may want to read it.

Supporting Details and Organizational Patterns

- What is a detail?
- How do you recognize levels of importance?
- What is a major detail?
- What is a minor detail?
- What organizational patterns are used in textbooks?
- How do transitional words signal organization?

Everyday Reading Skills: Selecting Magazines

What Is a Detail?

Details develop, explain, and prove the main idea. They are the facts, descriptions, and reasons that convince the reader and make the material interesting. Details answer questions and paint visual images so the reader has an experience with the author and sees what the author sees and understands. For example, in a passage on the validity of movie reviews, the supporting details might include information on the rating scale, the qualifications of the raters, and the influence of the production companies on the eventual reviews.

Details can be ranked by their level of importance in supporting a topic. Some details offer major support and elaboration, whereas others merely provide illustrations to relate the material to the reader's prior knowledge and make visualizing easier. All details play a part in our enjoyment of reading, but it is necessary to recognize their varying levels of importance.

Recognize Levels of Importance

To organize related words or ideas into levels of importance, the general topic is stated first, followed by subcategories of details, which may be further subdivided into specific examples. Either an outline or a diagram can be used to organize information into levels of importance.

EXAMPLE Notice that by using an outline and a diagram, the following list of words can be unscrambled to show relationships and levels of importance:

horses	grass	botany
zoology	cows	ants
bees	rabbits	entomology
branches of biology	flowers	mosquitoes
trees		

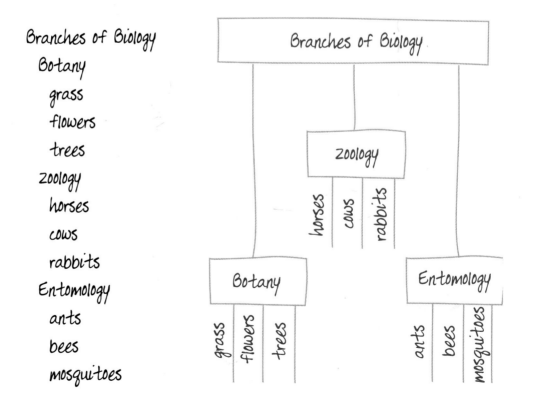

Branches of Biology
  Botany
    grass
    flowers
    trees
  Zoology
    horses
    cows
    rabbits
  Entomology
    ants
    bees
    mosquitoes

exercise 1

Major ideas and supporting details have been mixed together in the following lists of words. Think about how the ideas should be organized, and insert them in the outline or diagram form provided. The main idea or topic of each list appears either on the line above the outline or in the top box of the diagram.

List 1

elm, pine, conifers, maple, oak, deciduous, types of trees, spruce

Types of Trees

I. _____

    A. _____

    B. _____

II. Types of trees

    A. pine

    B. oak

    C. spruce

List 2

Maine, North Carolina, Southeastern, states in regions of the United States, New Mexico, Southwestern, Arizona, Rhode Island, Georgia, Connecticut, Florida, Northeastern

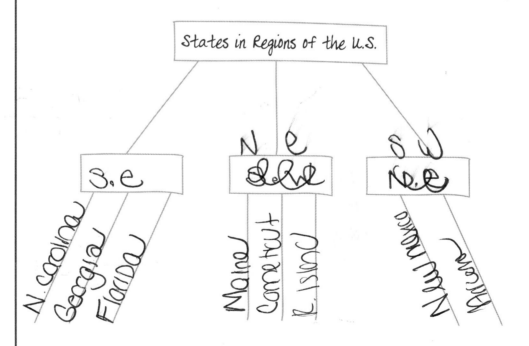

List 3

honest, personality, appearance, description of a person, shy, well dressed, blond, straightforward, tall

Description of a Person

I. _personality_

   A. _honest_

   B. _shy_

   B. _straight foward_

II. _appearence_

   A. _blond_

   B. _tall_

   C. _well dressed_

List 4

salsa, pasta, soy sauce, Mexican, ethnic foods, olive oil, fortune cookie, tacos, guacamole, Italian, egg rolls, Chinese

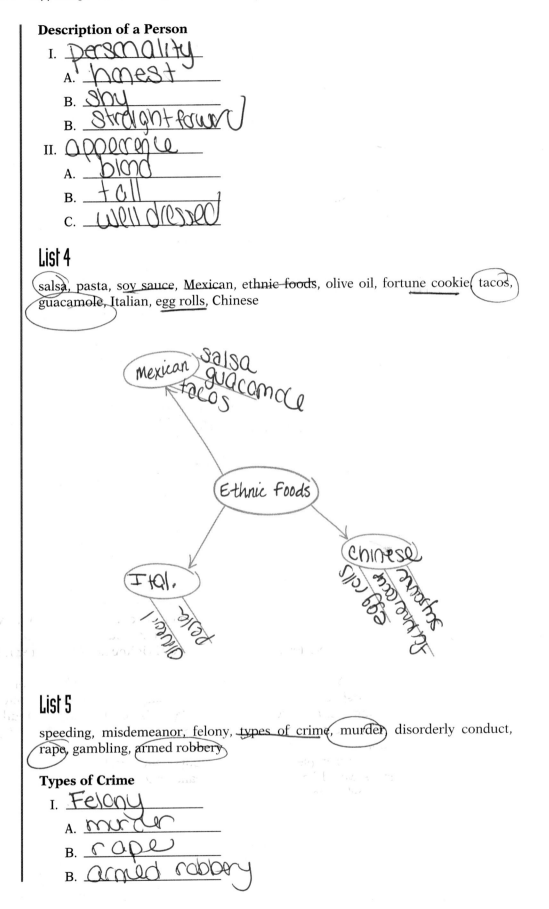

List 5

speeding, misdemeanor, felony, types of crime, murder, disorderly conduct, rape, gambling, armed robbery

Types of Crime

I. _Felony_

   A. _murder_

   B. _rape_

   B. _armed robbery_

II. _misdemeanor_

   A. _speeding_

   B. _disorderly conduct_

   C. _gambling_

List 6

Cameron Diaz, Michael Jordan, Christina Aguilera, Movies, Celebrities, Sammy Sosa, Ben Affleck, Lauryn Hill, Venus Williams, Sports, Enrique Iglesias, Denzel Washington, Music

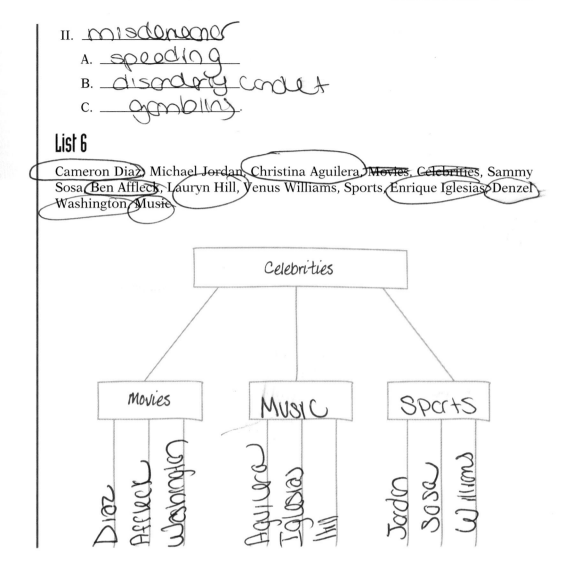

Distinguish Major and Minor Details

As demonstrated by the previous outlines and diagrams, all details are not of equal importance. When reading textbooks, you may sometimes feel you are receiving an overload of details. Not only is it impossible to remember all of them, but doing so can actually be a waste of time. With practice, you will learn that some details are major and should be remembered, whereas others are of only minor significance in supporting the main idea. How do you determine the importance of a particular detail? It depends on what point the author is making, and it depends on *what information is essential to develop, explain, or prove that point*.

For example, in a passage about communication by sound, the reason a bird sings would be of major significance and gives primary support for the main idea, whereas the particular species of a bird would be a minor detail the author included for interest and for secondary support. In a passage on the limitations of acupuncture, the date of origin of the technique would most likely be a minor detail, providing a secondary level of support. However, if the focus of the passage were on the history of acupuncture, the date of origin would be a major detail, giving primary support to the main idea.

Reader's TIP Distinguishing Major and Minor Details

To determine which details give major or minor support, first identify the author's main point and then ask yourself the following questions:

1. What details are needed to explain or prove the main idea? (These are major details that give primary support.)
2. What details are included just to make the passage more interesting? (These are minor details that provide a secondary level of support.)

Minor details add interest, help the reader understand by giving examples, create visual images, and generally fill out a passage. Perhaps the author could make the point without them, but minor details tend to enhance the quality of the work. Major details, however, directly support the main idea, regardless of whether it is directly or indirectly stated, and are vital to understanding the passage.

EXAMPLE Read the following paragraph. First determine the main point and then decide which details are major and which are minor.

> John Quincy Adams was a chip off the old family glacier. Short (5 feet 7 inches; 1.7 meters), thickset, and billiard-bald, he was even more frigidly austere than his presidential father, John Adams. Shunning people, he often went for early morning swims, sometimes stark naked, in the then pure Potomac River. Essentially a closeted thinker rather than a politician, he was irritable, sarcastic, and tactless. Yet few men have ever come to the presidency with a more brilliant record in statecraft, especially in foreign affairs. He ranks as one of the most successful secretaries of state, yet one of the least successful presidents.
>
> —*The American Pageant* by Thomas Bailey and David Kennedy

1. What point is the author trying to make? _____
   _____

2. Are the following details major or minor in their support of the author's point?

   Min. a. He was 5 feet 7 inches tall.

   Min. b. He was thickset and bald.

   Maj. c. He was a closeted thinker rather than a politician.

   Min. d. He swam naked in the Potomac River.

   Maj. e. He came to the presidency with a brilliant record in statecraft.

EXPLANATION The author's main point is that John Quincy Adams had been a brilliant secretary of state but was a socially inept politician and thus one of the least successful presidents. Items *a* and *b* on appearance are minor details that add interest but lend only secondary support. Item *c* is a major detail because it shows Adam's isolation as a socially inept politician. Swimming naked (*d*) is an interesting minor detail, and the last item (*e*) is a major detail because it develops the main point.

Transitional Words to Signal Levels of Importance. Sometimes the following connecting words signal the importance of details:

Major (primary support):   first / second   last / in addition
Minor (secondary support): for example / to illustrate

For each of the following topics, three details are given. Determine which details offer major (primary) support to the topic and which offer minor (secondary) support. Write the appropriate word in the blanks.

1. Reducing the Fur Trade

   Maj. a. Through advertising and publicity stunts, Peta, the world's largest animal rights group, has done much to convince the public that wearing fur is cruel.

   Maj. b. Over the last fifteen years people have come to realize the suffering of animals, and the fur industry has dramatically declined.

   Min. c. For example, Tyra Banks and Cindy Crawford will not model fur.

2. Dorothea Dix's Humanitarian Reform

   Maj. a. After visiting a jail to teach a Sunday school class to the female inmates and finding female patients in a mental hospital freezing in unheated, filthy cells, Dix started a lifelong campaign to improve conditions in such institutions.

   Min. b. From 1845 to 1885 she was directly responsible for establishing thirty-three mental hospitals at home and abroad.

   Min. c. Dix was born in Maine but moved to Boston at the age of 12 to live with her grandmother.

3. Diet of an Armadillo

   Maj. a. The armadillo enjoys scorpions, tarantulas, and grasshoppers, but its favorite food is ants, including the eggs and larvae.

   Min. b. If pursued, the armadillo can outrun a human and quickly dig itself into the ground.

   Min. c. Sometimes it will eat fungus and wild berries or catch a lazy lizard, but the belief that the armadillo raids henhouses is unfounded.

exercise 3

Distinguishing between major and minor details is important, whether you are studying a single paragraph, a chapter, or a whole book. After reading each of the following passages, first identify the author's main point. Then determine which of the details listed are major and which are minor in supporting that point. The skills you will use apply equally to these short readings and to the larger units of text you will be studying in college textbooks.

Passage 1

PRICE SETTING

The DeBeers Company of South Africa, a syndicate that controls most of the sales of raw diamonds, maximizes profits by determining what quantity of raw diamonds to offer on the world raw-diamond market. DeBeers markets diamonds through an unusual marketing procedure called a sight. About three weeks before each sight, DeBeers sends notices to the 300 largest diamond purchasers, who are asked to send in requests in carats for the amount of diamonds they wish to buy. Two days before the sight (held in London, Luzerne, and Kimberley, South Africa), the buyers are informed how many carats they have been allocated—an amount often below the quantity requested. At the sight each buyer is handed a container of raw diamonds. Buyers who refuse to purchase would run the risk of not being invited back. The market price of diamonds is regulated by the number of diamonds offered in each sight.

—*Essentials of Economics* by Paul Gregory

1. What point is the author trying to make? _____

   _____

2. Which details are major and which are minor in supporting the author's point?

   _____ a. The sight is held in London, Luzerne, and Kimberley.

   _____ b. DeBeers invites the 300 largest diamond buyers to the sight.

   _____ c. The buyers are offered fewer diamonds than the quantity requested.

Passage 2

THE FUTURE OF WAR

Will the future of war be cruise missiles and Stealth bombers or will it be computers and microchips? Many military analysts believe that the weaponry is changing from the "smart weapons" of the Persian War of 1991, and that future conflicts will be dominated by "cyberterrorism" and "netwars." Tactics will focus on disrupting information systems in order to confuse and control the enemy. Computers will be the preferred weapon of war for nations, revolutionaries, and criminals as well.

—*Society in Focus*, Third Edition, by William Thompson and Joseph Hickey

1. What point is the author trying to make? _____

   _____

2. Which details are major and which are minor in supporting the author's point?

   minor a. "Smart weapons" were used in the Persian War in 1991.

   major b. Tactics will focus on disrupting information systems in order to confuse and control the enemy.

   major c. Computers will be the new weapons of war for nations, terrorists, and criminals.

Passage 3

MARKET RESEARCH

Big companies figure out all sorts of stuff about us we don't even know ourselves—from how many headaches we get to how much dust we vacuum up. They know how many times we change our babies' diapers, how often we lose the cap to our toothpaste tube, and what we think about our local car dealer.

Of all businesses, the prize for research thoroughness may go to toothpaste makers. Among other things, they know that our favorite color for a toothbrush is blue and that only 37 percent of us are using one that is more than six months old. They know that 47 percent of us put water on our brush before we apply the paste, that 15 percent of us put water on after the paste, and that 24 percent of us do both. They also know that 14 percent of us don't wet the brush.

But that, of course, isn't all they know. They have also figured out that 21 percent of Americans have some difficulty handling one of their tubes, complaining of such problems as "trouble squeezing the last toothpaste out" (16 percent) and "tube breaks" (7 percent).

—*You Aren't Paranoid If You Think Someone Eyes Your Every Move* by John Koten

1. What point is the author trying to make? _____

_____

2. Which details are major and which are minor in supporting the author's point?

   MAJor a. Big companies know how many headaches we get.

   MAJor b. Toothpaste takes the prize for thoroughness in research.

   Minor c. The toothpaste tube breaks on 7 percent of us.

Passage 4

VACCINATION

Vaccination against a specific disease works by inducing the immune system to mount a primary immune response and to produce memory cells, ready to trigger a secondary response at the body's first real battle against the disease antigen. The practice of vaccination, however, began long before people understood how it works. Arabic and Chinese manuscripts more than a thousand years old refer to vaccination against smallpox. Lady Mary Wortley Montagu, wife of the British ambassador to Turkey, introduced this ancient custom into England in 1718. She had her children vaccinated by rubbing part of the scab from a healed smallpox sore into a small wound in the skin. This introduced a few live smallpox viruses into the body, stimulating a primary immune response and thereby conferring immunity to smallpox in later life. The snag was that vaccination with even a small amount of live virus sometimes caused a case of smallpox, which could be fatal.

—*A Journey into Life*, Second Edition, by Karen Arms and Pamela S. Camp

1. What point is the author trying to make? _____

_____

2. Which details are major and which are minor in supporting the author's point?

   Minor a. Lady Mary Wortley Montagu was the wife of the British ambassador.

   major b. Lady Montagu rubbed the scab of a healed smallpox sore on her children's skin to immunize them.

   major c. Live virus can sometimes cause a case of fatal smallpox.

Passage 5

THE VICE PRESIDENT

The role of the vice president of the United States is limited in power. In fact, Franklin Roosevelt's vice president, John Garner, claimed the job "isn't worth a pitcher of warm spit." The only formal responsibility is to preside over the United States Senate and cast a vote in case of a tie. Otherwise, the vice president's responsibilities and influence depend entirely upon the will of the president. As Vice President Hubert Humphrey put it, "He who giveth can taketh away and often does."

—*The New American Democracy*, Election Update Edition, by Morris Fiorina and Paul Peterson

1. What point is the author trying to make? _____

   _____

2. Which details are major and which are minor in supporting the author's point?

   major a. The vice president casts a vote in case of a tie in the Senate.

   major b. The president controls the influence of the vice president.

   minor c. John Garner was Franklin Roosevelt's vice president.

Follow Detailed Directions

Some of the normal rules of reading change dramatically when the task is to follow printed directions. Suddenly, all details are of equal importance, and you must switch gears to accomplish this new task. For example, every detail requires attention when you read the directions for a science experiment, a nursing procedure, or a computer program. You cannot read directions like you would a newspaper article.

Readers are not accustomed to attending to every single detail. For most reading, understanding the general idea and important details is adequate. However, this strategy does not work too well if you are assembling a bicycle or following travel directions to a party. When confronted with a set of directions, recognize that the task is different, even tedious, and then commit to reading step by step, and sometimes even word by word and phrase by phrase. Consult any diagram that accompanies the directions, and read aloud if necessary. Remember that some people are better than others at visualizing graphic designs, so consider finding a partner.

Reader's TIP   Following Directions

- Change your mindset from normal reading and commit to a different kind of task.
- Read to get an overview so you have a general idea of the task and can make a plan.
- Assemble the necessary equipment, estimate the time, and find a helper if needed.

- Read each step sequentially, and do as directed. Move from word to word and phrase to phrase for a clear understanding. Read aloud if necessary.
- Use numbers, letters, and guide words such as *first, next, before, after, then,* and *now* to maintain sequence. Insert your own numbers if steps are not sequenced.
- Visualize the process. Consult the diagram. Draw your own diagram if none exists.
- Think logically and keep your goal in mind.

EXAMPLE   Select a friend and follow these directions together for calculating pulse rate.

1. Select a pulse point that is comfortable for you and the other person. You can take pulse rate on the inner surface of the wrist, in the fold of the arm opposite the elbow, on the side of the throat a few inches from the center, or in the bend of the leg behind the knee.
2. Press two or three fingers gently down over the selected pulse point. Do not use the thumb because it has a pulse of its own that could be mistaken for the client's pulse.
3. Once the pulsations are felt, use the second hand on your watch to count the pulsations for 30 seconds.
4. Multiply the number of pulsations by two to calculate the pulse rate per minute. Write down the rate.
5. Wait a few minutes and repeat the procedure to obtain a second pulse rate. Write down the rate.
6. If the difference in the two pulse rates is more than two counts, repeat the procedure using a different pulse point. Write down this rate.

EXPLANATION   An overview of these directions indicates that you need a watch with a second hand, paper and a pen, and a willing friend. Find a comfortable

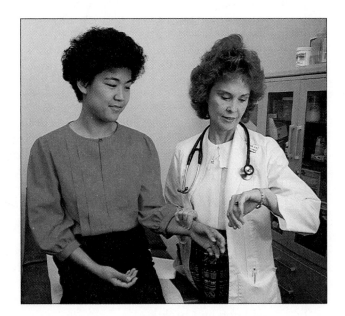

pulsation point and calculate the pulse rate. Evaluate your results by considering that a normal resting pulse rate for an adult is 80 pulsations per minute with a range from 60 to 100.

exercise 4

Directions 1

Use the following directions to put numbers and signs on the line below.

_____

1. Put the number 8 in the middle of the line.
2. On the left end of the line, write a 5 and on the right end put a 7.
3. Equidistant between the 8 and the 7 write down the sum of the two numbers.
4. Equidistant between the number on the far left of the line and the number in the middle, write down the sum of all the numbers on the line.
5. On either side of the number in the middle of the line insert a minus.
6. To the right of the first number on the line and to the left of the last number, insert a plus.
7. Put an equals sign after the last number on the line and use the signs to calculate the total of the numbers listed. What is your total?_____

Directions 2

Use the following directions to create an origami pecking crow out of paper.

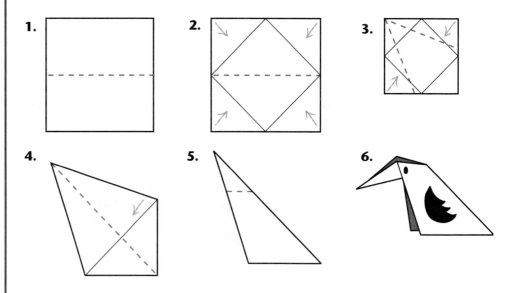

1. Begin this project with a square sheet of paper. Fold the square sheet of paper in half and then unfold it. Use the fold as a guide.
2. Now with your paper completely open again, fold each of the four corners inward to the center.
3. You now have a smaller square. Fold the top right corner and the bottom left corner both to the center line.
4. Fold in half so that each side is equal.
5. Fold the top corner back (approximately two fifths of the line) along the dotted line, unfold, and then fold inward to form the beak.
6. Draw eyes and wings as shown.
7. Have you now created a crow? Tap the tail of your pecking crow so that it will hop and peck.

Patterns of Organization

The logical presentation of details in textbooks tends to form several identifiable patterns. For example, introductory psychology texts tend to list many definitions and examples, whereas history texts present events in time order with numerous cause-and-effect conclusions. Recognizing these patterns helps you to read more efficiently and take notes for later study. They are blueprints for organizing your thinking.

Reader's TIP — Patterns of Organization and Signal Words

Addition (providing additional information): furthermore, again, also, further, moreover, besides, likewise

Cause and Effect (showing one element as producing or causing a result or effect): because, for this reason, consequently, hence, as a result, thus, due to, therefore

Classification (dividing items into groups or categories): groups, categories, elements, classes, parts

Comparison (listing similarities among items): in a similar way, similar, parallels, likewise, in a like manner

Contrast (listing differences among items): on the other hand, bigger than, but, however, conversely, on the contrary, although, nevertheless

Definition (initially defining a concept and expanding with examples and restatements): can be defined, means, for example, like

Description (listing characteristics or details): is, as, like, could be described

Generalization and Example (explaining with examples to illustrate): to restate, that is, for example, to illustrate, for instance

Location or Spatial Order (identifying the whereabouts of objects): next to, near, below, above, close by, within, without, adjacent to, beside, around, to the right or left side, opposite

Simple Listing (randomly listing items in a series): also, another, several, for example

Summary (condensing major points): in conclusion, briefly, to sum up, in short, in a nutshell

Time Order, Sequence, or Narration (listing events in order of occurrence): first, second, finally, after, before, next, later, now, at last, until, thereupon, while, during

---

Each organizational pattern can be predicted by key terms that signal the structure. Learn to use the patterns to mark your text and take notes for later study. Your markings and your notes are an organization of main ideas and major supporting details. The following are examples of the organizational patterns found most frequently in textbooks.

Simple Listing

To organize and condense material for the reader, introductory texts often enumerate key ideas. The listing technique may be used within one paragraph, or it may be used over three or four pages to pull material together. With a simple listing pattern, the items are of equal value and thus the order in which they are presented is of no importance.

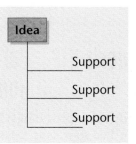

Transitional Words to Signal Listing. Listed items usually begin with general phrases, such as these:

Many of the items included were . . .

A number of factors were . . .

Signal words used as transitional words to link ideas include:

in addition   also   several   for example   a number of

Also used are numbers such as *one, two, three* (or *first, second, third*) or positions such as *next, last,* or *finally*, where numerical order is not relevant.

Mark Your Text. After reading a listing, circle the topic of the list, that is, the words that best describe what the list contains. Next, insert numbers for each listed item and underline any key words that help explain the details listed. The following is an example of this technique.

EXAMPLE

INTERVIEWING FOR A JOB

There are several tips one should remember (when interviewing for a job.) ¹Be sure to arrive on time and remember there is no excuse for being late. Attend to ²appearance and dress to look like a successful company employee. Also, ³do not smoke, chew gum, or accept candy, even if it is offered.

Your Notes on "Interviewing for a Job" would be as follows:

Topic: Tips for job interviewing

  1. Arrive on time.

  2. Attend to appearance.

  3. Don't smoke, chew gum, or eat.

exercise 5

For each of the following paragraphs, mark your text as if for later study. After reading insert a topic onto the blank at the beginning of the passage. Take notes by first recording the topic and then listing the items. Respond with *T* (true) or *F* (false) to the comprehension items.

Passage 1

_____

Business partnerships have several disadvantages. Unlimited liability is the greatest draw-back. For example, if any partner incurs a business debt (with or without the knowledge of the partnership), all partners may still be held liable. Another disadvantage is the potential lack of continuity. If one partner dies, the partnership dissolves. Surviving partners do have the option of forming a new business. In addition to theses concerns is the difficulty of transferring ownership. No partner, for example, may sell out without the consent of the others. Moreover, a partner who wants to retire or to transfer interest to a son or daughter must have the other partners' consent.

—*Business Essentials*, Third Edition, by Ronald Ebert and Ricky Griffin

1. Mark your text and then take notes.

   Topic: _____

   (1) _____

   (2) _____

   (3) _____

_____ 2. Unlimited liability means partners are responsible for business debts incurred by other partners.

_____ 3. A spouse could not automatically join a partnership after the death of the married partner.

Passage 2

_____

During elections to Congress there are a number of advantages of incumbency (being currently in office). One big one is that incumbents can issue "official" statements or make "official" trips to their district. They can get a lot of free publicity that their opponents would have to pay for. For another advantage, members of the House have office and staff budgets of approximately $350,000 a year; senators are given at least that and often considerably more if their states are large. Both receive 32 government-paid round trips to their districts each year. Also, facilities for making television or radio tapes are available in Washington at a low cost. In addition, there is the *frank,* the privilege of free official mailing enjoyed by Congress. Two hundred million pieces of mail, much of it quite partisan, are sent free under the frank every year.

—*The Basics of American Politics* by Gary Wasserman

1. Mark your text and then take notes.

   Topic: _____

   (1) _____

   (2) _____

   (3) _____

   (4) _____

_____ 2. A *frank* privilege is a government-paid trip home.

_____ 3. Incumbents receive publicity paid for by taxpayers.

Classification

In order to simplify a complex topic, authors frequently begin introductory paragraphs by stating that the information which follows is divided into a certain number of groups or categories. The divisions are then named and the parts are explained.

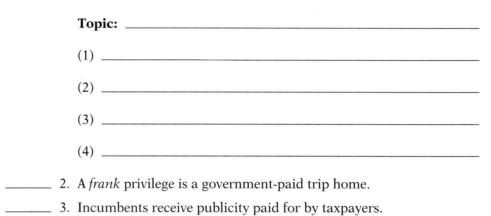

Transitional Words to Signal Classification. Signal words often used for classification are the following:

two divisions   three groups   four elements   five classes

Mark Your Text. After reading, circle the group that will be classified and the number of categories you can expect. Underline any key words that help explain the major details listed. The following is an example of this technique.

EXAMPLE   **FIVE KINGDOMS**

Today most scientists believe that living things should be divided into five kingdoms. We begin by describing the largest groups, the kingdoms, and then discuss various representatives at lower levels in the taxonomic scheme. The five kingdoms generally accepted by biologists are monera, protista, fungi, plantae, and animalia.

—*Biology: The World of Life*, Seventh Edition, by Robert Wallace

exercise 6

For each of the following paragraphs, mark your text as if for later study. After reading, insert a topic onto the blank at the beginning of the passage. Take notes by first recording the topic and then listing relevant supporting items. Respond with *T* (true) or *F* (false) to the comprehension items.

Passage 1

_____

A peaceful walk in a damp forest may bring you upon a most enchanting sight: a ring of delicate mushrooms, their little caps pushing up through the woodland floor. The beautiful little caps may be of various colors and different shapes, and some have bold markings. Mushrooms can be beautiful and taste great on steaks. A mushroom is a fungus, and athlete's foot is also a fungus.

Fungi were once placed in the kingdom with the true plants, but they are quite different from plants in a number of ways. In the mushroom group, as in the plants, phyla are called divisions and there are five of them. The divisions range from the first that includes mildews to the last that includes penicillium.

—*Biology: The World of Life*, Seventh Edition, by Robert Wallace

1. Mark your text and then take notes.

   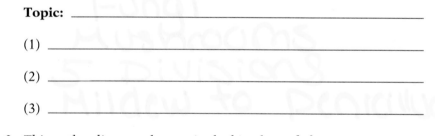

   Topic: _Fungi_____

   (1) _Mushrooms_____

   (2) _5 Divisions_____

   (3) _Mildew to Penicillin_____

_____ 2. This author lists mushroom in the kingdom of plants.

_____ 3. The fungi kingdom contains both edible and inedible members.

Passage 2

_____

We should first make it clear that, at present, we are not running out of even current forms of energy. The United States, for example, has vast deposits of coal. However, locating the coal is one thing: getting it out is another. There are heavy costs to our environment both in producing energy and in consuming it, and these costs must be weighed carefully in calculating the net benefits we receive. Should we use fossil fuels or the energy from atoms? Consider the following six categories in weighing the costs and benefits of energy sources.

—*Biology: The World of Life*, Seventh Edition, by Robert Wallace

1. Mark your text and then take notes.

   Topic: _____

   (1) _____

   (2) _____

_____ 2. The author believes fossil fuel is better than energy from atoms.

_____ 3. The United States is running out of coal.

Definitions with Examples

In each introductory course, you enter a completely new field with its own unique concepts and ideas. These courses frequently seem to be the hardest because of the overload of information presented. In a single beginning course, you are expected to survey the field from beginning to end. Beyond simply learning vocabulary, you must learn the terminology for major ideas that create a framework for the entire course. You must create a new schema. For example, in an introductory psychology textbook, several paragraphs might be devoted to describing *schizophrenia, paranoia,* or a *manic-depressive cycle.* To remember these terms, you would mark your text and take notes defining the conditions. You would also include examples to help you visualize the terms.

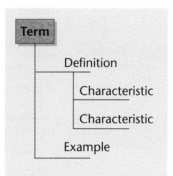

Transitional Words to Signal Definition and Examples. The new terms or concepts may appear as headings or they may appear in quotation marks, boldface, or italics. Connecting words include the following:

for example	in this case	to illustrate
more specifically	in more precise terms	in one instance

Mark Your Text. After reading the definition of a new term, circle the term and then underline the *key defining words.* A word of caution here: Only underline *key* words. Refrain from underlining sentence after sentence, which leaves you with too much highlighted material for later reference. Mark *Ex.* by the example that best helps you remember the term. The following paragraph illustrates this technique.

EXAMPLE   DISPLACEMENT

Father spanks son, who kicks the dog, who chases the cat. (Displacement) is the shifting of response from one object to another. The boss has yelled at the father, the father is angry at the boss but can't express it safely, so he *Ex* displaces his anger to his son and spanks him. The son is angry at his father, but can't express it safely, so he displaces his *Ex* anger to the dog and kicks it. The dog is "angry" at the son but can't express it safely, so he displaces his *Ex* "anger" to the cat and chases it. In the mechanism of displacement, a feeling is displaced to a safer substitute.

—Psychology: An Introduction to Human Behavior, Second Edition, by Morris Holland

Take Notes. For your study notes, jot down the term, define it in your own words, and list an example. Frequently, you will need to condense several sentences into a short phrase for your notes. If you think the text uses a clear and concise definition, it is permissible to use the same words, but don't let yourself fall into the "delayed learning" trap. If you simply copy textbook words that you do not understand, you won't be any better off weeks later when you study your notes for a midterm or final exam. The appropriate time to understand the term is when you first study and take notes on it.

Your notes on displacement might look like this:

Displacement: <u>Shifting the expression of a feeling from one object to</u>
<u>another safe substitute</u>

Example: <u>Son angry at father, so kicks dog</u>

---

exercise 7

Read the following paragraphs, and write a topic for the beginning of each passage. Circle the terms being defined, underline key phrases, and then write notes for later study. Respond to the comprehension items with *T* (true) or *F* (false).

Passage 1

_____

Thoughts and behavior during adolescence may appear to be egocentric. The *imaginary audience* refers to the adolescent's feeling of being onstage, that all eyes are focused on him or her. Much of the adolescent's time, then, is spent constructing, or reacting to, the imaginary audience. This audience is called imaginary because in reality the adolescent is not the object of such attention. In David Elkind's view, the construction of imaginary audiences helps account for a variety of adolescent behaviors and experiences, including the adolescent's sometimes excruciating self-consciousness. It is a minor tragedy of adolescent life that when these young people actually meet, each is likely to be more preoccupied with himself or herself than with observing the other.

—Adolescence and Youth by John Conger and Nancy Galambos

1. Mark your text and then take notes.

Imaginary audience: _____

Example: _____

_____

_____ 2. The author feels that when adolescents meet, each is usually focused on the other person.

_____ 3. The imaginary audience gives the adolescent a sense of security.

Passage 2

_____

Suppose you have just opened a quick copy-printing service in a new town, and you need contacts to develop your clientele. You might join a civic or social group with the sole purpose of meeting businesspeople and office personnel to whom you can sell your service. You are more interested in this unstated goal than in the goals or activities of the group itself.

When an individual conceals personal goals or needs in hopes of satisfying them through a group's interaction, the individual has a **hidden agenda**. A member with a hidden agenda can detract from a group's effectiveness because he or she will waste the group's time and energy for personal gain.

—*Effective Speech Communication* by John Masterson et al.

1. Mark your text and then take notes.

   Hidden agenda: _____

   Example: _____

_____ 2. Seeking customers can be a hidden agenda for joining a club.

_____ 3. The author suggests that members with hidden agendas tend to be positive for a club.

Description

Description is similar to listing; the characteristics that make up a description are no more than a definition or a simple list of details.

Transitional Words to Signal Description. Look for a list of defining details.

Mark Your Text. Circle the item being described and then underline the *key characteristic*. Only underline *key* words. The following paragraph illustrates this technique.

EXAMPLE   ▌ **LIZARDS**

(Lizards) are the most successful living group of reptiles. There are ^{1}3,100 different species of lizards in comparison to the snakes, which have 2,000 species. Lizards range in ^{2}size from a gecko at 1.2 inches to monitor lizards at 15 feet. The ^{3}speed of a lizard varies with where they live. The desert lizard is the fastest.

Take Notes. After marking your text, jot down the topic and underline the key characteristics. Your notes on the previous paragraph would be as follows:

Topic: Lizards

  1. Most successful reptiles—3,100 different species

  2. Size varies—gecko at 1.2 inches to monitor lizards at 15 feet

  3. Speed varies—desert lizard fastest.

▌ **exercise 8**

Read the following paragraphs, and write a topic for the beginning of each passage. Underline key phrases, and then write notes for later study. Respond to the comprehension items with *T* (true) or *F* (false).

Passage 1

_____

Vertebrates of class Mammalia have hair, a characteristic as diagnostic as the feathers of birds. Hair insulates the body, helping the animal maintain a warm and constant body temperature. Mammals are endothermic, and their active metabolism is supported by an efficient respiratory system. Mammary glands that produce milk are as distinctively mammalian as hair. All mammalian mothers nourish their babies with milk. Most mammals are born rather than hatched, and mammals have larger brains than other vertebrates of equivalent size.

—*Biology,* Fourth Edition, by Neil Campbell

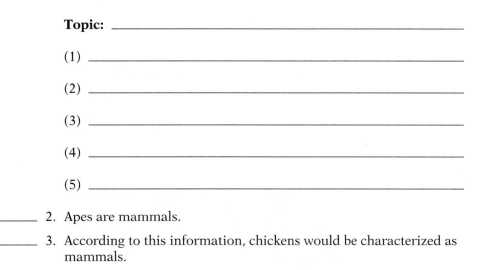

  1. Mark your text and then take notes.

   Topic: _____

   (1) _____

   (2) _____

   (3) _____

   (4) _____

   (5) _____

_____ 2. Apes are mammals.

_____ 3. According to this information, chickens would be characterized as mammals.

Passage 2

The shark is one of the most fabled, feared, and least understood large animals on earth. They have well-developed jaws and teeth and are reported to be totally humorless. The shark has a very short intestine and a large liver that helps with buoyancy. The body shape itself is quite streamlined, an important adaptation for coping with resistance.

—*Biology: World of Life*, Seventh Edition, by Robert Wallace

1. Mark your text and then take notes.

   Topic: _____

   (1) _____

   (2) _____

   (3) _____

   (4) _____

_____ 2. The author exhibits a sense of humor in claiming that sharks have none.

_____ 3. The shark's liver helps it float.

Time Order, Sequence, or Narration

Items in time order, sequence, or narration are listed in the order in which they occurred or in a specifically planned order in which they must develop. Changing the order would change the results. For example, events in history are typically organized in time order or narration. Novels, biographies, and anecdotes are usually developed chronologically, and instructions and directions are usually developed in sequence.

```
┌───────┐
│ Topic │
└───┬───┘
    │
    ├──── First
    │
    ├──── Second
    │
    └──── Third
```

Transitional Words to Signal Time Order or Sequence. Signal words often used for time order or sequence include:

first	second	afterward	after	before	when
until	at last	next	most important	finally	(dates)

Mark Your Text. After reading a time-ordered or sequenced section, first circle the topic and then decide on the significant events or steps and number them. Insert numbers for each important stage and underline key words that explain each one. By its nature, history is full of time-ordered or chronological events. Be aware that every event is not of equal significance. History textbooks also include many details that help you visualize but you do not need to remember. Use the subheadings in the text to help you judge the importance of events.

EXAMPLE

THE LOUISIANA PURCHASE

The events surrounding the (Louisiana Purchase) occurred as follows: In (1795) Spain granted western farmers the right to ship their produce down the Mississippi River to New Orleans, where their cargoes of corn, whiskey, and pork were loaded aboard ships bound for the East Coast and foreign ports. In (1800,) however, Spain secretly ceded the Louisiana territory to France and closed the port of New Orleans to American farmers, who exploded with anger. The president sent James Monroe to France to purchase the land. Circumstances played into American hands when, also in (1800,) slaves rebelled in Haiti, and France had to send troops to fight. After meeting with a determined resistance and mosquitoes carrying yellow fever, Napoleon exclaimed, "Damn sugar, damn coffee, damn colonies." He was then ready to sell. Finally, in (1803,) the United States officially purchased all of the Louisiana Province, a territory extending from Canada to the Gulf of Mexico and westward as far as the Rocky Mountains. The American negotiators agreed on a price of $15 million, or about 4 cents an acre.

—*America and Its People*, Third Edition, by James Martin et al.

Take Notes. After marking your text, jot down the topic and number the items that are relevant. Be brief. If these items need explanation, put key words underneath the item or in parentheses beside it. Your notes on the previous paragraph would be as follows:

Louisiana Purchase

1. 1795   Spain allowed shipping

2. 1800   Sold to France, which stopped shipping

3. 1800   France failed to win in Haiti

4. 1803   U.S. bought all land

exercise 9

Read the following paragraphs, and mark your text by writing a topic at the beginning of the passage, circling or numbering listed items, and underlining key phrases. Then write notes for later study. Respond to the comprehension items with *T* (true) or *F* (false).

Passage 1

On election day, 1963, hundreds of Mexican Americans in Crystal City, Texas, the "spinach capital of the world," gathered near a statue of Popeye the Sailor to do some-

thing that most had never done before: vote. Although Mexican Americans outnumbered whites two to one, whites controlled all five seats on the Crystal City council. For three years, organizers struggled to register Mexican American voters. When the election was over, Mexican Americans had won control of the city council. "We have done the impossible," declared Albert Fuentes, who led the voter registration campaign. "If we can do it in Crystal City, we can do it all over Texas. We can awaken the sleeping giant."

Since 1960 Mexican Americans have made impressive political gains. During the 1960s four Mexican Americans—Senator Joseph Montoya of New Mexico and representatives Eligio de la Garza and Henry B. Gonzales of Texas and Edward R. Roybal of California—were elected to Congress. In 1974, two Chicanos were elected governors—Jerry Apodaca in New Mexico and Raul Castro in Arizona—becoming the first Mexican American governors since early in this century. In 1981 Henry Cisneros of San Antonio, Texas, became the first Mexican American mayor of a large city.

—America and Its People, Third Edition, by James Martin et al.

1. Mark your text and take notes.

   Topic: _____

   1960 _____

   1963 _____

   1974 _____

   1981 _____

_____ 2. Albert Fuentes was elected governor of California.

_____ 3. The voting area in Crystal City was located near a statue of Popeye.

Passage 2

Criminals now have to worry about their own very unique DNA. Any cells will do, whether from blood, semen, teeth, hair follicle, or saliva. Samples are collected from the crime scene and suspect. The DNA is extracted, concentrated, and subjected to restriction enzymes, which chop the DNA into fragments. The fragments are then separated by gel electrophoresis. There are far too many different fragments in the gel to be of use, so the next step is critical. The gel layer is transferred to a sheet impregnated with nitrocellulose, which opens the strands up. Then radioactive DNA probe is added. The probe consists of short, single strands of radioactive DNA, whose sequence will match and join highly selected known human DNA sequences somewhere in the fragments. The selected fragments will form the fingerprint. To make the selected radioactive fragments visible, the nitrocellulose sheet is laid over X-ray film, and the desired pattern emerges. Since each person's DNA differs from all others (except for identical twins), the pattern becomes the "fingerprint." The odds of misidentification have been estimated one in a million and one in 70 billion.

—Biology: The World of Life, Seventh Edition, by Robert Wallace

1. Mark the text and then take notes.

    Topic: _____

    (1) _____

    (2) _____

    (3) _____

    (4) _____

    (5) _____

    (6) _____

_____ 2. The odds of making an error in DNA identification are one in a hundred.

_____ 3. The DNA pattern usually emerges on X-ray film.

Comparison and Contrast

Another pattern you will find in introductory texts is one that relates items according to existing comparisons and contrasts. To enrich your understanding of a topic, items are paired and then similarities or differences are listed.

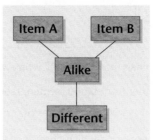

Transitional Words to Signal Comparison and Contrast. Signal words often used for comparison or contrast include:

Comparison: similar   like   in the same way   likewise

Contrast: different   on the other hand   but   nevertheless   however
       although   instead   conversely

Mark Your Text. After reading the passage, record the topic and then write an abbreviation for similarities or differences in the margin. Underline key words. The following paragraph illustrates the technique.

EXAMPLE

Diff.
Sim.
sim.
Diff.

CHICAGO AND CLEVELAND

Chicago, at the southern tip of Lake Michigan, is a port city and an important commercial and industrial center of the Midwest. It is also an important educational, cultural, and recreational center, drawing thousands to its concert halls, art museums, and sports arenas. Cleveland, on the south shore of Lake Erie, is also a port city and a commercial and industrial center important to its area. Like Chicago, it has several important colleges and universities, a distinguished symphony orchestra, one of the fine art museums of the world, and many recreational centers. The location of the two cities undoubtedly contributed to their growth, but this similarity is not sufficient to explain their wide social diversity.

—*Short Essays*, edited by Gerald Levin

Take Notes. First jot down the topics, and then write a heading for similarities or differences. Some passages will be mostly comparisons and some will be mostly contrasts. List how the topics are alike or different. Add key words needed for explanation. The following is an example.

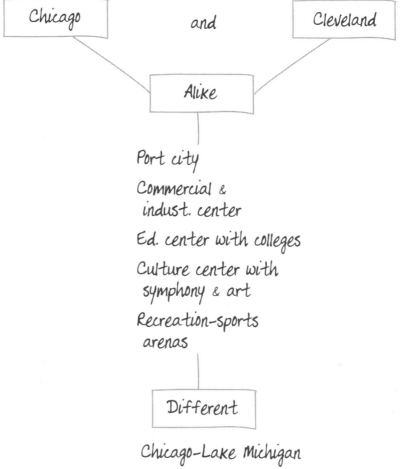

Read the paragraphs and write the topic at the beginning of the passage. Use an abbreviation to mark similarities or differences, underline key phrases, and then take notes for later study. Respond with *T* (true) or *F* (false) to the comprehension items.

Passage 1

During World War II, Roosevelt was president of the United States and Churchill was prime minister of England. Both men had similar styles of leadership and were skilled in the uses of power. Upon coming to office, Roosevelt asked Congress for broad executive powers to deal with a national emergency even before war was declared. Similarly, Churchill immediately centralized the war in his own hands by becoming both the prime minister and the defense minister. Both leaders had magnetic personalities that drew people to them. Roosevelt was sensitive to people and their dreams, perhaps having learned from his own battle with polio. Churchill was fired with imagination and a love of language. Both were gifted speakers, Roosevelt with his homely illustrations and Churchill with his emotion and vivid imagery.

1. Mark your text and then take notes. Describe each of the political labels.

    Topic: _____

    (1) _____

    (2) _____

    (3) _____

_____ 2. Churchill's sensitivity came from his battle with polio.

_____ 3. Roosevelt was both president and minister of defense.

Passage 2

_____

In the minds of many consumers, the Marlboro Man was the essence of masculinity, and the advertising image itself became an icon. The history of the Marlboro Man, however, suggests just how potent images of the West are. In 1954, Marlboro was the name brand of a filtered cigarette produced by Philip Morris and sold primarily to women. The cigarettes came in a white soft pack, had a red "beauty tip" filter to camouflage lipstick, and sold under the slogan, "Mild as May." Considered effeminate cigarettes, Marlboros had less than one-quarter of one percent market share. "Men will never smoke cigarettes with filters" was the common advertising wisdom.

Then Chicago advertiser Leo Burnett took over the Marlboro account. He changed the woman's cigarette into a man's cigarette, in fact a man's man's cigarette. The white soft pack become a strong red and white hard, flip-top pack. The "beauty tip" bit the dust, as did the "Mild as May" slogan, replaced by the image of a cowboy with a tattoo on the back of one hand. The original photographer of the series later recalled, however, that he used pilots, not cowboys, for models "because pilots seem to have little wrinkles around the eyes." The combination of rustic masculinity and a western setting—Marlboro Man and Marlboro Country—had an immediate appeal, and Burnett's campaign became the most financially successful in advertising history.

—*America and Its People*, Third Edition, by James Martin et al.

1. Mark your text and then take notes.

    Topic: _____

    _____

    _____

    _____

_____ 2. The original Marlboro package was soft.

_____ 3. The beauty tip for the cigarette was later dropped.

Cause and Effect

In this pattern, one of several factors, or causes, is shown to lead to or result in certain events, or effects. Cause-and-effect patterns can be complex because a single effect can have multiple causes and vice versa.

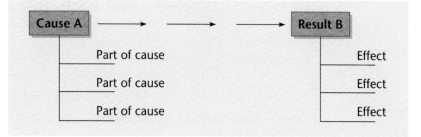

Transitional Words to Signal Cause and Effect. Signal words often used to indicate cause and effect include*:*

for this reason	consequently	on that account	thus
hence	because	made	therefore

Mark Your Text. Circle the topic, and remember there can be many causes and many effects. Therefore, give both labels and numbers to the causes and effects, as well as underlining key words to explain the items. The following paragraph illustrates the technique.

EXAMPLE

The cause: (1) *summer and* (2) *after-school jobs*

Effects:
1. *Money management*
2. *Skills*
3. *Belief in work*
   a. *Anxiety over free time*
   b. *Guilt over non-work activity*

(**EARLY JOBS**)

Aside from ¹ basic money management, *Eff* what did I actually learn from all my summer and *Cause* after-school jobs? Each one may have given me some ² small skills *Eff* but the cumulative effect was to deepen my ³ belief that work was the essential aspect *Eff* of grown-up life. Even now, I am sometimes filled with anxieties at the prospect of stretches of *free time.* When I do not immediately rush to fill that time with work, I have to fight off *guilt, Eff* struggling mentally against a picture of a Real Grown-up shaking a finger at me, someone with the droning voice of our high school career counselor, but with firm overtones of former employers, teachers, even my mother. "This," the voice beats relentlessly into my ear, "is your preparation for life."

—"Blooming: A Small-Town Girlhood" by Susan Allen Toth
from *The Compact Reader*, edited by Jane Aaron

Take Notes. Write the topic and then write headings to label causes and effects. List and number the causes and effects and add key words that are needed to explain. Here is an example.

Results of Early Jobs

Causes ⟶ ⟶	Results
Summer jobs	1. Money mgt.
After-school jobs	2. Skills
	3. Belief in work
	Anxiety over fun time
	Guilt over non-work

exercise 11 Read the following paragraphs. For each one, write the topic in the answer blank, label the causes and effects, underline key terms, and then take notes for later study. Respond with *T* (true) or *F* (false) to the comprehension items.

Passage 1

_____

Insects perform many roles vital to human life. Without bees and other insects, for instance, many flowering plants would never be pollinated—a prerequisite to producing crops such as apples, citrus fruits, berries, and cucumbers. Many beetles, ants, and flies are important decomposers, breaking down the dead bodies of plants and animals.

Nevertheless, people have devoted more time to killing insects than to praising them. It is perhaps unduly gloomy to conclude that we are losing the battle against insects, who will one day inherit the earth, but those who believe this have good reason for their opinion.

Insects destroy more than 10% of all crops in the United States, but the damage is even worse in the tropics, where hot weather throughout the year permits insects to grow and reproduce faster. In Kenya, officials estimate that insects destroy 75% of the nation's crops. A locust swarm in Africa may be 30 meters deep along a front 1500 meters long, and will consume every fragment of plant material in its path, leaving hundreds of square kilometers of country devastated.

Pesticides have not solved the insect problem. This is partly because pesticides act as selective pressures for the evolution of resistant strains of insects, which evolve too fast for expensive pesticide research to keep up.

—A Journey into Life, Second Edition, by Karen Arms and Pamela S. Camp

1. Mark your text and then take notes.

   Topic: _____

   _____

   _____

   _____

   _____

_____ 2. Bees are considered decomposers.

_____ 3. Locusts can probably be eradicated in Africa with pesticides.

Passage 2

_____

Americans are also more conscious of what they are eating. The desire to reduce cholesterol intake has caused a shift away from red meat and dairy products. The trend was substantial enough to cause beef producers to band together and mount an educational campaign to convince consumers that beef is healthful. The trend to healthier foods has primarily affected product rather than promotional strategies. Producers of dairy foods are coming out with lines of low-cholesterol products, cereal companies with high-fiber products, and liquor manufacturers with lower alcohol lines to reflect the trend away from hard liquor.

The combined effects of better medical care and greater health awareness have resulted in increased longevity in the past twenty years. From 1970 to 1990, life expectancy of the average American went from 70 to 76 years and should reach 80 by the turn of the century.

—*Consumer Behavior and Marketing Action,* Fourth Edition, by Henry Assael

1. Mark your text and then take notes.

   Topic: _____

   _____

   _____

   _____

   _____

   _____

_____ 2. Americans are eating fewer dairy products.

_____ 3. Eating beef tends to lower cholesterol levels.

exercise 12

Read the following beginning portions of paragraphs. Predict the dominant pattern of organization used by the author. Select from the following list:

Simple listing   Definition   Description   Time order   Comparison-Contrast

1. Alaska, located in the far northwest and unofficially called the Last Frontier, is mountainous, cold, and dark during the winter. Florida, on the other hand, nicknamed the Sunshine State, is flat, warm, and surrounded by beckoning beaches.

Organizational pattern: _____

2. Jupiter, the largest of the planets, is a very cold planet with an average temperature of −160°F. Sixteen known satellites rotate around the planet.

Organizational pattern: _____

3. The **fiscal year** is a 12-month period used for financial reporting. Many government agencies begin the fiscal year on July 1.

Organizational pattern: _____

4. Many different factors contribute to sales expertise. One is education; you must be able to answer questions about the product. Another is sincerity; the customer must believe you are giving honest answers.

Organizational pattern: _____

5. Cesar Chavez was born in Yuma, Arizona, in 1927. During the Great Depression his parents lost their land, and the family moved to California to labor as migrant workers. During the next years, Chavez attended over thirty elementary schools and finally dropped out of school in the seventh grade to work in the fields full time.

Organizational pattern: _____

Summary Points

- All details are not of equal importance (except when following directions).
- Major details are needed to explain or prove the main idea.
- Minor details are included to make the passage more interesting.
- A common organizational pattern in textbooks is to list ideas.
- In a classification pattern the divisions are named and the parts are explained.
- Another common pattern is to define an idea and give several examples.
- Events listed in the order in which they occur are in a chronological pattern or a sequence.
- A comparison or contrast pattern shows how items are alike or different.
- A cause-and-effect pattern shows how one event stimulated a particular result or results.

COLLABORATIVE PROBLEM SOLVING

Form a five-member group and select one of the following questions. Brainstorm and then outline your major points on a transparency. Choose a member to present the group findings to the class.

▶ Write step-by-step directions for leaving your classroom and going to a place on campus to eat lunch.

▶ Create a diagram that shows several categories and subcategories for elected state government officials.

▶ Create a list or diagram of ideas that compare and contrast your college with another college in the state.

▶ Provide two opening sentences stating the main idea for passages with a simple listing pattern of organization and two for a sequence pattern.

PERSONAL Feedback 1   Name _____

1. Describe a poster, painting, or photograph that you particularly like. What is the theme? How do the details support the theme? Why do you like it? _____

   _____

   _____

2. So far this term, have you collaborated on homework or products with other classmates? If so, describe your work. _____

   _____

   _____

3. In this class, who would you feel comfortable calling for assignment information? _____

   _____

4. What organizations have you joined? _____

   _____

   _____

5. What campus events or social functions have you attended? ___

   _____

   _____

6. When you have a break at school, where do you spend time? ___

   _____

   _____

7. What volunteer work have you recently done on or off campus?

   _____

   _____

   _____

8. What do you think "bonded to the college" means? _____

   _____

   _____

9. What would make you feel bonded to your college? _____

   _____

   _____

SELECTION 1   **PSYCHOLOGY**

THINKING BEFORE READING

Preview for content and organizational clues. Activate your schema and anticipate what you will learn.

What is the happiest part of your day?

Why do you like hugs?

I think this will say _____.

VOCABULARY PREVIEW

Are you familiar with these words?

pervasive	encounters	excessive	timidity	frailties
chronic	perspective	profoundly	competence	self-transcendence

What does the prefix *per* in *pervasive* and *perspective* mean?

How long does a chronic illness last?

Do you suffer from timidity?

Your instructor may give a true-false vocabulary review before or after reading.

THINKING DURING READING

As you read, use the five thinking strategies of a good reader: predict, picture, relate, monitor, and correct.

Refer to the
Reader's Tip
*for Psychology on
page 44.*

Becoming Healthy

How can you grow and eventually become fully functioning? How can you achieve that ideal stage of psychological health? You cannot be healthy simply by trying to be healthy; you cannot be happy simply by deciding to be happy.

5   Pleasure, happiness, and self-actualization cannot be effectively pursued; instead, they ensue, or automatically result, from your having satisfied a need, attained a goal, or grown toward health. Your deciding to be happy will not make you happy; happiness follows from what you *do*.

THREE THINGS TO AVOID

You have unpleasant feelings sometimes and this is quite natural. But if your unpleasant feelings are pervasive, unending, and tend to color your whole emotional life, then you
10   want to stop feeling so bad. We are all sometimes blue, but if you are blue most of the time, then you want to change. As you grow toward health, you tend to experience fewer and fewer persistent unpleasant feelings. Three of these unpleasant feelings are doubt, dread, and depression.

Doubt. Self-doubt makes you feel worthless, stupid, and dull. Many persons have ex-
15 cessive doubts about their physical appearance; they consider themselves unattractive,
ugly, and unlovable. They then retreat from dating and other interpersonal encounters
and remain highly self-conscious about their appearance. Other persons have excessive
doubts about their intelligence; they consider themselves uninteresting, ordinary, and
dull. They act with great shyness and timidity when among other people, believing that
20 no one would want to listen to their ideas. Excessive self-doubt, in general, comes from a
feeling that other people will not find you acceptable in some way; this feeling leads you
not to accept yourself. Understanding yourself and others is one way to avoid self-doubt;
you will discover that your frailties and fears are not unique. Being loved and prized by
someone is another way to escape excessive self-doubt; to be wholly accepted by some-
25 one else makes it easier for you to accept yourself.

Dread. Dread is a feeling of anxiety or worry. You feel afraid, but you are not sure
why. Dread makes you feel nervous, high-strung, restless, and irritable. The tension that
you feel may show up physically in nail-biting, in crying spells, in chain-smoking, in frequent headaches or neck aches, or in chronic fatigue. The persistent feeling of dread is a
30 message, and the message is this: Relax, reduce the pressures in your life, and try to resolve some of your conflicts.

Relaxing is something you may have to practice and learn how to do. Here is something for you to try: Go to a quiet darkened room. Sit or lie in a comfortable position.
Begin breathing deeply and slowly while you try to empty your mind of thoughts. Begin-
35 ning with your feet, tighten and then relax your muscles one by one, until all of the muscles of your body are relatively relaxed. Then close your eyes and imagine yourself float-
ing in a tub of warm water. The pressures of your life can sometimes be reduced by
getting away from them for a while—take a break and change your scene. For a change
of pace take a walk every day or do some light reading. You can sometimes be helped in
40 working out your problems and conflicts by talking to other people about them. As you
listen to yourself, you may gain some insights. The feedback of other people may also
give you a new perspective. Expressing your feelings to other people often in itself re-
duces the tension that you feel.

Depression. When you are depressed, you feel profoundly unhappy, blue, and sad.
45 You are moody and pessimistic; you don't feel that things will get better in the near future. You tend not to do things; your energy level is low. Things that once were significant now seem rather pointless. The persistent feeling of depression is a message, and the
message is this: Become active, get to work, begin to be involved. Get a part-time job,
start a project, volunteer as a helper in a clinic or community agency, join a club—do
50 something. Depression is the opposite of involvement.

THREE THINGS TO DO

What you do and what happens to you are under your control. You are in charge. And
what you do will determine whether you grow toward health or whether you stay as you
are now. While you cannot attain psychological health by pursuing it directly, you can
grow in the direction of health through certain kinds of experiences and these experi-
55 ences are under your control. Some experiences move you toward health; some move
you away from health. To learn about yourself and others, to love and to be loved, and to
live actively and productively—all are growth-producing.

Learn. To learn about others you must be involved with them. You must have a relationship with them of mutual trust. For how can I learn about you unless you trust me
60 enough to disclose your "inner self" to me? And how can you trust me unless I am willing to
reveal myself to you? You can help me understand myself, if I trust what you say about me.

Self-understanding cannot easily be achieved in isolation; other people help us to define who we are. Our impression of ourselves depends upon how other people consis-
tently react to us. My self-understanding and my knowledge of you thus depend upon

65 our relationship. If we do not have a trustful relationship, you may hide yourself from me. You may "mystify" me by trying to create an impression that you are different from what you really are. But if you allow me to know you, then you help me understand myself. Knowing others and understanding yourself leads to self-acceptance. You discover that the qualities in yourself that you have rejected are not unique to yourself; others are very
70 similar to you. And as you are accepted by others, you are led to accept yourself. Self-understanding and self-acceptance are experiences of growth that make possible a state of self-actualization.

Love. Experiences that confirm or validate who you are are health-producing experiences. Being loved by another is the most profound validation of yourself; for to be loved
75 means that someone knows you, that they accept the way you are, and that they value and prize you. To be loved, and therefore validated, is health-producing because it leads you to know, accept, and value yourself. And if you can do this, you are better able to function in life and more likely to experience a continual feeling of well-being.

The capacity for love is a symptom of health. The ability to love depends upon the
80 extent to which you value yourself, have faith in your own powers, and are not afraid of giving yourself.

Live. Living fully implies involvement with the world. When you actively do things, you experience your self, your power, and your capacity. When you become intensely involved in a job, hobby, cause, or other person, you tend to lose self-consciousness, de-
85 velop feelings of competence, and invest yourself in something "outside your own skin." You have feelings of purpose and meaningfulness and may taste the satisfaction of what has been called "meaning fulfillment." When you become absorbed in something outside yourself, you begin to experience a kind of self-transcendence, accompanied by a feeling of well-being. Thus the experience of active involvement is a growth experience.

(1,225 words)

—*Psychology: Introduction to Human Behavior*, Second Edition, by Morris Holland

THINKING AFTER READING

RECALL   Self-test your understanding. Your instructor may choose to give you a true-false review.

REACT   How does someone you know well create unhappiness? _____

_____

REFLECT   What makes you depressed? _____

_____

THINK CRITICALLY   Discuss how learning can help you achieve good health. Write your answer on a separate sheet of paper.

DETAILS AND ORGANIZATIONAL PATTERNS   Mark the following as major (M) or minor (m) details in support of the author's main point.

_____ 1. Self-doubt makes you feel worthless, stupid, and dull.

_____ 2. Tension may show up physically in nail-biting or headaches.

_____ 3. Learn about others.

_____ 4. Join a club to beat depression.

_____ 5. Live fully and be involved with the world.

6. What is the purpose of the first paragraph? _____

_____

7. What is the pattern of organization of the section entitled *Three Things to Avoid?* _____

8. What is the pattern of organization of the section entitled *Three Things to Do?* _____

Name _____

Date _____

COMPREHENSION QUESTIONS

Answer the following with *a, b, c,* or *d,* or fill in the blank. In order to help you analyze your strengths and weaknesses, the question types are indicated.

Main Idea _____ 1. The best statement of the main idea of this selection is:

    a. Negative and unpleasant feelings are natural but tend to ruin your emotional life.
    b. You can achieve health and happiness by avoiding negative feelings and focusing on certain positive experiences.
    c. In achieving good health, love and learning are more important than money.
    d. Pleasure, happiness, and self-actualization result as you grow toward health.

Inference _____ 2. The author's attitude toward becoming healthy is

    a. optimistic.
    b. pessimistic.
    c. sarcastic.
    d. sympathetic.

Inference _____ 3. The author believes that

    a. happiness can be pursued.
    b. happiness follows positive action.
    c. deciding to be happy can make you happy.
    d. setting realistic goals brings happiness.

Inference _____ 4. The author suggests that relaxation is a cure for

    a. self-doubt.
    b. anxiety.
    c. depression.
    d. timidity.

Inference 5. The author suggests that shyness is primarily a reflection of

_____

Detail _____ 6. The author views learning as

    a. getting a college degree.
    b. becoming involved in new hobbies.
    c. learning about yourself and others.
    d. always actively pursuing knowledge.

Inference _____ 7. The author feels that being loved

    a. is more important than loving.
    b. is not as important as involvement with the world.
    c. is the single key to good health.
    d. gives a feeling of self-worth.

Answer the following with *T* (true), *F* (False), or *CT* (can't tell).

Inference   _____   8. The author is more concerned with the psychological than the physiological contributions to health.

Inference   _____   9. According to the author, involvement and activity help to prevent depression.

Detail   _____ 10. Shy people can benefit from associating with self-confident, aggressive friends.

VOCABULARY

Answer the following with *a, b, c,* or *d* for the word or phrase that best defines the boldface word as used in the selection. The number in parentheses indicates the line of the passage in which the word is located.

_____ 1. "unpleasant feelings are **pervasive**" (8–9)

    a. upsetting
    b. uncharacteristic
    c. surprising
    d. prevalent

_____ 2. "other interpersonal **encounters**" (16)

    a. meetings
    b. groups
    c. friendships
    d. circumstances

_____ 3. "have **excessive** doubts" (17–18)

    a. endless
    b. needless
    c. more than usual
    d. inferior

_____ 4. "shyness and **timidity**" (19)

    a. nervousness
    b. meekness
    c. unreasonableness
    d. inconsistency

_____ 5. "your **frailties** and fears" (23)

    a. expectations
    b. unusual features
    c. hopes
    d. weaknesses

_____ 6. "**chronic** fatigue" (29)

    a. habitual
    b. unwanted
    c. difficult
    d. nervous

_____ 7. "give you a new **perspective**" (42)

    a. interest
    b. view
    c. tension
    d. desire

_____ 8. "feel **profoundly** unhappy" (44)

    a. slightly
    b. briefly
    c. deeply
    d. frankly

_____ 9. "feelings of **competence**" (85)

    a. love
    b. ability
    c. belonging
    d. need

_____ 10. "a kind of **self-transcendence**" (88)

    a. excelling
    b. rejection
    c. inner analysis
    d. admiration

VOCABULARY ENRICHMENT

A. The purpose of many **invented words** is to form shorter expressions that carry the same meaning. *Acronyms* are words made from the initial letters of other words. *Blends* are words formed by combining parts of other words. *Abbreviations* are shortened forms of longer words. Write the definitions and elongated forms of the following words:

> **scu·ba** \'skü-bə\ *n, often attrib* [self-contained underwater breathing *apparatus*] (1952) : an apparatus utilizing a portable supply of compressed gas (as air) supplied at a regulated pressure and used for breathing while swimming underwater

Source: Reprinted with permission from Merriam-Webster's *Collegiate Dictionary*, Tenth Edition. © 2000 by Merriam Webster, Incorporated.

(acronyms)

1. Scuba means _____

2. It comes from _____

> **medi·care** \'me-di-ˌker, -ˌkar\ *n, often cap* [blend of *medical* and *care*] (1955) : a government program of medical care esp. for the aged

Source: Reprinted with permission from Merriam-Webster's *Collegiate Dictionary*, Tenth Edition. © 2000 by Merriam Webster, Incorporated.

(blends)

3. *Medicare* means _____

4. It comes from _____

> ¹**ad** \'ad\ *n, often attrib* (1841)   **1** : ADVERTISEMENT 2   **2** : ADVERTISING
> ²**ad** *n* (1947) : ADVANTAGE 4

Source: Reprinted with permission from Merriam-Webster's *Collegiate Dictionary*, Tenth Edition. © 2000 by Merriam Webster, Incorporated.

(abbreviations)

5. *Ad* means _____

6. It comes from _____

B. Use an unabridged dictionary in your college library to find the definitions and origins of the following words.

Achilles' heel

7. Definition: _____

8. Origin: _____

    _____

maudlin

9. Definition: _____

10. Origin: _____

babel

11. Definition: _____

12. Origin: _____

   _____

C. Circle the similar-sounding word that is correct in each sentence.

anecdote: story   **access:** entrance   **moral:** honorable
antidote: medicine   **excess:** more than needed **morale:** spirit

13. The professor told an amusing (**anecdote, antidote**) about Queen
     Elizabeth.

14. The new key will give you easy (**access, excess**) to the computer room.

15. After the positive test grades were announced, the class (**moral,
     morale**) was high.

ASSESS YOUR LEARNING

Review confusing questions, seek clarification, and make notes in your text to
help you remember new information and vocabulary.

EXPLORE THE NET

● Locate and describe relaxation techniques that can help you reduce tension and
  relax quickly.

Relaxation Techniques
wso.williams.edu:8000/orgs/peerh//stress/relax.html
Relaxation Techniques
www.yourhealth.com/ahl/1847.html

● What are some alternative methods for treating depression? Describe three.

Depression.com
www.depression.com
Depression Central
www.psycom.net/depression.central.html

For additional readings and exercises, visit the *Breaking Through* Web site:

www.ablongman.com/smith

SELECTION 2   CRIMINAL JUSTICE

THINKING BEFORE READING

Preview for content and organizational clues. Activate your schema and anticipate what you will learn.

Do con artists prey on certain sectors of the population?

Why are many swindles not reported to the police?

I think this will say that _____.

VOCABULARY PREVIEW

Are you familiar with these words?

annals	guile	frailties	monetary	swindle
sleight	fraudulent	phony	affluent	perishable

Is greed a human frailty?

Is a fraudulent check phony?

How does sleight of hand make a card trick possible?

Your instructor may give a true-false vocabulary review before or after reading.

THINKING DURING READING

As you read, use the five thinking strategies of a good reader: predict, picture, relate, monitor, and correct.

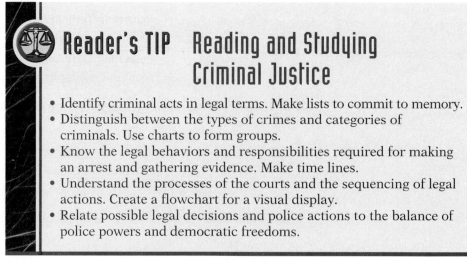

Reader's TIP Reading and Studying Criminal Justice

- Identify criminal acts in legal terms. Make lists to commit to memory.
- Distinguish between the types of crimes and categories of criminals. Use charts to form groups.
- Know the legal behaviors and responsibilities required for making an arrest and gathering evidence. Make time lines.
- Understand the processes of the courts and the sequencing of legal actions. Create a flowchart for a visual display.
- Relate possible legal decisions and police actions to the balance of police powers and democratic freedoms.

Confidence Games May Be a Shell Game Scene

The confidence artist is a recurring figure in history and in fiction, police annals, and the literature of criminology. The confidence artist steals by guile in a person-to-person relationship. Most confidence artists have insight into human nature and its frailties, not least among which is the desire to get something for nothing or for a bargain.

5   Many people who read the details of some of the confidence games below will find them hard to believe. How, they will ask, can anyone be so easily "conned"? But the police reports speak for themselves. The monetary loss and the number of confidence games very likely exceed the recorded figures because many victims are too embarrassed to make a police report.

THE PIGEON DROP

10   This swindle is operated by two people. A lone victim, usually elderly, is approached on the street by one of the swindlers, who strikes up a conversation. A wallet, envelope, or other item that could contain cash is planted nearby. The second swindler walks past, picking up the wallet or envelope within full view of the pair. The swindler approaches the partner and victim, saying that he or she has found a large sum of money and is will-

15   ing to divide it with them. But first the two must produce a large sum of money to show good faith. The victim is given no time to ponder and is urged to withdraw money from a savings account to show good faith. After withdrawing the money, the victim places it in an envelope provided by the first swindler. It is then shown to the second swindler who, by sleight of hand, switches envelopes, returning an identical envelope filled with

20   paper slips to the victim. Both swindlers then depart. The victim does not become aware of the con until he or she goes to deposit the newfound "money."

THE BANK EXAMINER SCHEME

The bank examiner scheme is one of the more sophisticated con games and requires knowing where targets bank. The con artist, usually a man, calls the victim—let us say an elderly woman—and introduces himself as a federal bank examiner, saying that there has

25   been a computer breakdown at the bank and that he wants to verify when she last deposited or withdrew money and her current balance. If she replies, for example, that there should be a deposit of $8,000 in the account, then the caller indicates that the bank records show a deposit of some lesser amount, perhaps $2,000. The caller then suggests that a dishonest teller may be tampering with the account and asks for help in ap-

30   prehending the teller. Once the victim agrees, the caller says that a cab will come and bring her to the bank. She is instructed that she should withdraw $7,000. One con man stays near the woman's house and observes her enter the cab. Another waits at the bank to verify the withdrawal and to be certain that bank officials or police are not alerted. After withdrawing the money, the woman gets back into the waiting cab and returns

35   home. One of the con men then telephones her to discuss the next phase of the bank's "investigation." While she is still on the phone, the second man knocks on the door. The man at the front door identifies himself as a bank employee, the woman lets him in, and lets him talk to the "bank examiner" on the telephone. After a short conversation, the con man hands the phone back to the woman. The caller instructs her to give her money

40   to the bank employee so that he can redeposit it with the suspected teller. Victim and money are soon parted—she may even be given a receipt.

INHERITANCE SCAM

In this scam, the victim's phone rings and, on the other end, a sweet-sounding person says, "You may be the recipient of a huge inheritance." But first some questions must be answered, such as birthday, birthplace, mother's maiden name, Social Security number—

45   all the information needed to withdraw money from the victim's bank account. When the victim answers the questions, the con artist says that he or she will deposit the inheritance in the victim's bank account. In the morning, a fraudulent check is deposited into the victim's account. In the afternoon, before the fraudulent check can be discovered, a withdrawal is made, and the victim has lost money.

50   One variation of the inheritance scam involves a victim who pays an inheritance tax before the inheritance is paid. Sometimes the caller tells the victim to mail the inheritance tax. Sometimes a well-dressed, official-looking gentleman collects the inheritance tax in cash before awarding the victim a phony cashier's check.

THREE-CARD MONTE

This scam is similar to the traditional shell game. The crook, using three "marked" play-
55 ing cards, shuffles the cards and coaxes the victim to pick the ace, queen of hearts, or
whatever. In this case, the hands of the crook are usually quicker than the eyes of the victims. The cards are "marked"—sometimes by feel, such as folded edges—in some way
that is recognizable to the shuffler. Initially permitted to win, thus receiving ego strokes,
the victim is then cheated out of his or her money.

C.O.D. SCAM

60 The suspects usually pose as delivery employees. In an affluent neighborhood, the suspect spots an empty house and finds the resident's name. After writing a phony mailing
label, the suspect goes next door and asks the neighbor to accept a perishable package
for the absent neighbor and to pay cash for C.O.D. charges.

A variant carried out on weekends involves demanding that a naïve teenage gas sta-
65 tion attendant take cash register funds to pay for a package the owner supposedly ordered. Hoping to please the boss, who is off work for the weekend, the young employee
pays the money. Of course, the boss ordered nothing, and the money is lost.

MONEY-MAKING-MACHINE SCAM

In this scam, a couple of con artists visit a local dice game to look for victims. They tell the
victim that they have smuggled a secret formula out of Germany (or some other foreign
70 country) that will bleach the ink on $1 bills. Then the blank paper can be pressed against
a $100 bill to form another $100 bill. In one case reported in Philadelphia, a victim
brought 150 hundred-dollar bills from his bank to a motel room, where the money was
washed and stuck in between pieces of tissue paper with "bleached" dollar bills. While
the victim went drinking with some of the con artists, one went back to the motel room
75 and took the money. Another promised to look for the thieves and kept the victim from
calling the police for a week. When the victim finally did call the police a week later, the
suspects were long gone.

NIGERIAN OIL CON

In the Nigerian oil con, the suspects place an advertisement in a newspaper, claiming to
have connections inside the Nigerian government. The price of oil that is quoted is usu-
80 ally just a few cents per barrel below the current market price. The victim's confidence in
the "good deal" is raised when the suspects dispatch to the victim "a succession of convincing telexes and documents," some even originating from the oil-carrying vessel itself.

The key to the con is the bill of lading. However, bills of lading are easy to fake. There
are few ways to check the authenticity of such documents, and the demand to see any ad-

85 ditional papers will be of little concern to shipping con artists. If it is only one document
that stands in the way of making a deal, then they will ask you what color you want it in.
    Soon after the buyer begins negotiating for the cargo, typically worth millions of dol-
lars, depending on the size of the oil tanker, the "supplier" will demand a cash advance of
$250,000 to defray port costs and other expenses. After payment is made, that is usually
90 the last time the buyer hears from the supplier. Both purchasers, the true purchaser and
the conned purchaser, often meet at the dock, awaiting the arrival of the same oil tanker.

(1,359 words)

—*Criminal Investigation*, Seventh Edition, by Charles Swanson,
Neil Chamelin, and Leonard Territo

THINKING AFTER READING

RECALL Self-test your understanding. Your instructor may choose to give you a
true-false review.

REACT Why do many people no longer put their names on their mailboxes? ___

_____

REFLECT How do police locate, arrest, and obtain verdicts against con artists?

_____

_____

THINK CRITICALLY The selection begins by asking how people can be so easily
conned. After reading the different scams, what factors do you think need to be
present in order for a successful scam to be accomplished? Write your answer on a
separate sheet of paper.

DETAILS AND ORGANIZATIONAL PATTERNS

1. What is the purpose of the first paragraph? _____

_____

2. After the first two paragraphs, what is the overall organizational pattern for
   the selection? _____

3. What is the organizational pattern of the section entitled *Three-Card Monte?*

_____

4. The description of the pigeon drop is told in what order? _____

Mark the following as major (M) or (m) details in support of the author's main
point.

_____ 5. In the pigeon drop the victim withdraws money from the bank to
          show good faith.

_____ 6. In the bank examiner scheme, a taxi waits while the victim with-
          draws money.

_____ 7. In the inheritance scam, the victim is assured of an inheritance.

_____ 8. In the Nigerian oil con, a bill of lading is produced to assure the
          victim.

Name _____

Date _____

COMPREHENSION QUESTIONS

Answer the following with *a, b, c,* or *d,* or fill in the blank. In order to help you analyze your strengths and weaknesses, the question types are indicated.

Main Idea _____ 1. The best statement of the main idea of the selection is:

    a. confidence artists steal money from unsuspecting victims through a variety of scams

    b. many victims are too embarrassed to report scams.

    c. in the literature of criminology confidence scams are the most difficult to believe.

    d. most confidence scams rely on two people to complete the swindle.

Inference 2. The word confidence in the phrase confidence artist suggests that

the "artist's" successful scam requires _____

_____

Detail _____ 3. In the pigeon drop swindle

    a. two people must show good faith money for the promise of a three-way split.

    b. three people must produce good faith money for a two-way split.

    c. the wallet that is planted contains the victim's money for a three-way split.

    d. the victim withdraws money from a bank account for a three-way split.

Detail _____ 4. In the bank examiner's scheme

    a. the con artists have bank records showing the victim's deposit amounts.

    b. the victim tries to deposit stolen money but is not successful.

    c. two con artists take the victim to the bank and deposit the victim's money in their account.

    d. the victim thinks that the money will be deposited but it is actually stolen.

Detail _____ 5. In one form of an inheritance scam described in the selection,

    a. the con artist wants to split the inheritance with the victim.

    b. the victim has a relative who has recently died, which prompts a call about an inheritance.

    c. the victim wants the inheritance and the con artist wants the victim's personal identification information.

    d. the con artist gives the victim a portion of the inheritance prior to getting the identification information.

Detail _____ 6. In the money-making machine scam example,

    a. the victim's $100 bills are bleached and duplicated.

    b. the victim's $100 bills are needed to press against bleached $1 bills.

    c. the victim delivers $100 bills and receives $1 bills.

    d. the victim delivers $1 bills and is promised $100 bills in return.

Detail   _____ 7. In the Nigerian Oil con example all of the following are true *except*

      a. a shipment of oil actually is being delivered to a port.
      b. the victim pays the con artist the total cost for the oil before delivery.
      c. the victim responds to an advertisement that suggests profits.
      d. the con artist supplies documents to validate the shipment.

Answer the following with *T* (true), *F* (false), or *CT* (can't tell).

Detail   _____ 8. In the three-card monte, the con artist first allows the victim to win money.

Inference   _____ 9. In both the C.O.D. scam and the pigeon drop, the victim is motivated by good intentions rather than greed.

Detail   _____10. In the pigeon drop, the swindler pretends to find money.

VOCABULARY

Answer the following with *a, b, c,* or *d* for the word or phrase that best defines the boldface word as used in the selection. The number in parentheses indicates the line of the passage in which the word is located.

_____ 1. "police **annals**" (1)

    a. rumors
    b. records
    c. conversations
    d. anecdotes

_____ 2. "steals by **guile**" (2)

    a. memory
    b. contracts
    c. cunning
    d. brain washing

_____ 3. "human nature and its **frailties**" (3)

    a. weaknesses
    b. secrets
    c. wisdom
    d. exceptions

_____ 4. "**monetary** loss" (7)

    a. instant
    b. financial
    c. temporary
    d. psychological

_____ 5. "**swindle** is operated" (10)

    a. meeting
    b. introduction
    c. transaction
    d. act of cheating

_____ 6. "**sleight** of hand" (19)

    a. hidden movement
    b. opening
    c. repetition
    d. return

_____ 7. "**fraudulent** check" (47)

    a. large
    b. fake
    c. unsigned
    d. hidden

_____ 8. "**phony** cashier's check (53)

    a. documented
    b. fake
    c. official
    d. convenient

_____ 9. "**affluent** neighborhood" (60)

    a. wealthy
    b. elderly
    c. suburban
    d. nearby

_____10. "**perishable** package" (62)

    a. stolen
    b. unexpected
    c. signature needed
    d. likely to spoil

VOCABULARY ENRICHMENT

Transitional Words

Transitions are signal words that connect parts of sentences and lead readers to anticipate a continuation or a change in the writer's thoughts. They are the same signal words that suggest patterns of organization and are categorized as follows:

Signal Addition: in addition   furthermore   moreover

Signal Examples: for example   for instance   to illustrate   such as

Signal Time: first   secondly   finally   last   afterward

Signal Comparison: similarly   likewise   in the same manner

Signal Contrast: however   but   nevertheless   whereas   on the contrary   conversely   in contrast

Signal Cause and Effect: thus   consequently   therefore   as a result

Choose a signal word from the following words to complete the sentences:

however	consequently	for example	likewise	furthermore

1. Betty Shabazz, the widow of Malcolm X, recognized the value of a college education; and _____, she returned to college to earn a doctorate and become a college teacher and administrator.

2. Anthropologists must be persistent. _____, Louis and Mary Leakey initially found primitive tools in Olduvai Gorge, but it was 28 years later that Mary discovered the first skull.

3. His real name was Samuel Longhorne Clemens; _____, millions know him as Mark Twain.

4. Plant hormones that regulate growth include auxins and gibberellins. _____, humans have important growth hormones.

5. People enjoy eating steaks rare. _____, some people use raw steak to cover an open wound as did the ancient Egyptians.

nevertheless	therefore	in this case	similarly	moreover

6. Some vitamins act as antioxidants, which means they neutralize free radicals and _____ reduce the risk of cancer.

7. Despite the benefits of antioxidants, new research _____ shows a danger because some minerals in multivitamins cause vitamin C to be released as a free radical.

8. More research on vitamins should be done. _____, doctors should be cautious in recommending vitamins that may not be needed.

9. At least five people were dead from botulism. _____, the poison could be traced to a swollen can of food that should have been discarded.

10. Hornwort is a bryophyta. _____, liverwort is also a bryophyta.

11. A cut in the skin breaks the protective covering around the body and _____ can be dangerous.

| on the contrary | for this reason | secondly |
| as an illustration | by the same token | |

12. To give CPR, first lift the neck and tilt the chin upward to open the airway. _____, check for breathing by holding your ear to the victim's mouth.

13. Dogs can be conditioned to respond to smell. _____, humans will sometimes salivate when smelling cookies baking.

14. Abnormal pituitary secretions can cause sudden increases in hormone production. Acromegaly, _____, is a condition known as dwarfism.

15. Plants store glucose in starch granules. Animals, _____, store glucose in glycogen molecules.

ASSESS YOUR LEARNING

Review confusing questions, seek clarification, and make notes in your text to help you remember new information and vocabulary.

EXPLORE THE NET

● Locate and print the top ten on the Federal Bureau of Investigation's "Most Wanted" List.

Federal Bureau of Investigation's Most Wanted List

www.fbi.gov/mostwanted.htm

● Locate information on additional types of financial scams. Describe two scams that are not listed in this selection. List tips to help people avoid being victims of crimes.

Financial Scandals

www.ex.ac.uk/~RDavies/arian/scandals

For additional readings and exercises, visit the *Breaking Through* Web site:

www.ablongman.com/smith

For a user name and password, see your instructor.

SELECTION 3 🔬 **SCIENCE**

THINKING BEFORE READING

Preview for clues to content. What do you already know about conflict resolution? Activate your schema and anticipate what you will learn.

What vaccinations should everyone have?

What is *Ebola*?

Under what circumstances have you experienced food poisoning?

This selection will probably tell me _____.

VOCABULARY PREVIEW

Are you familiar with these words?

mobilized	subsides	taxi	orifices	deranged
implemented	invincible	prominent	culprits	ingested

Why are culprits captured?

Is your ear an orifice?

Who is a prominent citizen in your community?

Your instructor may give a true-false vocabulary review before or after reading.

THINKING DURING READING

As you read, use the five thinking strategies of a good reader: predict, picture, relate, monitor, and correct.

Refer to the
Reader's Tip
for Science on
page 51.

The Nature of Infectious Diseases

Just by being human, you are a potential host for a great many pathogenic bacteria, viruses, fungi protozoans, and parasitic worms. When a pathogen has invaded your body and is multiplying in host cells and tissues, this is a an **infection**. Its outcome, disease, results if the body's defenses cannot be mobilized fast enough to prevent the pathogen's activities from
5 interfering with normal body functions. You may have heard of *contagious* diseases. This simply means that the pathogenic agents can be transmitted by direct contact with body fluids secreted or otherwise released (as by explosive wet sneezes) from infected individuals.

During an **epidemic**, a disease spreads rapidly through part of a population for a limited time, then the outbreak subsides. What happens when an epidemic breaks out in
10 several countries around the world at the same time? We call this a **pandemic**. AIDS, an incurable disease, is a prime example.

Sporadic diseases such as whooping cough break out irregularly and affect few people. *Endemic* diseases pop up more or less continuously, but they don't spread far in large populations. Tubercolosis is like this. So is impetigo, a highly contagious bacterial infec-
15 tion that often spreads no further than, say, a single day-care center.

EBOLA

Thanks to planes, trains, and automobiles, people now travel often and in droves all around the world. Human travelers can become infected within a matter of hours and taxi such pathogens far away, and eventually back home.

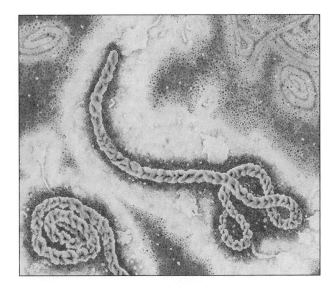

We know little about the deadly emerging pathogens. Maybe they have been around for a long time and only now are taking great advantage of the increased presence of the novel human hosts. Maybe they are newly mutated strains of existing species.

Consider *Ebola*, one of the deadliest of the viruses that cause hemorrhagic fever. It may have evolved from monkeys in tropical forests in Africa. By 1976 and possibly earlier, it was infecting humans. It kills between 70 and 90 percent of its victims. There is no vaccine against it. There is no treatment for the disease. Within a few days, nausea, vomiting, and diarrhea begin. Cells making up the lining of blood vessels are destroyed. Blood is free to seep out from the circulatory system, into the surrounding tissues, and out through all of the body's orifices. The liver and the kidneys may rapidly turn to mush. Patients often become deranged, and soon after that they die of circulatory shock. There have been four *Ebola* epidemics since 1976. Each time, government agencies around the world were mobilized; quarantine procedures were implemented to limit the spread of the disease.

DRUG-RESISTANT STRAINS

There is an old saying that, when you attack nature, it comes back at you with a pitchfork. Here we reinforce the point that infectious diseases are on the upsurge.

A mere twenty-five years ago, antibiotics and vaccines were considered invincible, and the Surgeon General of the United States announced we could "close the book on infectious diseases." There are now more than 5.8 billion people. Most live in crowded cities, and at any time, as many as 50 million are on the move within and between countries in search of a better life. Even putting aside the emerging pathogens, is it any wonder that pathogens responsible for cholera, tuberculosis, and other familiar diseases are striking with a vengeance?

Consider how one of these pathogens is having a field day. Because of economic pressures and social changes over the past several decades, the number of working mothers has skyrocketed in the United States. So has the number of preschoolers enrolled in day-care centers. In effect, each of these centers is a population of host individuals, whose immune systems are still developing and vulnerable to contagious diseases. Now think of *Streptococcus pneumoniae*. This bacterium causes pneumonia, meningitis, and middle-ear infections in people of all ages; about 40,000 to 50,000 cases end in death every year. The risk of infection is 36 times greater in large day-care centers than it is for children cared for at home. As recently as 1988, drug-resistant strains of *S. pneumoniae* were practically unheard of in the United States. Today, they are becoming the rule, not the exception.

PATHOGENS LURKING IN THE KITCHEN

Each year, food poisoning hits more than 80 million people in the United States alone. It kills about 9,000 of them, mainly the very young, the very old, or those with compro-

mised immune systems. People often dismiss their misery as "the 24-hour flu." *Salmonella enteritis* as well as certain strains of *E. coli* are prominent among the culprits. They typi-
55 cally are ingested with undercooked beef or poultry, contaminated water, unpasteurized milk or cider, and vegetables grown in fields fertilized with manure.

A few examples: In 1966, *S. enteritis* slipped into ingredients used to make a popular ice cream. In a single outbreak, possibly as many as 224,000 people suffered from stomach cramps, diarrhea, and other symptoms of *Salmonella*. In 1993 in Washington State,
60 more than 500 people became sick and three children died after eating restaurant hamburgers tainted with a pathogenic strain of *E. coli*. A recent outbreak of food poisoning was traced to unpasteurized apple juice.

Outbreaks such as these certainly grab our attention, yet pathogens lurking in the kitchen probably account for at least half of all cases of food poisoning. Examine wood or
65 plastic cutting boards or sleek, stainless steel knives with electron microscopes and you see nooks and crannies where microbes can lurk. Carlos Enriquez and his colleagues at the University of Arizona sampled 75 dishrags and 325 sponges in several homes. Most harbored colonies of *Salmonella* and *E. coli*, as well as *Pseudomonas* and *Staphylococcus*. Bacteria can live two weeks in a wet sponge. Use the sponge to wipe down the kitchen,
70 and you spread them about. Antibacterial soaps, detergents, and weak solutions of household bleach get rid of them. You can sanitize sponges simply by putting them through a dishwasher cycle.

Do you think food poisoning is a small concern? The annual cost of treating the infections caused by food-borne pathogens ranges between 5 and 22 *billion* dollars.

(1,017 words)

—*Biology: The Unity and Diversity of Life,* Eighth Edition, by Cecie Starr and Ralph Taggart

THINKING AFTER READING

RECALL   Self-test your understanding. Your instructor may choose to give a true-false review.

REACT   How much of what you eat is dependent on trust? Who are you trusting? _____

REFLECT   What can be done to protect the children at day-care centers from contagious diseases? _____

THINK CRITICALLY   Compare and contrast what you know about the spread and dangers of AIDS with the spread of computer viruses. Write your answers on a separate sheet of paper.

DETAILS AND ORGANIZATIONAL PATTERNS   Other than description, what is the overall pattern of organization for the logic and thought of this selection? _____

_____

Mark the following as major (M) or minor (m) details in support of the author's main point.

_____ 1. There is no vaccine against *Ebola*.

_____ 2. Risk of infection for children is greater in day-care centers as compared to homes.

_____ 3. *E. coli* can be spread in an unsanitary kitchen.

_____ 4. In the study, 75 dishrags were tested.

Name _____

Date _____

COMPREHENSION QUESTIONS

Answer the following with *a, b, c,* or *d,* or fill in the blank. In order to help you analyze your strengths and weaknesses, the question types are indicated.

Main Idea   _____   1. The best statement of the main idea of the selection is:

   a. *Ebola* is an emerging pathogen for which there is no known cure.
   b. Kitchens harbor hidden bacteria that cause food poisoning.
   c. Humans are increasingly endangered by pathogens that cause infectious and deadly diseases.
   d. Pathogens can be transmitted by direct contact with body fluids.

Detail   _____   2. The disease *Ebola* is characterized by all of the following except

   a. it originated in Malaysia.
   b. it begins with a high fever.
   c. the liver fails.
   d. the blood vessels are destroyed.

Inference   _____   3. The author implies that infectious diseases once presumed eradicated in the United States are resurfacing because

   a. children are not vaccinated.
   b. people are more crowded together.
   c. tuberculosis is contagious.
   d. vaccines are not made available to the poor.

Detail   _____   4. According to the author, day-care centers are particularly vulnerable to contagious diseases because of all the following except

   a. children have poorly developed immune systems.
   b. children are crowded together.
   c. fluids can be exchanged through sneezing and close contact.
   d. children do not get regular medical checkups.

Inference   5. Why is the dishwasher rather than the washing machine suggested

   for sanitizing sponges? _____

   _____

Inference   _____   6. The author's chief concern about manure to fertilize vegetables is that

   a. it does not stimulate growth as readily as commercial fertilizer.
   b. it depletes the soil of essential minerals.
   c. animal waste contaminates that can cause illness attach to the vegetables.
   d. farm workers are at risk for disease.

Detail   _____   7. The author suggests that bacteria is most likely initially introduced into the American kitchen through

   a. cooked pork.
   b. uncooked meat or poultry.
   c. packaged foods from the grocery store.
   d. knives and forks.

Answer the following with *T* (true), *F* (false), or *CT* (can't tell).

Detail _____ 8. According to the author, a pandemic is considered international, whereas an epidemic is considered regional.

Detail _____ 9. The author suggests that *Ebola* probably began with monkeys and then spread into the human population.

Inference _____ 10. The author suggests that *Salmonella* is more deadly than *E. coli*.

VOCABULARY

Answer the following with *a, b, c,* or *d* for the word or phrase that best defines the boldface word as used in the selection. The number in parentheses indicates the line of the passage in which the word is located.

_____ 1. "**mobilized** fast enough" (4)

    a. activated
    b. divided
    c. stretched
    d. multiplied

_____ 6. "procedures were **implemented**" (31)

    a. called
    b. limited
    c. started
    d. changed

_____ 2. "outbreak **subsides**" (9)

    a. resumes
    b. increases
    c. happens
    d. dies

_____ 7. "considered **invincible**" (34)

    a. unconquerable
    b. annoying
    c. hidden
    d. weak

_____ 3. "**taxi** such pathogens" (18)

    a. car
    b. transport
    c. auto
    d. driver

_____ 8. "*E. coli* are **prominent**" (54)

    a. dangerous
    b. evil
    c. unknown
    d. outstanding

_____ 4. "body's **orifices**" (28)

    a. muscles
    b. veins
    c. openings
    d. hands

_____ 9. "among the **culprits**" (54)

    a. flues
    b. causes
    c. solutions
    d. kitchen utensils

_____ 5. "became **deranged**" (29)

    a. insane
    b. ill
    c. nervous
    d. unconscious

_____ 10. "**ingested** with under-cooked beef" (55)

    a. cooked
    b. processed
    c. eaten
    d. mixed

VOCABULARY ENRICHMENT

A. Study the similar-sounding words, and then circle the one that is correct in each sentence.

| **alter:** change | **coarse:** not smooth | **dual:** two |
| **altar:** platform in church | **course:** studies or path | **duel:** fight |

1. You must (**alter, altar**) your study habits to make better grades.

2. To change a (**coarse, course**), you must go through a drop-add proce-dure.

3. The two senators fought a (**dual, duel**) at dawn.

B. Use context clues to mark *a, b, c,* or *d* for the meaning closest to that of the boldface word.

_____ 4. From listening to her talk about the trip, I got **vicarious** pleasure and felt as if I had been there.
   a. selfish
   b. enormous
   c. secret
   d. secondhand

_____ 5. The **cardiac** patient was waiting in surgery for a bypass operation.
   a. rested
   b. cancer
   c. emotion
   d. heart

_____ 6. Because of his **phobia**, he did not want to climb to the top of the tower and look down.
   a. rash
   b. fear
   c. disease
   d. mood

C. Use the indicated root to write words to complete each sentence in the groups.

vis, vid: see

7. When she plays tennis, she wears a _____ to keep the sun out of her eyes.

8. From the description you have given me, I cannot _____ the actor's face.

9. The rip was so well mended that the hole is now _____.

tin, ten, tent: hold, hold together

10. We cannot _____ the trip without stopping for gas.

11. The _____ crew cleans the floors at night when no one is in the building.

12. She has been _____ at her present job for a long time and is thus seeking other employment.

clud, clus: shut

13. She gradually became a _____ by staying in the house and not receiving any visitors.

14. To _____ the interview, the manager stood up and shook her hand.

15. A correct address should _____ the zip code.

ASSESS YOUR LEARNING

Review confusing questions, seek clarification, and make notes in your text to help you remember new information and vocabulary.

CONNECT

Read the following passage about **E. coli.** *Approximately 20,000 cases of* **E. coli** *contamination are recorded in the United States each year with about 250 resulting deaths. How vulnerable are you to this contamination? What do you do in the home and what can you do when eating out to prevent contamination?*

Hundreds of Tons of Ground Beef Recalled

Neil Sherman
HealthScout, August 1, 2000.

There's still a mystery about one death in Milwaukee. On July 29, a 3-year-old girl died from *E. coli* poisoning after eating at a restaurant, city officials say. They know she had a hamburger, but most of the 42 other people who also became ill at the restaurant had eaten watermelon. That may have been the main source of the *E. coli* poisoning, officials believe. They haven't established whether the girl had watermelon as well as a burger.

"Those who consumed watermelon at the restaurant were eight times more likely to be infected with *E. coli*. We do not know if the watermelon was contaminated before or after it entered the restaurant," according to Milwaukee's health commissioner, Dr. Seth Foldy.

Chuck Hungler, a spokesman for Jac Pac Foods, says *E. coli* "starts at the slaughterhouse."

The bacterium ordinarily lives harmlessly in the stomachs of cattle. Contamination occurs when cattle are confined to feed lots to be fattened for slaughter. The animals spread the germ by defecating and drooling into shared water troughs.

"No matter how much testing we do you can't test 100 percent of the meat," Hungler adds.

Hungler says grinding the meat into ground beef distributes the bacteria throughout the product. "When you grill a steak, you kill the bacteria on the outside, where it resides. But in ground beef, it gets ground in so you don't know where it is. So you can't eat it pink without a risk."

Hungler thinks food irradiation is the solution. "The public perception is that they are going to glow or something. But irradiation is a completely safe process and eventually, I think, it will be the way we get rid of this problem."

Irradiation, which uses electron beams to destroy *E. coli* and other bacteria, was approved by the USDA last year and is now being used at a handful of meat-processing plants in the Midwest.

The only sure-fire way of avoiding *E. coli* infection "is the safe handling of meat," says Blake. "It should be cooked to an internal temperature of 160°F.

Color is no indicator of internal temperature, Blake warns. "Studies have shown that some burgers can be brown on the inside but still not be at the proper temperature. And some burgers can be pink on the inside and be at 160°F."

EXPLORE THE NET

● Describe some of the treatment options that are now available to people infected with the AIDS virus.

The Body: An AIDS and HIV Information Source

www.thebody.com/treat/expdrugs.html

National AIDS Treatment Information Project

www.natip.org/index.html

● Locate information on food safety. List some things you can do to prevent food poisoning.

MEDLINE plus; Food Contamination/Poisoning

www.nlm.nih.gov/medlineplus/foodcontaminationpoisoning.html

FDA Consumer: The Unwelcome Dinner Guest: Preventing Food-Borne Illness

www.vm.cfsan.fda.gov/~dms/fdunwelc.html

For additional readings and exercises, visit the *Breaking Through* Web site:

www.ablongman.com/smith

PERSONAL Feedback 2   Name _____

1. Approximately how much time do you spend each day studying for this class? _____

   _____

2. Where do you typically study? _____

   _____

3. How do you manage telephone calls during your scheduled study time? _____

4. Describe a time this week that you have procrastinated. _____

   _____

5. What were the consequences of your procrastination? _____

   _____

EVERYDAY READING SKILLS

Selecting Magazines

Visit the magazine section of a large local bookstore, and you will see specialty magazines on an amazing array of topics from decorating to alternative medicine to scuba diving. Browse through the magazines to make your purchase choices. Publishers know that covers sell magazines, so check out the contents before paying your money for any of the following magazine types.

Newsmagazines

Newsmagazines are similar to newspapers in that they cover current events and areas of special interest such as business, science and technology, and the arts. Because they are usually published weekly, they cannot cover breaking stories with the same immediacy as newspapers and television. What they can offer, however, is more details and an analysis of events. The writers and editors of newsmagazines have more time than newspaper reporters to research their stories, examine how developments affect other related issues, and predict long-term consequences.

There are three main newsmagazines in the United States: *Time, Newsweek* and *U.S. News & World Report*. Although *Time* and *Newsweek* provide more coverage of popular culture than *U.S. News & World Report*, they all follow a similar format: reviews of international and national developments, as well as noteworthy events in business, science, the arts, lifestyle/social trends, and regular columnists' essays. *U.S. News & World Report* tends to be more politically conservative than the other two, but all contain the following elements.

News Stories

Newsmagazine stories present the same 5 *W's* and *H* as newspapers do, but they include more details, use more colorful and dramatic language, and add amusing or touching anecdotes. This is very different from the dry, "just the facts" style of newspaper writing.

Feature Stories

The feature story for the week is usually prominently displayed on the cover to attract your attention. Most features include background information to provide a history of the subject so you can understand how the current situation came to be. Colorful pictures, graphs, and survey results enrich the stories.

Editorials

The topics of these opinion essays in newsmagazines appeal to a broader national readership than those found in most newspapers. Rather than being isolated on a particular page, the editorials often appear beside the related stories.

Essays

Newsmagazines also include essays that can either cover very serious matters or be whimsical and humorous. These pieces can be written by professional journalists, politicians, or readers—anyone who has an opinion or experience they want to share.

Critiques

Newsmagazines include critiques or reviews of new movies, plays, music CDs, and books. The first paragraphs usually set the tone for the review and indicate a positive or negative bias. The middle section provides a summary of the work, appropriate background information, and examples to support the critic's opinion. The closing section summarizes the critic's view and predicts the impact of the work on the field.

exercise 1

Review current copies of *Time, Newsweek,* and *U.S. News & World Report* in your college library to answer the following questions.

1. Which magazine would you prefer to subscribe to and why?
2. What is the feature story in each, and why is each noteworthy?
3. Is *People* a newsmagazine? How would you categorize the stories in *People*?

Specialty Magazines

Specialty magazines cover almost every imaginable subject: fashion, business, technology, decorating, hobbies, health, and entertainment. Within these many categories, such publications can be very precise in their focus—not any type of guitar, but acoustic guitars. Specialty magazines cover their subjects in great detail and often use *jargon,* or specialized insider terminology, that might be unfamiliar to a new reader. Although much of the content may be difficult to follow at first, there are usually columns and articles devoted to beginners.

Feature Articles

Featured magazine articles are highlighted on the cover and in the table of contents. If you don't find the catchy summaries to be interesting, the articles probably won't be, either. Sometimes rather than one feature story, a featured theme is addressed throughout an entire issue. For instance, a travel magazine might focus exclusively on travel in Mexico or spas in the Southwest. Cooking magazines often center their publications on upcoming holidays and appropriate seasonal menus. If you already know you are interested in the specialty of the magazine, look to see if the themes and features in a given issue are intriguing.

Letters to the Editor

If you are unfamiliar with a particular magazine, read the Letters to the Editor section. These letters, sent in by readers, will refer to past stories and can give you an idea of the audience to which the magazine appeals. Can you identify with the ideas and issues that seem to be important to the letter writers?

News Update in Brief

Most magazines begin with short summaries that are comparable to headline news updates on television and radio. No more than a paragraph or two in length, these updates cover news in the field on upcoming events, research findings, celebrity news, products, and trends. The longer, in-depth articles can be profiles about relevant personalities, reviews of trends and books, how-to techniques, advice, technology, and processes.

Regular Columns

Columns appear regularly in magazines and are usually written by the same columnists each time, although guest writers can contribute as well. The columns are editorials about a current issue, event, or person in the magazine's field of interest, and reflect the writer's own biases.

Advertisements

Magazines make most of their revenue through selling advertising pages. The wider circulation a publication enjoys, the more advertisers it attracts. Be aware that an advertisement for a particular product does not imply an endorsement of that product by the magazine. Conflicts of interest can arise between the editorial content of a magazine and its major advertisers. If a major advertiser's products and services always receive overwhelmingly positive reviews, take extra care to decide for yourself whether the findings are warranted based on the material presented. With some magazines, particularly fashion magazines, ask yourself if the publication is more interested in informing its readers or in maintaining advertising dollars.

Reader's TIP   Choosing a Magazine

- Read the lead article headlines and the table of contents to find articles of interest to you.
- Flip through the magazine and read article titles and boxed article excerpts.
- Use article subheadings to preview.
- Read the captions of photos that interest you.
- Read several Letters to the Editor.
- Decide, purchase, and enjoy!

---

exercise 2

Visit a magazine stand or your community or college library and select four magazines that you would like to subscribe to if money were not an issue. For each magazine list the following:

1. Evaluate the quality of the feature articles.
2. Estimate the ratio or percentage of news and feature stories to advertisements.
3. Which regular articles are particularly appealing to you?

Textbook Learning

- What is annotating?
- What is the Cornell method of notetaking?
- How do you write a summary?
- How can you use outlining?
- What is mapping?

Everyday Reading Skills: Reading Reference Materials

Expect Knowledge to Exist

Expect to know something after you have read a textbook assignment. Don't just watch the words go by. Use learning strategies to select key elements and to prepare for remembering. In the previous chapter, we discussed two such strategies—marking the text and taking notes. In this chapter, our discussion of those strategies continues with coverage of annotating, summarizing, outlining, and mapping.

The process of reading, marking, and organizing textbook information takes time. Many students ask, "How much do I need to do?" The answer to that question is, "Typically, the more you do, the more you learn." In other words, it is better to read the text than not to read the text. What's more, it is better to read and mark than only to read. Finally, it is better to read, mark, and take notes in some form (summary, Cornell notes, outline, or map) than just to read and mark. Your choices depend on the amount of time you can dedicate to learning. "Time on task" is a critical element in college success.

Annotating

Annotating is a system of marking that includes underlining and highlighting. It is the first and most basic step for all of the other organizing strategies.

When to Annotate

Do annotating after a complete thought is presented. When you mark as you read, you may tend to mark too much, and overmarking wastes valuable review time. Wait until a complete thought has been presented to separate the most important ideas from the least important ones. Such a thought unit may be as short as one paragraph or as long as an entire section under a subheading.

How to Annotate

The word *annotate* is used to suggest a notation system for selecting important ideas that goes beyond straight lines and includes numbers, circles, stars, and written comments such as marginal notes, questions, and key words. With practice, students tend to form their own notation systems, which may include a variation of the following examples:

═══	Main idea (or write the topic in the margin beside the paragraph)	⎰ ⎱	Section of material to reread for review
───	Supporting material	(1), (2), (3)	Numbering of important details under a major issue
☆	Major trend or possible essay exam question	?	Didn't understand and must seek advice
✓	Important smaller point to know for multiple-choice item	*Topic, Def. or Ex.*	Notes in the margin
⬭	Word that you must be able to define	*How does it operate?*	Questions in the margin
▭	A key issue to remember	�	Indicating relationships

Unless you are reading a library book, always use some form of annotation for study reading. Let's consider textbooks, for example. Have you been annotating throughout this text as you have been reading? (The correct answer to this question should be "yes!") If your instructor were to say at this moment, "Take fifteen minutes to review what we have covered in this text for a quiz," would you be ready to study? Could you quickly review your annotations? Remember, it is a waste of time to read for the purpose of learning and not to annotate.

EXAMPLE

The following passage represents information typically found in college psychology books. Notice a mixture of two organizational patterns: (1) definitions with examples and (2) listing. Do you recognize signals that predict those patterns? Do the reader's markings help organize the material for later study?

PERSONALITY TYPES

According to Jung, Plato and Aristotle represent two fundamentally different tendencies in the human personality. Plato, concerned with the inner world, was an introvert, and *Introverts* Aristotle, focusing his energies on the outer world, was an extrovert. *Extroverts*

Introverts turn inward, seek isolation, and tend to withdraw from social engagements. They are reflective and introspective, absorbed with self-searching thoughts. They are self-critical and self-controlled, giving an outwardly cold appearance. They prefer to change the world rather than to adjust to it. Extroverts seek social contacts and are outgoing and accommodating. They appear friendly and outspoken and make friends easily. They are tolerant of others but relatively insensitive to the motivations and moods of their friends. They prefer to experience things rather than to read about them. Can you apply one of Jung's two personality types to yourself? How do you appear to others, as an introvert or an extrovert?

Most people are a mixture of introvert and extrovert, being neither wholly one nor the other. This is one of the problems of classifying people into types. Unlike rocks, few people can be easily sorted into boxes according to type. We are just not that simple; each of us has the potential for behaving in different ways in different circumstances.

—*Psychology: An Introduction to Human Behavior*, Second Edition, by Morris Holland

The learner's task is not just to read but also to earmark relevant ideas for future study. To be an efficient learner, do not waste time.

exercise 1

Read the following passage and use the suggested annotations to organize the material and mark key ideas for later study.

POPULAR MYTHS ABOUT MENTAL DISORDERS

The mentally ill are popularly believed to be extremely weird. In fact, most are far from greatly disturbed. This is the first of several common misconceptions. Only a few inmates of mental institutions spend their time cutting out paper dolls, screaming and yelling, talking to the air, or posing as kings or queens. Even among the most severely mentally ill—schizophrenics—the flamboyant symptoms of hallucinations and delusions are not the most important characteristics of their disorder. Instead, the less demonstrative symptoms of apathy and inertia constitute the core of schizophrenia (Boffey, 1986).

Mental illness is—to take up a second misconception—commonly regarded as hopeless, as essentially incurable. Even after people are discharged from a mental hospital as recovered, they are likely to be viewed with suspicion. In reality, the majority (some 70% to 80%) of hospitalized mental patients can recover and live relatively normal lives if their treatment has been adequate and received in time.

A third misconception is that there is a sharp, clear distinction between "mentally ill" and "mentally healthy." The dividing line between mental health and illness is mostly arbitrary (APA, 1994; Brody, 1997). This is not only because the behavior of different individuals ranges by imperceptible degrees from normal to abnormal, but also because an individual may shift at different times to different positions along that range, appearing normal at one time and abnormal at another.

The fourth point is that the mentally ill are often portrayed in news media, movies, and television programs as crazed, violent people. In fact, the great majority (about 90%) of mental patients are not prone to violence and criminality. They are more likely to engage in behavior harmful to themselves rather than to others.

The fifth popular myth is about midwinter depression, which psychiatrists call SAD (seasonal affective disorder). Many people assume that we are likely to become depressed in the middle of winter because of its coldness and lack of sunshine. Presumably, the summer is more likely to give us the blues because we spend less time with our loved ones than we do in the winter.

—*Deviant Behavior*, Sixth Edition, by Alex Thio

Check your annotations with a "study buddy." Could you study the essentials from the annotations without rereading the passage?

Notetaking

Notetaking involves using your own words and a separate notebook to condense the key ideas you have marked in your text while annotating. Simply jotting these ideas down on paper is notetaking. In more elaborate systems, important ideas are written in sentences, and then notes are inserted in the left margin for a quick topic reference.

When to Take Notes

Notetaking is useful for textbook study and class lectures. The marginal topic notes placed on the left are particularly helpful in organizing the study of a large body of material for a midterm or final exam.

How to Take Notes

The Cornell method, one of the most popular systems of notetaking, includes the following steps:

1. Draw a line down your paper 2.5 inches from the left edge to create a margin for noting key words and a wider area on the right for sentence summaries.
2. After reading a section, review your thoughts and write sentence summaries on the right side of your paper. Include the main ideas and key supporting details. Be brief and concise.
3. Review your summary sentences and underline key words. Write these key words in the column on the left side of your paper. These words can be used to stimulate your memory of the material for later study.

Abbreviations. Use short cuts. Develop your own system of abbreviations for notetaking, both for textbook and lecture notes. Some students mix shorthand symbols with their regular writing. Brainstorm with a "study buddy" and list abbreviations and symbols that can help you save time.

EXAMPLE   The following is an example of how the Cornell method might be used to organize notes on the passage about Jung's theories for future study.

	Jung's Personality Types
2 Types	*Jung believed in two types of personality and most people are a mixture of each.*
Introverts	*Introverts turn inward, seek isolation, are reflective, self-critical, and want to change the outside world.*
Ex.	*Plato is an example.*
Extroverts	*Extroverts are outgoing, friendly, tolerant of others, and prefer to experience things rather than to read about them.*
Ex.	*Aristotle is an example.*

exercise 2   Read the following passage, and then use the Cornell method to take notes for future use. Write your notes in the box that follows the selection.

MONEY LAUNDERING

Al Capone, the infamous gangster of the 1920s, is said to have amassed a fortune of $20 million in 10 years through bootlegging and gambling. Yet when Capone was sentenced to 11 years in prison in 1931, it was for income tax evasion. The conviction of Capone taught other organized-crime members an important lesson: Money not reported on an income tax return is money that cannot be spent or invested without risk of detection and prosecution.

Because most money collected by organized crime is from illegal sources, such as loan-sharking, prostitution, gambling, and narcotics, criminals are reluctant to report the income or its sources on tax returns. Before spending or otherwise using these funds, they must give the money an aura of legality. This conversion is known as *laundering*. To combat organized crime successfully, law enforcement officials must understand how money is laundered.

DOMESTIC LAUNDRIES

Certain businesses lend themselves to laundering money. For example, the business must be capable of absorbing a large volume of cash income, because most illicit income is received as cash. The purpose of laundering funds is to commingle licit and illicit monies so that they cannot be separated and to prevent the discovery of the introduction of illegal money into the business. Because most checks and credit card receipts are traceable by law enforcement officials, businesses such as restaurants, bars, and massage parlors, which take in a high proportion of cash, tend to be more desirable as laundries than businesses that receive most of their income as checks or other traceable instruments.

Another favorable characteristic for a laundry is expenses that do not vary with sales volume. An example of such a business is a movie theater that shows pornographic films. The expenses of such a business (rent, electricity, wages) are almost constant, regardless of whether the theater is full. Illicit income can be introduced and camouflaged in this type of business quite easily, because the additional sales do not increase expenses. Law enforcement officials who examine the records of such a theater would have trouble proving that the legitimate income generated by the theater was lower than that recorded.

Businesses that experience a high rate of spoilage or other loss of goods may also be used to launder money. Groceries and restaurants are good examples. Money is introduced into the business and recorded in its general income accounts as if it had been received from customers. Fraudulent invoices for produce or other perishable items are issued. The grocery or restaurant records the transaction as a cash payment. The undelivered produce or perishable items listed as spoiled and discarded are written off the books. The grocery store or restaurant thus avoids tax liability.

—*Criminal Investigation*, Seventh Edition, by Charles Swanson, Neil Chamelin, and Leonard Territo

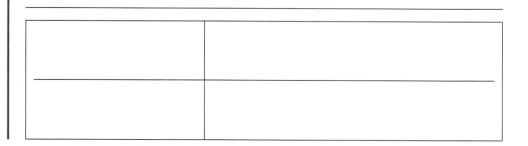

Summarizing

A **summary** is a short, concise method of stating the main idea and significant supporting details of the material. Think of it as the key words and phrases linked by complete sentences and presented in paragraphs.

When to Summarize

Professors frequently ask students to take notes in the form of a summary on assigned readings. Such readings, which are usually in the library, might include chapters from related texts, research articles from periodicals, or scholarly essays from books or periodicals. The preparation of a written summary can demonstrate to the professor that you have a clear understanding of the main points of the assignment. A summary can provide you with reference notes for later study; and it can be useful when you are compiling information from several sources for a long research paper.

How to Summarize

When you write a summary, put the ideas into your own words. If you need to quote an author directly, place quotation marks around the *exact* wording to avoid plagiarism. Keep in mind the purpose of your summary. The way you will use the information will influence the number of details you include. Generally, be brief but make your point. A summary should never be as long as the piece it is summarizing!

Reader's TIP   How to Write a Summary

- Remember your purpose; be brief.
- Underline the key ideas in the text you want to include.
- Begin your summary with a general statement that unites the key ideas.
- Include the key ideas that support the general statement. Link these ideas in sentences, and show their significance.
- Delete irrelevant or trivial information.
- Delete redundant information.
- Use your own words to show your understanding of the material. Don't try to camouflage a lack of comprehension.

EXAMPLE

The following is a summary of the passage on Jung's personality types (p. 213). Notice that the first sentence states the main ideas and the others concisely state the major supporting details.

> Jung believed in two types of personality and that most people are a mixture of each. Introverts turn inward, seek isolation, are reflective, self-critical, and want to change the outside world. Plato is an example.
>
> Extroverts, on the other hand, are friendly, tolerant of others, and prefer to experience things rather than to read about them. Aristotle is an example.

exercise 3

Annotate the following passage and then write a summary. Include only the most important details in your summary and exclude the irrelevant ones. For example, the first paragraph is an anecdote that dramatizes the problems of schizophrenia, but does the information belong in the summary?

PSYCHOSIS: LOSS OF CONTACT WITH REALITY

Jess was fired from his job in October. His parents told him he could move in with them till he found a new job. Jess moved in, but he didn't do anything about getting a new job. He sat around the house all day in his pajamas, smoking and watching TV. Both his parents worked, so it took them a while to notice that something was seriously wrong. Once his father became suspicious, he stayed home to see what was happening.

Jess didn't come out of his room that day, but his father could hear him talking. "No, that would be wrong," Jess said several times. "You don't know that's true!" he shouted. "How do you expect me to help it?" he cried out. Again, "No, no. That's all wrong. That's bad." There was no one in the room with Jess, but Jess wasn't talking to himself. He thought there was a Presence in the room with him.

SCHIZOPHRENIA

Jess's parents took him to the family doctor, who sent him to a psychiatrist. He placed Jess in a hospital, in the mental wing. Jess was diagnosed as suffering from *schizophrenia*. *Schizophrenia* is a whole group of mental disorders—*disorders of thinking, activity, feelings, and perceptions*. It is a *psychosis*, a word that means the *person is out of touch with reality*. Psychosis is a *distortion of thinking and feeling* that puts the person out of touch.

In the hospital, Jess seemed very excited and agitated. He paced around quite a bit and yelled at people. He talked to the voices he heard more and more. In psychological testing his thinking was distorted and unrealistic. For example, when the psychiatrist said: "Here's a proverb: New brooms sweep clean. Tell me what that means, please." Jess replied: "That's the trouble, always changing things. The weak get pushed around. You can't help it. It's wrong."

Jess was showing several typical symptoms of the group of disorders known as schizophrenia. What are they?

SYMPTOMS OF SCHIZOPHRENIA

Traditionally, psychiatry puts people into different *categories* of schizophrenia, depending on the symptoms of psychosis they showed. An entire classification system was worked out, and is still in use. Unfortunately, it is almost totally useless. The old divisions into types of schizophrenia are *worthless* for two reasons. First, there is very *little agreement* among psychiatrists as to what category a particular person falls into. Second, the various categories *overlap* so much that research often can't find differences among them. Instead of asking: "What are the different kinds of schizophrenia?" Let's ask: "What kinds of thoughts or behaviors are called schizophrenic?"

—*Psychology: What It Is/How to Use It* by David L. Watson

Written Summary

Schizophrenia is a group of mental disorders involving _____

_____

_____

_____

exercise 4   Annotate the following passage and write a summary.

COPING WITH JET LAG

Jet lag is the discomfort that you experience after traveling across several time zones. You probably know the feeling unless you have not traveled that far or are one of the lucky 15 percent who do not experience it. Jet lag can include some or all of the following symptoms: sleepiness, weakness, depression, insomnia, irritability, confusion, and loss of memory. Changes also occur in basic body functions, such as heart rate, blood pressure, and respiration. Jet lag is worst when you cross four or more time zones, when you lose time traveling west to east, and when you are older than 40 years of age. Recovery from jet lag occurs at the rate of about one time zone per day. This rule of thumb means that you will need about four days to recover from crossing four time zones. Obviously, jet lag can seriously hamper your fun if you are vacationing or affect your performance if you are traveling for business. Fortunately, there are steps you can take to minimize the disruption caused by jet lag. These steps have been outlined for flight crews, athletes, executives, military personnel, and vacationers (e.g., Chidester 1990; Redfern, 1989).

BEFORE YOUR TRIP

Control your mealtime so that on the day of your flight you are ready to eat at what would be appropriate times at your destination. Control your schedule of sleep and relaxation so that you are not strained or stressed at the beginning of your trip.

DURING YOUR FLIGHT

Dress comfortably, and loosen any restrictive clothing. As soon as you get settled on the plane, set your watch to the time at your destination, and start living by that time in your mind. If the destination time is the time you usually jog, then imagine jogging. You might also try some exercises in your seat. For example, you could press your head to the back of your seat for five counts to exercise your neck and upper back muscles. You could also tighten and relax your chest, stomach, and buttocks for five counts. Eat lightly, and, if at all possible, eat at the appropriate times according to your destination. Avoid candy, caffeine, and alcohol, which might make you restless. Furthermore, because caffeine and alcohol will increase dehydration effects of pressurized cabins, drink juice and water instead. Some experienced travelers try to drink a glass of juice or water for each hour that they fly. Finally, sleep or stay awake according to the schedule at your destination.

WHEN YOU ARRIVE

Follow the local sleeping, eating, and activity schedules. If you must sleep during the day, keep this rest period to less than 2 hours. Get out in the daylight as soon as you can for about 2 hours, if possible. Daylight will help your biological clock readjust faster. Finally drink a glass of milk or eat some ice cream before going to bed if you are having trouble sleeping. This recommendation sounds like an old folk remedy, and it is. However, this suggestion is also based on scientific evidence that dairy products have several properties that induce drowsiness.

—*Psychology: Principles and Applications,* Third Edition, by Stephen Worchel and Wayne Shebilske

Written Summary

Begin by writing a general statement about coping with jet lag. Link the key ideas and delete irrelevant information.

_____

_____

_____

_____

_____

_____

_____

_____

_____

Outlining

Outlining is a form of notetaking that gives a quick display of key issues and essential supporting details. Outlining uses indentations, numbers, and letters to show levels of importance. The outline forces you to sort out significant details and decide on levels of importance. Being able to outline shows that you understand main ideas and can distinguish between major and minor supporting details.

When to Outline

Outlining can be used to take notes on a textbook chapter or a class lecture or for brainstorming the answer for a possible essay question.

How to Outline

Letters, numbers, and indentations are used in an outline to show levels of importance. In a perfect outline, Roman numerals mark items of greatest importance and letters indicate supporting details. The greater distance from the left margin an item is listed, the less significance it is afforded. Your outline need not be picture perfect, but use indentation and some form of enumeration. Always remember that you are outlining to save time for later study and review. Don't cram all your facts on half a sheet of paper when you need several sheets. Give yourself plenty of room to write. You want to be able to look back quickly to get a clear picture of what is important and what supports it.

When taking notes in outline form, be brief and to the point. Use phrases rather than sentences. Record the main points, including key explanatory words, but leave out the insignificant details or "fillers."

Reader's TIP Creating an Outline

The following is the format for a model outline. Notice how the numbers, letters, and indentations show the importance of an idea.

Main Point or Topic
  I. Primary supporting detail
    A. Secondary supporting detail
    B. Secondary supporting detail
    C. Secondary supporting detail
  II. Second primary supporting detail
    A. Secondary supporting detail
    B. Secondary supporting detail
      1. Minor supporting detail or example
      2. Minor supporting detail or example
  III. Third primary supporting detail
    A. Secondary supporting detail
    B. Secondary supporting detail

Remember, making a picture-perfect outline is not critical; the important thing is to distinguish between the primary supporting ideas and the secondary supporting details. In an informal study outline, you can show the same levels of importance with indentations and bullets.

EXAMPLE The following example shows how the passage on Jung's theories (see p. 213) might be outlined for future study.

Jung's Personality Types

    I. Introverts

        A. turn inward, seek isolation

        B. reflective and introspective (self-searching)

        C. self-critical and self-controlled

        D. wish to change world rather than adjust

        E. ex. Plato

    II. Extroverts

        A. seek social contacts, outgoing

        B. friendly and outspoken

        C. tolerant of others

        D. prefer to experience than read about

        E. ex. Aristotle

EXPLANATION Notice that even though Plato and Aristotle are mentioned in the first paragraph, they fit logically as examples of each personality type. The "filler," such as the details in the last paragraph, is left out of the outline, but enough information is included so that rereading the passage won't be necessary.

exercise 5 Make a study outline for the following material. Annotate first and then organize your notes into an informal outline with numbers or bullets.

THE SIX TYPES OF LOVE

EROS: BEAUTY AND SENSUALITY

Erotic love focuses on beauty and physical attractiveness, sometimes to the exclusion of qualities you might consider more important and more lasting. The erotic lover has an idealized image of beauty that is unattainable in reality. Consequently, the erotic lover often feels unfulfilled. In defense of eros, however, it should be noted that both male and female eros lovers have the highest levels of reward and satisfaction when compared with all other types of lovers (Morrow, Clark, & Brock 1995).

LUDUS: ENTERTAINMENT AND EXCITEMENT

Ludus love is seen as fun, a game to be played. To the ludic lover, love is not to be taken too seriously; emotions are to be held in check lest they get out of hand and make trouble. Passions never rise to the point at which they get out of control. A ludic lover is self-controlled and consciously aware of the need to manage love rather than to allow it to control him or her. The ludic lover is manipulative and the extent of one's ludic tendencies has been found to correlate with the use of verbal sexual coercion (Sarwer, Kalichman, Johnson, Early, et al. 1993). Ludic-oriented sexually coercive men also experience less happiness, friendship, and trust in their relationships than do noncoercive men (Kalichman, Sarwer, Johnson, & Ali 1993). Ludic lover tendencies in women are likewise related to a dissatisfaction with life (Yancey & Berglass 1991).

STORGE LOVE: PEACEFUL AND SLOW

Like ludus love, **storge love** lacks passion and intensity. Storgic lovers do not set out to find lovers but to establish a companion-like relationship with someone they know and with whom they can share interests and activities. Storgic love develops over a period of time rather than in one mad burst of passion. Sex in storgic relationships comes late, and when it comes it assumes no great importance. Storgic love is sometimes difficult to separate from friendship; it is often characterized by the same qualities that characterize friendship: mutual caring, compassion, respect, and concern for the other person.

PRAGMA: PRACTICAL AND TRADITIONAL

The **pragma lover** is practical and wants compatibility and a relationship in which important needs and desires will be satisfied. In its extreme, pragma may be seen in the person who writes down the qualities wanted in a mate and actively goes about seeking someone who matches up. The pragma lover is concerned with the social qualifications of a potential mate even more than personal qualities; family and background are extremely important to the pragma lover, who relies not so much on feelings as on logic. The pragma lover views love as a necessity—or as a useful relationship—that makes the rest of life easier. The pragma lover therefore asks such questions about a potential mate as, "Will this person earn a good living?" "Can this person cook?" and "Will this person help me advance in my career?"

MANIC LOVE: ELATION AND DEPRESSION

The quality of mania that separates it from other types of love is the extremes of its highs and lows, its ups and downs. The **manic lover** loves intensely and at the same time worries intensely about and fears the loss of the love. With little provocation, for example, the manic lover may experience extreme jealousy. Manic love is obsessive; the manic lover has to possess the beloved completely—in all ways, at all times. In return, the manic lover wishes to be possessed, to be loved intensely. It seems almost as if the manic lover is driven to these extremes by some outside force or perhaps by some inner obsession that cannot be controlled.

AGAPE: COMPASSIONATE AND SELFLESS

Agape is a compassionate, egoless, self-giving love. Agape is nonrational and nondiscriminative. Agape creates value and virtue through love rather than bestowing love only on that which is valuable and virtuous. The agapic lover loves even people with whom he or she has no close ties. This lover loves the stranger on the road, and the fact that they will probably never meet again has nothing to do with it. Jesus, Buddha, and Gandhi practiced and preached this unqualified love. Agape is a spiritual love, offered without concern for personal reward or gain. The agapic lover loves without expecting that the love will be returned or reciprocated. For women, agape is the only love style positively related to their own life satisfaction (Yancy & Berglass 1991).

—*Human Communication*, Sixth Edition, by Joseph DeVito

Six Types of Love

I. Eros: Beauty and Sensuality

   A. Focus: _beauty and physical attractiveness_

   B. _often feels unfulfilled_

   C. _highest levels of reward and satisfaction._

   D. _idealized image of beauty._

II. Ludus: Entertainment and Excitement

   A. Focus: _not to be taken seriously_

   B. _self-controlled and minipulative_

   C. _fun - A game to be played._

   D. _Report disatisfaction_

III. Storge: Peaceful and Slow

   A. Focus: _lacks pation + intensity_

   B. _develops over time, sex is late_

   C. _very similar to friendship._

   D. _mutual caring + respect._

IV. Pragma: Practical and Traditional

   A. Focus: _practical, wants compatibility_

   B. _Concerned with social qualifications_

   C. _Viewes love as an necessity._

   D. _family background + Job important_

V. Manic: Elation and Depression

   A. Focus: _loves intensely, worries intensely_

   B. _fears loss of love_

   C. _may experience extreme jealousy_

   D. _wishes to be possessed._

VI. Agape: Compassionate and Selfless
    A. Focus: <u>nonrational, nondiscriminative</u>
    B. <u>Creates values and virtue through love</u>
    C. <u>Spiritual love</u>
    D. <u>Self-giving love.</u>

Mapping

Mapping visually condenses material to show relationships. A map is a diagram that places important topics in a central location and connects major points and supporting details in a visual display that shows degrees of importance. The previous study methods are linear in nature, whereas mapping uses space in a free and graphic manner.

When to Map

A map provides a quick reference for overviewing a chapter to stimulate prior knowledge, emphasize relationships, and aid recall. College students use maps or charts to reduce information for memorizing from lecture notes and the text.

How to Map

To prepare a map, do the following:

1. Draw a circle or a box in the middle of a page, and in it write the subject or topic of the material.
2. Determine the main ideas that support the subject, and write them on lines radiating from the central circle or box.
3. Determine the significant details and write them on lines attached to each main idea. The number of details you include will depend on the material and your purpose.

Maps are not restricted to any one pattern but can be formed in a variety of creative shapes, as the following diagrams illustrate:

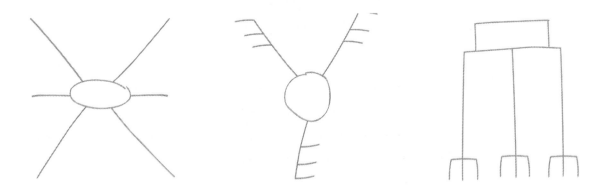

The following is an example of how the passage on Jung's theories might be mapped for future study:

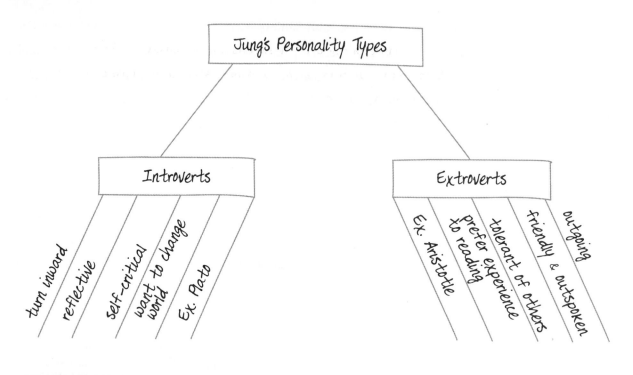

---

exercise 6

Read the following passage and map the key ideas for each. The structure of the maps is already provided. Insert the main idea first and arrange the supporting ideas to radiate appropriately.

RELIEF FOR INJURIES

For the past several hundred years many injuries were treated with heat—steaming baths where leisurely soaking was encouraged, hot water bottles, or electric heating pads or wraps. It was assumed that since heat speeded up metabolism, it would also speed the healing process. Today's researchers have proved that just the opposite is true. . . . Heat does speed up body processes but it also stimulates injured tissue and dilates blood vessels. In turn, this causes swelling to increase and enlarges the pools of blood and fluid, actually slowing healing. Even if there is no injury, heat after exercising can cause aches and pains. A quick, cool shower is recommended after your jog rather than a hot tub.

Four basic first aid procedures are used in treating the majority of runners' injuries.

STOP ACTIVITY

The first and most critical is to stop jogging as soon as the symptom appears. About the only pain you can run through is a side stitch. Joggers who insist on running with pain or walking off an injury usually incur further harm. Even though the pain does not become more intense, continuing the activity may aggravate the injury and prolong healing.

APPLY COLD

Cold packs are now universally accepted as the best first aid for virtually any jogging injury and constitute the second step in treatment. Chilling numbs the pain and minmizes swelling and inflammation by constricting blood and lymph vessels. Apply cold packs at least twice a day until the swelling and tenderness disappear. The ice pack should not be left in place longer than 30 minutes at one time. Muscle cramps are one of the few conditions associated with jogging where heat instead of cold should be applied.

IMMOBILIZE AND ELEVATE

Injuries that would benefit from being immobilized and/or given additional support should be wrapped with an elastic Ace-type bandage. This wrapping should be snug, but not tight enough to inhibit blood circulation. This third step should be taken before the final step of elevating the injured body part. Elevation not only helps drain fluid from the area, but also prevents blood and fluid from rushing to the area, thereby causing further swelling.

—*Jogging Everyone* by Charles Williams and Clancy Moore

 On a separate sheet of paper, make a study map or chart to diagram the essential information in the previous passage entitled *The Six Types of Love* (see Exercise 5).

Take Organized Lecture Notes

Develop an efficient system for organizing class lectures. Professors speak rapidly, yet expect students to remember important information. The Cornell system uses marginal notes to emphasize main points, whereas the outline format shows importance through indentation. Whichever system you use, allow yourself plenty of room to write. Considering your investment in college, paper is inexpensive. Use a pen to avoid smudges. Try writing on only one side of the paper so you can backtrack to add information when the professor summarizes. Compare your lecture notes with those of other students. Why would some professors say, "I can tell how much a student understood by looking at his or her lecture notes"?

exercise 8 Choose a study buddy and divide the work in order to compare the two notetaking systems, the Cornell method and the modified outline format. Ask permission and, if possible, both of you visit a regular history, psychology, sociology, or political science class. One of you should take notes using the Cornell method and the other using an informal version of the outline format. After class, compare notes and decide which method works better for you.

Summary Points

- Use a system of notations to annotate your text for future study.
- The Cornell Method of notetaking includes writing summaries and marginal notes.
- The summary is a short, concise method of stating the main idea and significant supporting details.
- Outlining gives a quick graphic display of key issues and can be used to brainstorm answers to essay exam questions.
- Mapping visually condenses material to show relationships.

COLLABORATIVE PROBLEM SOLVING

Form a five-member group and select one of the following questions. Brainstorm and then outline your major points on a transparency. Choose a member to present the group findings to the class.

- ▶ List ten tips for taking good lecture notes.
- ▶ List ten items you can purchase that will help you get organized for successful study.
- ▶ List ten shorthand terms or abbreviations that will help you take lecture notes rapidly.
- ▶ List ten reasons not to cut a class.

PERSONAL Feedback 1   Name _____

1. What format do you prefer for notetaking? Why? _____
   _____

2. What has been your experience with highlighting? How would you evaluate your own highlighting as compared with other methods of annotating? _____
   _____

3. Why should you take lecture notes only on one side of a notebook page? _____
   _____

4. How do you reward yourself during study breaks? _____

_____

_____

5. What is the most useful thing you have learned from this chapter?

_____

_____

_____

6. What is the most interesting thing you have learned so far from your instructor? _____

_____

_____

7. What do you feel are the five major differences in academic expectations between high school and college? _____

_____

_____

_____

SELECTION 1   HISTORY

THINKING BEFORE READING

Preview for content and organizational clues. Activate your schema and anticipate what you will learn.

Why are migrant workers needed?

Are migrant workers covered by minimum wage laws?

What is a scab?

I think this will say that _____

VOCABULARY PREVIEW

Are you familiar with these words?

impoverished	dilapidated	shunted	staunch	marred
intimidated	quell	escalating	atone	legacy

How does the word *escalating* relate to a word for a moving stairway?

Is a staunch supporter weak or strong?

If you have a legacy status with a college admissions office, what is your position?

Your instructor may choose to give a true-false vocabulary review before or after reading.

THINKING DURING READING

As you read, use the five thinking strategies of a good reader: predict, picture, relate, monitor, and correct.

ANNOTATING

Annotate the selection in order to make an outline or time line listing the significant events in the life of Cesar Chavez.

Refer to the
Reader's Tip
for History on
page 140.

Cesar Chavez and La Causa

In early April 1962, a 35-year-old community organizer named Cesar Estrada Chavez set out to single-handedly organize impoverished migrant farm laborers in the California grape fields. He, his wife, and their eight children packed their belongings into a dilapidated 9-year-old station wagon, and moved to Delano, California, a town of 12,000 that

5   was the center of the nation's table-grape industry. Over the next two years, Chavez spent his entire lifetime savings of $1200 creating a small social service organization for

Delano's field laborers; it offered immigration counseling, citizenship classes, funeral benefits, credit to buy cars and homes, assistance with voter registration, and a cooperative to buy tires and gasoline. As an emblem of his new organization, the National Farm Workers

10   Association, Chavez chose a black Aztec eagle inside a white circle on a red background.

Chavez's sympathy for the plight of migrant farmworkers came naturally. He was born in Yuma, Arizona, in 1927, one of five children of Mexican immigrants. When he was 10 years old, his parents lost their small farm; he, his brothers and sisters, and his parents hoed beets, picked grapes, and harvested peaches and figs in Arizona and California.

15   There were times when the family had to sleep in its car or camp under bridges. When young Cesar was able to attend school (he attended more than 30 schools as a child), he was often shunted into special classrooms set aside for Mexican-American children.

In 1944, when he was 17, Chavez joined the navy, and served for two years on a destroyer escort in the Pacific. After World War II ended, he married and spent two and a

20   half years as a sharecropper raising strawberries. That was followed by work in apricot and prune orchards and in a lumber camp. Then in 1952 his life took a fateful turn. He joined the Community Service Organization (CSO), which wanted to educate and organize the poor so that they could solve their own social and economic problems. After founding CSO chapters in Madera, Bakersfield, and Hanford, California, Chavez became

25   the organization's general director in 1958. Four years later, he broke with the organization when it rejected his proposal to establish a farmworkers union.

Most labor leaders considered Chavez's goal of creating the first successful union of farmworkers in U.S. history an impossible dream. Not only did farm laborers suffer from high rates of illiteracy and poverty (average family earnings were just $2000 in 1965),

30 they also experienced persistently high rates of unemployment (traditionally around 19 percent) and were divided into a variety of ethnic groups (Mexican, Arab, Filipino, and Puerto Rican). Making unionization even more difficult were the facts that farmworkers rarely remained in one locality for very long, and they were easily replaced by inexpensive Mexican day laborers, known as *braceros*, who were trucked into California and the

35 Southwest at harvest time.

Moreover, farmworkers were specifically excluded from the protection of the National Labor Relations Act of 1935. Unlike other American workers, farmworkers were not guaranteed the right to organize, had no guarantee of a minimum wage, and had no federally guaranteed standards of work in the fields. State laws requiring toilets, rest peri-

40 ods, and drinking water in the fields were largely ignored.

In September 1965, Chavez was drawn into his first important labor controversy. The Filipino grape pickers went on strike. "All right, Chavez," said one of the Filipino grape pickers' leaders, "are you going to stand beside us, or are you going to scab against us?" Despite his fear that the National Farm Workers Association was not sufficiently well orga-

45 nized to support a strike (it had less than $100 in its strike fund), he assured the Filipino workers that members of his association would not go into the field as strikebreakers. ¡*Huelga*!—the Spanish word for strike—became the grape picker's battle cry.

Within weeks, the labor strike began to attract national attention. Union, church groups, and civil rights organizations offered financial support for La Causa, as the farm-

50 workers' movement became known. In March 1966, Chavez led a 250-mile Easter march from Delano to Sacramento to dramatize the plight of migrant farm laborers. That same year, Chavez's National Farm Workers Association merged with an AFL-CIO affiliate to form the United Farm Workers Organization Committee.

A staunch apostle of nonviolence, Chavez was deeply troubled by violent incidents

55 that marred the strike. Some growers raced tractors along the roadside, covering the strikers with dirt and dust. Others drove spraying machines along the edges of their fields, spraying insecticides and fertilizer on the picketers. Some strikers, in turn, intimidated strikebreakers by pelting them with marbles fired from slingshots and by setting fire to packing crates. One striker tried to drive a car into a group of growers.

60 In an effort to quell the escalating violence and to atone for the militancy of some union members, Chavez began to fast on February 14, 1968. For five days he kept the fast a secret. Then, in an hour-long speech to striking workers, he explained that continued violence would destroy everything the union stood for. He said that the "truest act of courage, the strongest act of manliness, is to sacrifice ourselves for others in a totally non-

65 violent struggle for justice." For 21 days he fasted; he lost 35 pounds and his doctor began to fear for his health. He finally agreed to take a small amount of bouillon and

grapefruit juice and medication. On March 11, he ended his fast by taking communion and breaking bread with Senator Robert F. Kennedy.

70   The strike dragged on for three years. To heighten public awareness of the farmworkers' cause, Chavez in 1968 initiated a boycott of table grapes. It was the boycott that pressured many of the growers into settling the strike. An estimate 17 million American consumers went without grapes in support of the farmworkers' bargaining position. By mid-1970, two-thirds of California grapes were grown under contract with Chavez's union.

75   In the years following its 1970 victory, Chavez's union has been beset by problems from within and without. Union membership dwindled from a high of more than 60,000 in 1972 to a low of 5000 in 1974. (It has since climbed back to around 30,000). Meanwhile, public concern for the plight of migrant farmworkers declined.

Chavez died in 1993, at age 66. To commemorate his legacy, 25,000 people marched for more than two and a half hours to the spot where he had founded the
80   United Farm Workers Union. As a result of Chavez's efforts, the most backbreaking tool used by farmworkers, the short hoe, was eliminated, and the use of many dangerous pesticides in the grape fields was prohibited. His efforts also brought about a 70 percent increase in real wages from 1964 to 1980, and establishment of health-care benefits, disability insurance, pension plans, and standardized grievance procedures for farmworkers.
85   He helped secure passage of the nation's first agricultural labor relations act in California in 1975, which prohibited growers from firing striking workers or engaging in bad-faith bargaining. Thanks to his efforts, migrant farm laborers won a right held by all other American workers: the right to bargain collectively.

—*America and Its People*, Third Edition, by James Martin et al.

STUDY OUTLINE

Use your annotations to make an outline or time line listing the significant events in the life of Cesar Chavez.

THINKING AFTER READING

RECALL   Self-test your understanding. Your instructor may choose to give you a true-false review.

REACT   How did Chavez's early life prepare him for the ultimate leadership role that he would assume? _____

_____

REFLECT   Why did Chavez use fasting as a tactic to stop the strike?

THINK CRITICALLY   Compare and contrast the challenges, tactics, and the death of Martin Luther King, Jr. with those of Cesar Chavez. Write your answer on a separate sheet of paper.

Name _____

Date _____

COMPREHENSION QUESTIONS

Answer the following with *a, b, c,* or *d,* or fill in the blank. In order to help you analyze your strengths and weaknesses, the question types are indicated.

Main Idea _____ 1. The best statement of the main idea of the selection is:

    a. Chavez was the founder of the National Farm Worker's Association.
    b. Chavez learned the lessons of fighting for a cause during his military service in WWII.
    c. Chavez was disliked by farm owners but respected by migrant farm workers.
    d. Chavez's leadership helped improve the plight of migrant farm workers and help them win the right to collective bargaining.

Detail _____ 2. Chavez broke with the CSO because the organization

    a. ran out of money.
    b. wanted him to educate the poor.
    c. would not allow him to establish a farmworker's union.
    d. did not promote him to general director.

Detail _____ 3. Chavez's dream of creating a union for farmworkers was considered impossible because of all the following except

    a. farmworkers migrated frequently.
    b. day laborers could easily replace striking farmworkers.
    c. few workers were available to take jobs.
    d. farmworkers were ethnically diverse.

Detail _____ 4. Chavez's first significant labor strike was

    a. funded by the COS.
    b. started by Filipino grape workers.
    c. a direct reaction to poor working conditions for Mexicans.
    d. protected by the National Labor Relations Act of 1935.

Inference 5. In light of his military service in the navy, what about Chavez's life

after WWII seems ironic or surprising? _____

_____

_____

Detail _____ 6. The strike was finally ended by

    a. Chavez's fast.
    b. the AFL-CIO.
    c. a national grape boycott.
    d. the 250-mile Easter march to Sacramento.

Detail _____ 7. The chronological order, from first to last, of the organizations with which Chavez was affiliated is

    a. National Farm Workers Association, CSO, United Farm Workers Organization.
    b. United Farm Workers Organization, CSO, National Farm Workers Association.

    c. CSO, National Farm Workers Association, United Farm Workers Organization.

    d. CSO, United Farm Workers Organization, National Farm Workers Association.

Answer the following with *T* (true), *F* (false), or *CT* (can't tell).

Detail   _____ 8. Chavez used his own money to start the organization symbolized by the black Aztec eagle.

Detail   _____ 9. According to the passage, growers exposed workers to dangerous insecticides to break the strike.

Detail   _____ 10. In the years after the strike ended, Chavez's union doubled in membership.

VOCABULARY

Answer the following with *a, b, c,* or *d* for the word or phrase that best defines the boldface word as used in the selection. The number in parentheses indicates the line of the passage in which the word is located.

_____ 1. "**impoverished** migrant farm laborers" (2)

    a. worried
    b. wounded
    c. poor
    d. uneducated

_____ 2. "**dilapidated** 9-year-old station wagon" (4)

    a. remodeled
    b. shabby
    c. ancient
    d. large

_____ 3. "**shunted** into special classrooms" (17)

    a. promoted
    b. recommended
    c. allowed
    d. shifted

_____ 4. "**staunch** apostle" (54)

    a. weak
    b. faithful
    c. occasional
    d. knowledgeable

_____ 5. "**marred** the strike" (55)

    a. began
    b. harmed
    c. symbolized
    d. elevated

_____ 6. "**intimidated** strikebreakers" (57–58)

    a. killed
    b. avoided
    c. frightened
    d. escaped

_____ 7. "**quell** the escalating violence" (60)

    a. stop
    b. excite
    c. renew
    d. explain

_____ 8. "**escalating** violence" (60)

    a. repeated
    b. unnecessary
    c. unwanted
    d. increasing

_____ 9. "**atone** for the militancy" (60)

    a. revenge
    b. fight
    c. express regret
    d. answer

_____ 10. "commemorate his **legacy**" (78)

    a. gift to society
    b. pain
    c. knowledge
    d. children

VOCABULARY ENRICHMENT

A. **Context Clues:** Select the word from the list that best completes the sentences.

impoverished	dilapidated	shunted	staunch	marred
intimidated	quell	escalating	atone	legacy

1. Because of a late payment, the application was _____ to the bottom of the pile.

2. The wealthy heart surgeon started a charitable foundation as her late husband's _____ .

3. The real estate agent explained that the _____ house could be repaired for only a few thousand dollars.

4. The happiness of the holiday was _____ by a traffic accident that killed two teens.

5. At the political convention, the _____ Republicans cheered as their candidate was nominated.

6. In order to _____ the rebellion, the dictator used the military to enforce a curfew.

7. To avoid _____ rental prices, the student lived at home with his parents for most of his senior year.

8. Because of the famine, the _____ natives had to rely on rice that was provided by government agencies.

9. Not _____ by the barking dog, the veterinarian knew exactly how to safely subdue the animal for an examination.

10. To _____ for her rude outbursts, she brought a dozen roses to her friend.

B. **Thesaurus:** Use a thesaurus, either the computer or book version, to find four alternative words for each of the following:

1. indication _____

2. habit _____

3. beginning _____

4. agreement _____

5. respect _____

ASSESS YOUR LEARNING

Review confusing questions, seek clarification, and make notes in your text to help you remember new information and vocabulary.

CONNECT

Read the following passage about an organized effort to improve working conditions for farmworkers. How is this event similar to the events that Cesar Chavez organized? What are the critical issues in this demonstration? In what ways is the event consistent with Cesar's philosophies about organizing to improve working conditions?

Washington Farm Workers Rally

Associated Press, August 7, 2000

MATTAWA, Wash. (AP)—About 4,000 farm workers and religious, political and civil rights supporters called for better wages and working conditions during a 4 1/2-mile march between two south-central farm towns.

With temperatures in the mid-90s, the marchers—including a troupe of drum-beating Aztec dancers from Oregon—called for higher apple-picking wages, amnesty for undocumented workers and protection for labor organizers from reprisals by employers.

"We have literally millions of Latinos and people of other ethnicities performing the work that other people don't want to do," said Arturo Rodriguez, the national president of the United Farm Workers of America, "and they're treated like second-class citizens."

Rodriguez is the son-in-law of farm workers union founder Cesar Chavez.

In February, the AFL-CIO Executive Council passed a resolution calling for federal legislation granting amnesty to the 6 million undocumented workers in the United States. Most of Washington state's more than 100,000 agricultural workers are undocumented.

Many marchers on the way from Desert Aire to Mattawa, about 165 miles southeast of Seattle, said they make $6.50 an hour. Others said they got paid $9 or $10 per bin of apples—about $5 less than they got three years ago.

"We cannot feed our families with these low wages and we will stop working if necessary to get a fair wage," said farm worker Arnulfo Ramirez.

EXPLORE THE NET

- Locate the official Web site for the United Farm Workers. Where is the UFW national office? List some of the field offices. Describe an upcoming event that the UFW is involved in.

The Official Web Page of the United Farm Workers of America

www.ufw.org

- Search the Internet for speeches by Cesar Chavez. How would you describe the style of his speeches? What issues does he emphasize? Print one of the speeches.

Cesar E. Chavez Institute for Public Policy

www.sfsu.edu/%7Ececipp/cesar_chavez/chavezhome.htm

For additional readings and exercises, visit the *Breaking Through* Web site:

www.ablongman.com/smith

For a user name and password, please see your instructor.

SELECTION 2   BUSINESS

THINKING BEFORE READING

Preview for content and organizational clues. Activate your schema and anticipate what you will learn.

Do you have any beanie babies? If so, which one?

How can scarcity affect a product price?

Would you prefer to sell a toy product at Wal-Mart or a small specialty store?

After reading this I will probably know _____

VOCABULARY PREVIEW

Are you familiar with these words?

staggering	inevitable	craze	obsolete	obstacle
innovative	deceptively	forgo	restraint	congregate

What obstacles threaten your academic success?

Where do students at your college congregate?

What is the Pokemon craze?

Your instructor may give a true-false vocabulary review before or after reading.

THINKING DURING READING

As you read, use the five thinking strategies of a good reader: predict, picture, relate, monitor, and correct.

Reader's TIP   Reading and Studying Business

- Activate your schema with the introductory profiles and boxed materials that describe an actual company with a current business dilemma involving the chapter concepts.
- Connect business theories with a real company problem or solution to make learning easier. Use the business illustration to visualize the concept.
- Cross-reference your reading with the illustrative photographs, tables, flow charts, figures, and copies of real advertisements. Sketch your own models of business and marketing processes and concepts. Use these visual learning tools to enhance your learning.

- Apply theories and concepts to the case histories. Sometimes these are a continuing story in each chapter about the same company's use of the chapter concepts. One textbook, for example, has a continuing story of the Harley Davison Motorcycle Company and its rise to success. Other text may have many different case studies ranging from the success of Fisher-Price in the competitive toy market to the ethical issues of increasing global marketing of tobacco products when the dangers of tobacco are clearly delineated here at home.
- Use the exercises to reinforce chapter topics, strengthen your research skills, and expand your knowledge. An instructional software disk may come with your text with practice quizzes and other instructional help.
- Use the tips that suggest how to market yourself by applying the chapter's concepts in your career search. For example, tips may offer advice on how to identify and access the major employment pipelines (*distribution channels*) for your product (you) in your career search.

ANNOTATING AND OUTLINING

Annotate as you read and then make an informal study outline to answer the following essay exam question: List and describe Ty Warner's keys to success.

The Beanie Baby Business

Manufactured by Ty Inc., a privately held company in Oakbrook, Illinois, that specializes in stuffed animals, Beanie Babies have earned a fortune for the company and made staggering profits for tens of thousands of children and adults who trade them in secondary markets via the Internet. How Ty Inc. made this happen and how company executives

5   handled the inevitable business problems along the way is a story worth telling.

AN IDEA IS BORN

After graduating from college in 1962, future founder Ty Warner began working for Dakin Inc., an Illinois-based stuffed-animal manufacturer. He learned some important lessons during his 18 years with the company, especially in the marketing curriculum. "They taught me that it's better selling 40,000 accounts [to specialty gift shops] than it is

10   five accounts" to mass-market retailers such as Toys "R" Us and Wal-Mart. "It's more difficult to do," Warner admits, "but for the longevity of the company and the profit margins, it's better. [Beanie Babies] could be around for years just as long as I don't take the easy road and sell it to a mass merchant who's going to put it in bins."

Warner learned that in the stuffed-animal business, affordable, high-quality mer-

15   chandise is a must if you want children to spend their own money. Combining their

allowances, earnings, and gifts, children under 14 spend about $20 billion a year and influence adult spending to the tune of another $200 billion. When Warner began manufacturing Beanie Babies in 1993, this was the market he decided to corner.

MAKING THE BUSINESS WORK

Warner's first task was manufacturing. To keep production costs down, he contracted
20 with factories in China, where Beanie Babies were sewn and stuffed with polyvinyl chloride pellets. Then he began selling his product to independent gift shops for roughly $3 each. He already knew that an important benefit of working with such merchants as these was rapid cash flow: "Small retailers usually pay cash on delivery or write checks within 15 days, and that would affect our financial situation."

25   When the Beanie Babies craze took off in December 1995, Warner and a staff of about 100 clerks handled orders and shipments on what was quickly becoming an obsolete computer system. With as many as 100,000 calls a day coming into the company, Ty Inc. faced a serious information system crisis. The original system was designed for about 100 order-entry clerks to scroll through pages of forms for every customer and to enter
30 every bit of information manually. Chris Johnson, Ty director of management information systems, was assigned to find a replacement system that could start work immediately. Money, he was told, was no obstacle—as long as he solved the problem as fast as humanly possible.

        After compressing system planning time from 6 months to 2 months, Johnson chose
35 a system designed for high-volume businesses. The new system cut the number of ordering steps, automated shipping information and billing, conducted credit checks, gener-

ated separate invoices, and balanced inventory with orders. It promised to halve the time spent on many operations and to enter large chunks of data automatically, and, oddly enough, it was also easy to use. Order clerks, explains Johnson, "have to be able to look
40 up orders fast and click back and forth between windows. Customers need information on shipping fast, and the user interface needs to support that."

MARKETING GENIUS

The factor most responsible for turning Beanie Babies from a mere product to a craze was an innovative marketing strategy based on a deceptively simple three-step economic principle:

1. Provide stores with too few items to meet demand;
2. Stop production on individual items to induce permanent scarcity; and
3. Sit back and wait for demand to increase as word spreads.

By June 1997, Ty Inc. was limiting retailers to 36 pieces of each character per month.
45 Only single monthly orders were accepted. The perception of scarcity and exclusivity was increased further by Warner's decision to forgo television advertising. The hardest part of the strategy was imposing production restraint while demand increased. Although it would have been profitable in the short term to boost production, Warner was convinced that Beanie Babies would last longer if there were a permanent scarcity. The plan worked.
50 "I've been in the business 30 years," reports one toy store owner in Mamaroneck, New York, "and I've never seen an item like this."

To top off this strategy, Ty entered into a highly successful promotional relationship with McDonald's. The campaign broke all consumer-response records and increased Beanie Baby popularity immensely. Offering customers one of ten Teenie Beanie Babies
55 with the purchase of a Happy Meal, McDonald's sold nearly 200 million meals in 10 days (instead of the 35 days originally anticipated). In the process, Ty received about $45 million worth of free advertising for its full-size product.

BIRTH OF A SECONDARY MARKET

With the Beanie Babies priced at only $5, young children fueled demand, both by making purchases with allowance money and convincing parents to buy on impulse. Children
60 soon became avid collectors, and many owned the entire set. With some items out of production and others nearly impossible to find in retail stores, Beanie Babies soon became collectibles, and an active secondary market developed on the Internet. Ty Inc. encourages this market on its own Web site (www.Ty.com), which allows visitors to buy and sell and talk in chat rooms. Dozens of other Web sites have active marketplaces,
65 where prices are set by supply and demand.

Prices, of course, started to increase, but as they did, adults became the primary collectors of the most valuable items including Peanut the Elephant (in royal blue), which recently fetched $2,200, Rex the Tyrannosaurus ($1,750), and Peking the Panda ($1,295). Although children are priced out of this market, they congregate at Web sites with offer-

70 ings that start at about $10.

WILL IT LAST?

Things look very good for Ty Inc., at least for now. Although there are cheaper competitors, none has achieved the levels of design and quality that make Beanie Babies such a hot collectible. Moreover, Warner promptly sues the makers of knockoffs that are too close to Ty's designs. So far, three companies have been forced to recall their products

75 and hand over their profits to Warner.

As for Warner, he intends to stick with the strategy that's made his company a success. "Every time we make a shipment," he explains, "retailers want twice as many [Beanie Babies] as we can possibly get to them. And as long as kids keep fighting over them and retailers are angry at us because they can't get enough, I think those are good signs."

(1,100 words)

—*Business Essentials*, Third Edition, by Ronald Ebert and Ricky Griffin

THINKING AFTER READING

RECALL Self-test your understanding. Your instructor may choose to give you a true-false review.

REACT How did the company create a desire for return customers who wanted to own more than one Beanie Baby? _____

REFLECT How does the marketing of Pokemon products compare with the marketing strategies for Beanie Babies?

THINK CRITICALLY Ty Warner's strategy calls for controlling supply to increase demand. The case explained the benefits of this strategy. What are the potential pitfalls of such a strategy?

TEXTBOOK LEARNING Compare your study outline for the essay question with the outlines of other students. Change your outline, if appropriate.

Name _____

Date _____

COMPREHENSION QUESTIONS

Answer the following with *a, b, c,* or *d,* or fill in the blank. In order to help you analyze your strengths and weaknesses, the question types are indicated.

Main Idea _____ 1. The best statement of the main idea of the selection is

    a. Ty Warner used his past experience and clever marketing strategies to develop Ty Inc. into a successful company.
    b. Ty used the Internet to build a $200 billion Beanie Baby business.
    c. although Beanie Babies were once hot collectibles, future markets are uncertain.
    d. the central key to Ty Inc.'s success was spending the money to update the computer system.

Inference _____ 2. Which cliché might most accurately apply to Ty Warner's success with his Beanie Babies?

    a. Time flies when you are having fun.
    b. A bird in the hand is worth two in the bush.
    c. Less is more.
    d. Whatever can go wrong, will go wrong.

Detail _____ 3. For distribution, Ty Warner chose specialty stores over mass retailers because

    a. they are easier to sell.
    b. profit margins and product life are potentially higher.
    c. specialty stores attract customers with more money.
    d. the mass retailers will not advertise new products.

Detail _____ 4. The author suggests that mass retailers

    a. do not pay their bills.
    b. pay for merchandise quicker than specialty stores.
    c. pay for merchandise slower than specialty stores.
    d. pay cash at delivery.

Detail 5. The promotional relationship with McDonald's worked to the advantage of both Ty Inc. and McDonald's because _____

_____

_____

Detail _____ 6. The monthly number of Beanie Babies received by retailers was limited because

    a. more could not be manufactured at the rate of demand.
    b. more could not be shipped.
    c. Ty Warner chose this as a marketing strategy.
    d. the competition among specialty stores demanded limits.

Inference _____ 7. The author implies that the profit on a Beanie Baby to the specialty store is approximately

        a. $1.
        b. $2.
        c. $5.
        d. less than $1.

Answer the following with *T* (true) or *F* (false).

Detail _____ 8. Ty Inc. opposes the secondary Beanie Baby market.

Inference _____ 9. The author implies that the updated computer system allowed individual customers to place orders.

Detail _____10. According to the passage, Ty Inc. has produced at least 145 different Beanie baby characters.

VOCABULARY

Answer the following with *a, b, c,* or *d* for the word or phrase that best defines the boldface word as used in the selection. The number in parentheses indicates the line of the passage in which the word is located.

_____ 1. "made **staggering** profits" (2–3)

    a. understandable
    b. instant
    c. secondary
    d. huge

_____ 2. "**inevitable** business problems" (5)

    a. annoying
    b. unavoidable
    c. overwhelming
    d. growing

_____ 3. "Beanie Baby **craze**" (25)

    a. fight
    b. organization
    c. fad
    d. corporation

_____ 4. "**obsolete** computer system" (26–27)

    a. incomplete
    b. overloaded
    c. outdated
    d. frustrating

_____ 5. "was no **obstacle**" (32)

    a. barrier
    b. reward
    c. financial plan
    d. motivation

_____ 6. "**innovative** marketing strategy" (43)

    a. logical
    b. inventive
    c. fragile
    d. competitive

_____ 7. "**deceptively** simple" (43)

    a. slyly
    b. reasonably
    c. narrowly
    d. knowingly

_____ 8. "**forgo** television advertising" (46)

    a. seek
    b. favor
    c. facilitate
    d. pass up

_____ 9. "imposing production **restraint**" (47)

    a. limitations
    b. requests
    c. quality
    d. variety

_____10. "**congregate** at Web sites" (69)

    a. invest
    b. ask questions
    c. buy
    d. gather

VOCABULARY ENRICHMENT

A. **Words from Literature:** The names of certain characters in literature have dropped their capital letters and taken on special meaning in the English language. The following are from Spanish and English literature, respectively. Read the entries to determine their definitions and origins:

> **qui·xote** \ˈkwik-sət, kē-ˈhō-tē, -ˈō-\ *n, often cap* [Don *Quixote,* hero of the novel *Don Quixote de la Mancha* (1605, 1615) by Cervantes] (1648) : a quixotic person — **quix·o·tism** \ˈkwik-sə-ˌti-zəm\ *n* — **quix·o·try** \-sə-trē\ *n*
> **quix·ot·ic** \kwik-ˈsä-tik\ *adj* [Don *Quixote*] (1815) **1** : foolishly impractical esp. in the pursuit of ideals; *esp* : marked by rash lofty romantic ideas or extravagantly chivalrous action **2** : CAPRICIOUS, UNPREDICTABLE *syn* see IMAGINARY — **quix·ot·i·cal** \-ti-kəl\ *adj* — **quix·ot·i·cal·ly** \-ti-k(ə-)lē\ *adv*

Source: Reprinted by permission fom Merriam Webster's *Collegiate Dictionary*, Tenth Edition. ©2000 by Merriam Webster, Incorporated.

1. *Quixotic* means _____

2. It comes from _____

> **Lil·li·put** \ˈli-li-(ˌ)pət\ *n* : an island in Swift's *Gulliver's Travels* where the inhabitants are six inches tall
> **lil·li·pu·tian** \ˌli-lə-ˈpyü-shən\ *adj, often cap* (1726) **1** : of, relating to, or characteristic of the Lilliputians or the island of Lilliput **2 a** : SMALL, MINIATURE **b** : PETTY
> **Lilliputian** *n* **1** : an inhabitant of Lilliput **2** *often not cap* : one resembling a Lilliputian; *esp* : an undersized individual

Source: Reprinted by permission fom Merriam Webster's *Collegiate Dictionary*, Tenth Edition. ©2000 by Merriam Webster, Incorporated.

3. *Lilliputian* means _____

4. It comes from _____

B. Analogies

5. *Knife* is to *cut* as *gun* is to _____

    Relationship? _____

6. *Old* is to *ancient* as *recent* is to _____

    Relationship? _____

7. *Eye* is to *see* as *ear* is to _____

    Relationship? _____

8. *Go* is to *come* as *sell* is to _____

    Relationship? _____

9. *State* is to *governor* as *city* is to _____

    Relationship? _____

10. *Skin* is to *person* as *fur* is to _____

    Relationship? _____

11. *Smart* is to *intelligent* as *chilly* is to _____

   Relationship? _____

12. *Razor* is to *sharp* as *cement* is to _____

   Relationship? _____

13. *Winter* is to *summer* as *wet* is to _____

   Relationship? _____

C. Study the following definitions and then circle the similar-sounding word that is correct in each sentence.

   consul: foreign representative   **personal:** private
   council: elected officials   **personnel:** employees
   counsel: give advice

14. Many professors are willing to (**consul, council, counsel**) students with study problems.

15. Take your job application to the (**personal, personnel**) office.

ASSESS YOUR LEARNING

Review confusing questions, seek clarification, and make notes in your text to help you remember new information and vocabulary.

EXPLORE THE NET

- The market for new Beanie Babies has declined. However, the secondary collector's market is still active. Locate an article describing how the Beanie Baby market is changing. List and explain the reasons for the long-term popularity of the stuffed animals.

   www.abcnews.go.com/sections/business/DailyNews/beanies991225.html

   www.krause.com./corner/990212.html

- Visit the Web site for Ty Warner's company and explain how the company increases market demand in ways left unmentioned in the selection.

   www.ty.com

- Visit a Web site to check out the prices on retired Beanie Babies. Which are the most expensive ones and what are the prices?

   www.beaniex.com

   www.beanieprices.homepage.com

   www.wildaboutbeanies.com

For additional readings and exercises, visit the *Breaking Through* Web site:

   www.ablongman.com/smith

For a user name and password, please see your instructor.

SELECTION 3 🧠 **PSYCHOLOGY**

THINKING BEFORE READING

Preview the selection for clues to content. Activate your schema and anticipate what you will learn.

Who was Jack the Ripper?

Who was Son of Sam?

What recent mass murder tragedy has been in the news?

After reading this I will probably know _____

VOCABULARY PREVIEW

Are you familiar with these words?

carnage	lethal	alienated	arsenal	charismatic
credible	roam	elusive	lure	remorse

What is the roam charge on a mobile phone?

What is the lure on a fishing pole?

Why are powerful leaders usually charismatic?

Your instructor may give a true-false vocabulary review before or after reading.

THINKING DURING READING

As you read, use the five thinking strategies of a good reader: predict, picture, relate, monitor, and correct.

OUTLINING

Annotate the selection and then make an informal study outline to answer the following essay exam question: Describe the characteristics of mass and serial murderers.

Refer to the
Reader's Tip
for Psychology on
page 44.

Mass and Serial Murder

In 1997 Andrew Cunanan killed the famous fashion designer Gianni Versace in Miami Beach after having murdered four other men in other cities. In 1992 Jeffrey Dahmer of Milwaukee, Wisconsin, pleaded guilty to killing 15 young men, one after another. He reportedly had sex with some of the corpses, dismembered some of the bodies, and kept

5   in his refrigerator a severed head as well as a heart that he planned to eat later. Earlier, in 1985, another serial killer struck terror in the Los Angeles area. Called the Night Stalker, he sneaked into the homes of 19 people at night and killed them as they slept. Just a year

before, a mass murderer walked into a McDonald's restaurant in San Diego carrying a rifle, a shotgun, and a pistol with hundreds of rounds of ammunition. He opened fire on

10 everybody, killing 21 people—mostly children—and wounding 19 others. These types of killing—mass and serial murders—attract considerable attention from the media and public. Just the same, they are extremely rare.

Mass murder involves killing a number of people at about the same time and place. It usually ends with the murderer dying at the scene of the carnage. The murderer's

15 death results from either committing suicide or forcing the police to take lethal action. Despite the shocking nature of their crime, most mass murderers are not mentally ill. As sociologists Jack Levin and James Fox (1985) conclude after studying mass murderers, "The mass killer appears to be *extraordinarily ordinary*. He is indistinguishable from every-one else. Indeed, he may be the neighbor next door, a co-worker at the next desk, or a

20 member of the family."

Some mass murderers are *disgruntled employees* who want to get even with their boss who has wronged them in some way, by firing them, for example. But in the process of killing their boss, they end up murdering their coworkers as well. Other mass murderers are *heads of family* who kill their wives and children after having long felt

25 alone, alienated, helpless, and depressed, aggravated by heavy drinking. Some mass murderers are "*pseudocommandos*," who turn their homes into an arsenal and then lash out at what they consider to be an unjust or evil world. Finally, some mass murderers work as a team under the direction of a charismatic leader (Holmes and Holmes, 1992). Examples are those who participated in the 1993 bombing of the Word Trade Center in

30 New York City, or in the more recent killing of Muslims in Bosnia as well as many other terrorist acts against innocent citizens in other parts of the world.

Slightly more common than mass murder is serial murder, which involves killing a number of people one at a time. But the media has wildly exaggerated the incidence of serial murder by calling it an "epidemic." This exaggeration originated from the claim by a Justice Department official that serial murder accounts for about 20 percent of all homicides. Actually, the most credible figure, based on careful analysis by sociologists, is only 2 or 3 percent. Another myth about serial murder is that most (70 to 75 percent) serial murderers commit their crime in one city alone (Kappeler, Blumberg, and Potter, 1993).

35

While mass murderers are nearly always caught, serial killers are far more elusive because they are practiced and accomplished at what they do. First, they stalk their victims from a distance, studying the victims' routine activities and habits. Then they win the victims' confidence by befriending them, or gain entry into the victims' house that they have staked out for days. Next, they lure the victims into a trap or simply hold them captive by closing off all possibility of escape. Finally, they kill the victims. In the process of killing, they "often torture their victims, taking delight in the victims' agonies, expressions of terror, cries of despair, and reactions to pain" (Norris, 1989). This should not be surprising, because most serial killers have in their childhood tortured dogs and cats for the thrill of watching them suffer. They have also been subjected to a lot of physical and emotional abuse by their parents. Such experiences have apparently taught the serial killer to become a sociopath, incapable of feeling remorse or guilt for hurting others. Nonetheless, the vast majority of serial killers are not mentally ill. They appear as normal people who go to school or work, come home, and blend into their immediate neighborhood (Hickey, 1991; Norris, 1989).

40

45

50

(745 words)

—*Deviant Behavior,* Sixth Edition, by Alex Thio

STUDY OUTLINE

Use your annotations to make a study outline for this selection. Review your outline before answering the questions.

THINKING AFTER READING

RECALL   Self-test your understanding. Your instructor may choose to give a true-false review.

REACT   Why are serial killers so difficult to catch? _____

_____

REFLECT   What would be the motivation of the media to exaggerate the number of serial murders and call it an "epidemic"? _____

_____

THINK CRITICALLY   Devise a chart that compares and contrasts mass murderers and serial killers. How are they alike? How are they different? Construct your answer on a separate sheet of paper.

Name _____

Date _____

COMPREHENSION QUESTIONS

Answer the following with *a*, *b*, *c*, or *d*, or fill in the blank. In order to help you analyze your strengths and weaknesses, the question types are indicated.

Main Idea _____ 1. The passage is primarily concerned with

    a. tracing the history of mass and serial murders.
    b. explaining why and how mass and serial murderers kill.
    c. using psychological profiles to locate mass and serial murderers.
    d. showing the similarities of mass and serial murderers.

Detail _____ 2. All of the following were serial murderers except

    a. Andrew Cunanan.
    b. Jeffrey Dahmer.
    c. the Night Stalker.
    d. those who participated in the 1989 World Trade Center bombing.

Detail _____ 3. According to the passage, mass murders usually have all the following characteristics *except*

    a. the murderer wants to get even.
    b. people who are not connected to the murderer's conceived problems are killed.
    c. they observe the victims for months prior to the crime.
    d. the murderer's death is usually a result of the crime.

Inference _____ 4. In describing mass murderers, the phrase *extraordinarily ordinary*

    means _____

    _____

Detail _____ 5. According to the passage, serial murderers usually have all the following characteristics except

    a. they plan not to be captured.
    b. they learn the habits of their victims.
    c. they befriend their victims.
    d. they work as a team.

Detail _____ 6. Of all the homicides in the United States, according to the author, serial killing accounts for

    a. 20%.
    b. 2% or 3%.
    c. 70%.
    d. 75%.

Inference _____ 7. According to the passage, when police search for a serial killer, they should most likely look for someone

    a. who lives in the community.
    b. who has difficulties with the boss at work.
    c. who has an arsenal of guns.
    d. who belongs to a cult.

Answer the following with *T* (true) or *F* (false).

Inference   _____ 8. The author implies that a plea of insanity is a justifiable defense for mass and serial murderers.

Detail   _____ 9. The serial killer is more concerned with self-preservation than the mass murderer.

Inference   _____10. The author implies that serial killers are tormented by guilt.

VOCABULARY

Answer the following with *a*, *b*, *c*, or *d* for the word or phrase that best defines the boldface word as used in the selection. The number in parentheses indicates the line of the passage in which the word is located.

_____ 1. "scene of the **carnage**" (14)

    a. employment
    b. accident
    c. capture
    d. slaughter

_____ 2. "take **lethal** action" (15)

    a. deadly
    b. legal
    c. preventative
    d. immediate

_____ 3. "alone, **alienated**, and helpless" (25)

    a. powerful
    b. antisocial
    c. caring
    d. nervous

_____ 4. "homes into an **arsenal**" (26)

    a. office
    b. meeting hall
    c. computer headquarters
    d. arms depot

_____ 5. "**charismatic** leader" (28)

    a. evil
    b. dynamic
    c. selfish
    d. knowledgeable

_____ 6. "most **credible** figure" (36)

    a. noticeable
    b. repeated
    c. believable
    d. prestigious

_____ 7. "far more **elusive**" (39)

    a. popular
    b. intelligent
    c. slippery
    d. outgoing

_____ 8. "**stalk** their victims" (40)

    a. befriend
    b. kill
    c. follow
    d. hurt

_____ 9. "**lure** the victims" (43)

    a. capture
    b. attract
    c. command
    d. assault

_____10. "incapable of feeling **remorse**" (50)

    a. triumph
    b. success
    c. loneliness
    d. regret

VOCABULARY ENRICHMENT

A. Use context clues and word parts to write the meaning of the boldface words from a science text.

1. Animals have an **instinct** to protect their young from danger.

   _____

2. Some seeds need to be in the ground two weeks before they **germinate**.

   _____

3. If parts of a starfish are broken, it has the ability to **regenerate** itself.

   _____

4. Animals are **dependent** on the food supply for their livelihood.

   _____

5. The direction of the wind is a **variable** in determining future weather.

   _____

6. Many tropical plants are **adaptable** to indoor gardening.

   _____

7. By analyzing the supplied information, he solved the problem by
   deduction. _____

8. Fish and mammals fall into different categories in the animal **phylum**.

   _____

9. New concerns about pesticides indicate that they threaten our **ecological**
   balance. _____

   _____

10. Physical activity can affect a person's **metabolism**.

    _____

B. **Analogies:** Supply a word that completes the following analogies, and then state the relationship that has been established.

11. *Music* is to *piano* as *explosion* is to _____
    Relationship? _____

12. *Whale* is to *mammal* as *ant* is to _____
    Relationship? _____

13. *Bones* are to *leg* as *freckles* are to _____
    Relationship? _____

14. *Attract* is to *repel* as *pretty* is to _____

    Relationship? _____

15. *Tiger* is to *meat* as *cow* is to _____

    Relationship? _____

ASSESS YOUR LEARNING

Review confusing questions, seek clarification, and make notes in your text to help you remember new information and vocabulary.

EXPLORE THE NET

● Criminal profiling is an investigative technique that relies on making assumptions about a criminal's personality based on a crime. It is often used to apprehend serial killers. Visit The Crime Library Web site, and read articles on criminal profiling. Summarize its effectiveness and how it draws on psychology.

www.crimelibrary.com/criminology/criminalprofiling2

www.crimelibrary.com/serial4/criminalprofiling

● The popular television show, America's Most Wanted, has assisted in the apprehension of many dangerous criminals. Visit their Web site, and click on the link for *Archives*. How many criminals has the show assisted in apprehending?

www.amw.com.

For additional readings and exercises, visit the *Breaking Through* Web site:

www.ablongman.com/smith

For a user name and password, please see your instructor.

PERSONAL Feedback 2   Name _____

1. Would you describe yourself as a spontaneous person or a person who plans? _____

   _____

   _____

2. What type of noise bothers you when you study? _____

   _____

   _____

   _____

(continued)

3. Have you been generally happy or unhappy this week? Explain why. _____

_____

_____

4. What has happened this week to make you laugh at yourself?

_____

_____

_____

5. List a few questions that you have asked in any of your classes during the past two weeks. _____

_____

_____

6. What routine do you usually follow at night to get ready for the next day at school? _____

_____

_____

7. What has pleasantly surprised you about your college experience? _____

_____

_____

8. How did you waste time this past week? _____

_____

_____

EVERYDAY READING SKILLS
Reading Reference Materials

Whether you are researching a topic for a term paper or an automobile purchase decision, you want to find relevant and reliable data to support your final conclusions and recommendations. The material you use for support will depend on your project, your goals, and the research tools available to you.

Begin with Encyclopedias

Encyclopedias will provide you with background information about your topic, define key words used in the field, and, in certain cases, mention important researchers in the area under consideration. Many different encyclopedias are available for specific topics such as the *Encyclopedia of African American Religions*, *Encyclopedia of Earth Sciences*, and *The Cambridge Encyclopedia of Astronomy*. For college research, general encyclopedias such as *Americana*, *Colliers*, and *Britannica* may be helpful in your preliminary efforts at defining your research topic, but they probably will not include enough in-depth information to support your premise.

Your college or university library probably has a subscription to several encyclopedias on the Web. Some popular ones are the following:

Encarta   encarta.msn.com

Encyclopedia Britannica   www.eb.com

Grolier   www.grolier.com

Keep in mind that free general encyclopedias online are not as comprehensive as subscription-based online encyclopedias or encyclopedias in print.

 **exercise 1**

Visit your college library and locate two specialty encyclopedias, excluding general encyclopedias such as the **Encyclopedia Britannica**. Take notes on an interesting entry from each and share the notes with your classmates.

Use Indexes to Scholarly and Popular Publications

Most research topics can be approached from the viewpoints of several academic disciplines. For example, sexual assault can be addressed from a legal, medical, sociological, psychological, or educational vantage point. Decide on the academic discipline for your research paper, and ask a reference librarian to help you select an appropriate index. Then use the index to locate appropriate articles in the *periodical literature*. **Periodical** is a term used to describe all publications that come out on a regular schedule. These include popular sources and scholarly journals.

Reader's TIP   Defining Your Topic

To define your research topic, consider:

- **Geography:** Pick a specific area.
- **Time Frame:** Limit the time period under examination.
- **Interest Groups:** Narrow your research by appropriate descriptors such as age, gender, or occupation.
- **Academic Discipline:** What college or department would study this subject?

Articles in **popular sources** (usually newspapers and magazines) are aimed at the general public and written by professional journalists who are not specialists in the field. On the other hand, articles in **scholarly journals** contain research results of experts and always include a **bibliography**, or a list of the sources consulted by the author of the article. For most college research, you will need to use primarily scholarly journals.

Many articles that you find in indexes will not be relevant to your specific needs. Use the information that appears in the index entries to save time and make decisions. Each entry will display a **citation** to the article that includes the title, author(s), name of the periodical, volume and page numbers, issue date, and descriptive notes or key search terms. Usually the entry will also include an abstract (see the illustration that follows).

If the article title and the date look appropriate to your search, read the abstract. The **abstract** is a short paragraph that summarizes the article, stating the premise the authors set out to prove, the subjects or location of the project, and the conclusions (see the illustration opposite). If the abstract sounds as if the article will be relevant to your research, print the entry page or record the information so you can locate a copy of the article. In some cases the database provides a link to the complete text of the article. However, remember that the best articles for your topic may not be available electronically, but may be easily accessible in the library collection.

exercise 2

1. Would the article abstracted on the opposite page be relevant if you were giving a presentation to a teen peer group about healthy social behaviors? ____

2. For this field, would this article still be considered current enough to be useful? _____

3. What key words could you use to find articles on teenage alcohol abuse?

   _____

4. Where are the programs described offered? _____

   _____

TITLE: **Peer Pressure Can Be Useful**

AUTHOR: Graciella Russo

PUBLICATION: Journal of Developmental Psychology | v. 48(3) | June 99 | p. 35–41

NOTES: article | feature article | English | table | ISSN: 0020-4852

SUBJECTS: Drug abuse, Prevention. | Peer influence. | Peer teaching.

****

ABSTRACT: Peer pressure is usually viewed as an undesirable dynamic leading to drinking, smoking, early sexual activity, and undesirable social behaviors. A number of schools and civic/ social organizations, however, are offering programs in which peers demonstrate how positive behaviors offer desirable outcomes. Individuals who receive this peer input develop a more positive self-image and are likely to improve their academic/social skills and behaviors and, in turn, offer the same kind of assistance to other at-risk students.

Labels to be put on the citation
1 Title of article
2 Author of article
3 It is an article rather than a book
4 It is a feature article rather than a short paragraph or two.
5 It is written in English
6 A table is included in the article.
7 The ISSN number (International Standard Serial Number) is the counterpart to the book's ISBN. It is a unique number assigned to a journal and another method of identifying the "correct" journal when looking for a cited article.
8 The key terms or subjects under which this article is indexed.

Use the Internet

For researching, the Internet has both advantages and limitations. The advantages are the up-to-date coverage and the ease with which you can search, access, and download information. The Internet is often more informative and current than the library on topics relating popular trends, computer science, and government reports. You can use a **search engine**, an index of World Wide Web locations, to find a list of up-to-date Web sites that include your search term(s). The Web sites listed will vary with the search engine you use. See Chapter 1 for Internet search directions.

Each search engine works slightly differently: Some group links from the same site, some rank the links based on relevancy, and some allow you to limit your search by date, language, or domain type. Examples of search engines include Altavista, Excite, Hotbot, Go.com, and Lycos. There are dozens of search engines available, and a good list is available through *Yahoo!* (www.yahoo.com) or *Infomine* (infomine.ucr.edu).

Because the Internet is open to everyone, always question the accuracy, reliability, and bias of online information. With the Internet, there are no gatekeepers. By contrast, the scholarly journals previously mentioned have editors, usually a group of experts in the field, who decide what gets published and rejected.

Test-Taking Strategies

- Can your physical condition affect your test score?
- Are test questions predictable?
- How can you keep your mind on what you are reading?
- How are standardized test items made especially tricky?
- How do you organize an essay response?

Everyday Reading Skills: Using Mnemonics

Achieve Your Highest Potential

High test scores should reflect your knowledge and ability, not your use of tricks or gimmicks. Awareness of test-taking strategies, however, can help you achieve your highest potential.

In college you are basically faced with two types of tests: content exams and standardized tests. A content exam measures your knowledge on a subject that you have been studying. For example, the final exam in Psychology 101 measures your understanding and retention of what was taught throughout the course. The score becomes a major part of your final grade in the course. A standardized test, in contrast, measures your mastery of a skill that has developed over a long period of time, such as reading or doing mathematics. The scores on standardized tests usually help you qualify for entering or exiting specific college programs that are important to your academic success.

This chapter will help you improve your test scores by being aware of what is expected in the test-taking situation. Many of the following suggestions are obvious, but it is surprising how frequently students overlook them. Some relate to your physical and mental readiness for peak performance, whereas others explore means for coping with the challenging demands of the testing situation. Technical aspects of test construction are presented with opportunities for application and practice. Awareness and practice can indeed improve test scores and give you that winning edge!

Be Prepared

exercise 1

Read the passage, and then write *agree* or *disagree* for the statements that follow.

Ed was earning money for college by working at a local convenience store in the late afternoon and early evening. On Wednesday night his boss asked him to work long past midnight for an employee who had called in sick. Because Ed needed money for his car payments, he agreed. He did not tell his boss that he had an important test early the next morning.

Thursday morning Ed slept through the alarm but fortunately was awakened by the telephone a half-hour later. He arrived at the exam as the test booklets were being distributed, having missed the professor's introductory remarks and responses to students' questions. Ed spent the first part of the test settling down mentally and physically. He was surprised by some of the material on the test. As he began to read and answer questions, he worried that he would not do well.

_____ 1. Ed was mentally alert after a good night's sleep.

Ed made a poor decision in not telling his boss that he needed adequate sleep on the night before his big test. Being alert rather than drowsy can make the difference in answering correctly one item or more. That correct item, for example, could make the difference in a failing score of 68 or a passing score of 70. Don't take chances when the stakes are high. Being alert can make a difference. *Set yourself up for success, and get plenty of sleep the night before a test.*

_____ 2. Because Ed arrived while the test was being distributed, his lateness did not work against him.

Ed could not immediately begin to work on the test because he had to calm himself first. If you arrive late and flustered, you lose valuable time and begin at a disadvantage. Do your nerves a favor and avoid close calls. *Arrive five or ten minutes early for a test, and get settled.* Find a seat, greet your friends, and take out a pen or pencil.

_____ 3. Ed knew what to expect on the test.

Ed expressed surprise over some of the material on the test. Always check to be sure you know exactly what the test will cover. Know the format of the test. Will it be essay or multiple choice? Study with the format in mind. *Know what to expect on the test.*

_____ 4. Ed had probably asked how the test would be scored.

Because Ed arrived late and missed the professor's introductory remarks, he probably did not know about the scoring. Sometimes, but not very often, guessing is penalized in the scoring. When scores are based on answering all questions, you are better off guessing than leaving items blank. To be safe, ask if omitted items count against you. Also, sometimes some items are worth more points than others; this information is usually stated on the test itself. *Be aware of how the test will be scored.*

_____ 5. Ed approached the test with a positive mental attitude.

Ed had unnecessarily hurt himself and thus lost confidence. Preparation breeds self-confidence, and the lack of it breeds anxiety. Be prepared and plan for success. Give yourself good reasons to be optimistic. *Have confidence in your abilities.*

Stay Alert

exercise 2

Read the passage, and then write *agree* or *disagree* for the statements that follow.

After reading the first passage on the comprehension test, Julie realized that she had no idea what she had read. She had seen all the words, but her mind was not on the message. She was excited and wanted to do well, but was having trouble focusing on the material. She moved to the questions, hoping—erroneously—that they would provide clues to the meaning. They did not, and so she began rereading the passage with greater determination.

Julie finally gained control over the test and was doing fine until her classmates began to leave. She panicked. She was not finished, but saw others turning in their tests. She was stuck on an item that she had reread three times. She looked at her watch and saw she had ten minutes left. That would be plenty of time to finish the last passage, if she could only regain her composure.

_____ 1. Julie was unable to concentrate when she began the test.

Julie could not initially focus her attention and comprehend the material. She was anxious and excited. *Concentration is essential for comprehension.* If you are distracted, take a few deep breaths to relax and get your mind on track. Tune out internal and external distractions, and focus on the meaning. Visualize the message and relate it to what you already know. *Follow directions,* and proceed with confidence. Use your pen as a pacer to concentrate on the passage. (For more on this technique of rhythmically following the words, see Chapter 8.) If anxiety is a consistent problem, seek help from the campus counseling center.

_____ 2. Julie was smart to wear a watch to the test.

Time is usually a major consideration on a test, so always wear *and use* a watch. *Size up the task and schedule your time.* Look over all parts of the test when you receive it. Determine the number of sections to be covered and allocate your time accordingly. Check periodically to see if you are meeting your time goals.

On teacher-made tests, the number of points for each item sometimes varies. Spend the most time on the items that yield the most points.

_____ 3. Julie should be sure of her answer to each item before moving to another.

Do not waste time that you may need later by pondering an especially difficult question. Mark the item with a dot and move on to the rest of the test. If you have a few minutes at the end, return to the marked items. *On a test every minute counts, so work rapidly.* Be aggressive and alert in moving through the test.

_____ 4. Changing an answer usually makes it wrong.

If you have time at the end of the test, *go back to the items you were unsure about.* If careful rethinking indicates another response, change your answer. Research shows that scores can be improved making such changes.[1]

_____ 5. Students who finish a test early make the best grades.

The evidence indicates no correlation between high scores and the time taken to complete a test.[2] Speed does not always equal accuracy. *Don't be intimidated by students who finish early.* Schedule your time and meet your goals.

Seek Feedback

After a test, investigate your errors, if possible. On many standardized tests, only the score is reported, so you are unable to review the test itself. But when feedback is available, take advantage of the opportunity. Analyze your mistakes so you can learn from them and avoid repeating the same errors. Wrong answers give you valuable diagnostic information. If you do not understand the error in your thinking, seek advice from another student or the professor. Never merely look at your grade and forget the test if feedback is available.

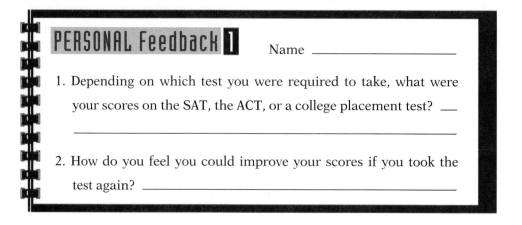

PERSONAL Feedback 1   Name _____

1. Depending on which test you were required to take, what were your scores on the SAT, the ACT, or a college placement test? ___

   _____

2. How do you feel you could improve your scores if you took the test again? _____

---

[1]Marshal A. Geiger, "Changing Multiple-Choice Answers: Do Students Accurately Perceive Their Performance?" *Journal of Experimental Educating* 59 (1991): 250–257.

[2]Robert K. Bridges, "Order of Finish, Time to Completion, and Performance on Course-Based Objective Examinations: A Systematic Analysis of Their Relationship on Both Individual Exam Scores and Total Score Across Three Exams," Annual Meeting of the Eastern Psychological Association, Baltimore, MD, April 1982.

3. What state- or college-mandated tests will you need to take before college graduation? _____

_____

4. What skills are included in those mandated tests? _____

_____

5. What class activities do you feel you need to help you improve your standardized test scores? _____

_____

6. What individual assistance could your instructor offer to help you improve? _____

_____

7. Review the comprehension questions you missed in previous chapters. What question types do you tend to miss most often? Why? _____

_____

8. What do you feel is the biggest misconception about standardized tests? _____

_____

Standardized Reading Tests

Students take standardized reading comprehension tests for a variety of reasons. Tests such as the SAT or the ACT are required for admission to many colleges. Computerized tests such as the Compass are used by many colleges for placement. Some states require additional testing for entering students, such as the TASP in Texas and the CLAST in Florida. In Georgia, students must take a test with a reading component, the Regents Exam, before they are allowed to graduate. Thus, for college students, performing well on standardized tests can be critical to success.

The following strategies will help you perform better on standardized reading tests.

Read to Comprehend

Read for the main idea of the passage. Don't fixate on details. Read to understand the author's message. Students ask, "Should I read the questions first and then the passage?" Experts differ in their opinions, but most advise reading the passage first and then answering the questions. If you read the questions first, you have five or six purposes for reading. Reading thus becomes fragmented and lacks focus. Read with one purpose: to understand the main idea. Avoid paying too much attention to detail.

Interact

Interact with the passage. Use the thinking strategies of good readers: Predict the topic and activate your schema. Visualize the message and relate it to what you already know. Monitor and self-correct. Apply what you already know about the reading process to each test passage.

Anticipate

Anticipate what is coming. Test passages are frequently untitled and thus offer no clue to content. To activate your schema before reading, glance at the passage for a repeated word, name, or date that might signal its subject.

Read the first sentence carefully. Reread if necessary. The first sentence usually sets the stage for what is to come. It sometimes states the central theme and sometimes simply stimulates your curiosity. In any case, the first sentence starts you thinking about what you will be reading. Continue to anticipate throughout the passage. Some of your guesses will be right and some will be wrong. Double-check information and self-monitor.

Relax

Don't allow yourself to feel rushed. Work with control and confidence. That anxious, pressured feeling tends to occur at the beginning, middle, and end of a test. In the beginning, you are worried about not being able to concentrate immediately and thus having to reread. In the middle, you may be upset because you are only half finished, which actually is where you should be. When the first student finishes the test, you may again feel rushed and lose your concentration. To combat this feeling, use your pen as a pointer to focus your attention both mentally and physically on the printed page. Plan your time, relax, and concentrate.

Read to Learn

Test passages are not all that dull. They may never compete with steamy novels, but some are quite interesting and informative. Anticipate having fun. Rather than reading with the artificial purpose of answering questions, read to learn and enjoy. You may surprise yourself!

Recall

Pull the passage together before pulling it apart. Remind yourself of the author's main point, rather than waiting for questions to prod you. This final monitoring step in the reading process only takes a few seconds.

exercise 3

Using the suggestions just outlined, read the following passage as if it were part of a reading comprehension test. The handwritten side notes will help make you aware of a few aspects of your thinking.

A what?
How could she get
out of there?

One of the most remarkable women in world history, famed for her vices as well as for her strong and able rule, governed China from about 660 to 705. The Empress Wu began her career as a concubine in the harem of the third T'ang emperor. When the emperor died, Wu and all the other concubines, according to custom, had their heads shaved and entered a Buddhist convent. Here they were expected to pass the remainder of their lives. Wu, however, was too intelligent and beautiful—as well as too unscrupulous—to accept such a fate. Within a year she had won the new emperor's heart and had become his

Where?

Reread to get her straight

Evil?

Puppets?

Full Power

Evil monks wanting power Manipulated scripture Does the author think it's O.K.? Surprise!

Expanded empire Weaknesses?

Lover?

One too many Downfall

concubine. According to a hostile tradition, she first met the new emperor in a lavatory when he was paying a ceremonial visit to the convent.

Wu rose steadily in the new emperor's favor until, after accusing the empress of engaging in sorcery, murdering her baby daughter, and plotting to poison her husband, she was herself installed as empress. According to the official history of the age, "The whole sovereign power passed into her hands. Life and death, reward and punishment, were determined by her word. The Son of Heaven merely sat upon his throne with hands folded."

After the death of the emperor twenty years later, Wu installed two of her sons as successive puppets. She ruthlessly employed secret police and informers to suppress conspiracies against her. Finally, in 690 at the age of sixty-two, she usurped the imperial title and became the only woman ever to rule China in name as well as in fact.

To legitimize her usurpation, the empress was aided by a group of unscrupulous Buddhist monks, one of whom is reputed to have been her lover. They discovered in Buddhist scriptures a prophecy that a pious woman was destined to be reborn as the ruler of an empire that would inaugurate a better age and to which all countries would be subject. Not only did the monks identify Wu as the woman in the prophecy, but they acclaimed her as a divine incarnation of the Buddha. The T'ang capital was renamed the Divine Capital, and Wu assumed a special title—"Holy Mother Divine Imperial One."

Despite her ruthlessness—understandable in the totally unprecedented situation of a woman seeking successfully to rule a great empire—the Empress Wu was an able ruler who consolidated the T'ang Dynasty. She not only avenged earlier Sui and T'ang defeats at the hands of the northern Koreans who had been subject to the Han, but she made all of Korea a loyal vassal state of China. Yet because she was a woman and a usurper, she found little favor with Chinese Confucian historians. They played up her vices, particularly her many favorites and lovers whom she rewarded with unprecedented honors.

Among those who gained great influence over the aging empress was a peddler of cosmetics, famous for his virility, who was first made abbot of a Buddhist monastery, then palace architect, and finally commander-in-chief of the armies on the northern frontier. At the age of seventy-two, her favorites—and reputed lovers—were two young brothers of a type known as "white faces" (men who were physically attractive but otherwise of no account), whose powdered and rouged faces were a common sight around the palace. When the empress appointed a younger brother of her two favorites to an important governorship, her leading ministers successfully conspired to put her son back on the throne. The two brothers were decapitated in the palace and the Empress Wu, the founder and only member of the Wu Dynasty, was forced to abdicate.

—*Civilization Past and Present* by Walter Wallbank et al.

Understand Major Question Types

Test questions follow certain predictable patterns. For example, almost all passages are followed by one question on the main idea. Learn to recognize the types of questions and understand how they are constructed. What techniques does the test writer use when creating correct answers and incorrect distractors? Well-written distractors are tempting incorrect responses that draw attention, cause confusion, and thus force the test taker to use knowledge and logic. This section discusses each major question type, offers insight into their construction, and gives you an opportunity to play the role of test writer.

Main Idea Questions

Main idea questions ask you to identify the author's main point. These questions are often stated in one of the following forms:

The best statement of the main idea is . . .

The best title for this passage is . . .

The author is primarily concerned with . . .

The central theme of the passage is . . .

Incorrect responses to main idea items fall into two categories: Some are too broad or general. They suggest that the passage includes much more than it actually does. For example, for a passage describing the hibernation of goldfish in a pond during the winter, the title "Fish" would be much too general to describe the specific topic. Other incorrect answers are too narrow. They focus on details within the passage that support the main idea. The details may be attention getting and interesting, but they do not describe the central focus. They are tempting, however, because they are direct statements from within the passage.

If you have difficulty understanding the main idea of a passage, reread the first and last sentences. Sometimes, but not always, one of these sentences will give you an overview or focus.

EXAMPLE
Answer the following main idea items on the passage about Empress Wu. Then read the handwritten remarks describing the student's thinking involved in judging whether a response is correct.

_____ 1. The best statement of the main idea of this passage is:

    a. Buddhist monks bring Wu to power.

      (Important detail, but the focus is on her.)

    b. Women in China were not equal to men.

      (Too broad and general, or not really covered.)

    c. Empress Wu's ambition for her young lovers leads to her downfall.

      (Very interesting, but a detail.)

    d. Empress Wu ruthlessly usurped power but became an able ruler of a great empire.

      (Yes, includes all and sounds great!)

_____ 2. The best title for this passage is:

    a. Confucians Defeat Wu.

      (Detail.)

    b. Empress Wu and Her Lovers.

      (Very interesting, but a detail.)

    c. Empress Wu, Ruler of China.

      (Sounds best.)

    d. Rulers of China.

      (Too broad; this is about only one woman.)

exercise 4
Read the following passage and answer the two main idea questions. Beside each possible answer, write why you did or did not choose that response. For main idea distractors, the reasons might be that the incorrect response is *too broad, a detail,* or *not in the passage.*

While the United States was involved in the Civil War, Napoleon III of France attempted to establish a Catholic monarchy in Mexico. He installed his puppet, Maximilian of Austria, on a Mexican throne and backed him with the French military. In 1866 Secretary of State Seward told France that its presence in Mexico was unacceptable, and 50,000 American troops were sent to the Rio Grande. That was enough, along with new problems in Europe, to persuade France to withdraw.

—*The United States* by Winthrop Jordan and Leon Litwack

_____ 1. The best title for this passage is

    a. Civil War in Mexico _____

         _____

    b. Maximilian Supported by French Military _____

    c. Mexican History in the 1800s _____

    d. Ending French Rule in Mexico _____

_____ 2. The best statement of the main idea of this passage is:

    a. Seward sent 50,000 American troops to the Rio Grande to

       protest French rule. _____

       _____

    b. An Austrian, Maximilian, was appointed by the French ruler to

       govern Mexico. _____

    c. Seward forced the end of French rule in Mexico. _____

    d. European governments face difficulties in the New World.

       _____

Detail Questions

Detail questions check your ability to understand material that is directly stated in the passage. To find or double-check an answer, note a key word in the question, and then quickly glance at the passage for that word or synonym. When you locate the term, reread the sentence for clarification. Detail questions fall in the following patterns:

The author states that . . .

According to the author . . .

According to the passage . . .

All of the following are true except . . .

A person, term, or place is . . .

Incorrect answers to detail questions tend to be false statements. Test writers like to use pompous or catchy phrases stated directly from the passage as distractors. Such phrases may sound authoritative but mean nothing.

EXAMPLE

Answer the following detail question on the passage about Empress Wu (see pages 264–265). Then note the handwritten remarks reflecting the thinking involved in judging whether a response is correct.

_____ 1. Empress Wu did all the following except

(Note the use of except; look for the only false item to be the correct answer.)

a. consolidate the T'ang Dynasty.

(True, this is stated in the fifth paragraph.)

b. accuse the empress of sorcery.

(True, this is stated in the second paragraph.)

c. appoint the brother of a young favorite to an important governorship.

(True, this is stated in the last paragraph.)

d. poison her husband.

(She did not do this, so this is the correct answer.)

exercise 5 Read the following passage, and answer the detail question. Indicate beside each response why you did or did not choose the item.

> Van Gogh left Paris for the southern provincial city of Arles. There he was joined briefly by the painter Paul Gauguin, with whom Van Gogh hoped to work very closely, creating perfect art in a pure atmosphere of self-expression. However, the two artists quarreled, and, apparently in the aftermath of one intense argument, Van Gogh cut off a portion of his ear and had it delivered to a prostitute living in a brothel. Soon after, Van Gogh realized that his instability had gotten out of hand, and he committed himself to an asylum, where—true to form—he continued to work prolifically at his painting. Most of the work we admire so much was done in the last two years at Arles. Vincent (as he always signed himself) received much sympathetic encouragement during those years, both from his brother and from an unusually perceptive doctor and art connoisseur, Dr. Gachet, whom he painted several times. Nevertheless, his despair deepened, and in July of 1890 he shot himself to death.
>
> —*Living with Art*, Fourth Edition, by William McCarter and Rita Gilbert

_____ 1. Van Gogh cut off his ear in

a. Paris. _____

b. an asylum. _____

c. Arles. _____

d. a brothel. _____

Implied Meaning Questions

An implied meaning is suggested but not directly stated. Clues in the passage lead you to make assumptions and draw conclusions. Items testing implied meaning deal with the attitudes and feelings of the writer that emerge as if from behind or between words. Favorable and unfavorable descriptions suggest positive and negative opinions toward a subject. Sarcastic remarks indicate the motivation of characters. Look for clues that help you develop logical assumptions. Implied meaning questions may be stated in one of the following forms:

The author believes (or feels or implies) . . .

It can be inferred (deduced from clues) from the passage . . .

The passage (or author) suggests . . .

It can be concluded from the passage that . . .

Base your conclusion on both what is known and what is suggested. Incorrect responses to implied meaning items tend to be false statements that lack logical support.

EXAMPLE Answer the following implied meaning questions on the passage about Empress Wu. Then note the handwritten remarks reflecting the thinking involved in judging whether a response is correct.

_____ 1. The author implies that Empress Wu

    a. was a devout Buddhist.

       (She was aided by them, but her religious zeal is not suggested.)

    b. killed the first empress's baby daughter.

       (No, she accused the former empress of doing this.)

    c. let her vices lead to her downfall.

       (True, rewarding her young lovers probably hurt the empire.)

    d. conquered Korea to satisfy the Confucian historians.

       (She did conquer Korea, but it is not suggested that she tried to satisfy the Confucian historians.)

exercise 6 Read the following passage, and answer the implied meaning question. In the blank, indicate the reason for your answer choice.

There are many species of truffles, boasting a variety of smells and tastes, ranging from nuts and cheese to sewer gas and rancid bacon grease. Those falling into the latter two groups are not particularly prized. Only a few of some 70 European species are sought after by gourmets, and none of the over 50 American species is remotely tolerable.

European truffle hunters have traditionally used pigs to sniff out truffles, sometimes buried 3 feet deep. The pigs work assiduously to dig out the truffles. The pigs work so hard that one wonders are the pigs' tastes so exquisitely refined that they appreciate the delicate taste of truffles so much? Actually, it turns out that they root them out for another reason. Truffles contain androstenol, a pig sex attractant. The hormone is released by boars and is exceedingly appealing to sows who then dig out the fungi.

—*Biology: The World of Life*, Seventh Edition, by Robert Wallace

_____ 1. The author implies that

    a. the pigs eat the truffles after they dig them.
    b. pigs are used to locate the 50 American species of truffles.
    c. the pigs hunt for all 70 of the European species of truffles.
    d. humans cannot locate the truffles that pigs can detect by smell.

    Reason for choice: _____

    _____

    _____

Purpose Questions

The purpose of a passage is not usually stated. Instead, it is implied and is related to the main idea. In responding to a purpose item, you are answering the question "What was the author's purpose in writing this material?" You might restate this question as, "What did the author do to or for me, the reader?"

EXAMPLE   Reading comprehension tests tend to include three basic types of passages, each of which suggests a separate set of purposes. Study the outline of the three types shown in the Reader's Tip box, and answer the question on the Empress Wu passage. Then note the handwritten remarks reflecting the thinking involved in judging whether an answer is correct.

Reader's TIP   Types of Test Passages

Factual Passages

What?	Science or history articles
How to read?	Read for the main idea, and do not get bogged down in details. Remember, you can look back.
Author's Purpose?	• To inform • To explain • To describe

Example: Textbooks

Opinion Passages

What?	Articles with a particular point of view on a topic.
How to read?	Read to determine the author's opinion on the subject. Then judge the value of the support included, and decide whether you agree or disagree.
Author's Purpose?	• To argue • To persuade • To condemn • To ridicule

Example: Newspaper editorials

Fiction Passages

What?	Articles that tell a story
How to Read?	Read to understand what the characters are thinking and why they act as they do.
Author's Purpose?	• To entertain • To narrate • To describe • To shock

Examples: Novels and short stories

_____ 1. The purpose of the passage on Empress Wu is

   a. to argue.

     (No side is taken.)

   b. to explain.

     (Yes, because the material is factual, like a textbook.)

   c. to condemn.

     (The reading is not judgmental.)

   d. to persuade.

     (No point of view is argued.)

exercise 7

Read the following passage, and answer the purpose question. In the blank, indicate the reason for your answer choice.

[A]nyone who has had a reasonable amount of contact with the federal government has encountered people who should be fired. There are, of course, some superb civil servants—maybe 10 percent of the total—who have every right to become indignant at blanket criticism of government workers. There are another 50 to 60 percent who range from adequate to good. Unfortunately, that leaves 30 to 40 percent in the range downward from marginal to outright incompetent.

Yet fewer than 1 percent are fired each year. This is because 93 percent are under some form of civil service and are therefore virtually impossible to fire.

Being able to fire people is important for two reasons: (1) to permit you to hire the people you want and to get rid of those you don't want, and (2) to make it possible for you to attract the kind of risk-takers who are repelled by the safe civil service and the political emasculation it entails.

—*Points of View: Readings in American Government and Politics*
by Robert E. DeClerico and Allan S. Hammock

_____ 1. The author's primary purpose in this passage is to

   a. narrate or tell a story.
   b. persuade, condemn, or argue.
   c. entertain.
   d. describe.

   Reason for response: _____

_____

Vocabulary Questions

Vocabulary items test your general word knowledge as well as your ability to figure out meaning by using context clues. Vocabulary items are usually stated as follows:

As used in the passage, the best definition of _____ is . . .

Both word knowledge and context are necessary for a correct response. Go back and reread the sentence before the word, the sentence with the word, and the sentence after the word to be sure that you understand the context and are not misled by unusual meanings. Be suspicious of common words such as *industry,* which seems simple on the surface but can have multiple meanings.

EXAMPLE Answer the following vocabulary question on the passage about Empress Wu (see page 264–265). Then note the handwritten remarks reflecting the thinking involved in judging whether an answer is correct.

_d_ 1. As used in the third paragraph of the passage, the best definition of _usurped_ is

(Reread the sentence. Look also at the use of "usurpation" in the fourth paragraph.)

a. earned.

(This is too positive to describe her ruthless behavior.)

b. won.

(Again, this is too positive for her negative actions.)

c. bought.

(No payoff is suggested.)

d. seized.

(Yes, she took control and then tried to make it legal.)

exercise 8 Read the following passage, and answer the vocabulary question. In the blank, indicate the reason for your answer choice.

Perhaps Mahatma Gandhi was one of the most aggressive men who ever lived, if one would wish to measure aggressiveness by motivation. This great chronicler of nonviolence aggressed against a social structure he believed was wrong and he won. Could a less aggressive, less assertive person have accomplished what he did? Yet his life is generally believed to be the antithesis of aggressiveness. The point is, aggression, especially among humans, may be hard to define, and thus the problem of investigating its motivation and historical origins becomes enormously complicated.

—_Animal Behavior_ by Robert Wallace

_____ 1. As used in the passage, the best definition of _antithesis_ is

a. denial.
b. dogma or doctrine.
c. opposite.
d. culmination.

Reason for choice: _____

_____

Hints for Taking Multiple-Choice and True-False Tests

Study the following hints, and answer the items on the passage about Empress Wu with _a, b, c,_ or _d,_ or _T_ (true) or _F_ (false), before reading the explanation in italics.

Read All Options

Even if the first answer seems undisputedly correct, read all the options. Be careful, and consider each answer. Multiple-choice tests usually ask for the _best_ answer, not for any one that is reasonable.

_____ 1. The author suggests that

    a. the empress wanted the emperor dead.
    b. the sons of the empress were disobedient.
    c. Wu's sons plotted against the emperor.
    d. the emperor gave the empress immense power.
    (Although the first option may be tempting, the last answer is
    implied by the quote describing her power and thus is correct.)

Predict the Correct Answer

As you read the stem (or beginning) of a multiple-choice item, anticipate what you would write for a correct response. Develop an answer in your mind before you read the options, and then look for a choice that corresponds to your thinking.

_____ 2. At the end of her reign, the Empress Wu was

    a. decapitated.
    b. married.
    c. pushed from power.
    d. imprisoned.
    (It says in the last sentence that she "was forced to abdicate." The
    third option most closely matches this answer.)

Avoid Answers with "100 Percent" Words

All and *never* mean 100 percent, without exception. In a true-false question, a response containing either word is seldom correct. Rarely can a statement be so definitely inclusive or exclusive. Other "100 percent" words to avoid are *no, none, only, every, always,* and *must.*

_____ 3. Empress Wu was hated by all the Chinese Confucian historians.
    (All means 100 percent, and thus is too inclusive. Surely one or two
    Confucians might not have felt so strongly against Wu.)

Consider Answers with Qualifying Words

Words such as *sometimes* and *seldom* suggest frequency, but do not go so far as to say *all* or *none.* Such qualifying words can mean more than none and less than all. By being so indefinite, they are difficult to dispute. Therefore, qualifiers are more likely to be included in a correct response to a true-false question. Other qualifiers are *few, much, often, may, many, some, perhaps,* and *generally.*

_____ 4. Empress Wu was hated by many of the Chinese Confucian historians.
    (The phrase "she found little favor" with Confucians and "They played
    up her vices" suggest dislike. The statement is true.)

Do Not Overanalyze

Try to follow the thinking of the test writer rather than overanalyzing minute points. Don't make the question harder than it is. Use your common sense, and answer what you think was intended.

_____ 5. Empress Wu fought Korea and won.
    (Naturally Empress Wu was not standing on the front line of battle
    with a sword but, as the leader of China, she was ultimately responsi-
    ble for the victory. Thus the answer is true.)

True Statements Must Be True Without Exception

A statement is either totally true or it is incorrect. Adding an incorrect *and, but,* or *because* phrase to a true statement makes it false and thus an unacceptable answer. If a statement is half true and half false, mark it false.

_____ 6. The Chinese Confucian historians plotted against Empress Wu because they were concerned about the welfare of the poor people of China.
(It is true that the Confucians plotted against Wu, but their reasons for doing so are not stated. The statement is half true and half false, so it is false.)

If Two Options Are Synonymous, Eliminate Both

If two items say basically the same thing but only one answer is possible, then neither can be correct. Eliminate the two and spend your time on the others.

_____ 7. The purpose of this passage is

    a. to argue.
    b. to persuade.
    c. to inform.
    d. to entertain.
    (Because "argue" and "persuade" are basically synonyms, you can eliminate both and move on to other options.)

Figure Out the Difference Between Similar Options

If two similar options appear, frequently one of them will be correct. Study the choices to see the subtle difference intended by the test maker.

_____ 8. Empress Wu was

    a. supported by many Buddhists.
    b. supported by all the Buddhists.
    c. beloved by the poor.
    d. the greatest ruler of the T'ang Dynasty.
    (The last two answers are not suggested. Close inspection shows that the word all *is the only difference between the first and second answers and is the reason that the second is untrue. Thus the first answer, with the qualifying word, is correct.)*

Use Logical Reasoning If Two Answers Are Correct

Some tests include the option *all of the above* and *none of the above*. If you see that two of the answers are correct and are unsure about a third, *all of the above* would be a logical response.

_____ 9. Empress Wu was a

    a. concubine.
    b. mother.
    c. wife.
    d. all of the above.
    (If you recall that Wu was a concubine and a mother but are not sure that she was a wife, "all of the above" would be your logical option because you know that two of the choices are correct.)

Look Suspiciously at Directly Quoted Pompous Phrases

In searching for distractors, test makers sometimes quote a pompous phrase from the passage that doesn't make much sense. Such a phrase may include lofty, ornate, and seemingly important language from the passage, yet still be incorrect. However, you may read the phrase and think, "Oh yes, I saw that in the passage. It sounds good, so it must be right." Be sure authoritative phrases make sense before choosing them.

_____10. Wu was installed as empress because

    a. the Son of Heaven folded his hands.
    b. the imperial title was suppressed in conspiracy.
    c. the prophecy in Buddhist scriptures identified her by name.
    d. the brilliant conniving of an ambitious woman was successful.
    (The first two are pompous and do not make any sense. The third is false because of the phrase "by name." The last is the correct answer.)

Simplify Double Negatives by Canceling Out Both

Double negatives are confusing and time consuming to unravel. Simplify a double-negative statement by first canceling out both negatives. Then reread the statement without the confusion of the two negatives, and decide on the accuracy of the statement.

_____11. Empress Wu was not unscrupulous.
    (Cancel out the two negatives, not *and* un. *Reread the sentence without the negatives: "Empress Wu was scrupulous!" This is a false statement.)*

Certain Responses Are Neither True Nor False

For some items, you are not given the clues necessary for judging their accuracy. There is not sufficient evidence to indicate whether they are true or false.

_____12. Empress Wu was loved by the Chinese people.
    (The passage does not provide any clues to indicate that she was loved or not loved by the Chinese people.)

Validate True Responses

If you are told that all of the answers are correct except one, verify each response and, by the process of elimination, find the one that does not fit.

_____13. Empress Wu was all of the following *except*

    a. a scheming concubine.
    b. a ruthless woman.
    c. the first woman to rule China.
    d. the founder of the T'ang Dynasty.
    (Always note the "except" and look for the response that is false. The first three answers are true and the last is untrue, so it is the correct answer.)

Recognize Flaws in Test Making

Professionally developed reading tests are usually well constructed and do not contain obvious clues to the correct answers. However, some teacher-made tests are hastily written and thus have errors in test making that can help you find the correct answer. Do not, however, rely on these flaws to make a big difference in your score, because such errors should not occur on a well-constructed test.

Grammar. Eliminate responses that do not have subject-verb agreement. The tense of the verb as well as modifiers such as *a* or *an* can also give clues to the correct response.

_____14. Wu's ambition was to become an

     a. concubine.
     b. empress.
     c. lover.
     d. Buddhist.
     (The an *suggests an answer that starts with a vowel. Thus "empress" is the obvious answer.)*

Clues from Other Parts of the Test. Information in one part of the test may help you with an uncertain answer in another section.

_____15. During Wu's reign, China defeated

     a. Vietnam.
     b. India.
     c. Russia.
     d. Korea.
     (A previous question has already mentioned the conquest of Korea.)

Length. On poorly constructed tests, longer answers are more frequently correct.

_____16. The author suggests that Wu promoted the cosmetics peddler to commander-in-chief because he

     a. was a good soldier.
     b. knew how to sell.
     c. had been a Buddhist monk.
     d. was her lover and she wanted to give him favors.
     (In an effort to be totally correct without question, the test maker has written the last—and longest—answer.)

Absurd Ideas and Emotional Words. Avoid distractors that contain absurd ideas or emotional words. The test maker probably got tired of trying to think of distractors and in a moment of weakness included a nonsense answer.

_____17. As used in the passage, the best definition of *concubine* is

     a. wife.
     b. child.
     c. mistress.
     d. dog.
     (The last answer is totally absurd. The test maker should take a break.)

Hints for Taking Essay Exams

In many ways, essay tests are more demanding than multiple-choice tests. Rather than simply recognizing correct answers, you must recall, create, and organize. You face a blank sheet of paper instead of a list of options, and, to write an appropriate response, you must remember ideas and present them in a logical and well-organized manner. The following suggestions can help you respond effectively.

Reword the Statement or Question

Sometimes the statement or question you are asked to discuss is written in a confusing or pompous manner. Be sure you understand the meaning, and then rephrase it in your own words. If it is a statement, put it in the form of a question. If it is a question, simplify it and, if possible, divide it into parts.

Decide on the approach you will use in making your response. Will you define, describe, explain, or compare? For example, suppose you were asked to support the following statement:

> Wu rose to power through unscrupulous deception, and she fell through her own vice and weaknesses.

First rephrase the statement as a question, using words such as *why, what,* or *how:*

> *How did Wu rise to power through unscrupulous deception and fall through her own vice and weaknesses?*

The question really contains two parts, which you can list separately:

1. *How did Wu rise to power through unscrupulous deception?*
2. *How did Wu fall from power through her own vice and weaknesses?*

How will you answer the question? Use two approaches:

1. List her unscrupulous acts of deception that put her in power.
2. Explain the reasons for her fall.

Answer the Question

Answer the question that is asked—not some other question. This may seem obvious, but students frequently get off track. Do not write a summary of the material, include irrelevant information, or repeat the same idea over and over again. Focus on the question and write with purpose.

The following is an example of an incorrect response to the question about Wu's rise and fall. It is a summary of the material rather than a direct answer:

> Empress Wu became the only woman to rule China in name as well as fact. Her rule lasted for 45 years. She began her rise to power as a concubine of the third Tang emperor.

Organize Your Answer

Think before you write. This is perhaps the most important step in test taking, but it is the one you may least want to take the time to do. Plan what you are going to say before you say it.

Brainstorm Ideas. Reread the question, and jot down a word or phrase to note the ideas you want to include in the answer. Number your ideas in the order in which you want to discuss them. On reconsidering, you may find that some of your brainstorming ideas overlap and others are an example of a larger idea. This is a chance for you to look at your possibilities and come up with a plan. When you use a plan, the writing is a lot easier and more logical.

Establish your purpose in the first sentence, and direct your writing to answer the question. List specific details that support, explain, prove, and develop your point. In a concluding sentence, reemphasize your arguments and restate your purpose. Divide your writing with numbers or subheadings whenever possible, because they simplify the answer for the reader and show the organization. If time runs short, use an outline or a diagram to express your remaining ideas.

The following example shows the plan for answering the question on Empress Wu. The brainstormed ideas have already been organized into a concise, working outline. Remember to think before you write; it is the most important step.

Rise	*Fall*
1. Left convent	1. Made ministers mad
2. Plots vs. wife (sorcery, daughter, poison)	2. Rewarding lovers & favorites Cosmetics peddler Young brothers (governorship)
3. Made empress	
4. After his death–2 sons	
5. Took power	
6. Monks made her divine ruler	

Use a Formal Writing Style

A college professor, not your best friend, will be reading and grading your answer. Be respectful, direct, and formal. Do not use slang expressions. Do not use phrases such as *as you know* or *well.* They may be appropriate in conversation but not in formal writing.

Avoid empty words and thought. Adjectives such as *good, interesting,* and *nice* say little. Be direct and descriptive in your writing.

State your thesis or main point, supply proof, and use transitional phrases to tie your ideas together. Words such as *first, second,* and *finally* add transition and help to organize your answer. Other terms, such as *however* and *in contrast,* show a shift in thought. Remember, you are pulling ideas together, so use phrases and words to help the reader see relationships.

The following example illustrates a poor response to the question on Empress Wu. Note the total lack of organization, the weak language, the slang phrase, and the failure to use transition words:

> Empress Wu was very sneaky. She did many dishonest things. She told lies about the empress that were so bad that the emperor dumped the empress. Well, then Wu rose like a bird to fill the new shoes.

Be Aware of Appearance

Research has shown that, on the average, essays written in a clear, legible hand receive a grade-level higher score than essays written somewhat illegibly.[3] Be

---

[3]Charles A. Sloan and Iris McGinnis, "The Effects of Handwriting on Teachers' Grading of High School Essays," Eric No. ED 220 836, 1978.

particular about appearance and considerate of the reader. Proofread for correct grammar, punctuation, and spelling.

Predict and Practice

Predict possible essay items by using the table of contents and subheadings of your text to form questions. Practice brainstorming to answer these questions. Review old exams for an insight into both the questions and the kinds of answers that received good marks. Outline answers to possible exam questions. Do as much thinking as possible to prepare yourself to take the test before you sit down to begin writing.

Notice Key Words

Following is a list of key words of instruction that appear in essay questions, with hints for responding to each word:

Compare: List the similarities.

Contrast: Note the differences.

Criticize: State your opinion and stress weaknesses.

Define: State the meaning and use examples so the term is understood.

Describe: State the characteristics so the image is vivid.

Diagram: Make a drawing that demonstrates relationships.

Discuss: Define the issue and elaborate on the advantages and disadvantages.

Evaluate: State positive and negative views and make a judgment.

Explain: Show cause and effect and give reasons.

Illustrate: Provide examples.

Interpret: Explain your own understanding of and opinions on a topic.

Justify: Give proof or reasons to support an opinion.

List: Record a series of numbered items.

Outline: Sketch the main points with their significant supporting details.

Prove: Use facts to support an opinion.

Relate: Connect items and show how one influences another.

Review: Give an overview with a summary.

Summarize: Retell the main points.

Trace: Move sequentially from one event to another.

Write to Earn Points

Essay exam grades seem much more subjective and mysterious than multiple-choice test grades. Some students feel they deserve to pass for filling the page with writing. They wonder what they did wrong if such a paper is returned with a substandard score.

Professors use objective measures to grade essay tests. They look for you to cover a certain number of points for a passing score. If you do not make the minimum number of points, the paper fails. Answer an essay question to earn points; do not waste your time including personal experiences or irrelevant facts. Stick to the question, and demonstrate to the professor that you know the material.

The following is the checklist the professor will use to score the essay on Empress Wu:

Rise (60 points)

1. Left convent
2. Plots against wife
3. Installed as empress
4. Sons on throne
5. Took power
6. Monks made her divine

Fall (40 points)

1. Ministers angry
2. Rewarding lovers
3. Examples—peddler and brothers

Grades

All passing exams must have items on both her rise and fall:

C = Minimum of 5 items

B = Minimum of 6 items

A = Minimum of 7 items

Read an "A" Paper for Feedback

When your professor returns a multiple-choice exam, reread the items and analyze your errors to figure out what you did wrong. An essay exam, however, is not so easy to review. Sometimes essay exams have only a grade on the front and no other comments. The professor may discuss in class what was needed for an "A" answer, but without seeing it pulled together, a perfect paper is difficult to visualize.

Ask to see an "A" paper. Maybe it will be yours. If so, share it with others. If not, ask your classmates or professor. The "A" paper becomes a model from which you can learn. Compare this paper with your own, and draw conclusions about the professor's expectations. Study and learn from the model so you will not repeat the same mistakes.

exercise 9

Read and assign a grade of A, B, C, D, or F to each of the following essay responses to the Empress Wu question. Explain your reasons for each grade and include any suggestions you would offer to the student who wrote the paper.

Paper 1

Empress Wu did many bad things in order to get the power. The things she did were against the people in power. She did not want to stay with the Buddhists because she wanted to be with the new emperor. He died and her sons became puppets. She worked against the people who did not like her.

She was finally forced out of power because she had lovers. One of the lovers became a governor. The two brothers that she liked were decapitated. She fell from power and thus was no longer the empress.

Paper 2

Empress Wu rose to power through tricks and deception. She was intelligent enough to devise a way to meet the new emperor, get him attracted to her, and thus escape her lifetime sentence in the convent. She rose in the new emperor's favor and plotted dishonestly against his wife. Wu falsely accused the emperor's wife of sorcery, murdering her own daughter, and plotting to poison her husband. Wu was soon made empress and given great power. When the emperor died, she ruled through her two sons. Finally, she took the throne herself. Buddhist monks helped her devise a scheme using the scriptures to validate her power. They said she was a divine incarnation of the Buddha.

Wu fell from power because of her weakness for men as lovers. She rewarded her lovers with power and thus angered her ministers. She made a cosmetics peddler an abbot, architect, and then commander-in-chief. Her final appointment of a younger brother of two of her favorites to an important governorship was too much for the ministers. They forced her from power.

Remember: Brainstorm before you write. Jot down the ideas you will use to answer the question and number them. Stick to the question, organize your response, and use logic.

Summary Points

- Gain points by learning how tests are constructed and what is expected of you in the test-taking situation.
- Get plenty of sleep the night before a test.
- Arrive early for a test and know what to expect.
- Concentrate and schedule your time.
- Seek feedback so you will not repeat the same mistakes.
- Use the five thinking strategies of good readers.
- Understand the major question types: main idea, details, implied meaning, purpose, and vocabulary.
- For essay exams, organize your response and answer the question directly.

COLLABORATIVE PROBLEM SOLVING

Form a five-member group and select one of the following questions. Brainstorm and then outline your major points on a transparency. Choose a member to present the group findings to the class.

▶ List ten feelings you have when you begin to take an important test.

▶ List ten tips for successfully writing essay exam responses in a history course.

▶ List ten reasons why you would not want to take a course that only had one test, the final exam.

▶ List standardized tests that you or your classmates may have to take in the future. Include tests for admission to professional schools, for graduate schools, and for jobs.

PERSONAL Feedback 2

Name _____

1. Do you prefer multiple-choice or essay exams? Why? _____
   _____

2. What are the weaknesses of your essay responses? _____
   _____

3. How did your last English course prepare you for essay exam responses? _____
   _____

(continued)

4. Describe an activity that could be done in this course to help you on essay responses. _____

_____

5. Name a student who writes excellent essay responses. _____

_____

6. Have you ever outlined a possible essay question before a test? If so, for what class? _____

_____

7. Describe the best paper you have ever written. _____

_____

8. Grading essay responses is more subjective than grading multiple-choice items. What system do you think professors use to arrive at accurate grades? _____

_____

EXPLORE THE NET

● Does your state have a required college skills exam? Use the following Web sites to locate and take a practice test of this type.

Texas Academic Skills Program (TASP)

www.tasp.nesinc.com/

New York State Regents Exam Preparation

www.barronsregents.com/

● Locate information about the exam required for people who want to work for the post office. What are the three types of tests on the postal exam? How are exam scores used to determine who will be interviewed?

Postal Jobs Exam and Study Guide Information

www.datasync.com/PostalJobs/exam.html

● What tests are required for admission to law school? What required tests must law school graduates pass before being certified to practice law?

Official LSAT Site of the Law School Admission Council

www.lsat.org/

About the Bar Exam

www.barbri.com/exam/about_bar_exam.html

For additional readings and exercises, visit the *Breaking Through* Web site:

www.ablongman.com/smith

For a user name and password, see your instructor.

EVERYDAY READING SKILLS

Using Mnemonics

Mnemonics are techniques to help you organize and recall. They work by incorporating your senses through pictures, sounds, rhythms, and other mental "tricks" to create extrasensory "handles" or hooks to make it easier for your brain to arrange and retrieve information. Given a list of 12 nouns to remember, students who link them in a story remember more than students who just try to memorize them as unrelated items. Weaving such a story is called *narrative chaining* because the technique links, organizes, and gives meaning to unrelated items. Following are some suggested mnemonic techniques for college learning:

Reading Out Loud

Although you may not think of this as a mnemonic, you use additional senses when you read out loud. Memory experts explain that your eyes *see* the material on the page, and your ears *hear* the information. Your mouth, tongue, lips and throat *feel* the sensation of speaking the words. This is particularly effective for studying lecture notes after class or before an exam.

Writing It Down

Writing works in a similar way to reading aloud because you feel your hand transcribing the information. Thus summarizing, annotating, notetaking, outlining, and mapping add sensory steps to learning. Always take class lecture notes to reinforce the spoken information. Also, when you write something down, make sure you understand the words you are using. In some cases you will be translating or paraphrasing what the professor says into your own words.

Creating Acronyms

Create words using the first letter of each word you want to remember. A well-known example of this technique is using HOMES to remember the great lakes: *H*uron, *O*ntario, *M*ichigan, *E*rie, *S*uperior.

Creating Acrostics

Form a sentence with the first letter of each word in your sentence corresponding to the first letter of each word in a list you want to remember. For example, *Members must promise justice unless neighbors enlist very soon* is an acrostic for remembering the nine planets in our solar system: *M*ercury, *M*ars, *P*luto, *J*upiter, *U*ranus, *N*eptune, *E*arth, *V*enus, *S*aturn. If you need to remember the planets in the order they orbit the sun, create a different sentence. Silly and unusual acrostics can be easy to remember.

Using Rhythms, Rhymes, and Jingles

Use rhythm, rhyme and jingles to create additional handles for your brain to use to process and retrieve. Most young students never forget the year Christopher Columbus came to America because of learning the rhythmic rhyme, "In fourteen-hundred-and-ninety-two/Columbus sailed the ocean blue."

Making Associations

Make a connection between seemingly unrelated ideas by using pictures, nonsense ideas, or connected bits of logic. For example, two easily confused words are *stationary,* which means standing still, and *stationery,* meaning letter-writing paper. To remember the difference, note that *station<u>a</u>ry* is spelled with an "a," which relates to the "a" in *st<u>a</u>nding* still; *station<u>e</u>ry is* spelled with an "e," which relates to *l<u>e</u>tters*.

Conjuring Mental Images

Create a picture, perhaps a funny picture, just as you would on a vocabulary concept card. Picture a *voracious* reader as a shark greedily eating a book.

Using Key Word Images

To learn foreign language vocabulary, use the sound of the new word to relate to an image of a known word. For example, the Spanish word for horse is *caballo,* which is pronounced *cab-eye-yo.* Associate *eye* as the key word and picture a horse with only one large eye.

EXAMPLE The residents of Alaska use several mental "tricks" to remember the five different types of salmon found in and around the state. These fish are very important to the economy of Alaska, and the colloquial names of the five types are sockeye, silver, pink, king, and chum. The mnemonic for remembering them is as follows.

Hold up your hand and associate a salmon type with each finger. First associate the chum salmon with your thumb because it rhymes. Next, your index finger is your pointing finger; in fact, you could hit yourself in the eye with it. Thus associate your dangerous pointing finger with the sockeye salmon. Your middle finger is the tallest, so associate it with the king salmon, the highest political position in a country. Associate the silver salmon with your ring finger, which very well might have a silver ring on it. Last, comes your pinkie finger, which naturally can be associated with the pink salmon. Now review each of your five finger salmon, commit them to memory, and feel like a proud Alaskan.

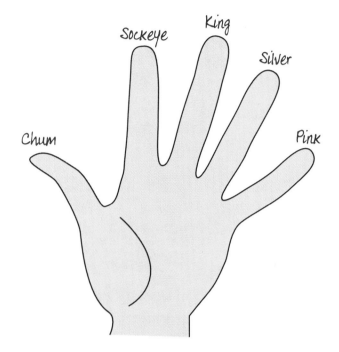

exercise 1

1. Create an association to remember that *cereal* is a breakfast food and *serial* is a numerical order. _____

   _____

2. Create an acrostic to remember the elements that make up the vast majority of molecules in living things: carbon, hydrogen, nitrogen, oxygen, phosphorus, and sulphur. _____

   _____

3. Create a rhyme or jingle to remember that World War II ended in 1945.

   _____

   _____

Reader's TIP   Remembering Information

- Hook it to mental signs that are easy to remember.
- Link it to other information or indicators you already know.
- Sense it by touching, writing, or speaking.
- Rehearse it by writing it or speaking it to yourself.

Efficient Reading

- What is your reading rate?
- How fast should you read?
- How can you increase your reading speed?

Everyday Reading Skills: Managing Workplace Reading

What Is Your Reading Rate?

If you are not zipping through a book at 1,000 words per minute, does it mean you are a slow reader? No, of course not. You do not need to be reading as fast as you can turn the pages, yet many college students are concerned about their reading rate. This chapter explains factors that contribute to a fast or slow reading rate and suggests techniques that can help you improve your reading efficiency.

Read the following selection at your normal reading speed. Time your reading so you can calculate your words-per-minute rate. Use a stopwatch or a watch with a second hand. Record your starting time in minutes and seconds. When you have completed the selection, record your finishing time in minutes and seconds. Answer the questions that follow and use the chart to determine your rate.

Starting time: _____ *minutes* _____ *seconds*

STEROIDS, THE DRUG OF "CHAMPIONS"

In 1988, at the Seoul Olympics, sprinter Ben Johnson of Canada burst out of the starting blocks to win the 100 meter dash, leaving American Carl Lewis in the dust. Three days later the gold medal was awarded to Lewis because traces of stanozolol were found in Johnson's urine. Stanozolol use is banned in international sports because it is an anabolic (tissue-building) steroid. Anabolic steroids burst upon the athletic scene in Olympic competition in the 1950s, when it was learned that Soviet weightlifters were using them to increase their strength. The Americans quickly followed suit and the drugs were soon being used in any sport that required strength (as does virtually every sport). At first steroids were used primarily by elite athletes looking for the final edge that might put them over the top. Soon, however, they found their way into local gyms where body builders of mediocre abilities and grand egos were wolfing down pills in hopes of looking good around the pool.

The major benefit of steroids seems to be to allow muscles to recover more quickly, so that the athlete can train harder. As athletes were reporting remarkable results with steroids, the medical community began testing the effects of the drugs and the drugs were soon banned. Medical researchers reported a variety of remarkable side effects of steroid use including liver cancer, heart disease, and kidney damage. One problem with the drugs is that, along with tissue building, they also "masculinize." The masculinization is particularly acute for women, who may grow facial hair as their voices deepen and their breasts decrease in size. They may, indeed, gain muscle mass, but the masculizing effects may be impossible to reverse. In adolescents, steroids hasten maturation and may cause growth to stop and the loss of hair in boys. Strangely, in men, the high levels of steroids in the body may cause the body's own production of male hormones to cease, resulting in enlarged breasts and shrunken testes.

Anabolic steroids also can cause behavioral changes by increasing the aggressiveness of the user. The aggressiveness may be manifest by more vigorous training but also by hostile and sometimes violent social interaction. Interestingly, much of what we know about steroid use comes from observations of abusers, since the medical community cannot administer such doses for athletes because of ethical considerations.

(387 words)

—*Biology: The World of Life,* Seventh Edition, by Robert Wallace

Finishing time: _____ *minutes* _____ *seconds*

Reading time in seconds = _____

Words per minute = _____ *(see Time Chart)*

TIME CHART

Time in Seconds and Minutes	Words per Minute
40	581
50	464
60 (1 min.)	387
120 (2 min.)	194
130	179
140	165
150	155
160	145
170	137
180 (3 min.)	129
190	122
200	116
210	110
220	106
230	101

Answer the following with *T* (true) or *F* (false).

_____ 1. Carl Lewis used steroids at the Seoul Olympics.

_____ 2. Steroid use was once accepted in international sports.

_____ 3. A high level of steroids in men may cause increased aggression.

_____ 4. A high level of steroids in women may cause enlarged breasts.

_____ 5. Liver cancer can be a side effect of steroids.

(Each scored item counts 20 points)

Comprehension = _____%

What Is an Average Reading Rate?

Rate calculations vary according to difficulty of the material. Research indicates, however, that on relatively easy material, the average adult reading speed is approximately 250 words per minute at 70 percent comprehension. For college students, the rate is sometimes estimated at closer to 300 words per minute.

Because this selection was not particularly difficult, the average adult reading speed of 250 words per minute at 70 percent comprehension would apply. If you are reading below this rate, you may have trouble finishing standardized tests and finishing assignments. The suggestions on page 290 can help you become a more efficient reader.

PERSONAL Feedback 1   Name _____

1. When you read the timed reading, how many times did you have to reread? _____

2. If your mind wandered during the timed reading, what were you thinking about? _____

(continued)

3. Describe why reading speed is or is not a problem for you. _____

_____

_____

4. What kind of easy reading would you choose for practicing and improving your reading rate? _____

_____

5. Describe any previous instruction that you have had on improving your reading rate. _____

_____

6. What do you think is the greatest misconception about reading speed? _____

_____

How Can You Increase Your Reading Speed?

Be Aggressive—Attack!

Grab that book, sit up straight, and try to get some work done. Don't be a passive reader who watches the words go by but lacks understanding and involvement. Be active. Look for meaning with a strong intellectual curiosity, and try to get something out of what you read. Drive for the main idea.

Faster reading does not mean poorer comprehension. Moderate gains in speed usually result in improved comprehension because you are concentrating and thinking more.

The following exercises will help increase your awareness of speed and give you a sense of haste. Time yourself on each exercise and then compare your time with those of other members of the class. If possible, do these exercises as a group, with one person calling out the time at five-second intervals.

exercise 2

In the lists here, the key word is in boldface in the column at the left. It is then repeated in the group of words to the right. As rapidly as possible, locate the identical word, check it, and then move to the next line. Try to do most of this visually rather than saying each word to yourself. When you have finished each list, record your time and compare your performance with that of fellow classmates.

List 1

1. **lip**	lid	long	left	lip	lap
2. **stand**	start	stand	strong	torn	stop
3. **wander**	willow	wanton	waiting	wander	worry
4. **vain**	vale	vain	vane	vague	value
5. **most**	mort	most	might	host	mast
6. **divide**	divine	devoted	divide	have	doing
7. **someone**	somewhere	someone	sooner	somehow	somebody

8. **week**	weak	meek	week	leak	seek
9. **hazy**	hazy	hazard	hamper	lazy	dizzy
10. **mold**	mole	mound	mold	mind	hold
11. **sight**	height	right	might	sight	light
12. **aide**	aid	aide	add	also	hide
13. **reform**	remake	reclaim	malformed	reform	form
14. **bubble**	raffle	baffle	bubble	rubber	blubber
15. **scarce**	source	sacred	scarce	scorn	serious
16. **fabulous**	famous	fabulous	fashion	false	fasten
17. **reservation**	preservation	occupation	realization	reservation	reserve
18. **reality**	really	reaction	finality	reality	rational
19. **tranquilizer**	transfer	relaxation	tranquilizer	transcribe	transit
20. **phenomena**	pneumonia	phenomena	paralysis	feminine	phrases

Time in seconds = _____

List 2

1. **wing**	wig	wring	wing	with	ring
2. **cram**	crash	carry	ram	ham	cram
3. **like**	mike	like	land	load	hike
4. **sandal**	saddle	sandal	ramble	soften	sweet
5. **prime**	proud	prim	prime	prissy	rime
6. **manage**	mingle	manager	mangle	manner	manage
7. **rash**	rash	rush	race	lush	rich
8. **trace**	trance	trace	trade	train	trail
9. **saline**	saloon	salmon	saline	short	slowly
10. **revenge**	regain	ravenous	rancid	revamp	revenge
11. **tired**	tried	trend	tread	tired	torn
12. **withdrawn**	without	withdraw	within	withdrawn	witness
13. **powerful**	power	potential	powerful	potent	palate
14. **indignant**	indigenous	indigent	distinguish	indignant	indulge
15. **remember**	dismember	remain	reminisce	remission	remember
16. **condescending**	condemning	condense	concise	coherent	condescending
17. **magnanimous**	magnificent	magnanimous	magnetic	malformed	magnify
18. **humorous**	human	hormone	hammock	hammer	humorous
19. **civilization**	civilized	citizenry	civic	civilization	centered
20. **ingenious**	ingenuous	injurious	ingenious	ignoble	engine

Time in seconds = _____

Concentrate

Our eyes cannot actually read. We read with our minds. Thus getting information from the printed page ultimately comes down to concentration. The faster you read, the harder you must concentrate. It is like driving a car at 80 miles per hour as opposed to 40 miles per hour. You are covering more ground at 80, and it requires total concentration if you are to keep the car on the road. Faster reading is direct, purposeful, and attentive. There is no time to think about anything except what you are reading.

As Professor Clayton Pinette at the University of Maine says, "Concentration requires lots of energy. Health, rest, and physical and mental well-being are necessary for good concentration. Rest breaks are important and so are personal rewards."[1]

_____

[1]Clayton Pinette, personal communication, February 1994.

Both external and internal distractions interfere with concentration. External distractions are the physical things around you. Are you in a quiet place? Is the television going? Can you hear people talking on the telephone? Are you being interrupted by someone asking you questions? You can control most external distractions by prior planning. Be careful in selecting your time and place to study. Choose a quiet place and start at a reasonable hour. Set yourself up for success.

Internal distractions, however, are much more difficult to control. They are the thoughts in your mind that keep you from concentrating. Again, prior planning will help. Keep a "To Do" list as mentioned in Chapter 1. Making a list and knowing that you will check back over it will help you stop worrying about your duties and responsibilities. Make an effort to spend more time *doing* something than *worrying* about something.

Visualizing can also help concentration. If you are reading about ostriches, visualize ostriches. As much as possible, try to see what you read as a movie. Use your imagination and all of your five senses to improve your comprehension.

exercise 3

In the lists here, the key word is in boldface. Among the words to the right, locate and mark the one most similar to the key word in meaning. In this exercise, you are not just looking at the shapes of words, but you are looking quickly for meaning. This will help you think fast and effectively. When you have finished each list, record your time, check your answers, and compare your performance with those of others in the class.

List 1

1. **recall**	read	guide	remember	fail	forgive
2. **sanitary**	new	fine	equal	clean	straight
3. **physician**	health	doctor	coward	elder	teacher
4. **motor**	car	horse	wagon	shine	engine
5. **first**	primary	last	finally	only	hard
6. **look**	stick	serve	glance	open	wait
7. **usual**	common	neat	best	cruel	kindness
8. **quick**	noisy	near	fast	finish	give
9. **annoy**	logic	make	win	disturb	set
10. **shout**	cry	action	most	fear	force
11. **friend**	family	mother	soldier	farmer	comrade
12. **carry**	plan	instruct	take	deal	rank
13. **sincere**	style	genuine	safe	future	simple
14. **valuable**	dear	unstable	truthful	ancient	broken
15. **diminish**	season	promote	forward	reduce	marry
16. **anxious**	appear	sight	nervous	mean	helpful
17. **liquid**	clear	running	pipes	kitchen	fluid
18. **prestige**	program	status	mission	natural	report
19. **core**	side	nation	heart	event	process
20. **harness**	control	appear	build	mark	attend

Time in seconds = _____

List 2

1. **ill**	sin	die	skill	sick	mind
2. **calm**	envy	breeze	peaceful	early	far
3. **nice**	pleasant	needed	new	smooth	plastic
4. **emotion**	drain	feeling	heat	silent	search
5. **close**	cost	tall	mild	flow	near
6. **gun**	knife	rifle	handle	metal	hold

7. **expert**	rule	sort	believer	follower	specialist
8. **obtain**	get	feature	delay	injure	adapt
9. **discuss**	sense	divide	order	talk	find
10. **moisture**	dampness	sample	screen	dark	dirty
11. **village**	mountain	town	river	country	moving
12. **bravery**	origin	voluntary	courage	means	social
13. **loyal**	client	faithful	definite	legal	scale
14. **convert**	swim	chief	movement	policy	change
15. **celebrate**	attain	learn	century	rejoice	statement
16. **argument**	fund	quarrel	meeting	democracy	voice
17. **preserve**	opportunity	solar	system	save	signal
18. **hilarious**	funny	horrible	drama	sensible	even
19. **imitate**	difficult	confer	strike	language	copy
20. **danger**	general	fair	position	risk	army

Time in seconds = _____

Stop Regressions

A **regression** is the act of going back and rereading what you have just finished. Does this ever happen to you? Certainly some textbook material is so complex that it requires a second reading, but most of us regress even when the material is not that complicated. The problem is simply "sleeping on the job." Your mind takes a nap or starts thinking about something else while your eyes keep moving across the page. Hence halfway down the page, you wonder, "What am I reading?" and you plod back to reread and find out. Then, after an alert rereading, the meaning is clear, but you have lost valuable time.

Regression can be a habit. You know you can always go back and reread. Break yourself of the habit. The next time you catch yourself going back to reread because your mind has been wandering say, "Halt, I'm going to keep on reading." This will put more pressure on you to pay attention the first time.

Sleeping through only one or two paragraphs in an entire chapter probably won't hurt your comprehension that much. Sleeping through much more than that, however, could be a problem. Remember, reading the assignment twice takes double the time. Try to reread only when it is necessary because of the complexity of the material.

Avoid Vocalization

Vocalization means moving your lips as you read. It takes additional time and is generally a sign of an immature reader. A trick suggested by specialists to stop lip movement is to put a slip of paper in your mouth. If the paper moves, your lips are moving, and you are thus alerted to stop the habit.

Subvocalization refers to the little voice in your head that reads out loud for you. Even though you are not moving your lips or making any sounds, you hear the words in your mind as you read. Some experts say that subvocalization is necessary for difficult material, and others say that fast readers are totally visual and do not need to subvocalize. The truth is probably in between the two. You may find that in easy reading you can eliminate some of your subvocalization and only hear the key words, whereas on more difficult textbook material, the subvocalization reinforces the words and gives you better reading comprehension. Because your work will be primarily with textbook reading, do not concern yourself with subvocalization at this time. In fact, you may need to read particularly difficult textbook passages out loud in order to understand them fully.

Expand Fixations

Your eyes must stop for you to read. These stops, which last for a fraction of a second, are called **fixations.** If you are reading a page that has twelve words to a line and you need to stop at each word, you have made twelve fixations, each of which takes a fraction of a second. If, however, you can read two words with each fixation, you will make only half the stops and thus increase your total reading speed.

You might say, "How can I do this?" and the answer has to do with peripheral vision. To illustrate, hold up your finger and try to look only at that finger. As you can see, such limited vision is impossible. Because of peripheral vision, you can see many other things in the room besides your finger. Research has shown that the average reader can see approximately 2.5 words per fixation.

Read the following phrase:

in the barn

Did you make three fixations, one on each word, or did you fixate once? Now read the following word:

entertainment

How many fixations did you make? Probably one, but as a beginning reader in elementary school, you most likely read the word with four fixations, one for each syllable. Your use of one fixation for *entertainment* dramatizes the progress you have already made as a reader and indicates the ability of the eyes to take in a number of letters at one time. The phrase *in the barn* has nine letters, whereas *entertainment* has thirteen. Does it make any sense to stop three times to read nine letters and once to read thirteen? Again, the reason we do so is habit and what we have taught ourselves to do. If you never expected or tried to read more than one word per fixation, that is all you are able to do.

The key to expanding your fixations is to read phrases or thought units. Some words seem to go together automatically and some don't. Words need to be grouped according to thought units. Your fixation point, as shown in the following example, will be under and between the words forming the thought unit, so your peripheral vision can pick up what is on either side of the point.

Read the following paragraph by fixating at each indicated point. Notice how the words have been divided into phrase units.

FASTER READING

A faster   reading speed   is developed   through practice
   ●   ●   ●   ●
and concentration.   Your reading rate   also depends
     ●   ●   ●
on how much   you know   about a subject.
    ●   ●   ●

exercise 4

In the lists here, the key phrase is boldface. Among the words on the line below, locate and mark the phrase that is most similar to the key phrase in meaning. Record your time, check your answers, and compare your performance with those of others in the class. This exercise will help you increase your eye span and grasp meaning quickly from phrases.

List 1

1. **to have your own**
   wish for more   share with others   to keep for yourself   harmed by fire
2. **finish a task**
   lessen the impact   cleaning the attic   turn on the lights   complete a job
3. **sing a song**
   hum a tune   work for pleasure   leave for vacation   wish on a star
4. **manage a business**
   lost your job   lock the door   seek employment   run a company
5. **sit for a while**
   make ends meet   rest in a chair   learn new ways   fall into bed
6. **clear and concise**
   engage in conversation   order a change   easy to understand   complex and difficult
7. **reach a goal**
   achieve an objective   call a meeting   change your mind   open a hearing
8. **free your mind**
   leave a spot   clear the head   turn the motor   remember a date
9. **walk down the road**
   meet in the car   support rapid transit   call the taxi   stroll in the street
10. **hold some money back**
    rush to the bank   drop a dime   accumulate savings   remain at work

Time in seconds = _____

List 2

1. **sense a disaster**
   sleep with ease   feel danger near   yearn for adventure   seek your fortune
2. **hurry to leave**
   walk in the rain   spill the coffee   lower the rent   rush out the door
3. **seek legal advice**
   engage an attorney   earn a living   move your address   give to charity
4. **forget to call**
   scream and yell   open an account   send by mail   neglect to phone
5. **offer your services**
   get in the way   ask to help   quit your job   waste your time
6. **listen to music**
   play in a band   buy a piano   hear a tune   turn off the radio
7. **notice a change**
   see a difference   buy a new shirt   work on a project   meet new people
8. **lose money gambling**
   pay for a product   not win a bet   cut expenses   make an offer
9. **clean up a spill**
   go in the kitchen   add more water   wipe away a stain   tear a rag
10. **leap with delight**
    sing a high note   turn the page   ask for help   jump for joy

Time in seconds = _____

Use a Pen as a Pacer

Using a pen to follow the words in a smooth, flowing line can help you set a rhythmical pace for your reading. In elementary school you were probably taught never to point at words, so this advice may be contrary to what you have learned. However, it can be an effective speed-reading technique.

The technique of using a pen as a pacer is demonstrated in the following paragraph. Use a pen to trace the lines shown, so it goes from one side of the column to the other and returns in a Z pattern. Because you are trying to read several words at a fixation, it is not necessary for your pen to go to the extreme end of either side of the column. After you have finished, answer the comprehension questions with *T* (true) or *F* (false) and compare your speed with that of others.

EXAMPLE   Breaking for Memory

Researchers have found that taking a series
of short breaks during a long
study period can enhance memory
and thus improve your recall
of the information. The breaks should be
a complete rest from the task
and should be no longer than
ten minutes. You may choose
to break every forty or fifty minutes.
During your break, you will experience
what experts call memory consolidation
as the new information is linked
and organized into knowledge networks.
According to some experts, deep breathing
and relaxation exercises can also help
by improving the flow of oxygen to the brain.

(100 words)

Time in seconds = _____

_____ 1. Fifty-minute breaks are recommended during long study periods.

_____ 2. Memory consolidation means improving the flow of oxygen to the brain.

EXPLANATION   The answers are (1) *false* and (2) *false*. Although it may seem awkward at first, practice using a pen to read in a Z pattern on light material such as the newspaper or magazines to get accustomed to the technique. It will not only force you to move your eyes faster, but also improve your concentration and keep you alert and awake.

Try using your pen as a pacer for the first five or ten minutes of your reading to become familiar with the feeling of a faster, rhythmical pace. When you tire, stop the technique, but try to keep reading at the same pace. If, later in the reading, you feel yourself slowing down, resume the technique until you have regained the pace. This is a simple technique that does not involve expensive machines or complicated instruction, and *it works!* Pacing with the Z pattern *will* increase your reading speed.

exercise 5

Read the following passage (using your pen as a pacer in the *Z* pattern in Passages 1, 2, and 3). Answer the comprehension question with *T* (true) or *F* (false), and then record your reading time and compare your performance with that of other students.

Passage 1

NATURAL GAS SAFETY

Natural gas   is odorless   so,   in the early days
of using   natural gas   to heat buildings   and cook,
someone would occasionally   light a match   without realizing that
a gas leak   had filled   the air   with gas.   Poof!
Inventors quickly   began designing devices   that would detect
the presence   of natural gas   in the air   and sound
an alarm.   However,   the best solution   was not
a detection device.   Instead,   a gas   that could be
easily smelled   was added   to the odorless   natural gas
so that   a leak   could be detected   easily   by a human's
built-in   gas detector,   the nose!

(69 words)

—*A Creative Problem Solver's Toolbox* by Richard Fobes

Time in seconds = _____

_____ 1. Another gas was mixed with natural gas to create a smell.

_____ 2. Originally natural gas was odorless.

Passage 2

NETIQUETTE

The rules   and guidelines   for acceptable behavior   on the Net
are called netiquette.   Be careful   to say   what you mean
and to say it   with care.   You cannot   double-click   and take
it back.   Keep your   messages short   and to the point.   People who
receive hundreds   of e-mails   each day are more likely   to respond
to short ones.   Although you   are hidden   from view,   appearances
are important.   Proofread   your messages.   Other people   will judge
your intelligence   and education   by the spelling,   grammar,   punctuation,

and clarity   of your messages.   If you   want your messages   to be taken
seriously,   present your   best face.

(100 words)

—Computer Confluence, Third Edition, by George Beekman

Time in seconds = _____

_____ 1. According to the author, once a message is sent you can double-click and retract it.

_____ 2. The author suggests that grammar and punctuation is not important in e-mail messages to close friends.

Passage 3

TYPING KEYBOARD

The earliest typewriters   usually jammed   when a key
was pressed   too soon   after the previous key
was released.   Most people   weren't willing
to tolerate   this flaw,   so early typewriters
were used   mostly by blind people   and others
who couldn't write   easily by hand.   Christopher Sholes
created a clever   supporting enhancement   that overcame
this jamming tendency.   He arranged   the letters
on the keys   awkwardly!   He put   the frequently
typed letters   E, T, O, N, R, and I   on keys
that required   finger movement   to reach them,
and assigned   frequently typed   pairs of letters,
such as E and D,   to the same finger.   His innovation worked!
It successfully   slowed down   a person's typing speed,
thereby reducing   the tendency for   his typewriters to jam.
Unfortunately,   because Sholes' typewriters   became so popular,
this awkward   keyboard arrangement   is the one
we still   use today!

(139 words)

—The Creative Problem Solver's Toolbox by Richard Fobes

Time in seconds = _____

_____ 1. Our present typing keyboard was adopted to enhance speed.

_____ 2. Early typewriters were used by blind people.

Passage 4

IS READING ENOUGH?

To learn effectively from textbooks, reading is never enough. Students from the University of Virginia read a passage from a biology textbook that contained fifty-four ideas. The students read it once and then immediately recalled it in their own words. The number of ideas recalled ranged from twenty (37 percent) to forty-four (81 percent), with an average of thirty-three (61 percent). This poor performance was obtained even though the passage was short and the students were bright. Robinson (1941) discovered that performance on objective tests is even worse, and it does not improve much with rereading. These results have been replicated many times (Vaughan & Estes, 1985). Generalizing from these data, we can predict your performance. If you read a chapter through carefully and immediately take an objective test, you will only get about 50 percent correct. Rereading will only improve your score slightly. Many students are shocked when a single reading and a quick review of their college textbooks is not enough. Do not panic, however, you just have to learn to study. Memory research indicates that the keys to remembering what you learn are organizing the material in your mind and relating new information to what you already know.

(204 words)

—*Psychology,* Third Edition, by Stephen Worchel and Wayne Shebilske

Time in seconds = _____

_____ 1. The studies predict that a careful reading of the material will give you a passing grade of 70 percent on an immediate objective test.

_____ 2. The material that was read and tested in the UVA experiment was a history passage.

Passage 5

LANGUAGE DEVELOPMENT

Frederick II, a king who lived almost 800 years ago in Europe, wanted to carry out an experiment. He was interested in learning what human language was the "most natural." He knew that as a child grew up, the child inevitably learned the language spoken by the people around it. Frederick thought this was hiding what would have been the "natural" language of the child. He reasoned that if he could get rid of the effects of this spoken language, the child would still speak, but would speak the "basic, natural" human language. Speaking a language, in his theory, was built in. You can see that the king wasn't all that well informed on the collaboration of environment and heredity. But, then, no one was in those days.

The king instructed a group of foster mothers not to speak at all to the babies they were caring for. It was okay to meet the baby's physical needs, but the foster mothers were not allowed to play with them, babble at them, sing to them, or speak to them. Frederick II figured that the children would "naturally" speak Hebrew, Greek, Latin, or perhaps Arabic. One of those was thought to be the "original" human language.

All the children spoke no language at all. They all died. "For they could not live without the petting and joyful faces and loving words of their foster mothers."

(232 words)

—*Psychology: What It Is/How to Use It* by David Watson

Time in seconds = _____

_____ 1. In his experiment Frederick II found that children will speak the original human language if left alone.

_____ 2. The children died from lack of food.

Preview Before Reading

Do not start reading without looking over the material and thinking about what you need to accomplish. Think about the title and glance over the material for key words and phrases. Read the boldface and italic type. Decide what you think the selection is going to be about and what you want to know when you finish it. A few minutes spent on such an initial survey will help you read more purposefully and thus more quickly.

Activate your schema. What is your prior knowledge on the subject? Pull out your computer chip and prepare to add new information or change existing ideas.

Set a Time Goal for an Assignment

For each of your textbooks, estimate the approximate number of words per page. Write this estimate in the front of your book so you can refer to it during the course. Knowing your reading rate, you can approximate how many minutes it will take you to read a page. Remember, your speed will vary with different textbooks according to the difficulty of the material. Toward the middle of the book, as you become more familiar with the subject, you will read faster than you did in the beginning.

Each time you sit down to do an assignment, count the number of pages you need to complete. Calculate the amount of time it will probably take you, and then look at the clock and write down your projected finishing time. Make your goal realistic and pace yourself so you can make it. Having an expectation will help you speed up your reading and improve your concentration. Do not become an all-night victim of Parkinson's law, which states that the job expands to fit the time available. Don't allow yourself all night or all weekend to read twenty-five pages. Set a goal and then try to meet it. Rather than leisurely sauntering through an assignment, develop a sense of urgency.

Be Flexible

Inefficient readers are overconscientious, too often giving equal time to all words and all types of reading. As mentioned, you should be able to read a newspaper article in much less time than it would take you to read a science or economics passage, especially if you have already heard the highlights on the news. One is more difficult and less familiar than the other. Don't read everything at the same rate. Be willing to switch gears and select the appropriate speed for the job.

Sometimes you may need to look over material for a detail or a specific point. In this case, don't read all the words. Skim until your eyes locate the information you need and then move on to the next task. This is a case of adjusting your speed to your purpose. For example, if you are told to read a history chapter for an exam, read it carefully and spend some time studying it. But, if you have been told to write a half-page summary of five articles in the library, you can probably just skim the material for the main ideas and a few supporting details. Again, adjust your speed to your purpose.

Practice

You cannot improve your running speed unless you get out and run. The same is true with reading. To learn to read faster, practice faster reading techniques every day. As explained in the following paragraph, *wishing* and *willing* are not the same:

> The *wish* to learn is diffuse and general. The *will* to learn is concentrated and specific. The wish to learn means that we repeat a thing again and again hoping for something to happen. The will to learn means that we dig down and analyze, that we try to find out exactly what is wrong and exactly how to put it right.
>
> —*Streamline Your Mind* by James Mursell

Summary Points

- The average adult reading speed is approximately 250 words per minute at 70 percent comprehension.
- Be an aggressive reader.
- Learn to control internal and external distractions so you can concentrate.
- **Regressing** is a crutch; don't do it.
- Rapid readers experience very little subvocalization.
- Expand your **fixations** into phrases or thought units.
- Use a pen as a pacer.
- Survey material before you read it.
- Pace yourself; set time goals for the completion of an assignment.
- Be flexible and adjust your speed to your purpose.
- Practice faster reading.

COLLABORATIVE PROBLEM SOLVING

Form a five-member group and select one of the following questions. Brainstorm and then outline your major points on a transparency. Choose a member to present the group findings to the class.

▶ Create a "Top Ten" list of suggestions for improving your reading speed.

▶ Create a "Top Ten" list of reasons why students have trouble concentrating on what they are reading.

▶ List reasons why prior knowledge influences reading rate.

▶ List reasons why you should not expect to read a textbook at the same reading rate as a novel.

TIMED READING 1   BUSINESS

Use your pen as a pacer and time your reading of the following selection.

Starting time: _____ *minutes* _____ *seconds*

www.Yahoo.com

Refer to the

Reader's Tip

for Business on page 238.

Yahoo! began as an exercise in procrastination. David Filo and Jerry Yang, then Ph.D. candidates at Stanford, were desperately seeking ways to avoid working on their computer science theses. Whereas other Stanford students found distraction in volleyball and Ultimate Frisbee, Jerry and David sought solace from the academic grind in surfing the Web,
5   which in late 1993 was just emerging as a place worth exploring. As they spent more time on the Web, the two both realized that their lists of favorite Web sites—maintained as bookmarks on Mosaic, an early Web browser—were becoming unmanageable. To make their lives easier, they decided to create a simple, "hot list" of their favorite sites, organize it by category, and post it to the Web for easy access.
10   What started as a pastime grew to an obsession. The directory became popular quickly, and people began sending Jerry and David digital fan mail to let them know how much they valued the fledgling Web guide. The two students were excited about the response to their initial efforts and decided to ramp up the pace (with their thesis advisor out of the country, Jerry and David had no pressure to do anything "productive"). They
15   tried to visit and categorize one thousand sites a day. Holed up in an old university trailer, David and Jerry worked like fiends. "Dave and I would sleep in the same spot," Jerry recalled. "He would sleep for about four hours, and I would work. And then he would get up and work and I would go to sleep."
      The directory grew. People noticed—and not just hard-core Web surfers. Jerry and
20   David soon connected with Michael Moritz, a partner at Sequoia Capital, who, like the

two entrepreneurs, thought that there might be a business to be built out of this whimsical, handcobbled directory of Web links. The business model was still unclear. What was apparent, however, was that the Web was growing at an outrageous pace. And in order to find their way around, people needed a guide.

25   In April 1995, Sequoia invested $1 million in Yahoo!, a modest injection of capital (by venture capital standards) that gave the young company the money it needed to move out of its trailer and into the fast lane. Had Sequoia partners retained their 25 percent of the company, their share would now be worth a fortune, for Yahoo! has become one of the most powerful brands on the Internet. With an average of 38 million unique

30   adult users per month, Yahoo! has an audience larger than that of almost any other Web site. It also has greater visibility than many conventional media brands. For example, more people visit Yahoo! each week than watch MTV, CNBC, or Nickelodeon. More people use Yahoo! each month than read *Newsweek, Time,* or *Life.*

Yahoo! spent $5 million to develop and air a series of irreverent TV commercials that

35   showed how everyday people might use Yahoo! to help them solve problems in their lives. John Yost, co-founder of Black Rocket, Yahoo!'s ad agency, got the inspiration for these ads by talking to a typical Yahoo! user during consumer research that the company was conducting:

This was a woman who had never done much with computers, as she didn't see

40   that they were very relevant to her life. She was an orchid grower, however, and when she discovered that through Yahoo!, she could track down all sorts of information about the flowers and exchange ideas with orchid growers throughout the world, she was ecstatic. This whole new world opened up to her. We began to refer to this experience as a "magic moment," and the campaign grew

45   from this idea.

After hearing the story of this woman's epiphany, Yahoo! and Black Rocket developed a series of commercials that played on the idea of Yahoo! as a service that enables everyday people to tap the Internet for solutions to life's dilemmas.

(653 words)

—*eBrands* by Phil Carpenter

Finishing time: _____ *minutes* _____ *seconds*

Total time: _____ *minutes* _____ *seconds*

Rate = _____ *words per minute (see time chart)*

TIME CHART

Time in Seconds and Minutes	Words per Minute	Time in Seconds and Minutes	Words per Minute
60 (1 min.)	653	180 (3 min.)	218
70	560	190	206
80	490	200	196
90	435	210	187
100	392	220	178
110	356	230	170
120 (2 min.)	327	240 (4 min.)	163
130	301	250	157
140	280	260	151
150	261	270	145
160	245	280	140
170	230	300 (5 min.)	131

Answer the following with *T* (true) or *F* (false).

_____ 1. While developing a list of favorite sites that became Yahoo!, Filo and Yang were supposed to be working on their Ph.D. theses in computer science at Stanford University.

_____ 2. Filo and Yang had only one bed in their original university trailer and thus took turns sleeping.

_____ 3. Sequoia Capital presently owns one third of Yahoo!

_____ 4. Yahoo! is a directory of Web links to guide searches.

_____ 5. According to the passage, Yahoo! has more hits each day than all of the other sites on the Internet put together.

_____ 6. The purpose of including the orchid grower example is to illustrate Yahoo!'s advertising strategy.

_____ 7. Black Rocket traded advertising expertise for a 20 percent ownership of Yahoo!

_____ 8. According to the passage, Filo and Yang began compiling their favorite sites as a recreational diversion.

_____ 9. As their work intensified, Filo and Yang set a goal of categorizing one thousand sites each week.

_____ 10. The author implies that the sites on Yahoo! have been compiled using code words and have not been visited personally.

Comprehension = (% correct) _____

TIMED READING 2 🧠 **PSYCHOLOGY**

Use your pen as a pacer and time your reading of the following selection.

Starting time: _____ *minutes* _____ *seconds*

Dr. Fossey and the Gorillas

Refer to the
Reader's Tip
for Psychology on page 44.

The villagers and the gorillas had always maintained a respectful separation and were not overly interested in one another. Dian Fossey, on the other hand, had become a living legend among the African people by living with the gorillas. She was especially known for defending the gorillas against poachers. Her defense included not only guns but also
5   Madison Avenue-style "witchcraft." The latter was probably her most effective weapon. Plastic Halloween skulls and masks, firecrackers, rubber snakes, and the slimy jelly available at any American toy store sent many poachers back to their villages with stories of horrible American sumu.[1] The unwordly defense reflected a misbegotten clash between species, cultures, and egos.

10   The conflict started for 35-year-old Dr. Dian Fossey on the evening of September 24, 1967. Within hours after she founded Karisoke, a research camp for studying mountain gorillas, she warned two Watusi herders and two Batwa poachers that she would tolerate neither cattle herding nor poaching in her part of Parc National des Volcans. Laws had prohibited these activities in the national park for several decades. The laws, however,
15   were weak in comparison with traditions. Tutsi and Twa people had depended on these lands since time immemorial. Tutsi grazed their cattle, and Batwa hunted for food and furs for themselves and Hutu farmers who purchased meat and hides.

The mountain gorillas were an endangered species whose very existence was at stake. The herders, Dr. Fossey argued, were destroying the gorillas' habitat because they
20   had more cattle than they needed. The poachers, Dr. Fossey discovered, were killing adult gorillas to sell their heads and hands for trophies, and their babies to zoos. For the next twenty-three years, therefore, the Karisoke camp was dedicated not only to studying gorillas but also to protecting their habitats and lives.

Dr. Fossey's intolerance toward those who endangered the mountain gorillas was ex-
25   ceeded only by her patience with the gorillas themselves. Dr. Fossey learned to capitalize on the gorillas' curiosity. She attracted them by imitating their own vocalizations and also imitated their self-grooming, submissive crouch and other behaviors. She learned by trial and error what did and did not work.

---
[1]*sumu*: witch

Eventually, Dr. Fossey's patience paid off, and she was able to join the gorilla "pic-
30 nics." She learned the gorillas' individual personalities and gave them names. She named
a young playful male Digit because he had a twisted broken finger and became close
friends with him. "He often invited play by flopping over onto his back, waving stumpy
legs in the air, and looking at me smilingly as if to say, 'How can you resist me?' At such
times, I fear, my scientific detachment dissolved" (Mowat, 1987, p. 101).

35 You can imagine Dr. Fossey's horror on January 1, 1978, when Ian, a young researcher, ran up to her and blurted out, "Oh, God, Dian! I hate to tell you this. Digit's
been murdered" (Mowat, 1987, p. 161). Dr. Fossey's distress escalated when she saw
Digit's mutilated body and heard a Twa poacher confess that he had done it.

Dr. Fossey buried Digit's remains near her cabin in a grave marked by a simple
40 wooden plaque, and she intensified her antipoaching war. On December 26, 1985, she
became a victim of that war. Her lifeless body was found in her bedroom with her skull
"split diagonally from her forehead across her nose and down one cheek to the corner of
her mouth" (Mowat, 1987, p. 336). Dr. Fossey was laid to rest near Digit and more than
a dozen other gorillas with whom she had lived and for whom she had died.

(599 words)

—*Psychology,* Third Edition, by Stephen Worchel and Wayne Shebilske

Finishing time: _____ *minutes* _____ *seconds*

Total time: _____ *minutes* _____ *seconds*

Rate = _____ *words per minute (see time chart)*

TIME CHART

Time in Seconds and Minutes	Words per Minute	Time in Seconds and Minutes	Words per Minute
60 (1 min.)	599	190	189
70	513	200	180
80	449	210	171
90	399	220	163
100	359	230	156
110	327	240 (4 min.)	150
120 (2 min.)	300	250	144
130	276	260	138
140	257	270	133
150	240	280	128
160	225	290	124
170	211	300 (5 min.)	120
180 (3 min.)	200		

Answer the following with *T* (true) or *F* (false).

_____ 1. The author suggests that Fossey wanted the villagers to think she was a witch.

_____ 2. Fossey's primary mission in Africa was to protect the gorillas from poachers.

_____ 3. Fossey was killed by a gorilla.

_____ 4. Fossey imitated the gorillas in order to get closer to them and observe their behaviors.

_____ 5. Digit was an old gorilla who became friendly with Fossey.

Comprehension = (% correct) _____

TIMED READING 1 ⚖ HISTORY

Use your pen as a pacer and time your reading of the following selection.

Starting time: _____ *minutes* _____ *seconds*

Eleanor Roosevelt

Refer to the
Reader's Tip
for History on
page 140.

Eleanor Roosevelt's emergence as a public figure was spurred on by family tragedy. In August 1921, Franklin Roosevelt was stricken with infantile paralysis, or poliomyelitis. While on vacation at their Campobello retreat in Maine, the family often went sailing. One day in August, they spotted a forest fire and put ashore to fight it. After the exhausting battle
5   was over, Franklin went swimming in a landlocked lake near the family home. Later that day he complained of chills and went to bed. The following day he developed a mild fever that worsened. Soon his arms and legs were paralyzed. When specialists arrived, they diagnosed him as having what was commonly called polio. If Franklin did survive, the family was told, he would probably be an invalid for the rest of his days. After the ini-
10   tial shock, Eleanor gathered her composure and saw to her husband's needs. With strong family support and extraordinary determination, Franklin Roosevelt began to recover, first regaining the use of his upper torso and arms. And though he never walked unaided again, within two years of his illness he was back in politics. Franklin and Eleanor now had a new relationship, probably unique in political history. Although they would never again
15   share the love of their earliest years together, they still needed one another. Franklin would work his way back into the political limelight, and Eleanor would be "his eyes and ears." [The following example illustrates her strength and commitment.]

The door to the hospital tent was so low that the tall woman, dressed in a standard Red Cross uniform, had to duck considerably to enter. It was good to be sheltered from

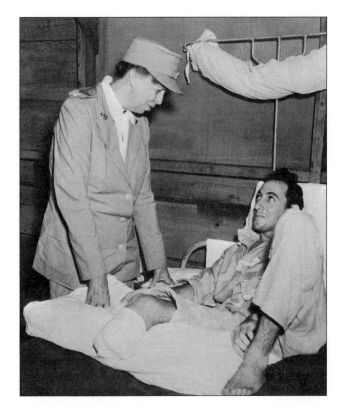

20   the blazing tropical sun of Christmas Island, in the South Pacific, on that fall day of 1943. But her senses were quickly overcome by the combined odors of antiseptic, bandages, and wounded men. There was little time on this stopover, yet it was important that she spend a few moments with a marine whose torso had been horribly mangled by a mortar shell blast. Extremely worried about the young man's survival, the doctors had asked First

25   Lady Eleanor Roosevelt to sit with him for a while and hopefully brighten his spirits and strengthen his will to live.

        Recovering her poise after the initial shock of the hospital scene, she smiled, adjusted her cap, walked to the bedside of the boy shrouded in bandages, and introduced herself as "Mrs. Roosevelt." Heavily drugged and barely conscious, the boy took the hand of the

30   kindly woman, who leaned forward to kiss him on the forehead. In the same unhurried, sincere, and caring manner with which she had spoken to hundreds of Allied soldiers fighting in World War II, Eleanor Roosevelt gently reassured the boy that he would fully recover and come home to the United States. The time was short, and the troop transport plane, on which she had traveled throughout the Pacific, was ready to depart for

35   Honolulu. But she stayed until the very last moment, holding the boy's hand and speaking softly to him. She even promised to visit his mother when she returned to the States. Only when he fell asleep did the first lady leave his bedside.

        Some months later, the same young soldier called on Eleanor Roosevelt at the White House to express his deep gratitude for her visit. Her remarkable impact on his recovery—

40   and on the morale of tens of thousands of Allied soldiers fighting in World War II—symbolizes the person who has been called the most important public woman of the twentieth century. The wife of President Franklin Roosevelt poured the same kind of boundless energy and tireless concern for the betterment of the world into all of her humanitarian interests. Eleanor Roosevelt was a pacesetter for the expansion of rights for minorities, the

45   disabled, and especially women. Still, she remained an embodiment of the characteristics that defined the traditional Victorian American woman.

(658 words)

—*From These Beginnings,* Sixth Edition, Volume Two,
by Roderick Nash and Gregory Graves

Finishing time: _____ *minutes* _____ *seconds*

Total time: _____ *minutes* _____ *seconds*

Rate = _____ *words per minute (see time chart)*

TIME CHART

Time in Seconds and Minutes	Words per Minute	Time in Seconds and Minutes	Words per Minute
60 (1 min.)	658	180 (3 min.)	219
70	564	190	208
80	494	200	197
90	439	210	188
100	395	220	179
110	359	230	172
120 (2 min.)	329	240 (4 min.)	165
130	304	250	158
140	282	260	152
150	263	270	146
160	247	280	141
170	232	300 (5 min.)	132

Answer the following with *T* (true) or *F* (false).

_____ 1. The author suggests that Eleanor Roosevelt performed the presidential tasks of mingling with the people while the president stayed close to home.

_____ 2. On the day Franklin Roosevelt became ill, he had helped fight a forest fire and swam in a cold lake.

_____ 3. After contracting polio, Franklin Roosevelt was never able to leave his wheelchair or travel away from home.

_____ 4. The wounded young man that Eleanor Roosevelt saw died after she left him.

_____ 5. Franklin Roosevelt was President of the United States during World War II.

Comprehension = (% correct) _____

EXPLORE THE NET

● Search the Internet for software that uses the computer to teach you techniques for faster reading. What are the claims of the advertisers, how much does such software cost, and what is your evaluation of its usefulness for you?

FReader Speed Reading Software

www.readingsoft.com/freader.html

Letter Chase Speed Reader

www.letterchase.com/read.htm

● Search for an online reading test that you can take to test your reading speed. How did you do? How well did you comprehend what you read?

Free Online Reading Test

www.readingsoft.com/

For additional readings and exercises, visit the *Breaking Through* Web site:

www.ablongman.com/smith

EVERYDAY READING SKILLS

Managing Workplace Reading

Everyone works at some point. Perhaps you had a full-time job before you entered college, or perhaps you work part time when you are not studying. In any event, all occupations demand some amount of reading. In fact, companies frequently hire expensive consultants to advise employees on efficient methods for meeting workplace reading demands. Typically, these consultants first urge employees to put their reading demands in perspective and set priorities. Memos, for example, may need to be read immediately, but annual reports can probably wait until later. As a next step, the experts strongly suggest handling a piece of paper only once. Their advice is "Do not open a letter and then set it aside to be handled later. If you open a letter, read it and take action." The three action options are respond to it, throw it in the trash, or file it to be used later with other material on the same subject.

> ### Reader's TIP   Managing Workplace Reading
> * Set priorities before reading.
> * Strive to handle a piece of paper only once.
> * Respond to it, discard it, or file it.

Types of Workplace Reading

Work-related documents usually make points quickly, have a serious tone, and are written to inform rather than to entertain. The importance of a document is determined by the way in which the information it contains can affect your job performance. Only you can answer this question, "Which of the following business documents is most important?"

Memos

A **memo** is a brief message used to update co-workers, announce meetings, ask questions, request assistance, or announce decisions. Memos are written in a concise, direct style and can be formal or informal, depending on the sender's level of seniority and the sender's relationship with the recipient. Used correctly, memos are intended for internal messages among company employees and are not generally used for communicating with those outside the organization.

Memos are usually only a few sentences long but can sometimes continue for several pages. The most important information is given at the beginning (see the illustration opposite). Notice dates, times, places, and requests for a response or action. Special formatting like numbered or bulleted lists may be applied to other important items to make them stand out.

TO: Market Designs Personnel
FROM: Sergio Rodriguez, Director of Personnel Services
DATE: March 1, 2001
CC: Veronica Menser, General Manager
RE: Direct Deposit of Paychecks

Please note that beginning with the second pay period in April, all non-salaried employees will have the option of direct deposit of their paychecks. In order to take advantage of this option, you must fill out a Direct Deposit Request Form (sample is attached) and return it to the Accounting Department by no later than March 15. Implementation of the direct deposit option will be delayed one month for those employees who submit their request after that date. If you have any questions, please contact me at extension 225.

---

exercise 1

1. What is the reason for the memo? _____

   _____

2. What is the necessary action? _____

Letters

A **letter** is somewhat more formal than a memo and therefore more appropriate for communication outside a company. Use a letter to give or request information, to congratulate or express appreciation, to register complaints, or to emphasize an action. Like memos, business letters are relatively short and written in a concise, direct manner.

Newsletters

Newsletters are documents published by businesses, organizations, clubs, or schools that combine news, editorial columns, letters, stories, and graphics on subjects of interest to group members. They look like mini-newspapers or multiple-page stapled letters. The purpose of a newsletter is to build group spirit, bind members together, recognize member achievement, and chronicle group events. Each member of the particular group usually receives the newsletter.

Newsletters are basically *propaganda* (persuasive public relations information) for the organization. They tend to report on the past and rarely have any critical information that demands action. If there is a table of contents, use it to guide your reading. If not, read the headings and beginning paragraphs to determine what you care to read.

Reader's TIP   Reading Newsletters

- Read selectively. You may want to read all of the newsletter or none of it.
- Read critically. You cannot consider the information in a newsletter to be objective because it contains information beneficial only to the company or organization. Unflattering information is not included, so the coverage is not balanced.
- Note items that are highlighted, set off by numbers, bullets, capital letters, or that appear in boldface or italic type.

Committee Minutes

At certain meetings, employees participate in creating policies, making reports, and developing plans of action. **Minutes** form the official records of these formal meetings. They list what happened in chronological order and usually have subheadings to indicate the different topics under discussion (see the illustration opposite). For an employee, committee minutes serve two purposes: (1) to verify what was decided for later reference if questions arise, and (2) to record what occurred at a meeting for the benefit of those who did not attend.

At the beginning of official meetings, minutes of the previous meeting are corrected and voted on for approval. Before voting as a committee member, read the minutes to make sure discussions and decisions were recorded accurately. Suggest appropriate corrections. Pay particular attention to statements attributed to you.

Reader's TIP   Reading Minutes

- Use subheadings to guide your reading.
- Confirm the accuracy of any statements attributed to you.
- Double-check the description of decisions that affect your department.

Minutes of the University Planning and Development Committee

Members Present: Angelo, Briggs, Cole, Hall, King, Lopez, Mann, Soto, Vega
October 14, 2001

The meeting was called to order at 1:00 PM by Chair Tony Angelo.

The minutes of the September 10 meeting were approved with one correction in the third paragraph to specify 15 new lights, rather than 12.

Classroom Renovation
Margaret Mann reported that the second floor of Jaramillo Hall is being renovated. Fourteen classrooms will be ready for use by spring semester. Nine of these will be equipped with 26 computer terminals each.

Banners
Foster King reported that the installation of banners with the university logo has been completed in the Student Center. Installation in the library, however, has been delayed because the poles that were shipped were defective. They will be replaced at no cost to the university and should arrive by November 1.

Science Building
Laura Cole reported that faculty and students are still discussing the plans for meeting and group study rooms in the new science building. The subcommittee will meet with the architects on October 18 and present a plan at the next meeting. Juan Soto requested that noise control should be considered in assigning space.

The meeting adjourned at 2:25 PM.

exercise 2

1. Who gave reports at the committee meeting? _____

_____

2. What seems to be the responsibility of this committee? _____

_____

_____

Analytical Reasoning

9

- What is good thinking?
- What are the characteristics of unsuccessful students?
- What are the characteristics of successful students?
- What is involved in good problem solving?
- How do graphic illustrations condense complex information?

Everyday Reading Skills: Reading Direct Mail Advertisements

Identify Analytical Thinking

According to researchers, good thinkers have developed a logical and sequential pattern of working through complex material, whereas poor thinkers lack this habit of analysis. Good thinkers work persistently, believing they will find the answer. They draw on their old knowledge to solve new problems and thus relate, interpret, and integrate what they already know with what they want to learn. Poor thinkers, in contrast, merely collect facts and are unaware of relationships. They cannot put old and new information together to draw conclusions. They seem to have no logical method for problem solving.

Each time you master a textbook, you have learned how to think about a subject. This process offers you both immediate and future benefits. For example, after you struggle through and finally understand an introductory biology text, the same habits of thinking and capturing meaning will transfer to the next biology course, which then will be easier to understand because of your experience. Another future benefit is the ability to apply your learned thinking skills to a new and different task. For instance, the very act of thinking through the complexities of biology will make it easier for you to tackle a chemistry, physics, or anthropology book. Thinking, like everything else, requires practice, and the more you do, the better you become. You gradually develop the ability to educate yourself.

Two researchers, Bloom and Broder, studied both academically successful and unsuccessful college students at the University of Chicago.[1] They described the thinking processes of each (see lists that follow).

Before reading further, think of a student you know personally who is not successful in school. Check to see if the following characteristics describe that student.

An Unsuccessful Student

1. Has no method of attacking new material.
2. Misunderstands or skips directions.
3. Fails to keep the purpose in mind.
4. Is unable to apply present knowledge to new situations.
5. Is passive in thinking and answers questions on the basis of few clues.
6. Uses "impression" or "feeling" to arrive at answers.
7. Is careless in considering details and jumps around from one to another.
8. After making a superficial attempt to reason, gives up and guesses.

Do you know a very successful student? How many of the following characteristics describe that student?

A Successful Student

1. Is careful and systematic in attacking the problem.
2. Can read directions and immediately choose a point at which to begin reasoning.
3. Keeps sight of goals while thinking through the problem.
4. Pulls out key terms and tries to simplify the material.
5. Breaks larger problems into smaller subproblems.
6. Is active and aggressive in seeking meaning.
7. Applies relevant old knowledge to the problem.
8. Is persistent and careful in seeking solutions.

---

[1]B. S. Bloom and L. Broder, *Problem-Solving Process of College Students* (Chicago: University of Chicago Press, 1950).

What kind of student are you? Go back to both lists and circle the characteristics that apply to you.

In studying these characteristics you will see that learning to comprehend what you read is learning to reason and to associate meaning. To understand the ideas in college textbooks, you have to work harder than you do when reading newspapers or magazines. Absorbing the meaning from college texts frequently requires a laborious, step-by-step analysis of details and their relationship to the whole. For example, understanding and explaining the functioning of a part of the body or the evolution of a volcano can be extremely complex.

Successful students attack their studying aggressively and systematically, and they persist to a logical conclusion. As you can see, Bloom and Broder's list of characteristics might just as easily apply to successful problem solving in everyday life as to success in the academic world. These characteristics thus contribute not only to college success but to the long-lasting personal success that is the ultimate reason for going to college. Start developing them!

The two lists by Bloom and Broder also describe test-taking characteristics. Too often students look for gimmicks in test taking, but a well-constructed test is not based on tricks. A high score should reflect the student's ability to think through the problems and come up with logical solutions. Again, the characteristics that describe the successful student also describe the successful test taker. After all, test taking is thinking.

PERSONAL Feedback 1

Name _____

1. If you won the lottery, what would you do with the money? ____
   _____
   _____

2. Why were you glad to leave high school? _____
   _____
   _____

3. What do you miss most about high school? _____
   _____
   _____

4. What does *delayed gratification* mean and how does it apply to
   college? _____
   _____
   _____

5. What causes you the most stress? _____
   _____
   _____

(continued)

6. How can a professor make you feel you are an important part of the class? _____

_____

7. Describe a problem at home, work, or school that you enjoyed attacking and solving systematically. _____

_____

_____

8. What do you feel is your greatest problem-solving strength? ___

_____

_____

Engage in Problem Solving

Another researcher, Whimbey, studied good and poor readers. He noted two prominent features of poor college readers.

> First, there is one-shot thinking rather than extended, sequential construction of understanding; and second, there is a willingness to allow gaps of knowledge to exist, in effect, an attitude of indifference toward achieving an accurate and complete comprehension of situations and relations.[2]

Whimbey and other researchers believe that all students can learn the characteristic behaviors of good readers by increasing their analytical reasoning skills through problem solving. Through analytical reasoning they break problems into small parts and use logic to arrive at a solution. Breaking a complex word problem into sequential steps for solution requires thinking skills similar to those used in breaking a paragraph down to get a main idea, draw a conclusion, or trace the details of a process.

EXAMPLE Read the following word problem and think about how you would figure out the answer.

> Mary is shorter than Carol but taller than Kathy. Sue is taller than Mary but shorter than Carol. Which girl is tallest?

Although the problem may seem rather confusing at first reading, when it is broken down in sequential steps, the answer is simple. The best way to solve this problem is to draw a diagram so you can visualize the relative height of each girl. Reread the problem and place each girl in a position on a vertical line:

---

[2]Arthur Whimbey, *Intelligence Can Be Taught* (New York: E. P. Dutton, 1975), 55.

Mary is shorter than Carol
⌐ Carol
└ Mary

but taller than Kathy.
⌐ Carol
├ Mary
└ Kathy

Sue is taller than Mary, but shorter than Carol.
⌐ Carol
├ Sue
├ Mary
└ Kathy

EXPLANATION The diagram indicates that the tallest girl is Carol.

Whimbey found that analytical reasoning skills can be taught through practice. He devised a variety of word problems similar to those that follow to help students learn. The thinking strategies used to solve these problems apply in every academic task, not just in reading textbooks. Break each problem in the exercise into parts and sequentially work toward a solution. You may want to do the first exercise with someone else so you can discuss the steps leading to a solution, and then try the rest on your own.

Make notes or diagrams to help you solve the following problems.

exercise 1

_____ 1. George and Scott are the same age. Beth is younger than George, and Jack is older than Scott. Tom is older than Scott but younger than Jack. Who is the oldest? (Do your figuring next to the diagram.)

_____ 2. Which set of letters is different from the other three?

a. LMOP   b. EFHI   c. RSTV   d. JKMN

_____ 3. According to the pattern, which letters should come next in the series?

B C D B E F B G __ __ __

_____ 4. An airplane left New York at 4:25 and arrived in Miami 4 hours and 45 minutes later. What time did it arrive in Miami?

_____ 5. According to the pattern, which numbers should come next in the series?

2 1 3 2 4 3 5 4 6 5 __ __ __

_____ 6. According to the pattern, what numbers and letters should come next in the series?

G H 2 K L 3 P Q 4 __ __ __

_____ 7. In how many days of the week are there more than three letters and less than five letters preceding the part of the word that is the same in all seven?

_____ 8. According to the pattern, what numbers should come next in the series?

1 2 3 6 4 5 6 15 7 8 9 24 10 __ __ __

9. Tim, Larry, and Dave got different scores on a history test. Tim scored higher than Larry but lower than Dave. Their last names, not in order, are Lewis, Davis, and Conners. Davis got the lowest score and Lewis got the highest. What are the last names of Tim and Larry?

_____10. How many letters are in either the rectangle or the square but not in both?

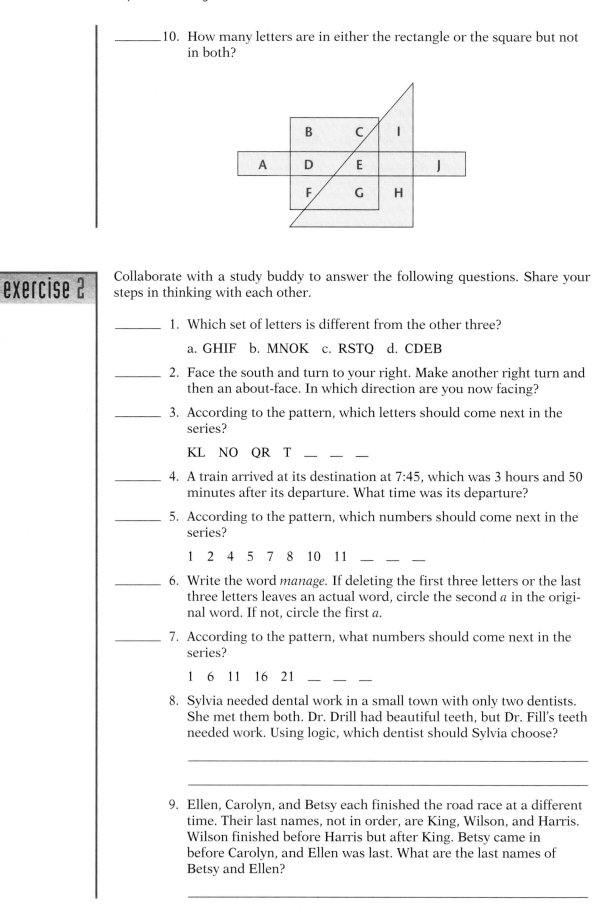

exercise 2

Collaborate with a study buddy to answer the following questions. Share your steps in thinking with each other.

_____ 1. Which set of letters is different from the other three?

a. GHIF   b. MNOK   c. RSTQ   d. CDEB

_____ 2. Face the south and turn to your right. Make another right turn and then an about-face. In which direction are you now facing?

_____ 3. According to the pattern, which letters should come next in the series?

KL   NO   QR   T __ __ __

_____ 4. A train arrived at its destination at 7:45, which was 3 hours and 50 minutes after its departure. What time was its departure?

_____ 5. According to the pattern, which numbers should come next in the series?

1   2   4   5   7   8   10   11 __ __ __

_____ 6. Write the word *manage*. If deleting the first three letters or the last three letters leaves an actual word, circle the second *a* in the original word. If not, circle the first *a*.

_____ 7. According to the pattern, what numbers should come next in the series?

1   6   11   16   21 __ __ __

8. Sylvia needed dental work in a small town with only two dentists. She met them both. Dr. Drill had beautiful teeth, but Dr. Fill's teeth needed work. Using logic, which dentist should Sylvia choose?

_____

_____

9. Ellen, Carolyn, and Betsy each finished the road race at a different time. Their last names, not in order, are King, Wilson, and Harris. Wilson finished before Harris but after King. Betsy came in before Carolyn, and Ellen was last. What are the last names of Betsy and Ellen?

_____

10. Fran, Sally, and Marsha collected old books from different countries. Together they had a total of eighteen books. Six of the books are from Spain, with one more than that being the total from Asia and one less being the total from Holland. Sally has two books from Spain, and Fran has an equal number from Asia. Marsha has twice as many books from Asia as Fran has. Both Marsha and Fran have only one book each from Holland, and Fran has only one from Spain. How many books does Sally have? How many does Marsha have?

	Holland	Spain	Asia	**Total**
Fran				
Sally				
Marsha				
Total				

Do you prefer working alone or did you benefit more from working with a study buddy?

Analytical Reasoning in Textbooks

Apply analytical reasoning to every page of every textbook you read. Reading is problem solving, and reading is thinking. Each time you answer a question about what you have read, you are displaying the characteristics of a successful student. Get in the habit of working through complex ideas carefully and systematically. Simplify the material, and break it into smaller, more manageable ideas. Draw on what you already know, and actively and aggressively seek to understand.

To help you visualize complex ideas, textbooks frequently include maps, charts, diagrams, and graphs. These illustrations condense a lot of information into one picture. Refer to such graphic illustrations while you read; the material will then be easier to understand.

Included in this chapter are several exercises on graphic illustrations and problems that require logical and sequential thinking. Before doing the exercises, read the hints in the Reader's Tip.

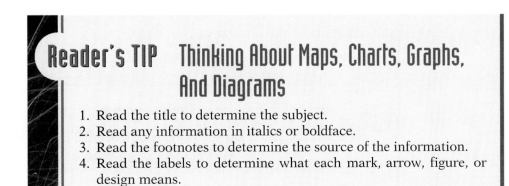

Reader's TIP Thinking About Maps, Charts, Graphs, And Diagrams

1. Read the title to determine the subject.
2. Read any information in italics or boldface.
3. Read the footnotes to determine the source of the information.
4. Read the labels to determine what each mark, arrow, figure, or design means.

5. Figure out the legend, the key on a map that shows what the markings represent.
6. Notice if numbers are written in some unit of measurement, such as percentages, dollars, thousands, millions, or billions.
7. Notice the trends and the extremes. What is the average, and what are the highs and lows?
8. Refer back and forth to the text to follow a process or label parts.
9. Draw conclusions based on the information.
10. Do not read more into the illustration than is supported by fact. In other words, don't draw conclusions that cannot be proved.

exercise 3

Collaborate with a study buddy to answer the following questions.

Female Representation in State Government*

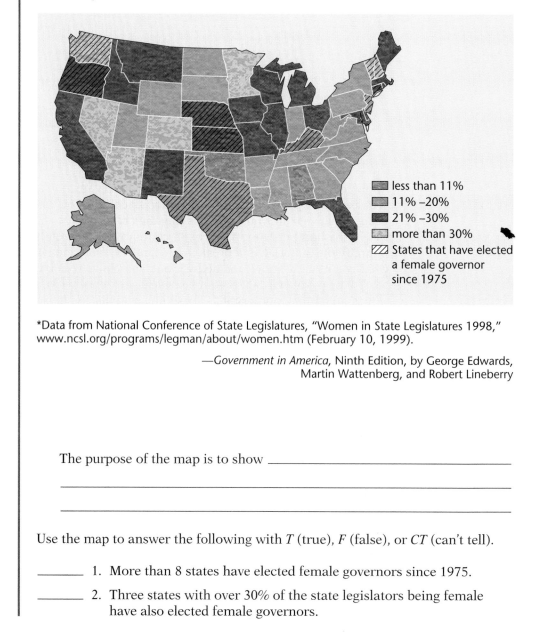

less than 11%
11% –20%
21% –30%
more than 30%
States that have elected a female governor since 1975

*Data from National Conference of State Legislatures, "Women in State Legislatures 1998," www.ncsl.org/programs/legman/about/women.htm (February 10, 1999).

—*Government in America*, Ninth Edition, by George Edwards, Martin Wattenberg, and Robert Lineberry

The purpose of the map is to show _____

_____

_____

Use the map to answer the following with *T* (true), *F* (false), or *CT* (can't tell).

_____ 1. More than 8 states have elected female governors since 1975.

_____ 2. Three states with over 30% of the state legislators being female have also elected female governors.

_____ 3. According to the map, California has a higher percentage of females in the state legislature than Florida or Maine.

_____ 4. The states with a higher percentage of female representatives have more females in the state population.

_____ 5. According to the map, there are no states in the Southeast with more than 30% female representation in the state legislatures.

6. Although the map does not show reasons, why do you think more states have not had female governors?

_____

exercise 4

Collaborate with a study buddy to review the chart and answer the questions that follow. Notice that numbers are in both thousands and percentages.

MINORITY POPULATIONS IN AMERICA IN 1994 AND PROJECTED FOR 2000 AND 2050*

	Number (Thousands)	Percentage of Population
1994		
African American	31,192	12.0
Latino	26,077	10.0
Asian American	8,438	3.2
American Indian	1,907	0.7
2000		
African American	33,741	12.2
Latino	31,166	11.3
Asian American	11,407	4.1
American Indian	2,055	0.7
2050		
African American	56,346	14.4
Latino	88,071	22.5
Asian American	38,064	9.7
American Indian	3,701	0.9

*Data from U.S. Bureau of the Census (1995a).

—*Sociology*, Second Edition, by Richard Appelbaum and William Chambliss

The purpose of this chart is to _____

_____

Use the chart to answer the following with *T* (true), *F* (false), or *CT* (can't tell).

_____ 1. By 2000 there were an estimated 2,549 more African Americans in the population than in 1994.

_____ 2. The greatest estimated minority group increase between the periods covered before and after 2000 is Latino.

_____ 3. The ranking of minority groups by percentage of the population is estimated to remain the same in 1994, 2000, and 2050.

_____ 4. Immigration is the primary force in the increase in the Latino population.

_____ 5. From 1994 to 2050 the estimated increase in the American Indian population is 2 percent.

6. Although the chart does not show reasons, why would you guess that the Latino population is predicted to increase by a greater percentage by 2050 than the African American population?

_____

exercise 5

Collaborate with a study buddy, first to explain the information on the graph and then to answer the questions.

The Coming Minority Majority. Based on the basis of current birthrates and immigration rates, the Census Bureau estimates that the demographics of the country should change as shown in the accompanying graph. Extend the lines a bit beyond the year 2050, and it is clear that the minority groups will soon be in the majority nationwide. Of course, should birth and immigration change, so will these estimates.

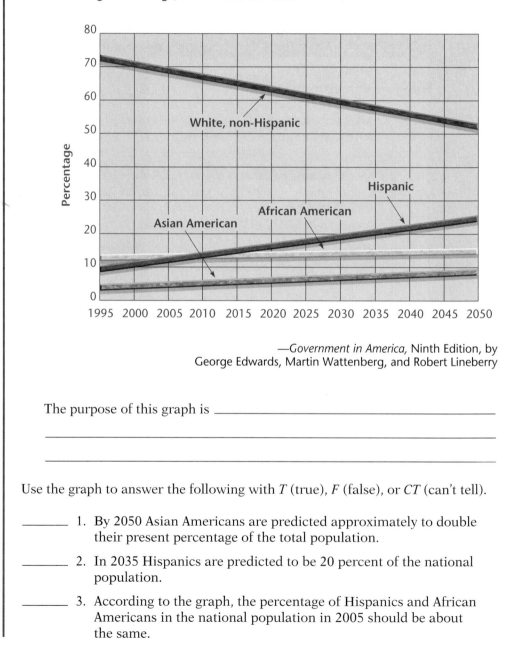

—*Government in America,* Ninth Edition, by
George Edwards, Martin Wattenberg, and Robert Lineberry

The purpose of this graph is _____

_____

_____

Use the graph to answer the following with *T* (true), *F* (false), or *CT* (can't tell).

_____ 1. By 2050 Asian Americans are predicted approximately to double their present percentage of the total population.

_____ 2. In 2035 Hispanics are predicted to be 20 percent of the national population.

_____ 3. According to the graph, the percentage of Hispanics and African Americans in the national population in 2005 should be about the same.

_____ 4. In the fifty years prior to 2050, the percentage of the non-Hispanic white population will decrease by over 30%.

_____ 5. By 2060 the Hispanic population will be in the majority.

6. Compare the estimated percentages for the year 2050 on this graph with the predicted changes on the previous chart. Which are the same, and which are different? Why might differences occur?

_____

exercise 6

Collaborate to study the graph and to answer the questions.

Time Served in State Prisons Versus Court Sentence for Selected Offenses*

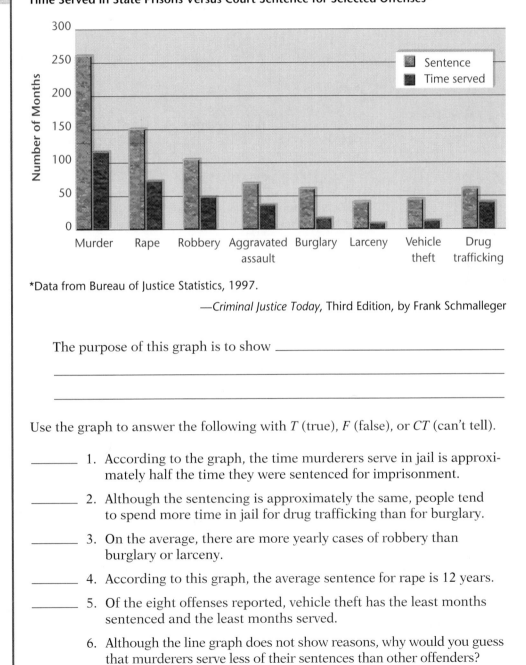

*Data from Bureau of Justice Statistics, 1997.

—*Criminal Justice Today*, Third Edition, by Frank Schmalleger

The purpose of this graph is to show _____

_____

_____

Use the graph to answer the following with *T* (true), *F* (false), or *CT* (can't tell).

_____ 1. According to the graph, the time murderers serve in jail is approximately half the time they were sentenced for imprisonment.

_____ 2. Although the sentencing is approximately the same, people tend to spend more time in jail for drug trafficking than for burglary.

_____ 3. On the average, there are more yearly cases of robbery than burglary or larceny.

_____ 4. According to this graph, the average sentence for rape is 12 years.

_____ 5. Of the eight offenses reported, vehicle theft has the least months sentenced and the least months served.

6. Although the line graph does not show reasons, why would you guess that murderers serve less of their sentences than other offenders?

exercise 7

Read the passage and use the drawing to help visualize your thoughts. Collaborate with a study buddy to answer the questions.

TYPES OF LAYERING

Layering may be described as modified cutting. The plant part to be cut is rooted before it is completely cut away from the parent plant. Roots or stems may be propagated by layering. The part of the plant that is eventually cut off to be grown independently is called the *layer*. Layering is accomplished in a variety of ways that may occur naturally or with the help of humans.

TIP LAYERING

Species such as boysenberry and black raspberry have been known to propagate naturally by *tip layering*. When the tips of the current season's long canes bend down and touch the soil, they turn around to grow upward once again. At the point of contact with the soil, roots start to develop, provided the portion is adequately covered with soil.

RUNNERS

Natural layering involving roots occurs in horticultural species such as the strawberry. As the plant grows, it produces *runners*, or *stolons* (above-ground creeping stems), in various directions. When the nodes on these structures come into contact with the soil, roots develop, and eventually new plants arise at these nodes.

SUCKERS

Suckers are adventitious shoots produced by species including spirea, red raspberry, and blackberry. These shoots arise from the horizontal roots produced by these plants. The result of this habit is that a single original plant may produce several new plants clustered together.

SIMPLE LAYERING

The simple layering method of propagation is easier to employ in species that produce long, flexible shoots that arise from the plant at ground level because it requires the part to be layered to bend to touch the ground. The selected stem is girdled or nicked about halfway through the portion that will be in contact with the soil. Nicking or girdling the stem causes auxins and carbohydrates to accumulate in the area of the stem for quick rooting.

SERPENTINE LAYERING

Several layers can be obtained from one shoot that is anchored to the ground. The flexible shoot is anchored to the soil at various sites rather than buried along the entire length.

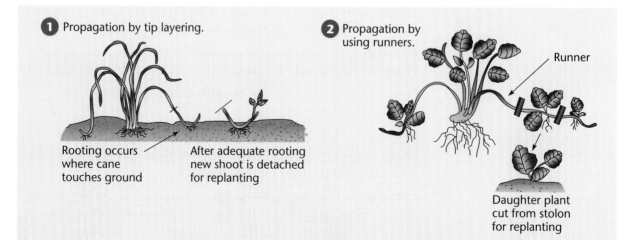

1 Propagation by tip layering.

Rooting occurs where cane touches ground

After adequate rooting new shoot is detached for replanting

2 Propagation by using runners.

Runner

Daughter plant cut from stolon for replanting

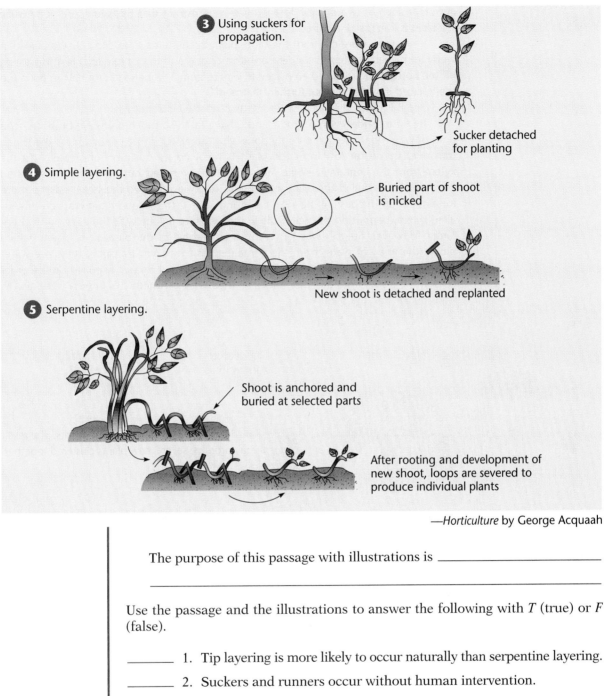

3 Using suckers for propagation.

Sucker detached for planting

4 Simple layering.

Buried part of shoot is nicked

New shoot is detached and replanted

5 Serpentine layering.

Shoot is anchored and buried at selected parts

After rooting and development of new shoot, loops are severed to produce individual plants

—*Horticulture* by George Acquaah

The purpose of this passage with illustrations is _____

_____

Use the passage and the illustrations to answer the following with *T* (true) or *F* (false).

_____ 1. Tip layering is more likely to occur naturally than serpentine layering.

_____ 2. Suckers and runners occur without human intervention.

_____ 3. A node must be nicked or girdled to stimulate growth.

_____ 4. Serpentine layering is basically multiple layering.

_____ 5. All of the methods of layering require a part of the plant to come in contact with the soil.

Read the passage and use the drawing to help visualize your thoughts.

exercise 8

THE KINDEST CUT

After thanking the donor for a bouquet of flowers and sniffing them appreciatively, the next step is to find a vase and put them in water. The florist usually sends a message to cut off an inch or two of stem first; purists even instruct that this should be done while the stem is immersed in water.

Three stems were cut from the same plant at the same time. Stem 1 was placed in water immediately. Stem 2 was left for half an hour, and then a two-inch length was cut off the bottom end. It was then placed in water. Stem 3 was also left for half an hour and then placed in water without further treatment.

Stem 3 is distinctly wilted, whereas the other two look normal.

The figure shows why Stems 1 and 2 have fared so much better: in both, the column of water in the xylem is continuous with the water in the container. As the leaves transpire, the water lost from the plant is replaced by pulling more water into the xylem from the container. While Stems 2 and 3 were left out of water, transpiration from the leaves pulled the water column in the xylem up into the stem, leaving room for air to enter the base of the xylem. Cutting Stem 2 the second time removed this air-filled xylem, permitting the water still in the xylem to link up with the water in the container. However, Stem 3 was left with an air bubble at the base of its xylem, which blocks the entry of water from the container. As the leaves transpire, they lose water faster than the dwindling xylem contents can replace it. Water is pulled out of other cells in the leaves until they no longer fill their walls. Without this internal support the walls buckle and the plant wilts.

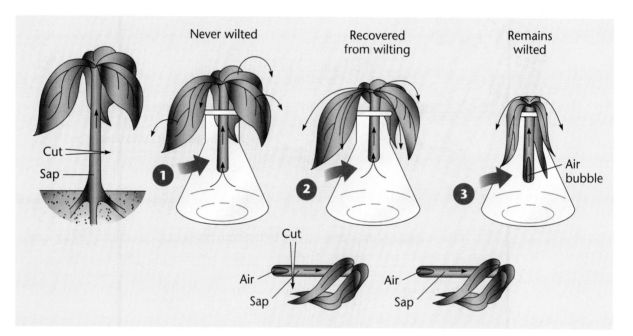

—*A Journey into Life*, Second Edition, by Karen Arms and Pamela Camp

Use the passage and the diagram to answer the following questions with *T* (true) or *F* (false).

_____ 1. Stem 2 would not be receiving water unless it had been cut a second time.

_____ 2. The flow of water in Stem 1 is not blocked by an air bubble.

_____ 3. The xylem is in the stem of the plant.

_____ 4. The xylem of Stem 2 was blocked before the second cut.

_____ 5. If cut immediately above the air bubble and placed in water, Stem 3 might recover freshness.

exercise 9

Answer the following questions and then analyze your responses in order to learn about yourself.

PSYCHOLOGICAL TIME

Attitudes toward time vary from one culture to another. In one study, for example, the accuracy of clocks was measured in six cultures—Japan, Indonesia, Italy, England, Taiwan, and the United States. Japan had the most accurate and Indonesia had the least accurate clocks. A measure of the speed at which people in these six cultures walked found that the Japanese walked the fastest, the Indonesians the slowest.

WHAT TIME DO YOU HAVE?

For each statement, indicate whether the statement is true (*T*) or untrue (*F*) of your general attitude and behavior.

_____ 1. Meeting tomorrow's deadlines and doing other necessary work comes before tonight's partying.

_____ 2. I meet my deadlines and due dates.

_____ 3. I complete projects on time by making steady progress.

_____ 4. I am able to resist temptations when I know there is work to be done.

_____ 5. I keep working at a difficult, uninteresting task if it will help me get ahead.

_____ 6. If things don't get done on time, I don't worry about it.

_____ 7. I think that it's useless to plan too far ahead because things hardly ever come out the way you planned anyway.

_____ 8. I try to live one day at a time.

_____ 9. I live to make better what *is* rather than to be concerned about what *will* be.

_____ 10. It seems to me that it doesn't make sense to worry about the future, since fate determines that whatever will be, will be.

_____ 11. I believe that getting together with friends to party is one of life's important pleasures.

_____ 12. I do things impulsively, making decisions on the spur of the moment.

_____ 13. I take risks to put excitement in my life.

_____ 14. I get drunk at parties.

_____ 15. It's fun to gamble.

_____ 16. Thinking about the future is pleasant to me.

_____ 17. When I want to achieve something, I set subgoals and consider specific means for reaching those goals.

_____ 18. It seems to me that my career path is pretty well laid out.

_____ 19. It upsets me to be late for appointments.

_____ 20. I meet my obligations to friends and authorities on time.

_____ 21. I get irritated at people who keep me waiting when we've agreed to meet at a given time.

_____ 22. It makes sense to invest a substantial part of my income in insurance premiums.

_____23. I believe that "A stitch in time saves nine."

_____24. I believe that "A bird in the hand is worth two in the bush."

_____25. I believe it is important to save for a rainy day.

_____26. I believe a person's day should be planned each morning.

_____27. I make lists of things I must do.

INTERPRETATION

This time test measures seven different factors. If you selected true (*T*) for all or most of the questions within any given factor, you are probably high on that factor. If you selected untrue (*F*) for all or most of the questions within any given factor, you are probably low on that factor.

Count the number of true (*T*) responses for each area.

1–5_____, 6–10_____, 11–15_____, 16–18_____, 19–21_____,

22–25_____, 26–27_____

The first factor, measured by questions 1–5, is a future, work motivation, perseverance orientation. These people have a strong work ethic and are committed to completing a task despite difficulties and temptations. The second factor (questions 6–10) is a present, fatalistic, worry-free orientation. High scorers on this factor live one day at a time, not necessarily to enjoy the day but to avoid planning for the next day or anxiety about the future.

The third factor (questions 11–15) is a present, pleasure-seeking, partying orientation. These people enjoy the present, take risks, and engage in a variety of impulsive actions. The fourth factor (questions 16–18) is a future, goal-seeking, and planning orientation. These people derive special pleasure from planning and achieving a variety of goals.

The fifth factor (questions 19–21) is a time-sensitivity orientation. People who score high are especially sensitive to time and its role in social obligations. The sixth factor (questions 22–25) is a future, practical action orientation. These people do what they have to do—take practical actions—to achieve the future they want.

The seventh factor (questions 26–27) is a future, somewhat obsessive daily planning orientation. High scorers on this factor make daily "to do" lists and devote great attention to specific details.

—*Essentials of Human Communication*, Third Edition, by Joseph DeVito

Using your rankings on the scale, write a brief description of your attitude and behavior regarding time.

I am _____

_____

_____

COLLABORATIVE PROBLEM SOLVING

Form a five-member group and select one of the following questions. Brainstorm and then outline your major points on a transparency. Choose a member to present the group findings to the class.

▶ Record the month in which each class member was born. Create a bar graph showing the number of class birthdays in each month. Put the months on the horizontal line and indicate the number of birthdays in each month on the vertical line.

▶ Record the month in which each class member was born. Create a bar graph showing the number of class birthdays in each month. Indicate the number of birthdays on the horizontal line and put the months on the vertical line.

▶ Record the date of the month on which each class member was born. Create a bar graph showing the number of class birthdays on each date. Put the dates on the horizontal line and indicate the number of birthdays on each date on the vertical line.

▶ Record the date of the month on which each class member was born. Create a bar graph showing the number of class birthdays on each date. Indicate the number of birthdays on the horizontal line and put the dates on the vertical line.

Summary Points

- Reading is thinking.
- Good thinkers have developed a logical and sequential pattern of working through complex material.
- Good thinkers work persistently, believing they will find the answer.
- Good thinkers draw on old knowledge to solve new problems.
- Good thinkers are active and aggressive in seeking meaning.
- Good thinkers break larger problems into smaller problems.
- Good thinkers pull out key terms and simplify problems.

THINKING BEFORE READING

Preview for content and organizational clues. Activate your schema and anticipate what you will learn.

What type of natural disaster most threatens your area?

What was the name of last year's most destructive hurricane?

Why is Florida so vulnerable to hurricanes?

THINKING DURING READING

As you read, predict, picture, relate, monitor, and correct.

tranquil	rotary	precipitation	deceptive	liberated
aloft	barrage	debris	torrential	advent

What does the prefix in *advent* mean?

Why is the pronunciation of *debris* unexpected?

What is the opposite of *torrential*?

Refer to the
Reader's Tip
for Sciences on
page 51.

Profile of a Hurricane

Most of us view the weather in the tropics with favor. Places like Hawaii and the islands of the Caribbean are known for their lack of significant day-to-day variations. Warm breezes, steady temperatures, and rains that come as heavy but brief tropical showers are expected. It is ironic that these relatively tranquil regions sometimes produce the most vio-
5   lent storms on Earth.

These intense tropical storms are known in various parts of the world by different names. In the western Pacific, they are called *typhoons*, and in the Indian Ocean, including the Bay of Bengal and Arabian Sea, they are simply called *cyclones*. In the following discussion, these storms will be referred to as hurricanes. The term *hurricane* is derived
10   from Huracan, a Carib god of evil.

Although many tropical disturbances develop each year, only a few reach hurricane status. By international agreement a hurricane has wind speeds of at least 119 kilometers[1] per hour and a rotary circulation. Mature hurricanes average about 600 kilometers across, although they can range in diameter from 100 kilometers up to about 1500 kilometers.
15   From the outer edge of the hurricane to the center, the barometric pressure has sometimes dropped 60 millibars, from 1010 to 950 millibars. The lowest pressures ever recorded in the western hemisphere are associated with these storms.

At the very center of the storm is the eye of the hurricane. This well-known feature is a zone where precipitation ceases and winds subside. The eye offers a brief but deceptive
20   break from the extreme weather in the enormous curving wall clouds that surround it. The air within the eye gradually descends and heats by compression, making it the warmest part of the storm. Although many people believe that the eye is characterized by

---

[1]1 kilometer is equal to approximately 0.62 mile.

clear blue skies, this is usually not the case because the subsidence in the eye is seldom strong enough to produce cloudless conditions. Although the sky appears much brighter
25 in this region, scattered clouds at various levels are common.

A hurricane is a heat engine that is fueled by the latent heat liberated when huge quantities of water vapor condense. The amount of energy produced by a typical hurricane in just a single day is truly immense—roughly equivalent to the entire electrical energy production of the United States in a year.

30 Hurricanes develop most often in the late summer when ocean waters have reached temperatures of 27°C or higher and are thus able to provide the necessary heat and moisture to the air. This ocean-water temperature requirement is thought to account for the fact that hurricanes do not form over the relatively cool waters of the South Atlantic and the eastern South Pacific.

35 Hurricanes diminish in intensity whenever they (1) move over ocean waters that cannot supply warm, moist tropical air, (2) move onto land, or (3) reach a location where the large-scale flow aloft is unfavorable. In addition, because the land is usually cooler than the ocean, the low-level air is chilled rather than warmed. Moreover, the increased surface roughness over land results in a rapid reduction in surface wind speeds.

STORM SURGE

40 Without question, the most devastating damage in the coastal zone is caused by the storm surge. It not only accounts for a large share of coastal property losses, but it is also responsible for 90 percent of all hurricane-caused deaths. A storm surge is a dome of water 65 to 80 kilometers wide that sweeps across the coast near the point where the eye makes landfall. If all wave activity were smoothed out, the storm surge is the height of the
45 water above normal tide level. In addition, tremendous wave activity is superimposed on the surge. We can easily imagine the damage that this surge of water could inflict on low-lying coastal areas.

Wind speeds recorded by a data buoy in the eastern Gulf of Mexico during the passage of Hurricane Kate on November 20 and 21, 1985. The substantially lower wind speeds associated with the eye of the storm are clearly shown.*

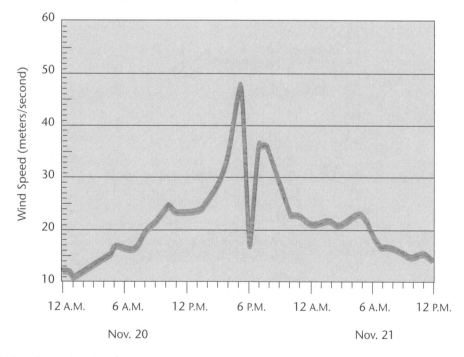

*After the National Hurricane Center/NOAA.

WIND DAMAGE

Destruction caused by wind is perhaps the most obvious of the classes of hurricane damage. For some structures, the force of the wind is sufficient to cause total ruin. Mobile
50 homes are particularly vulnerable. In addition, the strong winds can create a dangerous
barrage of flying debris.

INLAND FLOODING

The torrential rains that accompany most hurricanes represent a third significant threat—
flooding. Whereas the effects of storm surge and strong winds are concentrated in
coastal areas, heavy rains may affect places hundreds of kilometers from the coast for sev-
55 eral days after the storm has lost its hurricane-force winds.

DETECTING HURRICANES

The advent of weather satellites has largely solved the problem of detecting tropical
storms and has significantly improved monitoring. However, satellites are remote sensors,
and it is not unusual for wind-speed estimates to be off by tens of kilometers per hour.

(773 words)

—*The Atmosphere,* Seventh Edition, by Frederick Lutgens and Edward Tarbuck

THINKING AFTER READING

RECALL Self-test your understanding. Your instructor may choose to give you a
true-false review.

REACT Why are mobile homes particularly vulnerable to hurricane damage?

REFLECT Under what conditions might an area benefit from a hurricane?

THINK CRITICALLY With satellite technology, the tracking of hurricanes has become more accurate. How can improved predicting of hurricane patterns save
live, property, and money? Write your answer on a separate sheet of paper.

ANALYTICAL REASONING

Use the graph on page 333 to answer the following items with *T* (true) or *F*
(false).

_____ 1. The graph covers a 72-hour period.

_____ 2. Wind speed increased steadily without any decreases from 12 a.m.
to 4 p.m. on November 20.

_____ 3. The calm in the eye of the hurricane lasted approximately three
hours.

_____ 4. Wind speeds recorded after the eye were not as fast as those
recorded before the eye.

_____ 5. Prior to the eye, winds reached speeds of approximately 48 meters
per second.

Name _____

Date _____

COMPREHENSION QUESTIONS

Answer the following with *a, b, c,* or *d,* or fill in the blank. In order to help you analyze your strengths and weaknesses, the question types are indicated.

Main Idea _____ 1. The best statement of the main idea of the selection is

    a. calm places can produce intense tropical storms.
    b. hurricanes cause intense damage and leave many people homeless each year.
    c. a hurricane is an intense tropical storm that develops over warm tropical waters and can cause extreme damage from winds and water on land.
    d. a hurricane is a heat engine that produces electricity.

Detail _____ 2. By international agreement, a hurricane is defined by all of the following *except*

    a. wind speed of 119 kilometers per hour.
    b. rotary circulation.
    c. a drop in barometric pressure.
    d. an eye with a clear blue sky.

Detail _____ 3. The eye of a hurricane

    a. has the most damaging winds.
    b. produces torrential rains.
    c. is the warmest part of the storm.
    d. signals the end of the storm.

Inference _____ 4. According to the passage, hurricanes probably begin developing in late summer because

    a. the season will soon be changing to autumn.
    b. the ocean water temperature is highest.
    c. cool winds from the South Atlantic reach the Caribbean.
    d. typhoons and cyclones occur during the winter.

Detail _____ 5. All of the following will diminish the intensity of a hurricane except

    a. cold ocean water.
    b. land.
    c. warm ocean air.
    d. cold land air.

Detail 6. What is the purpose of the graph on page 333? _____

_____

_____

Detail _____ 7. The storm surge is characterized by all of the following except

    a. it pushes ocean water across coastal property.
    b. it occurs where the eye of the hurricane hits land.
    c. it occurs at low tide.
    d. it surges and floods.

Answer the following with *T* (true), *F* (false), or *CT* (can't tell).

Inference _____ 8. The author implies that typhoons, cyclones, and hurricanes are all about the same.

Detail _____ 9. High winds from a hurricane usually kill more people than the storms surges.

Detail _____ 10. The storm surge can be as much as 80 kilometers high.

VOCABULARY

Answer the following with *a*, *b*, *c*, or *d* for the word or phrase that best defines the boldface word as used in the selection. The number in parentheses indicates the line of the passage in which the word is located.

_____ 1. "**tranquil** regions "
(4)

a. warm
b. calm
c. breezy
d. tropical

_____ 6 "large-scale flow **aloft**" (37)

a. below
b. around
c. overhead
d. downhill

_____ 2. "**rotary** circulation"
(13)

a. intense
b. random
c. rapid
d. circular

_____ 7. "dangerous **barrage**"
(50–51)

a. circle
b. wall
c. blast
d. barrier

_____ 3. "**precipitation** ceases" (19)

a. rain
b. heat
c. temperature
d. winds

_____ 8. "flying **debris**" (51)

a. dirt
b. insects
c. water
d. trash

_____ 4. "**deceptive** break" (19–20)

a. fearful
b. uneventful
c. turbulent
d. deceiving

_____ 9. "**torrential** rains" (52)

a. sudden
b. frequent
c. annoying
d. fierce

_____ 5. "heat **liberated**"
(26)

a. added
b. freed
c. mixed
d. multiplied

_____ 10. "**advent** of weather satellites" (56)

a. advertisement
b. appearance
c. location
d. idea

VOCABULARY ENRICHMENT

Context Clues

Select the word from the list that completes the sentences.

tranquil	rotary	precipitation	deceptive	liberated
aloft	barrage	debris	torrential	advent

1. After the storm, the shore was littered with _____

2. When the summer tourists come to Maine, the small coastal towns are no longer _____

3. _____ women do not mind speaking out on issues, even if the opinions are unpopular.

4. Five days of _____ rain created flooding in the fields and threatened the livestock.

5. The forecast for the evening is for _____ in the form of snow or sleet.

6. With the _____ of the new millennium, people are hoping for peace and prosperity.

7. The pickpocket had a _____ way of smiling and asking unsuspecting tourists for directions.

8. The scientists sent a weather balloon _____ to record data for the experiment.

9. The speaker was hit by a _____ of questions about the human rights policies in China.

10. The _____ fan over the bed moves the air enough to keep the room cool on moderate spring nights.

ASSESS YOUR LEARNING

Review confusing questions, seek clarification, and make notes in your text to help you remember new information and vocabulary.

EXPLORE THE NET

● List the top ten deadliest, costliest, and most intense hurricanes to occur in the United States since 1900.

National Hurricane Center Tropical Prediction Center Past Hurricane History

www.nhc.noaa.gov/pastall.html

● Hurricanes can be detected through the use of satellite imagery. Search for satellite imagery of current conditions in the Gulf of Mexico hurricane region, the Atlantic hurricane region, and the Pacific hurricane region.

Tropical Prediction Center/National Hurricane Center

www.nhc.noaa.gov/

For additional readings and exercises, visit the *Breaking Through* Web site:

www.ablongman.com/smith

SELECTION 2 🧠 **PSYCHOLOGY**

THINKING BEFORE READING

Preview for content and organizational clues. Activate your schema and anticipate what you will learn.

Do fraternity and sorority members engage in group activities that they would not participate in as individuals?

Did German citizens know about Nazi death camps?

What happened at Jonestown?

I think this selection will say that _____

VOCABULARY PREVIEW

Are you familiar with these words?

underlings	adjacent	ominous	legitimate	anguish
vividly	communal	incomprehensible	mock	solitary

What is the root of *communal*?

Is breaking a mirror considered an *ominous* sign?

What is real about a *mock* trial?

Your instructor may choose to give a true-false vocabulary review before or after reading.

THINKING DURING READING

As you read, use the five thinking strategies of a good reader: predict, picture, relate, monitor, and correct.

Refer to the
Reader's Tip
for Psychology on page 44.

Obedience

Although it's possible to get a group of high school students to conform to Nazi-like values and beliefs, it's still a long way from there to the death camps and the murder of millions of people. Or is it? During the Nuremberg trials, in which the Nazi war criminals were brought to account, one phrase was heard so often that it has come to be associated with the German underlings even by people who are not old enough to remember World War II. The phrase is, "I was just following orders." As the court records show, this excuse was not well received. The lowest-ranking officers, it was conceded, might possibly use such an excuse. But certainly the higher-ranking officers had a choice.

THE MILGRAM EXPERIMENT

In 1961 social psychologist Stanley Milgram investigated **obedience** in a study that is now considered a classic. Milgram began by using students from Yale University as sub-

5

10

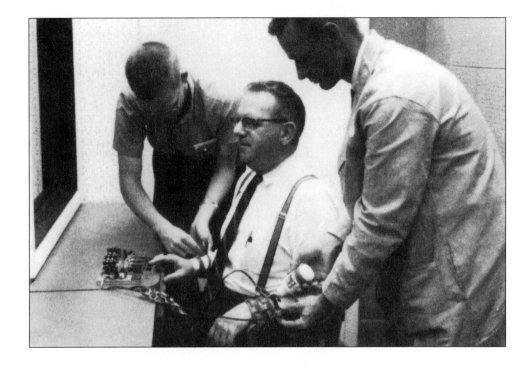

jects and later expanded his research to include a cross section of people of different ages, occupations, and educational levels.

Two subjects were ushered into an experimental room and were told that they were part of an investigation to test the effects of punishment, in the form of an electric shock,
15   on memory. An experimenter, dressed in a white lab coat, would oversee the experiment. The subjects would draw lots to find out who would be the "learner" and who would be the "teacher." Unknown to the real subject, the other subject, "Mr. Wallace," a gentle-looking, friendly 50-year-old man, was really an actor working for Milgram. The lots were rigged so that the real subject would be assigned the role of teacher.

20   The teacher was given a sample shock of 45 volts to find out what it would feel like—it stung. The learner, Mr. Wallace, was then strapped into the electric chair as the subject chosen to be the teacher watched. The teacher-subject was then taken into an adjacent room and put in front of an array of switches ranging from "Slight shock, 15 volts," to "Danger: severe shock, 450 volts." The learner was instructed to repeat a list of words.
25   Every time he made an error, the teacher was to administer a shock, starting with the lowest level and gradually increasing. The actor playing the role of learner had been given a script to follow for each voltage level, since the teacher would be able to hear him from the next room. As the shock level rose, the learner would begin to protest. The stronger the shock, the louder he was to protest. At 75 volts he would moan; at 150 volts
30   he would demand to be released from the chair. At 180 volts he would yell that he could no longer stand the pain. At 300 volts he would protest that he had a heart condition and begin to scream. If the teacher complained at any time, the experimenter would say, "Teacher, you have no other choice; you must go on!" (Milgram, 1963, p. 374). After the 300-volt level, it was planned that there would be an ominous silence from the learner's
35   room, as though he were unconscious or even dead. Unknown to the teacher, the learner received no real shocks.

Milgram's aim was to find out how much pressure to obey would be created by the experimenter in the lab coat when he said, "Teacher, you have no other choice; you must go on!" How far would subjects go under these circumstances? Before conducting the
40   experiment, Milgram interviewed 40 psychiatrists, describing the procedure you have just read. He asked them to estimate the behavior of most subjects. The psychiatrists agreed that the majority would not go beyond 150 volts, and that perhaps only one in a

thousand, those who were very deviant or sadistic, would go all the way to 450 volts. How far would you have gone?

45 To everyone's horror, when the experiment was conducted, 62 percent of the teacher-subjects went all the way to 450 volts! None of them seemed to enjoy it. For example, after delivering 180 volts, one subject said,

> He can't stand it! I'm not going to kill that man in there. You hear him hollering? He's hollering. He can't stand it. What if something happens to him? . . . I mean,
> 50 who is going to take the responsibility if anything happens to that gentleman?

At that point the experimenter said that he would take responsibility. The subject replied, "All right," and continued delivering shocks.

Of the 38 percent of the subjects who were not willing to go to 450 volts, many went to high levels (see graph). All who refused to continue simply walked out of the ex-
55 periment. Not one of them tried to see how Mr. Wallace was. Interestingly, the personality tests that were administered to the subjects failed to reveal any differences between the subjects who obeyed and those who refused.

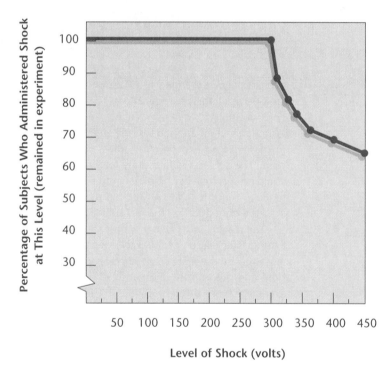

Level of Shock (volts)

Variables Influencing Obedience. Social psychologists have identified at least three variables in this experiment that may help to explain the high rate of obedience. First, a
60 legitimate authority, the experimenter, was present and was willing to take responsibility. Second, the victim was in another room, and this distance may have lessened the teacher's stress by eliminating the need to see the learner's anguish. Third, the teacher-subject accepted the subordinate role, applying all the rules the subject had ever learned about being a good follower. Perhaps, as social psychologist Philip Zimbardo has sug-
65 gested, such follower training in public situations begins on the first day of school, when the teacher says, "Stay in your seat no matter what."

It should be stressed that obedience does not happen only under these select conditions. Even if the learner is directly in front of the teacher-subject, the latter may still obey. In a variation of the Milgram experiment, the teacher-subject actually had to force the

70   learner's hand down onto an electric shock plate. Obedience under these conditions, although less frequent, was still much higher than anyone had predicted.

By today's standards, the Milgram experiment may not be considered ethical because of the stress placed on the teacher-subject. Some of the subjects were shaking and weeping as they pressed the 450-volt lever. How do you debrief such a subject after the experi-
75   ment? Do you say, "Don't feel bad—the learner is only an actor. I just wanted to see if you would electrocute a stranger just because I told you to." No serious after-effects were observed among the teacher-subjects, but even after a careful debriefing many felt that they had discovered an evil side of themselves. Some of the volunteer experimenters who helped Milgram to conduct the research were called to account by university authorities,
80   who asked why they had continued the experiment when they could plainly see that the teacher-subjects were under stress. The frightening answer: "Milgram told us to!"

The Milgram findings are not specific to the United States. Similar results have been obtained in many other countries, including Germany and Australia. The same results even were found among three groups of children, aged 7, 11, and 15 years, who were
85   ordered to shock an innocent victim.

The Jonestown tragedy vividly demonstrated the potential consequences of conformity and blind obedience to authority. In 1978 almost 900 members of the California-based People's Temple died in a ritual mass suicide in Jonestown, Guyana, at the command of their leader, Reverend Jim Jones. Jones believed that his communal group was
90   under attack from the outside by forces bent on destroying it. (This outside force was, in reality, nothing more than one congressman, Leo Ryan, who had come to Guyana to check on people from his district and who was leaving there with 14 of them.) After Jones's men had murdered the congressman and several of his party, Jones ordered his followers to kill themselves by taking cyanide. The mass death shocked the world and left
95   people wondering how such a thing could have happened.

Although a few members disobeyed Jones and ran into the jungle, most complied. The final tape recordings of Jonestown are horrifying to hear. The people went to their self-administered deaths crying and screaming for help. Most were not happy to die, which makes their deaths even more incomprehensible.

100   Now that you have learned something about conformity and obedience, you may begin to appreciate the powerful influences that were in effect that day in Jonestown. The people in Jones's community were followers; they had learned through much practice and training to obey their leader, even carrying out mock suicides. Like Milgram's teacher-subjects, many of them cried and were under great stress at the end, but they
105   obeyed. Social comparison certainly had an effect. We would predict that a person surrounded by hundreds of other people committing suicide would be much more likely to do the same than would a solitary person ordered to kill himself. By their actions, the people in Jonestown were also complying with reference group norms. Jones's followers had no other group to which they could refer. They were not only completely dependent
110   on the group, but also isolated in a dense South American jungle, far from their homes.

Would you have been one of the few who escaped? It's easy to feel invulnerable to social forces when they aren't directly working on you. Most people believe that, in all except extreme circumstances, such as a gun held to their head, their own internal values and belief systems would override external social forces. But social psychologists are find-
115   ing that this is in fact a rarity. More often the opposite is true; the social forces turn out to be stronger than our personal values, beliefs, and feelings.

(1,603 words)

—*Psychology*, Third Edition, by John Dworetzky

THINKING AFTER READING

RECALL   Self-test your understanding. Your instructor may choose to give you a true-false review.

REACT Do you consider the Milgram experiment ethical? _____

_____

REFLECT How do colleges protect the rights of students who volunteer to participate in experiments? _____

_____

THINK CRITICALLY Explain how the research studies prove that the Nazi officers'
behavior in the death camps was not a fluke. Write your answer on a separate
sheet of paper.

ANALYTICAL REASONING

Use the preceding graph to answer the following items with *T* (true) or *F* (false).

_____ 1. Of the subjects who remained in the experiment, 100 percent were
willing to administer a shock of approximately 275 volts.

_____ 2. Less than half of the subjects who remained in the experiment were
willing to administer a shock of 450 volts.

_____ 3. Almost 90 percent of the subjects who remained in the experiment
were willing to administer a shock over 300 volts.

_____ 4. From 300 to 450 volts, subjects who were willing to administer the
shocks dropped out at a rate of approximately 30 percent.

_____ 5. No subjects were willing to administer the maximum shock of 450
volts.

Name _____

Date _____

COMPREHENSION QUESTIONS

Answer the following with *a, b, c,* or *d,* or fill in the blank. In order to help you analyze your strengths and weaknesses, the question types are indicated.

Main Idea   _____   1. The best statement of the main idea of this selection is

   a. research shows that many variables influence obedience.
   b. research shows a high rate of obedience to commands that result in harm to others.
   c. research indicates that Nazi officers were not responsible for their actions in the death camps.
   d. Milgram's research shows that people are basically evil.

Detail   _____   2. Milgram's subjects were told that the experiment was investigating

   a. punishment.
   b. obedience.
   c. electric shock.
   d. memory.

Detail   _____   3. The forty psychiatrists who were asked to predict the results of the experiment

   a. overestimated the power of obedience.
   b. underestimated the power of obedience.
   c. gave answers that closely resembled the actual findings.
   d. portrayed a more negative view of human nature than the research itself.

Inference   4. The major objection of the subject who said, "He can't stand it!"

   seems to have been _____

   _____

Inference   _____   5. Today the Milgram experiment might be considered inhumane or unethical because

   a. the subjects were upset by their own actions.
   b. the learner could have been injured.
   c. experimenters cannot make subjects perform.
   d. it investigates the dark side of human nature.

Inference   6. The answer, "Milgram told us to!" shows that the volunteer experimenters

   _____

   _____

Detail   _____   7. In the Jonestown tragedy, the religious followers

   a. killed each other.
   b. fought Jim Jones.
   c. were tricked by Leo Ryan.
   d. poisoned themselves.

Answer the following with *T* (true) or *F* (false).

Inference _____ 8. Although two subjects entered the experimental room, only one was an actual subject.

Detail _____ 9. In experiments similar to Milgram's, the level of obedience drops when the teacher is in close physical contact with the learner.

Inference _____ 10. The community in Jonestown was a satanic cult that believed in evil deeds.

VOCABULARY

Answer the following with *a, b, c,* or *d* for the word or phrase that best defines the boldface word as used in the selection. The number in parentheses indicates the line of the passage in which the word is located.

_____ 1. "German **underlings**" (5)

   a. children
   b. persons of lesser rank
   c. enemies
   d. citizens

_____ 2. "into an **adjacent** room" (22–23)

   a. adjoining
   b. convenient
   c. soundproof
   d. comfortable

_____ 3. "an **ominous** silence" (34)

   a. oppressive
   b. sudden
   c. painful
   d. foreboding

_____ 4. "a **legitimate** authority" (60)

   a. university
   b. lawful
   c. convincing
   d. diplomatic

_____ 5. "the learner's **anguish**" (62)

   a. desire
   b. objections
   c. distress
   d. protests

_____ 6. "**vividly** demonstrated" (86)

   a. clearly
   b. hopelessly
   c. sadly
   d. carefully

_____ 7. "his **communal** group" (89)

   a. religious
   b. hard-working
   c. collective
   d. fanatic

_____ 8. "even more **incomprehensible**" (99)

   a. tragic
   b. unintelligible
   c. cruel
   d. ruthless

_____ 9. "**mock** suicides" (103)

   a. multiple
   b. recent
   c. illegal
   d. fake

_____ 10. "a **solitary** person" (107)

   a. simple
   b. brave
   c. single
   d. trusting

VOCABULARY ENRICHMENT

A. Context Clues

Select the word from the list that completes the sentences.

underlings	adjacent	ominous	legitimate	anguish
vividly	communal	incomprehensible	mock	solitary

It was Maria's first day in her new job. She entered the room and walked beyond the large desk. In her own mind she believed that she was the _____ person who could turn this company from debt to profit. On her new desk was an _____, poorly written letter from the manager. He had made mistakes. Rather than treat the employees like associates, he had treated them like mere _____ who were there to serve him. His antics and temper tantrums had been _____ described to her on the day that she interviewed for the job. The secretary, who was located in the _____ office, said his harsh criticism caused her great _____ and unhappiness. He had even refused to use the _____ coffeepot, insisting instead on having his own. She recognized this refusal as an _____ sign of events to come. Because of his personality, most of the employees did not respect him. After discovering that he was the son of the president's new spouse, the sales staff would _____ his credentials, saying he had no _____ right to be there.

B. Thesaurus

Use a thesaurus, either the computer or book version, to find four alternative words for each of the following:

1. indication _____

2. habit _____

3. beginning _____

4. agreement _____

5. respect _____

ASSESS YOUR LEARNING

Review confusing questions, seek clarification, and make notes in your text to help you remember new information and vocabulary.

CONNECT

Read the following reaction to the Milgram experiment. How would you have felt if you had taken part in the experiment? In most colleges, professors conduct experiments on human research subjects. What are the rules in your college on such experiments? How are students protected? Collaborate in groups to find out about the procedures and policies regarding human research subjects. Ask group members to report those policies to the class. If possible, find out and report on current research being conducted at your college. Describe to the class any research project in which you have participated and evaluate its effects on you.

Criticisms of the Milgram Experiment

Josh Gerow
Essentials of Psychology

In reading about Milgram's research, it should have occurred to you that putting subjects in such a stressful experience might be considered morally and ethically objectionable. Milgram himself was quite concerned with the welfare of his subjects. He took great care to debrief them fully after each session had been completed. He told them that they had not really administered any shocks and explained why deception had been necessary.

Milgram reported that the people in his studies were not upset over having been deceived and that their principal reaction was one of relief when they learned that no electric shock had in fact been used. Milgram also indicated that a follow-up study performed a year later with some of the same subjects showed that no long-term adverse effects had been created by his procedure.

Despite these precautions, Milgram was severely criticized for placing people in such an extremely stressful situation. Indeed, one of the effects of this research was to establish in the scientific community a higher level of awareness of the need to protect the well-being of human research subjects. It is probably safe to say that because of the nature of Milgram's experience, no one would be allowed to perform such experiments today.

EXPLORE THE NET

● Find biographical information about Stanley Milgram. Where did he grow up? Where did he study psychology? How do you think his background influenced his interest in social psychology?

Stanley Milgram

www.muskingum.edu/~psychology/psycweb/history/milgram.htm

www.stanleymilgram.com/

● Locate information about the Jonestown tragedy. What theories are offered to explain the mass suicide? Discuss how many and how people survived the tragedy by disobeying Jim Jones.

Alternative Considerations of Jonestown and People's Temple

www-rohan.sdsu.edu/~remoore/jonestown/

For additional readings and exercises, visit the *Breaking Through* Web site:

www.ablongman.com/smith

SELECTION 3   BUSINESS

THINKING BEFORE READING

Preview for content and organizational clues. Activate your schema and anticipate what you will learn.

Why are you motivated to make good grades in college?

If you were a millionaire, would you get a college degree?

This selection will probably tell me _____

VOCABULARY PREVIEW

Are you familiar with these words?

stifled	inspire	proponent	premise	pinnacle
crux	deemphasis	hygienic	grievances	verbalizing

How do the prefixes *pre* and *pro* differ?

Are people who get to the *pinnacle* usually inspired?

What committees in your college are set up to hear student *grievances*?

Your instructor may give a true-false vocabulary review before or after reading.

THINKING DURING READING

As you read, predict, picture, relate, monitor, and correct.

Refer to the
Reader's Tip
*for Business on
page 238.*

Motivating Yourself[1]

"It is asking too much to suggest that people motivate themselves in the work environment. Motivation should come from the supervisor, special rewards, or the job itself."

Many people would disagree with the above quotation. They would claim that self-motivation is an absolute necessity in many work environments. They would also claim
5   that the more you can learn about motivation, the more you understand yourself and, as a result, the more you will be in a position to inspire your own efforts.

Let's assume that you find yourself in a job where things are not going well. You feel stifled and "boxed in." You may, for example, be much more capable than the job demands. Perhaps too, the pay and benefits are only average, your immediate supervisor
10   is difficult to deal with, and some other factors are not ideal. Even so, you consider the organization a good one and you recognize that by earning promotions your long-term future can be excellent.

How can you inspire yourself to do a better-than-average job despite the temporary handicaps? How can you motivate yourself to live close to your potential despite a nega-

---

[1]From *Your Attitude Is Showing*, Ninth Edition by Elwood N. Chapman, © 1987. Adapted by permission of Prentice-Hall, Inc., Upper Saddle River, NJ.

15 tive environment? How can you keep your attitude from showing? How can you keep from injuring important human relationships?

There are many theories or schools of thought on why people are motivated to achieve high productivity on the job. Most of these are studied by managers so that they will be in a better position to motivate the employees who work for them. In this chapter we are
20 going to reverse the procedure. We are going to show you how to motivate yourself. *If your supervisor can be trained to motivate you, why can't you learn to motivate yourself?*

THEORY 1: SELF-IMAGE PSYCHOLOGY

This is frequently called the PsychoCybernetics School. The proponent of this theory is Dr. Maxwell Maltz, a plastic surgeon. The basic idea is that, in order to be properly moti-vated to achieve certain goals, an individual must recognize the *need* for a good self-
25 image. Dr. Maltz discovered in his work as a plastic surgeon that some patients became much more self-confident and far more motivated after having their faces greatly im-proved. Why? Maltz came to the conclusion that the image the individual had of himself (or herself) *inside* was more motivating than the changes he had made *outside*. In short, the way an individual *thinks* he or she looks can be more important than the way he or
30 she actually looks to others.

How Can You Use This Theory to Motivate Yourself? Learn to picture yourself in a more complimentary way. First, research has shown that most people who have poor self-images actually *do* look better to others than they do to themselves. If this is true of you, you might try concentrating on your strong features instead of the weak ones, thus
35 developing a more positive outlook and a better self-image.

Second, you might consider improving yourself on the outside as well as on the in-side. You may not want to go as far as plastic surgery, but you could change your hair-style, dress differently, lose or gain weight, exercise, and many other things. According to the theory, however, unless you recognize and accept the improvement, nothing may
40 happen. PsychoCybernetics is, of course, a do-it-yourself project. You do all the work—and you get all the credit, too!

THEORY 2: MASLOW'S HIERARCHY OF NEEDS

This is a very old theory developed by Abraham Maslow in his book *Motivation and Personality.* The premise here is that you have certain needs that must be fulfilled if you are to be properly motivated. These needs are built one on top of the other as in a pyramid.

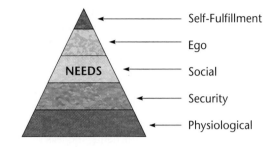

45   The bottom need is physiological—food, good health. The next is safety and security. The third from the bottom is social needs: one needs to be accepted and enjoy the company of others. Next are ego needs—recognition from others. Finally, at the pinnacle, is one's need for self-fulfillment or self-realization.

The crux of this theory is that the bottom needs must be fulfilled before the others
50   come into play. In other words, you must satisfy your need for food and security *before* social needs become motivating. You must satisfy social and ego needs before self-fulfillment is possible.

How Can You Use This Idea to Motivate Yourself to Reach Goals? If you believe Maslow is right, it would be self-defeating to reverse the pyramid or "skip over" unsatis-
55   fied needs to reach others. Chances are good, however, that your first two needs are being adequately satisfied so you could make a greater effort to meet new people and make new friends. This could, in turn, help to satisfy your ego needs. With both your social and ego needs better satisfied you might be inspired to attempt greater creative efforts which could eventually lead you to greater self-realization.

THEORY 3: PSYCHOLOGICAL ADVANTAGE

60   This school was founded by Saul W. Gellerman. It contends that people constantly seek to serve their own self-interests, which change as they grow older. People can make their jobs work for them to give them a psychological advantage over other people at the same level. The way to create a psychological advantage in a starting job that is beneath your capacity is to learn all there is about that job. That way, you can use the job as a spring-
65   board to something better, a position that will give you more freedom and responsibility.

How Could You Use This to Inspire Yourself? The best way, perhaps, is to be a little selfish about your job. Work for the organization and yourself at the same time. Instead of letting your job control you, perhaps pulling you and your attitude down, use it as a launching pad. Use it to build human relations that will be important later on. Study the
70   structure of your organization so you will understand the lines of progression better than the other employees. Study the leadership style of your supervisor and others so that you will have a better one when your turn comes.

THEORY 4: MOTIVATION-HYGIENIC SCHOOL

This theory was developed by Professor Frederick Herzberg. Basically it claims that undesirable environmental factors (physical working conditions) can be dissatisfiers. Factors of
75   achievement, recognition, and freedom, on the other hand, are satisfiers. All working environments have both negative and positive factors.

How Can You Take Advantage of This Theory? People who maintain positive attitudes under difficult circumstances do so through attitude control. They concentrate *only* on the positive factors in their environment. You can, for instance, refuse to recognize the
80 demotivating factors in your job and concentrate only on those things that will satisfy your needs better.

This could mean a deemphasis on physical factors and more emphasis on psychological factors such as social, ego, and self-fulfillment needs. One individual puts it this way: "I work in a very old building with poor facilities. Even so I have learned that I can be
85 happy there because of the work I do and the great people I work with. One quickly gets used to fancy buildings and facilities and begins to take them for granted anyway."

THEORY 5: THE MAINTENANCE-MOTIVATION THEORY

This school is much like Herzberg's hygienic approach and was developed by M. Scott Myers of Texas Instruments, Inc. His research found that employees usually fall into one of two groups: motivation-seekers and maintenance-seekers. In short, some people look
90 for those factors that are motivating to them and are constantly pushing themselves toward fulfillment. Others are concerned with just staying where they are. Maintenance-seekers spend much time talking about working conditions, wages, recreational programs, grievances, and similar matters and do little or nothing to motivate themselves. Motivation-seekers, on the other hand, look beyond such matters.

95 ***How Might You Use This to Improve Your Own Motivation?*** The obvious answer is, of course, to keep yourself out of the maintenance-seeker classification. To do this you should try not to overassociate with those in the maintenance classification. Without your knowing it, they could pull you into their camp. Try also to talk about positive things instead of being a complainer. Verbalizing negative factors often intensifies the dissatis-
100 faction one feels. Turn your attention to things you can achieve on the job—not to the negative factors.

(1,338 words)

THINKING AFTER READING

RECALL   Self-test your understanding. Your instructor may choose to give you a true-false review.

REACT   If you could have plastic surgery, what would you have done and what do you think it would do for you?

REFLECT   For each of Maslow's five levels of needs, name and describe a person that you know who fits the level.

THINK CRITICALLY   Why would a plastic surgeon be the author of a book on self-image and motivation? Write your answer on a separate sheet of paper.

ANALYTICAL REASONING

Use your analytical reasoning skills on the following business problem.

After having worked for the same corporation for over three years, Norman decided that he had made a major mistake. He had been accepted into a formal management training program directly out of college. He had received his first supervisory role before his first year was up, but after that nothing else happened. He had been on a plateau for over two years. In recent months he had been feeling extremely frustrated, stifled, and somewhat hostile. He admitted that his attitude was showing. He admitted that his personal productivity had stagnated.

Norman knew the primary reason for his lack of upward progress. His company had been going through a consolidation process and had put a freeze on hiring new employees. Very few middle- and upper-management positions were opening. Nevertheless, Norman finally came to the uncomfortable conclusion that he had to do something about his situation. He had to force some kind of action, even if it was difficult.

He then sat down and listed the advantages and disadvantages of his role with the company:

Advantages	Disadvantages
Good geographical location	Corporation not expanding
Good benefits	Salary only fair
Job security	Limited learning opportunities
Good personnel policies	Overconservative management
Good physical working conditions	Poor supervisor
Little commuting time	Already made some human relations mistakes
Good home neighborhood	Limited opportunities for upward communication with management
Enjoyable type of work	Boring fellow supervisors

After carefully going over the pros and cons of his job—and considering his three-year investment—Norman decided he had the following options:

1. Go to the personnel department and discuss his frustration about being on a plateau.
2. Submit a written request for a transfer involving a promotion.
3. Start a serious search for a new job in a new company.
4. Resign with two weeks' notice and start looking for a new job.
5. Talk to his supervisor and ask for more responsibility.
6. Motivate himself so that management will recognize a change in attitude and consider him for the next promotion.
7. Relax, continue present efforts, and wait it out.
8. Motivate himself for three months. Then if nothing happens, resign.
9. After telling his boss his intentions, go to the president of the company with the problem.
10. Go to the president of the company to discuss his personal progress.

Assume you are Norman. First, on a separate sheet of paper, list which of the listed options you would consider. Second, put them in the order in which you would undertake them. Third, add any steps you would take that are not on the list. Fourth, justify your decisions.

Name _____

Date _____

COMPREHENSION QUESTIONS

Answer the following with *a, b, c,* or *d,* or fill in the blank. In order to help you analyze your strengths and weaknesses, the question types are indicated.

Main Idea _____ 1. The best statement of the main idea is

a. motivation comes from within and cannot be taught.
b. people can use different theories of motivation to motivate themselves.
c. people who are not motivated lose their jobs.
d. motivation in an organization is the responsibility of management.

Purpose _____ 2. The purpose of this selection is to

a. improve management.
b. criticize supervisors.
c. encourage self-motivation.
d. analyze mistakes.

Detail _____ 3. According to Maltz's theory, many people make mistakes by

a. thinking they look worse than others think they do.
b. trying to look as good as others.
c. thinking they look better than they do.
d. trying to hide their weaknesses from others.

Inference _____ 4. In Maslow's hierarchy of needs, winning sales trophies satisfies the

a. security need.
b. social need.
c. ego need.
d. self-fulfillment need.

Conclusion _____ 5. Gellerman's theory of psychological advantage is based primarily on

a. competition.
b. self-interest.
c. group cooperation.
d. the needs of management.

Conclusion _____ 6. According to the motivation-hygienic theory, a person should

a. work only in a positive environment.
b. motivate supervisors to clean up the environment.
c. ignore the negative factors in the environment and focus on the positive factors.
d. seek a job with only positive factors.

Inference 7. According to the maintenance-motivation theory, someone who

wants to stay in a position for a few more years until retirement is

a _____.

Answer the following with *T* (true) or *F* (false).

Inference _____ 8. The author seems to agree with the quotation at the beginning of the selection.

Inference _____ 9. In Maslow's hierarchy, the need to feel that you are using all of your talents to the best of your ability is the self-fulfillment need.

Conclusion _____10. Maltz's theory is exactly the opposite of Herzberg's theory.

VOCABULARY

Answer the following with *a, b, c,* or *d* for the word or phrase that best defines the boldface word as used in the selection. The number in parentheses indicates the line of the passage in which the word is located.

_____ 1. "feel **stifled**" (7–8)

    a. useless
    b. smothered
    c. angry
    d. sick

_____ 2. "**inspire** yourself" (13)

    a. motivate
    b. force
    c. command
    d. instruct

_____ 3. "**proponent** of this theory" (22)

    a. scholar
    b. attacker
    c. supporter
    d. manager

_____ 4. "The **premise** here" (43)

    a. signal
    b. mistake
    c. meaning
    d. supposition

_____ 5. "at the **pinnacle**" (47–48)

    a. bottom
    b. crucial time
    c. peak
    d. most noticeable point

_____ 6. "The **crux** of this theory" (49)

    a. crucial point
    b. beginning
    c. solution
    d. reward

_____ 7. "**deemphasis** on physical factors" (82)

    a. renewed response
    b. less stress
    c. complete drop
    d. minor stress

_____ 8. "**hygienic** approach" (87)

    a. scientific
    b. analytical
    c. healthful
    d. resourceful

_____ 9. "**grievances**, and similar matters" (93)

    a. successes
    b. contests
    c. enrichments
    d. complaints

_____10. "**Verbalizing** negative factors" (99)

    a. hiding
    b. talking about
    c. overlooking
    d. remembering

VOCABULARY ENRICHMENT

A. Study these easily confused words and circle the correct one for each sentence.

ware: goods sold	**decent:** morally good	**allusion:** reference
wears: puts on clothes	**descent:** move downward	in literature
where: a place	**dissent:** disagreement	**illusion:** false idea

1. The bookstore surprised us with some new (**wares, wears**).

2. The (**decent, descent, dissent**) between the two countries grew into a major confrontation.

3. He is operating under the (**allusion, illusion**) that I am going to help him with homework.

B. Refer to Appendix 2 and use the doubling rule to complete the following words.

4. regret + ing = _____

5. swim + ing = _____

6. excel + ent = _____

7. ship + ment = _____

C. Suffixes: Use the boldface suffix to supply an appropriate word for each group of sentences.

ment: act of, state of, result of action

8. Another _____ to the constitution was proposed by the legislature.

9. Growing children need to eat the right foods so their bodies get the proper _____.

10. My _____ with the manager was postponed until tomorrow at two o'clock.

ence: action, state, quality

11. The therapist showed great _____ in working with the man for hours to achieve a tiny degree of success.

12. The behavior of seemingly untrainable dogs can improve when the dogs are sent to _____ school.

13. Who had the greatest _____ over your life as you were growing up?

able, ible: can do, able

14. To get elected, political candidates must mix with the public and make themselves highly _____.

15. I need a _____ car that I can count on to start each morning.

ASSESS YOUR LEARNING

Review confusing questions, seek clarification, and make notes in your text to help you remember new information and vocabulary.

EXPLORE THE NET

● Describe two motivational strategies advocated by the popular speaker Tony Robbins.

Dream Life
www.dreamlife.com/

Anthony Robbins & Associates
www.anthonyrobbins-assoc.com/

● You are the head of human resources for a large company. The president of the company believes all of the employees would benefit from motivation training and has asked you to provide her with information on three motivational speakers. Prepare a memo that provides this information, and recommend which speaker you think would be best, and why.

Republic Speakers Bureau
www.republicspeakers.com/

The Ozols Business Group
www.ozols.com/

Life Success Productions
www.bobproctor.com/

For additional readings and exercises, visit the *Breaking Through* Web site:

www.ablongman.com/smith

EVERDAY READING SKILLS

Reading Direct Mail Advertisements

How much "junk" mail do you receive each week? If you have no interest in a piece of advertising, throw it away. If you are interested, always remember the old saying, "If it sounds too good to be true, it probably is."

Do not succumb to the glitz. Recognize that if you do not really need the product or service, saving 40 percent will not be beneficial. If you are intrigued, however, read to clarify your total commitment and exactly what you will receive in return. Read the fine print.

Credit Cards

Credit card promotions (see figure) have become such a problem at colleges that some institutions are banning the advertisers from campuses. You have probably already received many promotions saying that you are preapproved for a certain credit limit. Some students, enticed by the easy credit and low monthly payments, charge themselves into serious debt with crippling finance charges that take years to repay. Thus the misuse of credit cards can be deadly.

Proper use of a credit card, however, can be extremely convenient. Before committing to one, know first that you have the means and the discipline to pay your bill before the due date. If always paid promptly, your only cost for this financial convenience will be the annual fee, which is typically $50 or less (and for many cards there is no annual fee).

Reader's TIP Evaluating a Credit Card Offer

- How much is the annual fee for the card?
- What is the finance charge rate? Annual rates run 18% to 22%, so finance charges can add up quickly.
- Does the rate start low and change after an initial introductory period? The balance may be subject to a higher interest rate after the initial period at the low rate expires.
- Why do you need it? If you already have one card, why do you need another one?

exercise 1

1. How long will the introductory rate be available on this credit card? _____

_____

2. After the introductory period, what is the best annual percentage rate (APR) you could get if your account balance is less than $2,500? _____

3. If your application is transferred to Hamilton Southwest, what is the highest fixed annual percentage rate (APR) you might have to pay? _____

(NOTE: ALL OF THIS INFORMATION IS VALID EVEN IF THE OFFER INDICATES YOU HAVE BEEN PRE-APPROVED)

3.99%
Introductory APR

THE CARD YOU'VE BEEN WAITING FOR
THE BENEFITS YOU NEED
THE RATE YOU WANT

Dear Stephanie Albert,

This card is not for everyone. It's for people like you who are just starting out and have already demonstrated responsibility with their credit. Because you've shown that kind of special care, Hamilton Bank can make this special offer to you—a Hamilton Premier MasterCard.

The rate shown above is one of the lowest of any major credit card issuer. There's no gimmick here—the fixed rate of 3.99% is yours for nine months and will not increase if the Prime Rate changes.* After nine months, you'll still save with a variable Annual Percentage Rate as low as Prime +5.49%—right now that's only 13.24%.*

This rate saves you money on new purchases and on outstanding balances, too. Move those high rate balances to your Hamilton Premier MasterCard—who knows how much you'll save?

With a Hamilton Premier MasterCard, you'll also enjoy these benefits:
- Credit line up to $100,000
- No annual fee
- Optional Travel Accident Insurance, Lost Luggage Insurance, Auto Rental Insurance, Credit Card Registration and Merchandise Protection

*By filling out the following application, you agree that we reserve the right, based upon your evaluation, to open a Hamilton Standard MasterCard account if you do not qualify for a Hamilton Premier MasterCard account or, if you do not qualify, not to open any account. If we do not open an account, we may submit your application to our subsidiary, Hamilton Southwest, which will consider you for an Excel or Regular MasterCard account with the pricing terms shown below.

HAMILTON BANK SUMMARY OF TERMS

Annual Percentage Rate for Purchases	Variable Rate Information
Preferred Pricing: 3.99% Introductory APR for 9 months. Thereafter, for Hamilton MasterCard: 13.24% if your balances are greater than or equal to $2,500/15.24% if your balances are less than $2,500. For Hamilton MasterCard: 17.24%. *Non-Preferred Pricing:* 22.74%	Annual Percentage Rate is fixed at 3.99% for the first 9 months your account is open. Thereafter, your Annual Percentage Rate may vary. For Hamilton Premier MasterCard, the rate is determined monthly by adding 5.49% if your balances are greater than or equal to $2,500 or 7.49% if balances are less than $2,500 (for Hamilton Standard MasterCard: 9.49% for all balances), to the Prime Rate as published in *The Wall Street Journal.* *Non-Preferred Pricing:* Your Annual Percentage Rate may vary. The rate is determined monthly by adding 14.99% to the Prime Rate. This rate will not be lower than 19.8%.

HAMILTON SOUTHWEST SUMMARY OF TERMS

Annual Percentage Rate for Purchases	Variable Rate Information
Preferred Pricing: For Excel MasterCard: 23.15%. For Regular MasterCard: 27.15%. These rates will not be lower than 21.9% or higher than 29.9%. *Non-Preferred Pricing:* Fixed 29.9% APR.	*Preferred Pricing:* Your Annual Percentage Rate may vary. For Excel MasterCard accounts, the rate is determined quarterly by adding 15.4% to the Prime Rate as published in *The Wall Street Journal.* For Regular MasterCard accounts, the rate is determined quarterly by adding 19.4% to the Prime Rate.

CD, Tape, and Book Clubs

These promotions offer attractive packages. Who wouldn't want to get 10 or 15 CDs for a penny? In reality, these introductory items are "loss leaders." In other words, the company loses money by giving you so much up front, but they make it back (and more) by requiring you to purchase other merchandise in the future. In the traditional CD, tape, and book clubs, you are sent a new selection every month. If you don't want it, you send it back within a limited time period. However, if you neglect to send it back or are late, you are charged for it. After shipping and handling fees are added, you often pay a higher price than you would at a local retailer.

If you are considering membership in one of these clubs, do the math and determine whether the number of so-called free (or almost free) items you get up front will still be a bargain after you figure in the price of additional items you will have to buy in the future. Carefully examine the types of music or books the club has to offer. Is there a large selection of the type of music you listen to or books you read? Also, pay attention to how current the selections are. Often the most desirable releases will not be available through the clubs until well after they have been shipped to regular retail stores.

exercise 2

Locate a CD, tape, or book club promotion. You may find one in a magazine or in your mailbox. Examine the advertisement and answer the following questions.

1. What is your long-term contract? How many purchases are required and for what dollar amount?
2. What is the average price for each item over the life of the contract? Do the math and include the shipping fees. Is this a bargain or are local stores cheaper?
3. How current are the selections? Will the club have new releases before or after retailers do?

Inference

10

- What is implied meaning?
- Why would meaning be implied rather than stated directly?
- What is slanted language or connotation of words?
- What kinds of clues imply meaning?
- How do good readers draw conclusions?

Everyday Reading Skills: Reading News

What Is an Inference?

An *inference* is a meaning that is suggested rather than directly stated. Inferences are implied through clues that lead the reader to make assumptions and draw conclusions. For example, instead of making a direct statement, "These people are rich and influential," an author could imply that idea by describing an impressive residence, expensive heirlooms, and prominent friends. Understanding an inference is what we mean by "reading between the lines" because the suggestion, rather than the actual words, carries the meaning.

Inference from Cartoons

Cartoons and jokes require you to read between the lines and make a connection. They are funny because of the unstated, rather than the stated. When listeners catch on to a joke, it simply means they have made the connection and recognize the unstated inference. For example, what inference makes the following joke funny?

> **Sam:** Do you know how to save a politician from drowning?
> **Joe:** No.
> **Sam:** Good.

Taxpayers like to dislike politicians, and this joke falls into that category. As a rule, when you have to explain the inference in a joke, the fun is lost. You want your audience to make the connection and laugh uproariously.

EXAMPLE Look at the following cartoon. What do you know about a jury? What is being implied about this one?

"*Eleven hamburgers, one frank. Eleven coffees, one tea. Eleven apple pies, one chocolate cake. . . .*"

—*Elements of Public Speaking* by Joseph DeVito

EXPLANATION A jury is composed of twelve people who are trying to reach consensus on a verdict of guilty or not guilty. The implication in this cartoon is that eleven of the jurors are in agreement on everything, including what to eat, and one juror is totally opposed. Ordering food implies that the discussion may drag on for a long and difficult time. Frequently, a point that takes some figuring out and taps our imagination has a greater impact on us than one that is obviously stated.

exercise 1 The following cartoon contains many suggestive details that imply meaning. Use the details to figure out the meaning of the cartoon and answer the questions.

—Jack Ohman. *The Oregonian,* © 1999.
Reprinted by permission. All rights reserved.

1. Who is Hitler and what is *Mein Kampf*? _____

   _____

2. Who is Tim McVeigh? _____

3. Why is the fertilizer significant? _____

   _____

4. Why is the computer significant? _____

   _____

5. What do the mother's words say about the parents? _____

   _____

   _____

6. What is the main point of the cartoon? _____

   _____

   _____

Recognizing Suggested Meaning

In reading, as in everyday life, information may or may not be stated outright. For example, someone's death would seem to be a fact beyond question. An author could simply state, "He is dead," but often it is more complicated than that. In literature and in poetry such a fact might be divulged in a more dramatic manner, and the reader is left to put the clues together and figure out what happened. Read the following excerpt from a story about a shipwrecked crew's struggle to shore. What clues tell you that the oiler is dead?

> In the shallows, face downward, lay the oiler. His forehead touched sand that was periodically, between each wave, clear of the sea.
>
> —*The Open Boat* by Stephen Crane

The oiler's head is face down in the shallow water. When the waves rush in to shore, his face is in the water, and when they wash out, his face or forehead touches the sand. He is bobbing at the water's edge like a dead fish and cannot possibly be alive with his face constantly underwater or buried in the sand. The man must be dead, but the author doesn't directly state that.

Two paragraphs later in the story the author writes:

> The welcome of the land to the men from the sea was warm and generous; but a still and dripping shape was carried slowly up the beach, and the land's welcome for it could only be the different and sinister hospitality of the grave.
>
> —*The Open Boat* by Stephen Crane

The "still and dripping shape" and the "sinister hospitality of the grave" support your interpretation of the clues, even though the author still has not directly stated, "The oiler is dead." Implying the idea is perhaps more forceful than making a direct statement.

PERSONAL Feedback 1
Name _____

1. Who supplied your references for college admission or for your last job? _____
   _____

2. What professor would you ask to write you a letter of reference for an award or scholarship? Why would you choose that particular professor? _____
   _____
   _____

3. Describe how textbooks differ from literature books. _____
   _____
   _____

4. Katharine Hepburn told Barbara Walters that she would describe herself as an oak tree. What plant would you choose to describe yourself as? _____

_____

5. Describe the personal dynamics of your reading class. _____

_____

_____

6. What have you added to the class? _____

_____

7. What have you done to investigate courses for next term? What do you plan to take and why? _____

_____

Connecting with Prior Knowledge

Authors, like cartoonists, use inferences that require linking old knowledge to what is being read at the time. Clues that imply meaning may draw on an assumed knowledge of history, current issues, or social concerns. Just as in making the connection to understand the punch line of a joke, the reader must make a connection in order to understand the inference.

EXAMPLE   **THE TREE**

It was 390 feet tall. Nothing on earth could match it. It had stood as a slender sapling in the cool coastal air, perhaps moving slightly in a light breeze, on the very day Caesar finally decided to move against Britain. But all that happened a long way from the area that would be called California. Great leaders were born as the tree grew. And they died as the tree became stronger and taller. Wars came and went, as well as plagues and famine. There were great celebrations and deep mourning here and there over the earth. The tree lived through it all.

—*Biology: The World of Life,* Seventh Edition, by Robert Wallace

1. Although not directly stated, what kind of tree is this?
2. How old is the tree?
3. Is the tree still there?

EXPLANATION From the age, height, and location, the reader could infer that the tree is a giant redwood. The tree dates back to Caesar—about two thousand years ago. The word *was* in the first sentence implies the tree is no longer there. The following exercises illustrate how authors expect readers to connect with prior knowledge.

exercise 2

Answer the questions that follow each passage.

Passage 1

THE BEGINNING OF THE SHOOTING

After seeing the light in the North Church, Paul Revere and William Dawes rode through the countryside alerting the colonists that British troops were out moving across the back bay. In Concord and Lexington, trained militiamen were waiting to respond.

Where and approximately when is this? _____

_____

_____

Passage 2

MANDATORY TESTING

Mandatory testing can further wreak havoc in the lives of those who test positive. Individuals who have tested positive from voluntary testing have been known to say: "Hardly an hour goes by when I don't think about it," "I feel like a leper," or "I am frightened of being rejected." Some have even killed themselves or tried to do so. Many carry their burden secretly for fear of losing friends, lovers, jobs, homes, and health insurance.

—*Sociology*, Third Edition, by Alex Thio

Although not directly stated, this article refers to mandatory testing for

what? _____

Passage 3

TELLING THE STORY

The account of that morning some weeks later belongs to history. Three planes take off during the night of 6 August from Tinian in the Mariana Islands. Paul Tibbets is the group's commander. Eatherly opens the formation. There are no bombs in his plane; as for the others, no one suspects what a terrible device is hidden inside the *Enola Gay*. A bigger contrivance, they think, nothing more. Eatherly's job is to pinpoint the target with maximum accuracy. He must establish whether weather conditions allow for the center to be Hiroshima, Kokura or Nagasaki, or whether they should continue towards secondary targets. He tells the story of that morning's events in a voice devoid of emotion which suggests that the recitation is the thousandth one.

—"The Man from Hiroshima" by Maurizio Chierici,
in *One World, Many Cultures* by Stuart Hirschberg

1. Although not directly stated, what is the "bigger contrivance"? _____

_____

2. What was the mission assignment of Tibbets and Eatherly? _____

_____

Recognizing Slanted Language

Writers choose words to manipulate the reader and thus to control the reader's attitude toward a subject. Such words are referred to as having a particular **con-**

notation or **slant.** The dictionary definition of a word is its *denotation,* but the feeling or emotion surrounding a word is its *connotation.* For example, a real estate agent showing a rundown house to a prospective buyer might refer to the house as "neglected" rather than "deteriorated." Both words mean rundown. *Neglected* sounds as if a few things have been forgotten, whereas *deteriorated* sounds as if the place is rotting away and falling apart.

Some words in our society seem to have an automatic positive or negative slant. Words such as *socialist, cult member,* and *welfare state* have a negative emotional effect; words such as *the American worker, democracy,* and *everyday people* have a positive effect. The overall result of using slanted language is to shift the reader's attitude toward the point of view, positive or negative, advocated by the author.

Label the following phrases as either *P* (slanted positively) or *N* (slanted negatively).

_____ 1. a well-dressed man

_____ 2. a ruthless despot

_____ 3. freedom of the press

_____ 4. a larger-than-life leader

_____ 5. corporate raiders

_____ 6. give sympathy and understanding in return

_____ 7. ignorant of common courtesy

_____ 8. efficient office management

_____ 9. corporate greed

_____10. further extension of authoritarian rule

_____11. keen insight and infectious wit

_____12. a pillar of the community

_____13. massacres of the Holocaust

_____14. stooped to serving a cruel master

_____15. the temperament of an angel

_____16. reminded her of home and hearth

_____17. an unpredictable candidate with a short memory

_____18. the home folks of rural America

_____19. the warm flow of family comfort

_____20. spoken with malice toward all

exercise 4

Indicate whether the boldface words in the following passages are positive (*P*) or negative (*N*), and explain your answer.

_____ 1. Surprisingly well read—especially in history and biography—

Truman possessed **sound** judgment, the ability to reach decisions quickly, and a fierce and uncompromising sense of right and wrong. _____

—America: Past and Present by Robert Divine et al.

_____ 2. To classify the Presleys as "dirt poor" would not be an overstatement. Elvis was born in a "**shotgun-style** house," meaning that one could fire a gun at the front door and shoot out the back door. Only ten paces separated the front door from the back in the two-room dwelling. _____

—From the Beginnings, Sixth Edition, Volume Two
by Roderick Nash and Gregory Graves

_____ 3. Benjamin Franklin was born in Boston in 1706, the next-to-the-last of the 13 children of Josiah Franklin, a candle and soap maker, and Abiah Franklin. Although early on he exhibited a "**Thirst for Knowledge**" and a "Bookish Inclination," he was taken out of school when he was 10 in order to help his father. _____
_____

—America: Past and Present by Robert Divine et al.

_____ 4. "It is not every company chairman who bakes cookies for management trainees or rewards top salespeople with furs, jewels, vacations, and pink Cadillacs. But Mary Kay Ash, 64, founder of Mary Kay Cosmetics Inc., does all these things—and such tangible inspiration has paid off **phenomenally.**" _____
_____

—Marketing by Patrick Murphy and Ben Enis

_____ 5. "The Democrats rallied behind Carter, although the convention delegates displayed a **notable lack of enthusiasm** in renominating him." _____

—America: Past and Present by Robert Divine et al.

exercise 5

Write a word or phrase with a negative connotation that could be substituted for each of the following neutral words. For example, negative substitutes for the word *said* could be *shouted, screamed,* or *threatened.*

1. food _____

2. news _____

3. go away _____

4. antiques _____

5. walk _____

6. house _____

7. to help _____

8. supervise _____

9. interest _____

10. think _____

Drawing Conclusions

Readers use both stated and unstated ideas to logically draw conclusions. They use the facts, the hints, and prior knowledge to piece together meaning. The facts and clues lead to assumptions, which then lead to conclusions. Read the following passage and explain how the conclusion is suggested.

EXAMPLE

MY HOUSE

My master still went to school every day and, coming home, he'd still bottle himself up in his study. When he had visitors he'd continue to complain about his job.

I still had nothing to eat so I did not become very fat but I was healthy enough. I didn't become sick like Kuro and, always, I took things as they came. I still didn't try to catch rats, and I still hated Osan, the maid. I still didn't have a name but you can't always have what you want. I resigned myself to continue living here at the home of this schoolteacher.

—From a story by Natsume Soseki, in *One World,
Many Cultures* by Stuart Hirschberg

Conclusion: The narrator of the story is a cat.

What clues suggest this conclusion? _____

EXPLANATION The term *my master* may lead to an initial suspicion of a pet, but the "try to catch rats" clearly suggests a cat. The option of continuing to live in the home supports the idea of a cat. The story, as you might guess, is titled "I Am a Cat."

exercise 6

In passages 1 through 5, identify the clues that lead to the stated conclusions. In passage 6, state the conclusion and identify the clues.

Passage 1

CULTS: THE PEOPLE'S TEMPLE

A **cult** is usually united by total rejection of society and extreme devotion to the cult's leader. The People's Temple is a dramatic example. In the 1970s their leader, Jim Jones, preached racial harmony, helped the poor, established drug-rehabilitation programs, staged protest demonstrations against social injustices, and helped elect sympathetic politicians. He moved his cult from San Francisco to Jonestown, Guyana, because, he said, evil people in the United States would try to destroy the Temple. He told his flock that to build a just society required a living God—namely, himself. To prove his deity, he "healed parishioners by appearing to draw forth cancers" (which actually were bloody chicken gizzards). He claimed that he had extraordinary sexual gifts, required Temple members to turn over all their possessions to him, and insisted that they call him "Dad" or "Father." Then the People's Temple shocked the world. In November 1978 more than 900 members committed mass suicide at the order of their leader.

—*Sociology*, Third Edition, by Alex Thio

Conclusion: Jim Jones brainwashed cult members into total submission.

What clues suggest this conclusion? _____

_____

_____

Passage 2

THE TOBACCO CRAZE

The first European smoker, Rodrigo de Jerez, was with Columbus. Jerez was jailed by the Spanish Inquisition for seven years because of his bad habit, but he was the wave of the future. Slowly, inexorably, the practice of "drinking" tobacco smoke spread throughout Europe. James I, who found smoking "Loathsome" and forbade it in his presence, could not stop it. Nor could the Sultan of Turkey, who threatened to execute puffers.

The lure of the exotic—the trendy—has always been potent among the leisured classes, and some European physicians seized on tobacco as a miracle drug—"the holy, healing herb," "a sovereign remedy to all diseases"—prescribing it liberally to their patients. Throughout the 1500s, the Spanish were pleased to meet Europe's demand from their West Indian plantations.

—*The American Past*, Fifth Edition, by Joseph Conlin

Conclusion: Although initially rejected by political leaders, tobacco became an accepted and sought after commodity.

What clues suggest this conclusion? _____

_____

_____

Passage 3

ELIZABETH, THE SURVIVOR

England's monarch after Bloody Mary was one of the shrewdest politicians ever to wear a crown. Her father beheaded her mother as an adultress and a witch when Elizabeth was three. When she was fourteen, the English church embraced Protestantism and the official sentiments of the royal court took an anti-Spanish turn. Elizabeth went along. When she was twenty, England proceeded back to Rome under Mary and became an ally, almost a client state of Spain.

Thus, when King Philip II rushed to England to propose marriage to her, Elizabeth waffled. To wed his Most Catholic Majesty, the scourge of the Reformation, would surely set English Protestants to plotting against her. To humiliate Philip by rejecting him abruptly, however, might plunge Elizabeth into a war with Spain for which England was not prepared. Elizabeth seemed to say yes to Philip's suit, then no, then maybe. In fact, she said nothing at all. She wore Philip down (he found a wife in France), and had her way.

— *The American Past*, Fifth Edition, by Joseph Conlin

Conclusion: Elizabeth's early life in court taught her to be shrewd politician and to protect her power and throne.

What clues suggest this conclusion? _____

_____

_____

_____

Passage 4

NICHOLAS II (1894–1917)

Last of the Romanov tsars, Nicholas II was in almost every respect an unfortunate man. Besides having been influenced by a reactionary father and a strong-willed mother, he was dull, weak, stubborn, insensitive, and totally devoid of the qualities required for successfully administering a great empire. The day following his coronation, in conformity with tradition, he scheduled a banquet celebration for the people of the capital. A huge throng, possibly half a million souls, turned out for the great event. At one point the crowd surged forward and more than a thousand people were trampled to death. But Nicholas and the tsarina attended a ball at the French embassy that night and apparently spent a most enjoyable evening.

—*A History of the Western World* by Solomon Modell

Conclusion: Nicholas and the tsarina had a total lack of concern for the welfare of the people.

What clues suggest this conclusion? _____

_____

_____

Passage 5

LANDMINES

Cheap and easy to deploy, many fighting forces routinely use mines to defend a frontier, deny opponents the use of a road, and many other purposes. Often these landmines remain active long after the fighting has ceased, posing a significant threat to the safety of the civilian population. The magnitude and horror of his problem sparked a grassroots effort to ban landmines.

The campaign received a major boost in 1996 when Diana, Princess of Wales, joined in the effort, going to places most affected by land mines, comforting victims, and bringing the issue to the attention of millions. When Princess Diana died in a car crash in August 1997, sorrow often turned into commitments to support her charitable interests, including the effort to ban mines. Only a few nations remain opposed to the landmine convention.

—*American Government,* 1999 Edition, by Karen O'Connor and Larry Sabato

What conclusion does the author imply? _____

_____

_____

What clues suggest this conclusion? _____

_____

_____

exercise 7

Use a combination of inference skills to read the following passages and answer the questions.

Passage 1

TEXAS TOUGH

Lyndon Baines Johnson was a complex man—shrewd, arrogant, intelligent, sensitive, vulgar, vain, and occasionally cruel. He loved power, and he knew where it was, how to get it, and how to use it. "I'm a powerful sonofabitch," he told two Texas congressmen in 1958 when he was the most powerful legislator on Capitol Hill. Everything about Johnson seemed to emphasize or enhance his power. He was physically large, and seemed even bigger than he was, and he used his size to persuade people. The "Johnson Method" involved "pressing the flesh"—a back-slapping, hugging sort of camaraderie. He also used symbols of power adroitly, especially the telephone which had replaced the sword and pen as the symbol of power. "No gunman," remarked one historian, "ever held a Colt .44 so easily" as Johnson handled a telephone.

A legislative genius, Johnson had little experience in foreign affairs. Reared in the poverty of the Texas hill country, educated at a small teachers' college, and concerned politically with domestic issues, before becoming president LBJ had expressed little interest in foreign affairs. "Foreigners are not like the folks I am used to," he often said, and whether it was a joke or not he meant it. He was particularly uncomfortable around foreign dignitaries and ambassadors, often receiving them in groups and scarcely paying attention to them. "Why do I have to see them?" he once asked. "They're [Secretary of State] Dean Rusk's clients, not mine."

—*America and Its People*, Third Edition, by James Martin et al.

Answer with *T* (true) or *F* (false).

_____ 1. LBJ had an enormous ego.

_____ 2. LBJ used the telephone to influence votes.

_____ 3. LBJ quickly learned to perform in international situations.

_____ 4. LBJ's background is reflected in both his genius and his flaws.

_____ 5. LBJ was the right person to be president during the Vietnam War.

_____ 6. The phrase *replaced the sword* suggests a negative connotation.

Passage 2

THE REIGN OF LOUIS XVI (1774–1793)

A plain, fat, rather stupid young man, who loved to hunt and tinker with locks, Louis XVI succeeded his grandfather (whose one legitimate son, Louis XVI's father, died in 1765) at the age of twenty. His modesty and inherent kindness did not serve him well. He was far too simple, possessed an almost total lack of self-confidence, and could be made to change his mind with relative ease. His wife, Marie Antoinette, an Austrian princess, was pretty, not well educated, shallow, and selfish. Totally unconcerned with the people's welfare, she devoted herself to jewels and costly clothes, gambling and flirtation, masques and balls. Not completely satisfied with court life, she insisted on interfering in governmental affairs and sabotaged, to the extent that she could, whatever chance existed for the reformation of French life. Her liberal emperor-brother, Joseph II of Austria, reprimanded her, but his words went unheeded.

—*A History of the Western World* by Solomon Modell

Answer with *T* (true) or *F* (false).

_____ 1. Louis XVI and his wife were probably loved and respected by his people.

_____ 2. Despite his wife's influence, Louis XVI had many of the qualities of a great leader.

_____ 3. Louis XVI was firm in his decisions.

_____ 4. Marie Antoinette's extravagance was probably resented by the people.

_____ 5. Joseph II understood the possible repercussions of Marie Antoinette's actions.

_____ 6. The reformation of French life would probably have been a benefit to the people.

_____ 7. The phrase *tinker with locks* suggests hard work.

Passage 3

"LIZZIE BORDEN TOOK AN AX"

Andrew [Borden] was rich, but he didn't live like a wealthy man. Instead of living alongside the other prosperous Fall River citizens in the elite neighborhood known as The Hill, Andrew resided in an area near the business district called the flats. He liked to save time as well as money, and from the flats he could conveniently walk to work. For his daughters Lizzie and Emma, whose eyes and dreams focused on The Hill, life in the flats was an intolerable embarrassment. Their house was a grim, boxlike structure that lacked comfort and privacy. Since Andrew believed that running water on each floor was a wasteful luxury, the only washing facilities were a cold-water faucet in the kitchen and a laundry room water tap in the cellar. Also in the cellar was the toilet in the house. To make matters worse, the house was not connected to the Fall River gas main. Andrew preferred to use kerosene to light his house. Although it did not provide as good light or burn as cleanly as gas, it was less expensive. To save even more money, he and his family frequently sat in the dark.

The Borden home was far from happy. Lizzie and Emma, ages thirty-two and forty-two in 1892, strongly disliked their stepmother Abby and resented Andrew's penny-pinching ways. Lizzie especially felt alienated from the world around her. Although Fall River was the largest cotton-manufacturing town in America, it offered few opportunities for the unmarried daughter of a prosperous man. Society expected a woman of Lizzie's social position to marry, and while she waited for a proper suitor, her only respectable social outlets were church and community service. So Lizzie taught a Sunday School class and was active in the Woman's Christian Temperance Union, the Ladies' Fruit and Flower Mission, and other organizations. She kept herself busy, but she wasn't happy.

In August 1892, strange things started to happen in the Borden home. They began after Lizzie and Emma learned that Andrew had secretly changed his will. Abby became violently ill. Abby told a neighborhood doctor that she had been poisoned, but Andrew refused to listen to her wild ideas. Shortly thereafter, Lizzie went shopping for prussic acid, a deadly poison she said she needed to clean her sealskin cape. When a Fall River druggist refused her request, she left the store in an agitated state. Later in the day, she told a friend that she feared an unknown enemy of her father's was after him. "I'm afraid somebody will do something," she said.

On August 4, 1892, the maid Bridget awoke early and ill, but she still managed to prepare a large breakfast of johnnycakes, fresh-baked bread, ginger and oatmeal cookies with raisins, and some three-day-old mutton and hot mutton soup. After eating a hearty meal, Andrew left for work. Bridget also left to do some work outside. This left Abby and Lizzie in the house alone. Then somebody did something very specific and very grisly. As Abby was bent over making the bed in the guest room, someone moved into the room unobserved and killed her with an ax.

Andrew came home for lunch earlier than usual. He asked Lizzie where Abby was, and she said she didn't know. Unconcerned, Andrew, who was not feeling well, lay down on the parlor sofa for a nap. He never awoke. Like Abby, he was slaughtered by someone with an ax. Lizzie "discovered" his body, still lying on the sofa. She called Bridget, who had taken the back stairs to her attic room: "Come down quick; father's dead; somebody came in and killed him."

Experts have examined and reexamined the crime, and most have reached the same conclusion: Lizzie killed her father and stepmother. In fact, Lizzie was tried for the gruesome murders. However, despite a preponderance of evidence, an all male jury found her not guilty. Their verdict was unanimous and was arrived at without debate or disagreement. A woman of Lizzie's social position, they affirmed, simply could not have committed such a terrible crime.

Even before the trial started, newspaper and magazine writers had judged Lizzie innocent for much the same reasons. As one expert on the case noted, "Americans were certain that well-brought-up daughters could not commit murder with a hatchet on sunny summer mornings."

Jurors and editorialists alike judged Lizzie according to their preconceived notions of Victorian womanhood. They believed that such a woman was gentle, docile, and physically frail, short on analytical ability but long on nurturing instincts.

Too uncoordinated and weak to accurately swing an ax and too gentle and unintelligent to coldly plan a double murder, women of Lizzie's background simply had to be innocent because of their basic innocence.

—*America and Its People*, Third Edition, by James Martin et al.

Answer with *T* (true) or *F* (false).

_____ 1. Andrew Borden's family suffered from his efforts to save money.

_____ 2. Abby was probably correct in telling the doctor that her illness was due to poison.

_____ 3. Andrew was killed when he discovered his wife dead.

_____ 4. The jury did not carefully consider the evidence against Lizzie.

_____ 5. The Victorian stereotyping of women worked in Lizzie's favor.

_____ 6. The author believes that Lizzie was not guilty.

_____ 7. The quotation marks around the word *discovered* change the connotation of the word.

PERSONAL Feedback 2   Name _____

1. What characteristics do you have that are important for leadership? _____

_____

2. During this term, what have your leadership roles been? _____

_____

3. As the term has progressed, how has your thinking about college changed? _____

_____

_____

4. How are your friends and loved ones affecting your academic success? _____

_____

_____

5. What is most irritating about your roommates or people you live with? _____

_____

_____

6. What will you remember the most from this class? _____

_____

_____

_____

COLLABORATIVE PROBLEM SOLVING

Form a five-member group and select one of the following questions. Brainstorm and then outline your major points on a transparency. Choose a member to present the group findings to the class.

▶ Use details, dialogue, and characters to create a cartoon about poorly performing public high schools that blames *teachers* for the problems.

▶ Use details, dialogue, and characters to create a cartoon about poorly performing public high schools that blames *students* for the problems.

▶ Use details, dialogue, and characters to create a cartoon about poorly performing public high schools that blames *parents* for the problems.

▶ Use details, dialogue, and characters to create a cartoon about poorly performing public high schools that blames a *lack of money* for the problems.

Summary Points

- Implied meaning is not directly stated but can be deduced from clues.
- Jokes and cartoons are funny because of implied meaning.
- Inferences require linking old knowledge to what is being read at the time.
- Slanted language manipulates the reader's attitude toward a subject.
- Conclusions allow you to generalize meaning based on clues and incorporate what you already know with what you have just discovered.

EXPLORE THE NET

● Find and print three jokes that are appropriate for class discussion. Explain the inference that makes each joke funny. Conduct your own search, or begin with the following sites:

Cool-Jokes.com

www.cool-jokes.com/

Joke Express

www.jokeexpress.com/

Jokes.com

www.jokes.com/

● Find and print three different editorial cartoons that make a statement about the same topic. Discuss the inferences made in each, and how their main points differ.

The Association of American Editorial Cartoonists

www.detnews.com/AAEC/AAEC.html

For additional readings and exercises, visit the *Breaking Through* Web site:

www.ablongman.com/smith

For a user name and password, see your instructor.

SELECTION 1 **SPEECH**

THINKING BEFORE READING

Preview the selection for content and organizational clues. Activate your schema and anticipate the story.

What type of speech would you expect from a graduation speaker?

Where is Notre Dame ?

Who was Mother Teresa?

THINKING DURING READING

As you read, predict, picture, relate, monitor, and correct.

> **Reader's TIP   Reading and Studying an Essay or Speech**
>
> Ask yourself the following questions:
>
> - What is the theme, thesis, or main idea?
> - How do the details and examples develop the theme?
> - How does the title aid in understanding the essay?
> - What is the author's attitude toward the subject?
> - What images contribute to the theme of the essay?
> - What is the conclusion? How is it significant?

Commencement Address: Living Up To Your Fullest Potential

While today celebrates the end of one phase, it also marks the beginning of the many experiences you will choose to undertake. While the word "retirement" seems increasingly limited, the term "commencement" has become even more appropriate as we move into what is now known as the "Knowledge Economy." "Commencement" indicates to us
5 that all the years of study are about preparation so that we may "begin," "launch," "initiate," "originate," or "bring forth,"—all synonyms of the verb "to commence."

I remember being in your shoes and wondering: this is all very exciting but will I succeed? What will I need to do? Is there anything I can be sure of? I believe there are two things you must do, and if you give your heart to these, you will succeed. The most im-
10 portant two things are: living up to your fullest potential, and developing the potential of your team or community.

LIVE UP TO YOUR FULLEST POTENTIAL

I am reminded of a story of a man walking around in a circus. He saw the troupe of elephants; each was tied to a stake in the ground. He asked the elephant keeper; how long

must this stake be to hold the elephant to his spot? The elephant keeper pulled it out and
15   it was only a normal stake you would use for any tent; no more than about 15 inches.

It was the idea of the stake, the picture of the stake that sometimes holds us back. I am
sure each of us has our stake and we imagine it deeper in the ground than what it really is.

I also recall the story of one of my students. She had a major mishap that caused her
to lose the whole grade on a project in one course. When she came to see me, she was
20   devastated: convinced that her career was over before it started. I logically did the calcu-
lation and showed her that this mishap carried the weight of less than one percent in her
total GPA. This did not console her. She extended this to probable failure in getting an internship and, of course, probable failure in everything afterwards. After half an hour
when my efforts went nowhere, I finally said, you are indeed right—you will probably en-
25   counter total failure. For the scariest thing about life is that it is a self-fulfilling prophecy.
You will go exactly as high or as low as you think you will go. She was stunned by my
comments, picked herself up and went on to a very successful internship.

Living up to our fullest potential requires at least four things:

A. In the "Knowledge Economy," the most important source of competitive advan-
30   tage for the company and source of power for the individual is knowledge. Based on a report by the National Alliance of Business, a high school graduate earns 53% more than
one who does not complete high school. A person with a two-year degree earns 37%
above a high school graduate—an additional two years of college will bring a similar increase. This gap nearly doubled in the last 15 years.

35   The barriers to learning are disappearing quickly. But one thing remains the same—
the onus for learning is still on the individual learner. It is completely up to each one of
you to cultivate his or her curiosity for new knowledge and to have the discipline to engage in these programs.

B. In addition to learning we must also be willing to take risks. We know the future
40   holds many uncertainties and that we must be adaptable, versatile and flexible. As companies move into new areas and re-design processes and structure, we find ourselves in
new territories: creating, experimenting, improvising, modifying and changing. All these
require us to take risks, and not be afraid of what we don't know, what we have not
done, and what we cannot predict. A recent card I got said: Get out on a limb; that's
45   where the fruit is.

C. Taking risks means facing possibility of something that is not working out—that
means setbacks and flops. Mary Pickford once said: "You may have a fresh start any moment
you choose, for this thing that we call 'failure' is not falling down, but the staying down."

I have learned that if I put aside the questions "what do people think?" or "do I look
50   foolish?" I recover more quickly and become bolder. I find that taking risk requires something as deep as inner strength and as pragmatic as a "nest egg," or the "rainy day
fund." I have learned that equally important, I must be humble enough to ask for the
support of good friends and supportive colleagues. In the end, a strong dose of self-
confidence and humor will go a long way. I am reminded of what Linda Ellerbee once
55   said, "Laughter in the face of reality is probably the finest sound there is. In fact, a good
time to laugh is any time you can."

   D. Finally, living up to our potential requires a tremendous amount of energy, discipline, and sacrifice. It is hard to give at that level unless you are driven by a sense of passion for causes and work you feel deeply about.

60   E. I want to move from the notion of "Building You" to "Building Us."

   The notion of "Building Us" is as simple and as humbling as what is noted in this Irish
proverb, "It is in the shelter of each other that the people live." All of us would agree that
little is done except in collaboration with each other.

   "Building us" or building community is about creating a sense of the common good
65   and fostering ownership by all members for the success of the group. It requires a commitment to "win-win" solutions and decision making, which does not create persistent
winners and losers.

   Building community is based on the recognition of our interdependence and a deep
respect for each other. I recall from my own commencement speaker a definition of
70   charisma: "To take people as we find them, to like them for what they are and not to de-
spise them for what they are not." To me, leadership is that ability to bring out the best in
people, to unite and build trust, and to forge collaboration among people for meaningful
and significant endeavors.

   In conclusion, I am excited about the possibilities you face. Your analyses, efforts,
75   and decisions will collectively shape our tomorrow. On this journey forward, there will be
many satisfying and glorious moments; there will be ones that bring disappointment and
hopefully re-assessment and renewal.

   But always remember that we are never alone on our journey, but in the presence of
God as His children. I would like to end with a quote from Mother Teresa, "I know God
80   will not give me anything I can't handle. I just wish he didn't trust me so much."

   God bless you and make joy a part of each day.

(1,168 words)

Carolyn Woo, Dean of the University of Notre Dame's College
of Business Administration, Commencement Speech at Holy
Cross College, South Bend, Indiana, May 9, 1998

THINKING AFTER READING

RECALL   Self-test your understanding. Your instructor may choose to give a true-false review.

REACT   Are you moved by the speech? What might you do differently after reading this speech? _____

REFLECT   What "elephant stakes" do you have that are limiting your vision?

_____

THINK CRITICALLY   Although this selection is powerful to read, it was written as a carefully crafted speech, not as an essay. What aspects of style make this work as a speech but would not be as advantageous in an essay? Elaborate on the impact of each. Write your answer on a separate sheet of paper.

INFERENCE

1. What does the author mean by saying that "life is a self-fulfilling prophecy"?

   _____

2. What does the author mean by the phrase "Knowledge Economy"? _____

   _____

   _____

3. What is the meaning of "Get out on a limb; that's where the fruit is"?

   _____

4. What does Linda Ellerbee mean by "Laughter in the face of reality is probably the finest sound there is"? _____

   _____

5. What is meant by the Irish proverb, "It is in the shelter of each other that the people live"? _____

Name _____

Date _____

COMPREHENSION QUESTIONS

Answer the following with *a, b, c,* or *d,* or fill in the blank. In order to help you analyze your strengths and weaknesses, the question types are indicated.

Main Idea _____ 1. The best statement of the main idea of this selection is

    a. strive to reach for your fullest potential and build a sense of community with others.
    b. graduation is a milestone with many joys and pitfalls.
    c. your success in life depends on your determination.
    d. use your creativity to build a successful life.

Inference _____ 2. In the anecdote about the stakes and the elephants, the author suggests that

    a. the stakes were strong enough to hold the elephants if they tried to pull away.
    b. the elephant keeper could not pull out the stakes.
    c. the stakes formed a psychological barrier that held the elephants.
    d. elephants are innately gentle and thus easily trained for the circus.

Inference _____ 3. In the story about the student who lost the major project grade, the author suggests that

    a. the student was consoled by tallying her GPA.
    b. attacking the student's attitude was more successful than presenting facts and figures.
    c. encouraging words were more successful than confrontational talk.
    d. the student did not get the desired internship because of the failed project.

Inference _____ 4. Based on the data from the National Alliance of Business, the earnings of a person with a two-year degree exceed a person who does not finish high school by

    a. 53%.
    b. 37%.
    c. 15%.
    d. 90%.

Inference _____ 5. By referring to a "nest egg" and a "rainy day fund," the author suggests that the inner strength to take risks can also come from

    a. love.
    b. friends.
    c. money.
    d. God.

Detail   _____ 6. The author's commencement address speaker defined *charisma* as the ability to

        a. change people for the common good.
        b. form collaborations.
        c. lead people.
        d. accept people as they are.

Inference   7. In the concluding quote, Mother Teresa implies that _____

      _____

      _____

Answer the following with *T* (true), *F* (false), or *CT* (can't tell).

Inference   _____ 8. The author uses the words "commencement" and "retirement" as synonyms.

Detail   _____ 9. In the phrase "the onus for learning is still on the individual learner," the word onus is synonymous with responsibility.

Inference   _____ 10. Mary Pickford, in her quotation, condemns the initial mistake.

VOCABULARY ENRICHMENT

Idiom

An *idiom* is a phrase used mainly in conversation that has meaning other than the literal meaning of the words themselves. For example, the phrase "My eyes were bigger than my stomach" is an idiom. The exact, literal meaning of the words is anatomically impossible. In our culture, however, the phrase is a creative way of saying, "I took more food on my plate than I can possibly eat." Other languages may not have this exact same expression, but they may have different idioms to express the same idea. Students who learn English as a second language find our idioms confusing when they look for an exact translation.

Idioms are slang phrases, clichés, and regional expressions. Their popularity changes with the times. Grandparents may use idioms that would make a college student shudder. Professional writers try to avoid idioms because they are considered informal.

Write the meaning of the boldface idioms in the following sentences.

1. She is **making a mountain out of a molehill** in continuing to stress the importance of that one test. _____

2. I knew Lucy could not keep a secret, and now she has **spilled the beans.**

  _____

3. Lewis successfully quit smoking this time, but he said he had to stop **cold turkey.** _____

4. The fraternity overspent last month, and the treasurer reported that the budget was a hundred dollars **in the red.** _____

5. I will tell you about the surprise party, but you must **button your lip** when Harold comes into the room. _____

6. They all went to the mountains this weekend and left me **holding the bag.**

   _____

7. The computer problem was a **piece of cake,** so we had time to play baseball. _____

8. If I can't get the money from Dad, I still have an **ace in the hole.** _____

   _____

9. We are going to the beach over Labor Day to **catch some rays.** _____

   _____

10. Jerome is **in the doghouse** with his girlfriend because of last weekend.

    _____

ASSESS YOUR LEARNING

Review confusing questions, seek clarification, and make notes in your text to help you remember the new information and vocabulary.

SELECTION 2 📚 **LITERATURE**

THINKING BEFORE READING

Preview the selection for content and organizational clues. Activate your schema and anticipate the story.

What is an alchemist?

Were alchemists viewed positively or negatively? Why?

VOCABULARY PREVIEW

Are you familiar with these words?

| alchemist | baser metals | autopsy | insomnia | hot grog |

Can chemists turn *baser metals* into gold?

What ingredients are in *hot grog*?

THINKING DURING READING

As you read, predict, picture, relate, monitor, and correct.

Refer to the
Reader's Tip
for Literature on
page 132.

The Alchemist's Secret

Sitting quietly in his little herb shop on a crooked street in the shadow of Notre Dame, Doctor Maximus did not look like a very remarkable man. But he was. Five hundred years before, he might have busied himself changing the baser metals into gold. But in Paris of the nineties, it is said, he worked at a more subtle alchemy. He changed dreams into real-
5   ities—provided, of course, you could pay.

The man who came into the gaslit shop this early October evening in 1891 was pre-pared to pay. He stood just inside the door, blotting his forehead with a silk handkerchief although actually the weather was rather cool. He was holding a heart-shaped package tightly under one arm. "You are Monsieur le Doctor Maximus?"
10   The Doctor bowed respectfully.

"I have a problem," said the visitor nervously. "I am told you might help me with it."

"Indeed?" said the Doctor mildly. "Who told you that?"

The newcomer glanced around uneasily at the dim shelves, the leathery tortoise dan-gling from a string, the small stuffed crocodile with its dust-filmed eyes. "Last night we
15   had a dinner guest. A foreign diplomat. First secretary of the—"

"Ah, yes, Pechkoff. It is true I did him a small service."

"He was not very specific, you understand. But after a few glasses of cognac he talked rather freely. I got the impression . . ."

"Yes?"
20   "That if it weren't for your—er—assistance he would still be married, most unhap-pily, to his first wife."

Doctor Maximus took off his glasses and polished the spotless lenses. "She died, I be-lieve, poor woman. Quite suddenly."

"Yes," said the visitor, "she did. So suddenly that there was an autopsy. But they dis-
25   covered nothing wrong."

"Of course not," said Doctor Maximus, smiling gently.

"My wife," said the visitor with a certain agitation, "is a very beautiful woman. Naturally, she has many admirers. She has always ignored them until recently, but now there is one—I don't know which one—a younger man, no doubt. She admits it! She demands
30   that I make some settlement. I will not—"

Doctor Maximus raised his hand. "The details," he murmured, "do not concern me."

The visitor's face was tight and dangerous. "I am not a man to be made a fool of!"

"No," said the Doctor, "I can see that."

"Madame," said the visitor abruptly, "is very fond of candy." He unwrapped the
35   heart-shaped package and placed it on the counter. It was a box of chocolates. "I thought perhaps you might—ah—improve the candies at your convenience and then post them to her. She would be very pleased. I have even prepared a card to enclose." He took out a small rectangle of cardboard. On it was printed in neat capitals: FROM AN ADMIRER.

Doctor Maximus took the card and sighed. "My fees are not inconsiderable."

40   "I did not expect them to be," the visitor said stiffly. He did not flinch when the price was named. He paid it, in gold coins. He blotted his forehead once more with the silk handkerchief. "Will you be able to send the candy tonight?"

"Perhaps," said the Doctor noncommittally. "We shall see. And where should it be sent?"

45   "Ah, yes," said the visitor. "Of course." And he gave Madame's name and address.

Doctor Maximus wrote the information on a slip of paper. Then he scribbled three digits on another slip and handed it over. "You sir, are customer 322. If there are any difficulties, kindly refer to that number. Not," he added, "that there will be any."

With one hand on the doorknob, the visitor hesitated. "It won't be—" he wet his
50   lips—"it won't be painful, will it?"

"Not at all," said Dr. Maximus. He peered over his spectacles in a benign and sympathetic fashion. "You seem rather upset. Do you want me to give you something to make you sleep?"

"No, thank you," said his visitor nervously. "I have my own prescription for insom-
55   nia: a hot grog before going to bed."

"Ah, yes," said Dr. Maximus. "An excellent habit."

"Good night," said the visitor, opening the door into the narrow, ill-lit street.

"Good-bye," murmured Dr. Maximus.

60 Taking the box of chocolates in one hand and the slip of paper in the other, he went into the little room at the rear of the shop. From the shelf above his test tubes and retorts he took a big black book, opened it, and looked at the record of the previous transaction. There it was, entered only that afternoon in his spidery handwriting: *Customer 321. Complaint: the usual. Remedy: six drops of the elixir, to be administered in husband's hot grog at bedtime . . .*

65 Dr. Maximus sighed. Then, being a man who honored his commitments, he opened the box of chocolates and went to work. There was no great rush. He would post the parcel in the morning.

In the herb shop, as in life, you got just about what you paid for. But his motto was, First come, first served.

(867 words)

—"The Alchemist's Secret" by Arthur Gordon

THINKING AFTER READING

Inference Questions

1. Where did the couple learn of Dr. Maximus? _____
   _____

2. How was Dr. Maximus connected to Pechkoff's wife? _____
   _____

3. Why was the husband who drank grog unhappy with his wife? _____
   _____

4. How did Dr. Maximus realize that the husband was his next victim? _____
   _____
   _____

5. What can be concluded about Customer 321? _____

6. Why is the motto, "First come, first served," ironic in this story? _____
   _____
   _____

7. Why is the phrase "being a man who honored his commitments" sarcastic?
   _____

8. What is the theme of this story? _____
   _____

VOCABULARY ENRICHMENT

Literary Devices

A. **Personification.** In personification, an inanimate object is given human characteristics. Personification can embellish an image and create a mood. In the sentence, "The wind sang through the trees," the word *sang* gives the wind a human characteristic that adds a soft, gentle mood to the message.

Write the meaning, mood, or feeling the boldface personification adds to the message in the following sentences.

1. Her skin **crawled** when the music played. —————

2. The glowing fireplace was the **heart** of the mountain lodge. —————
————————

3. The sun **kissed** the flowers in the meadow. —————

4. The house **stretched** to make room for their new baby brother. ———
————————

5. The stars **flirted** with the drifting sand. —————

B. **Irony.** Irony is saying one thing but meaning another. It may be used to show humor or to be sarcastic and ridicule others. The trick in irony is to be able to recognize that the speaker does not really mean what he or she says. The context in which the statement is made gives clues to the speaker's true attitude. Gullible people have trouble picking up irony and are subsequently sometimes fooled and embarrassed. For example, after a basketball game, someone may say to a player who scored only once in seventeen tries, "You're a great shot." Here irony is used to ridicule the poor shooting.

Complete the story in each of the following sentences by choosing the response that best shows irony.

———— 6. Each time the professor called on Larry to answer a question, he gave the wrong response. After class Frances said to Larry,

   a. "We need to study hard."
   b. "Here's the guy with the brains."
   c. "I hope you weren't embarrassed."

———— 7. Sue missed only one item on a chemistry exam that almost everyone else failed. When congratulated, Sue retorted,

   a. "Maybe next time I'll study."
   b. "I'm glad I studied."
   c. "My major is chemistry."

———— 8. As newlyweds, Betsy and Fred moved to a tiny New York apartment. When their parents came to visit, a sign on the door said,

   a. "Welcome to our new place."
   b. "Welcome to the Caribbean Hilton."
   c. "Welcome to our friends and family."

———— 9. Because George's apartment was so dirty, his friends called him

   a. the Slob.
   b. George the Unclean.
   c. Mother's Helper.

————10. Chris was known to be cheap, so friends started calling him

   a. Mr. Rockefeller.
   b. Mr. Scrooge.
   c. Mr. Chips.

THINKING BEFORE READING

Preview for content and organizational clues. Activate your schema, and anticipate the author's opinion.

What does the title suggest?

What does *irony* mean? Give an example.

What is watercress?

After reading this, I will probably want to _____.

VOCABULARY PREVIEW

Are you familiar with these words?

indispensable	cavernous	eminent	brusquely	dubious
sanctum	wan	beatific	nominal	sublime

What root word do you see in *cavernous*?

Would you like to pay a *nominal* fee for a summer vacation?

Is a toothbrush *indispensable*?

Your instructor may give a true-false vocabulary review before or after reading.

THINKING DURING READING

As you read, predict, picture, relate, monitor, and correct.

Refer to the
Reader's Tip
for Literature on page 132.

The Doctor's Heroism

To kill in order to cure!—Official Motto of the Broussais Hospital

The extraordinary case of Doctor Hallidonhill is soon to be tried in London. The facts in the matter are these:

On the 20th of last May, the two great waiting rooms of the illustrious specialist were
5   thronged with patients, holding their tickets in their hands.

At the entrance stood the cashier, wearing a long black frock coat; he took the indispensable fee of two guineas from each patient, tested the gold with a sharp tap of the hammer, and cried automatically, "All right."

In his glassed-in office, around which were ranged great tropical shrubs, each grow-
10   ing in a huge Japanese pot, sat the stiff little Doctor Hallidonhill. Beside him, at a little round table, his secretary kept writing out brief prescriptions. At the swinging doors, covered with red velvet studded with gold-headed nails, stood a giant valet whose duty it was to carry the feeble consumptives to the lobby whence they were lowered in a luxurious elevator as soon as the official signal, "Next!" had been given.
15   The patients entered with dim and glassy eyes, stripped to the waist, with their clothes thrown over their arms. As soon as they entered they received the application of the plessimeter and the tube on back and chest.

"Tick! tick! plaff! Breathe now! . . . Plaff . . . Good . . . "

Then followed a prescription dictated in a second or two; then the well-known,
20 "Next!"

Every morning for three years, between nine o'clock and noon, this procession of sufferers filed past.

On this particular day, May 20th, just at the stroke of nine, a sort of long skeleton, with wild, wandering eyes, cavernous cheeks, and nude torso that looked like a parch-
25 ment-covered cage lifted occasionally by a racking cough—in short a being so wasted that it seemed impossible for him to live—came in with a blue-fox skin mantle thrown over his arm, and tried to keep himself from falling by catching at the long leaves of the shrubs.

"Tick, tick, plaff! Oh, the devil! Can't do anything for you!" grumbled Doctor Halli-
30 donhill. "What do you think I am—a coroner? In less than a week you will spit up the last cell of this left lung—the right is already riddled like a sieve! Next!"

The valet was just about to carry out the client, when the eminent therapeutist sud-denly slapped himself on the forehead, and brusquely asked, with a dubious smile:

"Are you rich?"

35 "I'm a millionaire—much more than a millionaire," sobbed the unhappy being whom Hallidonhill thus peremptorily had dismissed from the world of the living.

"Very well, then. Go at once to Victoria Station. Take the eleven-o'clock express for Dover! Then the steamer for Calais. Then take the train from Calais to Marseilles—secure a sleeping car with steam in it! And then to Nice. There try to live on watercress for six
40 months—nothing but watercress—no bread, no fruit, no wine, nor meats of any kind. One teaspoonful of iodized rainwater every two days. And watercress, watercress, water-cress—pounded and brayed in its own juice . . . that is your only chance—and still, let me tell you this: this supposed cure I know of only through hearsay; it is being dinned into my ears all the time; I don't believe in it the least bit. I suggest it only because yours
45 seems to be a hopeless case, yet I think it is worse than absurd. Still, anything is possible . . . Next!"

The consumptive Croesus was carefully deposited in the cushioned car of the eleva-tor; and the regular procession commenced through the office.

Six months later, the 3rd of November, just at the stroke of nine o'clock, a sort of
50 giant, with a terrifying yet jovial voice whose tones shook every pane of glass in the doc-tor's office and set all the leaves of all the tropical plants a-tremble, a great chubby-cheeked colossus, clothed in rich furs—burst like a human bombshell through the sor-

rowful ranks of Doctor Hallidonhill's clients, and rushed, without ticket, into the sanctum of the Prince of Science, who had just come to sit down before his desk. He seized him
55 round the body, and, bathing the wan and worn cheeks of the doctor in tears, kissed him noisily again and again. Then he set him down in his green armchair in an almost suffocated state.

"Two million francs—if you want," shouted the giant. "Or three million. I owe my breath to you—the sun, resistless passions, life—everything. Ask me for anything—any-
60 thing at all."

"Who is this madman? Put him out of here," feebly protested the doctor, after a moment's prostration.

"Oh, no you don't," growled the giant, with a glance at the valet that made him recoil as from a blow. "The fact is," he continued, "I understand now, that even you, you
65 my savior, cannot recognize me. I am the watercress man, the hopeless skeleton, the helpless patient. Nice. Watercress, watercress, watercress! Well, I've done my six months of watercress diet—look at your work now! See here—listen to that!"

And he began to drum upon his chest with two huge fists solid enough to shatter the skull of an ox.
70 "What!" cried the doctor, leaping to his feet, "you are—my gracious, are you the dying man who I . . ."

"Yes, yes, a thousand times yes!" yelled the giant. "I am the very man. The moment I landed yesterday evening I ordered a bronze statue of you; and I will secure you a monument in Westminster when you die."
75 Then dropping himself upon an immense sofa, whose springs creaked and groaned beneath his weight, he continued with a sigh of delight, and a beatific smile:

"Ah, what a good thing life is!"

The doctor said something in a whisper, and the secretary and the valet left the room. Once alone with his resuscitated patient, Hallidonhill, stiff, wan and glacial as ever,
80 stared at the giant's face in silence for a minute or two. Then, suddenly:

"Allow me, if you please, to take that fly off your forehead!"

And rushing forward as he spoke, the doctor pulled a short "Bulldog revolver" from his pocket, and quick as a flash fired into the left temple of the visitor.

The giant fell with his skull shattered, scattering his grateful brains over the carpet of
85 the room. His hands thrashed automatically for a few moments.

In ten cuts of the doctor's scissors, through cloak, garments, and underwear, the dead man's breast was laid bare. The grave surgeon cut open the chest lengthwise, with a single stroke of his broad scalpel.

When, about a quarter of an hour later, a policeman entered the office to request
90 Doctor Hallidonhill to go with him, he found him sitting calmly at his bloody desk, examining with a strong magnifying glass, an enormous pair of lungs that lay spread out before him. The Genius of Science was trying to find, from the case of the deceased, some satisfactory explanation of the more than miraculous action of watercress.

"Constable," he said as he rose to his feet, "I felt it necessary to kill that man, as an
95 immediate autopsy of his case might, I thought, reveal to me a secret of the gravest importance, regarding the now degenerating vitality of the human species. That is why I did not hesitate, let me confess, *to sacrifice my conscience to my duty.*"

Needless to add that the illustrious doctor was almost immediately released upon a nominal bond, his liberty being of far more importance than his detention. This strange
100 case, as I have said, is shortly to come up before the British Assizes.

We believe that this sublime crime will not bring its hero to the gallows; for the English, as well as ourselves, are fully able to comprehend *that the exclusive love of the Humanity of the Future without any regard for the individual of the Present is, in our own time, the one sole motive that ought to justify the acquittal under any circumstances, of the mag-*
105 *nanimous Extremist of Science.*

(1,361words)

—"The Doctor's Heroism" by Villiers de L'isle-Adam
from *75 Short Masterpieces*, edited by Roger B. Goodman

THINKING AFTER READING

RECALL   Self-test your understanding. Your instructor may choose to give a true-false review.

REACT   What was wrong with the man? Why do you think the cure worked?

_____

REFLECT   Why is the final part of the last sentence written in italics? What does it mean? Restate the message in your own words. _____

_____

THINK CRITICALLY   Although this is an old story, explain why this story might have been written by a modern animal rights activist. What point might such an activist make with this story? Write your answer on a separate sheet of paper.

INFERENCE

1. What is the irony of the title of the short story? _____

   _____

2. Why is the motto, "To kill in order to cure!" placed at the beginning of the story? _____

   _____

3. What is ironic about the patient's gratitude? _____

   _____

   _____

   _____

4. What is the connotation of the phrase, "stiff little Doctor Hallidonhill"? ____

   _____

5. What is meant by the phrase, *"to sacrifice my conscience to my duty"*? ____

   _____

   _____

Name _____

Date _____

COMPREHENSION QUESTIONS

Answer the following with *T* (true) or *F* (false).

Inference _____ 1. The first sentence suggests an alleged illegal action will follow.

Inference _____ 2. The description of the cashier suggests that the doctor is only interested in money, but that does not prove to be true.

Inference _____ 3. The cashier suspects that some of the guineas might be counterfeit.

Inference _____ 4. The patients stood outside the glassed-in office for the doctor to examine them.

Inference _____ 5. The blue-fox skin mantle over the patient's arm implies wealth.

Inference _____ 6. The doctor's expression of faith and confidence in the watercress method motivated his patient to believe in it.

Inference _____ 7. The doctor lost millions by shooting the patient.

Inference _____ 8. The story implies the cliché, "The end justifies the means."

Inference _____ 9. The author implies that the doctor should be punished.

Inference _____ 10. The use of the word *grateful* in "scattering his grateful brains over the carpet of the room" suggests sarcasm and irony rather than sympathy.

VOCABULARY

Answer the following with *a, b, c,* or *d* for the word or phrase that best defines the boldface word as used in the selection. The number in parentheses indicates the line of the passage in which the word is located.

_____ 1. "**indispensable** fee" (6–7)

    a. small
    b. large
    c. necessary
    d. impossible

_____ 2. "**cavernous** cheeks" (24)

    a. red
    b. hollow
    c. infected
    d. itchy

_____ 3. "**eminent** therapeutist" (32)

    a. rude
    b. blunt
    c. sensitive
    d. distinguished

_____ 4. "**brusquely** asked" (33)

    a. abruptly
    b. loudly
    c. sympathetically
    d. nervously

_____ 5. "with a **dubious** smile" (33)

    a. endearing
    b. kind
    c. suspicious
    d. joyful

_____ 6. "**sanctum** of the Prince of Science" (53–54)

    a. enthusiasm
    b. confusion
    c. sanctuary
    d. hate

_____ 7. "**wan** and worn cheeks" (55)   _____ 9. "**nominal** bond" (99)

    a. pale   a. insignificant
    b. old   b. outrageous
    c. tired   c. high
    d. hearty   d. undisclosed

_____ 8. "**beatific** smile" (76)   _____10. "**sublime** crime" (101)

    a. knowing   a. evil
    b. manly   b. shocking
    c. handsome   c. horrible
    d. heavenly   d. noble

VOCABULARY ENRICHMENT

Figurative Language

Writers and speakers use figurative language to spark the imagination and make the message more sensual and visual. The words create images in the mind and activate associations stored in memory. Figurative language is challenging because figuring out the meaning demands logical and creative thinking.

A. **Simile.** A simile uses the words *like* or *as* to compare two unlike things. The purpose of a simile is to strengthen the message by adding a visual image. Similes usually dramatize the characteristics of nouns. As a reader, you must figure out the unique characteristic the simile is describing. In the sentence, "the new teacher stood like a statue in front of the class," what does the simile add to the meaning? "Like a statue" describes the teacher as "stiff and unmoving." The simile adds humor and visual interest to the sentence.

Write the meaning of the boldface similes in the following sentences.

   1. Matthew ran **like the wind.** _____

   2. The children rose **like bubbles of carbonated water.** _____

       _____

   3. The late teenager crept to her room **like an autumn leaf that falls**

       without a sound. _____

   4. The overcooked bread was as hard **as the table.** _____

   5. Earleen wept through the movie **like an injured child.** _____

B. **Metaphor.** Whereas a simile uses the words *like* or *as* to compare two unlike things, a metaphor does not use those words but instead states the comparison directly. For example, "The soccer player was a tiger" is a metaphor that dramatizes the player's aggressive spirit. If the statement had been, "The girl plays soccer like a tiger," the figure of speech would be a simile, but the meaning would remain the same.

Write the meaning of the boldface metaphors in the following sentences.

   6. Grandpa had a head of **snow** and a warm smile. _____

7. My roommate was a **pig** when it came to housecleaning. _____

8. Sam was the **dove** at the meeting. _____

9. Her troubles were a **stone** around her neck. _____

   _____

10. The storm was the **thief** of the enchanting summer night. _____

   _____

ASSESS YOUR LEARNING

Review confusing questions, seek clarification, and make notes in your textbook to help you remember the new information and vocabulary.

EVERYDAY READING SKILLS

Reading News

Editorials. Unlike news stories, **editorials** are one of the few types of articles in newspapers that are subjective—that is, they express the opinion of a person or organization. A newspaper's editorial pages feature the views of its management and editors. Subjects for these pieces are usually related to particular local, national, or international news stories.

Although the style of editorials vary as widely as people's opinions, the basic format is usually the same: Two or three brief paragraphs describe a scene or provide historical background leading up to the main theme the writer intends to discuss. After stating a position, the writer follows up with examples, data, and analysis to support the position. Once the case has been made, alternative ideas and solutions may be provided and may also include the writer's belief as to what will happen if the current situation is not changed. The final paragraphs summarize and restate the main idea of the editorial.

Remember that editorials *always express opinions* and regardless of how persuasive the writer's argument might be, you are free to reject it. Newspapers encourage readers to express their own opinions—either for or against editorials—in Letters to the Editor. Selected letters are published in the newspaper, usually in the same section with the editorials, and often feature the views of readers who disagree with recent editorials or with the way in which a news story has been reported.

Reader's TIP   Reading Editorials

While reading editorials, ask yourself the following questions:

- What event prompted the editorial?
- What is the thesis or opinion being promoted by the author?
- Do the details prove the thesis?
- Is the author liberal or conservative?
- What is left out?
- Are the sources, facts, and other support credible?

exercise 1

1. What event does the writer describe to introduce the main idea? _____
_____
_____

2. What is the writer's main idea? _____
_____

3. What one example does the writer give that would help the mayor better
understand this position? _____
_____

Tuesday, April 25, 2000

EDITORIAL PAGE

Political Poverty

In a recent speech to the Linville Chamber of Commerce, Mayor Anderson praised the city council for its "new direction" and its efforts to eliminate city programs that "throw money" at social problems. The audience found this statement to their liking and responded enthusiastically.

However, one phrase in the mayor's speech was quite revealing. He believes it is wrong to expect "governments . . . to take over the upbringing of all who choose the low road to poverty."

What sort of misguided thinking is this—not only to blame those who are "grossly neglected" (as the Mayor characterized them) and who have "special needs for their predicaments," but to further stigmatize them by calling theirs "the low road"?

People do not choose poverty. People do not choose the obstacles they must overcome any more than they choose the family into which they are born. The physically challenged, the culturally deprived, and those lacking sufficient education can certainly take the responsibility for changing their circumstances, but cannot be blamed for those circumstances—no matter how convenient it may be for addressing the city's fiscal difficulties.

A moral society bears responsibility for providing aid and education to the less fortunate. We all contribute to this effort by paying our taxes. However, all too often our culture also rushes to blame victims for their own predicaments. This is because we have an unrealistic sense of our own immunity and invulnerability, believing we can avoid or surmount any challenge—in other words, always thinking "that could never happen to me." Perhaps we would feel more humble if we were the ones trying to overcome catastrophic illness without adequate medical care, trying to find a job without the skills provided by a sound public education system, or trying to feed a family on a minimum-wage salary. In such circumstances, the luxury of being as smug and self-assured as the mayor, the city council, and the Chamber members are would certainly be lost.

Proponents of this so-called new direction absolve themselves too easily of moral responsibility when the low road that they have chosen is one of convenience and callous indifference toward those already burdened and less fortunate than themselves.

---

4. Is the author liberal or conservative? _____

5. Is the main idea supported primarily by facts or opinions? _____

exercise 2

Locate an editorial that interests you in a local, city, or national newspaper. Cut out the editorial and answer the following questions:

1. What event prompted the editorial?
2. What is the author's opinion on the issue?
3. Do the details prove the thesis and are they credible?
4. What is left out?

Critical Reading

- What is an author's purpose or intent?
- What is point of view?
- What is bias?
- What is tone?
- How do you distinguish between fact and opinion?
- What are fallacies?

Everyday Reading Skills: Evaluating Internet Information

What Do Critical Readers Do?

Critical readers evaluate what they read. They use direct statements, inferences, prior knowledge, and language clues to assess the value and validity of what they are reading. Critical readers do not accept the idea that "If it's in print, it must be true." They do not immediately accept the thinking of others. Rather, they think for themselves, analyze different aspects of written material in their search for truth, and then decide how accurate and relevant the printed words are.

Recognize the Author's Purpose or Intent

Authors write with a particular **purpose** or **intent** in mind. For example, you might be instructed to write a scientific paper on environmental pollution with the ultimate purpose of inspiring classmates to recycle. In writing the paper, you must both educate and persuade, but your overriding goal is persuasion. Therefore, you will choose and use only the facts that support your argument. Your critical reading audience will then carefully evaluate your scientific support, recognizing that your purpose was to persuade and not really to educate, and thus decide whether to recycle all or some combination of paper, glass, aluminum, and plastic. The author's reason for writing can alert the reader to be accepting or suspicious. These are three common purposes for writing:

- **To inform.** Authors use facts to inform, to explain, to educate, and to enlighten. The purpose of textbooks is usually to inform or explain, but sometimes an author might venture into persuasion, particularly on topics such as smoking or recycling.
- **To persuade.** Authors use a combination of facts and opinions to persuade, to argue, to condemn, and to ridicule. Editorials in newspapers are written to argue a point and persuade the reader.
- **To entertain.** Authors use fiction and nonfiction to entertain, to narrate, to describe, and to shock. Novels, short stories, and essays are written to entertain. Sometimes an author may adopt a guise of humor in order to entertain and achieve a special result.

EXAMPLE For each of the following topic sentences, decide whether the main purpose is to inform (*I*), to persuade (*P*), or to entertain (*E*).

_____ 1. Telling secrets in the form of public confessions on television talk shows is detrimental to building healthy, satisfying relationships. Such talk shows reveal the worst in human behavior and should be taken off the air.

_____ 2. Self-disclosure in communication means revealing information about yourself, usually in exchange for information about the other person.

_____ 3. Daytime viewers don't seem too surprised to find that Sam has been married to two other women while he has been dating Lucinda who is carrying his third child and is having an affair with Sam's best friend.

EXPLANATION The purpose of the first sentence is to persuade or condemn such programs for the harm they can cause the participants. The purpose of the second sentence is simply to inform or educate by giving a definition. The last sentence exaggerates in order to entertain.

exercise 1

Identify the main purpose of the following as to inform (*I*), to persuade (*P*), or to entertain (*E*).

_____ 1. Lucy and Rachel were both 11 years old when they met in the textile mill for work. When they were not changing the bobbins on the spinning machines, they could laugh with each other and dream of trips back home.

_____ 2. Samuel Slater opened a new textile mill in Rhode Island in 1790 and employed seven boys and two girls between the ages of 7 and 12. The children were whipped with a leather strap and sprayed with water to keep them awake and alert. Consolidating such a work force under one roof, the children could produce three times as much as whole families working at home.

_____ 3. The textile mills of the late eighteenth century in America were not unlike the sweat shops of Central America today. Children were employed for pennies under the supervision of an adult who was concerned about profit. Today, however, enlightened Americans are buying the product of the labor of foreign children. Perhaps Americans should think before buying.

_____ 4. To be successful in the future, retail companies must embrace e-commerce and establish creative Web sites that are easy for customers to use. Explore Internet options for advertising, marketing, and retailing.

_____ 5. In response to a drop in profits, Gap, Incorporated opened Old Navy stores targeted at discount shoppers. This created a three-tiered organization. The company's Banana Republic is designed to appeal to high-end shoppers, The Gap to a middle market searching for quality casual clothing, and Old Navy for the bargain hunters.

_____ 6. She quickened her pace as the footsteps behind her became louder. Was he following her or did he just happen to be turning down Grove Street also?

exercise 2

Read the passages and identify the author's purpose for each by responding with *a, b, c,* or *d.*

Passage 1

VOTING BY E-MAIL?

If people can register by computer, the next step is naturally voting by e-mail. A growing trend in the Pacific Coast states has been voting by mail. In 1998, Oregon voters approved a referendum to eliminate traditional polling places and conduct all future elections by mail. In California, approximately 25 percent of the votes cast currently come in via the post office. Again, as e-mail takes the place of regular mail, why not have people cast their votes through cyberspace? It would be less costly for the state, as well as easier for the average citizen—assuming that computer literacy reaches near-universal proportions some time in the future. The major concern, of course, would be ensuring that no one votes more than once and preserving the confidentiality of the vote.

—*Government in America,* Ninth Edition, by George Edwards,
Martin Wattenberg, and Robert Lineberry

_____ 1. The primary purpose of this passage is to

    a. support voting by e-mail.
    b. argue against voting by e-mail.
    c. explain how voting by e-mail would leave out the poor.
    d. compare voting by e-mail with voting by mail.

_____ 2. The author uses the examples of voting by mail in Oregon and California to show that

    a. these states register voters by computer.
    b. states can reduce costs by establishing a system of voting by mail.
    c. states are already successfully moving away from the traditional polling place system.
    d. Pacific Coast states are more aggressive than East Coast states at seeking voting solutions.

Passage 2

JANE ADDAMS

Without knowing why, Jane Addams opened her eyes. It was pitch-black in her bedroom, and at first, she heard nothing more than the muted night noises of the Chicago streets surrounding Hull House. Then she saw what had disturbed her sleep. A burglar had pried open the second-story window and was rifling her bureau drawers. Jane spoke quietly, "Don't make a noise." The man whirled around, then prepared to leap out the window. "You'll be hurt if you go that way," Jane calmly observed. A conversation ensued in the darkness. Addams learned that the intruder was not a professional thief, but simply a desperate man who could find no employment that winter of 1890 and had turned to crime to survive. Hull House had been founded the previous fall as a social "settlement" to serve just such people. It testified to Jane Addams's belief that only unfavorable circumstances stood between the innate dignity and worth of every individual and their realization. Moreover, Addams believed that as a well-to-do, cultivated lady she had a special responsibility for alleviating the social ills accompanying the nation's growth. So she was in earnest when she promised her unexpected visitor that if he would come back the next morning, she would try to help. The burglar agreed, walked down the main stairs, and left by the front door. At 9 A.M. he returned to learn that Jane Addams had found him a job.

—From These Beginnings, Sixth Edition, Volume Two,
by Roderick Nash and Edward Graves

_____ 1. The primary purpose of this passage is to

    a. explain how Hull House operated on a daily basis.
    b. illustrate Jane Addams's courage and commitment to her cause.
    c. argue the need for social settlements to assist the needy.
    d. educate the public on the reasons for crime.

_____ 2. The author implies that Hull House was designed primarily to serve

    a. drug users.
    b. the mentally ill.
    c. criminals after release from jail.
    d. people down on their luck.

Passage 3

IMPACT OF CONSUMPTION

Because of our technological advances, those of us in developed nations have become mass consumers. The United States, for example, has less than 5% of the global population but consumes far more than 5% of the world's resources. The average U.S. citizen consumes almost 14 times as much energy as the average person in China and 36 times the amount consumed by the average person in India. Overall, the United States consumes more energy than the total population of Central and South America, Africa, India, and China combined. The high rate of resource use compounds the danger imposed by the human population explosion.

—*Biology*, Fourth Edition, by Neil Campbell, Lawrence Mitchell, and Jane Reece

_____ 1. The primary purpose of this passage is to

    a. outline methods to curb consumption.
    b. inform readers of the dangerously high consumption rates of developed nations.
    c. explain why developed nations have higher consumption rates.
    d. persuade readers to share consumption rates with underdeveloped nations.

_____ 2. The author implies that the human population explosion will mean that

    a. the consumption rate per person in the United States will change.
    b. the average person in the United States will no longer consume 36 times as much as the average person in India.
    c. people in underdeveloped countries will increase their per person resource consumption.
    d. the number of people consuming resources in all countries will increase.

Recognize the Author's Point of View or Bias

If you were reading an article analyzing George W. Bush's achievements as president, you would ask, "Is this written by a Republican or a Democrat?" The answer would help you understand the point of view or bias from which the author is writing and thus help you evaluate the accuracy and relevance of the message.

Point of view refers to the opinions and beliefs of the author or of the reader, and a critical reader must recognize how those beliefs influence the message. Students sometimes find the term *point of view* confusing because, when discussing literature, point of view refers to the first, second, or third grammatical person that the author is using as the narrative voice. In this chapter, however, point of view refers to an opinion or position on a subject. For example, if you were reading an article on UFOs you would ask, "Does the author write from the point of view of a believer or a nonbeliever in aliens?"

Bias is a word closely related to point of view. However, the term *bias* tends to be associated with prejudice, and thus it has a negative connotation. A bias, like a point of view, is an opinion or a judgment. Either may be based on solid facts or on incorrect information, but a bias suggests that an author leans too heavily to one side in unequally presenting evidence and arguments. All authors write from a certain point of view, but not all authors have the same degree of bias.

Because both writers and readers are people with opinions, their biases interact on the printed page. Thus critical readers need to recognize an author's bias or point of view as well as their own. For example, a reader might fail to understand an author's position on legalizing prostitution because the reader is totally opposed to the idea. In such a case, the reader's bias or point of view on the subject can interfere with comprehension.

EXAMPLE   Respond to the following statement by describing the author's point of view or bias, as well as your own.

> African animals are endangered and should not be used for fur coats. Minks, however, are a different story and should be considered separately. Minks are farmed animals that are produced only for their fur.

Explain the author's point of view/bias. _____

Explain your own position on the topic. _____

EXPLANATION   The author implies that minks are not endangered and should be used for fur coats. Your position may be the same, or you may think that being on the endangered list is not the only issue. You may feel that animals should not be used for clothing.

exercise 3   The following statements adamantly express only one side of an issue. Read each statement, and mark whether you agree (*A*) or disagree (*D*). Then describe the point of view/bias of the author and your own position.

_____ 1. Teenage drinking causes accidents and deaths. The legal drinking age in all states should be raised to 21. The fact that citizens can be drafted into the military at 18 years of age has no connection with the age at which they can legally consume alcohol.

Explain the author's point of view/bias. _____

_____

Explain your own point of view/bias. _____

_____

_____ 2. The billions of dollars allocated to the space program would be better spent relieving the suffering of the poor and sick here on earth. We have not solved our problems on this planet, so why should we be eager to expand to other worlds?

Explain the author's point of view/bias. _____

_____

Explain your own point of view/bias. _____

_____

_____ 3. An overwhelming amount of this nation's land is owned by the government in the form of national parks and forests. This is especially true in the West. Much of this land is not needed for public recreation and could be sold to private enterprise, with the proceeds going to pay off part of the national debt.

Explain the author's point of view/bias. _____

_____

Explain your own point of view/bias. _____

_____

_____ 4. Is a parent responsible for a child's actions? Because some parents neglect their parental duties when signs of danger are obvious, public interest in parental duty laws is increasing. Under such laws, parents can no longer look the other way while society suffers the consequences.

Explain the author's point of view/bias. _____

_____

Explain your own point of view/bias. _____

_____

_____ 5. Cities that have teen curfews violate the rights of responsible teens. Those teens who obey are forced to curtail wholesome activities while violators continue as if there was no curfew.

Explain the author's point of view/bias. _____

_____

Explain your own point of view/bias. _____

_____

Read the following description of Napoleon Bonaparte from a freshman history textbook. Keep in mind that Napoleon is generally considered one of the great heroes of France and one of the greatest conquerors of the world. Does this passage say exactly what you would expect? Analyze the author's point of view, and answer the questions that follow with *T* (true) or *F* (false).

exercise 4

Passage 1

Napoleon was a short, swarthy, handsome man with remarkable, magnetic eyes. Slender as a youth, he exhibited a tendency toward obesity as he grew older. He was high-strung, and his manners were coarse. Militarily, he has been both denigrated and extolled. On the one hand, his success has been attributed to luck and the great skill of his professional lieutenants; on the other, he has been compared with the greatest conquerors of the past. Politically, he combined the shrewdness of a Machiavellian despot with the majesty of a "sun king." It is generally conceded that he was one of the giants of history. He had an exalted belief in his own destiny, but as an utter cynic and misanthrope felt only contempt for the human race. He once exclaimed, "What do a million men matter to such as I?" The world was Napoleon's oyster. He considered himself emancipated from moral scruples. Yet this man, who despised humanity, was worshiped by the millions he held in such contempt. To his soldiers he was the invincible hero, a supreme ruler over men, literally a *demi-god*. He came from nowhere, but was endowed with an extraordinary mind and the charisma required for masterful leadership. He used democracy to destroy democracy. He employed the slogans of revolution to fasten his hold on nations. His great empire collapsed, but his name will never be forgotten.

—*A History of the Western World* by Solomon Modell

_____ 1. The author wants to present Napoleon as a demigod.

_____ 2. The author shows Napoleon as the greatest military leader in history.

_____ 3. The author feels that Napoleon effectively used propaganda for his own benefit.

_____ 4. The author wants to show the differences between the public and the private views of Napoleon.

_____ 5. The author feels that Napoleon adhered to a strict moral code.

_____ 6. The author feels that Napoleon matured into a handsome, well-mannered gentleman.

_____ 7. The author believes that Napoleon's success was due primarily to good luck.

_____ 8. The author feels that Napoleon had little regard for the average person.

_____ 9. The author feels that Napoleon is undeserving of a prominent place in history.

_____ 10. The author feels that Napoleon used ruthless tactics to get what he wanted.

The author gives a cynical description of Napoleon. For example, he relates a quote attributed to Napoleon that shows him in an unfavorable light. The critical reader needs to be aware that other accounts show Napoleon as a great leader who was concerned for his soldiers and wanted the best for France.

Read Passage 2 for a somewhat different view of Napoleon. Then answer the questions that follow.

Passage 2

Few men in Western history have compelled the attention of the world as Napoleon Bonaparte did during the fifteen years of his absolutist rule in France. Schooled in France and at the military academy in Paris, he possessed a mind congenial to the ideas of the Enlightenment—creative, imaginative, and ready to perceive things anew. His primary interests were history, law, and mathematics. His particular strengths as a leader lay in his ability to conceive of financial, legal, or military plans and then to master their every detail; his capacity for inspiring others, even those initially opposed to him; and his belief in himself as the destined savior of the French. That last conviction eventually became the obsession that led to Napoleon's undoing. But supreme self-confidence was just what the French government lacked since the first days of the revolution. Napoleon believed both in himself and in France. That latter belief was the tonic France now needed, and Napoleon proceeded to administer it in liberally revivifying doses.

—*Western Civilizations* by Edward McNall Berns et al.

_____ 1. This author has a more positive opinion of Napoleon than the previous author.

_____ 2. This author believes that Napoleon's initial self-confidence was unwelcome in France.

_____ 3. This author suggests that Napoleon developed a mental obsession about being a destined savior that led to his decline.

_____ 4. This author does not imply that Napoleon hated humanity.

_____ 5. This author believes that Napoleon failed to attend to details and thus lost power.

Recognize the Author's Tone

The author's **tone** describes the writer's attitude toward the subject. An easy trick to distinguish tone is to think of tone of voice. When someone is speaking, voice sounds usually indicate whether the person is angry, romantic, or joyful. In reading, however, you cannot hear the voice, but you can pick up clues from the choice of words and details.

As a critical reader, tune in to the author's tone, and thus let attitude become a part of evaluating the message. For example, an optimistic tone on water pollution might make you suspicious that the author has overlooked information, whereas an extremely pessimistic article on the same subject might overwhelm you, causing you to discount valuable information.

EXAMPLE   Identify the tone of the following passage.

> Tiger Woods doesn't just play golf well, he plays better than anyone in the world. His father Earl taught 1-year-old Tiger to putt, and the next year Tiger beat Bob Hope at putting on a national television show. By age 3, the amazing Tiger shot a 48 for 9 holes, and at age 8 he won an international junior tournament.

_____ 1. The author's tone is

     a. nostalgic.
     b. ironic.
     c. admiring.

EXPLANATION The details chronicle Tiger's amazing early success with wonder and admiration. The tone is admiring of his exceptional talent.

Reader's TIP   Recognizing the Author's Tone

The following list of words with explanations can describe an author's tone or attitude:

- **Absurd, farcical, ridiculous**: laughable or a joke
- **Ambivalent, apathetic, detached**: not caring
- **Angry, bitter, hateful**: feeling bad and upset about the topic
- **Arrogant, condescending**: acting conceited or above others
- **Awestruck, admiring, wondering**: filled with wonder
- **Cheerful, joyous, happy**: feeling good about the topic
- **Compassionate, sympathetic**: feeling sorrow at the distress of others
- **Complex**: intricate, complicated, and entangled with confusing parts
- **Congratulatory, celebratory**: honoring an achievement or festive occasion

- **Cruel, malicious**: mean spirited
- **Cynical**: expecting the worst from people
- **Depressed, melancholy**: sad, dejected, or having low spirits
- **Disapproving**: judging unfavorably
- **Distressed**: suffering strain, misery, or agony
- **Evasive, abstruse**: avoiding or confusing the issue
- **Formal**: using an official style
- **Frustrated**: blocked from a goal
- **Gentle**: kind or of a high social class
- **Ghoulish, grim**: robbing graves or feeding on corpses; stern and forbidding
- **Hard**: unfeeling, strict, and unrelenting
- **Humorous, jovial, comic, playful, amused**: being funny
- **Incredulous**: unbelieving
- **Indignant:** outraged
- **Intense, impassioned**: extremely involved, zealous, or agitated
- **Ironic**: the opposite of what is expected; a twist at the end
- **Irreverent**: lack of respect for authority
- **Mocking, scornful, caustic, condemning**: ridiculing the topic
- **Objective, factual, straightforward, critical**: using facts without emotions
- **Obsequious**: fawning for attention
- **Optimistic**: looking on the bright side
- **Outspoken**: speaking one's mind on issues
- **Pathetic**: moving one to compassion or pity
- **Pessimistic**: looking on the negative side
- **Prayerful**: religiously thankful
- **Reticent**: shy and not speaking out
- **Reverent**: showing respect
- **Righteous**: morally correct
- **Romantic, intimate, loving**: expressing love or affection
- **Sarcastic**: saying one thing and meaning another
- **Satiric**: using irony, wit, and sarcasm to discredit or ridicule
- **Sensational**: overdramatized or overhyped
- **Sentimental, nostalgic**: remembering the good old days
- **Serious, sincere, earnest, solemn**: being honest and concerned
- **Straightforward**: forthright
- **Subjective, opinionated**: expressing opinions and feelings
- **Tragic**: regrettable or deplorable mistake
- **Uneasy**: restless or uncertain
- **Vindictive**: seeking revenge

exercise 5

Mark the letter that identifies the tone for each of the following sentences.

_____ 1. Baseball was invented as an urban game in order for owners to make money, players to become arrogant, and spectators to drink overpriced beer.

    a. objective
    b. nostalgic
    c. humorous

_____ 2. The Puritans came to the new land for religious freedom, yet they allowed their followers little freedom. Anne Hutchinson was banished from the colony for preaching that salvation can come through good works.

    a. optimistic
    b. ironic
    c. sentimental

_____ 3. When I study now, I'm in a lab with fifty noisy computers. What happened to the quiet chair in a corner with a table for your books, papers, and pencils?

    a. objective
    b. bitter
    c. nostalgic

_____ 4. According to a recent study in a book called *Living Well,* sexually active partners who do not use contraceptives stand an 85 percent chance of conceiving within a year.

    a. subjective
    b. objective
    c. sarcastic

_____ 5. If given the funding, scientists could trace most aggressive behavior, crime, and violence to either too much testosterone or low blood sugar.

    a. sentimental
    b. subjective
    c. objective

_____ 6. On hot summer days, the health risks increase as auto exhaust from rush hour traffic pollutes the air, threatens our lungs, and damages the ozone layer.

    a. disapproving
    b. reverent
    c. incredulous

_____ 7. Aging can be isolating and lonely. As mobility becomes more limited, the elderly patiently wait for the excitement of a friend's call or a child's next visit.

    a. evasive
    b. righteous
    c. sympathetic

_____ 8. LASIK eye surgery may soon make glasses and contacts obsolete. Although long-term studies are still needed, the immediate results are convincing professional athletes to have the computer-controlled laser correction.

    a. sarcastic
    b. optimistic
    c. frustrated

exercise 6

Read the passages and answer the questions that follow by writing in the blanks, answering with *a*, *b*, *c*, or *d*, or by responding with *T* (true) or *F* (false).

Passage 1

TECHNO-BORES

Techno-bores are like chemically altered bores in that their condition (infatuation with technology—often computers) blinds them to the possibility that *your* reality simply isn't theirs. Details about the latest software or synthesizer are lost on you.

The curious thing about computer-obsessed bores is that their behavior appears to have been directly influenced by the machines they love—you can see little floppy disks spinning in their eyes when they speak; their sentences come out in a robotic cadence. Don't even consider launching a personal question in the direction of a techno-bore— you may cause a short circuit.

—"The Ten Most Memorable Bores" by Margot Mufflin

1. What is the tone of the passage? _____

2. What clues reveal the author's tone? _____

_____

Passage 2

STONE CRABS

One of the more regrettable circumstances attendant upon the tourist invasion of Dade County, Florida, of recent winters, was the discovery by visitors of the stone crab.

The home folks in Dade County, Florida, have long esteemed the stone crab, the greatest of native delicacies, and can remember when they were so numerous that a man could dip a foot anywhere in Biscayne Bay and come up with a stone crab hanging on each toe. Or lacking the energy to dunk a pedal he could buy more stone crabs for a few bits than a horse could lug.

Since the winter visitors got on to the stone crab, however, the crustaceans have become scarce and costly. They now sell by the karat. They are so expensive that the home folks are inclined to leave them off their menus. The visitors eat more of the stone crab nowadays and this is all the more deplorable when you reflect that stone crabs are really too good for visitors. A certificate of at least four years residence in Dade County should be required of every person desiring stone crabs.

—"The Brighter Side," by Damon Runyon

_____ 1. The author's tone is

    a. bitter.
    b. serious.
    c. humorous.
    d. sympathetic.

_____ 2. The author's primary purpose is to

    a. educate.
    b. entertain.
    c. narrate.
    d. shock.

Passage 3

TAKING THE TEST

For the next two weeks I ate bacon cheeseburgers almost daily, a series of last meals. Every time the phone rang, at home or at the office, I felt an electric anxiety. My doctor had promised he would not call, but I kept hoping he'd break our agreement and phone to say I was negative. That way I could sleep at night. He didn't call. I grew more obsessed daily. Even though for hours at a time I'd forget to anticipate my test results, my fear would ambush me like a bowel-loosening punch in the gut. I told myself that I wouldn't die the very day the doctor told me the bad news. My HIV-positive friends, and those who had been diagnosed with AIDS, were still alive—mostly. They'd coped. I'd cope too. Cold comfort.

—"Taking the Test" by David Groff

———— 1. The author's tone is

    a. bitter.
    b. fearful.
    c. sarcastic.
    d. intellectual.

———— 2. The author's primary purpose is

    a. to argue.
    b. to criticize.
    c. to describe.
    d. to entertain.

Passage 4

POPULATION GROWTH AND RESOURCES

In 1988, a billion and a half people inhabited the earth. Now the population exceeds five billion and is growing fast—in essence, the world must accommodate a new population roughly equivalent to that of the United States and Canada *every three years.* Understanding ecosystems and how civilization is living on capital provides the appropriate context for analyzing the population problem. It immediately exposes the myth that the impact of the population stems primarily from poor people in poor countries who do not know enough to limit their reproduction. Numbers per se are not the measure of overpopulation; instead it is the *impact* of people on ecosystems and nonrenewable resources. While developing countries severely tax their environments, clearly the populations of rich countries leave a vastly disproportionate mark on the planet. The birth of a baby in the United States imposes more than a hundred times the stress on the world's resources and environment as a birth in, say, Bangladesh. Babies from Bangladesh do not grow up to own automobiles and air conditioners or to eat grain-fed beef. Their life-styles do not require huge quantities of minerals and energy, nor do their activities seriously undermine the life-support capability of the entire planet.

—"Population, Growth, and Resources" by Paul Ehrlich and Anne Ehrlich

———— 1. The authors' tone is

    a. sarcastic.
    b. humorous.
    c. hopeful.
    d. serious.

_____ 2. The authors' point about how the few consume the most is ironic.

_____ 3. The authors' purpose is to condemn poor countries for not putting limits on reproduction.

Distinguish Fact from Opinion

The reader who cannot distinguish between fact and opinion will always remain gullible. By contrast, the critical reader realizes that most writing contains a combination of facts and opinions and is able to tell one from the other. A **fact** is a statement that can be proven true or false, whereas an **opinion** is a statement of feeling that cannot be proven right or wrong.

EXAMPLE   Mark the following statements as *F* (fact) or *O* (opinion).

_____ 1. George Washington was the first president of the United States.

_____ 2. George Washington was the best president of the United States.

_____ 3. The author states that George Washington was the best president of the United States.

_____ 4. It is a fact that George Washington was the best president of the United States.

The first and third are statements of fact that can be proven, but the second and fourth are opinions, even though the fourth tries to present itself as a fact. In psychology, for example, it is a fact that Freud believed the personality is divided into three parts; however, it is only an opinion that there are three parts of the human personality. Others may believe the personality should be divided into two parts or ten parts.

Dr. Beatrice Mendez-Egle, a professor at the University of Texas-Pan American, further clarifies the distinction between fact and opinion with the following definitions and table:

> A **fact** is an observation that can be supported with incontrovertible evidence. An **opinion,** on the other hand, is a commentary, position, or observation based on fact but that represents a personal judgment or interpretation of these facts.

Fact	Opinion
3/4 of the students in this class are making A's.	This class is really smart.
The temperature in the class is 78°.	This classroom is always hot and stuffy!
George W. Bush won the presidency with fewer popular votes than Al Gore in 2000.	George W. Bush doesn't deserve to be president because fewer than half the voters who voted in the 2000 presidential election voted for him.

The first two opinions are clearly judgments that would probably be obvious to most readers. The third opinion, however, is mixed with fact and thus the judgment portion of "doesn't deserve to be president" needs the sharp eye of a critical reader to recognize it as an opinion. In order to achieve a certain purpose, a writer can support a particular bias or point of view and attempt to confuse the reader by blending facts and opinions so that both sound like facts.

exercise 7

Mark the following statements from textbooks as *F* (fact) or *O* (opinion).

_____ 1. "Much of our lives, in fact, is spent filling out questionnaires, taking tests, and being interviewed."

> —*Psychology and You* by David Dempsey and Philip Zimbardo

_____ 2. "Veins, by definition, are blood vessels that carry blood back toward the heart from capillary beds."

> —*Biological Principles* by Gideon Nelson

_____ 3. "If Adams was inept politically, he was deft diplomatically, and in foreign affairs he was expected to shine."

> —*The American Pageant* by Thomas Bailey and David Kennedy

_____ 4. "To register as a taste, molecules of a substance must dissolve in the mucus of a taste bud and trigger off nerve impulses in the hair cells."

> —*Biological Principles* by Gideon Nelson

_____ 5. "Adler, too, believed that early childhood experiences shaped the human personality, but he emphasized the social nature of the child's urges and believed that they could, for the most part, be brought under rational control."

> —*Psychology and You* by David Dempsey and Philip Zimbardo

_____ 6. "Several Southern states adopted formal protests; in South Carolina flags were lowered to half-mast."

> —*The American Pageant* by Thomas Bailey and David Kennedy

_____ 7. "An applicant who is publicly shy and withdrawn, for example, would probably not be hired as a sales representative or an airline flight attendant."

> —*Psychology and You* by David Dempsey and Philip Zimbardo

_____ 8. "The hedonistic theory was first set forth by the Greek philosopher Epictetus, who believed that all human action could be explained by the desire to seek pleasure or avoid pain."

> —*Psychology and You* by David Dempsey and Philip Zimbardo

_____ 9. "A great deal of knowledge about the structure of the brain has accumulated through the years, and more is probably known about the human brain than about any other vertebrate's brain."

> —*Biological Principles* by Gideon Nelson

_____ 10. "Despite this trend toward the diffusion of power, it would be naive to believe that wealth and power are no longer linked."

> —*Sociology: Human Society* by Melvin DeFleur et al.

exercise 8

The following passage from a history textbook describes Thomas Jefferson. Notice the mixture of facts and opinions in developing a view of Thomas Jefferson. Mark the items that follow as fact (*F*) or opinion (*O*).

Jefferson hardly seemed cut out for politics. Although in some ways a typical, pleasure-loving southern planter, he had in him something of the Spartan. He grew tobacco, but did not smoke, and he partook only sparingly of meat and alcohol. Unlike most planters he never hunted or gambled, though he was a fine horseman and enjoyed dancing, music, and other social diversions. His practical interests ranged enormously—from architecture and geology to natural history and scientific farming—yet he displayed little interest in managing men. Controversy dismayed him, and he tended to avoid it by assigning to some thicker-skinned associate the task of attacking his enemies. Nevertheless, he wanted to have a say in shaping the future of the country, and once engaged, he fought stubbornly and at times deviously to get and hold power.

—*American Nation*, Tenth Edition, by John Garraty and Mark Carnes

_____ 1. Jefferson hardly seemed cut out for politics.

_____ 2. Jefferson was a typical, pleasure-loving southern planter.

_____ 3. Jefferson grew tobacco, but did not smoke.

_____ 4. Controversy dismayed Jefferson.

_____ 5. Jefferson fought deviously to get and hold power.

Recognize Valid and Invalid Support for Arguments

When evaluating persuasive writing, critical readers realize that support for an argument or a position can be in the form of both facts and opinions. For example, valid reasons for a career change or a vacation destination can be a combination of both facts and feelings. The trick is to recognize which reasons validly support the point and which merely confuse the issue with an illusion of support.

A **fallacy** is an error in reasoning that can give an illusion of support. On the surface, a fallacy can appear to add support, but closer inspection shows it to be unrelated and illogical. For example, valid reasons for buying running shoes might be comfort and price, whereas invalid reasons might be that "everybody has them" and a sports figure said to buy them.

Fallacies are particularly prevalent in **propaganda,** a form of writing designed to convince the reader by whatever means possible. Propaganda can be used to support a political cause, advertise a product, or engender enthusiasm for a college event.

Experts have identified and labeled over 200 fallacies or tricks of persuasion. The following list contains some of the most common ones.

Testimonials: Celebrities who are not experts state support.
  Example: Tiger Woods appears in television advertisements endorsing a particular credit card.

Bandwagon: You will be left out if you do not join the crowd.
  Example: All the voters in the district support Henson for senator.

Transfer: A famous person is associated with an argument.
  Example: George Washington indicated in a quote that he would have agreed with us on this issue.

Straw Person: A simplistic exaggeration is set up to represent the argument.
  Example: The professor replied, "If I delay the exam, you'll expect me to change the due dates of all papers and assignments."

Misleading Analogy: Two things are compared as similar that actually are distinctly different.
  Example: Studying is like taking a shower; most of the material goes down the drain.

Circular Reasoning: The conclusion is supported by restating it.
> *Example:* Papers must be turned in on time because papers cannot be turned in late.

exercise 9

Identify the letter for the fallacy in each of the following statements: (a) testimonial, (b) bandwagon, (c) transfer, (d) straw person, (e) misleading analogy, (f) circular reasoning.

_____ 1. The monument of Joaquin Murieta should be restored because Michelangelo created monuments.

_____ 2. The first semester of college is like the premiere of a Batman movie because both require the use of imagination.

_____ 3. Customs booklets warn that Cuban cigars are not legally allowed in the United States because the government will not let you bring them into the country.

_____ 4. The soft drink must be good because Sinbad's ads say that he enjoys it.

_____ 5. Purchase tickets immediately because everyone in school has signed up for the event and soon it will be sold out.

_____ 6. A student who is late for class would probably be late for a job interview and thus be a failure.

_____ 7. Use the cosmetics advertised by Jennifer Lopez because she says they work for her.

_____ 8. Writing a term paper is like brewing coffee when your crushed beans turn into a flow of ideas.

_____ 9. Join a club to meet new friends because you will meet people that you do not know.

_____ 10. George W. Bush points out that the first president of the United States was another George W.

exercise 10

To practice your critical thinking skills, read the textbook passages, and then answer the questions that follow.

Passage 1

ELIZABETH OF RUSSIA (1741–1762)

Elizabeth was Peter the Great's daughter. She is said to have been ignorant, charming, extravagant, capricious, and nymphomaniacal. She ascended the throne as a result of a palace revolution and ruled for some twenty-two years. Because of her dependence on the service nobility, the class from which members of the palace guard were chosen, their power increased considerably during her reign. To the same degree, German influence at court was drastically reduced. One reason, among others, was Elizabeth's hatred for Frederick the Great of Prussia, who is reputed to have made rather uncomplimentary remarks about her moral character. Legend has it that he was not far wrong; the empress apparently made a practice of selecting handsome young men from her palace guard as her lovers. She also felt a great need for ostentatious display. It is said that while her peasants went hungry Elizabeth accumulated fifteen thousand gowns. She knew little, however, about geography; she thought one could travel from Russia to Britain entirely by land.

—A History of the Western World by Solomon Modell

Answer the following with *T* (true) or *F* (false), or with *a, b, c,* or *d*.

_____ 1. The author wishes to show Elizabeth as a selfish ruler, interested in herself rather than the people.

_____ 2. The author suggests that the status of the service nobility increased, in part due to Elizabeth's sexual desires.

_____ 3. The author's tone is primarily objective.

_____ 4. The author respects Elizabeth's accomplishments.

_____ 5. The author uses the example about geography to verify Elizabeth's extravagance.

_____ 6. All of the following words have a negative connotation *except*

    a. ostentatious.
    b. capricious.
    c. charming.
    d. nymphomaniacal.

Mark the following statements as *F* (fact) or *O* (opinion).

_____ 7. "She ascended the throne as a result of a palace revolution. . . ."

_____ 8. "To the same degree, German influence at court was drastically reduced."

_____ 9. "She also felt a great need for ostentatious display."

Passage 2

KILLING BOBCATS

The reasons for killing such an endangered species are varied. Ranchers often cite the bobcat as a chicken killer (while choosing to overlook its role in controlling rodents). Among many cultures, including our own, such killing is often taken to be a symbol of maleness or manhood. If the cats were run down on foot and then throttled with bare hands, perhaps a case could be made for this argument, but they have very little chance of escaping trained hounds and high-powered rifles. Sometimes the reason given for such killing is economic. Perhaps the hides can be sold. If the demand exists, it will be met, whether the poachers are African tribesmen killing the last of the rhinos or Louisiana citizens spotlighting alligators at night. The sale of such skins is not restricted throughout most of the world and one can find all sorts of spotted-cat skin on the proud backs of status-conscious Europeans any cool Saturday afternoon. They are also showing a resurgence in the United States. A Siberian lynx coat was recently advertised in Los Angeles for over $70,000. The high price was stated to be due to the fact that the animal was so rare.

—*Biology: The World of Life,* Seventh Edition, by Robert Wallace

Answer the following with *T* (true) or *F* (false).

_____ 1. The author's purpose is to ridicule people who kill rare animals.

_____ 2. The author implies that the bobcat serves no useful purpose for society.

_____ 3. The author implies that killing animals with high-powered rifles is connected with a false sense of manhood.

_____ 4. The author's tone is sympathetic to people who killed bobcats.

_____ 5. The author suggests that the buyer of the $70,000 lynx coat is as guilty as the hunter.

_____ 6. In using the phrase "Louisiana citizens spotlighting alligators at night," the author intends for the slant to be positive.

Mark the following statements as *F* (fact) or *O* (opinion).

_____ 7. "Ranchers often cite the bobcat as a chicken killer. . . ."

_____ 8. "The sale of such skins is not restricted throughout most of the world. . . ."

_____ 9. "The high price was stated to be due to the fact that the animal was so rare."

Passage 3

A DEAD LAKE

Lake Erie was once one of the world's most beautiful lakes. Its waters were pure and abounded with life. It provided food, and lent its beauty to man for literally thousands of years. What man, camped beside it in earlier times, spending leisurely days swimming and fishing and reveling in its quiet sunrises, could have guessed its fate? The growing human population, however, was demanding new goods. The production of those goods required great amounts of water. So factories were set up along the banks of the immense lake—factories that would use the water as a coolant, and the lake itself as a dump. Thus millions of tons of poisons of all sorts were poured directly into the water. After all, this was the cheapest means of disposal. Cheap production increased profits. But the question is, did the industrialists have the *right* to pour their garbage into a lake they didn't own? As their profits increased, the lake was changed to the extent that it became dangerous to swim in it or drink from it. The industrialists, of course, when threatened with belated lawsuits in recent years, argued that their dumping of poisons into the lake resulted in cheaper goods for people, and *that,* after all, is what the people *really* wanted. You can immediately see that the question can be extended to apply to industries that vomit their poisonous fumes into the air. Whose air is it, after all?

Because of new demands being placed on the earth's fresh water, it is very likely that you will come to change your feelings toward the uses of fresh water before long. Whereas you may have, somewhere around the second grade, learned that water is something people drink and plants need, you may soon come to think of it in terms of its mining and allocation.

—*Biology: The World of Life,* Seventh Edition, by Robert Wallace

Answer the following with *T* (true) or *F* (false).

_____ 1. The author's purpose is to warn the reader of a very real threat.

_____ 2. The author's tone is humorous.

_____ 3. The author implies that Lake Erie was sacrificed for greed.

_____ 4. The author suggests that the industrialists shifted the blame unfairly in their response to the Lake Erie lawsuits.

_____ 5. The author feels that a larger portion of the air and water supply should be allocated for industrial needs than for human needs.

_____ 6. In using the phrase "vomit their poisonous fumes into the air," the author intends for the slant to be negative.

Mark the following statements as *F* (fact) or *O* (opinion).

_____ 7. "Lake Erie was once one of the world's most beautiful lakes."

_____ 8. "... factories were set up along the banks of the immense lake. ..."

_____ 9. "Cheap production increased profits."

Passage 4

SIMPLICITY

Clutter is the disease of American writing. We are a society strangling in unnecessary words, circular constructions, pompous frills and meaningless jargon.

Who really knows what the average businessman is trying to say in the average business letter? What member of an insurance or medical plan can decipher the brochure that tells him what his costs and benefits are? What father or mother can put together a child's toy—on Christmas Eve or any other eve—from the instructions on the box? Our national tendency is to inflate and thereby sound important. The airline pilot who wakes us to announce that he is presently anticipating experiencing considerable weather wouldn't dream of saying that there's a storm ahead and it may get bumpy. The sentence is too simple—there must be something wrong with it.

But the secret of good writing is to strip every sentence to its cleanest components. Every word that serves no function, every long word that could be a short word, every adverb which carries the same meaning that is already in the verb, every passive construction that leaves the reader unsure of who is doing what—these are the thousand and one adulterants that weaken the strength of a sentence. And they usually occur, ironically, in proportion to education and rank.

During the late 1960's the president of Princeton University wrote a letter to mollify the alumni after a spell of campus unrest. "You are probably aware," he began, "that we have been experiencing very considerable potentially explosive expressions of dissatisfaction on issues only partially related." He meant that the students had been hassling them about different things. As an alumnus I was far more upset by the president's syntax than by the students' potentially explosive expressions of dissatisfaction. I would have preferred the presidential approach taken by Franklin D. Roosevelt when he tried to convert into English his own government's memos, such as this blackout order of 1942:

> Such preparations shall be made as will completely obscure all Federal buildings and non-Federal buildings occupied by the Federal government during an air raid for any period of time from visibility by reasons of internal or external illumination.

"Tell them," Roosevelt said, "that in buildings where they have to keep the work going to put something across the windows."

—*On Writing Well,* Sixth Edition, by William Zinsser

Answer the following with *T* (true) or *F* (false), or with *a, b, c,* or *d.*

_____ 1. The author's main purpose is to criticize wordy writing.

_____ 2. The author quotes Roosevelt to show how simply the blackout order could have been stated.

_____ 3. The author quotes the president of Princeton to show that educated people usually communicate clearly.

_____ 4. The author feels that the airline pilot avoids using the word *storm* because it may frighten the passengers.

_____ 5. The overall tone of the passage is serious.

_____ 6. All of the following words are negatively slanted *except*

      a. clutter.
      b. jargon.
      c. decipher.
      d. brochure.

Mark the following statements as *F* (fact) or *O* (opinion).

_____ 7. "Clutter is the disease of American writing."

_____ 8. "We are a society strangling in unnecessary words. . . ."

_____ 9. " . . . the secret of good writing is to strip every sentence to its cleanest components."

Passage 5

THEODORE ROOSEVELT AND THE ROUGH RIDERS

Brimming with enthusiasm, perhaps a bit innocent in their naiveté, the Rough Riders viewed Cuba as a land of stars, a place to win great honors or die in the pursuit. Like many of his men, TR believed "that the nearing future held . . . many chances of death, of honor and renown." And he was ready. Dressed in a Brooks Brothers uniform made especially for him and with several extra pairs of spectacles sewn in the lining of his Rough Rider hat, Roosevelt prepared to "meet his destiny."

In a land of beauty, death often came swiftly. As the Rough Riders and other soldiers moved inland toward Santiago, snipers fired upon them. The high-speed Mauser bullets seemed to come out of nowhere, making a *z-z-z-z-z-eu* as they moved through the air or a loud *chug* as they hit flesh. Since the Spanish snipers used smokeless gunpowder, no puffs of smoke betrayed their positions.

During the first day in Cuba, the Rough Riders experienced the "blood, sweat and tears" of warfare. Dr. Church looked "like a kid who had gotten his hands and arms into a bucket of thick red paint." Some men died, and others lay where they had been shot dying. The reality of war strikes different men differently. It horrifies some, terrifies others, and enrages still others. Sheer exhilaration was the best way to describe Roosevelt's response to death and danger. Even sniper fire could not keep TR from jumping up and down with excitement.

On July 1, 1898, the Rough Riders faced their sternest task. Moving from the coast toward Santiago along the Camino Real, the main arm of the United States forces encountered an entrenched enemy. Spread out along the San Juan Heights, Spanish forces commanded a splendid position. As American troops emerged from a stretch of jungle, they found themselves in a dangerous position. Once again the sky seemed to be raining Mauser bullets and shrapnel. Clearly the Heights had to be taken. Each hour of delay meant more American casualties.

The Rough Riders were deployed to the right to prepare to assault Kettle Hill. Once in position, they faced an agonizing wait for orders to charge. Most soldiers hunched behind cover. Bucky O'Neill, however, casually strolled up and down in front of his troops, chain-smoked cigarettes, and shouted encouragement. A sergeant implored him to take cover. "Sergeant," Bucky remarked, "the Spanish bullet isn't made that will kill me." Hardly had he finished the statement when a Mauser bullet ripped into his mouth and burst out of the back of his head. Even before he fell, Roosevelt wrote, Bucky's "wild and gallant soul has gone out into the darkness."

—*America and Its People*, Third Edition, by James Martin et al.

Answer the following with *T* (true) or *F* (false) or with *a, b, c,* or *d.*

_____ 1. The author's main purpose is to persuade.

_____ 2. The author feels that the Rough Riders had a glorified view of war.

_____ 3. The author shows sarcasm in mentioning the "Brooks Brothers uniform."

_____ 4. In view of his subsequent death, Bucky O'Neill's remark about a Spanish bullet was ironic.

_____ 5. The overall tone of the passage is humorous.

_____ 6. All of the following phrases are negatively slanted *except*

    a. sheer exhilaration.
    b. jumping up and down.
    c. sternest task.
    d. casually strolled.

Mark the following statements as *F* (fact) or *O* (opinion).

_____ 7. ". . . the Spanish snipers used smokeless gunpowder. . . ."

_____ 8. "Dr. Church looked 'like a kid who had gotten his hands and arms into a bucket of thick red paint.'"

_____ 9. "Some men died, and others lay where they had been shot dying."

Passage 6

MEANWHILE, HUMANS EAT PET FOOD

The first time I witnessed people eating pet foods was among neighbors and acquaintances during my youth in the South. At that time it was not uncommon or startling to me to see dog-food patties sizzling in a pan on the top of a stove or kerosene space heater in a dilapidated house with no running water, no refrigerator, no heat, no toilet and the unrelenting stench of decaying insects. I simply thought of it as the unfortunate but unavoidable consequence of being poor in the South.

The second time occurred in Cleveland. Like many other Southerners, I came to seek my fortune in one of those pot-at-the-end-of-the-rainbow factories along Euclid Avenue. Turned away from one prospective job after another ("We didn't hire hillbillies," employers said), I saw my nest egg of $30 dwindle to nothing. As my funds diminished and my hunger grew, I turned to pilfering food and small amounts of cash. With the money, I surreptitiously purchased, fried and ate canned dog and cat food as my principal ration for several weeks.

I was, of course, humiliated to be eating something that, in my experience, only "trash" consumed. A merciless pride in self-sufficiency kept me from seeking out public welfare or asking my friends or family for help. In fact, I carefully guarded the secret from everyone, because I feared being judged a failure. Except for the humiliation I experienced, eating canned pet food did not at the time seem to be particularly unpleasant. The dog food tasted pretty much like mealy hamburger, while the cat food was similar to canned fish that I was able to improve with mayonnaise, mustard or catsup. My later experience as a public assistance caseworker in Richmond, a street-based community worker in South Philadelphia, and my subsequent travels and studies as a medical sociologist throughout the South, turned up instances of people eating pet food because they saw it as cheaper than other protein products. Throughout the years, similar cases found in the Ozarks, on Indian reservations and in various cities across the nation have also been brought to my attention.

My experience and research suggest that human consumption of pet food is widespread in the United States. My estimate, one I believe to be conservative, is that pet foods constitute a significant part of the diet of at least 225,000 American households, affecting some one million persons. Who knows how many more millions supplement their diet with pet food products? One thing that we can assume is that current economic conditions are increasing the practice and that it most seriously affects the unemployed, poor people, and our older citizens.

There are those who argue that we do not have enough hard data on the human consumption of pet foods. Must we wait for incontrovertible data before we seriously seek to solve the problems of hunger and malnutrition in America? I submit that we have data enough.

—"Meanwhile, Humans Eat Pet Food" by Edward H. Peeples, Jr.

Answer the following with *T* (true) or *F* (false).

_____ 1. The author's purpose is to change laws governing the sale of pet food.

_____ 2. The author's overall tone is humorous.

_____ 3. The author has probably been referred to as a hillbilly.

_____ 4. The author writes from the point of view of one who has been poor, as well as from that of a professional caseworker.

_____ 5. The term *trash* is used to refer to people.

COLLABORATIVE PROBLEM SOLVING

Form a five-member group and select one of the following questions. Brainstorm and then outline your major points on a transparency. Choose a member to present the group findings to the class.

▶ List five facts and five opinions that could be used to support the argument that people should not smoke.

▶ Write five different statements regarding rap music, each with one of the following tones: humorous, angry, ironic, sarcastic, and nostalgic.

▶ Create a fallacy for each of the six types listed in this chapter: testimonial, bandwagon, transfer, straw person, misleading analogy, and circular reasoning.

▶ List five points that you would make in an argument for capital punishment and five points that you would make in an argument against capital punishment.

Summary Points

● Critical readers evaluate the accuracy and relevance of the printed word before accepting it.
● Authors write with a particular *purpose* or *intent* in mind.
● *Point of view* refers to the writer's opinions and beliefs.
● Both writers and readers bring *bias* to the printed page.
● *Tone* refers to the author's attitude toward the subject.
● A *fact* is a statement that can be proven true or false.
● An *opinion* is a statement of feeling that cannot be proven right or wrong.
● A *fallacy* is an error in reasoning designed to give the illusion of support.
● *Propaganda* is a form of writing that uses fallacies to convince readers.

SELECTION 1   **NARRATIVE ESSAY**

THINKING BEFORE READING

Preview for content and organizational clues. Activate your schema and anticipate what you will learn.

What celebrities have died of drug-related causes?

Were drugs sold in your high school?

What are the social consequences of drugs in a community?

I want to learn _____.

VOCABULARY PREVIEW

Are you familiar with these words?

ambivalence	stupefied	convulse	miraculously	audibly
gnashing	irreverent	freak	speculated	casualty

What does the prefix in *ambivalence* mean?

What is property and casualty insurance?

What does the root word in *speculated* mean?

Your instructor may give a true-false vocabulary review before or after reading.

THINKING DURING READING

As you read, use the five thinking strategies of a good reader: predict, picture, relate, monitor, and correct.

Refer to the
Reader's Tip
*for an Essay or
Speech on page
375.*

As They Say, Drugs Kill

The fastest way to end a party is to have someone die in the middle of it.

At a party last fall I watched a 22-year-old die of cardiac arrest after he had used drugs. It was a painful, undignified way to die. And I would like to think that anyone who shared the experience would feel his or her ambivalence about substance abuse dissolving.

5   This victim won't be singled out like Len Bias as a bitter example for "troubled youth." He was just another ordinary guy celebrating with friends at a private house party, the kind where they roll in the keg first thing in the morning and get stupefied while watching the football games on cable all afternoon. The living room was littered with beer cans from last night's party—along with dirty socks and the stuffing from the 10 secondhand couch.

And there were drugs, as at so many other college parties. The drug of choice this evening was psilocybin, hallucinogenic mushrooms. If you're cool, you call them "shrooms."

This wasn't a crowd huddled in the corner of a darkened room with a single red 15 bulb, shooting needles into their arms. People played darts, made jokes, passed around a joint and listened to the Grateful Dead on the stereo.

VIOLENT FALL

Suddenly, a thin, tall, brown-haired young man began to gasp. His eyes rolled back in his head, and he hit the floor face first with a crash. Someone laughed, not appreciating the violence of his fall, thinking the afternoon's festivities had finally caught up with another
20   guest. The laugh lasted only a second, as the brown-haired guest began to convulse and choke. The sound of the stereo and laughter evaporated. Bystanders shouted frantic suggestions:

"It's an epileptic fit, put something in his mouth!"

"Roll him over on his stomach!"

25   "Call an ambulance; God, somebody breathe into his mouth."

A girl kneeling next to him began to sob his name, and he seemed to moan.

"Wait, he's semicoherent." Four people grabbed for the telephone, to find no dial tone, and ran to use a neighbor's. One slammed the dead phone against the wall in frustration—and miraculously produced a dial tone.

30   But the body was now motionless on the kitchen floor. "He has a pulse, he has a pulse."

"But he's not breathing!"

"Well, get away—give him some f—ing air!" The three or four guests gathered around his body unbuttoned his shirt.

35   "Wait—is he OK? Should I call the damn ambulance?"

A chorus of frightened voices shouted, "Yes, yes!"

"Come on, come on, breathe again. Breathe!"

Over muffled sobs came a sudden grating, desperate breath that passed through bloody lips and echoed through the kitchen and living room. "He's had this reaction be-
40   fore—when he did acid at a concert last spring. But he recovered in 15 seconds . . . ," one friend confided.

The rest of the guests looked uncomfortably at the floor or paced purposelessly around the room. One or two whispered, "Oh my God," over and over, like a prayer. A friend stood next to me, eyes fixed on the kitchen floor. He mumbled, just audibly, "I've
45 seen this before. My dad died of a heart attack. He had the same look. . . ."

I touched his shoulder and leaned against a wall, repeating reassurances to myself. People don't die at parties. People don't die at parties.

Eventually, no more horrible, gnashing sounds tore their way from the victim's lungs. I pushed my hands deep in my jeans pockets wondering how much it costs to
50 pump a stomach and how someone could be so careless if he had this reaction with another drug. What would he tell his parents about the hospital bill?

Two uniformed paramedics finally arrived, lifted him onto a stretcher and quickly rolled him out. His face was grayish blue, his mouth hung open, rimmed with blood, and his eyes were rolled back with a yellowish color on the rims.

55 The paramedics could be seen moving rhythmically forward and back through the small windows of the ambulance, whose light threw a red wash over the stunned watchers on the porch. The paramedics' hands were massaging his chest when someone said, "Did you tell them he took psilocybin? Did you tell them?"

"No, I . . ."
60 "My God, so tell them—do you want him to die?" Two people ran to tell the paramedics the student had eaten mushrooms five minutes before the attack.

It seemed irreverent to talk as the ambulance pulled away. My friend, who still saw his father's image, muttered, "That guy's dead." I put my arms around him half to comfort him, half to stop him from saying things I couldn't believe.

65 The next day, when I called someone who lived in the house, I found that my friend was right.

My hands began to shake and my eyes filled with tears for someone I didn't know. Weeks later the pain has dulled, but I still can't unravel the knot of emotion that has moved from my stomach to my head. When I told one friend what happened, she shook
70 her head and spoke of the stupidity of filling your body with chemical substances. People who would do drugs after seeing that didn't value their lives too highly, she said.

NO LESSONS

But others refused to read any universal lessons from the incident. Many of those I spoke to about the event considered him the victim of a freak accident, randomly struck down by drugs as a pedestrian might be hit by a speeding taxi. They speculated that the stu-
75 dent must have had special physical problems; what happened to him could not happen to them.

Couldn't it? Now when I hear people discussing drugs I'm haunted by the image of him lying on the floor, his body straining to rid itself of substances he chose to take. Painful, undignified, unnecessary—like a wartime casualty. But in war, at least, lessons are
80 supposed to be learned, so that old mistakes are not repeated. If this death cannot make people think and change, that will be an even greater tragedy.

(1,004 words)

—Laura Rowley from *Models for Writers,* Fourth Edition, edited by
Alfred Rosa and Paul Eschholz

THINKING AFTER READING

RECALL Self-test your understanding. Your instructor may choose to give a true-false review.

REACT How would this incident have affected you? _____

_____

REFLECT What type of drug awareness programs would be most effective for high school students? _____

_____

_____

THINK CRITICALLY Are you convinced by what the author says about drugs? Why or why not? Write your answer on a separate sheet of paper.

CRITICAL READING

Answer the following with *T* (true) or *F* (false), or with *a, b, c,* or *d.*

_____ 1. The story is told from the victim's point of view.

_____ 2. The author's purpose is to persuade.

_____ 3. The author's tone is disgust.

_____ 4. All of the following words are negatively slanted *except*

    a. secondhand couch.
    b. gnashing sounds.
    c. ordinary guy.
    d. speeding taxi.

Mark the following statements as *F* (fact) or *O* (opinion).

_____ 5. "The fastest way to end a party is to have someone die. . . ."

_____ 6. "The living room was littered with beer cans. . . ."

_____ 7. "People who would do drugs after seeing that don't value their lives. . . ."

Name _____

Date _____

COMPREHENSION QUESTIONS

Answer the following with *a, b, c,* or *d,* or fill in the blank. In order to help you analyze your strengths and weaknesses, the question types are indicated.

Main Idea _____ 1. The best statement of the main idea of this selection is

      a. drugs are addictive.
      b. drug users should seek professional help.
      c. drugs are destroying our society.
      d. drugs are dangerous.

Inference _____ 2. The author mentions Len Bias, who was a talented basketball player, to indicate that

      a. drug abuse is a problem for the rich and famous.
      b. the victim she describes will not be considered important.
      c. both the famous and the unknown are affected by drugs.
      d. drug victims teach us a lesson.

Inference _____ 3. The author's description suggests that the people at the party were

      a. unstable drug addicts.
      b. high school students experimenting with drugs.
      c. average young people.
      d. close friends that she had known for years.

Inference   4. The author dramatizes the partygoers' hesitance to tell the para-

medics about the psilocybin to _____

_____

Inference _____ 5. The author mentions the hospital bills to emphasize

      a. the fear of parents.
      b. what runs through the mind in a crisis.
      c. the high cost of medical attention for drug abusers.
      d. the group's need to share financial responsibility.

Detail _____ 6. When the author told her friends about the overdose, most were

      a. convinced not to take drugs.
      b. unaffected.
      c. consumed by grief.
      d. eager to fight against drugs.

Inference   7. The phrase "he chose to take" is particularly meaningful because

_____

_____

Answer the following with *T* (true) or *F* (false).

Inference _____ 8. The friend whose father had died of a heart attack was correct in his assessment of the situation.

Inference _____ 9. The author feels that the victim had been forewarned of the danger of drugs to his system.

Inference _____ 10. The author is optimistic about the lessons to be learned from the victim's death.

VOCABULARY

Answer the following with *a, b, c,* or *d* for the word or phrase that best defines the boldface word as used in the selection. The number in parentheses indicates the line of the passage in which the word is located.

_____ 1. "her **ambivalence**" (4)

    a. hatred
    b. uncertainty
    c. attraction
    d. belief

_____ 6. "**gnashing** sounds" (48)

    a. depressing
    b. grinding
    c. surprising
    d. deadly

_____ 2. "get **stupefied**" (7)

    a. groggy
    b. argumentative
    c. aggressive
    d. defensive

_____ 7. "**irreverent** to talk" (62)

    a. unnecessary
    b. not applicable
    c. disrespectful
    d. insane

_____ 3. "began to **convulse**" (20)

    a. swallow
    b. breathe heavily
    c. cough
    d. contract muscles

_____ 8. "**freak** accident" (73)

    a. abnormal
    b. sudden
    c. horrible
    d. major

_____ 4. "**miraculously** produced" (29)

    a. immediately
    b. finally
    c. marvelously
    d. hesitantly

_____ 9. "They **speculated**" (74)

    a. wished
    b. guessed
    c. thought
    d. were told

_____ 5. "just **audibly**" (44)

    a. barely heard
    b. religiously
    c. nervously
    d. quietly

_____ 10. "wartime **casualty**" (79)

    a. assignment
    b. hero
    c. battle
    d. death

VOCABULARY ENRICHMENT

A. Study the similar-sounding words and circle one for each sentence.

accent: speech pattern   **elicit:** draw out   **eminent:** well known
ascent: climb upward   **illicit:** improper   **imminent:** about to happen

1. My roommate speaks with a slight (**accent, ascent**).

2. The police suspected (**elicit, illicit**) activities in the apartment.

3. The guest speaker was an (**eminent, imminent**) geologist from Russia.

B. Use context clues, word parts, and, if necessary, the dictionary, to write the meaning for each of the boldface words from a sociology textbook.

4. Immigrant children were **assimilated** into American society through the school system. _____

5. In order to live together in harmony, society demands **conformity** from its members. _____

6. The study investigated the **correlation** between intelligence and wealth.

_____

7. For his leadership in the community, he was held in high **esteem.** _____

_____

8. Rather than being members of her own **peer** group, most of her friends were ten years older. _____

9. Society has become increasingly more **urban** as people leave the farms to look for jobs. _____

10. Through money, some people hope to achieve a higher social **status.**

_____

C. Identify the boldface phrase as simile, metaphor, or personification and explain the meaning.

11. George Washington was the **father of the country** but he had no children of his own. _____

12. Glaciers are melting **like warm ice cream** because pollution is trapping heat to the earth. _____

13. Some birds migrate over two continents, perhaps **singing their songs** in both English and Spanish. _____

_____

14. In order to avoid 200 mph winds that strike **like tornadoes,** climbers can ascend Mount Everest only during two months of the year. _____

_____

15. Poetry **speaks to** both the heart and the brain. _____

_____

ASSESS YOUR LEARNING

Review confusing questions, seek clarification, and make notes in your text to help you remember new information and vocabulary.

CONNECT

Experiments have shown that, even in the face of an obviously correct decision, group members will conform to go along with an incorrect group decision. Read the following and reflect on your experiences with group conformity. Describe a group in which you are a member and explain the group's values. List five examples, either positive or negative, of ways in which you feel you conform with the group.

Conformity
Henry Roediger et al.
Psychology, Second Edition

Social pressure is not confined to explicit attempts to convince you of something (persuasion) or to get you to do something by asking or telling you to do it (compliance or obedience). **Conformity** is yielding to group pressure when there is no direct order to do so. Every group has social norms, or implicit rules, that its members obey. Although we may prefer to see ourselves making our own choices, most of our behavior is dictated by group norms. Although adolescents typically take pride in rebelling against their parents' values and behavior patterns, the more thoughtful rebels recognize that the rebel group itself imposes constraints of speech, dress, and action.

Experiments have demonstrated how others' opinions can affect individuals' behavior. A powerful demonstration was devised by Asch (1956). Subjects saw a standard line, and had to decide which of the other lines was the same length as the standard. Typically, the subject made his or her decision after a number of other subjects announced theirs; and following a few trials in which the first few subjects (actually experimental confederates) made the obviously correct decision, there followed some trials in which the confederates unanimously chose the wrong alternative. A large percentage of the actual subjects (75 percent) went along with the group on at least one trial, despite the evidence of their own senses, whereas subjects who performed alone hardly ever erred.

EXPLORE THE NET

● List the names and phone numbers of five national drug abuse hotlines.

Alcohol and Drug Abuse Hotlines

www.hivpositive.com/f-Resources/f-20-AbuseHotlines/AlcoholDrug.html

Drug Abuse Information: Hotlines, Helplines, and Information Centers

www.corporatedrugtesting.com/cdtlinks.htm

● Locate information on drug treatment centers in your state. Describe the types of treatment provided.

The National Center on Addiction and Substance Abuse

www.casacolumbia.org/

For additional readings and exercises, visit the *Breaking Through* Web site:

www.ablongman.com/smith

| SELECTION 2 | 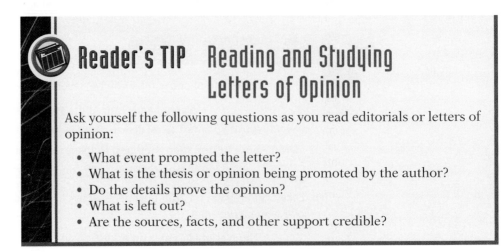 | LETTERS OF OPINION |

THINKING BEFORE READING

Preview for content and organizational clues. Activate your schema and anticipate what you will learn.

Why do women change their last names in marriage?

What marriage couples do you know who have different last names?

As a woman, if you were married three times, would you change your name each time?

This selection will probably tell me _____.

VOCABULARY PREVIEW

Are you familiar with these words?

| litany | vestige | harkens | veiled | patriarchal |
| differentiates | interjected | controversial | virtually | scarring |

Would you repeat a *litany* in church?

Is American society *patriarchal* or matriarchal?

What is presently a *controversial* topic on your campus?

THINKING DURING READING

As you read, use the five thinking strategies of a good reader: predict, picture, relate, monitor, and correct.

> ### Reader's TIP   Reading and Studying Letters of Opinion
>
> Ask yourself the following questions as you read editorials or letters of opinion:
>
> - What event prompted the letter?
> - What is the thesis or opinion being promoted by the author?
> - Do the details prove the opinion?
> - What is left out?
> - Are the sources, facts, and other support credible?

Women Selecting Names

The *Philadelphia Inquirer*, as part of a series called "Community Voices," invited readers to respond to these questions: "Did you take your husband's last name when you married?

Why or why not? Whose name did you give your children?" The following letters are a sample of the diverse responses.

LETTER FROM CHARLENE MCGRADY

5   When my husband-to-be, Doug Fearn, and I announced our intention to marry a dozen years ago, we thought we might get some push-back because he's white and I'm black. But my decision to keep my birth name (I hate the term *maiden name*) has generated far more controversy. When the issue comes up, Doug and I handle it in characteristically different ways.

10   I resort to a litany of long-winded, logical arguments, noting that I was 33 when we married and owned property (my home as well as an investment property and other investments) in my own name and was well-established personally, professionally and financially as Charlene McGrady. My life got better when I married Doug, but I certainly didn't become a new person, and I saw no reason for my established identity to disappear. Be-
15   sides, no state in the union requires women to change their names after marriage. It's simply a vestige of English common law—a custom that harkens back to the times when women were considered property and men put their names on anything they owned. I usually finish with some veiled reference to the scene in *Roots* when the slave master has Kunta Kinte beaten in an effort to make him answer to Toby, his slave name.

20   My wise and wonderful husband, on the other hand, simply smiles and explains, "I married her; I didn't adopt her."

Our nine-year-old daughter, Hannon Fearn, uses her dad's last name. She doesn't have a problem with having a different last name from mine (her first name is my mother's birth name) because many of her friends are children of first marriages and have
25   last names that are different from their remarried moms (who adopted the second husband's last name).

And I didn't have a problem with giving her Doug's last name; what's important is that she knows she can remain Hannon Fearn for the rest of her life, if she chooses.

Charlene McGrady, West Chester

LETTER FROM LIZA M. RODRIGUEZ LAVERGNE

My grandmother, Maria Eugenia Suris de Rodriguez, kept her maiden name after mar-
30 riage. My mother, Michelle Lavergne de Rodriguez, also kept hers after marrying my father. It was not until I attended college in Durham, N.C., that I became aware of the
"keep or drop" name debate taking place in feminist (and not-so-feminist) circles.

In Puerto Rico, where I was born and raised, women traditionally have kept their
family name (their father's) even after they take their marriage vows. Although keeping
35 our fathers' last names as our maiden names still reflects a patriarchal tradition, the fact
that our children use both the father's and the mother's last names differentiates our culture from the practice of adopting the husband's last name and passing that name on to
the children.

As a child, I remember my parents teaching us our eight last names (which I can still
40 recite)—four from my mother's side and four from my father's. This was a way of remembering our ancestors as far back as four generations and recognizing that we came from
the union of two families.

Therefore, it was never a question for me whether I would keep my maiden name.
However, I added a personal twist to this family tradition.

45 Although women from my grandmother's and mother's generations kept their
maiden names, they adopted their husband's by adding the word *de*, which means *of*. So
even if the mother's family name was recognized after marriage, the preposition *of* was
interjected, which implied *belonging to*.

In reflection of this practice, I decided not to adopt my husband's last name at all. I
50 simply use my maiden name (Rodriguez). But for all official documents, such as diplomas,
marriage certificates and licenses, I add my mother's name (Lavergne). It's a way of honoring her and my ancestors from my mother's side.

As for children, my husband and I agree that they should use both our names, Torres
and Rodriguez. We just haven't decided which one will come first. The last time the issue
55 came up, we discussed the possibility of leaving it up to chance. Maybe we'll just flip a coin.

Liza M. Rodriguez Lavergne, Philadelphia

LETTER FROM AMY VERSTAPPEN

When my husband and I decided to give our daughter my last name, it seemed like a
sensible plan. Having grown up in a blended family, in which different last names were
the norm, keeping my own name at marriage was an easy choice.

When I became pregnant, we considered our options. Each of our last names was al-
60 ready a mouthful, and hyphenation seemed out of the question. We considered picking a
new name, but because our names link us to our family history, that seemed artificial and
beside the point. My husband had dozens of relatives with his name, whereas mine was
due to die out with my sisters and me. Why not give our child my name? My husband
was completely comfortable with the choice, pointing out that women had been doing
65 this for centuries.

Little did we know how controversial our decision would be. Routinely, people assume
that my daughter is not my husband's—and when it is explained, they look at us in utter
shock. They ask my husband, "Didn't you want your kid to have your name?" and say to
me, "Your husband must be a really nice guy!" The idea that the man would give up the
70 privilege of "passing down his name" is virtually unthinkable; the assumption that women
will give up this privilege unquestioned. Although I know many women who kept their
name at marriage, I know no other women who have shared that last name with their children. In our age of choices, it is interesting to see how unacceptable this choice still is.

Amy Verstappen, Philadelphia

LETTER FROM SPENCER CLAYTON

If I were to get married, I would want my wife to take my last name. Not because I'm old-
75 fashioned, but because it would be easier for our children. Sure, it's the '90s, but it's also

the age when many children are born out of wedlock. By my wife not taking my last name, a different image than that of a married couple would be projected.

Nothing is more scarring for a child than being teased about their parents. I should know. My parents are divorced. All through nine years of school, people have asked
80 about my father. Teachers, friends and kids I didn't like asked about him. When I would tell my teachers about my medical problems, they would say, "Your dad's a doctor; get him to write a note." They didn't understand that he wasn't there.

I wouldn't want to give people another reason to tease my child. If they found out that my wife and I had different last names, they'd say to our child, "Your parents aren't
85 married."

If my wife didn't take my last name, my child would—simply because it is customary for a child of marriage to have his/her father's last name. However, I hope I never have to deal with this. Hopefully, my wife will take my last name—even if she keeps hers along with it.

Spencer Clayton, Philadelphia

—*Mirror on America*, edited by Joan T. Mims and Elizabeth M. Nollen

THINKING AFTER READING

RECALL   Self-test your understanding. Your instructor may choose to give a true-false review.

REACT   Which author has written the best letter in your opinion and why? Is your choice affected by your bias on the issue? _____

_____

_____

REFLECT   What facts are used to support these four arguments? List them.

_____

_____

THINK CRITICALLY   What is your position on the name that a wife should take after marriage and the name that a child should have? Write a response, similar to the previous ones, stating your opinions and listing your reasons for your position. Write your answer on a separate sheet of paper.

Name _____

Date _____

COMPREHENSION QUESTIONS

For each letter of opinion, the first three questions require filling in the blank; the others require a *T* (True) or *F* (False) answer.

(*Questions 1–6 refer to the letter by Charlene McGrady.*)

Main Idea

1. What is the author's position on her last name? _____

_____

Detail

2. List the reasons she gives for her choice. _____

_____

_____

_____

Detail

3. What is her position on her child's name, and why does she think the child accepts it? _____

_____

Inference _____ 4. The author implies that she is more concerned with explaining her name decision than her husband.

Inference _____ 5. The author includes the reference to *Roots* to show that she is not owned by her husband.

Inference _____ 6. The author implies that she has attempted to change the English common law.

(*Questions 7–12 refer to the letter by Liza M. Rodriguez.*)

Main Idea

7. What is the author's position on her last name? _____

_____

Detail

8. List the reasons she gives for her choice. _____

_____

Detail

9. What is her position on her child's name? _____

_____

Inference _____ 10. The author kept the tradition of her mother and grandmother by interjecting a preposition into her name.

Inference _____ 11. The author implies that the name-changing issue is not a feminist debate in Puerto Rico.

Detail _____ 12. Rodriguez is the author's husband's name.

(Questions 13–18 refer to the letter by Amy Verstappen.)

Main Idea 13. What is the author's position on her last name? _____

_____

Detail 14. List the reasons she gives for her choice. _____

_____

Detail 15. What is her position on her child's name, and what are her

reasons? _____

_____

Inference _____16. The author considered giving her daughter a hyphenated name.

Inference _____17. The author's tone is angry when she describes the reactions of
other people.

Inference _____18. The author implies that her husband's name is difficult to say.

(Questions 19–25 refer to the letter by Spencer Clayton.)

Main Idea 19. What is the author's position on his wife's last name? _____

_____

Detail 20. List the reasons he gives for his choice. _____

_____

Detail 21. What is his position on his child's name, and what are his reasons?

_____

Inference _____22. The author feels that his reasoning is macho.

Inference _____23. This author's opinion is more traditional than the previous authors.

Detail _____24. This author is the only male author.

Detail _____25. This is the only author who does not yet have children.

VOCABULARY

Answer the following with *a, b, c,* or *d* for the word or phrase that best defines the boldface word as used in the selection. The number in parentheses indicates the line of the passage in which the word is located.

_____ 1. "**litany** of . . . _____ 2. "**vestige** of English
arguments" (10) common law" (16)

a. essay a. mistake
b. narrative b. joke
c. repetitive chant c. fault
d. false statement d. remainder

_____ 3. "**harkens** back to the times" (16)

    a. draws attention
    b. repeats
    c. limits
    d. censors

_____ 7. "preposition *of* was **interjected**" (47)

    a. translated
    b. manipulated
    c. invented
    d. inserted

_____ 4. "**veiled** reference" (18)

    a. literary
    b. partially concealed
    c. hereditary
    d. sensitive

_____ 8. "**controversial** our decision would be" (66)

    a. quarrelsome
    b. rejected
    c. popular
    d. sad

_____ 5. "**patriarchal** tradition" (35)

    a. ancient
    b. spiritual
    c. relating to female domination
    d. relating to male domination

_____ 9. "**virtually** unthinkable" (70)

    a. essentially
    b. humanly
    c. randomly
    d. secretly

_____ 6. "**differentiates** our culture" (36–37)

    a. discloses
    b. separates
    c. symbolizes
    d. transforms

_____ 10. "**scarring** for a child" (78)

    a. frightening
    b. damaging
    c. shocking
    d. unusual

VOCABULARY ENRICHMENT

A. Use context clues and word parts to write the meaning of the boldface words in the following paragraph from a psychology book.

An organism can **replenish** its water **deficit** in two ways—by drinking and by recovering water from the kidneys before it is **excreted** as urine. A water deficit motivates the organism to drink and also sets off a homeostatic mechanism by stimulating the release of the antidiuretic hormone (ADH) from the pituitary gland. ADH regulates the kidneys so that water is reabsorbed into the bloodstream and only very concentrated urine is formed. (After a night's sleep, you may notice that your urine is a darker color and has a stronger odor than it does at other times of the day; your body has recovered water from your kidneys to **compensate** for the fact that you have not consumed fluids while you were sleeping.) This **homeostatic** mechanism can maintain the body's water balance only to a certain point, however. When the water deficit is too great, thirst becomes intense and the organism is **impelled** to find water.

—*Introduction to Psychology* by Rita Atkinson et al.

1. replenish: _____

2. deficit: _____

3. excreted: _____

4. compensate: _____

5. homeostatic: _____

6. impelled: _____

B. Create your own analogies for each type of relationship. Think of a second word that establishes the indicated relationship, and then finish the analogy with a similar comparison.

7. Degree: *Damp* is to _____ as _____ is to

_____.

8. Part to whole: *Toes* are to _____ as _____ is to

_____.

9. Cause and effect: *Careless* is to _____ as _____ is to

_____.

10. Classification: *Airplane* is to _____ as _____ is to

_____.

C. Choose one of the following transitional words or phrases to complete each sentence.

| however | for instance | thus | in addition | in a like manner |

11. Freud was the first to conceptualize a theory of personality, _____ he is considered the father of psychoanalysis.

12. Freud's theories were considered by many to be too sexual and caused some of his followers to leave; _____, a group of his followers who broke away were known as neo-Freudians.

13. Karen Horney was a neo-Freudian who, _____, became the first American female psychologist.

14. Carl Jung began with Freud studying personality; _____, later in life he focused on learning theory.

15. Although the neo-Freudians discarded some of the negativity of Freud, they retained Freud's belief that the subconscious affects the personality and, _____, popularized their own theories through research and publication.

ASSESS YOUR LEARNING

Review confusing questions, seek clarification, and make notes in your text to help you remember new information and vocabulary.

EXPLORE THE NET

● The Internet has made it possible for you to sit at home and research your family name. You can trace your family back for many generations. Locate three Web sites that provide how-to information for beginners in genealogical research. How do you get started? List suggestions that these sites give for initiating genealogical research.

Beginner's Guide to Family History Research

biz.ipa.net/arkresearch/guide.html

Genealogy Primer

www.sky.net/~mreed/primer.htm

● One way to do genealogical research is to use databases such as of military records. Locate and provide the Web site addresses of two military record databases. Are any of your ancestors listed in the databases?

WWII Civilian Draft Registration Database

ancestry.excite.com/search/rectype/inddbs/3172a.htm

Civil War Research Database

ancestry.excite.com/search/record/military/civil.html

For additional readings and exercises, visit the *Breaking Through* Web site:

www.ablongman.com/smith

SELECTION 3 **BUSINESS**

THINKING BEFORE READING

Preview for content and organizational clues. Activate your schema and anticipate what you will learn.

Who do you know who has a female boss?

Are female bosses more likely to be nitpickers than male bosses?

This selection will probably tell me _____.

VOCABULARY PREVIEW

Are you familiar with these words?

disdain	conventional	competent	apparent	shuns
clout	echelons	expertise	flounder	relentless

What does the noun form of *flounder* mean?

What does taking out a *conventional* loan on a house mean?

What is your area of *expertise*?

Your instructor may give a true-false vocabulary review before or after reading.

THINKING DURING READING

As you read, use the five thinking strategies of a good reader: predict, picture, relate, monitor, and correct.

Refer to the
Reader's Tip
for Business on
page 238.

The Job Makes the Person

"I'd never work for a woman," a woman draftsman told me. "They are too mean and petty."

Research on female workers has for years looked for sex differences on the job. Women, the surveys show, have lower aspirations than men, less commitment to work, and more concern with friendships than with the work itself. And many people assume that women make poor leaders because their personalities do not allow them to be assertive. Women who do make it to management positions are presumed to fit the mold of the dictatorial, bitchy boss.

To explain why more women don't seek or find career success, many people concentrate on supposed personality differences between the sexes: women's "motive to avoid success" or incapacity to handle power. Or they look at childhood training and educational training: how women learn to limit their ambitions and hide their accomplishments. Because women learn that high achievement means a loss of traditional femininity, they choose to preserve the latter and sacrifice the former.

When I began to study women in work organizations three years ago, I also was looking for sex-related individual differences that would explain women's absence from

high-status, powerful jobs. If women were ever going to make it in a man's world, the conventional wisdom said, we would have to get them when they're young and make sure they don't pick up any motives to avoid success or other bad habits. When I looked
20 more closely at how real people in organizations behave, however, the picture changed. I could find nothing about women in my own research and that of others that was not equally true of men in some situations. For example, some women do have low job aspirations, but so do men who are in positions of blocked opportunity. Some women managers are too interfering and coercive, but so are men who have limited power and
25 responsibility in their organizations. Some women in professional careers behave in stereotyped ways and tend to regard others of their sex with disdain, but so do men who are tokens—the only member of their group at work.

So I dropped my search for sex differences, and I concentrated instead on three aspects of a business organization that do the most to explain the conventional wisdom
30 about women: opportunity, power, and tokenism.

OPPORTUNITY

Are women less ambitious and committed to work than men? According to one large corporation I investigated, they are. This company has surveyed 111 hourly employees in white-collar jobs about their attitudes toward promotion. Sure enough, the men showed greater motivation to advance in rank than the women, and the men had higher self-
35 esteem, considering themselves more competent in the skills that would win them promotions. The women seemed much less interested in advancement, sometimes saying that they cared more about their families.

Yet in this company, like many, there were dramatic differences in the actual opportunities for promotion that men and women had. Men made up only a small proportion
40 of white-collar workers; most were clustered in professional roles with steps toward management positions. Over two thirds of the women were secretaries or clerks in dead-end jobs. They could hope to advance two or three steps up to executive secretary, and there they would stop. Only rarely had a secretary moved up into professional or managerial ranks. No wonder the women found promotion a far-fetched idea.

45   If the company had looked at women in high-ranking jobs, the apparent sex difference in work attitudes would have vanished utterly. In my interviews, I found that ambition, self-esteem, and career commitment were all flourishing among women in sales jobs, which are well-paid and on the way to top management. Indeed, one successful young woman in the sales force told me she hoped someday to run the company.

50   Lack of opportunity to succeed, not a personality style that shuns success, is often what separates the unambitious from the climbers—and the women from the men. The great majority of women hold jobs that have short, discouraging career ladders—secretarial, clerical, factory work. When the jobs include opportunities for advancement, women want to advance. But jobs without such opportunities depress a person's ambi-
55 tion and self-esteem, for men as well as women.

GOSSIP AT THE DEAD END

Opportunity also determines what kinds of relationships a person forms on the job. Workers who have few prospects of moving up and out compensate by making close friends. The very limitations of the job ensure that those friends will be around for a while, and one better make sure that at least the social side of an unchallenging job is pleasurable.
60 Being well-liked becomes another meaning of success to people in dead-end work, and if you've got the best stories to offer the office, you can add a bit of excitement to mundane work. So it often looks as if women are "talk-oriented," not "task-oriented," in their jobs. Some employers point to the gossipy office coffee klatch as a direct result of women's natural concern with people, rather than with achievement. Instead, I think it is
65 more accurate to say that female socializing reflects the jobs they have.

Highly mobile jobs demand that a person be most concerned with the work. Such jobs make close friendships with co-workers less likely. The corporate world requires its participants to be willing to relocate, to surpass rivals without hesitation, to use other people to advance in status. The aggressive, striving junior executive is as much a cre-
70 ation of his place in the organization hierarchy as is the talkative, unambitious secretary.

POWER

One of the reasons given to explain why so few women have organizational authority is that people don't like female bosses. In a 1965 *Harvard Business Review* survey of almost 2,000 executives, few respondents of either sex said that they or others would feel comfortable about working for a woman, although the women were more ready to do so
75 than the men. Over half of the men felt that women were "temperamentally unfit" for management, echoing the stereotype of the ineffective lady boss who substitutes pickiness about rules for leadership.

In fact, there is no solid evidence of lasting differences in the leadership styles of men and women. Nor is there evidence that people who work for women have lower morale.
80 Research points in the other direction: those who have worked for a woman boss are much more likely to be favorably disposed toward female leaders.

One clear factor distinguishes good leaders from bad, effective from ineffective, liked from disliked. It is not sex, but power. It is not a matter of personality, but of clout.

Just because people have been given formal authority by virtue of position and title,
85 they do not necessarily have equal access to power in the organization. It is not enough to be the most skillful handler of people in the world. One also needs system-granted power to back up one's demands and decisions and to ensure the confidence and loyalty of subordinates.

System power comes from having influence in the upper echelons of the organiza-
90 tion, through membership in informal inner circles and by having high status. As a number of social-psychological studies have shown, people who bring such signs of status and influence into a group tend to be better liked—not resented—and to get their way

more often. Organization members, as my interviews revealed, prove to be very knowledgeable about who is in and who is out, and when I asked them to describe desirable
95 bosses, they decidedly preferred those with power to those with style or expertise.

TOKENISM

I studied what happens to women when they do manage to get closer to the top, and I
uncovered a range of familiar situations. Male managers who could not accept a woman
as a colleague without constantly reminding her that she was "different." Women who
could not make themselves heard in committee meetings and who felt left out. Bright
100 women who hid their accomplishments. A female sales executive who felt that most
women should not be hired for jobs like hers. A woman scientist who let another woman
in her unit flounder without help. A woman faculty member who brought cookies to department meetings and mothered her colleagues.

All the characters were there, dressed in their sex roles. Yet I saw that even so the
105 play was not about sex. It was about numbers. These women were all tokens, alone or
nearly alone in a world of male peers and bosses. When people take on a token status—
whether they are female scientists or male nurses or black executives in a white company—they share certain experiences that influence their behavior.

Tokens, by definition, stand out from the crowd. In one company I studied, the first
110 12 women to go to work among 400 men set the rumor mill in motion. They caused
more talk and attracted more attention, usually for their physical attributes, than new
male employees. The men tended to evaluate the women against their image of the ideal
female rather than the ideal colleague, and the women, under relentless scrutiny, felt
they could not afford to make mistakes.

THE JOB MAKES THE WOMAN

115 What I am suggesting is that the job makes the man—and the woman. People bring
much of themselves and their histories to their work, but I think we have overlooked the
tremendous impact of an organization's structure on what happens to them once they
are there.

If my approach is right, it suggests that change will not come from changing person-
120 alities or attitudes, and not from studying sex or race differences. Change will come only
from interrupting the self-perpetuating cycles of blocked opportunity, powerlessness, and
tokenism.

Take the case of Linda S., a woman who had been a secretary in a large corporation
for 16 years. Five years ago, she would have said that she never wanted to be anything
125 but a secretary. She also would have told you that since she had recently had children she
was thinking of quitting. She said secretarial work was not a good enough reason to leave
the children.

Then came an affirmative-action program, and Linda was offered a promotion. She
wavered. It would mean leaving her good female friends for a lonely life among male
130 managers. Her friends thought she was abandoning them. She worried whether she
could handle the job. But her boss talked her into it and promised to help, reassuring her
that he would be her sponsor.

So Linda was promoted, and now she handles a challenging management job most
successfully. Seeing her friends is the least of her many reasons to come to work every
135 day, and her ambitions have soared. She wants to go right to the top.

"I have 15 years left to work," she says. "And I want to move up six grades to corporate vice president—at least."

(1,810 words)

—Rosabeth Moss Kanter from *Understanding Diversity* by
Carol P. Harvey and M. June Allard

THINKING AFTER READING

RECALL Self-test your understanding. Your instructor may choose to give a true-false review.

REACT What has been your experience with knowing, observing, or working for a female boss? _____

_____

_____

REFLECT List the assumptions about women workers that are stated in the beginning, and beside each, list evidence presented that substantiates or refutes those assumptions. _____

_____

_____

THINKING CRITICALLY As a new manager of a business organization, what strategies would you use to motivate employees in dead-end jobs?

CRITICAL READING

1. Why does the author begin the selection with "'I'd never work for a woman,' a woman draftsman told me. 'They are too mean and petty'"? _____

   _____

2. What is the purpose of the first five paragraphs? _____

   _____

3. What is the purpose of the anecdote about Linda S. at the end of the selection? Does the story offer valid proof of the argument? _____

   _____

4. What is the author's bias on female bosses? What is your bias? _____

   _____

5. How would you evaluate the statement, supported by the 1965 *Harvard Business Review* survey, that people do not like female bosses? _____

   _____

Name _____

Date _____

COMPREHENSION QUESTIONS

Answer the following with *a, b, c,* or *d.* In order to help you analyze your strengths and weaknesses, the question types are indicated.

Main Idea _____ 1. The best statement of the main idea of this selection is

    a. more women than men work in jobs that lack advancement opportunities.
    b. surveys have shown that people do not want to work for female bosses.
    c. work attitudes are molded more by the job itself than by sex or racial differences.
    d. men have not given women credit for their ability to succeed in high-ranking jobs.

Inference _____ 2. The tone of the passage is

    a. angry.
    b. objective.
    c. sarcastic.
    d. humorous.

Inference _____ 3. The author feels that the major problem with the company's method of surveying 111 hourly white-collar workers was

    a. more women than men were surveyed.
    b. the women cared more about their families than the men.
    c. the opportunities for advancement were not equal for the men and women surveyed.
    d. the men had higher self-esteem and would thus be more likely to win promotions.

Inference _____ 4. The author feels that the major reason women workers are often considered more talk oriented than task oriented is because

    a. women bring a strong sense of community to the workplace.
    b. women make close friends easily and have a natural concern for others.
    c. female socializing is acceptable on the job.
    d. women use friendship to compensate for lack of advancement opportunities in dead-end jobs.

Detail _____ 5. The author defines the system-granted power that a leader needs to be successful within an organization as

    a. being an informal member of the top group of decision makers.
    b. being a skillful handler of people.
    c. having the courage to back up one's demands and make decisions.
    d. having the style, personality, and desire to lead.

Inference _____ 6. The author implies all of the following about women *except*

      a. they must work harder to advance.
      b. they are regarded by colleagues as different.
      c. they are hired because the majority of the employees want change.
      d. their experiences as tokens influence their behaviors.

Inference _____ 7. The conclusion, "Women are in dead-end jobs, therefore most women are not ambitious in seeking professional advancement," is an example of an error in reasoning called

      a. straw person.
      b. transfer.
      c. misleading analogy.
      d. circular reasoning.

Mark the following as a statement of fact (*F*) or opinion (*O*).

_____ 8. Highly mobile jobs demand that a person be most concerned with the work.

_____ 9. Research points in the other direction: Those who have worked for a woman boss are much more likely to be favorably disposed toward female leaders.

_____ 10. Opportunity also determines what kinds of relationships a person forms on the job.

VOCABULARY

Answer the following with *a, b, c,* or *d* for the word or phrase that best defines the boldface word as used in the selection. The number in parentheses indicates the line of the passage in which the word is located.

_____ 1. "regard . . . with **disdain**" (26)

      a. anger
      b. scorn
      c. competition
      d. uncertainty

_____ 4. "**apparent** sex difference" (45–46)

      a. obvious
      b. unwanted
      c. unnoticed
      d. natural

_____ 2. "explain the **conventional** wisdom" (29)

      a. traditional
      b. scientific
      c. unspoken
      d. incorrect

_____ 5. "**shuns** success" (50)

      a. courts
      b. overlooks
      c. avoids
      d. loses

_____ 3. "more **competent** in the skills" (35)

      a. qualified
      b. highly paid
      c. interested
      d. flexible

_____ 6. "Not . . . personality, but of **clout**" (83)

      a. influence
      b. charm
      c. education
      d. intelligence

_____ 7. "upper **echelons** of the organization" (89–90)

    a. limits
    b. values
    c. ranks
    d. point of view

_____ 8. "style or **expertise**" (95)

    a. experience
    b. know-how
    c. leadership
    d. personality

_____ 9. "**flounder** without help" (102)

    a. quit
    b. get fired
    c. struggle
    d. beg

_____ 10. "under **relentless** scrutiny" (113)

    a. unnecessary
    b. persistent
    c. needless
    d. untimely

VOCABULARY ENRICHMENT

Select the word from the following list that best completes each sentence.

disdain	conventional	competent	apparent	shuns
clout	echelons	expertise	flounder	relentless

1. The couple chose a _____ wedding format with a white dress and formal attire.

2. Few employees in a large corporation have the _____ to be able to comfortably call the president and ask for advice.

3. The protesters showed their _____ for the flag by cutting and burning it.

4. The paparazzi were _____ in their pursuit of Princess Diana for pictures to sell to the tabloids.

5. Workers who are _____ can get the job done without supervision and do not need to look for excuses.

6. Often a professional athlete has a high level of _____ in more than one sport.

7. Success is more likely to come to a person who welcomes work rather than _____ it.

8. The clues indicated an _____ accident rather than suggesting a devious murder.

9. Mentors are frequently assigned to new students so they will not _____ without someone to call for help.

10. In a sport such as golf, only a few players in the top _____ make the cut to play in the major tournaments.

ASSESS YOUR LEARNING

Review confusing questions, seek clarification, and make notes in your text to help you remember new information and vocabulary.

EXPLORE THE NET

- Search for current books about women in the workplace. List the titles, general content, and prices for three books that sound interesting.

Amazon.com

www.amazon.com/

Barnes & Noble.com

www.bn.com/

- Find information on women who are the CEOs of major companies. List three women CEOs and the companies they head up.

CEO Help—Women CEOs

www.ceohelp.com/womenceos.html/

WITI—CEO Recognition Awards

www.witi.com/center/witimuseum/ceorecognitiona/

For additional readings and exercises, visit the *Breaking Through* Web site:

www.ablongman.com/smith

EVERYDAY READING SKILLS

Evaluating Internet Information

For researching anything from recent movie reviews to Shakespearean interpretations, the Internet offers easy access to up-to-date information. The disadvantage of Internet information, however, is that you must always question its reliability and credibility. Unlike the periodicals in libraries that are reviewed by experts, there are no gatekeepers on the Internet. Anyone from a Nobel Prize scientist to a paramilitary fanatic can purchase a Web site for approximately $100, self-publish, sound like an expert, and turn up in your search.

Be prepared to use your critical reading skills to evaluate Internet material. Question not only what is said, but also who wrote it and who paid for it.

Reader's TIP Critically Evaluating Electronic Material

Ask the following questions to evaluate:

- What are the author's credentials in the field? Is the author affiliated with a university? Check this by noting professional titles in the preface or introduction, finding a biographical reference in the library, or searching the Internet for additional references to the same author.
- Who paid for the Web page? Check the home page for an address, as well as the end of the electronic address for *edu, gov, org,* or *com.* Depending on the material, this could lend credibility or raise further questions.
- What is the purpose of the Web page? Is the purpose to educate or to sell a product, a service, or an idea? Check the links to investigate any hidden agendas.
- How do the biases of the author and the sponsor affect the material? Is the reasoning sound? Check the tone, assumptions, and evidence. What opposing views have been left out?

Refer to the Web site on the opposite page to complete Exercise 1.

exercise 1

1. What is the purpose of this site? _____

2. What are the credentials of the author? _____

3. Who paid for the site? _____

4. Why are you inclined to believe or not believe the information in the letter?

_____

SanRafael.com

San Rafael
Nutrition Company, Inc.

Welcome to the new world of health and fitness, to the incredible benefits of looking great and feeling fantastic! Forget about sweating at the gym, tedious treadmills and crowded aerobic classes. What I have to offer is a no-hassle, easy way to drop unwanted pounds for a healthier, more energetic YOU!!

This is all made possible by the San Rafael Program™, my amazing combination of all natural ingredients, including Translite™ and ZX-12™. Until now, the patented formula in the San Rafael Program™ has been the secret of **Hollywood celebrities** and others whose careers depend on a youthful, healthy appearance. The **three simple steps** of the program have been clinically proven not only to help you lose weight fast and boost your energy level, but also to help rid your body of unhealthy toxins that upset your natural metabolic balance.

To find out more about the astounding results made possible by the San Rafael Program™, click on *Info*. To order samples or to get your own supply of this fantastic product, click on *Shopping*. To find out how you can enjoy the advantages of better health as well as the financial benefits of becoming a distributor of the San Rafael Program™, click on *Network*.

Whatever option you choose, I want to welcome you to a better, healthier life and to becoming a member of the San Rafael family!

Sincerely,

Marilyn Obado

Marilyn Obado
President
San Rafael Nutrition Co., Inc.

| Info | Shopping | Network |

exercise 2

Search the Internet for a Web site that sells antiaging products such as creams that claim to prevent wrinkles or vitamin concoctions that claim to enhance vitality. Print the page, and then make a list of the claims you feel are exaggerated and not supported by facts.

Independent Textbook Assignments

- Can you apply what you have learned?
- Can you organize for textbook study?
- How well can you prepare for an exam?

Apply What You Have Learned

Do you know now how to study an actual textbook chapter on your own, prepare for a test on the chapter, and then do well on the exam? This chapter provides two longer textbook selections for you to show what you have learned. Your job as an efficient independent learner is to read, study, and learn. For each selection, your instructor has provided both multiple-choice and essay questions for your exams.

Take control and organize your study according to the strategies outlined in this text. Preview, set goals, and activate your schema before you begin to read. Use the five thinking strategies of good readers while you are reading, annotating, and taking notes. After reading, recall what you have read and predict possible exam questions. Study and use time management techniques to make sure you are 100 percent prepared on each examination date.

INDEPENDENT ASSIGNMENT 1 COMMUNICATIONS

THINKING BEFORE READING

Preview the chapter by reading the subheadings, boldface print, and inserted questions.

What focus do you predict this chapter will take on smoking?

How much time do you predict you will need to read, annotate, and take notes on this chapter?

Do you plan to take notes using an informal outline format or a system of note-taking?

To activate your schema and stimulate thinking, explain the wisdom of the following quotes:

"The test of a man's or woman's breeding is how they behave in a quarrel."—George Bernard Shaw

"Never go to bed mad. Stay up and fight."—Phyllis Diller

"You cannot shake hands with a clenched fist."—Indira Gandhi

THINKING DURING READING

As you read, predict, picture, relate, monitor, and correct. In addition, because you will need to study this material for an exam, annotate and take notes on what you want to remember in each section. As a study aid, pause to answer the questions inserted within the chapter. When you have finished the chapter, compare your notes with those of fellow classmates.

Reader's TIP   Reading in Communications

Ask yourself the following questions as you read a communications text:

- How can I improve as a communicator and a conversationalist?
- How do I react to other people? Am I open to ideas?
- How can I become a more valuable group member or a more productive group leader?
- Am I afraid to speak in public? How can I lessen that fear?
- What actions and expressions should be avoided in opening and closing a speech?

Conflict Management

Tom wants to go to the movies and Sara wants to stay home. Tom's insisting on going to the movies interferes with Sara's staying home and Sara's determination to stay home interferes with Tom's going to the movies. Randy and Grace have been dating. Randy wants to get married; Grace wants to continue dating. Each couple is experiencing interpersonal conflict, a situation in which the people (Hocker & Wilmot, 1985; Folger, Poole, & Stutman, 1997):

- are interdependent; what one person does has an effect on the other person
- perceive their goals to be incompatible; if one person's goal is achieved the other's cannot be
- see each other as interfering with his or her own goal achievement

The types and nature of conflict can be further described by reference to the concepts of content and relationship.

CONTENT AND RELATIONSHIP CONFLICTS

Content conflict centers on objects, events, and persons in the world that are usually, but not always, external to the parties involved in the conflict. These include the millions of issues that we argue about every day—the value of a particular movie, what to watch on television, the fairness of the last examination or job promotion, and the way to spend our savings.

Relational conflicts are equally numerous and include such situations as a younger brother refusing to obey his older brother, partners who each want an equal say in making vacation plans, and a mother and daughter who each want to have the final word concerning the daughter's lifestyle. Here conflicts do not arise as much from an external object as from relationships between individuals, with such issues as who is in charge, the equality of a primary relationship, and who has the right to establish rules of behavior.

Like many such concepts, content and relationship conflicts are easier to separate in a textbook than they are in real life, where many conflicts contain elements of both. However, it helps in understanding and in effectively managing conflict, if you can recognize those issues that pertain to content (primarily) and those that pertain to relationship (primarily).

- *Question:* How do content and relationship conflicts differ?

MYTHS ABOUT CONFLICT

One of the problems in dealing with interpersonal conflict is that we may be operating with false assumptions about what conflict is and what it means. For example, do you think the following are true or false?

- If two people in a relationship experience conflict, it means their relationship is in trouble.
- Conflict hurts an interpersonal relationship.
- Conflict is bad because it reveals our negative selves, for example, our pettiness, our need to control, our unreasonable expectations.

As with most things, simple answers are usually wrong. The three assumptions above may all be true or may all be false. It depends. In and of itself, conflict is neither good or bad. Conflict is a part of every interpersonal relationship, between parents and children, brothers and sisters, friends, lovers, and co-workers. If it isn't, then the relationship is probably dull, irrelevant, or insignificant. So, it's not so much the conflict that creates a problem as the way in which you deal with the conflict. Because of this, the major portion of this chapter focuses on ways of managing conflict rather than avoiding it.

THE NEGATIVES AND POSITIVES OF CONFLICT

Conflict can lead to both negative and positive effects. Among the potential negative effects is that it may lead to increased negative feelings for your "opponent" (who may be your best friend or lover). It may cause a depletion of energy better spent on other areas. Or, it can lead you to close yourself off from the other person, to shrink the size of your open self. When you hide your true self from an intimate, you prevent meaningful communication.

The major positive value of interpersonal conflict is that it forces you to examine a problem that you may otherwise avoid and work toward a potential solution. If productive conflict strategies are used, a stronger, healthier, and more satisfying relationship

"What's amazing to me is that this late in the game we still have to settle our differences with rocks."

may well emerge from the encounter. The very fact that you're trying to resolve a conflict means that you feel the relationship is worth the effort—otherwise you'd walk away from such conflict. Through conflict you learn more about each other and with that knowledge comes understanding.

- *Question:* What are the negative and positive effects of conflict?

CULTURAL CONTEXT

The cultural context is important in understanding and in effectively managing conflict. Culture influences the issues that people argue about as well as what are considered appropriate or inappropriate strategies for dealing with conflict. For example, cohabiting 18-year-olds are more likely to experience conflict with their parents about their living style if they lived in the United States than if they lived in Sweden where cohabitation is much more accepted. Similarly, male infidelity is more likely to cause conflict among American couples than among southern European couples.

- *Question:* Give an example from your experience of how culture affects conflict.

BEFORE AND AFTER THE CONFLICT

If you're to make conflict truly productive, you'll need to consider a few suggestions for preparing for the conflict and for using the conflict as a method for relational growth.

Before the Conflict. Try to fight in private. In front of others, you may not be willing to be totally honest; you may feel you have to save face and therefore must win the fight at all costs. You also run the risk of incurring resentment and hostility by embarrassing your partner in front of others.

Although conflicts typically arise at the most inopportune times, you can choose the time when you will try to resolve them. Confronting your partner when she or he comes home after a hard day of work may not be the right time for resolving a conflict. Make sure you're both relatively free of other problems and ready to deal with the conflict at hand.

Know what you're fighting about. Only when you define your differences in specific terms, can you begin to understand and resolve them. Fight about problems that can be solved. Fighting about past behaviors or about family members or situations over which you have no control is usually counterproductive.

After the Conflict. Learn from the conflict and from the process you went through in trying to resolve it. For example, can you identify the fight strategies that aggravated the situation? Does your partner need a cooling-off period? Do you need extra space when upset? Can you tell when minor issues are going to escalate into major arguments? Does avoidance make matters worse? What issues are particularly disturbing and likely to cause conflicts? Can these be avoided?

Keep the conflict in perspective. Be careful not to blow it out of proportion where you begin to define your relationship in terms of conflict. Avoid the tendency to see disagreement as inevitably leading to major blow-ups. Conflicts in most relationships actually occupy a very small percentage of the couple's time and yet, in their recollection, they often loom extremely large.

Attack your negative feelings. Negative feelings frequently arise because unfair fight strategies were used to undermine the other person—for example, personal rejection, manipulation, or force. Resolve surely to avoid such unfair tactics in the future, but at the same time let go of guilt and blame, for yourself and your partner. If you think it would help, discuss these feelings with your partner or even a therapist.

Increase the exchange of rewards and cherishing behaviors to demonstrate your positive feelings and that you are over the conflict. It's a good way of saying you want the relationship to survive and flourish.

- *Question:* List some guidelines to follow before and after conflicts.

EFFECTIVE CONFLICT MANAGEMENT

Throughout the process of resolving conflict, avoid the common but damaging strategies that can destroy a relationship. At the same time, consciously apply the strategies that will resolve the conflict and even improve the relationship. Here we consider seven general strategies each of which has a destructive and a productive dimension.

WIN-LOSE AND WIN-WIN STRATEGIES

In any interpersonal conflict, you have a choice. You can look for solutions in which one person wins, usually you, and the other person loses, usually the other person (win-lose solutions). Or you can look for solutions in which you and the other person both win (win-win solutions). Obviously, win-win solutions are the more desirable, at least when the conflict is interpersonal. Too often, however, we fail to even consider the possibility of win-win solutions and what they might be.

For example, let's say that I want to spend our money on a new car (my old one is unreliable) and you want to spend it on a vacation (you're exhausted and want to rest). Through conflict and its resolution, we hope to learn what each really wants. We may then be able to figure out a way for each of us to get what we want. I might accept a good used car and you might accept a less expensive vacation. Or we might buy a used car and take an inexpensive road trip. Each of these solutions will satisfy both of us—they are win-win solutions—each of us wins, and gets what we want.

• *Question:* Describe a win-win solution and a win-lose solution from your experience.

AVOIDANCE AND FIGHTING ACTIVELY

Avoidance is physical or psychological withdrawal from the conflict situation. Sometimes it involves physical flight—you leave the scene of the conflict (walk out of the apartment

"Let me finish! You always say, 'You win' before I've won!"

or go to another part of the office.) Sometimes it involves setting up a physical barrier like blasting the stereo or locking the door. Sometimes it takes the form of emotional or intellectual avoidance. In this case you leave the conflict psychologically by not dealing with any of the arguments or problems raised, much like the gentleman in the cartoon who'd rather end the discussion before it begins.

Instead of avoiding the issues, take an active role in your interpersonal conflicts. This is not to say that a cooling-off period is not at times desirable. It is to say, instead, that if you wish to resolve the conflict, you should take responsibility for your thoughts and feelings. For example, when you disagree with your partner or find fault with her or his behavior, take responsibility for these feelings, use I-messages. For example, you can say, "I disagree with . . ." or "I don't like it when you . . ." Avoid statements that deny your responsibility, for example, "Everybody thinks you're wrong about . . ." or "Chris thinks you shouldn't . . ."

- *Question:* What is an avoidance strategy, and what is the effect?

FORCE AND TALK

When confronted with conflict, many people prefer not to deal with the issues but rather to emotionally or physically force their positions on the other person. In either case, however, the conflict at hand is avoided and the person who "wins" is the one who exerts the most force. This technique is commonly used by warring nations, children, and even some normally sensible and mature adults. This is surely one of the most serious problems confronting relationships today, but many approach it as if it were of only minor importance or even something humorous.

More than 50% of both single and married couples reported that they had experienced physical violence in their relationship. If we add symbolic violence (for example, threatening to hit the other person or throwing something), the percentages are above 60% for singles and above 70% for marrieds (Marshall & Rose, 1987). In another study, 47% of a sample of 410 college students reported some experience with violence in a dating relationship. In most cases, the violence was reciprocal—each person in the relationship used violence. In cases in which only one person was violent, the research results are conflicting. For example, Deal and Wampler (1986) found that in cases where one partner was violent, the aggressor was significantly more often the female partner. Other research, however, has found that the popular conception of men being more likely to use force than women is indeed true (DeTurck, 1987): Men are more apt than women to use violent methods to achieve compliance.

One of the most puzzling findings is that many victims of violence interpret it as a sign of love. For some reason, they see being beaten, verbally abused, or raped as a sign that their partner is fully in love with them. Many victims, in fact, accept the blame for contributing to the violence instead of blaming their partners (Gelles & Cornell, 1985; Ehrensaft & Vivian, 1996).

The only real alternative to force is talk. Instead of force, talk and listen. The qualities of openness, empathy, and positiveness, for example, discussed earlier are suitable starting points.

- *Question:* Why do you think victims interpret force as a sign of love?

GUNNYSACKING AND PRESENT FOCUS

Gunnysacking refers to the practice of storing up grievances (as in a gunnysack, a large bag usually of burlap) so we may unload them at another time. The immediate occasion may be relatively simple (or so it might seem at first), such as someone's coming home late without calling. Instead of arguing about this, the gunnysacker unloads all past grievances. The birthday you forgot 2 years ago, the time you arrived late for dinner last month, the hotel reservations you forgot to make are all noted. As you probably know from experience, when one person gunnysacks, the other person often reciprocates. As a result two people end up dumping their stored-up grievances on one another. Frequently the original problem never gets addressed. Instead, resentment and hostility escalates.

A present focus is far more constructive. Focus your conflict on the here-and-now rather than on issues that occurred in the past (as in gunnysacking). Similarly, focus your conflict on the person with whom you're fighting, not on the person's mother, child, or friends.

- *Question:* How did gunnysacking get its name?

FACE-ENHANCING AND FACE-DETRACTING STRATEGIES

Another dimension of conflict strategies is that of face orientation. Face-detracting or face-attacking strategies involve treating the other person as incompetent, untrustworthy, or bad (Donahue & Kolt, 1992). Such attacks can vary from mildly embarrassing the other person to severely damaging his or her ego or reputation. When such attacks become extreme they may be similar to verbal aggressiveness—a tactic explained in the next section.

Face-enhancing techniques help the other person maintain a positive image, one of a person who is competent, trustworthy, and good. There is some evidence to show that even when you get what you want, for example, at bargaining, it's wise to help the other person retain positive face. This makes it less likely that future conflicts will arise (Donahue & Kolt, 1992). Not surprisingly, people are more likely to make a greater effort to support the listener's "face" if they like the listener than if they don't (Meyer, 1994).

- *Question:* What tactics are designed to make others lose face?

ATTACK AND ACCEPTANCE

An attack can come in many forms. In *personal rejection*, for example, one party to a conflict withholds love and affection. He or she seeks to win the argument by getting the other person to break down in the face of this withdrawal. In withdrawing affection, the individual hopes to make the other person question his or her own self-worth. Once the other is demoralized and feels less than worthy, it's relatively easy for the "rejector" to get his or her way. The "rejector," in other words, holds out the renewal of love and affection as a reward for resolving the conflict in his or her favor.

When you attack someone by hitting below the belt, a tactic called *beltlining*, you can inflict serious injury. When you hit above the belt, however, the person is able to absorb the blow. With most interpersonal relationships, especially those of long standing, you know where the belt line is. You know, for example, that to hit Pat with the inability to have children is to hit below the belt. You know that to hit Chris with the failure to get a permanent job is to hit below the belt. Hitting below the beltline causes added problems for all persons involved. Keep blows to areas your opponent and your relationship can absorb and handle.

Express positive feelings for the other person and for your relationship. Communication is irreversible; the words cannot be unsaid or uncommunicated, but they can be partially offset by the expression of positive statements.

- *Question:* How are personal rejection and beltlining connected?

VERBAL AGGRESSIVENESS AND ARGUMENTATIVENESS

Verbal aggressiveness is a method of winning an argument by inflicting psychological pain—by attacking the other person's self-concept. It's a type of disconfirmation that seeks to discredit the person's view of himself or herself and is often the talk that leads to physical force (Infante & Wigley, 1986; Infante, Sabourin, Rudd, & Shannon, 1990; Infante, Riddle, Horvath & Tumlin, 1992).

Argumentativeness, on the other hand and contrary to popular usage, refers to a quality that is productive in conflict resolution. It refers to your willingness to argue for a point of view—your tendency to speak your mind on significant issues. It's the preferred alternative to verbal aggressiveness for dealing with disagreements.

To cultivate argumentativeness and prevent it from degenerating into aggressiveness, treat disagreements as objectively as possible. Avoid assuming that because someone takes issue with your position or your interpretation, that they're attacking you as a person (Infante, 1988). Avoid attacking the other person (rather than the person's arguments) even if this would give you a tactical advantage; it will probably backfire at some later time and make your relationship more difficult. Center your arguments on issues rather than people.

Reaffirm the other person's sense of competence; compliment the other person as appropriate. Allow the other person to save face; never humiliate the other person. Avoid interrupting; allow the other person to state her or his position fully before you respond. Stress equality and the similarities that you share; stress your areas of agreement before attacking the disagreements. Throughout the conflict episode, express interest in the person's position, attitude, and point of view.

- *Question:* Why is argumentativeness considered positive?

—*Essentials of Human Communication,* Third Edition, by Joseph DeVito

THINKING AFTER READING

Recall what you have read with a study buddy and prepare to take an examination on the material.

1. What are the major points in this chapter? _____

   _____

   _____

2. What essay questions might be asked about this chapter? _____

   _____

   _____

3. What multiple-choice or true-false questions might be asked? _____

   _____

   _____

4. What will be your time schedule for studying the material in this chapter?

   _____

   _____

   _____

5. When is the exam and how much will it count toward your final grade?

   _____

   _____

   _____

Exam Description: The exam prepared for this textbook chapter includes 9 multiple-choice and 11 true-false items, as well as an essay question. Be sure you know the definitions of destructive and productive conflict management strategies and can also recognize applications of those strategies.

THINKING AFTER THE EXAM

PERSONAL Feedback 1 Name _____

1. How would you evaluate your grade on the exam? _____
   _____
   _____

2. Did you make the grade that you studied to get? Why or why not?
   _____
   _____

3. What on the exam came as a surprise to you? _____
   _____
   _____

4. What was on the exam that was not included in your notes? ___
   _____
   _____

5. How will you study differently next time? _____
   _____
   _____

6. How will you manage your time differently next time? _____
   _____
   _____

7. Did you work with a study buddy? Why or why not? _____
   _____
   _____

INDEPENDENT ASSIGNMENT 2   HISTORY

THINKING BEFORE READING

Preview the chapter by reading the subheadings. Write down your time plan for reading, annotating, notetaking, and studying this chapter.

THINKING DURING READING

As you read, predict, picture, relate, monitor, and correct. In addition, because you will need to study this material for an exam, annotate and take notes on what you want to remember in each section. Use the study questions in the bulleted lists to test your comprehension.

Refer to the **Reader's Tip** *on History on page 140.*

The Surge Westward

Early in April 1846, 87 pioneers led by George Donner, a well-to-do 62-year-old farmer, set out from Illinois for California. As this group of pioneers headed westward, they never imagined the hardship that awaited them. The pioneers' 27 wagons were loaded not only with necessities, but with fancy foods, liquor, and such luxuries as built-in beds and stoves.

In Wyoming, the party decided to take a shortcut, having read in a guidebook that pioneers could save 400 miles by cutting south of the Great Salt Lake. At first the trail was "all that could be desired," but soon huge boulders and dangerous mountain passes slowed the expedition to a crawl. During one stretch, the party traveled only 36 miles in 21 days. In late October, the Donner party reached the eastern Sierra Nevada and prepared to cross the Truckee Pass, the last remaining barrier before they arrived in California's Sacramento Valley. They climbed the high Sierra ridges in an attempt to cross the pass, but early snows blocked their path.

Trapped, the party built crude tents covered with clothing, blankets, and animal hides, which were soon buried under 14 feet of snow. The pioneers intended to slaughter their livestock for food, but many of the animals perished in 40-foot snowdrifts. To survive, the Donner party was forced to eat mice, their rugs, and even their shoes. In the end, surviving members of the party escaped starvation only by eating the flesh of those who died.

Finally, in mid-December, 17 men and women made a last-ditch effort to cross the pass to find help. They took only a six-day supply of rations, consisting of finger-sized pieces of dried beef—two pieces per person per day. During a severe storm two of the group died. The surviving members of the party "stripped the flesh from their bones, roasted and ate it, averting their eyes from each other, and weeping." More than a month passed before seven frostbitten survivors reached an American settlement. By then, the rest had died and two Native-American guides had been shot and eaten.

Relief teams immediately sought to rescue the pioneers still trapped near Truckee Pass. The situation that the rescuers found was unspeakably gruesome. Surviving members of the Donner party were delirious from hunger and overexposure. One survivor was found in a small cabin next to the cannibalized body of a young boy. Of the original 87 members of the party, only 47 survived.

It took white Americans a century and a half to expand as far west as the Appalachian Mountains, a few hundred miles from the Atlantic coast. It took another 50 years to push the frontier to the Mississippi river. By 1830, fewer than 100,000 pioneers had crossed the Mississippi.

During the 1840s, however, tens of thousands of Americans ventured beyond the Mississippi River. Inspired by the new vision of the West as a paradise of plenty, filled with fertile valleys and rich land, thousands of family chalked GTT ("Gone to Texas") on their gates or painted "California or Bust" on their wagons and joined the trek westward. By 1850 pioneers had pushed the edge of American settlement all the way to Texas, the Rocky Mountains, and the Pacific Ocean.

- *Questions:* What happened to the Donner party?

  How did the survivors reach California?

  Trace the route of the Donner party on a current map.

PATHFINDERS

In 1803, the year that the United States purchased the Louisiana territory from France, President Thomas Jefferson appointed his personal secretary, Meriwether Lewis, and William Clark, a former U.S. military officer, to explore the area's northern portion. Between 1804 and 1806, Lewis and Clark and about 45 other men traveled up the Missouri River, across the Rocky Mountains, and along the Columbia River as far as the Pacific before returning to St. Louis.

In 1806, as Lewis and Clark returned from their 8000-mile expedition, a young army lieutenant named Zebulon Pike left St. Louis to explore Louisiana territory's southern portion. Traveling along the Arkansas River, Pike saw the towering peak that bears his name. He and his party then traveled into Spanish territory along the Rio Grande and Red River. Pike's description of the wealth of Spanish towns in the Southwest attracted American traders to the region.

Pike's report of his expedition, published in 1810, helped to create one of the most influential myths about the Great Plains; that is, that the plains were nothing more than a "Great American Desert," a treeless and waterless land of dust storms and starvation. "Here," wrote Pike, is "barren soil, parched and dried up for eight months of the year . . . [without] a speck of vegetation."

- *Questions:* What did Lewis and Clark do?

  What areas did Zebulon Pike explore?

MOUNTAIN MEN

Fur traders and trappers quickly followed in the footsteps of Lewis and Clark, who brought back reports of rivers and streams teeming with beaver and otter in the northern Rockies. Starting in 1807, keelboats ferried fur trappers up the Missouri River. By the mid-1830s these "mountain men" had marked out the overland trails that would lead pioneers to Oregon and California.

The Rocky Mountain Fur Company played a central role in opening the western fur trade. Instead of buying skins from the Native Americans, the company ran ads in St. Louis newspapers asking for white trappers willing to go to the wilderness. In 1822, it sent a hundred trappers along the upper Missouri River. Three years later the company introduced the "rendezvous" system, under which trappers met once a year at an agreed-upon meeting place to barter pelts for supplies. "The rendezvous," wrote one participant, "is one continued scene of drunkenness, gambling, and brawling and fighting, as long as the money and the credit of the trappers last."

- *Question:* How did the Rocky Mountain Fur Company open the western fur trade?

TRAILBLAZING

The Santa Fe and Oregon trails were the two principal routes to the far West. William Becknell, an American trader, opened the Santa Fe Trail in 1821. His 800-mile journey from Missouri to Santa Fe took two months. When he could find no water, Becknell drank blood from a mule's ear and the contents of a buffalo's stomach. Ultimately, the trail tied the New Mexican Southwest economically to the United States and hastened American penetration of the region.

The Santa Fe Trail served primarily commercial functions. From the early 1820s until the 1840s, an average of 80 wagons and 150 traders used the trail each year. Mexican settlers in Santa Fe purchased cloth, hardware, glass, and books. On their return east, American traders carried Mexican blankets, beaver pelts, wool, mules, and silver. By the 1830s, traders had extended the trail into California with branches reaching Los Angeles and San Diego.

- *Question:* What is the historical importance of the Santa Fe Trail?

SETTLING THE FAR WEST

During the 1840s thousands of pioneers headed westward toward California and Oregon. In 1841, the first party of 69 pioneers left Missouri for California, led by an Ohio schoolteacher named John Bidwell. The members of the party knew little about western travel: "We only knew that California lay to the west." The hardships the party endured were nearly unbearable. They were forced to abandon their wagons and eat their pack animals, "half roasted, dripping with blood." But American pioneering of the far West had begun. The next year another 200 pioneers went west. Over the next 25 years, 350,000 more made the trek along the overland trails.

- *Question:* Outline the order, according to approximate years, in which significant western settlement occurred.

LIFE ON THE TRAIL

Each spring, pioneers gathered at Council Bluffs, Iowa, and Independence and St. Joseph, Missouri, to begin a 2000-mile journey westward. For many families, the great spur for emigration was economic. The financial depression of the late 1830s, accompanied by floods and epidemics in the Mississippi Valley, forced many to pull up stakes and head west. Said one woman: "We had nothing to lose, and we might gain a fortune." Most settlers traveled in family units. Even single men attached themselves to family groups.

At first, pioneers tried to maintain the rigid sexual division of labor that characterized early nineteenth-century America. Men drove the wagons and livestock, stood guard duty, and hunted buffalo and antelope for extra meat. Women got up before dawn, collected wood and "buffalo chips" (animal dung used for fuel), hauled water, kindled campfires, kneaded dough, and milked cows. The demands of the journey forced a blurring of gender-role distinctions for women who, in addition to domestic chores, performed many duties previously reserved for men. They drove wagons, yoked cattle, and loaded wagons. Some men did such things as cooking, previously regarded as women's work.

Accidents, disease, and sudden disaster were ever-present dangers. Diseases such as typhoid, dysentery, and mountain fever killed many pioneers. Emigrant parties also suffered devastation from buffalo stampedes, prairie fires, and floods. At least 20,000 emigrants died along the Oregon Trail.

Still, despite the hardships of the experience, few emigrants ever regretted their decision to move west. As one pioneer put it: "Those who crossed the plains . . . never forgot the ungratified thirst, the intense heat and bitter cold, the craving hunger and utter physical exhaustion of the trail. . . . But there was another side. True they had suffered, but the satisfaction of deeds accomplished and difficulties overcome more than compensated and made the overland passage a thing never to be forgotten."

- *Questions:* Why did settlers go west?
  What were the hardships and divisions of labor for pioneers on the trail west?

MANIFEST DESTINY

In 1845 an editor named John L. O'Sullivan referred in a magazine to America's "manifest destiny to overspread the continent allotted by Providence for the free development of our yearly multiplying millions." One of the most influential slogans ever coined, the term *manifest destiny* expressed the romantic emotion that led Americans to risk their lives to settle the far West.

The idea that America had a special destiny to stretch across the continent motivated many people to migrate west. Manifest destiny inspired a 29-year-old named Stephen F. Austin to talk of grandly colonizing the Mexican province of Texas with "North American population, enterprise and intelligence." It led expansionists—united behind the slogan "54°40' or fight!"—to demand that the United States should own the entire Pacific Northwest all the way to Alaska. Aggressive nationalists invoked the idea to justify the displacement of Native Americans from their land, war with Mexico, and American expansion into Cuba and Central America. More positively, the idea of manifest destiny also inspired missionaries, farmers, and pioneers, who dreamed only of transforming plains and fertile valleys into farms and small towns.

- *Questions:* What is manifest destiny?
  What is the historical significance of manifest destiny?

—*America and Its People*, Third Edition, by James Martin et al.

THINKING AFTER READING

Recall what you have read with a study buddy and prepare to take an examination on the material.

1. What are the major points in this chapter? _____

   _____

2. What essay questions might be asked about this chapter? _____

   _____

3. What multiple-choice or true-false questions might be asked? _____

_____

_____

4. What will be your time schedule for studying the material in this chapter?

_____

_____

5. When is the exam and how much will it count toward your final grade?

_____

_____

Exam Description: The exam prepared for this textbook chapter includes 20 true-false items and one essay question. Be sure that you know the detail of the westward expansion and cause and effect nature of the events.

THINKING AFTER THE EXAM

PERSONAL Feedback 2   Name _____

1. How would you evaluate your grade on the exam? _____

_____

2. Did you make the grade that you studied to get? Why or why not?

_____

3. What on the exam came as a surprise to you? _____

_____

4. What was on the exam that was not included in your notes? _____

_____

5. How will you study differently next time? _____

_____

6. How will you manage your time differently next time? _____

_____

7. Did you work with a study buddy? Why or why not? _____

_____

8. How did your studying and performance on this exam differ from the previous exam on conflict management? _____

_____

Appendix 1
Pronunciation Review

There are twenty-six letters in the English alphabet. These letters, however, make many more than twenty-six sounds. When you are trying to sound out a new word, knowing a few principles of phonics will help.

Phonics is the use of letter–sound relationships in pronouncing unknown words. With a knowledge of phonics, you can sound out parts of a word and then blend the parts to make a whole. The whole usually approximates the sound of the word. If the word is already in your speaking vocabulary, the approximation may be sufficient to trigger your recall of the exact pronunciation. If you need an exact pronunciation, check the dictionary for the phonetic spelling.

Principles of Phonics

Do All Letters Make Sounds?

Say *time*. How many sounds do you hear? How many letters are there? There are four letters, but only three sounds because the final *e* is not heard. Sometimes the number of sounds and the number of letters are the same, and sometimes they are not.

Slowly say each word that follows, and listen for the sounds. In the blank next to the word, write the number of sounds you hear.

ball __3__   heel _____   hen _____   ride _____

ate __2__   sand _____   con _____   play _____

can _____   top _____   boy _____   snow _____

The Short Vowel Sounds

The letters *a, e, i, o,* and *u* are vowels.[1] You will always remember the short vowel sounds if you memorize the beginning sound of the following keyword pictures.

a = apple

---

[1]The letter *y* can serve as a consonant or vowel. When *y* comes at the beginning of a word as in *yellow*, it is a consonant. The letter *y* in the middle of a word usually stands for a short *i* vowel sound as in *gym*. As the last sound in a short word such as *my*, the letter *y* usually stands for a long *i* vowel sound. In a longer word such as *baby*, the final *y* usually stands for a long *e* vowel sound.

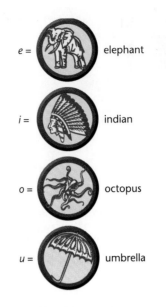

e = elephant

i = indian

o = octopus

u = umbrella

Say each of the following words, and put a check next to each word that has a short vowel sound.

flag _____   cup _____   hair _____   pig _____

feed _____   meat _____   top _____   nine _____

can _____   egg _____   flip _____   us _____

The Long Vowel Sounds

Notice the difference in the *o* sound in *got* and *go*. The *o* in *got* is short, as in *octopus*, whereas the *o* in *go* is a long vowel sound.

When a vowel says its name, as the *o* in *go*, it is called the *long sound* of the vowel. These long sounds are formed in several ways.

Compare the sound of *a* in *man* and in *main*. The first *a* is short and the second *a* is long. Study the following word pairs. How does the additional letter change the sound of the vowel?

ran   rain
got   goat
met   meat
bat   bait
fed   feed

When a word has two vowels together, usually the first vowel is long and the second is silent.

Now compare the sound of the *a* in *at* and in *ate*. The first *a* is short and the second *a* is long. Study these word pairs. How does the final *e* affect the preceding vowel?

us   use
pin   pine
rip   ripe
mad   made
not   note

When a word has a vowel followed by a consonant, the final e is silent and the preceding vowel is long.

Mark the following vowels as short (ăt) or long (āt¢). Cross out the silent vowels.

māil	pie	boat	but
pĕt	kite	dime	coal
fast	milk	leaf	did

The Consonant Sounds

The letters other than *a, e, i, o,* and *u* are consonants. A vowel can be pronounced by itself, but a consonant needs a vowel to make a complete sound. Study the first sound of the following words to learn the sound of the consonants.

ball	sun	tap	pipe	vase
fish	rat	moon	kite	wagon
lamp	hat	dog	jug	zipper

Tricky Consonant Sounds

1. *C* (*cat* versus *cigar*): When *c* is followed by *e, i,* or *y,* it usually has the soft sound of the *s* in *sun,* as in *cell, city, bicycle, ace,* and *cent.* When *c* is followed by *a, or,* or *u,* it usually has the hard sound of the *k* in *kite,* as in *cast, cocoa, curb, Dracula,* and *come.*
2. *G* (*gate* versus *giraffe*): When *g* is followed by *e, i,* or *y,* it usually has the soft sound of the *j* in *jump,* as in *germ, ginger, cage,* and *giant.* When *g* is followed by other letters, it has the hard sound of the *g* in *gate,* as in *drug, gag, tugboat,* and *piglet.*
3. *Q* (*queen*): The *u* always follows the *q* to make the *kw* sound, as in *quart, quick,* and *quiz.*
4. *X* (*box*): When *x* is at the end of a word, is usually has a *ks* sound, as in *ax, ox,* and *fox.*
5. *Y* (*yard* versus *gym*): When *y* begins a word, it is a consonant, as in *yellow* and *yell.* At the end of a word, however, *y* is a vowel, as in *very, sadly,* and *many.*

Consonant Blends

Two or three consonant letters that appear together and keep their own sounds are called *consonant blends.* When you say the word, you can hear each consonant in the blend. Blends can be found in the beginning, middle, or end of a word. Study the following blends and listen to the sounds.

black	brown	prize	snip	spring
clean	crab	train	spider	square
fly	dry	scum	still	string
glee	fry	skip	sweet	hunt
plum	green	smoke	scrub	thank
			sand	held

Consonant Digraphs

When two consonants are next to each other but make only one speech sound, they are called *consonant digraphs*. Some digraphs take the sound of a single letter, whereas others form a new sound.

shell	laugh	church
that	phone	
what		

Silent Consonants

In several unusual cases, a consonant can be silent. Study the following examples, and note the letter combinations in which only one consonant is heard.

putt	gnat	autumn
lamb	sight	psalm
debt	ghost	isle
duck	knit	castle
scene	calf	wrap

Double Vowel Sounds

When two vowels appear next to each other in a word, they can have only the sound of the first vowel, a new single sound, or more than one single sound.

Sound of the First Vowel Only	New Single Sound	More Than One Sound
aid	haul	out
tray	boy	dough
sea	coin	cousin
dead		soup
week		room
soap		foot

Compound Words

When small words are put together to make a longer word, the result is called a *compound word*. Study the examples.

after + noon = afternoon
to + day = today
birth + day = birthday

Show the parts of the following compound words by drawing a line between the short words.

everything	underpass	watchman	landslide
crossroad	butterfly	sometime	moonlight
cowboy	peanut	pocketbook	oatmeal

Counting the Syllables in a Word

A syllable is a part of a word. Each syllable has a vowel sound. To tell how many syllables a word has, count the vowels that make sounds. Remember that final *e*'s are usually silent. If two vowels come together, they usually count as only one sound. In addition, remember that *y* at the end of a word is usually a vowel. Study the following examples, and note the number of syllables in each word.

contest	__2__	baggage	__2__	complain	__2__	dictionary	__4__
kindergarten	__4__	ambulance	__3__	foundation	__3__	victory	__3__

Count the number of syllables in the following words.

injury	__3__	diplomatic	____	democracy	____
organization	____	refreshments	____	kangaroo	____
disappointment	____	establishment	____	discovery	____
correspondent	____	scissors	____	combination	____

Dividing Words Between Syllables

To divide a word into syllables, first mark the vowel and consonant sounds in the word. Be sure to allow for consonant blends. Then follow one of the two basic patterns:

Pattern 1. Vowel consonant/consonant vowel (vc/cv)

dinner
vc|cv

children
vc|cv

sister
vc|cv

garden
vc|cv

basket
vc|cv

entertainment
vc|cvc|cvc |cv

Pattern 2. Vowel/consonant vowel (v/cv)

before
v|cv

music
v|cv

lady
v|cv

reason
v|cv

hotel
v|cv

baby
v|cv

Divide the following words into syllables using the vc/cv and v/cv patterns.

over	window	prepare
December	recess	potato
yesterday	doctor	gravy

Long versus Short Vowels

No rule will enable you to pronounce all words correctly, but two rules can help you.

1. If a syllable ends with a consonant sound, the vowel sound in the syllable is usually short. It is called a *closed syllable*.

   dĭn|nĕr   fŏr|gĕt
   vc|cv   vc|cv

   wĭn|dŏw   hăp|pĕn
   vc|cv   vc|cv

2. If a syllable ends with a vowel sound, that vowel sound is usually long. It is called an *open syllable*.

   hō|tĕl   ō|pĕn
   v|cv   v|cv

   hā|lō   mō|lăr
   v|cv   v|cv

Divide the following words into syllables using the vc/cv and v/cv patterns. Mark the long and short vowel sounds using the rule for open and closed syllables.

yellow	volcano	vacant
Mohawk	November	label
hello	passenger	simmer
annotate	plentiful	traffic

Using Phonics to Decode and Pronounce Words

Use what you have learned about phonics to pronounce the following words. Many may be new to you. Use the vc/cv and v/cv patterns to divide them into syllables. Be aware of blends and silent letters. Then rewrite the word and mark each vowel sound as long or short.

prenatal	prē nā tăl	hallucinogen	_____
avert	_____	fiscal	_____
engram	_____	rubella	_____
castigate	_____	peptide	_____
scurrilous	_____	mitosis	_____
olfactory	_____	inadvertent	_____
independent	_____	aspirant	_____

Using the Dictionary's Phonetic Spelling

The phonetic spelling of a word in the dictionary may seem like a foreign language at first. The symbols represent sounds that are all explained in a key. After you learn a few basic principles, the symbols will help you rather than confuse you.

Pronunciation Key

Every dictionary contains a pronunciation key. In a standard dictionary, a short form of the key is usually found at the bottom of each page spread, and the complete list of symbols is in the front of the book. Many of the sounds, especially the short and long vowels, will be familiar to you. For the letters with unfamiliar marks, sound out the sample word to understand the sound and duplicate it in your new word. The following is the short pronunciation key. Say each sample word and listen for the sound of the letters in bold.

a hat	**i** it	**oi** oil	**ch** child	⎡ a in about
ā age	**ī** ice	**ou** out	**ng** long	⎢ e in taken
ä far	**o** hot	**u** cup	**sh** she	**ə** = ⎢ i in pencil
e let	**ö** open	**u̇** put	**th** thin	⎢ o in lemon
ē equal	**ô** order	**ü** rule	**ŦH** then	⎣ u in circus
ėr term			**zh** measure	

Accents

An accent mark placed after a syllable tells you to stress that syllable when you pronounce the word. For example, the word *minute* can have one of two meanings, depending on how you pronounce it. With the accent on the first syllable, *min' it*, the word means sixty seconds. With the accent on the second, *min nut'*, it means very tiny. This heavy accent mark is called the *primary accent*. Some words contain a secondary accent mark, which means that another syllable receives some stress but not as much as the one with the primary accent. The word *playoff* (*plā' of'*) is an example.

The Schwa

The schwa is an upside-down *e*. It stands for a weak vowel sound that is like the short *u* in *up*. The schwa can stand for all five vowel letters. It is an unstressed sound and usually is an unaccented syllable. Say the following words and listen for the schwa sound.

tomato	tə mā´tū
plaza	plaz´ə
pencil	pĕn´səl

Use the pronunciation key provided to help you pronounce each of the following familiar words presented in phonetic spelling. Then write the correct spelling of each word.

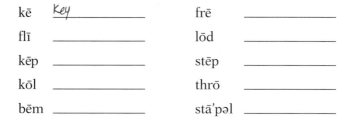

kē	*Key*	frē	_____
flī	_____	lōd	_____
kēp	_____	stēp	_____
kōl	_____	thrō	_____
bēm	_____	stā´pəl	_____

Appendix 2
Spelling Confusing Words

A U.S. president once said, "Damn a man who can't spell a word but one way." Nevertheless, college professors tend to expect one official spelling for a word. Unfortunately, no "golden rules" of spelling yield perfect results. There are a few spelling rules, but none is without exception. The following four rules may help you get through some rough spots.

RULE 1   Use *i* before *e* except after *c*:

believe	ceiling	receipt
grief	conceited	priest
cashier	yield	piece

Exceptions: Height, either, leisure, efficient

RULE 2   Drop the final *e* when adding a suffix that begins with a vowel:

hope + ing = hoping

believe + ing = believing

nice + est = nicest

Keep the final *e* when adding a suffix that begins with a consonant:

use + ful = useful

retire + ment = retirement

lone + ly = lonely

RULE 3   When a word ends in a consonant plus *y*, change the *y* to *i* to add a suffix:

lazy + ness = laziness

penny + less = penniless

marry + es = marries

RULE 4   Double the final consonant when all of the following apply:

a. The word is one syllable or is accented on the last syllable.
b. The word ends in a consonant preceded by a vowel.
c. The suffix begins with a word.

hop + ing = hopping

skip + ing = skipping

repel + ent = repellent

Appendix 3
Word Parts: Prefixes, Roots, and Suffixes

WORD PART	MEANING	EXAMPLE
Prefixes		
a-, an-	without, not	atypical, anarchy
ab-	away, from	absent, abnormal
ad-	toward	advance, administer
ambi-, amphi-	both, around	ambiguous, amphibious
anna-	year	annual
anti-, contra-, ob-	against	antisocial, contradict
bene-, eu-	well, good	benefactor, eulogy
bi-, du-, di-	two or twice	bicycle, duet, dichotomy
cata-, cath-	down, downward	catacombs
cent-, hecto-	hundred	centipede
con-, com-, syn-	with, together	congregate, synthesis
de-	down, from	depose, detract
dec-, deca-	ten	decade
demi-, hemi-, semi-	half	hemisphere, semicircle
dia-	through	diameter, diagram
dis-, un-	not, opposite of	dislike, unnatural
dys-	ill, hard	dystrophy
ex-	out, from	exhale, expel
extra-	beyond, outside	extralegal
hyper-	above, excessive	hyperactive
hypo-	under	hypodermic
il-, im, in-	not	illogical, impossible
in-	in, into	inside, insert, invade
infra-	lower	infrared
inter-	between	intercede, interrupt
intra-	within	intramural
juxta-	next to	juxtaposition
mal-, mis-	wrong, ill	malformed, mislead
mill-	thousand	milligram
nove-, non-	nine	novena, nonagon
oct-, octo-	eight	octopus
omni-, pan-	all	omnipotent, pantheist
per-	through	perennial, pervade
peri-, circum-	around	perimeter, circumvent
poly-, multi-	many	polygamy, multiply
post-	after	postscript
pre-, ante-	before	prepared, antebellum
pro-	before, for	promoter
proto-	first	prototype
quad-, quatra-, tetra-	four	quadrilateral, tetrad

WORD PART	MEANING	EXAMPLE
quint-, penta-	five	quintuplet
re-	back, again	review, reply
retro-	backward	retrogress, retrospect
sequ-	follow	sequence
sex-, hexa-	six	sextet
sub-	under	submarine, subway
super-	above, over	supervise
temp-, tempo-, chrono-	time	tempo, chronological
trans-	across	translate, transcontinental
tri-	three	triangle
uni-, mono-	one	unicorn, monocle
vice-	in place of	viceroy

Roots

alter, hap	to change	alteration, mishap
ama, philo	to love	amiable, philosophy
amina	breath, spirit	animate
aqua	water	aquarium, aqualung
aster, astro	star	disaster, astronomy
aud	to hear	audible, auditory
auto, ego	self	autonomy, egotist
bio	life	biology
cap	head	caption, capitulate
cap, capt	to take	capture
card, cor, cord	heart	cardiac, core, cordial
cosmo	order, universe	cosmonaut
cresc	to grow, increase	crescendo
cryp	secret, hidden	cryptogram
dent	teeth	dental
derma	skin	dermatologist
duc, duct	to lead	reduce, conduct
equ, iso	equal	equivocal, isometric
err, errat	to wander	erratic
ethno	race, tribe	ethnic
fac, fact	to do, make	manufacture
fract	to break	fracture
frater	brother	fraternity
gene	race, kind, sex	genetics, gender
grad, gres	to go, take steps	graduation, digress
gyn	woman	gynecologist
hab, habi	to have, hold	inhabit, habitual
helio, photo	sun, light	heliotrope, photograph
homo	man	homo sapiens
lic, list, liqu	to leave behind	derelict, relinquish
lith	stone	monolith
loc	place	location, local
log	speech, science	logic, dialogue
loquor	to speak	loquacious, colloquial
lum	light	illuminate
macro	large	macrocosm
manu	hand	manual, manuscript
mater	mother	maternity
med	middle	mediate

WORD PART	MEANING	EXAMPLE
meter	to measure	barometer
micro	small	microscope
miss, mit	to send, let go	admit, permission
morph	form	morphology
mort	to die	immortalize
mut, mutat	to change	mutation
nat	to be born	natal, native
neg, negat	to say no, deny	negative, renege
nym, nomen	name	synonym, nomenclature
ocul	eye	oculist, monocle
ortho	right, straight	orthodox, orthodontist
osteo	bone	osteopath
pater	father	paternal
path	disease, feeling	pathology, antipathy
phag	to eat	esophagus, phagocyte
phobia	fear	claustrophobia
phon, phono	sound	symphony, phonics
plic	to fold	duplicate, implicate
pneuma	wind, air	pneumatic
pod, ped	foot	tripod, pedestrian
pon, pos	to place	depose, position
port	to carry	porter, portable
pseudo	false	pseudonym
psych	mind	psychology
pyr	fire	pyromaniac
quir	to ask	inquire, acquire
rog	to question	interrogate
scrib, graph	to write	prescribe, autograph
sect, seg	to cut	dissect, segment
sol	alone	solitude
soma	body	somatology, psychosomatic
somnia	sleep	insomnia
soph	wise	sophomore, philosophy
soror	sister	sorority
spect	to look at	inspect, spectacle
spir	to breathe	inspiration, conspire
tact, tang	to touch	tactile, tangible
tele	distant	telephone
ten, tent	to hold	tenant, intent
tend, tens	to stretch	extend, extension
the, theo	god	atheism, theology
therma	heat	thermometer
tort	twist	torture, extort
ven, vent	to go, arrive	convention, advent
verbum	word	verbosity, verbal

Suffixes

-able, -ible	capable of	durable, visible
-acy, -ance, -ency, -ity	quality or state of	privacy, competence, acidity
-age	act of, state of	breakage
-al	pertaining to	rental
-ana	saying, writing	Americana
-ant	quality of, one who	reliant, servant

WORD PART	MEANING	EXAMPLE
-ard, -art	person who	wizard, braggart
-arium, -orium	place for	auditorium
-ate	cause to be	activate
-ation	action, state of	creation, condition
-chrome	color	verichrome
-cide	killing	homicide
-er, -or	person who, thing which	generator
-esque	like in manner	picturesque
-fic	making, causing	scientific
-form	in the shape of	cuneiform
-ful, -ose, -ous	full of	careful, verbose
-fy, -ify, -ize	to make, cause to be	fortify, magnify, modify
-hood, -osis	condition or state of	childhood, hypnosis
-ics	art, science	mathematics
-ism	quality or doctrine of	conservatism
-itis	inflammation of	appendicitis
-ive	quality of, that which	creative
-latry	worship of	idolatry
-less	without	homeless
-oid	in the form of	tabloid
-tude	quality or degree of	solitude
-ward	in a direction	backward
-wise	way, position	clockwise

Appendix 4
ESL: Making Sense of Figurative Language and Idioms

- What is ESL?
- What is figurative language?
- What are common English idioms?

What is ESL?

How many languages can you speak? Are you a native English speaker who has learned Spanish or are you a native Farsi speaker who has learned English? If you have acquired skill in a second or third language, you know it takes many years and plenty of patience to master the intricacies of a language. Not only do you learn new words, but you must also learn new grammatical constructions. For example, the articles habitually used in English such as *a, an* or *the* do not appear in Russian, Chinese, Japanese, Thai, or Farsi. In Spanish and Arabic, personal pronouns restate the subject, as in *My sister she goes to college.* In Spanish, Greek, French, Vietnamese, and Portuguese, "to words" are used rather than "ing words," as in *I enjoy to play soccer*. These complexities, which are innately understood by native speakers, make direct translation difficult. The English language has many unusual phrases and grammatical constructions that defy direct translation.

To assist students with these complexities, most colleges offer courses in ESL (English as a Second Language) designed to teach language skills to non-native speakers of English. If you are an ESL student, you may have been recruited through an international exchange program with another college, you may be a newly arrived immigrant, or you may be a citizen with a bilingual background. You bring a multicultural perspective to classroom discussions and campus life that will broaden the insights of others. Not only are some of your holidays different from those of others, but your sense of family life, work, and responsibility may also be different. Share your thoughts and ideas with native English speakers as they share the irregularities of the language with you.

What Is Figurative Language?

One aspect of the English language that defies direct translation and confuses non-native speakers, and sometimes even native speakers, is **figurative language**. This is the manipulation of the language to create images, add interest, and draw comparisons by using figures of speech (see Chapter 10, "Inference"). The two most commonly used, *simile* and *metaphor*, are defined as follows:

Simile: a stated comparison using *like* or *as* (*example:* The baby swims like a duck.)

Metaphor: an implied comparison (*example:* The baby is a duck in water.)

Many figurative expressions have become commonplace in the English language. As in the previous metaphor, the *baby* is not actually a *baby duck*, but the meaning is that *the baby swims very well*. However, neither direct translation nor a dictionary will unlock that meaning. When you encounter comparisons that seem out of the ordinary or ill chosen, ask yourself whether a figure of speech is being used, and look within the sentence for clues to help you guess the meaning.

The following practice exercises contain figurative language. Read each dialogue passage for meaning and then use the context clues to match the number of the boldfaced figure of speech with the letter of the appropriate definition. To narrow your choices, the answers to 1–5 are listed within a–e and the answers to 6–10 are listed within f–j.

practice 1

Maria: I am not going to be the one to stand in line for concert tickets this time. It is a (1) **pain in the neck**. Last time Fran left me (2) **holding the bag** on a $40 ticket for about a month.

Lynne: You did (3) **bend over backward** to organize the last outing. I would have (4) **jumped down Fran's throat** when she said she didn't have the cash to pay you. There is no reason (5) **to beat around the bush** with someone who doesn't pay promptly. Some people will (6) **walk all over you** if you let them.

Maria: I (7) **broke my neck** to get in line early. Those tickets were (8) **selling like hotcakes**. I think they (9) **jacked up** the price because they knew the demand would be high.

Lynne: I had to **bite my tongue** not to say something to Fran about your efforts and her lack of gratitude.

_____ 1. pain in the neck	a. owed money
_____ 2. holding the bag	b. avoid a clear answer
_____ 3. bend over backward	c. criticize angrily
_____ 4. jumped down Fran's throat	d. bothersome
_____ 5. to beat around the bush	e. make a great effort
_____ 6. walk all over you	f. selling quickly
_____ 7. broke my neck	g. raised prices
_____ 8. selling like hotcakes	h. keep from speaking
_____ 9. jacked up	i. take advantage of you
_____10. bite my tongue	j. tried hard

practice 2

Ron: I've got (1) **to take my hat off to** the group that organized the charity drive for the children's hospital.

Eric: They started out with (2) **two strikes against them** because most people had just made a contribution to the American Red Cross drive.

Ron: The president of the organization is a real (3) **go-getter**. He tried to educate people before asking for a contribution.

Eric: Until he outlined the situation in the Friday meeting, I did not know the hospital was (4) **in a jam**. Purchasing equipment for the cancer unit put them (5) **in the red**.

Ron: When the 15-year-old boy spoke at the meeting, I was ready to (6) **open my wallet**. He said he had come through the cancer treatment and (7) **passed with flying colors**.

Eric: I gave $5 and was happy to know that my money would help a good cause. Not all charitable solicitations are (8) **on the level**. I like to (9) **double-check** to make sure that the charity is not a (10) **fly-by-night** operation. Now I'm thinking about doing some volunteer work at the hospital.

_____ 1. to take my hat off to   a. in trouble

_____ 2. two strikes against them   b. losing money

_____ 3. go-getter   c. with little chance of success

_____ 4. in a jam   d. admire

_____ 5. in the red   e. ambitious worker

_____ 6. open my wallet   f. investigate thoroughly

_____ 7. passed with flying colors   g. give money

_____ 8. on the level   h. untrustworthy

_____ 9. double-check   i. honest

_____ 10. fly-by-night   j. succeeded

practice 3

Ross: I heard (1) **through the grapevine** that you had a (2) **fender bender** and put a dent in your car.

Howard: Ross, please don't (3) **breathe a word** about that. My parents will not be happy. I was really (4) **out to lunch** at the time and have been (5) **kicking myself** for not being more alert. I want to keep it (6) **hush-hush** for a while.

Ross: Do you have a plan for getting it fixed, or should we (7) **put our heads together** to create one?

Howard: I am waiting for final grades to come out. If I have all A's, I will then (8) **put my cards on the table** with them.

Ross: Man, that is really (9) **using your noodle**.

Howard: If that doesn't work, I'll be (10) **back to the drawing board** and could use your help.

_____ 1. through the grapevine   a. regretting

_____ 2. fender bender   b. inattentive

_____ 3. breathe a word   c. by gossip from other people

_____ 4. out to lunch   d. tell, talk

_____ 5. kicking myself   e. minor accident

_____ 6. hush-hush   f. thinking

_____ 7. put our heads together   g. ready to start over

_____ 8. put my cards on the table   h. confer

_____ 9. using your noodle   i. secret

_____10. back to the drawing board   j. confess all

What Are Common English Idioms?

An idiom is an expression with a special meaning that cannot be understood by directly translating each individual word in the idiom. Because of years of exposure, the meaning is usually understood by native speakers but is confusing if you are learning English as a second language.

Idioms are more common in spoken and informal language than in formal writing. In fact, most idiomatic expressions can usually be replaced by a single formal word. To add to the confusion, some idioms have dual meanings, and many idioms are grammatically irregular.

EXAMPLE What does the idiomatic expression *go over* mean in the following sentences?

(a) How did my speech *go over*?

(b) I want to *go over* the exam paper with the professor.

EXPLANATION In both sentences, the use of the idiom is informal. A more formal version of each would be as follows:

(a) *How was my speech **received** by the audience?*

(b) *I want to **review** the exam paper with the professor.*

Notice the grammatical irregularity in the first sentence. *Over* is not followed by a noun (name of a person, place, or thing) as a preposition (connecting words like *in*, *out*, and *at*) normally would be according to the rules of grammar; *over* becomes part of the verb phrase (words showing action). Thus the translation requires a change in wording, whereas the second use of the idiom is grammatically correct and can be directly translated by the single word *review*.

Nobody says that understanding idioms is easy. Entire books have been written about categorizing, recognizing, and translating thousands of them. To help clear up the confusion, some books group idioms according to families like root words, and others categorize them according to grammatical constructions. Either way, understanding idiomatic expressions depends more on using context clues to deduce meaning and familiarity with the informal, spoken language than with learning rules.

Reader's TIP Categorizing Idioms

Idioms are sometimes categorized into the following groups:

- Word families: grouping around a similar individual word
  Down as in *step down, take down, pipe down, narrow down, nail down, run down, tear down, knock down, let down, die down, cut down*

- Verb + Preposition: action word plus a connecting word
  Hammer away means *persists, stand for* means *represents,* and *roll back* means *reduce.*

- Preposition + Noun: connecting word plus the name of a person, place, or thing
  On foot means *walking, by heart* means *memorized,* and *off guard* means *surprised.*

- Verb + Adjective: action word plus a descriptive word
  Think twice means *consider carefully, hang loose* means *be calm,* and *play fair* means *deal equally.*

- Pairs of Nouns: two words naming a person, place, or thing
  Flesh and blood means *kin, part and parcel* means *total,* and *pins and needles* means *nervous.*

- Pairs of Adjectives: two descriptive words
  Cut and dried means *obvious, fair and square* means *honest, short and sweet* means *brief.*

In the following practice exercises, idioms are grouped according to a common word. Use the context clues within each sentence to write the meaning of the boldfaced idiom in the blank.

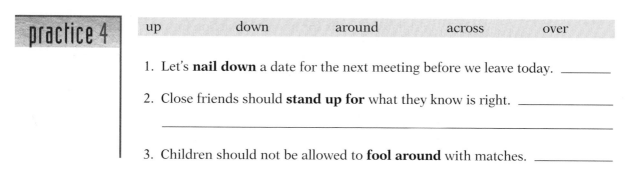

practice 4

| up | down | around | across | over |

1. Let's **nail down** a date for the next meeting before we leave today. _____

2. Close friends should **stand up for** what they know is right. _____
   _____

3. Children should not be allowed to **fool around** with matches. _____

4. With a quick example the student was able to **get across** the application of the theory. _____

5. They had a big **blowup** over who was responsible for the telephone bill.

_____

6. Yesterday I **ran across** an old friend at the airport. _____

7. Because we are having a party, I asked a few friends in my psychology class to **drop over**. _____

8. The new grocery store is open **around the clock**. _____

9. If the class president would **step down** in March, we could get a more dynamic person into the position. _____

10. After winning the free concert tickets, she was **bubbling over** with excitement. _____

---

practice 5

in	about	for	off	out

1. Before school starts, we need to **see about** renting an apartment. _____

_____

2. The manager stayed late at work to **break in** the new employee. _____

3. If you need to shorten the paragraph, **leave out** the last sentence. _____

4. What do the school colors **stand for**? _____

5. Although the designer's name was displayed, the purse was actually a cheap **knockoff**. _____

6. As soon as class is over, we are going to **take off** for a weekend at the beach. _____

7. Because I have a car this semester, **getting about** is much easier. _____

8. This latest demand **calls for** immediate action from our coalition. _____

_____

9. Let's all **chip in** to buy our professor a gift. _____

10. When cleaning, you do not want to **throw out** something that you may need later. _____

practice 6

free and easy	part and parcel	give-and-take	null and void
touch and go	spick-and-span	day in and day out	
little by little	high and low	sooner or later	

1. If you continue to drive with your gas gauge on empty, **sooner or later** you will be stuck on the side of the road. _____

2. By decreasing the medication **little by little**, the body can adjust without a painful reaction. _____

3. Overcooked food and slow service are the complaints restaurant managers hear **day in and day out**. _____

4. The peace negotiations were **touch and go** until the rebels accepted the compromise. _____

5. When I eat in a restaurant, I am more confident about cleanliness if the rest room is **spick-and-span**. _____

6. The opportunity to be with family is **part and parcel** of any holiday celebration. _____

7. After an appeal to a higher court, the previous decision to grant millions in damages could be declared **null and void**. _____

8. We will never decide which band to book for the party unless club members engage in a little **give-and-take**. _____

9. When she starts making her own money, she won't continue to spend with such a **free and easy** attitude. _____

10. After searching **high and low** for my keys, I found them under the computer. _____

Reader's TIP   Internet Sites to Explore

Dave's ESL Cafe
www.eslcafe.com/
Emphasis in this site is on English as it is spoken in the United States. It includes search tools for ESL books and a general discussion forum for ESL students and teachers.

EF Englishtown

englishtown.ef.com/en/default.asp

Englishtown is translated into eight languages and has learning games, bulletin boards where you can ask grammar and culture questions, a location for ESL/EFL teachers, a pen pal club, and a school where you can take classes online.

ESL Flow

www.homestead.com/ESLflow/Index.html

On this site, grammar concepts are organized into elementary, preintermediate, and intermediate categories. Resources are organized both for students and teachers and include grammar, speaking, dialogues, readings, handouts, and lesson plans.

English Zone

members.home.net/englishzone/index.html

This is a site for students who are learning English as a Second Language or studying English in general. It provides instruction and exercises on idioms, verbs, grammar, and writing.

Tower of English

members.tripod.com/%7Etowerofenglish/index.htm

Tower of English allows students to integrate lots of Web sources into their learning experience. It provides links to online ESL courses, tutors, and pen pals.

Appendix 5
Weekly Vocabulary Lessons

Expand your vocabulary by linking new words with familiar word parts. Learn over two hundred words in the following ten vocabulary lessons using a word family approach. Plan to master one lesson each week.

Directions

Begin by learning the word parts and definitions highlighted at the beginning of each lesson. Take a moment to brainstorm any words that you already know using those prefixes, suffixes, or roots. Read the initial sentence for each word part and underline the related word or words. Study the bulleted family of words and the sentences in which they are used. At the end of each list, create an additional word using the highlighted prefix, suffix, or root.

Use the review exercises to quiz yourself and reinforce your learning. Be flexible in adding suffix variations to the bulleted words.

Your instructor may assign an additional quiz to review your progress.

Lesson 1: See, Hear, and Voice Your Concerns

Roots	*Vis, vid*: see	*aud, aus*: hear or listen	*voc, vok*: voice or call

Words with *vis* or *vid* = *see*

Julius Caesar wrote, "Veni, vidi, vici," meaning "I came, I saw, I conquered."

- Visible: can be seen

  On a clear night the stars are more *visible* in the countryside than in an urban area with city lights.

- Visionary: one who sees visions or dreams of the future

  You have to be both a *visionary* and a good businessperson to create a successful dot-com company.

- Visor: a brim to protect the eyes so you can see better

  Wear a *visor* when playing tennis so the sun doesn't interfere with your performance.

- Evident: can easily be seen

  The solution was *evident* to those who had previously encountered the problem.

● Visa: an endorsement on a passport giving the bearer the right to enter a country

Prior to visiting certain countries, tourists must apply for a *visa*.

● Vista: a view from a distance

The *vista* from a mountaintop on an autumn day can be breathtaking.

● Envision: to see in one's mind

Try to *envision* the furniture in the empty room.

● _____: cannot be seen

The secret ink in the spy document was _____ without special glasses.

Words with *aud* or *aus* = *hear or listen*

The audience listened to the stage production in the auditorium.

● Audible: can be heard

Because she speaks so softly, her voice is barely *audible*.

● Audition: a hearing to try out for a role

The actor nervously began the *audition* for a part in the Broadway musical.

● Audio: sound made by electronic or mechanical reproduction

The *audio* on my television is not clear.

● Auditory: relating to hearing

The *auditory* nerves are damaged and thus hearing is impaired.

● Audit: a formal examination of accounts made by an accountant

Citizens fear an *audit* by the Internal Revenue Service.

● _____: an instrument to measure hearing

The doctor used an _____ to test for a hearing aid.

● _____: cannot be heard

The speaker was rendered _____ because of the background music.

Words with *voc* or *vok* = *voice or call*

Give voice to your ideas in your vocabulary.

● Evoke: call out from the past

The ceremony was designed to *evoke* the memory of past heroes.

● Vocation: a call to serve in a particular profession

Although my plans may change, I am presently preparing for a *vocation* in nursing.

- Vociferous: making a noisy outcry

  The supporter of change made *vociferous* objections to the opponent's remarks.

- Avocation: a hobby or second calling

  Music is my *avocation,* but I know I cannot make enough money playing a musical instrument to support myself.

- Convocation: an assembly or calling together

  The *convocation* celebrated the 75th anniversary of the college.

- Invocation: solemn prayer or divine blessing

  The religious service began with an *invocation.*

- Invoke: to call forth

  The witness sought to *invoke* the Fifth Amendment to avoid answering the question.

- _____: to call forth anger

  Unmercifully teasing a person can _____ an argument.

- _____: spoken or voiced

  The celebrity was very _____ about the need for security at the concert.

Review

Part I

Choose the best word from the list to complete each of the following sentences.

invocation	audience	vocation	vista	visor
vocal	convocation	audit	avocation	visa

1. If customers are _____, they can usually make their complaints heard.

2. From the cruise ship, the travelers could see a _____ of the mountainous island surrounded by the sea.

3. Our chorus was honored to sing at the _____ honoring our new college president.

4. A company _____ indicated that funds had been listed in the wrong column rather than stolen.

5. The _____ clapped after the performance.

6. The priest gave a brief _____ at the beginning of the assembly.

7. A _____ is required to enter Israel.

8. Recreational golfing can become a serious and challenging _____.

9. After thirty years, the electrical engineer retired with a pension from his lifelong _____.

10. Wear a _____ to protect your eyes from the sun.

Part II

Answer the following with true (*T*) or false (*F*).

_____11. Parents invoke their authority to get their children to go to bed.

_____12. A vociferous group is quiet and orderly.

_____13. A visionary might seek to envision a better future.

_____14. The tail lights on a motor vehicle should be visible at night.

_____15. To promote a cause, a group of activists usually wants a vocal spokesperson.

_____16. For most people, gardening is an avocation rather than a vocation.

_____17. Landing a part in a play usually takes more than one audition.

_____18. Financial records are reviewed in a company audit.

_____19. The person who provokes an argument is sometimes called a troublemaker.

_____20. Teens usually prefer background music to be inaudible.

Lesson 2: Not, Not, and Not

Prefixes	*in, im*: not	*dis*: not	*un*: not

Words with *in* or *im* = not

Can invisible fences be used to restrain pets?

● inadequate: not enough

Having *inadequate* health care causes many flu victims to go untreated.

● inaccessible: not able to be reached

Some mountain areas are *inaccessible* except by foot.

● inclement: not mild

Keep an umbrella handy for *inclement* weather.

● intolerable: not bearable

Children learn by suffering consequences for *intolerable* behaviors.

● inhospitable: not welcoming

The *inhospitable* island was cold, windy, and barren.

- insatiable: cannot be satisfied

  Young readers have an *insatiable* desire for more Harry Potter stories.

- improbable: not likely to occur

  Because the doctor is overbooked today, it is *improbable* that I will get an appointment.

- immoral: not of good character

  The politician's *immoral* actions were scorned by the voters.

- impassable: blocked

  With the bridge washed out from the flood, the road was *impassable*.

- immortal: cannot die

  An *immortal* flame burns to honor the assassinated president.

- immobilized: cannot be moved

  The zookeepers had to *immobilize* the lion before treating its infected foot.

- _____: not having the ability

  His _____ to read music did not keep him from singing.

Words with dis = not

Do stories in the tabloids dishonor the memory of Princess Diana?

- disarm: take weapons away

  The troops were *disarmed* after the surrender.

- disadvantage: handicap

  The major *disadvantage* of the sofa was the light-colored fabric easily got dirty.

- discredit: not believe

  To *discredit* his character, the opposition circulated a rumor of drug addiction.

- disgrace: shame

  With the indictment pending, the mayor resigned in *disgrace*.

- disloyal: unfaithful

  The *disloyal* employee revealed company secrets.

- distrust: doubt

  If you *distrust* the management, don't invest your money in the company.

- disconcerted: upset

  The computer virus caused the workers to be *disconcerted* and angry.

- disregard: not to pay attention to

  If you have already paid, please *disregard* the last bill.

- dissolved: melted away
  The sugar *dissolved* into the hot espresso.

- disinherit: to deny an inheritance
  Few parents will actually *disinherit* a child.

- _____: not claim

  After hearing the negative comments, I wanted to _____ my cousin.

Words with *un* = not

I took an uneducated guess about the cause of the unfinished manuscript.

- unable: not having the skill

  Because of a shortage, the company was *unable* to ship the software.

- unabridged: not shortened

  For the derivation of words, use an *unabridged* dictionary.

- unaffected: not touched

  Although we saw the funnel, our house was *unaffected* by the tornado.

- unaltered: not changed

  No one had been working on the projects and thus the plans remained *unaltered* from the last meeting.

- untouchable: cannot be touched

  The children were told that the food was *untouchable* until the guests arrived.

- _____: not said
  Our _____ rule was that we split the cost of the gas on the trip.

Review

Part I

Answer the following with true (*T*) or false (*F*).

_____ 1. An abridged dictionary contains more information that an unabridged one.

_____ 2. When voting locations are designated, counties seek inaccessible buildings.

_____ 3. A disinherited relative receives no gift from the deceased.

_____ 4. An invisible correction can be easily detected.

_____ 5. To discredit a source is to cast doubt on its worth.

_____ 6. Renters usually desire intolerant landlords.

_____ 7. An immobilized elephant is unlikely to charge.

_____ 8. An unaltered proposal remains in its original format.

_____ 9. Disloyal fans boost the morale of a team.

_____10. Powdered milk will dissolve in water.

Part II

Choose the best word from the list to complete each of the following sentences.

inadequate	disregard	unaffected	immoral	disgrace
impassable	disarm	inclement	untouchable	disconcerting

11. The three-foot snow left the roads _____.

12. Humor can sometimes be used to _____ the anger of a complaining customer.

13. The _____ weather did not stop the snow skiers from reaching the top of the mountain.

14. The _____ actions of the spouse were the grounds for the divorce.

15. In a museum, signs indicate that the paintings are _____.

16. Because they lived on the river, they were _____ by the water shortage.

17. The _____ protestors caused the speaker to lose her train of thought.

18. Spenders who _____ money may soon be in debt.

19. If you want to make good grades, do not take a test with _____ preparation.

20. As their child was convicted of the crime, the parents hung their heads in _____.

Lesson 3: Before and After

Prefixes	*ante*: before	*pre*: before	*post*: after

Words with *ante* = *before*

Can antenuptial counseling help marriages become stronger?

- Antebellum: existing before the war

    The *antebellum* home with the white columns was built before the Civil War.

● Antecede: to go before

Queen Elizabeth should *antecede* Prince Philip at state events.

● Antecedent: the word coming before the pronoun to which the pronoun refers

The name *Valerie* is the *antecedent* of *her* in the sentence.

● Antediluvian: belonging to the time before the flood; very old

She ignored the advice and regarded it as *antediluvian*.

● Antennae: feelers on the head of an insect used as organs of touch

The insect's *antennae* inspected the food.

● Antescript: a note added before something such as a prefix to a letter

The *antescript* indicated why the letter would be late arriving.

● _____: waiting room or room before another

She waited in a small _____ with chairs before being summoned into the president's office.

Words with *pre = before*

Use the meaning of the prefix to predict the meaning of a new word.

● Preamble: an introduction

Schoolchildren learn the *Preamble* to the Constitution.

● Precede: to go before

Your good name can *precede* your presence.

● Predecessor: one who preceded another in office

Her *predecessor* helped orient the new chairperson to the job.

● Preeminent: supreme, before all others

Our professor is the *preeminent* scholar in contemporary Russian literature.

● Prelude: a musical or dramatic introduction

As the *prelude* began, the remaining ticket holders were seated in the audience.

● Premonition: a forewarning or omen

When I heard the barking dog, I had a *premonition* that trouble was around the corner.

● Prejudice: judgment before proof is given

A lawyer will try to avoid choosing a potential juror who shows signs of *prejudice*.

● Precocious: having early development

The *precocious* child could read at 2 years of age.

● _____: care taken beforehand

A flu shot is a _____ against getting the flu.

Words with *post = after*

How do you indicate whether the time is ante meridian or post meridian?

● Posterity: descendants who come after

Leave a gift for *posterity* and donate money to the college library.

● Posthumous: after death

The *posthumous* award was given to the widow of the soldier.

● Postnatal: the time immediately after birth

A *postnatal* examination monitors the health of the new mother.

● Postpone: delay or set the date back

Let's *postpone* the meeting until tomorrow after lunch.

● Postscript: a note added to a letter after it has been signed

Karen scribbled an afterthought in the *postscript* of her long letter.

● _____: studies after graduation.

Many students work for a year after graduation before starting a _____ program.

Review

Part I

Choose an appropriate word from the list to complete each of the following sentences.

precocious	premonition	antebellum	prelude	postscript
predecessor	posthumous	preamble	postponed	preeminent

1. The ambassador is a _____ scholar in the history of Nigeria.

2. Shorten the _____ and begin the main point of your speech.

3. As a _____ athlete, Tiger Woods demonstrated his skills by putting on television against adults.

4. The threat of a tornado caused the game to be _____ for three hours.

5. A _____ award honors a dead hero.

6. The couple is restoring the _____ home to its original 1860s appearance.

7. The musical _____ set the mood for the romantic stage production that followed.

8. Bill Clinton was the _____ of George W. Bush.

9. A superstitious person would see a black cat as a _____ of danger.

10. Sara added her quickly remembered thoughts as a _____ at the end of the letter.

Part II
Answer the following with true (*T*) or false (*F*).

_____11. A prejudiced listener has trouble fairly evaluating both sides.

_____12. An antediluvian outfit is up to date.

_____13. A postnatal exam checks the growth of the fetus.

_____14. Ante meridian refers to the afternoon.

_____15. The antennae of an insect is usually attached to its tail.

_____16. The antescript is positioned in the main body of the letter.

_____17. An antecedent is a person, place, or thing.

_____18. Antenuptual arguments occur after the wedding day.

_____19. A presumed appointment needs to be double-checked for certainty.

_____20. Environmental regulations consider both the present and posterity.

Lesson 4: Turn and Throw

Roots	*vers, vert*: turn	*jac, jec, ject*: throw, lie

Words with *vers* or *vert* = turn

Could the use of criminals in a clothing advertisement become a controversial topic?

● Convert: win over; persuade

Through mind-controlling strategies, the young man was *converted* to cult beliefs.

● Revert: turn back to

Reformed smokers are frequently tempted to *revert* to old habits.

● Divert: turn away from

The driver's attention was *diverted* by the traffic accident on the side of the highway.

- Invert: turn upside down

  If you want to divide a fraction, you need to *invert* and multiply.

- Averse: turned against

  Although they were no longer married, she was not *averse* to seeing him at social functions.

- Introvert: shy and quiet; introspective

  Being an *introvert*, the writer rejected offers to read his poems in public.

- Extrovert: outgoing; gregarious

  An *extrovert* like Oprah Winfrey enjoys the energy of a large studio audience.

- Ambivert: having both introverted and extroverted tendencies

  Many of us are *ambiverts* because we enjoy being with people but also need some quiet time to ourselves.

- Pervert: turned to an improper use

  Because of a shoe fetish, the thief was regarded as a *pervert*.

- Obverse: facing the opponent; front surface

  The head of the president was depicted on the *obverse* side of the coin.

- Conversant: knowledgeable to talk about a subject

  After another semester of economics, I hope to be more *conversant* on the euro.

- Versatile: having many skills; can turn from one thing to another

  A *versatile* jacket can be worn with several different pants and shirts.

- Subversive: undermining

  The terrorists were engaged in *subversive* activities.

- Vertigo: a dizzy spell when things seem to be turning

  Avoid roller-coasters if you have a tendency toward *vertigo*.

- Version: an adaptation or translation of the original form

  The children's *version* of the Bible had pictures and large print.

- Versus: against

  The next trial was the *State of Texas versus John Doe*.

- Vortex: both a whirling and suction motion as in a whirlpool

  Watching the whirling water from the cliff, he threw a log into the *vortex* and watched it disappear.

- _____: can be reversed

  Because the raincoat is _____, it can be either yellow or black.

• _____: cannot be reversed

After careful consideration, my decision is _____.

Words with jac, jec, ject = throw or lie

Would you have an objection to leaving class early?

- inject: insert

  Students appreciate professors who *inject* humor into lectures.

- eject: to throw out

  If the plane is shot, the fighter pilot can push the *eject* button.

- dejected: low in spirits

  After failing two tests, the *dejected* student finally sought help in the lab.

- adjacent: next to

  Consumers save time when a dry cleaner is *adjacent* to a grocery store.

- conjecture: to form an opinion; guess

  The statement that the new president will step down is merely *conjecture*.

- interject: throw a word in between others

  Because the two renters were constantly talking, I could not *interject* a word about a deposit for damages.

- projection: thrown forward

  At the year's end, the company had not met its profit *projections*.

- abject: degraded

  In the Rio Barrio the children live in abject poverty.

- _____: refusal

  The company threatened a _____ of the proposal because of the cost.

Review

Part I

Answer the following with true (*T*) or false (*F*).

_____ 1. A conjecture is a fact rather than an opinion.

_____ 2. If a proposal is rejected, it is no longer under consideration.

_____ 3. Subversive activity is clearly evident.

_____ 4. Water in the vortex sprays up like a fountain.

_____ 5. If it is stated as *Wiley versus Rogers*, the two sides are in opposition.

_____ 6. If you are conversant in Spanish history, you know the subject well.

_____ 7. A versatile athlete can play several sports well.

_____ 8. If you invert a cup of coffee, the liquid is likely to spill.

_____ 9. A dejected worker is not a happy employee.

_____10. A controversial topic draws little disagreement.

Part II

Choose the best word from the list to complete the following sentences.

diverted	averse	projections	pervert	extroverted
converted	vertigo	version	adjacent	introverted

11. Inner ear problems can cause loss of balance and _____.

12. The _____ sculptor enjoyed his meditative time alone in the garden admiring the forms of nature.

13. The developer _____ the stream so it no longer ran through the middle of the property.

14. The _____ professor gave lively lectures and enjoyed meeting students for lunch or office hours.

15. The sex offender was labeled a _____ because of the unacceptable nature of the reported behavior.

16. By remodeling with glass windows, the screen porch was _____ to a room that could be used all year.

17. Because the walls are not soundproof, I can hear the television in the apartment _____ to mine.

18. The population _____ for 2025 will influence current mass transit decisions.

19. The sign indicated that the home owners were _____ to cigarette smoking on the premises.

20. Depending on what _____ of the story you heard, the new neighbor is either a rock singer or a movie star.

Lesson 5: Come Together, Hold Together, and Shut

Roots   *greg*: come together, group   *ten, tent, tain, tinu*: hold together, hold
clud, clus: shut

Words with greg = come together, group

The congregation sang hymns of praise.

- Congregate: to flock together

  Students were instructed to *congregate* in the gym prior to the first class period.

● Gregarious: outgoing; enjoying groups

Gregarious people enjoy parties.

● Aggregation: a collection or union

The steering committee was an *aggregation* of six different sororities.

● Egregious: conspicuous, the worst out of the group

The *egregious* error was easy to detect but costly to fix.

● Segregate: to separate from the group

Before eating M & M's, do you *segregate* the colors?

● _____: doing away with segregation

For business reasons, the men's club voted to _____ and accept women as members.

Words with *ten, tent, tain, tinu* = hold together, hold

For safe maintenance, use a lock to secure the *contents* of the case.

● Tenant: one who holds a lease on a house or apartment

The present *tenant* pays his rent early.

● Tenacity: quality of holding together for a purpose

Do you have the drive and *tenacity* to run for public office?

● Contented: easy in mind or satisfied

A *contented* dog is usually well fed.

● Contentment: satisfaction with one's lot

Money is not essential for *contentment*, but it does help.

● Intent: purpose, concentration, holding one's mind on a single matter

What is the *intent* of this lengthy proposal?

● Retain: to hold secure

With a majority in the Senate, the Republicans can *retain* power.

● Continuously: without stopping

The waters of the Niagara River *continuously* flow over Horseshoe Falls to the delight of summer visitors.

● Tenable: able to be held or defended

Your paying for the damage is a *tenable* solution to the accident.

● Untenable: cannot be held

Continuing a relationship after abuse is *untenable*.

● _____: not content

I am _____ with my midterm exam grades, because I know I can do better.

Words with *clud* or *clus* = shut

Conclusive evidence should get a conviction in court.

● Recluse: one who shuts himself or herself away from others, a hermit

The *recluse* only left the deserted island for provisions.

● Exclude: to shut out

Do not *exclude* your friends from your joys or sorrows.

● Inclusive: counting everything

The quoted price is *inclusive* of tax and shipping.

● Seclude: to remove, shut off

In order to recuperate, he wanted to *seclude* himself from visitors.

● Preclude: to close beforehand or hinder

Having a mobile phone does not *preclude* the need for an answering machine on your home telephone.

● _____: the final statement.

At the end of a term paper, the author states a _____.

Review

Part I

Answer the following with true (*T*) or false (*F*).

_____ 1. Gregarious students usually are shy.

_____ 2. If you segregate pairs of socks by colors, you mix them together in one group.

_____ 3. If students congregate in the doorway, entrance into the building may be more difficult.

_____ 4. An egregious boor is usually a desirable companion.

_____ 5. Desegregated cows and horses roam the pasture together.

_____ 6. Contented babies cry excessively.

_____ 7. If you retain your job, you keep your position.

_____ 8. A winning lawyer has a tenable case.

_____ 9. To seclude yourself is to join the group for the celebration.

_____ 10. An inclusive organization welcomes entry to many.

Part II

Choose the best word from the list as a synonym for the following.

intent	tenacity	contents	recluse	conclusion
maintenance	aggregation	tenant	congregation	contentment

11. Hermit   _____

12. Renter   _____

13. Happiness   _____

14. Collection   _____

15. Purpose   _____

16. Final statement _____

17. Flock   _____

18. Determination   _____

19. Upkeep   _____

20. Belongings   _____

Lesson 6: One Too Many

Prefixes	*mono, mon*: one	*bi, bin, bis*: two	*poly*: many

Words with *mono* or *mon* = one

The monomaniac is addicted to the Internet.

● Monarchy: a government with only one ruler

 The power of the English *monarchy* has changed since the time of Elizabeth I.

● Monocle: an eyeglass for only one eye

 A *monocle* of the 1800s was more difficult to wear than the eyeglasses of today.

● Monogamy: marriage to one person only

 In the United States, *monogamy* is the legally accepted form of marriage.

● Monologue: a discourse by one person

 Jay Leno starts his late night show with a humorous *monologue*.

● Monochromatic: only one color

 A home decorated in beige has a *monochromatic* color scheme.

● Monotony: sameness

Talking to customers breaks the *monotony* of working as a cashier.

● _____: one tone of unvaried pitch

The professor speaks in a _____ voice that puts the class to sleep.

Words with *bi, bin,* or *bis* = two

If you have the cheapest concert seats, carry binoculars.

● Bimonthly: occurs every two months

Regular *bimonthly* reports are required six times each year.

● Bifocal: having two lenses

Initial use of *bifocal* lenses can be a difficult adjustment.

● Bigamy: marrying one person while already married to another

Bigamy is illegal in the United States.

● Bilingual: using two languages

In the United States most *bilingual* speakers know Spanish as well as English.

● Bipartisan: representing two parties

A *bipartisan* committee would include both Democrats and Republicans.

● Biennial: something that occurs at two-year intervals or lasts two years

Rather than every year, the class decided to have *biennial* reunions.

● _____: something that occurs every two weeks

Our committee meets _____.

Words with *poly* = many

The polytechnic institute accepted early applications.

● Polygon: closed figure with many angles

A square is a *polygon* with four equal sides.

● Polyglot: a linguist who knows many languages

Having lived in many countries, the investor returned home as an accomplished *polyglot*.

● Polygamy: custom of plural spouses

In cultures that practice *polygamy*, the additional wives may function as house servants.

● Polyandry: custom of plural husbands

Polyandry is the exclusively female version of polygamy.

● Polychromatic: having many colors

The *polychromatic* fabric emphasized the reds and blues against the yellow background.

● Polydactyl: having more than the normal number of fingers or toes.

The *polydactyl* abnormality was evident in three generations of family members.

● Polymorphic: having many forms

A *polymorphic* cartoon character can change from a cat to a tiger.

● _____: inhabited by many races

The inner-city restaurant district offered a diverse number of _____ treats.

Review

Part I

Answer the following with true (*T*) or false (*F*).

_____ 1. A polyglot is more than bilingual.

_____ 2. Two people talk to each other in a monologue.

_____ 3. A black piano has a monochromatic surface.

_____ 4. Bimonthly meetings occur twice each month.

_____ 5. Bipartisan politics suggests that two parties are willing to negotiate.

_____ 6. The biennial reports were due every January and July.

_____ 7. If white is a color, the U.S. flag is polychromatic.

_____ 8. An exclusively Italian area in a city constitutes a polyethnic neighborhood.

_____ 9. Exciting people tend to enjoy monotony.

_____ 10. Bifocal lenses contain two separate eyeglass prescriptions.

Part II

Choose the best word from the list to fit the following descriptions.

monarch	monocle	monogamy	bilingual	polymorphic
bigamy	monotone	polyandry	polygon	polydactyl

11. More than ten toes   _____

12. One tone of voice   _____

13. Having two wives   _____

14. Having two husbands   _____

15. One eyeglass   _____

16. Many forms   _____

17. Speaking two languages   _____

18. A queen   _____

19. One spouse   _____

20. A rectangle   _____

Lesson 7: Call Out and Remember to Send

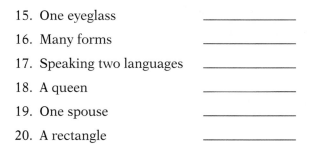

Roots   *claim, clam*: declare, call out   *mem*: remember   *mitt, miss*: send

Words with *claim* or *clam* = declare or call out

When do you use an exclamation mark at the end of a sentence?

- Clamor: a racket

  The suitcase made a loud *clamor* as it fell off the rack.

- Reclaim: regain or demand the return of

  After recovering from minor injuries, the tennis player *reclaimed* the tournament championship.

- Disclaim: cut off, deny

  If you insult the host, I will *disclaim* ever knowing you.

- Exclaim: cry out

  The patriots *exclaimed* joys of victory at the celebration.

- Irreclaimable: cannot be restored

  The moving company declared that the broken furniture was *irreclaimable*.

- Proclamation: a notice to the public

  A *proclamation* concerning taxation was published in the newspaper.

- Claimant: one who makes a claim

  The *claimant* told the insurance company that a tree hit the car during the hurricane.

- _____: lost items not called for

  Lost and found items that are _____ are eventually given to charity.

Words with *mem* = remember

Send a memo to jog my memory.

- Memento: something to make one remember

  The small statue is a *memento* of my trip to Italy.

- Memoir: a record to remember

  The soldier's *memoirs* gave a personal perspective to the war.

- Memorandum: a note or reminder

  Because a *memorandum* is a business correspondence, make the message short and direct.

- Memorable: worth remembering

  Having the whole family together made the Thanksgiving dinner a *memorable* occasion.

- Memorabilia: thing worth remembering

  Elvis *memorabilia* is sold at Graceland.

- Commemorate: to observe and remember

  Display a flag to *commemorate* Independence Day.

- Memorial: a reminder of a great event

  The fountain was a *memorial* to the founder of the city.

- _____: not remembered

  Holidays can jog our _____ feelings.

Words with *mitt or miss* = send

Do you admit when you make an error?

- Missile: something sent through the air

  The *missile* was directed toward enemy territory.

- Emissary: a messenger sent on a mission

  She sent an *emissary* to the French government.

- Remiss: careless

  I would be *remiss* if I did not remind you that the gates close at midnight.

- Remit: pay back

  The phone company asked me to *remit* another thirty dollars.

- Submit: surrender

  He had to *submit* to a body search at the airport.

- Emit: to send out

  The car seems to be *emitting* pollution.

- _____: allow

  Will you _____ me to use your name as a reference?

Review

Part I

Answer the following with true (*T*) or false (*F*).

_____ 1. An exhaust emissions check measures auto pollution.

_____ 2. Veterans Day commemorates those who served in the armed services.

_____ 3. In order to receive an insurance payment, the claimant must suffer a loss.

_____ 4. Irreclaimable goods are fixed rather than replaced.

_____ 5. A "We are not responsible for" statement is a company disclaimer.

_____ 6. To reclaim checked goods, you usually need a ticket.

_____ 7. To be remiss is to neglect a duty.

_____ 8. A memoir is or should be nonfiction.

_____ 9. Olympic memorabilia includes collectors' pins that commemorate the games.

_____10. If you remit money, you refuse to pay.

Part II

Choose the best word from the list as a synonym for the following.

memorandum	emissary	proclamation	exclamation	memoir
clamor	memorial	remittance	missile	memento

11. Book _____

12. Washington Monument _____

13. Person _____

14. Keepsake _____

15. Correspondence _____

16. Noise _____

17. Explosive _____

18. Official announcement _____

19. Cry _____

20. Payback _____

Lesson 8: For or Against?

Prefixes   *pro*: for, forward, forth   *Anti, ant*: against   *contra*: against

Words with *pro* = for, forward, forth

Do medical procedures frequently require signed forms?

- Prochoice: for abortion rights

  The *prochoice* rally was held on the steps of the state capital.

- Proponent: supporter

  Are you a *proponent* of building another oil pipeline in Alaska?

- Procure: to get or gain

  Campers need to *procure* supplies a week prior to departure.

- Profess: to openly admit

  I *profess* to enjoying double fudge chocolate brownie cake.

- Prolific: bring forth young or fruit

  The *prolific* young couple had six small children.

- Proficient: showing skill

  To be *proficient* in Spanish requires a knowledge of grammar.

- Proliferate: to bring forth by rapid production

  Fast-food restaurants seem to *proliferate* along interstate highway exits.

- _____: to go forward

  If you already have a ticket, you can _____ to the entrance.

Words with *anti* or *ant* = against

Can antiabortion signs be used in a demonstration?

- Antacid: a counteracting agent for acidity of the stomach

  Take an *antacid* tablet for a burning stomach.

- Antagonism: a strong feeling against a person or idea

  After sharing several funny jokes, the *antagonism* between them evaporated.

- Antarctic: the opposite of the North Pole

  The *antarctic* region is south of the Arctic.

- Anticlimax: a letdown from a greater event

  After the previous night's celebration, the New Year's luncheon was an *anticlimax*.

- Antipathy: a strong feeling of dislike

  As the scandal unfolded, the business partner's *antipathy* toward the accused was evident.

- Antithesis: a contrast of ideas

  The son's liberal ideas are the *antithesis* of his father's conservative policies.

- Antibody: a substance in the body opposing diseases

  The scientists worked to create an *antibody* for the new flu strain.

- Antidote: a remedy for poison

  Jungle travelers carry an *antidote* for snake bites.

- Antifreeze: a substance to slow the freezing process

  Check your car for *antifreeze* before the first frost.

- _____: hindering the coagulation of blood

  After the stoke, the patient took an _____.

Words with *contra* = against

Does sex education increase the use of contraceptives?

- Contraband: illegal

  Contraband items can be seized by the police.

- Contradict: to speak against

  To *contradict* a speaker, you must be sure of your facts.

- Contrarian: person who takes contrary views

  Reasoning with a *contrarian* is not always possible.

- _____: to go against usual thinking

  A _____ issue can be argued forever.

Review

Part I

Answer the following with true (*T*) or false (*F*).

_____ 1. An antidote is an amusing story.

_____ 2. A prolific plant bears many fruits.

_____ 3. Supplies can be procured by illegal means.

_____ 4. A contrarian would most likely be comfortable in a role that involves questioning.

_____ 5. Prochoice advocates demonstrate against abortion clinics.

_____ 6. If you contradict the evidence, you disagree with the facts.

_____ 7. An athlete must be proficient to be on a professional team.

_____ 8. A sick person usually welcomes an antibody.

_____ 9. A controversial news story would be unlikely to generate further discussion.

_____ 10. For a peaceful relationship, mutual antagonism should be resolved.

Part II

Choose the best word from the list as a synonym for the following.

| profess | antacid | antithesis | proponent | antifreeze |
| procedure | controversy | anticlimax | contraband | antipathy |

11. Liquid solution for machines   _____

12. Feeling of dislike   _____

13. Smuggled drugs   _____

14. Admit   _____

15. Pill   _____

16. Plan   _____

17. Opposite   _____

18. Disagreement   _____

19. Supporter   _____

20. Disappointment   _____

Lesson 9: Know, Flow, and Wander

Roots   *gnosi, cognosc*: know   *fluc, flu, fluv, flux*: flowing   *migra*: wander

Words with *gnosi, cognosc* = know

The accused was released on bail on her own recognizance.

● Cognition: act of knowing

    Cognition includes both awareness and judgment.

● Agnostic: one who professes not knowing of the existence of God

    The beliefs of an atheist differ from those of an *agnostic*.

● Cognizant: knowing, being aware

    Are you *cognizant* of the dangers involved with offshore oil drilling?

● Incognito: not known

    The celebrity wore a wig and sunglasses in order to appear *incognito*.

● Prognosis: forecast

    With the medical treatments available, the *prognosis* for your complete recovery is excellent.

- _____: to know again

  Since you cut your hair, I hardly _____ you.

Words with *fluc, flu, fluv, flux* = flowing

Can influence be used to sell computers?

- Fluent: flowing easily in speech

  After living in Mexico for a semester, she is *fluent* in Spanish.

- Fluctuate: to shift or change

  The outside temperature will *fluctuate* from morning to noon.

- Flue: a passageway for the flow of air

  Open the *flue* to let the smoke escape.

- Fluidity: free flowing

  The *fluidity* of her ideas convinced the company to sign the advertising contract.

- Flume: an inclined channel with a stream running through

  Take the canoes out of the river before you reach the *flume*.

- Affluent: wealthy

  Many *affluent* Americans build fabulous mansions.

- Effluent: flowing out

  The *effluent* river widened as it neared the ocean.

- _____: a liquid

  The medicine is available in both pill and _____ form.

Words with *migra* = wander

Do migratory birds fly from California to Chile?

- Migrant: one who wanders from place to place

  The *migrant* assisted in the apple harvest in the fall.

- Migration: movement from place to place

  Birds undertake an extensive *migration* to avoid harsh winters.

- Immigrant: a settler in a new land

  Many *immigrants* to the United States later apply for citizenship.

- Emigrant: one who leaves a country

  Because of economic opportunities, the United States has more immigrants than *emigrants*.

● _____: coming into a country

Over the years our country's _____ laws have changed.

Review

Part I

Answer the following with true (*T*) or false (*F*).

_____ 1. An agnostic believes there is no God.

_____ 2. If your blood pressure fluctuates, it does not remain steady.

_____ 3. New settlers from Mexico into Arizona are called immigrants.

_____ 4. Migratory birds tend to stay in Florida year round.

_____ 5. The ghetto is usually populated by affluent residents.

_____ 6. The prognosis for a disease is usually made before the examination.

_____ 7. The fluidity of a waterfall can be changed by freezing weather.

_____ 8. Fluent linguists must frequently pause for translations.

_____ 9. A neighbor who moves to Spain has emigrated out of this country.

_____ 10. If you are cognizant of the rules, you can't use ignorance as an excuse for breaking them.

Part II

Choose the best word from the list as a synonym for the following.

prognosis	fluid	migration	recognize	influence
migrant	flume	incognito	flue	affluent

11. Wanderer   _____

12. Chimney channel   _____

13. Prediction   _____

14. Rich   _____

15. Undercover   _____

16. Liquid   _____

17. Persuasive power   _____

18. Ravine of falling water _____

19. Accept   _____

20. Movement   _____

Lesson 10: Bend, Born, and Body

| **Roots** | *flex, flect*: bend | *nat, nasc*: born | *corp*: body |

Words with *flex* or *flect* = bend

Do ballet dancers need to be flexible?

- Flex: to bend

  Flex your muscles to show your strength.

- Deflect: bend away from

  The politician was able to *deflect* the vicious questions and move to an agenda discussion.

- Genuflection: bending the knees, bowing

  My arrogant boss seems to expect total submission and *genuflection*.

- Inflection: the rise and fall of the voice

  The *inflection* in his voice suggests he is from England or South Africa.

- Reflect: to think back to

  Reflect on literary readings through a discussion with others.

- Reflective: thoughtful

  Quiet, *reflective* moments can give a sense of inner peace.

- Reflector: that which sends back light

  Wear a *reflector* when you walk at night.

- _____: image thrown back

  Do you see your _____ in the pond below?

Words with *nat* or *nasc* = born

Do July 4th celebrations create a sense of nationalism?

- Native: belonging to by birth

  Are palm trees *native* to your area?

- Naïve: acting as one born yesterday

  The *naïve* respondent thought she had won a prize.

- Naturalize: to give citizenship to one foreign born

  Gisela has been a *naturalized* citizen in this country for two years.

- Innate: inborn

  Can you control the *innate* urge to eat chocolate candy at Halloween?

- Renaissance: a rebirth or revival

  The inner-city neighborhood is experiencing a *renaissance* with young urban pioneers renovating houses.

- Nationality: country of origin

  Her *nationality* is either Mexican or Costa Rican.

- _____: between different countries

  Because of the many embassies represented, Washington, D.C., is a very _____ city.

Words with *corp* or *corpor* = *body*

Who would you expect to find at corporate headquarters?

- Corporal: relating to the body

  The scars indicated *corporal* punishment.

- Corporation: business people united legally

  The president of the *corporation* received stock bonuses.

- Incorporate: to unite legally, add

  You need to *incorporate* a visual display into the oral presentation.

- Corps: group organized for a common cause

  The Peace *Corps* members are sent to remote areas to help people.

- Corpuscle: a cell that flows in the blood

  A *corpuscle* can be a red or white blood cell.

- Corpse: a dead body

  An autopsy was performed on the *corpse* because of the mystery surrounding the death.

- Corpulent: excessively fat

  Santa Claus is *corpulent* and jolly.

- _____: the ability to incorporate, quality of being corporate

  After lengthy discussions with both owners, the attorney realized the two businesses were _____.

Review

Part I

Answer the following with true (*T*) or false (*F*).

_____ 1. A reflective thinker seldom recalls the past.

_____ 2. Flexible clay can still be molded.

_____ 3. A corpulent corpse will probably be difficult to move.

_____ 4. Spanking a child is corporal punishment.

_____ 5. Corpuscles are found in many plants.

_____ 6. If you look in a mirror, you can see your reflection.

_____ 7. An innate talent is a genetic gift.

_____ 8. Companies traded on the New York Stock Exchange are incorporated businesses.

_____ 9. A deflected arrow is repelled from the target.

_____10. Immigrants must apply to become naturalized citizens.

Part II

Choose the best word from the list to complete the following sentences.

näive	corps	reflectors	nationalism	inflection
flex	renascence	genuflect	native	nationality

11. His final voice _____ indicated that he was asking a question rather than stating a fact.

12. On Halloween night parents are cautioned for safety to attach _____ to children's costumes.

13. Although the flower is _____ to the mountains of Peru, California growers are now producing plants that can tolerate warmer summers.

14. The army called on the _____ of engineers to replace the bridge.

15. The freshman was _____ to think that the late paper would not be penalized.

16. When the king entered the room, the servants were expected to _____ to show respect.

17. The music of the military band heightened our feelings of _____ as the fighter planes flew by in perfect formation.

18. The _____ of the speaker was actually Colombian, although she had spent the last two years in Mexico City as a consultant.

19. When you lift weights, you _____ your muscles.

20. With art shops and restaurants opening on Hill Street, city planners hoped for a _____ of the previously downtrodden warehouse area.

Glossary

abstract Short paragraph that summarizes an article, stating the author's premise, the subject or location of the project, and the conclusions.

acronym Abbreviation pronounced as a word and contrived to simplify a lengthy name and gain quick recognition for an organization or agency. For example, *UNICEF* is the abbreviation for the United Nations International Children's Emergency Fund.

addition pattern Pattern of paragraph organization that includes additional information.

analogies Comparisons that measure not only word knowledge, but also ability to see relationships.

annotating Method of highlighting main ideas, significant supporting details, and key terms using a system of symbols and notations so the markings indicate pertinent points to review for an exam.

applied level of reading This level calls for reaction, reflection, and critical thinking and involves analyzing, synthesizing, and evaluating.

argument Assertion or set of assertions that supports a conclusion and is intended to persuade.

bar graph Graph comprising a series of horizontal or vertical bars in which the length of each bar represents a particular amount. Often, time is represented by the vertical scale and quantity is measured by the horizontal scale.

bias Author's attitude, opinion, or position on a subject suggesting the facts have been slanted toward the author's personal beliefs. As commonly used, *bias* has a negative connotation suggesting narrow-mindedness and prejudice.

bibliography List of the sources consulted by the author of a scholarly article or paper.

biography The story of a person's life or a portion of it as told by another person.

bookmarking Save-the-site technique that lets the user automatically return to the designated Web site with just one or two mouse clicks.

browser Software that searches to find the URL.

build meaning Good readers develop an understanding of what they read by using the following five thinking strategies: predict, picture, relate, monitor, and correct.

cause-and-effect pattern Pattern of paragraph organization showing one element as producing or causing a result or effect.

characters In a story, the main people; they should be consistent in behavior and should grow and change according to their experiences.

citation In an index entry, a reference to an article that includes the title, author(s), name of the periodical, volume and page numbers, issue date, and descriptive notes or key search terms.

classification pattern Pattern of paragraph organization dividing items into groups or categories.

cliché Overworked phrase that should be avoided in formal writing (e.g., *working like a dog*).

climax In literature, the turning point near the end of a story in which conflict intensifies to a peak.

comparison pattern Pattern of paragraph organization listing similarities among items.

conclusion Logical deduction from both stated and unstated ideas using the hints as well as the facts to interpret motives, actions, and outcomes. Conclusions are drawn on the basis of perceived evidence, and because perceptions differ, conclusions can vary from reader to reader.

conflict Clash of ideas, desires, or actions as incidents in a plot build progressively.

connotation Feeling or emotion associated with a word that goes beyond its dictionary definition.

contrast pattern Pattern of paragraph organization listing differences among items.

Cornell system System of notetaking in which you put questions on one side of a vertical line and notes that answer the questions on the other side.

creative thinking Ability to generate many possible solutions to a problem.

512

critical thinking Deliberating in a purposeful, organized manner in order to assess the value of old and new information.

critique Review that judges the merits of a work.

databases Computer-based indexes to assist research. A single article may be listed under several topics and may appear in several different indexes.

deductive reasoning Method by which one starts with a conclusion from a previous experience and then applies it to a new situation.

definition pattern Pattern of paragraph organization initially defining a concept and expanding with examples and restatements.

denotation Dictionary definition of a word.

details Specifics in a passage that develop, explain, and support the main idea such as reasons, incidents, facts, examples, steps, and definitions.

diagram Outlined drawing or illustration of an object or a process.

directory path Particular location within the Web site's host computer.

domain name Name registered by the Web site owner.

domain type Category to which the site owner belongs.

download Method of saving or viewing an attachment by e-mail or importing programs from other sources.

editorials Subjective articles that express the opinion of a person or organization. A newspaper's editorial pages feature the views of its management and editors.

electronic mail (e-mail) Message sent from one person or organization to another person or group of people using the World Wide Web. These messages can be read, printed, saved, forwarded to someone else, and/or discarded.

encyclopedias Reference books that give comprehensive coverage of a subject. Many different encyclopedias are available for specific topics such as the *Encyclopedia of African American Religions*, *Encyclopedia of Earth Sciences*, and *The Cambridge Encyclopedia of Astronomy*.

essay Short work of nonfiction that discusses a specific topic. Does not develop as a story does and it lacks characters and a plot.

etymology Study of word origins involving the tracing of words back to their earliest recorded appearance.

fact Statement based on actual evidence or personal observation. It can be checked objectively with empirical data and proved to be either true or false.

fallacy Inference that appears to be reasonable at first, but closer inspection proves it to be unrelated, unreliable, or illogical. Tool used in constructing a weak argument.

feature stories In journalism, human interest stories that differ from typical news stories in their timeliness, style, and length.

fiction Writing invented by the imagination.

figurative language Words intentionally used in a different way—out of their literal context—so they take on new meaning.

file name Specific file within the host's directory.

fixations Stops lasting a fraction of a second that eyes make in order to read. On the average, 5 to 10 percent of reading time is spent on fixations.

generalization and example pattern Pattern of paragraph organization explaining a concept by illustrating with examples.

historical novel Story that blends using both real and invented characters against a backdrop of documented historical events.

home page Main page for a Web site through which other areas of the site can be reached.

hypertext links In the World Wide Web, phrases that are often distinguished by a different color and are underlined. Clicking on them will not only move you from one page to another within the Web site, but can also send you to other related Web sites. The words chosen and underlined as the link describe the information likely to be found at that destination.

idioms Expressions that have taken on a generally accepted meaning over many years of use but do not make sense on a literal level. Idioms can be similes and metaphors. For example, *sleeping like a log* is both a simile and also an idiom because it is an accepted and often used expression that is not literally true.

index Research tool that contains listings of articles organized by the topics within the articles. Most libraries have electronic periodical indexes.

inductive reasoning Method by which one gathers data and then, after considering all available material, formulates a conclusion.

inference Meaning that is not directly stated but suggested through clues that lead one to make assumptions and draw conclusions.

intent Reason or purpose for writing, which is usually to inform, persuade, or entertain.

Internet Electronic system of more than 25,000 worldwide computer networks. The Internet is the networked system that allows the World Wide Web to function.

interpretive level of reading At this level the reader makes assumptions and draws conclusions by considering the stated message, the implied meaning, the facts, and the author's attitude toward the subject.

inverted pyramid Format of news writing that begins with a summary paragraph and continues with paragraphs that explain details in a descending order of importance.

issue An assertion or position statement in an argument. It is what the author is trying to convince you to believe or to do.

lateral thinking A way of thinking *around* a problem or even redefining the problem.

lead In a news story, the first paragraph that catches the reader's attention, establishes a focus, and summarizes the essential points of the story.

letter Formal communication appropriate for outside the company.

line graph Graph incorporating a continuous curve or *frequency distribution*. The horizontal scale (or *axis*) measures one aspect of the data (or *variable*), and the vertical scale measures another aspect, making it easy to see the relationship between the variables at a glance. As the data fluctuate, the line changes direction and, with extreme differences, becomes very jagged.

links See *hypertext links*.

LISTSERV Subscription service that sends out news, discussion, and research on particular topics by e-mail. You can post your own opinion as well as request assistance with specific questions related to the focus of the group.

literal level of reading At this level the reader might be able to answer detail questions asking *who, what, when*, and *where*, but not understand the overall purpose of the passage.

location or spatial order pattern Pattern of paragraph organization identifying the whereabouts of objects.

main idea Central message the author is trying to convey about the material.

map Visual representation of a geographic area.

mapping Visual system of condensing ideas or cognitive material through diagramming of major points and significant subpoints to show relationships and importance.

memo Short, informal business note usually for internal business purposes.

metacognition Knowledge of the processes involved in reading and the ability to regulate and direct them.

metaphor Direct comparison of two unlike things that does not use the words *like* or *as*. A metaphor and a simile can communicate the same idea and are only differentiated by the presence or absence of the words *like* or *as*.

minutes Official record of the business decisions for a meeting.

mnemonics Techniques to help the brain organize and recall information by incorporating the senses through pictures, sounds, rhythms, and other mental tricks to create extrasensory handles or hooks.

mood Overall feeling of the work, often conveyed by the author's emotional attitude toward the subject.

multiple meanings Some words are confusing because they have several different meanings. For example, the dictionary lists over thirty meanings for the word *run*.

newsgroup Topic-specific Web site where the user can review news on a particular subject and post and read one's own and others' opinions, discussions, and questions.

newsletter Mini-newspaper published within an organization to build group spirit.

news stories Front page articles that report the facts of news events in descending order of importance.

notetaking Method of jotting down important ideas for future study from a lecture or text.

novel Extended fictional work that has all of the elements of a short story. Because of its length, a novel usually has more character development and more conflicts than a short story.

opinion Statement of personal feeling or a judgment. It reflects a belief or an interpretation rather than an accumulation of evidence, and it cannot be proved true or false.

outline Method of organizing major points and subordinating items of lesser importance with Roman numerals, numbers, letters, and indentations to quickly show how one idea relates to another and how all aspects relate to the whole.

paragraph Group of sentences about a single topic that expresses a single main idea.

patterns of organization Organizational structure of a passage that can be a simple listing, time order, definition with examples, comparison-contrast, or cause and effect.

periodical Publications that come out on a regular schedule, including popular sources and scholarly journals.

personification Attributing human characteristics to nonhuman things.

pie graph Circle divided into wedge-shaped slices, with each slice representing a percentage of the whole. The complete pie or circle represents 100 percent.

plot Action in a story or a play. Sequence of incidents or events linked in a manner that suggests causes for the events.

point of view In reading, point of view is the author's attitude, opinion, or position on a subject. In literature, point of view describes who tells the story and is indicated most commonly by the third person (in which the author is the all-knowing observer). Alternatively, the first person (in which the main character tells the story by using the word *I*) or second person (in which the story is told through the use of the word *you*) may be used.

popular sources Newspapers and magazines aimed at the general public and written by professional journalists who are *reporters* rather than specialists in the field and thus focus on *who, what, where, when, why,* and *how.*

prefix Group of letters with a special meaning added to the beginning of a word.

premise Reasons provided in support of the thesis of an argument.

previewing First stage of reading: a method of looking over the material to guess what it is about, assess what you already know about the topic, decide what you will probably want to know after you read, and make a plan for reading.

primary sources Public and private documents of a period, used by historians to research the times.

prior knowledge What is already known about a subject, which is the single best predictor of reading comprehension.

protocol Short for *hypertext transfer protocol,* a type of language computers networked via the Internet use to communicate with each other.

purpose Reason or intent for writing, which is usually to inform, persuade, or entertain.

recalling Telling oneself what has been learned after reading, relating it to what is already known, and reacting to it to form an opinion.

reference bibliographies Book-length lists of research material related to a particular subject.

regression Rereading sentences or paragraphs because one's mind was wandering during the initial reading of the material.

root Stem or basic part of a word derived primarily from Latin and Greek.

scanning Process of searching for a single bit of information. Reader merely needs to pinpoint a specific detail, rather than comprehend the general meaning of the material.

schema Concept of a compartment similar to a computer chip in the brain that holds all that is known on a subject.

scholarly journals Regularly scheduled publications aimed at scholars, specialists, and students. They contain detailed research results written by specialists in the academic field of study and are frequently theoretical.

search engine Program that searches the Internet for information. Can be found at such Web sites as Yahoo!, AltaVista, Excite, Go.com, or Lycos.

secondary sources Nonprimary sources such as textbooks that interpret or retell historical events.

server name Indicates the computer network over which the user travels to reach the desired location (in most cases, the World Wide Web).

setting Backdrop for a story and the playground for the characters. Setting may include the place, the time, and the culture.

short story Brief work of narrative fiction with a beginning, a middle, and an end that ranges from 500 to 15,000 words.

simile Comparison of two unlike things using the words *like* or *as* (e.g., "His words were like sharp knives to my heart").

simple listing pattern Pattern of paragraph organization randomly listing items in a series.

situational irony Events occur contrary to what is expected, as if in a cruel twist of fate (e.g., Juliet awakens and finds that Romeo has killed himself because he thought she was dead).

skimming Technique of selectively reading for the main idea and quickly overviewing material. Involves skipping words, sentences, paragraphs, and even pages.

subvocalization Inaudible voice in one's mind that reads.

suffix Group of letters with a special meaning added to the end of a word. Can alter the meaning of a word as well as the way the word can be used.

summary Brief, concise statement of the main idea of a piece of writing and its significant supporting details. The first sentence states the main idea or thesis, and subsequent sentences incorporate the significant details.

suspense As conflict builds in a plot, the reader's anxious concern about the characters' well-being.

symbolism Object, action, person, place, or idea that carries a condensed and recognizable meaning (e.g., an opened window might symbolize an opportunity for a new life).

table Organized listing of facts and figures in columns and rows to compare and classify information for quick and easy reference.

theme Heart, soul, or central insight of—or universal truth expressed by—a work. Message is never preached but revealed to the emotions, senses, and imagination through powerful shared experiences.

time order, sequence, or narration pattern Pattern of paragraph organization listing events in the order of occurrence.

tone Writer's attitude toward the subject or the audience. For example, an author's word choice may suggest humor, cutting remarks suggest sarcasm, and ironic remarks show the gap between the actual and the expected.

topic General rather than specific term that forms an umbrella under which the author can group the specific ideas or details in a passage.

topic sentence Sentence that condenses the thoughts and details of a passage into a general, all-inclusive statement of the author's message.

transitions Signal words that connect parts of sentences and lead readers to anticipate a continuation or a change in the writer's thoughts.

Uniform Resource Locator (URL) On the Web, specific directions for finding your way to a specific site, just as an address and zip code are required to mail a letter. A URL is similar to an e-mail address, except that it routes the user to a source of information called a *Web page* or *Web site* rather than to the mailbox of an individual person.

verbal irony Use of words to express a meaning that is the opposite of what is literally said. In other words, it is saying one thing and suggesting another. If the intent is to ridicule, the irony can also be called *sarcasm*.

vertical thinking Straightforward and logical way of thinking that would typically result in a solution. It involves deeper exploration of the same idea for a problem solution (e.g., continuing to develop stronger poisons to kill insects).

vocalization moving one's lips as one reads.

Web directory Type of search engine that organizes hypertext links into categories like libraries organize books into categories.

Web pages Locations or "sites" of information provided by individual people, businesses, educational institutions, or other organizations on the Internet.

World Wide Web (WWW) Electronic information network that is similar to an enormous library, with Web sites like books and Web pages like the pages in the books.

Acknowledgments

Text Credits

Acquaah, George. From *Horticulture* by George Acquaah, copyright © 1999. Reprinted by permission of Prentice-Hall, Inc., Upper Saddle River, NJ.

Appelbaum, Richard. From *Sociology*, 2nd Edition, by Richard Appelbaum, copyright © 1998. Reprinted by permission of Prentice-Hall, Inc., Upper Saddle River, NJ.

Arms, Karen and Camp, Pamela S. Excerpts from *Biology: A Journey Into Life*, Second Edition by Karen Arms and Pamela S. Camp, copyright © 1991 by Saunders College Publishing. Reprinted by permission of the publisher.

Associated Press. From "Washington Farm Workers Rally" from Associated Press, August 7, 2000. Reprinted with permission of The Associated Press.

Beekman, George. From *Computer Confluence*, 4th Edition, by George Beekman, copyright © 2000. Reprinted by permission of Prentice-Hall, Inc., Upper Saddle River, NJ.

Brown, Les. From *Live Your Dreams* by Les Brown, copyright © 1992 by Les Brown Unlimited, Inc. Reprinted by permission of HarperCollins Publishers, Inc.

Campbell, Neill. From *Biology*, 4th Edition, by Neill Campbell, copyright © 1987, 1990, 1993, 1996 by The Benjamin/Cummings Publishing Company, Inc. Reprinted by permission of Addison-Wesley Educational Publishers, Inc.

Carpenter, Phil. Reprinted by permission of Harvard Business School Press. From *eBrands* by Phil Carpenter, Boston, MA, pages 153–154, 163–164. Copyright © 2000 by President and Fellows of Harvard College.

Certo, Samuel. From *Modern Management*, 8th Edition, by Samuel Certo, copyright © 2000. Reprinted by permission of Prentice-Hall, Inc., Upper Saddle River, NJ.

Chapman/O'Neil. From *Your Attitude Is Showing*, 9th Edition, copyright © 1999. Adapted by permission of Pearson Education., Upper Saddle River, NJ.

Conger, John Janeway and Galambos, Nancy L. From *Adolescence and Youth*, 5th Edition, by John Janeway Conger and Nancy L. Galambos, copyright © 1997 by Allyn & Bacon. Reprinted/adapted by permission.

Conlin, Joseph. From *The American Past*, 5th Edition, by Joseph R. Conlin, copyright © 1997 by Harcourt, Inc. Reprinted by permission of the publisher.

DeVito, Joseph. From *Essentials of Human Communication*, 3rd Edition, by Joseph DeVito, copyright © 1993 by HarperCollins College Publishers. Reprinted by permission of Addison-Wesley Educational Publishers, Inc.

DeVito, Joseph. From *Human Communication*, 6th Edition, by Joseph DeVito, copyright © 1994 by HarperCollins College Publishers. Reprinted by permission of Addison-Wesley Educational Publishers, Inc.

Dworetzky, John. From *Psychology*, 3rd Edition, by J. Dworetzky, © 1988. Reprinted with permission of Brooks/Cole, an imprint of the Wadsworth Group, a division of Thomson Learning. Fax (800) 730–2215.

Ebert, Ronald and Griffin, Ricky. From *Business Essentials*, 3rd Edition, by Ronald Ebert and Ricky Griffin, copyright © 2000. Reprinted by permission of Prentice-Hall, Inc., Upper Saddle River, NJ.

Edwards, George. From *Government In America*, 9th Edition, by George Edwards *et al.*, copyright © 2000 by Addison-Wesley Educational Publishers, Inc. Reprinted by permission of Addison-Wesley Educational Publishers, Inc.

Fabes, Richard and Martin, Carol Lynn. From *Exploring Child Development* by Richard Fabes and Carol Lynn Martin. Copyright © 2000 by Allyn & Bacon. Reprinted/adapted by permission.

Fink, Jerry. From "The Do's and Don'ts of Dealing with Killer Bees" by Jerry Fink, Las Vegas Sun, May 15, 2000. Copyright © 2000 by the Las Vegas Sun. Reprinted by permission.

Fiorina, Morris and Peterson, Paul. From *The New American Democracy*, Election Update Edition, by Morris Fiorina and Paul Peterson, copyright © 2000 by Allyn & Bacon. Reprinted/adapted by permission.

Fobes, Richard. From *The Creative Problem Solver's Toolbox* by Richard Fobes. Copyright © 1993 by Richard Fobes. Reprinted by permission of Solutions Through Innovation.

Garraty, John. From *American Nation*, 10th Edition, by John A. Garraty, copyright © 2000 by John A. Garraty. Reprinted by permission of Addison-Wesley Educational Publishers, Inc.

Gerow, Josh. From *Essentials of Psychology* by Josh Gerow, copyright © 1993. Reprinted by permission of Prentice-Hall, Inc., Upper Saddle River, NJ.

Goodman, Roger B. "The Doctor's Heroism," translated by Roger B. Goodman, from *75 Short Masterpieces—Stories from The World's Literature* by Roger B. Goodman, copyright © 1961 by Bantam

Books. Used by permission of Bantam Books, a division of Random House, Inc.

Google Inc. Usenet listing for the Latin translation of the Seven Deadly Sins reprinted by permission of Google Inc.

Gordon, Arthur. "The Alchemist's Secret" by Arthur Gordon. Copyright © 1952 Arthur Gordon. Reprinted by permission.

Hellmich, Nanci. From "Effects of Skipping Sleep Can Be a Real Eye-opener" by Nanci Hellmich in USA Today, March 22, 1999. Copyright © 1999 USA Today. Reprinted with permission.

Holland, Morris. From *Psychology: An Introduction to Human Behavior*, Second Edition, by Morris Holland. Copyright © 1978 by D.C. Heath and Company. Used with permission of Houghton Mifflin Company.

Kanter, Rosabeth Moss. Copyright © 1993 by Rosabeth Moss Kanter, from "The Job Makes the Person," which first appeared in *Psychology Today* magazine and was drawn from *Men and Women of the Corporation* (Perseus Books). Reprinted also in *Understanding Diversity* by Carol Harvey and M. June Allard. Reprinted by permission of the author.

Kassin, Saul. From *Psychology*, 2nd Edition, by Saul Kassin, copyright © 1997. Reprinted by permission of Prentice-Hall, Inc., Upper Saddle River, NJ.

Kishlansky, Mark. From *The Unfinished Legacy* by Mark Kishlansky et al., copyright © 1993 by Harper-Collins College Publishers. Reprinted by permission of Addison-Wesley Educational Publishers, Inc.

Koten, John. Republished with permission of the *Wall Street Journal* from "You Aren't Paranoid If You Think Someone Eyes Your Every Move" by John Koten, the *Wall Street Journal*, March 29, 1985, copyright © 1985 Dow Jones & Company, Inc. Permission conveyed through Copyright Clearance Center, Inc.

Lutgens, Frederick and Tarbuck, Edward. From *The Atmosphere*, 7th Edition, by Frederick Lutgens and Edward Tarbuck, copyright © 1989. Reprinted by permission of Prentice-Hall, Inc., Upper Saddle River, NJ.

Macionis, John J. From *Sociology*, 8th Edition, by John J. Macionis, copyright © 2000. Reprinted by permission of Prentice-Hall, Inc., Upper Saddle River, NJ.

Martin, James Kirby. From *America and Its People* by James Kirby Martin et al., copyright © 2001 by James Kirby Martin, Randy Roberts, Steven Mintz, Linda O. McMurry, and James H. Jones. Reprinted by permission of Addison-Wesley Educational Publishers, Inc.

McCarter, William. From *Living With Art*, 4th Edition, by William McCarter et al., copyright © 1995. Reprinted by permission of The McGraw-Hill Companies.

McGraw, Phillip. From *Life Strategies* by Phillip C. McGraw. Copyright © 1999 by Phillip C. McGraw, Ph.D. Reprinted by permission of Hyperion.

Merriam-Webster Collegiate Dictionary. By permission. From *Merriam-Webster's Collegiate Dictionary*, Tenth Edition, © 2000 by Merriam-Webster, Incorporated.

Miller, Roger Leroy. From *Economics Today* 1999–2000 Edition, copyright © 1999 by Addison-Wesley Publishing Company, Inc. Reprinted by permission of Pearson Education Inc.

Mims, Joan T. and Nollen, Elizabeth M. From *Mirror on America*, edited by Joan T. Mims and Elizabeth M. Nollen, copyright © 2000 by Bedford/St. Martin's. Reprinted with permission of Bedford/St. Martin's.

Morehead, Philip D. and Morehead, Andrew T. From *The New American Roget's College Thesaurus* by Philip D. Morehead and Andrew T. Morehead, copyright © 1958, 1962 by Albert H. Morehead. Copyright © 1978, 1985, renewed 1986 by Philip D. Morehead and Andrew T. Morehead. Used by permission of Dutton Signet, a division of Penguin Putnam Inc.

Nash, Roderick and Graves, Gregory. From *From These Beginnings*, 6th Edition, by Roderick Nash and Gregory Graves, copyright © 2000 by Addison-Wesley Longman, Inc. Reprinted by permission of Addison-Wesley Educational Publishers, Inc.

O'Connor, Karen and Sabato, Larry. From *American Government*, 1999 Edition, by Karen O'Connor and Larry Sabato, copyright © 2000 by Addison-Wesley Longman, Inc. Reprinted by permission of Addison-Wesley Educational Publishers, Inc.

Peeples, Jr., Edward H. From " . . . Meanwhile Humans Eat Pet Food" by Edward H. Peeples, Jr., *New York Times*, December 16, 1975. Copyright © 1975 by The New York Times Company. Reprinted by permission.

Rice, Laura Williams and Rice, Jr., Robert P. From *Practical Horticulture*, 4th Edition, by Laura Williams Rice and Robert P. Rice, Jr., copyright © 2000. Reprinted by permission of Prentice-Hall, Inc., Upper Saddle River, NJ.

Roediger, Henry L. From *Psychology*, 2nd Edition, by Henry L. Roediger et al., copyright © 1987. Reprinted by permission of Prentice-Hall, Inc., Upper Saddle River, NJ.

Rowley, Laura. From "As They Say, Drugs Kill" by Laura Rowley, copyright © 1992 by Bedford/St. Martin's. From *Models For Writers*, 4th Edition, by Alfred Rosa and Paul Eschholz. Reprinted with permission of Bedford/St. Martin's.

Runyan, Damon. "The Brighter Side" by Damon Runyan, 1940. Reprinted with special permission of King Features Syndicate.

Salinas, Marta. "The Scholarship Jacket" by Marta Salinas from *Nosotras: Latina Literature Today*, edited by Maria del Carmen Boza, Beverly Silva, and Carmen Valle. Copyright © 1986 by Bilingual Press/Editorial Bilingüe, Arizona State University, Tempe, AZ. Reprinted by permission of the publisher.

Schmalleger, Frank. From *Criminal Justice Today*, 3rd Edition, by Frank Schmalleger, copyright © 1996. Reprinted by permission of Prentice-Hall, Inc., Upper Saddle River, NJ.

Sherman, Neil. From "Hundreds of Tons of Ground Beef Recalled" by Neil Sherman from *HealthScout*,

August 1, 2000, copyright © 2001 by *HealthScout.* Reprinted by permission of *HealthScout.*

Starr, Cecie and Taggart, Ralph. From *Biology: The Unity and Diversity of Life with Infotrac and 2.1 CD*, 8th Edition, by C. Starr and R. Taggart, © 1998. Reprinted with permission of Wadsworth, an imprint of the Wadsworth Group, a division of Thomson Learning. Fax (800) 730–2215.

Swanson, Charles. From *Criminal Investigation*, 7th Edition, by Charles Swanson et al., copyright © 1996. Reprinted by permission of The McGraw-Hill Companies.

The American Heritage Dictionary of the English Language. Copyright © 1994 by Houghton Mifflin Company. Reproduced by permission from *The American Heritage Dictionary of the English Language*, Third Paperback Edition.

Thio, Alex. From *Deviant Behavior*, 6th Edition, by Alex Thio, copyright © 2001 by Allyn & Bacon. Reprinted/adapted by permission

Thio, Alex. From *Sociology*, 3rd Edition, by Alex Thio, copyright © 1992 by Allyn & Bacon. Reprinted/adapted by permission.

Thompson, William E. and Hickey, Joseph V. From *Society in Focus*, 3rd Edition, by William E. Thompson and Joseph V. Hickey, copyright © 1999 by Allyn & Bacon. Reprinted/adapted by permission.

Wallace, Robert. From *Biology: The World of Life*, 7th Edition, by Robert Wallace, copyright © 1997 by Addison-Wesley Educational Publishers, Inc. Reprinted by permission of Addison-Wesley Educational Publishers, Inc.

Wasserman, Gary. From *The Basics Of American Politics* by Gary Wasserman, copyright © 2000 by Gary Wasserman. Reprinted by permission of Addison-Wesley Educational Publishers, Inc.

Watson, David. From *Psychology* by David L. Watson. Copyright © 1996 by David L. Watson. Reprinted by permission of Kendall/Hunt Publishing Company.

Wolf, Robin. From *Marriage and Families in a Diverse Society* by Robin Wolf, copyright © 2000. Reprinted by permission of Prentice-Hall, Inc., Upper Saddle River, NJ.

Woo, Carolyn. From "Living Up to Your Fullest Potential" by Carolyn Woo, Vital Speeches of the Day 64, 8/15/98, pages 670–672. Reprinted by permission of the author.

Worchel, Stephen and Shebilske, Wayne. From *Psychology: Principles and Applications*, 3rd Edition, by Stephen Worchel and Wayne Shebilske, copyright © 1997. Reprinted by permission of Prentice-Hall, Inc., Upper Saddle River, NJ.

Yahoo! Inc. "Star-Spangled Banner" screen shot reproduced with permission of Yahoo! Inc., © 2000 by Yahoo! Inc. *Yahoo!* and the *Yahoo!* logo are trademarks of Yahoo! Inc.

Zinsser, William. From *On Writing Well*, 6th Edition, by William Zinsser, copyright © 1976, 1980, 1985, 1988, 1990, 1994, 1998 by William K. Zinsser. Published by HarperCollins Publishers, Inc. Reprinted by permission of the author.

Photo Credits

Page: 1: © Frozen Images/The Image Works; **15**: © Bill Lai/The Image Works; **17**: © 2000 Jose Luis Pelaez Inc./The Stock Market; **29**: © LWA – Sharie Kennedy/The Stock Market; **46**: Oscar Burriel/Science Photo Library/Photo Researchers, Inc.; **52**: © Joe Raedle/Liaison/Newsmakers/Online USA; **58**: © Clay Patrick McBride/Photonica; **67**: © R. Lord/The Image Works; **70 Left & Right, 77**: Cartoon taken from "Vocabulary Cartoons, SAT Word Power" published by New Monic Books, www.vocabularycartoons.com; **101**: © Wally McNamee/CORBIS; **108**: *Double Take* by Norman Rockwell. Printed by permission of the Norman Rockwell Family Trust. Copyright © 1941 the Norman Rockwell Trust. Collection of The Norman Rockwell Museum at Stockbridge, Massachusetts; **121**: © K.C. Tanner/Superstock; **125**: © Will & Deni McIntyre/Science Source/Photo Researchers, Inc.; **133**: Diego Rivera. Museu de Arte, Sao Paulo, Brazil. © 2001 Banco de México Diego Rivera & Frida Kahlo Museums Trust. Av. Cinco de Mayo No. 2, Col. Centro, Del. Cuauhtémoc 06059, Mexico, D.F./Instituto Nacional de Bellas Artes y Literature/Art Resource, NY; **141**: © Matt Herron/Take Stock; **151**: © Hans Wolf/Imagebank; **161**: © David R. Frazier Photolibrary/Photo Researchers, Inc.; **174**: Zuma Press, Inc.; **186**: © R. Lord/The Image Works; **194**: Imagebank; **201**: A. Gragera, Latin Stock/Science Photo Library/Photo Researchers, Inc.; **211**: © Flip Chalfant/The Image Bank; **231**: © Matt Herron/Take Stock; **240**: © Carolyn A. Herter/Gamma Liaison; **248**: *Fort Worth Star*/Tom Pennington/Sipa Press; **259**: © Jim Harrison/Stock Boston; **287**: © Chuck Keeler, Jr./The Stock Market; **302**: Photograph by Danielle Weil. Reproduced with permission of Yahoo! Inc. © 2000 by Yahoo! Inc. *Yahoo!* and the *Yahoo!* logo are trademarks of Yahoo! Inc.; **305**: © Robert I. Campbell/National Geographic Image Collection; **307**: © Bettmann/CORBIS; **315**: © Matt Zumbo/ Imagebank; **339**: Copyright 1965 by Stanley Milgram. From the film "Obedience," distributed by Penn State, Media Sales; **348**: © Simons, Chip, 1997/FPG International; **359**: René Magritte, *La Condition Humaine*, Gift of the Collectors Committee, Photograph © 2001 Board of Trustees, National Gallery of Art, Washington, 1933; **360**: © Sieron; **361**: Jack Ohman, The Oregonian © 1999, from Brooks, *The Best Editorial Cartoons of the Year*, 2000 edition, Pelican Publishing; **376**: © Steve Raymer/CORBIS; **383**: Super-Stock; **387**: Jules Leonard, *The Doctor of the Poor*. Musee des Beaux-Arts, Valenciennes, France. Art Resource, NY; **395**: Jacob Lawrence, *The Library*, 1960. © Smithsonian American Art Museum, Washington, DC/Art Resource, NY; **419**: © VCG/FPG; **427**: F. Cruz/Superstock; **436**: A. Vengo/Superstock; **447**: © Adam Smith, 1997/FPG International; **450**: © Jack Ziegler. The *New Yorker* Collection. The Cartoon Bank. All Rights Reserved; **452**: Reprinted with permission from *Modern Maturity*. Copyright 1996 American Association of Retired Persons; **457**: Detail. Albert Bierstadt, *The Oregon Trail*, 1869. Oil on canvas, 31" x 49". Courtesy The Butler Institute of American Art, Youngstown, Ohio.

Index

Progress Record for Reading Selections

Directions: Maintain a record of your progress on the longer reading selections throughout the textbook. In the appropriate spaces, record your total percent correct for the comprehension and vocabulary items on each selection. Further analyze your comprehension results by noting the number of items included for each skill area and then indicating the number of items missed in that skill area.

SELECTION	COMPREHENSION	MAIN IDEA	DETAILS	INFERENCE	VOCABULARY
	(Total %)		(Total items) (Number missed)		(Total %)
CHAPTER 2					
Hypnosis	_____	(1) (-__)	(2) (-__)	(7) (-__)	_____
The Killers Are Coming!	_____	(1) (-__)	(6) (-__)	(3) (-__)	_____
Problems in Schools	_____	(1) (-__)	(5) (-__)	(4) (-__)	_____
CHAPTER 4					
Sleeping and Dreaming	_____	(1) (-__)	(4) (-__)	(5) (-__)	_____
The Scholarship Jacket	_____	(1) (-__)	(3) (-__)	(6) (-__)	_____
The Dream of Nonviolent Reform	_____	(1) (-__)	(5) (-__)	(4) (-__)	_____
CHAPTER 5					
Becoming Healthy	_____	(1) (-__)	(7) (-__)	(2) (-__)	_____
Confidence Game	_____	(1) (-__)	(2) (-__)	(7) (-__)	_____
The Nature of Infectious Diseases	_____	(1) (-__)	(5) (-__)	(4) (-__)	_____
CHAPTER 6					
Cesar Chavez	_____	(1) (-__)	(8) (-__)	(1) (-__)	_____
The Beanie Baby Business	_____	(1) (-__)	(6) (-__)	(3) (-__)	_____
Mass and Serial Murder	_____ !	(1) (-__)	(3) (-__)	(6) (-__)	_____
CHAPTER 8					
www.Yahoo.com	_____	(0) (-__)	(8) (-__)	(2) (-__)	_____
Dr. Fossey and the Gorillas	_____	(0) (-__)	(3) (-__)	(2) (-__)	_____
Eleanor Roosevelt	_____	(0) (-__)	(4) (-__)	(1) (-__)	_____
CHAPTER 9					
Hurricanes	_____	(1) (-__)	(7) (-__)	(2) (-__)	_____
Obedience	_____	(1) (-__)	(4) (-__)	(5) (-__)	_____
Motivating Yourself	_____	(1) (-__)	(1) (-__)	(9) (-__)	_____
CHAPTER 10					
Commencement Speech	_____	(1) (-__)	(1) (-__)	(8) (-__)	_____
The Alchemist's Secret	_____	(0) (-__)	(0) (-__)	(8) (-__)	_____
The Doctor's Heroism	_____	(0) (-__)	(0) (-__)	(10) (-__)	_____
CHAPTER 11					
As they Say, Drugs Kill	_____	(1) (-__)	(1) (-__)	(8) (-__)	_____
Women Selecting Names	_____	(4) (-__)	(11) (-__)	(10) (-__)	_____
The Job Makes the Person	_____	(1) (-__)	(1) (-__)	(5) (-__)	_____
CHAPTER 12					
Conflict Management	_____				
The Surge Westward	_____				